CRISIS, WAR, AND THE HOLOCAUST IN LITHUANIA

Lithuanian Studies without Borders

Series Editor—**Darius Staliūnas** (Lithuanian Institute of History)

Editorial Board
Zenonas Norkus (Vilnius University)
Shaul Stampfer (Hebrew University)
Giedrius Subačius (University of Illinois at Chicago)

Other Titles in this Series

The Shaken Lands: Violence and the Crisis of Governance in East Central Europe, 1914–1923. Edited by Tomas Balkelis and Andrea Griffante

The Storytelling Human: Lithuanian Folk Tradition Today. Compiled and edited by Lina Būgienė

Entangled Interactions between Religion and National Consciousness in Central and Eastern Europe. Edited by Yoko Aoshima

The Lithuanian Metrica: History and Research. Artūras Dubonis, Darius Antanavičius, Raimonda Ragauskienė, and Ramunė Šmigelskytė-Stukienė

Between Rome and Byzantium: The Golden Age of the Grand Duchy of Lithuania's Political Culture. Second Half of the Fifteenth Century to First Half of the Seventeenth Century. Jūratė Kiaupienė

The Literary Field under Communist Rule. Edited by Aušra Jurgutienė and Dalia Satkauskytė

The Creation of National Spaces in a Pluricultural Region: The Case of Prussian Lithuania. Vasilijus Safronovas

Spatial Concepts of Lithuania in the Long Nineteenth Century. Edited by Darius Staliūnas

The Art of Identity and Memory: Toward a Cultural History of the Two World Wars in Lithuania. Edited by Giedrė Jankevičiūtė and Rasutė Žukienė

For more information on this series, please visit:
https://www.academicstudiespress.com/lithuanian-studies-without-borders-series/

CRISIS, WAR, AND THE HOLOCAUST IN LITHUANIA

Saulius Sužiedėlis

2025

Library of Congress Cataloging-in-Publication Data

Names: Sužiedėlis, Saulius, 1945- author.
Title: Crisis, war, and the Holocaust in Lithuania / Saulius Sužiedėlis.
Description: Boston : Academic Studies Press, 2024. | Series: Lithuanian studies without borders | Includes bibliographical references.
Identifiers: LCCN 2024001651 (print) | LCCN 2024001652 (ebook) | ISBN 9798887194905 (hardback) | ISBN 9798887194912 (adobe pdf) | ISBN 9798887194929 (epub)
Subjects: LCSH: Jews—Persecutions—Lithuania—History—20th century. | Holocaust, Jewish (1939-1945)—Lithuania. | World War, 1939-1945—Lithuania. | Lithuania—History—German occupation, 1941-1944. | Lithuania—History—20th century. | Collective memory--Lithuania.
Classification: LCC DS135.L5 S89 2024 (print) | LCC DS135.L5 (ebook) | DDC 940.53/18094793--dc23/eng/20240213
LC record available at https://lccn.loc.gov/2024001651
LC ebook record available at https://lccn.loc.gov/2024001652

Copyright © 2025, Academic Studies Press. All rights reserved

ISBN 9798887194905 (hardback)
ISBN 9798887194912 (adobe pdf)
ISBN 9798887194929 (epub)

Book design by Tatiana Vernikov
Cover design by Ivan Grave
On the cover: The monument to the victims of the Nineth Fort, Kaunas, Lithuania. Sculpture by A. Vincentas Ambraziūnas (1984).

Published by Academic Studies Press in association with the United States Holocaust Memorial Museum.
The US Holocaust Memorial Museum's Jack, Joseph, and Morton Mandel Center's mission is to ensure the long-term growth and vitality of Holocaust Studies. To do that, it is essential to provide opportunities for new generations of scholars. The vitality and the integrity of Holocaust Studies requires openness, independence, and free inquiry so that new ideas are generated and tested through peer review and public debate. The opinions of scholars expressed before, during the course of, or after their activities with the Mandel Center do not represent and are not endorsed by the Museum or its Mandel Center.

Academic Studies Press
1007 Chestnut St.
Newton, MA 02464, USA
press@academicstudiespress.com
www.academicstudiespress.com

Contents

Preface and Acknowledgments	VII
Abbreviations	XIV

Part One: Before the Shoah

1. Tradition, Accommodation, Conflict: Jews and Lithuanians from the Grand Duchy to the End of the First Republic	2
2. The Stalinist Cauldron: Lithuanians, Jews, and Soviet Power, June 1940–June 1941	90

Part Two: Destruction

3. The Specter of Genocide: Invasion, Insurrection, and the Assault on the Jews, June 22–July 31, 1941	157
4. Concentration and Destruction: The Mass Murder Campaign in Lithuania, August–December 1941	238
5. Survival, Destruction, Struggle: Ghettos and Jewish Resistance	323

Part Three: Response, Memory, Legacy

6. Images of Blood: Perpetrators, Observers, Bystanders, Rescuers	405
7. The Past as Legacy and Conflict: Wartime and Holocaust Narratives in Lithuania	478
Appendix 1. The Jäger Report	551
Appendix 2. Ghettos in Belarus	562
Sources and Bibliography	563
Index	599

Preface and Acknowledgements

This study is the result of years of interaction with historians, journalists, and writers from Lithuania, Latvia, Estonia, the United States, Poland, Germany, the United Kingdom, and Israel. The inspiration and encouragement to complete the book emerged from discussions among the eleven-member Sub-Commission on Nazi Crimes, one of two research groups constituting the International Commission for the Evaluation of the Crimes of the Nazi and Soviet Occupation Regimes in Lithuania (henceforth the IHC) established in 1997.[1] The commission sponsored reports and conferences on various aspects of the Nazi occupation of Lithuania, but it soon became apparent that there was a need for a single-volume history of the Holocaust in Lithuania—accessible to the general public—which, at the same time, would be an academic study written in accordance with standards of scholarship as understood in democratic societies. In a 2016 meeting in Vilnius of the sub-commission, of which I was then chair, the group decided that such a history would be written by a single author subject to peer review but without editorial control by any governmental entity. The need for comprehensive national histories dealing with the Holocaust was further underscored at a meeting with specialists in Baltic history at the Consultation on Current Issues and Future Directions for Holocaust Studies in the Baltic States held at the Mandel Center for Advanced Holocaust Studies of the United States Holocaust Memorial Museum in Washington, D.C. (USHMM) in 2017.

This book describes the fate of a community that lived for centuries in Lithuania. It was obvious at the outset that any serious study of the Shoah in Lithuania would have to incorporate the substantial scholarship of the post-Soviet era, particularly the work of researchers with access to previously restricted collections in archives and libraries. Since independence, Lithuanian scholars have published a large body of work dealing with the history of the First Republic (1918–1940) and the ensuing half-century of foreign occupation (1940–1990). However, the majority of these monographs and articles, including research

---

1 Formally, Tarptautinė komisija nacių ir sovietinio okupacinių režimų nusikaltimams Lietuvoje įvertinti; shorter name, Tarptautinė istorinio teisingumo komisija. In English short form, simply the International Historical Commission (IHC).

on the history of Lithuania's Jews, are in Lithuanian and thus largely inaccessible to readers outside the country. At the same time, scholars from outside Lithuania with the linguistic skills necessary to mine the relevant sources have also published noteworthy studies. This book owes much to their work and collegial advice.

The German occupation of Lithuania constituted the most violent event in modern Lithuanian history, resulting in the destruction of more than 90% of the country's Jewry. The savagery that erupted in the summer of 1941 marked the initial phase of the European-wide Holocaust. The fact that this genocide occurred under some conditions unique to Lithuania is not to suggest that the Holocaust here was the end result of predictable historic continuity, a kind of *Sonderweg*, the "special path" proposed by some authors to explain the rise of the Third Reich.

In the first chapter I present an overview of how Lithuanians and especially Lithuanian Jews responded to the challenges of the interwar period and in the second chapter, the subsequent Soviet occupation, a crisis that thrust the nation headlong into the most violent decade of its history (1940–1950), an experience that commenced what historian Robert Gellately has aptly called "the age of social catastrophe."[2] In the following four chapters, I recount the brutal destruction of Lithuanian Jewry, the stages of mass murder, as well as the responses of victims, perpetrators, bystanders, more distant observers, and contemporary commentators. The final chapter summarizes the aftermath of the Holocaust in Lithuania as both a problem of historiography and as an evolving, contentious narrative in society. The end of World War II was followed by years of guerilla warfare and massive dislocation which affected mostly ethnic Lithuanians, an experience which deflected collective memory away from what had happened to the Lithuanian Jews. The widespread amnesia regarding collaboration in the Holocaust became difficult to sustain in the aftermath of Lithuania's post-1990 encounter with the West. The ensuing conflict over responsibility for crimes committed during the Nazi occupation continues to agitate Lithuanians and has become a significant factor in the country's ongoing cultural and political struggles.

Situating the Holocaust within Lithuania's twentieth-century social catastrophe helps us to understand some of the dynamics of collaboration,

---

2   Robert Gellately, *Lenin, Stalin, and Hitler: The Age of Social Catastrophe* (New York: Vintage Books, 2008).

especially regarding motivation and intent. But it cannot answer all questions; most importantly, it does not explain how Jews, who had existed alongside Gentile neighbors for centuries, were virtually annihilated in a stunningly short time. Historic anti-Judaism and antisemitism undoubtedly drove people to commit crimes and were factors in the indifference of much of society in the face of mass persecution and murder. But such prejudices cannot explain why in Lithuania more Jews were killed in a single week in 1941 than in all the anti-Jewish attacks over the preceding (and one should stress, markedly turbulent) three centuries of the country's history. Antisemitism was a necessary but insufficient cause of the destruction of the Lithuanian Jews. As historians we must also search for answers in the specific conditions of time and place that gave rise to the horror.

Absent the German occupation, the Holocaust in Lithuania is inconceivable. The Wehrmacht's commandants issued the very first official anti-Jewish measures in the country's modern history within days of the German invasion, including decrees on the establishment of ghettos and the wearing of the infamous yellow patches. Some officers of the German security forces encouraged the pogroms. The German Civil Administration (Zivilverwaltung) established in late July 1941 played a decisive role in coordinating the concentration and destruction of the Jews. The most salient issues when addressing responsibility for the destruction process itself are the institutional interactions between the different German military and police organizations which had operational command of the killing process, and the Lithuanian police and administrative structures which accepted their lead and, at times, acted on their own. The latter are particularly relevant to this history since militarized Lithuanian police units provided the majority of the killers not only during the destruction of provincial Jewry in the late summer and fall of 1941, but also at the trenches of Paneriai (Ponar/Ponary) and the Ninth Fort.

While it is important for historians to emphasize the structural factors and social and political circumstances of mass murder, there is also a risk. The reader may get the impression that a particular atrocity was a tragedy caused by impersonal forces rather than by people possessing moral agency. The Holocaust was not a natural disaster. Historic circumstances may have set the stage, but it is important to keep in mind that the mass murder of the Jews was, above all, a crime of staggering scale, the premeditated result of decisions made by politicians, police officials, and military officers who held power over vulnerable populations. Even if they did not directly participate in murder, the victims' neighbors had numerous, often life-or-death, choices to make. They could hide persecuted

Jews or turn away people seeking shelter; they could protest or remain silent; they could stand by and watch or reach out a helping hand; they could resist or assist the occupiers. To bring to light the agency of the people of that time, I have frequently allowed historical actors to present, in their own words, their thoughts, impressions, and justifications for their actions, even when what they say is inconsistent, counterintuitive, and even contradictory.

Antisemitic ideology and historical animosities may circulate widely during periods of relative social peace, but they need to be activated to produce mass violence. Nazi leaders consciously weaponized anti-Jewish stereotypes, primarily by the imposition of a narrative of collective guilt which constitutes the essential motive behind all genocides. When teachers tell their students that the Nazis "killed Jews simply because they were Jews," they are voicing a widely repeated meme that sounds, and is, compelling but does not, in the end, explain very much. As bizarre as it is to imagine, the Nazi leadership actually believed Jews to be a mortal threat to the survival of the German nation. For the Nazis, Jews as a group really were guilty—not because they simply existed, but because in Hitler's eyes, they were, by their very nature, a constant threat to the "Aryan" peoples of Europe and were certain to continue posing an existential danger in the future. The antisemites of the Lithuanian Activist Front (LAF) also weaponized collective blame by invoking the trope that most Jews were Bolsheviks; they knew this falsehood would resonate under the conditions of the Soviet occupation of 1940–1941, particularly when added to the allegation that Jews betrayed Lithuania to the foreign invaders. Later, some intellectuals took up Nazi racial themes which until the German occupation had largely been on the margins of Lithuanian discourse. This kind of ideological incitement provided an impetus to murder, and to those who needed it, rationalization after the fact.

The inclusion here of research conducted during the past three decades will hopefully force a reexamination of some assumptions that circulate in popular narratives and even in some scholarly accounts. A few corrections can be listed here:

(1) Jews were not a majority in the Lithuanian Communist Party in 1940–1941;
(2) The Lithuanian perpetrators, a minority of the population, to be sure, were not a tiny rabble of misfits and lowlifes but represented different strata of society;
(3) As a rule, the collaborating police were not threatened if they refused orders to kill, particularly during the first months of the German occupation;

(4) In most cases, Lithuanian officials who left their posts rather than continue their duties were not punished;
(5) Jews were not significantly overrepresented among the Soviet deportees of June 14–17, 1941;
(6) Thousands of Jews were not killed in pogroms in the Lithuanian countryside before the Germans arrived on the scene, although instances of spontaneous violence have been reliably recorded;
(7) There were numerous examples of egregious intercommunal violence in Nazi-occupied Europe, but most Jews who died in the Holocaust were not killed by their neighbors in any literal sense;
(8) Lithuania's rescuers were not a mere handful but, in proportion to the total population, constituted the second highest percentage of Righteous Among the Nations (after the Netherlands).

It is not likely that popular misconceptions will easily disappear, but historians engage in malpractice if they do not challenge them when the evidence requires a reconsideration of historical storylines. Unfortunately, there is a growing divide between what specialists know and what much of the public thinks it knows about the Holocaust. Anyone who has followed the acrimonious public debates on the American Civil War should not find this surprising. Nonetheless, it is important to attempt to close the gap.

Lithuania's history presents a multinational kaleidoscope. Even the terms "Lithuania" and "Lithuanian" have, in the past, meant different things at different times to different people. Until the early twentieth century, most chroniclers of the country's history wrote in languages other than Lithuanian; hence different versions of toponyms, personal names, and institutional designations appear in the archives and published works. As a general rule, I choose the present-day spellings of place names as utilized by the National Geographic Society, which means employing the current official language of each region: Vilnius, not Vilna or Wilno; Kaunas, not Kovno; Suwałki, not Suvalkai; Ashmyany, not Oszmiana. However, I retain the names Vilna Ghetto and Kovno Ghetto, since these two important historic sites, the largest ghettos of the region, designate uniquely Jewish spaces and deserve to be remembered as such. Where useful, I have also provided alternative versions of terms often encountered in the literature (see also the list in "Abbreviations, Terms, Places"). In presenting surnames, I have tried to adhere to the spelling particular to a given person's nationality, while indicating alternative versions where necessary. Translations into English from Lithuanian, Russian, Polish, and German sources are my own, except in cases where I chose available published versions as referenced in the notes.

This work could not have been completed without the assistance and generosity of many friends who, over the years, corrected errors, opened new avenues of inquiry, and invited me to participate in international conferences and meetings. Much of what I learned at these gatherings has found its way into this study. Lithuanian institutions, scholars, and researchers in particular provided crucial assistance. The office of the IHC in Vilnius assisted with books, materials, and travel. My thanks to the IHC: Chairman Emanuelis Zingeris, Executive Director Ronaldas Račinskas, Program Coordinator Ingrida Vilkienė, and Administrative Assistant Eglė Šukytė-Malinauskienė. The members of the IHC's Sub-Commission on Nazi Crimes provided not only suggestions, reviews, and useful criticism but books and archival materials as well. My thanks go to Andrew Baker, Arūnas Bubnys, Christoph Dieckmann, Šarūnas Liekis, Jürgen Matthäus, Norman Naimark, Antony Polonsky, Dina Porat, Joachim Tauber, and Arkadi Zeltser. The Lithuanian Institute of History in Vilnius gave me access to important resources, and for this I thank Alfonsas Eidintas, Alvydas Nikžentaitis, Mindaugas Pocius, Gediminas Rudis, Vytautas Žalys, and especially Darius Staliūnas, who as editor of the Lithuanian Studies without Borders series published by Academic Studies Press read and criticized early drafts of the manuscript.

My thanks to Lara Lempert (Lempertienė), head of the Judaica Division of the National Heritage Research Department of the National Library of Lithuania, for providing the diary of Yitzhak Rudashevski. I am grateful to Sergey Kanovich, Milda Jakulytė-Vasil, and Irina Pocienė of the Lost Shtetl Museum for relevant materials on Šeduva. Laima Vincė helped me present Matilda Okinaitė's fascinating story. Alfredas Rukšėnas assisted with copies of testimonies obtained from Yad Vashem and assisted in collecting statistical data on the victims of the operations of the summer and fall of 1941. Andrius Kulikauskas provided an electronic trove of documents from Lithuanian archives. The helpful staff of the Lithuanian Central State Archive and the Lithuanian Special Archive assisted in my search for records in Vilnius. Vytautas Magnus University of Kaunas (Vytauto Didžiojo universitetas, VDU) generously supported my 2011 undergraduate course there on war and genocide, which gave me a better understanding of how to present difficult themes to a broader audience. Dr. Linas Venclauskas of the VDU History Faculty shared his pioneering work on the evolution of Lithuanian antisemitism.

A generous grant from the Pennsylvania State System of Higher Education supported my research in Lithuania during a sabbatical leave. The Academic

Grants Program of Millersville University of Pennsylvania funded travel to Stockholm for an important conference on collaboration and resistance in the Baltics. The university's history department furnished me with secretarial assistance and travel funds. I am grateful to the Hoover Institution at Stanford University for assisting my visit there and for giving me access to materials from the Edvardas Turauskas Collection. The director of YIVO, Jonathan Brent, kindly invited me to discuss my work with scholars and students in New York. I am also indebted to Ina Navazelskis of the USHMM Oral History Archive who helped me locate some relevant testimonies. Charles Perrin of Kennesaw State University allowed me to read his research on some interesting aspects of antisemitism in the late 1930s. Prof. Mordechai Zalkin of Ben-Gurion University of the Negev was an invaluable advisor on the history of Lithuanian Jewry before the Shoah and kindly corrected some of my misconceptions. Daria Nemtsova, Ekaterina Yanduganova, Stuart Allen, and Alana Felton at Academic Studies Press were very understanding about numerous delays in the writing. Claire Rosenson, the special projects editor for new research at the USHMM, was wonderfully patient when helping me with copyright issues and other problems related to publication. Many thanks to the late Mel Hecker, the publication officer for academic publications at the USHMM Mandel Center, who provided invaluable editorial assistance during the review process.

I should note that one of the few rewards in the process of researching some of the most depraved aspects of human behavior has been the opportunity to engage with younger scholars who have shared their work with me and have been valued partners in examining a difficult past. I owe a debt to Stanislovas Stasiulis, Justas Stončius, Zigmas Vitkus, Aurimas Švedas, and Julija Šukys. I am grateful to my wife, Carol Sperry-Sužiedėlis, who endured my numerous absences and encouraged me to stick with the project. This list of people and institutions would be woefully incomplete without acknowledging a dear friend and advisor: Irena Veisaitė (1928–2021), scholar, teacher, Holocaust survivor, and speaker of inconvenient, but essential, truths. Her experience, wisdom, and moral compass were gifts that motivated and encouraged me to continue writing. Irena's life embodied Vilna and Vilnius in equal measure, and it is to her memory that I dedicate this book.

While I acknowledge the enormous assistance I enjoyed when writing this book, I remain solely responsible for any omissions, inconsistencies, or errors.

Abbreviations

Names and Terms

ap.	L. apyrašas, archival inventory
b.	L. byla, archival file
CPSU	Communist Party of the Soviet Union
EG	G. Einsatzgruppen, Special Action Group
EK	G. Einsatzkommando, Special Action Commando
EU	European Union
f.	L. fondas, archival collection
FPO	Y. Fareynikte Partizaner Organizatzie, United Partisan Organization
G.	German language
Gestapo	G. Geheime Staatspolizei, German Security Police
GK	G. Generalkommissariat, General Commissariat
GBK	G. Gebietskommissariat, District Commissariat (subordinate to GK)
IHC	International Commission for the Evaluation of the Crimes of the Nazi and Soviet Occupation Regimes in Lithuania, also International Historical Commission
KGB	R. Komitet gosudarstvennoi bezopasnosti, Committee for State Security
L.	Lithuanian language
l.	L. lapas, archival page
LAF	Lithuanian Activist Front
LCVA	L. Lietuvos centrinis valstybės archyvas, Lithuanian Central State Archive
LCP	Lithuanian Communist Party
LGGRTC	L. Lietuvos gyventojų genocido ir rezistencijos tyrimų centras, Research Center on the Genocide and Resistance of the People of Lithuania
LMAVB RS	L. Lietuvos mokslų akademijos Vrublevskio bibliotekos Rankraščių skyrius, Lithuanian Academy of Sciences Vrublevskis Library, Manuscript Section
LNP	Lithuanian Nationalist Party
LYA	L. Lietuvos ypatingasis archyvas, Lithuanian Special Archive
NATO	North Atlantic Treaty Organization
NKGB	R. Narodnyi kommissariat gosudarstvennoi bezopasnosti, People's Commissariat of State Security
NKVD	R. Narodnyi kommissariat vnutrennikh del, People's Commissariat of Internal Affairs
NSDAP	G. Nationalsozialistische Deutsche Arbeiterpartei, National Socialist German Workers' Party

P.	Polish language
PG	Provisional Government
R.	Russian language
RAD	G. Reichsarbeitsdienst, Reich Labor Service
RKO	G. Reichskommisssariat Ostland, Reich Commissariat for the Baltic States and Belarus
RSHA	G. Reichssicherheitshauptamt, Main Office of Reich Security
SA	G. Sturmabteilung, Storm Trooper Unit
SD	G. Sicherheitsdienst, Security Service
SS	G. Schutzstaffel, Security Staff
SSR	Soviet Socialist Republic
USSR	Union of Soviet Socialist Republics
VLIK	L. Vyriausias Lietuvos išlaisvinimo komitetas, Supreme Committee for the Liberation of Lithuania
VPMLL	L. Valstybinė politinės ir mokslinės literatūros leidykla, State Publishing House for Political and Scholarly Literature
VSD	L. Valstybės saugumo departamentas, Department of State Security
Y.	Yiddish
YIVO	Y. Yidisher Visnshaftlekher Institut, Institute for Jewish Research
ZV	G. Zivilverwaltung, German Civil Administration

Cities and Towns by Language

Lithuanian	Polish	Russian	German	Yiddish
Alytus	Olita	Olita	Aliten	Alite
Biržai	Birże	Birzhai	Birsen	Birzh
Eišiškės	Ejszyszki	Eishyshki	Eischischken	Eishishok
Jurbarkas	Jurbork	Yurbark	Georgenburg	Yurburg
Kaunas	Kowno	Kovno	Kauen	Kovne
Kėdainiai	Kejdany	Kedaynyay	Gedahnen	Keidan
Klaipėda	Kłaijpeda	Klaipeda	Memel	Memel
Kretinga	Kretynga	Kretinga	Krottingen	Kretinge
Lazdijai	Łoździeje	Lazdiyai	Lasdien	Lazdei
Marijampolė[1]	Mariampol	Maryampol	Mariampol	Mariampol
Mažeikiai	Mażejki	Mazheikyai	Mosscheiken	Mazheik
Panevėžys	Poniewież	Ponevezh	Poniewiesch	Ponevezh

1   1955–1989, Kapsukas.

Lithuanian	Polish	Russian	German	Yiddish
Plungė	Płungiany	Plunge	Plungen	Plungyan
Raseiniai	Rosienie	Rossieny	Raseinen	Rasayn
Rokiškis	Rakiszki	Rokishkis	Rokischken	Raikishok
Šakiai	Szaki	Shakyay	Schaken	Shaki
Šiauliai	Szawle	Shavl	Schaulen	Shavl
Švenčionys	Święcany	Shvenchyany	Schwintzen	Svintsyan
Taurage	Taurogi	Tauragi	Tauroggen	Tovrig
Telšiai	Telsze	Telshyay	Telschen	Telz
Trakai	Troki	Troki	Tracken	Trok
Ukmergė	Wilkomierz	Ukmerge	Ukmerge	Vilkomir
Utena	Uciana	Utyana	Utena	Utyan
Vilkaviškis	Wyłkowiszki	Vilkavishkis	Wilkowischken	Vilkovishk
Vilnius	Wilno	Vilna	Wilna	Vilne
Zarasai[2]	Jeziorosy	Zarasyay[3]	Ossersee	Ezherene

---

2   1919–1929, Ežerėnai.
3   1836–1918, Novoaleksandrovsk.

Part One

BEFORE THE SHOAH

1.

Tradition, Accommodation, Conflict: Jews and Lithuanians from the Grand Duchy to the End of the First Republic

On October 28–29, 1941, nearly 9,200 men, women, and children, about a third of the Jewish population of Kaunas, were marched to the tsarist-era Ninth Fort, where they were massacred by the Nazis and their accomplices. What became known as the Great Action[1] was the violent crest of a nearly three-month wave of mass murder. Historian Algimantas Kasparavičius stresses its importance: "The greatest tragedy of Lithuania's twentieth century occurred not in June 1940 when the nation lost its freedom and statehood, but one year later, when the Holocaust began in Nazi-occupied Lithuania." He reminds Lithuanian readers, for whom the loss of independence is at the center of a painful history, that "after a nation has lost its independence in critical historical circumstances, it is possible to restore statehood under changing and favorable geopolitical conditions. Meanwhile, the community of Lithuania's Jews . . . can never be restored."[2] Many Lithuanians have had difficulty accepting the historic weight of the Shoah, in part because it competes with the Stalinist crimes that preoccupied much of society following the independence movement of the late 1980s. Nevertheless, the country's historians, journalists, and human rights activists have devoted increasing attention to the "vanished world" of Lithuanian Jewry,

---

1   As presented in the Ninth Fort Museum in Kaunas (L. Didžioji akcija).
2   Algimantas Kasparavičius, "Lietuvių politinės iliuzijos: Lietuvos laikinosios vyriausybės 'politika' ir Holokausto pradžia Lietuvoje," Izb.lt, accessed June 30, 2018, http://www.lzb.lt/2017/01/11/lietuviu-politines-iliuzijos-lietuvos-laikinosios-vyriausybes-politika-ir-holokausto-pradzia-lietuvoje-1941-metais/.

including the story of the "lost shtetls."³ This emphasis on the Jewish past is essential, since grasping the enormity of the Holocaust requires knowledge of what was destroyed: the unique world of the Litvaks,⁴ a distinct Jewish society with roots in the Grand Duchy of Lithuania which once included Belarus and parts of Ukraine and which, until the Nazi occupation, constituted one of Lithuania's historic national communities. Litvak cultural and social life evolved during periods of turbulent change from the late medieval period onwards, including tsarist rule (1795–1915), the Great War, and the subsequent revolutionary upheavals that led to the emergence of successor nation-states built on the ruins of the empires of Eastern and Central Europe. Before the Shoah, the region's Jewish lives occupied a continuously changing space filled with promises and perils, as exemplified in the journey of a young poet and her family.

Matilda Olkinaitė (1922–1941): The Unrealized Promise of Litvak Life in the First Republic

In 1987 Alfredas Andrijauskas, a graduate student of German studies, brought Irena Veisaitė, his academic advisor, a frayed notebook of Lithuanian verses from the pen of Matilda Olkinaitė, a young Jewish woman from Panemunėlis, a small community in northeastern Lithuania with a 1940 population of an estimated 550 souls. During the Nazi occupation, Rev. Juozapas Matelionis (1893–1964), the pastor of the town's Catholic parish, had preserved the manuscript by hiding it under the main altar; eventually, it found its way into the hands of Andrijauskas, the church organist. Years later, Dr. Veisaitė, a Holocaust survivor, university professor, literary critic, and co-founder of Lithuania's Open Society Foundation, recalled that Olkinaitė's poetry brought her to tears. Here was a unique relic of modern Litvak culture which, along with its people, had been

---

3   Alvydas Nikžentaitis, Stefan Schreiner, and Darius Staliūnas. eds., *The Vanished World of Lithuanian Jews* (Amsterdam: Rodopi, 2004). See also the reference to the Lost Shtetl Project of the Šeduva Jewish Memorial Fund.

4   The complexities that form Litvak identity are well described in Vladimir Levin and Darius Staliūnas, "*Lite* on the Jewish Mental Maps," in *Spatial Concepts of Lithuania in the Long Nineteenth Century*, ed. Darius Staliūnas (Boston: Academic Studies Press, 2016), 312–370. See also Mordechai Zalkin, "Lithuanian Jewry and the Concept of 'East European Jewry,'" *Polin* 25 (2013): 57–70, which emphasizes the Litvaks' reputation for rationalism, the influence of the Lithuanian environment, and their oft-reported inimical attitudes to Polish Jews.

destroyed in the Holocaust. Veisaitė's search for the poet led to unexpected convergences. Archival records revealed that in 1940, as a student at the University of Vilnius, Olkinaitė had roomed in Veisaitė's apartment building (Matilda's flat was no. 32, the professor was a longtime resident of no. 49). The next discovery: one of Veisaitė's former classmates was a childhood friend of the poet's younger sister. The quest to discover more of Olkinaitė's poetry led the professor to Colonel Eduardas Matulionis (1912–1987), a Soviet army officer who had known the Olkinas family before the war. Unexpectedly, he gave Veisaitė the young woman's diary encased in a tooled leather notebook, complete with its then-fashionable lock and key.[5] The story of the discovery of Olkinaitė's writings is itself a microcosm of Lithuania's conflicted twentieth century. Two Lithuanians sharing a near-identical surname had proved instrumental in uncovering a unique fragment of Jewish culture: one, a veteran of the Communist Party since the 1930s and an officer in the Red Army's Sixteenth Lithuanian Riflemen's Division;[6] the other, a Catholic priest, accused of aiding the postwar anti-Soviet resistance, deported to Siberia in 1951.

In April 1989 Veisaitė published a selection of the poet's verse in the country's premier literary newspaper,[7] but it was only three decades later that Olkinaitė's story achieved wider recognition in Lithuania, in part because of growing interest in Jewish history and the Holocaust but also due to the efforts of the Lithuanian American writer and translator Laima Vincė.[8] In 2018 the American journalist Matthew Shaer followed up Vincė's research and traveled to Panemunėlis to investigate Olkinaitė for part of *Smithsonian* magazine's series "The Unforgotten: New Voices of the Holocaust," which featured recently discovered diarists of the Shoah. Shaer's extensive report focused in large part on the murder of the Olkinas family and Lithuania's subsequent reckoning with the

---

5   Irena Veisaite, "Pajutau, kad ji man—likimo sesuo," *Matilda Olkinaitė, Atrakintas dienoraštis: kūrybos rinktinė*, comp. Mindaugas Kvietkauskas (Vilnius: Lietuvių literatūros ir tautosakos institutas, 2019), 49–53. Readers may wish to consult the English version: *Matilda Olkinaitė, The Unlocked Diary: Collected Works*, trans. Laima Vincė and ed. Mindaugas Kvietkauskas (Vilnius: Institute of Lithuanian Literature and Folklore, 2021).

6   On the Sixteenth Division, see below, Chapter 5.

7   Irena Veisaitė, "Matilda Olkinaitė," *Literatūra ir menas*, April 1, 1989: 8–9.

8   Ann Diamond, "The Translator Who Brought a Lost Jewish Poet's Words to the English-Speaking World," *Smithsonian Magazine*, October 24, 2018, https://www.smithsonianmag.com/arts-ulture/translator-brought-jewish-poet-words-english-speaking-world-180970555/.

past, or as the author put it, society's confrontation with "trenchant questions about wartime collaboration," problems that are prominent in post-Soviet discussions of historic memory and trauma in both academe and the popular press. Some came to see Olkinaitė as "Lithuania's Anne Frank," although the life and death stories of the two young women are markedly different.[9]

Matilda's father was an atypical transplant in the local Jewish community of Olkinaitė's birth. Noachas Olkinas (Noah Olkin, 1891–1941) came of age in a doctor's family in Vilnius, where he finished his schooling and worked at one of the city's apothecaries during the Great War. It is not clear why Noachas moved to Kaunas, where in 1919 he completed his pharmaceutical studies and received a license to practice, although one explanation might be that the constant battles over Vilnius between Polish forces and the Red Army persuaded some Jews that Lithuanian-controlled areas provided a safer haven. In 1920 Noachas arrived in Panemunėlis to open the town's first modern pharmacy and settled there for his remaining years, one of many Jews who had studied medicine while in Russian exile, had returned to Lithuania, and then, faced with a surfeit of medical professionals in Kaunas, moved to the country's smaller towns and villages.[10] Olkinas found the local Jewish population of his adopted community much diminished. In the fall of 1915, the Russian military had forcibly evacuated all two hundred of the township's Jews who joined thousands of other displaced persons during the tsarist army's disastrous retreat. Only twenty-two Jewish families returned to the Panemunėlis rural county (*valsčius*) after the founding of the Lithuanian state: the 1923 census of the republic counted 102 Jews there, less than 2% of the population, most of whom lived in the township.[11]

Noachas and his wife Asna raised four children: Elijah, the oldest (born in 1919), was followed by Matilda (1922) and two more daughters, Mika (1925) and Grunia (1930). By all accounts, Noachas Olkinas was widely respected by

---

9   Matthew Shaer, "The Words of a Young Jewish Poet Provoke Soul Searching in Lithuania," *Smithsonian Magazine*, November 2018, https://www.smithsonianmag.com/history/young-jewish-poet-words-provokes-soul-searching-lithuania-holocaust-180970540/; Laima Vincė, "The Silenced Muse: The Life of a Murdered Jewish Lithuanian Poet," *Deep Baltic: Inside the Lands Between*, May 8, 2018, https://deepbaltic.com/2018/05/08/the-silenced-muse-the-life-of-a-murdered-jewish-lithuanian-poet/.

10 I owe this insight into the social history of Lithuania's Jewish medical practitioners to Prof. Mordechai Zalkin.

11 The *valsčius* was the basic rural administrative unit from the early modern period until 1950 and forms the root of the Lithuanian term for "peasant" (*valstietis*). The township, or literally a "small town" (*miestelis*), was the smallest urban unit of administration.

his Lithuanian and Jewish neighbors: contemporaries remembered that he often refused fees from financially distressed townspeople. The family were native speakers of Yiddish, fluent in Russian and Lithuanian, conversant in Polish and German. The Olkinas children attended Lithuanian-language government schools, a growing practice among secular Jews in the cities, less common in the shtetls. Pastor Matelionis was a frequent guest at the Olkinas house: neighbors recall that, as a token of their friendship, Noachas donated a confessional carved of oak to St. Joseph's Church. In 1939 Matilda ("Matlė" to her classmates and friends) graduated from the secondary school in Rokiškis and, in the fall,

IMAGE 1.1. Clockwise: The Olkinas family in front of their pharmacy in Panemunėlis, undated (Courtesy of Ivaškevičius Family Archive). Thirteen-year-old Matilda Olkinaitė's Kupiškis State Middle School graduation photo, June 1935 (Courtesy of Lithuanian Central State Archive). Students from the J. Tumas Vaižgantas Gymnasium ca. 1939, Matilda seated second from left. (Courtesy of Private Archive of Irena Veisaitė.)

enrolled in the Faculty of Humanities at the University of Kaunas to pursue a degree in French language and literature.[12]

The first entry in Olkinaitė's diary dates from August 15, 1940, but there is evidence of her literary talent well before then. In February 1940, the cultural section of the Lithuanian daily *Lietuvos žinios* (Lithuanian news) published a poem by a seventeen-year-old student, one M. Olkinaitė, titled "Cain and the Abels," a reference to the blood-soaked biblical tale warning of the horrors of mass violence. The paper later published two more of Olkinaitė's poems, one a lyrical poem "The Cerulean Bird," the other "The Word," a short poem expressing antiwar sentiments.[13] Except for her family and friends, most readers of *Lietuvos žinios* knew little or nothing of the author, but back in Panemunėlis and Rokiškis they knew all about their local prodigy. Since the age of nine she had published Lithuanian verse, first in mimeographed school journals, then in national youth magazines. At ten she wrote patriotically about her country ("It's always best in my homeland") and, in another poem, celebrated Lithuania's heroic aviators ("To remember heroes").[14] As she grew older, Olkinaitė's writing progressed from "childish" to mature themes. In 1938, in the spirit of the twentieth anniversary of the First Republic and in praise of the authoritarian president Antanas Smetona (1874–1944), she published the ode "To the Leader of the Nation," that read in part: "We are marching! Take us forward, Leader / Along Lithuania's Path!"[15] In the same year another poem, "Two Mothers," evoked a different spirit, addressing the heartbreak of Japanese and Chinese mothers mourning their sons gone to battle.[16]

After her graduation from Rokiškis secondary school, Olkinaitė thanked her editor of seven years, Stasys Tijūnaitis (1888–1966), a Catholic pedagogue and promoter of youth literature, the man who had encouraged her talent. He was pleased with the end of Matilda's childhood phase and published a farewell

---

12 Mindaugas Kvietkauskas, "Mėlynas Matildos talento paukštis," in *Olkinaitė, Atrakintas*, 16–47.

13 M. Olkinaitė, "Kainas ir Abeliai," *Lietuvos žinios*, February 3, 1940, 5; "Mėlynas paukštis," *Lietuvos žinios*, March 30, 1940, 6; "Žodis," *Lietuvos žinios*, May 11, 1940, 6.

14 M. Olkinaitė, "Tėvynėje geriausia," *Žvaigždutė* 18 (September 15, 1933): 274; also, "Didvyriams paminėti," *Žvaigždutė* 16 (August 15, 1933): 243. The latter poem is dedicated to the celebrated transatlantic New York—Kaunas flight of Stepas Darius and Stasys Girėnas in July 1933, which ended in tragedy just short of their destination.

15 M. Olkinaitė, "Tautos vadui," *Mokslo dienos* 11 (1938): 585.

16 M. Olkinaitė, "Dvi motinos," *Mokslo dienos* 1 (1938): 10.

titled "To M. Olkinaitė in Panemunėlis" in the August 1939 issue of *Kregždutė* (The little swallow), a magazine that nurtured aspiring young poets. He addressed Olkinaitė in formal language: "I am thrilled with Your achievements, graduation from school, how You have grown up and matured. Even though we have never met in person, I feel closely the beating of Your good heart, just as You had acknowledged my own.... I wish You to go forward with the same diligence that You have shown until now, and I pray to heaven for blessings upon You."[17] Within a month Germany invaded Poland and Olkinaitė began her university studies in Kaunas.

We can reconstruct some of Olkinaitė's student life during the last months of independent Lithuania by examining her academic records. In January 1940, the University of Kaunas Faculty of Humanities moved to Vilnius after the city came under Lithuanian rule as a result of the Soviet-Lithuanian mutual assistance pact negotiated the previous October. Olkinaitė was registered on February 2 as a resident in an apartment building occupying today's 16 Basanavičius Street, an address popular with Jewish tenants and well-known to historians of Litvak culture. Simon Dubnow (1860–1941), the renowned historian and promoter of Jewish cultural autonomy, had lived there in the late 1920s. The first office of YIVO, the Jewish Scientific Institute, was located at this very site in the apartment of the institute's co-founder, philologist Max Weinreich (1894–1969). The Vilnius-born French novelist Romain Gary (1914–1980) spent his childhood years in the apartment complex's large courtyard (today: Basanavičius 18) which he described in his 1960 autobiographical novel *Promise at Dawn*. Olkinaitė later moved to a house across from the city's main synagogue, where she rented rooms with her brother, Elijah, and his fiancée, Liza Abramson.

Olkinaitė's professors included the country's foremost literati, Vincas Krėvė-Mickevičius (1882–1954) and Vincas Mykolaitis-Putinas (1893–1967). Fellow classmates later made their mark as acclaimed poets, among them Vytautas Mačernis (1921–1944) and Alfonsas Nyka-Niliūnas (1919–2015). In addition to her classes in French, she now took up Slavic studies. It was during her Vilnius period that Olkinaitė published in the national daily *Lietuvos žinios*. We know that she was an avid participant in student literary circles and that her readings were warmly received.[18] She hoped to publish a book of poetry. In

---

17   Stasys Tijūnaitis, "M. Olkinaitei Panemunėlyje," *Kregždutė* 8 (1939): 2.
18   Diary entry from November 17, 1940, in *Olkinaitė* (diary entries are not paginated).

March 1940 Olkinaitė wrote one of her few poems dedicated to Jewish themes ("The Jewish Lullaby").[19] Her student days were also complicated by a love affair with a young man, Arūnas, whose name appears but once in her diary, even though she recorded many of her inner struggles.[20]

Judging by what interested correspondents at *Smithsonian*, it seems that to the world outside Lithuania, Olkinaitė's death mattered more than her life. In some sense, this is understandable: a young Jewish woman's journey as a literary talent, working in her society's dominant language, would not in itself be a notable achievement in any Western European country or in the United States. Perhaps, hers was simply a normal life of promise. The imprint of the Holocaust conceals much of the history that enveloped her family, particularly the radical changes in Litvak society that followed World War I and presented a web of adjustments, possibilities, and dangers. Nothing in the centuries-long arc of Litvak history pointed to the existence of the cultural marvel that was Matilda Olkinaitė. The lived experience of this pharmacist's daughter from Panemunėlis would have perplexed her grandparents. But this is obvious only if we examine, however briefly, the history of Lithuania's Jews.

The Litvaks under the Grand Dukes and Tsars

By the mid-eighteenth century, the Ashkenazi settlements of the Polish-Lithuanian Commonwealth constituted the largest Jewish diaspora in the world, a culture rooted in the Yiddish language and adherence to religious practices that had developed over centuries.[21] The influx of Jews into Poland and Lithuania resulted in large part from the deteriorating situation in Western and Central Europe: expulsion from England (1290); the Black Death and numerous massacres during the Crusades; the persecution of the Jewish community in Spain; and evictions from Austria and Silesia. There were some Jews among the merchants and artisans who arrived during the reign of Grand Duke Gediminas (ruled ca. 1316–1341), the ruler who expanded the Lithuanian state and founded the Jagiellonian dynasty that ruled over much of Central and Eastern

---

19 "Žydiška lopšinė," in *Olkinaitė*, 274.
20 See below, Chapter 2.
21 Antony Polonsky, *The Jews in Poland and Russia*, vol. 1, *1350–1881* (Oxford: The Littman Library of Jewish Civilization, 2010), 9–11.

Europe until 1572. There is evidence of Jewish communities in Grodno, Lutsk, Vladimir (Volhynia), Brest, and Trakai by the end of the fourteenth century (only the latter settlement was located within the current Lithuanian borders). The charters granted by Grand Duke Vytautas to the Jews of Brest and Grodno in 1388–1389 formed the legal foundation for the state's Jewish communities.[22] The Lithuanian rulers granted Jews extensive economic rights, protected the autonomy of Jewish religious and communal institutions, and forbade Gentiles from engaging in the blood libel (the accusation that Jews used Christian blood in religious rituals). In 1495 Grand Duke Alexander I expelled Jews from Lithuania, but the exile was short-lived, and in 1507 Sigismund I reconfirmed the rights Jews had previously enjoyed,[23] which were incorporated into the Lithuanian Statute in 1529. The third version of the statute promulgated in 1588 remained in force until 1840.

By the mid-sixteenth century an estimated ten thousand Jews lived in the Grand Duchy of Lithuania in fifteen autonomous communities, the majority in what are today Ukraine and Belarus.[24] In 1598 King of Poland and Grand Duke of Lithuania Sigismund Vasa granted Jews permission to reside in Vilnius, a city that attracted ever more Jewish migrants and ultimately gained fame as the "Jerusalem of Eastern Europe." Jews suffered grievously during the uprising of the Cossack chieftain Bohdan Khmelnytski (Chmelnicki) and the subsequent Muscovite invasions which brought to Lithuania a decade (1648–1658) of unprecedented destruction. The plague of 1709–1711 and the Great Northern War (1700–1721) killed nearly a third of the grand duchy's inhabitants, but during the second half of the eighteenth century the economy recovered and population growth resumed. Jewish newcomers settled in towns and villages that had been devastated, eventually outnumbering the Germans, Poles, and Scots who had previously made up most of the region's ethnically non-Lithuanian urban

---

22 As prince, Vytautas was de facto ruler of Lithuania even before the period of his formal reign (1392–1430). A recent study of the Brest privileges is Jurgita Šiaučiūnaitė-Verbickienė, "Vytauto Didžiojo 1388m. privilegija Brastos žydams. Nauji atsakymai į atsakytus klausimus," *Lietuvos istorijos metraštis* 2 (2021): 5–25.

23 Polonsky, The Jews in Poland and Russia, 42–44. More details are in Solomonas Atamukas, *Lietuvos žydų kelias nuo XIV a. iki XXI a. pradžios* (Vilnius: Alma littera, 2007), 23ff.

24 See Jurgita Šiaučiūnaitė-Verbickienė, "The Jewish Living Space in the Grand Duchy of Lithuania: Tendencies and Ways of Its Formation," in *Jewish Space in Central and Eastern Europe*, ed. Larisa Lempertienė and Jurgita Šiaučiūnaitė-Verbickienė (Newcastle: Cambridge Scholars Publishing, 2007), 7–26.

MAP 1. The Polish-Lithuanian Commonwealth
after the Union of Lublin (1569) (Saulius Sužiedėlis, *Historical Dictionary
of Lithuania*, 2nd ed. [Lanham, Md: Scarecrow Press, 2011].)

demographic.[25] The Polish-Lithuanian Commonwealth's 1764–1765 census estimated the number of Jews at 750,000, of whom nearly two hundred thousand lived in the grand duchy. Many Jewish households engaged in the alcohol trade, primarily as renters on landed estates, but the business declined drastically with the introduction of the Russian state liquor monopoly in 1896.[26]

---

25 See Atamukas, *Lietuvos žydų kelias*, 34–35.
26 Vladimir Levin, "Socialiniai, ekonominiai, demografiniai bei geografiniai žydų bendruomenės Lietuvoje bruožai," in *Lietuvos žydai: istorinė studija*, ed. Vladas Sirutavičius, Darius Staliūnas, and Jurgita Šiaučiūnaitė-Verbickienė (Vilnius: baltos lankos, 2012), 153, 160, 165.

The grand duchy's statutes governing Jewish life addressed five principal areas: the authority of municipalities over Jewish life; economic protections; assurances of security; religious rights; and legal proceedings involving Christian subjects. The basic unit of Jewish self-government was the *kehilah*, the local community, which was governed by a committee (*kahal*) headed by a chairman (*parnas*). Archival sources provide considerable information on the Jewish administration of religious, social, and economic activities in Vilnius, such as relief for the poor; the maintenance of synagogues, cemeteries, communal property, and the water system; support for education; and supplying flour for matzahs during Passover.[27] The local communities also elected representatives to provincial and state councils. In 1623 King Sigismund III Vasa convened the Jewish Council of Lithuania (Vaad Medinat Lite). The major responsibility of the Jewish councils was to apportion the poll tax among the various communities, but their writ soon expanded to include judicial, religious, and commercial matters, as well as arbitration among the kehilah.[28]

The tradition of autonomy was one of the most important developments in the history of East European Jewry, aptly summarized by Antony Polonsky:

> [Self-government] gave the Jews a sense of rootedness. . . . [I]n those places where some modernized form of Jewish self-government was retained, the transformation of the Jews from a religious and cultural community linked by a common faith into citizens or subjects of the countries where they lived was most successful. Similarly, the communal self-government which was exercised by the *kehillah*, for all its imperfections, is one important element in the democratic tradition of the State of Israel. In this sense, the legacy of Jewish self-government was one of the most fundamental legacies of the Jewish experience in Poland-Lithuania.[29]

In view of the protections granted to the state's Jewish, Muslim, and Karaim subjects, Lithuanians have at times been tempted to idealize the grand duchy as a society of tolerance, a peaceable "assembly of nations," perhaps even a historic bridge to the later process of European integration. The remarkable mosaic of cultures in premodern Vilnius should not, however, be confused with

---

27 See Polonsky, *The Jews in Poland and Russia*, 49–50.
28 Jurgita Šiaučiūnaitė-Verbickienė, "The Jews," in *The Peoples of the Grand Duchy of Lithuania*, ed. Grigorijus Potašenko (Vilnius: aidai, 2002), 57–68.
29 Polonsky, *The Jews in Poland and Russia*, 67.

twenty-first-century notions of multiculturalism. Historically, the concepts of nation (a community, a *Volk*) and state (a political entity) in Central and Eastern Europe, a region where the borders of national communities and states did not much overlap until well into the twentieth century, have differed from the way these ideas are understood in Western Europe and the United States.[30] In historic Vilnius, religious affiliation, closely linked to language and ethnicity, constituted the markers of what passed for national identity: Catholics (Poles and Lithuanians); Protestants (Germans); Orthodox and Uniate (East Slavs); Muslims (Tatars); and followers of Judaism (Jews and Karaim). This "city of strangers" encompassed a world of ritualized coexistence based on custom and civic codes developed over generations. Recent studies of Vilnius society during the seventeenth and eighteenth centuries make clear that litigation, economic conflicts, and even rioting between the confessions were not uncommon. But Lithuania avoided the horrendous European religious wars which followed the Reformation, even as discrimination against the state's non-Catholic subjects increased under the reign of the Vasa monarchs (1587–1668).[31]

The Partitions of the Polish-Lithuanian Commonwealth (1772–1795) carried out by Austria, Prussia, and Russia annihilated what had been the largest polity in East Central Europe. The tsars seized the lion's share of the loot, expanding their western border to the heart of the continent, and in the process transformed the demographic structure of their empire. Russia now contained millions of Catholics (Poles, Lithuanians, Belarusians, Uniates), Protestants (Baltic Germans, Latvians, Estonians), and Jews. Many of these new subjects, particularly the Polish-Lithuanian gentry, never reconciled themselves to Russian rule, even though the imperial government initially left much of the old economic and social order intact.

During the long tsarist century (1795–1915) the Litvak population increased nearly six-fold. The 1897 imperial census reported about one and one-half million Jewish inhabitants in the lands of the former grand duchy. Approximately one-third of the Litvaks lived in the gubernias of Vilnius (Vilna), Suwałki

---

30 In Britain and the United States commentators tend to use the terms "nation," "country," and "state" interchangeably which can cause confusion to citizens of political entities such as the former USSR and Yugoslavia who saw themselves as members of historic *nations* within a *state* structure.

31 See Laimonas Briedis, *Vilnius: City of Strangers* (Vilnius: baltos lankos, 2009) and David Frick, *Kith, Kin & Neighbors: Communities and Confessions in Seventeenth-Century Wilno* (Ithaca: Cornell University Press, 2013).

MAP 2. Under the Tsars: The Lithuanian governorates (gubernias) and districts (uyezds) in the Russian Empire 1867–1914. Public domain.

1. Tradition, Accommodation, Conflict | 15

MAP 3. The Pale of Settlement in the nineteenth century. (Note: Congress Poland, including the Suwałki gubernia, was not included in the Pale.)
Public domain.

(Suvalki), and Kaunas (Kovno), with nearly 370,000 residing within what are now the borders of the Republic of Lithuania.[32] All told, as many as 5,250,000 Jews were subjects of the Russian Empire on the eve of the Great War. Linguistically, Lithuanian Jews were a homogenous group: 98–99% reported Yiddish as their mother tongue. According to the 1897 imperial census, Jews comprised 13.8% of the population (212,666 persons) in Kaunas gubernia, of whom only 168 reported Lithuanian as their first language.

Jews were restricted, with some exceptions, to the infamous Pale of Settlement which Catherine the Great established in 1791, a territory whose eastern limits corresponded roughly to the current internationally recognized western border of the Russian Federation. To be sure, the Pale was an onerous badge of discrimination, but restricting Jews to lands which they had inhabited for centuries had less of an impact on the life of Litvaks than the Russian policies that aimed to transform Jews into "useful subjects." Most tsarist bureaucrats believed that Jewish society consisted of parasites who disdained the backbreaking labor of the peasants and manipulated the greedy instincts of the gentry. Initially, however, the imperial authorities did not substantially alter the system of communal autonomy, since they needed the institution to collect taxes and maintain order. Tsar Alexander I (1801–1825) proposed numerous reforms, such as limitations on traditional dress, intended, at least, to partially integrate Jews into Russian society, but most of these measures proved difficult to implement.

Over time, however, Russian rule considerably undermined the legal structures, communal governance, and cultural/religious practices that defined traditional Litvak society. The empire's Jews regarded the reign of the reactionary Nicholas I (1825–1855) as one of the darkest periods of their history. The tsar's most brutal policy was the imposition in 1827 of military conscription on Jewish communities requiring the delivery of so-called "recruits." As most of these inductees for the mandated twenty-five-year service in the Russian army were minors, some as young as twelve, families understandably saw conscription as a life sentence. Jewish communal leaders and rabbis often aggravated social tensions by selecting the victims from the poorest, most vulnerable strata.[33] Nicholas promulgated further decrees intended to "modernize" Jewish life

---

32 Levin, "Socialiniai," 163.

33 For more on social tensions within the Jewish community during this period, see Dawid Fajnhauz, "Konflikty społeczne wśród ludności żydowskiej na Litwie i Białorusi w pierwszej połowie XIX wieku," *Biuletyn Żydowskiego Instytutu Historycznego* 52 (1964): 3–15.

by formally abolishing the kehilah in 1844, although a limited form of Jewish self-government continued in religious and economic matters within a somewhat contradictory legal context. The tsar also prohibited distinctive Jewish dress. Nicholas's harsh provisions were never fully realized, but his policies did much to undermine the authority of Jewish leaders.

Sergei Uvarov (1786–1855), the deputy minister of education and the author of the reactionary doctrine of Official Nationality,[34] sought to transform Jews into "useful subjects of the Fatherland." In an 1840 letter to the superintendent of schools in Belarus, the administration of the Vilnius gubernia communicated the spirit of Uvarov's pedagogical purpose: "to correct Jewish morality and eliminate their fanatical hatred of Christianity . . . thus bringing them closer to the other inhabitants . . . , and to completely uproot the harm which the Jews present to the majority population."[35] On the other hand, the processes of modernization of Jewish education in Lithuania had begun already as early as the beginning of the nineteenth century, and the increase in the numbers of modern Jewish schools indicates that a significant part of society did not view the changes as destructive.[36]

Initially, the reign of the reform-minded Alexander II (1855–1881) promised some reprieve. In 1865 the wealthy Litvak merchant David Luria, the founder of the first modern Jewish school in Minsk, published an ode to Tsar Alexander, exulting that "Israel rejoices at the genius of its king."[37] While such praise of the rulers of states was not uncommon throughout Jewish history, Alexander's government did abolish certain restrictions on Jewish economic activities, which allowed wealthier Jews, particularly graduates of universities,

---

34 The doctrine rested on the three pillars of orthodoxy, autocracy, and nationality as the unifying ideology of the Russian Empire.

35 Cited in Aušra Pažėraitė, "Žydų kultūrinių ir politinių orientyrų pokyčiai Aleksandro II laikais," in *Žydų klausimas Lietuvoje XIX a. viduryje*, ed. Vladas Sirutavičius and Darius Staliūnas (Vilnius: LII, 2004), 54–55, 62; also, on the conflicts within the Jewish community regarding education, see Aušrelė Kristina Pažėraitė, "Išsaugoti savastį ar supanašėti? Žydų mokyklų reformos Lietuvoje Nikalojaus laikais," *Darbai ir dienos* 34 (2003): 235–253.

36 For this latter perspective, see Eliana Adler, *In Her Hands: The Education of Jewish Girls in Tsarist Russia* (Detroit: Wayne State University Press, 2011) and Mordechai Zalkin, *Modernizing Jewish Education in Nineteenth-Century Eastern Europe: The School as the Shrine of Jewish Enlightenment*, Studies in Jewish History and Culture 50 (Leiden: Brill, 2016). Also, see Michael Stanislawski, *Tsar Nicholas I and the Jews: The Transformation of Jewish Society in Russia 1825–1855* (Philadelphia: The Jewish Publication Society of America, 1983).

37 As quoted in Pažėraitė, "Žydų kultūrinių," 53.

retired soldiers, and certain craftsmen to live and work in Russia proper. Yet life for most Jews confined to the Pale worsened, partly as the result of the economic impact of the abolition of serfdom and growing anti-Judaism both in government circles and among the populace, stimulated by lurid ritual murder accusations and reports of Jews among the terrorists who assassinated the emperor on March 13, 1881. The accession of the reactionary Alexander III (1881–1894) was accompanied by a wave of pogroms. The ultraconservative chief procurator of the Holy Synod, Konstantin Pobedonostsev (1827–1907), was the main architect of the so-called "May Laws" which restricted Jewish settlement in rural areas. Russia's last Romanov ruler, Nicholas II (1894–1917), reaffirmed his predecessor's antisemitic policies.

Within the Pale of Settlement, the situation of the Jews in the Lithuanian lands was somewhat different. Here, until the early 1900s mass violence against Jews was virtually unheard of and agricultural Jewish settlements were still relatively widespread. Southwestern Lithuania, the so-called Trans-Niemen region (Užnemunė or Suvalkija in Lithuanian, Suwałszczyzna in Polish) enjoyed a special status within the empire. This territory of the ethnically Lithuanian lands had been part of the Duchy of Warsaw (1807–1815) established by Napoleon and was then included in the semi-autonomous Kingdom of Poland (1815–1867) under the Russian crown. The Emancipation Act proclaimed by the kingdom in 1862 meant that the process of Jewish integration there differed from that in the rest of the tsarist empire.[38]

The Polish-Lithuanian insurrections of 1831 and 1863–1864 against tsarist rule placed Jews in a quandary: a minority supported the rebels, especially during the second outbreak, while others preferred Russian law and order. In a disturbing portent of future twentieth-century scapegoating, Jews suffered physical attacks at the hands of insurgents who accused them of spying for the Russian forces, particularly during the uprising of 1831, as recounted in the sources mined by historian Augustinas Janulaitis. Some of the gentry used the opportunity to rid themselves of troublesome Jewish renters and competitors in the alcohol trade and to turn any potential social unrest directed against the upper classes onto the Jews.[39] Through it all, many Jews took the sensible view that "Russia is the father and Poland is the mother. When [the parents—S. S.]

---

38 Polonsky, *The Jews in Poland and Russia*, 315.
39 Augustinas Janulaitis, *Žydai Lietuvoje: bruožai iš Lietuvos visuomenės istorijos XIV–XIX amž.* (Kaunas: A. Janulaitis, 1923), 136–144, 168–169.

fight, children must stay out of their quarrel."⁴⁰ What was missing in this piece of folk wisdom was any mention of Lithuanians.

The spiritual and cultural life of the Jewish community underwent extensive change during the late grand duchy and tsarist periods. At the end of the eighteenth century, the Hasidic movement began spreading rapidly throughout Eastern Europe, posing a challenge to rabbinical authority. The resistance against Hasidism was particularly strong in Lithuania where opponents of the movement (known as the mitnagedim/misnagdim) cited the works of Elijah ben Solomon Zalman (1720–1797), the famous Vilna gaon, who inspired a rational and scholarly approach to the study of the Talmud and Old Testament. The gaon issued a formal excommunication of the Hasidim in 1781 and, after his death, Chaim ben Isaac (Yitzhak) (1749–1821) continued the critique of Hasidism, albeit in a less militant spirit, and founded the Volozhin Yeshiva which revolutionized the study of the Torah. Volozhin became the model for higher Jewish religious education in Lithuania and was a forerunner of the yeshivas of Mir, Eišiškės, Baranavichy, Panevėžys, Slabada/Slobodka (L. Vilijampolė), and Telšiai, which were to achieve worldwide renown.⁴¹

By the end of the nineteenth century several major branches came to represent the Orthodox/Conservative strand of Judaism in Lithuania, including the relatively small Hasidic communities, adherents of the Mitnagedim legacy of the Gaon, and the Mussar movement founded by Israel Lipkin Salanter (1810–1883) who hailed from the town of Žagarė. During his decade-long stay in Kaunas (1847–1857), Salanter established a comprehensive program of study stressing ethical precepts (musar) as a path towards perfection. After Salanter left for Prussia, his followers established themselves in the Slabada yeshiva and recruited hundreds of new adherents to their teacher's methods of study in Telšiai, Kelmė, and other Lithuanian towns. They sought to both counter the influence of the Haskalah movement and reinvigorate religious studies which had become, in their view, stagnant and devoid of spiritual/ethical meaning.⁴² The renowned Kaunas-born French philosopher Emmanuel

---

40 As quoted in Atamukas, *Lietuvos žydų kelias*, 61.
41 Marcinas Vodzinskis, "Chasidai ir mitnagedai," in *Žydai Lietuvoje: Istorija. Kultūra. Paveldas*, comp. Larisa Lempertienė and Jurgita Šiaučiūnaitė-Verbickienė (Vilnius: R. Paknio leidykla, 2009), 123.
42 Aušra Pažėraitė, "Musaro sąjūdis," in Lempertienė and Šiaučiūnaitė-Verbickienė, *Žydai Lietuvoje*, 125-129. See also Immanuel Etkes, *Rabbi Israel Salanter and the Musar Movement: Seeking the Torah of Truth*, trans. Jonathan Chipman (Philadelphia: Jewish Publication Society, 1993).

Levinas (1906–1995) acknowledged the influence of the teachings of Chaim of Volozhin and Salanter on his intellectual development.[43] However, the Mussar movement encountered fierce rabbinical opposition and had limited influence.

The greatest challenge to Orthodox Judaism in Europe came from the Haskalah, the modern Jewish Enlightenment propagated by early thinkers like Moses Mendelsohn (1729–1786), who advocated Jewish participation in the cultural life of host nations. The secular elite of urban Polish Jewry came to describe themselves as "Poles of the Mosaic faith." The Jewish community in Vilnius played a key role in the processes of enlightenment and modernization of Jewish society in Lithuania and in Eastern Europe long before the banker Joseph Ginzberg established the Society for the Dissemination of the Enlightenment among Russian Jews in 1863. Inasmuch as this group urged closer ties to the Gentile cultural environment, the tendency was towards a Russian orientation. An extreme but rare example was Uri Tsvi Kovner, who left his native Vilnius for Odesa, abandoned Hebrew-language works, and devoted himself entirely to Russian literature. Most Jews rejected assimilation and channeled their efforts into maintaining a Jewish identity. For example, Peretz Smolenskin (1842–1885), a Litvak from Belarus active in Odesa and Vienna, rejected both the "superstitions" of rabbinical Orthodoxy and Hasidism as well as the appeal of Russification. Historian Michael Casper notes: "At a time of rapid Russification of Jewish communities in other parts of the Russian Empire, Lithuania emerged as a center of Yiddishism and Hebraism."[44]

The Vilnius-born poet and journalist Judah Leib Gordon (1830–1892) famously described the Haskalah program in one of his poems as the notion of "being a Jew at home and a man in the streets." In Lithuania, the Hebrew-language weekly *Hakarmel*, edited by Samuel Joseph Finn, encouraged the movement.[45] The Lithuanian Haskalah fostered the literary use of the Hebrew language, which the Vilnius poet A. D. B. Lebenson (pen

---

43 Pažėraitė, "Žydų kultūrinių," 83–84.

44 Michael Casper, "Strangers and Sojourners: The Politics of Jewish Belonging in Lithuania, 1914-1940" (PhD diss., University of California, Los Angeles, 2019), 9.

45 For an overview see Atamukas, *Lietuvos žydų kelias*, 84–87 and Marcinas Vodzinskis, "Socialinis ir kultūrinis bendruomenės modernėjimas," in Lempertienė and Šiaučiūnaitė-Verbickienė, *Žydai Lietuvoje*, 131–133. On the battles between the traditionalists and Haskalah supporters see Mordechai Zalkin, "Tarp Haskalos ir tradicionalizmo," in Sirutavičius, Staliūnas, and Šiaučiūnaitė-Verbickienė, *Lietuvos žydai: istorinė studija*, 205–217.

name: Adam Hakohen) described as the "beautiful celestial idiom" and "God's first language." The Kaunas writer Abraham Mapu's historical novel *Ahavat tsion* (The Love of Zion), published in Vilnius in 1853, became hugely popular in the Russian Empire and beyond.[46] The Lithuanian maskilim aroused bitter opposition from traditionalist rabbinical circles, notably in the person of Jacob Halevi Lifshitz, a melamed from Kėdainiai, who moved to Kaunas in 1870 and became the assistant of the renowned Talmudist and chief rabbi of the city, Yitzchak Elchanan Spektor (1817–1896). Lifshitz published numerous attacks against the perceived implacable enemies of Judaism: the Haskalah, Zionism, and all forms of secularism.

No amount of clerical resistance, however, could halt the arrival of new political ideologies. The newspaper *HaMaggid*, published in East Prussia to avoid Russian censorship, was the first significant indication of Zionist influence in Lithuania. The editors, Eliezer Lipman Silverman (1819–1882), who grew up in Kretinga, and David Gordon (1831–1886), who was born in Pamėrkiai, turned their periodical into the most important platform for public discussion of Zionism. Gordon was also one of the leaders of the Hibbat Zion movement which was founded in the early 1880s. Moshe Leib Lilienblum (1843–1910), from Kėdainiai, published an article advocating a "Jewish rebirth in the land of their forefathers." Isaac Leib Goldberg (1860–1935), from Šakiai, and Samuel Jacob Rabinovich (1857–1921), a prominent Talmudic scholar from Panevėžys, were among the Lithuanian Jews represented at the First Zionist Congress in Basel in 1897. In 1902 the Religious Zionist movement HaMizrachi was founded in Vilnius. August 16, 1903, Theodore Herzl, the founder of the movement, addressed a crowd of thousands in Vilnius, an event he described as "unforgettable" in his diary.[47] According to historian David E. Fishman, the land of the Litvaks "became both the birthplace and center of the two branches, religious and socialist, of the Zionist movement."[48] In January 1905 Vilnius hosted a conference of Russia's Zionist activists. The weekly *Haolam* (The World),

---

46 For more on the literature of the period, see Larisa Lempertienė, "Žydų spauda ir literatūra," in Sirutavičius, Staliūnas, and Šiaučiūnaitė-Verbickienė, *Lietuvos žydai: istorinė studija*, 219.

47 Quoted in Atamukas, *Lietuvos žydų kelias*, 94.

48 As quoted in his article "Nuo štadlanų iki masinių partijų: žydų politiniai judėjimai Lietuvoje," in Sirutavičius, Staliūnas, and Šiaučiūnaitė-Verbickienė, *Lietuvos žydai: istorinė studija*, 260.

the organ of the World Zionist Organization, was published there from 1907 until 1912.

Lithuania was also the birthplace of the General Jewish Workers' Union (Yiddish: Algemayner Yidisher Arbeter Bund), established in Vilnius in the same year as the Zionist Congress. The Bund published the Yiddish-language *Di Arbeter Shtime* (Voice of the Workers) and in 1898 joined the Russian Social Democratic Worker's Party (RSDWP) as an autonomous organization led by Litvak socialists, such as Arkadi Kremer (1865–1935), from Švenčionys, and Vilnius-born Mikhail Goldman-Liber (1880–1937). During its first decade, the Bund constituted the largest and most effective revolutionary socialist movement in the tsarist empire. However, at the second RSDWP Congress in Brussels and London in 1903, Lenin engineered their expulsion, accusing them of nationalism and rejecting their claim to be leaders of the Jewish proletariat. Some members of the Bund joined the Bolshevik wing of the RSDWP, but the majority gravitated towards the Menshevik faction of Russian Marxists and continued to act as an autonomous body. The Bund movement promoted Yiddish as the preferred medium within the Jewish community, a practice that encouraged Jewish national identity, even as many Bundists criticized Zionism as a bourgeois nationalist ideology.

The Bund socialists were not entirely averse to a largely secular current of Eastern European Jewry known as Jewish autonomism. The recognized ideologue of the movement, the Belarusian-born historian Simon Dubnow (1860–1941), was the father-in-law of noted Bundist leader Henryk Ehrlich (1882–1942) and was well acquainted with the situation in Lithuania from the time spent in Vilnius and Kaunas. Dubnow was skeptical of the prospects for a Jewish state in Palestine but also opposed assimilation, favoring in its stead the preservation of Jewish cultural life within the Eastern and Central European diaspora. Dubnow perished in the Holocaust, as did his vision of a modern Jewish community coexisting with the other European nations.

Litvaks and Their Neighbors before the Great War

Modernization and the social upheavals of the late imperial period disrupted once familiar patterns of social interaction among Russia's nations. Until the mid-nineteenth century most of Lithuania's tsarist subjects lived within a predominantly agrarian world which was home to social and ethno-religious groups whose mutual relations were regulated by laws, customs, and norms

1. Tradition, Accommodation, Conflict | 23

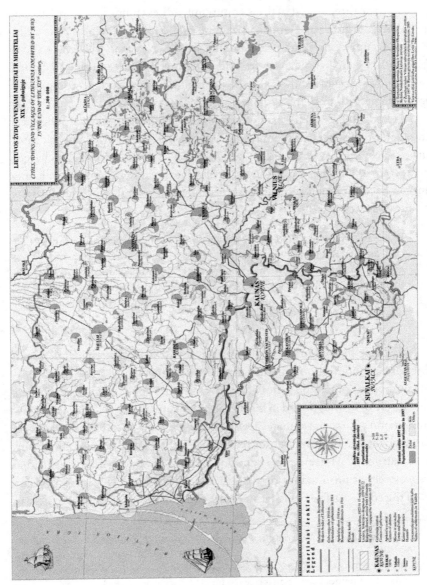

MAP 4. Lithuanian cities and towns with substantial or majority Litvak populations in 1897. (Courtesy of IHC.)

developed over the centuries.⁴⁹ The Polonized landowners and townspeople, the Lithuanian- and Belarusian-speaking peasants and petty gentry, and Litvaks constituted the three largest of these communities. Less numerous were Russian Old Believers, Lutheran Germans, Karaim, and Muslim Tatars. Historically, the Jews occupied a unique place among the other estates: viewed as social inferiors, they were beholden to the landed aristocracy but, as a rule, occupied an economic space above the villagers, many of whom performed compulsory labor for their lords until the abolition of serfdom in the 1860s.

Jews constituted a vital part of economic life, despite the vast religious/cultural gulf that separated them from Christian society. In 1778 English tutor William Coxe journeyed through Lithuania as part of his aristocratic charge's Grand Tour of Europe. Coxe was struck by how the region's Jews not only managed necessary mercantile and travel arrangements but contributed to the agricultural sector as well:

> If you ask for an interpreter, they bring you a Jew; if you come to an inn, the landlord is a Jew, if you want post-horses, a Jew procures them and a Jew drives them; if you wish to purchase, a Jew is your agent: and this is the only country in Europe where Jews cultivate the ground: in passing through Lithuania, we frequently saw them engaged in sowing, reaping, mowing, and other works of husbandry.⁵⁰

Tsarist rule pushed many rural Jews into the towns where they functioned in the rural economy as middlemen, small-time moneylenders, and artisans, as well as providers of mundane but essential consumer goods to Gentile villagers (matches are often mentioned in the memoirs and literature). According to nineteenth-century Russian estimates Jews constituted more than 90% of traders in Kaunas gubernia. The 1897 census reported less than 8% of ethnic Lithuanians in that category.⁵¹ However, the common perception among Lithuanians that Jews were either unsuited for or avoided agricultural labor is incorrect: nearly 10% of the country's Jews were farmers at the turn of the century. While Russian

---

49 See Zygmunt Bauman, *Modernity and the Holocaust* (Ithaca, NY: Cornell University Press, 1992), 35–37.

50 As quoted in Briedis, *Vilnius: City of Strangers*, 69. For more on Jewish relations with the Gentile communities before tsarist rule see Jurgita Šiaučiūnaitė-Verbickienė, *Žydai Lietuvos Didžiosios Kunigaikštystės visuomenėje: sambūvio aspektai* (Vilnius: Žara, 2009).

51 See Aelita Ambralevičiūtė, "Economic Relations between Jewish Traders and Christian Farmers in the Nineteenth-Century Lithuanian Provinces," *Polin* 25 (2013): 71–91.

authorities discouraged Jews from living in Gentile villages, they were not averse to Jews tilling the land separately or in their own rural settlements.[52]

The symbiotic, but also conflicting, interactions between Jews and peasants at times played out in quasi-ritualistic fashion, depicted by a traveler in this colorful 1857 account of a confrontation at a market toll barricade in southwestern Lithuania:

> [A] loaded wagon is flying at great speed toward the town in the hope of avoiding the roadblock and the required market levy. At this very moment, a war-like command reverberates: "Halt!"—in an instant, the wagon is stopped. The Lithuanian [driver], caught in a reckless deed, scratches his head, then pleads that he has nothing with which to pay, that he has barely enough money for the market. He climbs down from the wagon, a whip in his hand, bargaining with the unyielding lookouts. Sometimes, he even refuses to obey, woe then to the impudent! A dozen Jews cluster around him, while the Lithuanian staves them off as best he can with his riding crop—a little Jewish fellow, kneading the peasant constantly with his knees and mussing his hair, keeps crying: "Pay! Pay!" The Lithuanian ... seeks to lift his arms to beat off the unwelcome "guest," when a new rattle of arriving wagons and a dozen fists under his nose, or, on occasion, even a shove, applied from a careful distance, deflects his attention from his ruffled head. Willy-nilly, he reaches into his breast pocket and pulls out a small bag. . . . Confused and unable to quickly regain his composure, the peasant finally pays the few cents (*groszy*) with great difficulty. Turning away, he puts back his bag and wants to finally rid himself of the little nuisance fastened on him, but the little Jewish fellow isn't stupid—with one leap he is already several steps away from the peasant, and is hanging onto another Lithuanian, reaching for the latter's head. There's just nothing to be done; one must drive on. The peasant settles into his wagon, spurs on his horses, all the while shaking his head in dissatisfaction. However, once he arrives in the town square and looks around at the many white peasant overcoats and hears the greeting: *Sveikas, drūtas* [Lithuanian: Hello and good health!] ..., a smile returns to his face. He greets his brothers happily and forgets about his tousled hair.[53]

---

52 On the occupations of rural Jews in Lithuania, see Hirsz Abramowicz, *Profiles of a Lost World: Memoirs of East European Jewish Life before World War II*, trans. Eva Zeitlin Dobkin, ed. Dina Abramowicz and Jeffrey Shandler (Detroit: Wayne State University Press, 1999), 41–58; cf. Rūta Binkytė, Milda Jakulytė-Vasil, and Giedrius Jakubauskas, "The Jewish Village of Degsnė: A Case Study," in Lempertienė and Šiaučiūnaitė-Verbickienė, *Jewish Space*, 185–193.

53 "Korespondencya Gazety Warszawskiéj. Sejny," *Gazeta Warszawska* 206 (August 8, 1857), 4.

A more spiteful depiction of a toll collector, replete with resentment against townsfolk, was published in a textbook for Lithuanian students learning Polish: "the ugly Jew was searching [my] wagon with an iron club in his hand. The devil knows what he was looking for; then he ordered me to pay for the entrance to the market, the bridge toll, and the pavement levy.... Well, that's the way it is in the towns, what can you do?"[54]

Situated within the framework of a stratified agrarian society, the relations of Lithuanian villagers and Jews were essentially "premodern." Jews and Lithuanians lived in proximity without engendering deeper mutual understanding: the two societies lived alongside, but not *with*, each other, and close lifelong friendships were rare. There was little interest in the Other's cultural and spiritual worlds.[55] Knowledge of each other's languages was confined to vocabulary useful for trade and interactions on the street. Aside from the petty gentry of Samogitia and the relatively thin layer of the emergent Lithuanian intelligentsia, the peasantry constituted most of the country's Lithuanian speakers before the Great War. In contrast to the populace in the countryside, educated Jews and Lithuanians who escaped the rural and small-town milieu tended to assimilate into one of the region's linguistic "high cultures": Russian proved attractive to Jews, Polish appealed to Lithuanians.

The peasants tended to view all those who did not till the soil as outsiders, including urban Poles and Germans, but villagers singled out the Jews as a distinctly alien element. Well known to the peasant as a trader, craftsman, and retailer, pigeonholed as a swindler and pushy salesman, the Jew also emerged in folklore as a pagan-like opaque element, an observer of bizarre religious rituals that bordered on the diabolical. In village culture, the devilish image survives to this day in the "Jewish" masks that revelers wear during pre-Lenten carnivals. As Mordechai Zalkin has noted, even as the economy modernized during the nineteenth and twentieth centuries, Lithuanian-Jewish relations developed within "a whole world of mutual negative images as well as suspicions composed mainly of stereotypes and prejudices." Jewish views of their Gentile neighbors were hardly more nuanced than the peasant superstitions:

---

54 Franciszek Marciński, *Grammatyka polska dla Litwinów uczących się jezyka polskiego* (Suwałki: Drukarnia wojewódzka, 1833), 124.
55 For a somewhat different view see Abramowicz, *Profiles of a Lost World*, 94.

For their part, many Jews perceived the native Lithuanians as a primeval, undeveloped, primitive rural society. A typical illustration of this attitude is the following description of Boris Schatz, who was born in Varniai in 1866 and was known as one of the most famous Jewish sculptors in [the] late nineteenth century: "The Christians from the nearby villages arrived every week on market day, wearing garments made of sheep's leather, big leather hats and simple straw sandals. They would offer their products using a very strange language that I did not understand; [it] sounded somewhat wild [...] they seemed to me like the Philistines, the Amalekites and some other half-wild tribes from time immemorial, that my ancient forefathers constantly struggled with."[56]

One scholarly work fittingly summed up the traditional Lithuanian view of the Jew as "a quite familiar stranger," an outsider and yet, at the same time, an "indispensable part of the life cycle in the countryside."[57] This latter depiction provides a corrective to the simplistic general picture based on contemporary reports of estrangement: on some level, despite their differences Jews and Lithuanians of the largely premodern countryside needed each other, a form of mutual interdependence described by historian Eric Goldstein:

> The close residential proximity and economic interaction between Jews and Lithuanians in Darbėnai suggests that members of the two groups also experienced a certain degree of social interaction. Often, writers who discuss Jewish-Lithuanian interaction specify that contact was limited to the economic sphere and did not include social relations. This may be true of more intimate forms of socializing (social visiting, strong friendships, participation in the same organizations), but it does not take into account the myriad ways in which Jews and Lithuanians did interact simply by sharing certain spaces. Despite the clear boundaries of language, culture and religion that separated Jews and Lithuanians, the

---

56 Mordechai Zalkin, "Sharunas, Prince of Dainava, in a Jewish Gown: The Cultural and Social Role of Hebrew and Yiddish Translations of Lithuanian Literature and Poetry in Interwar Lithuania," *Jahrbuch für Antisemitismusforschung* 21 (2012): 149–150; cf. Levin and Staliūnas, "*Lite*," 349–350.

57 See Laima Anglickienė, "Svetimas, bet neblogai pažįstamas: žydo įvaizdis lietuvių liaudies kultūroje," *Darbai ir dienos* 34 (2003): 213–234; also, Nerijus Udrėnas, "Book, Bread, Cross, and Whip: Imperial Russia and the Construction of Lithuanian Identity" (draft copy of PhD diss.), 366.

conduct of good business relied on a degree of cordiality, familiarity and development of relationships with returning customers.[58]

Lithuania's Catholic clergy nurtured long-standing anti-Jewish prejudices reinforced by social and political animosities. Bishop Motiejus Valančius (1801–1875), a forerunner of the Lithuanian national movement, stressed the harmful impact which Jewish tavern-keepers and merchants ostensibly exercised on the moral and social life of the peasantry. Furthermore, in the eyes of the clergy, Jews' perceived support for the tsar made them allies of Catholicism's rival, Russian Orthodoxy. Christian anti-Judaism was somewhat mitigated by the Church's admonitions concerning the dignity of all human beings: even as Valančius warned peasants about dishonest Jewish traders, he cautioned them against violence towards "God's children."[59] The writings of Rev. Justinas Pranaitis (1861–1917) proved more malevolent. In 1892 he published the anti-Judaic tract *Christianus in Talmude Iudaeorum* (The Christian in the Jewish Talmud), which emphasized the supposed undying Jewish hatred of Christians. In 1912 Pranaitis appeared as the government-appointed "expert" in the infamous Beilis case. On the other hand, the beatified Jurgis Matulaitis (1871–1927), the bishop of Vilnius and modern Lithuania's most ethical hierarch, condemned anti-Jewish pogroms.[60] It is difficult to explain the stark difference in attitude: both Matulaitis and Pranaitis were children of prosperous peasant households in Suvalkija and were affiliated with the prestigious Theological Academy in St. Petersburg, the former as student, the latter as a professor.

Aside from religious and ethnic differences, the long-standing hostility between village and town provided another nexus of conflict. Despite the

---

58 Eric L. Goldstein, "The Social Geography of a *Shtetl*: Jews and Lithuanians in Darbėnai, 1760-1940," in Lempertienė and Šiaučiūnaitė-Verbickienė, *Jewish Space*, 36.

59 See Jonas Boruta, "Katalikų bažnyčia ir lietuvių-žydų santykiai XIX–XX a.," *Lietuvių Katalikų mokslo akademija. Metraštis* 14 (1999): 1–23; cf. Vygantas Vareikis, "Tarp Valančiaus ir Kudirkos: žydų ir lietuvių santykiai katalikiškosios kultūros kontekste," *Lietuvių Katalikų mokslo akademija. Metraštis* 14 (1999): 81–82; Vladas Sirutavičius, "Katalikų Bažnyčia ir modernaus lietuvių antisemitizmo genezė," *Lietuvių Katalikų mokslo akademija. Metraštis* 14 (1999): 69–75; Vytautas Toleikis, "Žydai Vyskupo Motiejaus Valančiaus raštuose," *Darbai ir dienos* 70 (2018): 179–233.

60 Genovaitė Gustaitė, "Vyskupas Jurgis Matulaitis ir žydai Vilniaus vyskupijoje 1918–1925," *Lietuvių Katalikų mokslo akademija. Metraštis* 14 (1999): 105–113. See Jurgis Matulaitis, *Užrašai*, ed. Paulius Subačius, Institutum Historicum Marianorum, Fontes Historiae Marianorum (Vilnius: aidai, 1998), 199–200.

commercial utility of the towns, peasants viewed them as inhospitable places, disrespectful of the villagers' culture and language. In the logic of their estate, rural folk considered that "only the work of the land was fit for human labor." Yet the very nature of traditional interaction within a conservative social hierarchy ensured some stability and a measure of violence-mitigating security.[61] The mutual stereotypes of the different communities were often negative but hardly murderous: while incidents such as confrontations over market tolls were commonplace and mutual religious prejudices were centuries-old in Lithuania, mob violence directed against Jews was infrequent and never approached the scale of the lethal pogroms seen, for example, in Kishinev (1903) and Odesa (1905).[62] Jews themselves remarked on the weakness of antisemitism and the paucity of pogroms in Lithuania.[63] Nevertheless, reports of minor anti-Jewish disturbances and "fist fights" appeared in the press of the early 1900s and small-scale clashes erupted in several places during the revolutionary upheavals of 1905–1907. The Easter 1905 riot in the town of Dusetos resulted in a Jewish fatality, a rare case in Lithuania at the time. Both the secular and clerical media generally took a dim view of such outbreaks.[64]

Lithuania's Polonized landowners and urbanites often asserted primitive anti-Judaic stereotypes that tended to portray Jews as interlopers from afar, publishing biased, starkly negative impressions of Jewish life. They noted the bizarre clothing, the strange beards, the ubiquitous peyot, the constant whiff of garlic and onion that emanated from Jewish dwellings and inns, the ambience of filth and dirt—all in addition to the supposedly parasitical nature of Jewish commercial

---

61 For more on Jewish-Lithuanian relations in the countryside and shtetls see Ignas Končius, *Žemaičio šnekos* (Vilnius: Vaga, 1996), 63; Saulius Sužiedėlis, "Užnemunės miestų ir miestelių socialekonominės problemos XIX amžiaus pirmojoje pusėje (iki 1864 m. reformos)," in *Lituanistikos instituto 1977 metų suvažiavimo darbai*, ed. Janina K. Reklaitis (Chicago: Lituanistikos institutas, 1979), 93–105. On popular antisemitism from a cultural and literary perspective see Vytautas Kavolis, *Sąmoningumo trajektorijos: lietuvių kultūros modernėjimo aspektai* (Chicago: A&M Publishers, 1986).

62 On the comparative aspects of this history see Darius Staliūnas, *Enemies for a Day: Antisemitism and Anti-Jewish Violence in Lithuania under the Tsars* (Budapest: Central European University Press, 2015).

63 Two examples are quoted in Azriel Shochat, "The Beginnings of Antisemitism in Independent Lithuania," *Yad Vashem Studies* 2 (1958): 38.

64 Examples are cited in Udrėnas, "Book, Bread, Cross, and Whip," 358–360. The pogrom in Dusetos is analyzed in Darius Staliūnas, "Dusetos, Easter 1905: The Story of One Pogrom," *Journal of Baltic Studies* 43, no. 4 (2012): 495–514.

practices and the community's innate aversion to manual labor. Others reflected on the "Eastern" physical features common to the "children of Israel." The painter Wincenty Smokowski's travelogue-memoir of historic Trakai published in 1841 noted "such a striking nature of the facial features of Lithuanian Jews, that they can be easily recognized even with their skin peeled." To this repellant image, he contrasted his favorable impression of the local Karaim "who speak very pure Polish and do not mangle its pronunciation like the lazy local Jews."[65]

The gentry decried Jewish "exploitation" of the peasantry, citing the pernicious corruption of villagers' morals by Jewish tavern keepers, a transparently hypocritical stance. Since the early modern period Jews had come to constitute the majority of leaseholders of the ubiquitous inns (L. *karčema*), important gathering places and waystations for travelers, and thus sellers of hard liquor to the peasantry. The agrarian elite profited greatly from a privilege known as *propinacja* (P.)—the landowners' exclusive right to distill and sell, tax-free, grain alcohol on their estates, primarily to the resident serfs who were often coerced into mandatory purchase quotas of their masters' production. Until the mid-nineteenth century, the Church also profited from the enterprise, since Jews often sold alcohol on lands rented from parishes, dioceses, and monasteries.[66] Envious petty gentry sought to penetrate the market by leasing smaller distilleries and local inns to Jews, arousing the opposition of the landed estates which, in turn, sought to prohibit Jewish settlement and employment in the countryside. Litigation between Jews and the nobility over the right to distill and sell alcohol was not uncommon.

The Jewish role in the alcohol trade became a particularly divisive issue during the mass temperance movement of the mid-nineteenth century, which arose as a response to the plague of peasant drunkenness. At times, the Jewish tavern keepers, like other small traders, found themselves trapped by economic forces over which they had little control.[67] Nonetheless, the idea of the evil social

---

65 Wincenty Smokowski, "Wspomnienie Trok w 1822 r.1," *Athenaeum* 5 (1841): 162. An overview of the nobility's attitudes towards Jews based on contemporary accounts is in Zita Medišauskienė, "Atkarus, bet būtinas: žydai ir bajoriškoji Lietuvos visuomenė," in Sirutavičius and Staliūnas, *Žydų klausimas*, 85–106.

66 Vygantas Vareikis, "Žemaičiai ir žydai: sugyvenimas, komunikacija, svetimumas," in *Žemaitijos žydų kultūros paveldo atspindžiai*, ed. Hektoras Vitkus and Jolanta Skurdauskienė, (Klaipėda: Klaipėdos universiteto leidykla, 2019), 25–26.

67 Kazimierz Gieczys, *Bractwa trzeźwości w diecezji żmudzkiej w latach 1858–1864*, Studia Teologiczne 4 (Wilno: Ksieg. św. Wojciecha, 1935), 6, 154. See also Janulaitis, *Żydai Lietuvoje*,

influence of the Jewish innkeeper persisted. One Catholic priest insisted in his 1935 doctoral dissertation that "one reason for widespread drunkenness was the hegemony of Jewry."[68]

The opinions of Polonized elites, however, had limited influence on the attitudes of ethnic Lithuanians. During the second half of the nineteenth century most Polish-speaking landowners and townspeople rejected Lithuanian national aspirations, deriding the intelligentsia who supported them as "mad Lithuanians" (P. *litwomani*). For its part, the Lithuanian national movement reflected a spectrum of attitudes towards the Other, which sprang from the intelligentsia's social roots. Before World War I nearly three-fourths of the educated children (mostly sons) of peasants came from the region of southwestern Lithuania, which had been part of the autonomous Kingdom of Poland. Here the early abolition of serfdom in 1807 and the subsequent 1864 land reform (P. *uwłaszczenie*, or "enfranchisement") facilitated the emergence of relatively prosperous landed farmers who were able to provide their children access to education.[69]

The village-born students saw themselves as representatives of the country's majority population and considered unjust the historic exclusion of Lithuanian speakers from commerce, higher education, the clerical hierarchy, and the professions. By the early twentieth century the national movement, which had begun as an apolitical linguistic and cultural renaissance in the early nineteenth century, had fractured into social democratic, secular/liberal, and conservative Catholic currents. The political diversity of Lithuanian nationalism affected attitudes towards Jews. The social democrat Steponas Kairys (1879–1964) addressed anti-Jewish bias in a rhetorical question: "Did the *varpininkai*[70] intelligentsia bring their clearly negative stance towards the Jews to the *Varpas* [journal] from childhood days, from the attitudes acquired under the villager's

---

102–105. On Jewish-Lithuanian economic conflicts and the inn as an institution, see Saulius Sužiedėlis, "The Lithuanian Peasantry of Trans-Niemen Lithuania, 1807–1864: A Study of Social, Economic and Cultural Change" (PhD diss., University of Kansas, 1977), 332–348.

68 Gieczys, *Bractwa trzeźwości w diecezji żmudzkiej w latach 1858–1864*, 5.

69 Miroslav Hroch, *Die Vorkämpfer der nationalen Bewegung bei den kleinen Völkern Europas: eine vergleichende Analyse zur gesellschaftlichen Schichtung der patriotischen Gruppen*, Acta Universitatis Carolinae Philosophica et Historica 24 (Prague: Universita Karlova, 1968), 70.

70 The monthly journal *Varpas* (Bell) founded in 1889 was the first major Lithuanian periodical to adopt a liberal nationalist perspective critical of tsarism. The followers of the journal's ideology were known as *varpininkai*.

roof, and then, further stoked by the not infrequent sermons in the churches, all of which made it impossible to gain insight into the life of Lithuanian Jews and their obvious social stratification?" Kairys suggested that the national activists of *Varpas* were more prone to hold anti-Jewish attitudes than "our common people who were objective and far more favorably disposed towards the Jews."[71]

Political polarization and the dynamics of a changing economy contributed to anti-Jewish attitudes. Some Lithuanian leaders claimed that Jewish clannishness and solidarity constituted a de facto monopoly of the rural economy and urged "Christians," that is, the peasants, to enter the crafts, petty trade, and other "Jewish" occupations and to buy "from their own" whenever possible. Vincas Kudirka (1858–1899), a physician and one of the founders of modern Lithuanian nationalism, was convinced that Jewish doctors had driven him to near poverty by undermining his medical practice in Šakiai. Kudirka's first published work was a folksy, primitive tale of the origins of the Jewish restriction against pork, concluding with the stanzas: "Everyone everywhere knows the Jewish way / That a Jew does no harm to his own, whether rich or poor."[72] Kudirka assailed the Jews as a danger to the peasants' Catholic faith, railing against them as "the most vicious wolves dressed in sheep's wool," and praised the notoriously antisemitic Adolf Stöcker, one of Kaiser Wilhelm II's court chaplains, as an example of a righteous Christian leader spearheading the struggle against Jewish malevolence.[73] In 1886 Petras Vileišis (1851–1926), an industrialist identified as "the first Lithuanian millionaire," published a booklet titled "Our Jews and How We Must Defend Ourselves against Them," in which he urged his readers "to look at the Jews who are strong because they have unity." Vileišis counseled villagers to expel the Jewish liquor trade from the countryside and to establish Christian shops and credit unions.[74]

Modern antisemitic ideas from abroad injected pseudoscientific racial notions into homespun negative stereotypes. Kudirka cited Edouard Drumont's argument about the inborn and immutably malignant nature of the Jews which

---

71 Steponas Kairys, *Lietuva budo* (New York: Amerikos lietuvių socialdemokratų sąjungos literatūros fondas, 1957), 238–240.
72 Vinc. Kapsas [pseud.], "Dėl ko žydai nevalgo kiaulėnos," *Auszra* 6 (1885): 160–161.
73 "Mes ir żydai," *Varpas* 8 (1891): 127–128.
74 Ramojus [pseud.], *Musu żydai, ir kaip nū anu turime gitiesi* (New York: Lietuwiszkojo Balso, 1886), 22–23.

could not be ameliorated through assimilation.[75] In 1914 the physician Antanas Maliauskas published the treatise "Jews from an Economic and Social Perspective," citing the supposedly scientific arguments of British, German, and other writers that "from an anthropological perspective . . . Jews are not a purely Semitic nation, but a creation from a mixture of several peoples." Maliauskas argued that Jews were cheaters by nature, morally corrupting the societies in which they were embedded, exerting a malicious influence in politics, literature, and culture. As authorities, he cited, among others, A. H. Sayce's *Races of the Old Testament* (1891), as well as German professor W. H. Riehl's notion that "the most important feature of the Jewish character is the constant search for profit." Perhaps because Maliauskas's work was published by the Catholic journal *Ateitis*, he cautioned that "although we must defend ourselves from their double-dealing, it is not permissible to hate the Jews as a nation: that would be immoral and utterly unfit for Christians." The author admired the Zionist program as a "beautiful idea," since, as he wrote, "once all the Jews go off to Palestine, the Jewish question will be solved." In the meantime, Maliauskas urged the state to turn the "energy of the Jews . . . [away from] the exploitation of others and . . . to accustom them towards productive work, so they would be satisfied with an honest wage."[76] But such racialized texts were relatively few and had marginal influence among Lithuanian intellectuals at the turn of the century. In addition, as Kairys had noted, villagers were more "objective" in their views and tended to be more pragmatic in their approach. There is some anecdotal evidence suggesting that Lithuanian peasants gladly accepted treatment from Jewish doctors and did not share Kudirka's antipathies towards his competitors.[77]

More liberally inclined leaders discouraged anti-Jewish violence and superstitious stereotypes, notably Petras Leonas (1864–1938), Lithuania's first minister of justice, who derided the blood libel in the weekly *Lietuvos ūkininkas* (Lithuanian farmer) in November 1913. But there was popular backlash: in response to letters unhappy with such a "defense of the Jews," the editors assured readers that while Jews were innocent of the "cannibalistic blood

---

75 As argued in Q. D. ir K. [pseud.], "Tėvyniszki varpai," *Varpas* 10 (1890): 152.

76 Quotes are in Antanas Maliauskas, *Žydai ekonomijos ir visuomenės žvilgsniu* (Kaunas: Saliamono Banaičio spaustuvė, 1914), 5–54.

77 Mordechai Zalkin, "*Mūsų gydytojas*: The Social and Cultural Aspects of the Jewish Medical Doctor in Lithuanian Countryside before the Second World War," in Lempertienė and Šiaučiūnaitė-Verbickienė, *Jewish Space*, 183.

libel . . . we know very well that among the Jews are not a few who harm us and we will address this in the future."[78] Although some intelligentsia, such as Antanas Staugaitis (1876–1954), could not imagine organizing cooperatives and peasant commerce without challenging "Jewish domination," others, like Povilas Višinskis (1875–1906), urged Lithuanians to work for the economic improvement of the village not at the expense of the Jews or by invoking "Jew hatred," but through their own efforts.[79]

While important, relations with Jews were not the singular preoccupation of the emerging national intelligentsia: of greater concern were the social dominance of Polonized elites and the oppression of the tsarist autocracy. In December 1905 nearly two thousand Lithuanian political activists gathered in Vilnius amidst industrial unrest and anti-Russian protests in the countryside. This gathering, christened later christened the Great Diet of Vilnius (Didysis Vilniaus seimas), was the first political conference representing Lithuania's majority nation. The future president Antanas Smetona (1874–1944) recognized that the members of this Diet had adopted a key transformation in their thinking: for them, the concept of "Lithuania" no longer corresponded to the historic borders of the old grand duchy but only to the three gubernias of Vilnius, Kaunas, and Suwałki and, even there, only in regions where "we find living signs of our language."[80] On December 7, 1905 (November 24, 1905) the delegates announced the "Decisions of the First Assembly of the Lithuanian Nation's Representatives," denouncing tsarism and calling for an autonomous political entity within the borders of an ethnographically defined Lithuania, in which "the other nations living in Lithuania could enjoy full freedoms." The political

---

78 Petras Leonas, "Žydo Beilio byla ir kunigo Pranaičio niektikėjimas," *Lietuvos ūkininkas*, n.s., 45 (November 20, 1913), 462–463; editorial response is in "Kunigo Pranaičio nietiktėjimas," *Lietuvos ūkininkas*, n.s., 46 (November 27, 1913), 474–476. See also Darius Staliūnas, "Lithuanian Antisemitism in the Late Nineteenth and Early Twentieth Centuries," *Polin* 25 (2013): 135–149.

79 For a survey of Lithuanian-language antisemitic narratives and the intelligentsia's response, see Linas Venclauskas, *Tekstų byla: lietuvių antisemitinis diskursas nuo XIX a. antros pusės iki 1940 metų* (Vilnius: Versus, 2022), 44–218; cf. Klaus Richter, "Antisemitismus und litauische Intelligentzija (1900–1914)," *Jahrbuch für Antisemitismusforschung* 21 (2012): 89–114.

80 Quoted in Darius Staliūnas, "Lietuvių ir žydų politinio bendradarbiavimo epizodai XX a. pradžioje," in Sirutavičius, Staliūnas, and Šiaučiūnaitė-Verbickienė, *Lietuvos žydai: istorinė studija*, 271–282. On the contrasting Jewish idea of "Lithuania," see Abba Strazhas, "Der nationale Erwachen des litauischen Volkes und Judenheit," *Acta Universitatis Stockholmiensis-Studia Baltica Stockholmiensia* 2 (1985): 179.

1. Tradition, Accommodation, Conflict — 35

leaders proposed a parliament (Seimas) "elected by direct, secret ballot . . . , without regard to gender, nationality or religious affiliation."[81] The ensuing conclusion of a "pragmatic alliance" between Jewish and Lithuanian leaders during the elections to the Duma in 1906–1907, a seemingly positive development, was largely tactical: anti-Polish calculations, based on the rationale of the "lesser evil," played a more important part in political cooperation than any sense of common purpose.[82] Tensions between Lithuanians and Jews took the shape of occasional street-level confrontations.[83]

World War I and Nation-Building in the "Shattered Zone": Founding the First Republic (1914–1920)

On August 1, 1914, Germany declared war on Russia after the Tsar refused the Kaiser's demand to halt mobilization in response to Austria-Hungary's invasion of Serbia. After some initial successes, the Russian army suffered defeats and began a retreat, adopting a scorched earth policy, which resulted in the expulsion eastward of hundreds of thousands of Lithuania's inhabitants. This severe dislocation affected all nationalities, but Jews suffered an exceptional level of violence from the tsarist forces. There are numerous records detailing the looting, rapes, and killings carried out by the military, particularly the Cossacks. At times, local peasants took part in sharing the spoils. Records indicate that by May 5, 1915, the Russians had completed the exile of nearly two hundred thousand people from forty-four sites in Kaunas gubernia and eighteen collection points in Courland. Another source claims that nearly 150,000 Jews were evacuated from Kaunas gubernia in two weeks in May 1915. There are estimates that the total wartime displacement from Lithuania may have been as high as a half-million.

---

81   "Pirmojo Lietuvių Tautos Atstovų susivažiavimo nutarimai," *Vilniaus žinios*, n.s., 276 (November 24, write out Old Style, December 7, 1905), 1–2; Saulius Sužiedėlis, "A Century After: The 'Great Diet of Vilnius' Revisited," *Journal of Baltic Studies* 38, no. 4 (2007): 419–432.

82   Darius Staliūnas, "Collaboration of Lithuanians and Jews during the Elections to the First and Second Dumas," in *A Pragmatic Alliance: Jewish-Lithuanian Political Cooperation at the Beginning of the Twentieth Century*, ed. Darius Staliūnas and Vladas Sirutavičius (New York: CEU Press, 2011), 45–75.

83   As recounted in Darius Staliūnas, "Antisemitic Tension during the 1905 Revolution in Lithuania," *Jahrbuch für Antisemitismusforschung* 21 (2012): 54–88. A general overview of the historiographic problem is in François Guesnet and Darius Staliūnas, "No Simple Stories: Die litauisch-jüdischen Beziehungen im 19. und 20. Jahrhundert," *Jahrbuch für Antisemitismusforschung* 21 (2012): 17–25.

Whatever the real number, the Russian expulsions set the stage for transformative demographic changes. There is no reliable data on how many Lithuanian Jews found their way back, but it can be assumed that many of the evacuees never returned.[84]

Much of the Lithuanian intelligentsia initially adopted a strong anti-German stance and, despite favoring national autonomy, supported the Russian war effort as loyal subjects of the tsar. But this position soon lost any connection to the military and political realities on the ground. The war and the accompanying revolutionary upheavals destroyed the Russian Empire and, at the same time, hastened the demise of what remained of Lithuania's old socio-ethnic order. In May 1917 leaders of Russia's Lithuanian refugees held a political conference in Petrograd where, despite struggles between conservative and socialist factions, they agreed on the goal of a sovereign state rather than a vague autonomous polity. Concurrently, Lithuanian leaders back home sought to initiate negotiations concerning the country's future status with the Ober Ost, the German military occupation authority. In September 1917, a conference held under German auspices and composed almost entirely of ethnic Lithuanians elected the twenty-member Council of Lithuania, known as the Taryba, which proclaimed the goal of an "independent, democratically organized state" with a capital in Vilnius. Most of the country's Polish minority greeted the announcement with outright hostility. Amidst concerns about the unrepresentative national composition of the Taryba and the prospect of an "ethnographically Lithuanian state," the Jewish attitude could best be described as one of anxiety and unease.[85] Most Jewish leaders of the period had little interest in the Lithuanian national movement and failed to appreciate the extent to which Lithuanian leaders were mobilizing society in support of independence.[86] Over time the situation changed: in the words of historian Šarūnas Liekis, "although both Lithuanians and

---

84   See Tomas Balkelis, *War, Revolution, and Nation-Making in Lithuania, 1914–1923* (Oxford: Oxford University Press, 2018), 19–24; also, Semen Goldin, *Russkaya armiya i evrei 1914–1917* (Moscow: Mosty kultury, 2018), 218–291, 404–408, and Eric Lohr, "The Russian Army and the Jews: Mass Deportation, Hostages, and Violence during World War I," *Russian Review* 60, no. 3 (2001): 404–419.

85   See the primary sources as published in Darius Staliūnas, "The Lithuanian-Jewish Dialogue in Petrograd in 1917," in Sirutavičius and Ataliūnas, *Pragmatic Alliance*, 231–243.

86   See Šarūnas Liekis, "Documents on the Lithuanian Council in the Central Zionist Archive in Jerusalem," in Sirutavičius and Staliūnas, *Pragmatic Alliance*, 245–270, and Mordechai Zalkin, "Lithuanian Jewry and the Lithuanian National Movement," in Sirutavičius and Staliūnas, *Pragmatic Alliance*, 21–44. Cf. Shochat, "Beginnings," 13.

Jews ... had started out being deaf to one another, a long-lasting period of dialogue and institutional cooperation subsequently developed."[87] But this change came about only after an intense period of nation-building, social upheaval, and the violent rearrangement of state borders.

The Taryba declared Lithuania's independence on February 16, 1918. Following negotiations, a minister for Jewish affairs (without portfolio), Jokūbas Vygodskis (Jakub Wygodzki) (1857–1942), and two Jewish deputy ministers were appointed to the first cabinet of the Republic of Lithuania on November 11, 1918. The fledgling Lithuanian government immediately confronted existential threats from without and within. Since the outbreak of the war, Lithuania had entered what has been called a "shattered zone" which replaced the relative stability of Russian imperial power and, after 1915, the German military administration.[88] As the war continued, and even after the end of hostilities on the Western front, violence, economic insecurity, and social strife became endemic, abating only at the end of 1920. During the German occupation, Jews had been accused by their neighbors of conniving with the detested Ober Ost authorities whose requisitions had driven many villagers close to famine.[89] In the struggle for Vilnius during the spring of 1919 Bolshevik and Polish forces carried out antisemitic pogroms in the city.[90] Lithuania's wars of national liberation in 1918–1920 witnessed a number of anti-Jewish outbreaks in areas where the newly organized national army confronted invading Bolshevik, Polish, and Bermondtist[91] forces. The most serious anti-Jewish violence outside Vilnius was recorded in May and early June of 1919 following the capture of Panevėžys from the Red Army by Lithuanian and German troops, some of whom proceeded to loot Jewish shops and hunt Bolshevik suspects. Claims of Jewish sniper fire in support of the Communists drove some of the local populace to engage in pogroms causing an undetermined number of fatalities in the city.

---

87 Šarūnas Liekis, "Lithuanians and Jews in 1914-1918: Motives for Political Cooperation," *Jahrbuch für Antisemitismus* 12 (2012): 132.
88 Balkelis, *War*, 3, 33–34.
89 Shochat, "Beginnings," 9–11.
90 An account is in the diary of Matulaitis, *Užrašai*, 144ff.
91 The Bermondtists, officially the West Russian Volunteer Army created in 1918–1919 under General Pavel Bermondt-Avalov, were a German-sponsored anti-Bolshevik army that was widely viewed as an attempt to perpetuate German hegemony in the Baltics.

In the countryside the notoriously brutal commander of the Second Infantry Regiment, Vincas Grigaliūnas-Glovackis (1885–1964), executed as many as several hundred suspected Bolsheviks, including Jews.[92] Another fatal incident was recorded on July 10, 1919, when a squad of twenty-five to thirty Lithuanian soldiers led by Sergeant Aleksandras Vilavičius opened fire on a Zionist meeting in Ukmergė. The resulting court martial held that some of the soldiers who had observed the gathering were angered by the anti-Lithuanian tone of one of the speakers and had then organized an action to suppress "a revolt against the Lithuanian government." The military found no evidence of a Jewish uprising and indicted Vilavičius for "attacking the meeting for no reason, having no right to do so, and without a government order. As a consequence, several Jews were wounded, and one, Joselis Želdaf, mortally wounded."[93] The anti-Jewish violence clearly took place in the context of a kind of "White Terror," but events in Lithuania never approached the scale of the killings that characterized the Russian Civil War of 1918–1921.[94]

At the first Lithuanian Jewish Congress in Kaunas in January 1920 delegates protested the pogroms as well as the lack of Jewish participation in the bureaucracy; there were allegations that virtually all Jewish railroad workers had been dismissed.[95] Jewish protests against the excesses to the Allied Military Mission and other international bodies ensured that events such as those in Panevėžys could not be swept under the rug. Lithuania's leaders were acutely aware of the need to convince the international community of the viability of their state and sought support by presenting themselves as paragons of democracy and advocates for national minorities. On August

---

92 An account based on contemporary sources is in Eglė Bendikaitė, "'Lai kalba žygiai ir faktai': Panevėžio krašto žydai Nepriklausomybės kovose," in *Iš Panevėžio praeities: Lietuvos nepriklausomybės gynėjai ir puoselėtojai*, ed. Donatas Pilkauskas and Zita Pikelytė (Panevėžys: Panevėžio kraštotyros muziejus, 2018), 64–83.

93 As quoted in the Indictment of the Military Procurator of October 26, 1920, published in Vladas Sirutavičius and Darius Staliūnas, eds., *Kai ksenofobija virsta prievarta: lietuvių ir žydų santykių dinamika XIX a.–XX a. pirmojoje pusėje* (Vilnius: LII 2005), 246–248.

94 See Balkelis, *War*, 6–7, 114–118. Balkelis argues that Russo-centric historiography, which sees the period as primarily an ideological struggle between "Reds" and "Whites," is a simplified narrative which vastly understates the role of the nationalist revolutions and other social upheavals of the period.

95 As presented in Lietuvos centrinis valstybės archyvas [Lithuanian Central State Archive, Vilnius—henceforth LCVA], f. 1437, ap. 100, l. 1–2, 28–33.

5, 1919, the Lithuanian delegation to the Paris Peace Conference adopted a comprehensive declaration on Jewish national rights, which formed the basis for the short-lived Jewish national autonomy (1918–1925).[96] On January 10, 1920, the conservative daily *Lietuvos aidas* called the Jews "faithful old friends."[97]

Competing political projects for a new Lithuania proliferated amidst the wars and revolutionary movements. Many Poles longed for the restoration of the Polish-Lithuanian Commonwealth, including its Ukrainian lands, as an inclusive federal solution for the nations of the region. Some Jewish leaders opposed to social revolution preferred a modernized version of the old grand duchy in which Lithuanians, Poles, Jews, and Belarusians would coexist as autonomous Swiss-style ethnic cantons with four official languages.[98] A multinational commonwealth may have appealed to liberal sentiment, but it was obvious that such an arrangement would tend to favor the still entrenched landowning class and educated urbanites (Poles and Jews) at the expense of the peasant masses (that is, Lithuanians and Belarusians). The older concept of Lithuanian autonomy within a new Russia based on historic borders, which would include the Litvak-inhabited lands of Belarus, would place ethnic Lithuanians in the minority. Not surprisingly, for most Lithuanian leaders, a nation-state separated from Russia and Poland located within a Lithuanian ethnographic space was the indispensable condition for the future economic betterment of the peasantry as well as the establishment of majority rule.

As it turned out, the embattled Republic of Lithuania survived. The center-left government of Mykolas Sleževičius (1882–1939) persevered during the trying months of early 1919 as the new Lithuanian state gradually consolidated its position, protected by a growing Lithuanian army and, for a time,

---

96 See Šarūnas Liekis, *A State within a State? Jewish National Autonomy in Lithuania 1918–1925* (Vilnius: Versus Aureus, 2003); Atamukas, *Lietuvos žydų kelias*, 134–140.; Zenonas Ivinskis, "Lietuva ir žydai istorijos šviesoje," *Aidai* 1 (1972): 24–27; Shochat, "Beginnings," 7–48; Samuel Gringauz, "Jewish National Autonomy in Lithuania," *Jewish Social Studies* 14 (1952): 225ff.; Paul Radensky, "Žydų reikalų ministerija ir žydų tautinė autonomija Lietuvoje 1919–1923 metais," *Lietuvos istorijos metraštis* (1995): 84–97; Raimundas Valkauskas, "Žydų tautinės autonomijos klausimas," *Lietuvos istorijos studijos* 3 (1996): 57–74.

97 Quoted in Vladas Sirutavičius, "Valdžios politika žydų atžvilgiu," in Sirutavičius, Staliūnas, and Šiaučiūnaitė-Verbickienė, *Lietuvos žydai; istorinė studija*, 301.

98 See the editorial statements in *Unser Tag*, October 15 and October 24, 1920, as recorded by the Press Department of Lithuania's Ministry of Jewish Affairs, in LCVA, f. 1437, ap. 1, b.100, l. 18–19.

a deteriorating German military umbrella. The Constituent Assembly, elected by universal suffrage, convened in May 1920 and took on the challenge of creating a modern democracy. At the same time, the international situation stabilized. The Polish-Lithuanian battle over Vilnius ended with an armistice brokered by the League of Nations in November 1920. Despite the end of hostilities and the recognition of Polish sovereignty over the Vilnius region by the Conference of Ambassadors in 1923, a formal state of war between Poland and Lithuania continued until March 1938.[99]

As part of Europe's "shattered zone," Lithuania suffered a period of state disintegration, revolution, and social chaos during World War I and its immediate aftermath. It is tempting to see these violent years as a prelude to what happened a generation later, but a search for causal connections or analogues is bound to fail when considered in terms of the historic impact of what followed. As violence abated after 1920, Lithuania's national communities entered a period of

MAP 5. The Republic of Lithuania, 1918–1940.
(Saulius Sužiedėlis, *Historical Dictionary of Lithuania*, 2nd ed.
[Lanham, Md: Scarecrow Press, 2011].)

---

99 An older and still useful survey is Alfred Erich Senn, *The Emergence of Modern Lithuania* (New York: Columbia University Press, 1959). A more thorough and incisive analysis based on the latest archival research is in Balkelis, *War*.

transformative readjustments within a modernizing society, bringing years of both promise and peril. The historical record, much enlarged by new research, shows that the crises of the early twentieth century produced changes that bore only passing resemblance to the events that followed the outbreak of the Second World War.

Lithuanians, Jews, and Political Challenges in the New Lithuania

As the politicians representing Lithuania's once marginalized villagers took control of the state, it became clear that the advent of majority rule signaled a revolution in interethnic relations.[100] For the country's minorities, dealing directly with the Lithuanian-speaking majority without the intervening agencies of the past, such as the tsarist bureaucracy, the Polish aristocracy, or the Ober Ost, was, at best, a disconcerting experience. Would Jews consider the new Lithuania of peasant upstarts *their* state as well? At least initially, most Jews had less faith than their Lithuanian countrymen in the permanence of the new republic. Polish and Jewish condescension concerning the new "peasant" state is recorded in many sources.[101] Territorial conflicts with Poland over Vilnius, and with Germany over Klaipėda/Memel, created problems with the new state's Polish and German minorities. Lithuania's land reform of the early 1920s was widely understood not only as an economic measure but as the overthrow of the historic social and cultural influence of the country's Polonized landowners. The republic's attempts to integrate (or "Lithuanianize") the historically Prussian Klaipėda Territory encountered the resistance of ethnic Germans who looked for support to Berlin.[102]

---

100 What is meant by majority rule here is "the control of the state by the numerically largest national community in the context of an accession to power by a group previously subjected to a linguistic or ethnic minority's legal, social and cultural domination," as in Saulius Sužiedėlis, "A Century After": 430. In the Lithuanian case, this model applies primarily to the position of ethnic Lithuanians vis-à-vis the Polonized landowning and urban elites.

101 For example, a group of Jewish and Polish socialists attacked the Lithuanian Taryba as representing "a small and very backward nation," as reported in Shochat, "Beginnings," 19.

102 In January 1923 insurgents supported by the Lithuanian government seized control over Klaipėda (Memel). The conflict between Lithuanians and local Germans was only partly mitigated by the Klaipėda Convention of 1924 guaranteed by the Conference of Ambassadors (France, Britain, Italy, and Japan) which granted German speakers considerable autonomy within the territory.

A minister of Jewish affairs was part of the Lithuanian cabinet until 1924. During the period between the Constituent Assembly (Seimas) of 1920 and the Third Seimas of 1926–1927, Jewish deputies constituted the most active political group among the minorities, at times working in concert with Polish and German colleagues. Significant Jewish participation in national politics was, however, short-lived. The Lithuanian government's initially positive attitude towards minority rights aroused opposition in more radical nationalist circles, which attacked the establishment of Polish-language schools as a sop to former oppressors and criticized Jewish autonomy as a "state within a state." The Christian Democrats accused Jewish politicians of siding with the secular left. The Catholic bloc's political influence between 1922 and 1926 coincided with a progressive curtailment of Jewish self-government. When a center-left coalition of Social Democrats, Peasant Populists, and national minorities came to power in May 1926 the opposition, led by the Christian Democrats, claimed that the new government was "soft on Bolshevism" and coddled anti-Lithuanian elements.

During the electoral agitation of the mid-1920s primitive xenophobic appeals roused fears of Bolshevism, subversion by disloyal minorities, and Jewish "domination."[103] The Lithuanian edition of the *Protocols of the Elders of Zion* was published in Panevėžys in 1924. Antisemitic articles appeared in *Trimitas* (The Bugle), the journal of the paramilitary Lithuanian Riflemen's Union (Lietuvos šaulių sąjunga), which stereotyped Jews as insufficiently patriotic economic parasites, and illegal traffickers in prostitution. Moderates within the union condemned such propaganda.[104] Students were particularly active in demonstrations that demonized social democracy as a "foreign" threat to the Lithuanian nation. On December 14, 1926, the University of Kaunas briefly closed the Department of Medicine after Lithuanian students protested the refusal of Jews to provide "their share" of cadavers for classroom dissection, a supposedly

---

103 An anti-government leaflet of July 5, 1926, charged that the "new Seimas is ruled by Jews, Social Democrats, Germans ..., Polish spies." Other antisemitic leaflets were circulated by a shadowy group called Fighters Against the Jews. See LCVA, f. 1556, ap. 3, b. 211, l. 3, 11. Cf. Vytautas Žalys and Alfonsas Eidintas, *Lithuania in European Politics: The Years of the First Republic, 1918–1940* (New York: St. Martin's Press, 1997), 51–55.

104 Vytautas Jokubauskas, Jonas Vaičenonis, Vygantas Vareikis, and Hektoras Vitkus, *Valia priešintis: paramilitarizmas ir Lietuvos karinio saugumo problemos* (Klaipėda: Klaipėdos universiteto Baltijos regiono istorijos ir archeologijos institutas, 2015), 50–52.

"Jewish privilege" which, to the protesters, implied disrespect for Gentile bodies.[105]

The rightist military coup of December 17, 1926, brought down the government of President Kazys Grinius (1886–1950) and Prime Minister Sleževičius, propelling Antanas Smetona and his Nationalist Union (Tautininkų Sąjunga) to power. The new regime disbanded the Seimas, prohibited public activities of the other political parties, and outlawed what it considered extreme ideological movements. The proscribed left-wing movements included the Lithuanian Communist Party (LCP), but the government also suppressed the fascistic Iron Wolf (Geležinis vilkas) and the pro-Nazi front organizations of the Klaipėda region's Germans.[106] The abolition of Jewish national autonomy in 1925 and the Nationalists' takeover effectively ended any significant Jewish role in the central administration (the several diplomats and government officials who remained were an exception to the rule). The Fourth Seimas (1936–1940) under Smetona was a legislative veneer consisting of forty-nine "representatives of the nation," all ethnic Lithuanian men, elected indirectly and with limited advisory functions.

The regime did permit local elections to rural, town, and district councils, the only bodies in which Jews still exercised authority in public affairs. Inasmuch as ethnic Lithuanians made up more than 90% of the country's farmers, Jewish representation in local government was limited to the municipalities. Jews and other minority members formed a majority of the Kaunas city council until 1934. At the same time Jews made up nearly 30% of the membership in the country's twenty-one municipal councils and a majority in two (Šakiai and Jonava), but less than 1% served as appointed civil servants.[107] During the first years of independence Jews had played a role in the military: an estimated three

---

105 Dangiras Mačiulis, "'Žydų lavonų klausimas' Lietuvos universitete 1926–1927 metais," *Lietuvos istorijos metraštis* 2 (2002): 159–166. The issue of dissections was a standard canard in anti-Jewish outbreaks at Polish universities as well.

106 On Smetona's regime see Piotr Łossowski, "The Ideology of Authoritarian Regimes (The Baltic States 19261934–1940)," in *Dictatorships in EastCentral Europe*, ed. Janusz Żarnowski (Warsaw: PAN, 1983), 181–202. The Nationalist Union maintained that it was an organization of national unity and thus did not formally constitute a political party.

107 See Kaubrys, *National Minorities*, 105–113. After the 1934 local elections, Jewish city and town council members made up five of twenty-five representatives in Kaunas; five of twenty-one in Šiauliai; six of twelve in Vilkaviškis; five of nine in Šakiai; and six of nine in Jonava. Cf. Vladas Sirutavičius, "'A Close, but Very Suspicious Stranger': Outbreaks of Antisemitism in Inter-War Lithuania," *Polin* 25 (2013): 248.

thousand Jews served in the Lithuanian army during the struggle for independence (1918–1920) of whom about five hundred were listed as volunteers. As citizens, Jews were subject to the draft, but it is estimated that more than 90% of Jewish conscripts served in the infantry, and only a handful were ever commissioned as officers.[108]

Under Smetona's dictatorship, Lithuania's Jews maintained a measure of communal self-rule, and as counterintuitive as it may seem, the regime initiated a more moderate official discourse towards minorities than that of the previous democratically elected Catholic bloc. Not all proponents of a Lithuanian-dominated state considered Jews the most dangerous element: a nationalist memorandum in 1926 emphasized the need for an "ethnic national state" but also noted that the Jews could be allowed to "participate in the government . . . without harm to the state's independence," since, unlike Poles and Germans, they had neither dangerous foreign sponsors nor irredentist demands.[109] In 1933 two antisemitic newspapers, *Lietuvio žodis* (The Lithuanian's word) and *Tautos žodis* (The nation's word), appeared but were quickly banned.[110] The government continued contributions to rabbinical salaries: in the late 1920s its per capita subsidy to the Jewish religious community exceeded that assigned to the Catholic Church.[111]

The Litvaks of the First Republic: Demography, Education, and Culture

Political, economic, and social changes led nearly twenty thousand Lithuanian Jews to leave the country between 1920 and 1940, a majority departing for South Africa and Palestine. Jews constituted about a fifth of the Republic's emigrants during the two decades (tellingly, about one-third of the exodus during the 1930s). Nonetheless, the demographics of the Jewish community remained

---

108 Jonas Vaičenonis, "Prisiekė Adonojo vardu: žydai pirmosios Lietuvos Respublikos kariuomenėje," *Darbai ir dienos* 34 (2003): 273–283.
109 LCVA, f. 1557, ap. 1, b. 208, l. 1–2.
110 Vladas Sirutavičius, "Antisemitizmo proveržiai," in Sirutavičius, Staliūnas, and Šiaučiūnaitė-Verbickienė, *Lietuvos žydai: istorinė studija*, 412.
111 Vladas Mironas, "Tikybos Nepriklausomoje Lietuvoje," in *Pirmasis Nepriklausomos Lietuvos dešimtmetis 1918–1928*, ed. Vyriausias Lietuvos Nepriklausomybės 10 metų sukaktuvėms ruošti komitetas (Kaunas: Šviesa, 1990), 390 [reprint of 1930 edition]. Russian Orthodox and Protestant denominations also received higher per capita subsidies.

stable. The first Lithuanian census of 1923 provided an official figure of 153,743 Jewish citizens (7.5% of the population).[112] This figure did not change much until Lithuania's takeover of Vilnius and its environs from Poland in October 1939 which added some ninety thousand Jews to the country's population, including an influx of refugees from Nazi- and Soviet-occupied territory, thus raising the resident Jewish population under Lithuanian rule from an estimated 160,000 to nearly a quarter of a million.[113] Although there were substantial differences between Polish and Lithuanian governmental policies towards the Jews, there was no historic cultural chasm separating the Litvaks of the Vilnius region from their historic brethren in what was often termed "Kaunas Lithuania." The one exception was the strong preference of the former for Polish as their second language, rather than Lithuanian or Russian, as was the practice among the Jews of the First Republic.

There is a vast photographic record of Lithuanian shtetls of the interwar period that would look familiar to an observer from the late tsarist period: a panorama of synagogues and of people in traditional garb engaged in trade, worship, and other time-honored activities. These pictures are authentic but represent only a part of the changing landscape of Lithuania's Jewish society between the wars. Without minimizing the problem of persistent anti-Jewish attitudes, most Jews recognized that the Lithuanian state provided a relatively secure haven for their community, a welcome contrast to the official interwar antisemitism in Poland, Hungary, and Romania (not to speak of Germany after 1933). Litvak memories of the period may be selective,[114] but an overview of the educational, cultural, and social life of the predominantly Orthodox and Zionist Jewish community of interwar Lithuania reveals a vital and modernizing civil society, albeit one lacking significant access to political influence.

---

112 For a more detailed survey of the 1923 census see Saulius Kaubrys, *National Minorities in Lithuania: An Outline*, trans. Milda Dyke (Vilnius: Vaga, 2002), 40–60.

113 *Lietuvos gyventojai: 1923 m. rugsėjo 17 d. gyventojų surašymo duomenys* (Kaunas: Lietuvos Respublika, Finansų ministerija, Cent. statistikos biuras, 1924), 30. The 1923 census excluded the approximately seven thousand Jews of the Klaipėda region. See also, Alfonsas Eidintas, "The Emigration Policy of the Tautininkai Regime in Lithuania, 1926–1940," *Journal of Baltic Studes* 16, no. 1 (Spring 1986): 65–66; *Lietuvos statistikos metrastis 1938*, vol. 11 (Kaunas: Centralinis statistikos biuras, 1939): 55; Atamukas, *Lietuvos žydų kelias*, 155, 205.

114 For example, the rosy picture in the memoir of Frieda Frome, *Some Dare to Dream: Frieda Frome's Escape from Lithuania* (Ames: Iowa State University Press, 1988), 7: "Germans, Russians, Jews, and many others, in addition to the native Lithuanians, lived together in tolerance and peace."

The only Jewish post-primary educational institution in Kaunas before independence was the Hebrew-language secondary school founded in 1915 during the German occupation. The First Republic's constitutions of 1922 and 1928 mandated public support for the education of national minorities in their native language, a policy affecting not only Jews but Poles, Russians, and Germans. While the traditional cheder elementary schools and the yeshivas were still prominent, a network of modern Jewish education expanded rapidly. The Tarbut schools stressed a Zionist program that emphasized the history and geography of Israel and mandated, where possible, Hebrew as a language of instruction. By the early 1920s this system encompassed the majority of Jewish youth in the five to eighteen age group. In 1938 Tarbut operated 108 establishments from kindergarten through the secondary level with nearly thirteen thousand students, but the apex of the system were the eleven Zionist-operated gymnasiums (advanced secondary schools). The Yavneh schools of Lithuania's Orthodox community sought to combine modernized pedagogy with religious instruction. This network established four gymnasiums during the 1920s, three for girls and only one for boys, a result of the reluctance on the part of the traditional community to abandon the cheders and yeshivas as the primary mode of schooling. In contrast to the Tarbut and Yavne organizations, Yiddish-language schools declined, particularly after they came under the influence of the socialist Kultur-Lige which the government suppressed in 1924. In all, fourteen Jewish private gymnasiums of all ideological stripes enrolled more than two thousand students during the 1939–1940 school year.

During the 1920s a smaller number of Jewish students attended Russian- and German-language schools because of the strong academic reputation they had enjoyed before the Great War, but Lithuanian-language institutions attracted a growing number of Jews during the 1930s.[115] In 1933, antisemitic policies in the Reich had aroused public demonstrations among Lithuanian Jews, some of whom had previously enrolled their children in traditionally respected German-language institutions. As an alternative, a group of parents whose children had a limited command of Hebrew raised the novel idea of establishing the

---

115 Dov Levin, *The Litvaks: A Short History of the Jews in Lithuania* (Jerusalem: Yad Vashem, 2009), 144–149. Cf. Mordechai Zalkin, "Žydų mokyklų idėjinė diferenciacija," in Sirutavičius, Staliūnas, and Šiaučiūnaitė-Verbickienė, *Lietuvos žydai: istorinė studija*, 357–370; also, Saulius Kaubrys, "Žydų mokyklų tinklas: kiekybinių pokyčių charakteristikos," in Sirutavičius, Staliūnas, Šiaučiūnaitė-Verbickienė, *Lietuvos žydai: istorinė studija*, 371–385.

first Jewish secondary school with Lithuanian as the language of instruction, something considered a breakthrough at the time. This gymnasium in Kaunas received modest subsidies from the Ministry of Education in Kaunas and recorded an enrollment of 230 students by 1939.[116]

Under the authoritarian rule of Antanas Smetona (1926–1940) political expression was curtailed, but the press and social organizations were given considerable latitude as forums for communal issues. Lithuania's Jewish press reflected a diverse spectrum of religious-cultural outlooks and political views. During the 1920s a large part of the urban secular Jewish community were avid readers of Lithuania's Russian-language press, but these publications proved less popular among the younger generation. Between 1921 and 1931 sixty Hebrew- and Yiddish-language magazines appeared in Lithuania. In 1935 the First Republic's Jews supported six daily newspapers and four weekly periodicals. One estimate is that during the 1930s the printing presses issued three hundred Yiddish- and nearly 230 Hebrew-language publications.[117] The Yiddish-language daily *Di Yiddishe Shtime* (The Jewish Voice) founded in 1919 by the Lithuanian Zionist Federation was the most widely read interwar Jewish newspaper, covering Lithuanian domestic issues and foreign policy in depth and urging readers to participate, as citizens, in the life of the country.[118] The Smetona government generally viewed the Zionist movement favorably. Some Lithuanians considered Zionists "fellow nationalists"; others, less kindly, saw the Hechaluz (He-Halutz) youth movement, which encouraged emigration to a Jewish homeland in Palestine, as a solution to the "Jewish problem." The authorities kept a closer eye on the daily *Das Vort* (The Word), the mouthpiece of the Zionist Socialists

---

116 Benediktas Šetkus, "Kauno žydų gimnazija dėstomąja lietuvių kalba: vokiečių ir žydų konfrontacijos darinys," *Lituanistica* 65, no. 2 (2019): 74–87.

117 See Larisa Lempertienė, "Tapukario Lietuvos politinių ir socialinių aktualijų pateikimas žydų dienraštyje *Di Jidiše štime*," in *Abipusis pažinimas: lietuvių ir žydų kultūriniai saitai*, ed. Jurgita Šiaučiūnaitė-Verbickienė (Vilnius: Vilniaus universiteto leidykla, 2010), 229–244; cf. Pavel Lavrinec, "Žydų bendruomenė, lietuvių kultūra ir rusų spauda," in Šiaučiūnaitė-Verbickienė, *Abipusis pažinimas*, 201–227; Levin, *Litvaks*, 150–156; Mordechai Zalkin, "Lietuvos žydų bendruomenės kultūrinės transformacijos," in Sirutavičius, Staliūnas, and Šiaučiūnaitė-Verbickienė, *Lietuvos žydai: istorinė studija*, 351.

118 A history of Lithuanian Zionism from 1906–1940 utilizing Lithuanian archival sources and materials from YIVO is Eglė Bendikaitė, *Sionistinis sąjūdis Lietuvoje* (Vilnius: LII, 2006).

published between 1932 and 1940, and occasionally detained the more radical Marxist members of the movement.[119]

The popular religious periodical *Der Yiddishe leben* (Jewish life) opposed the Zionists and, by contrast, showed little interest in Lithuanian affairs outside the confines of the Orthodox Jewish community. The *Folksblat* (The People's Paper), which represented the ideology of the Folkist movement and moved closer to the radical left during the 1930s, clashed with the Zionists on issues of language (Yiddish vs. Hebrew) and whether the future of the Jewish nation lay in the diaspora or emigration to Palestine.[120] Jewish periodicals in the Lithuanian language emerged slowly. In 1924–1925 *Yidishe Shtime* issued a biweekly Lithuanian-language supplement *Mūsų garsas* (Our voice), but the only long-term interwar Lithuanian-language Jewish periodical was the weekly *Apžvalga* (Review), published from 1935 to 1940 by the Association of Jewish Soldiers of Lithuania's Independence Wars (LŽKS). The association, which counted nearly 2,500 members in over forty-three chapters during the mid-1930s, followed a pro-Smetona line, but, when the editors deemed necessary, defended Jewish interests and criticized public manifestations of antisemitism.[121]

Aside from the educational system and the press, Lithuania's Jews sponsored a variety of cultural organizations ranging from theatrical and musical companies to the popular network of the internationally renowned Maccabi sports clubs, which, at its peak, gathered 5,800 members in eighty-two clubs throughout the country. Lithuania's Jewish community, subsidized in part by the OZE and the Joint, supported eight Jewish hospitals with six hundred beds, including the large Bikkur-Holim in Kaunas. In all, 215 Jewish organizations, institutions, and associations were registered with the Ministry of the Interior in 1938.[122]

---

119 Atamukas, *Lietuvos žydų kelias*, 174. For an overview of the contentious trends in Lithuanian Zionism, see Levin, *Litvaks*, 160–173.

120 See Eglė Bendikaitė, "Dvi ideologijo—vienas judėjimas: sionistinis socializmas nepriklausomoje Lietuvoje," *Darbai ir dienos* 34 (2003): 255–271 and her "Walking a Thin Line: The Successes and Failures of Socialist Zionism in Lithuania," *Polin* 25 (2013): 207–227.

121 See Anna Verschik, "The Lithuanian-Language Periodicals *Mūsų garsas* (1924–1925) and *Apžvalga* (1935–1940): A Sociolinguistic Evolution," *Polin* 25 (2013): 293–303.

122 Zalkin, "Lietuvos žydų bendruomenės," in Sirutavičius, Staliūnas, and Šiaučiūnaitė-Verbickienė, *Lietuvos žydai: istorinė studija*, 354; Levin, *Litvaks*, 151–154, 178–181. The OZE (R. Obshchestvo okhraneniya zdorovya evreiskogo naseleniya) was founded in

The Jews of Vilnius, the city known as the "Jerusalem of the North" faced different challenges from their brethren in Kaunas. Polish rule proved more violently antisemitic: in terms of scale, there were no analogues in Lithuania to the Easter pogroms of 1919 or the 1931 riots at Stefan Batory University. The Jews here maintained a diverse social and cultural life, not unlike that in "Kaunas Lithuania," reflected in the conflicting Zionist, Orthodox, and Folkist parties. In 1931 the Jewish community in Vilnius supported five dailies and some 224 Hebrew and Yiddish publications.[123] Vilnius had been the center of the Jewish workers' movement at the turn of the twentieth century and, despite a decline after the Great War, once again grew in strength during the late 1930s.[124] The YIVO (Yidisher Visnshaftlekher Institut) library and research institute founded in 1925 became, and is still today one of the foremost centers of Yiddish scholarship in the world. YIVO, relocated to New York in 1940, was to inherit what remained of the famous Strashun Library of Judaica. The Jung Vilne writers' movement, which came of age in the 1930s under the stewardship of Chaim Grade (1910–1982), Avraham Sutzkever (1913–2010), and others, became one of the best-known Yiddish literary groups. Following the restoration of Polish-Lithuanian diplomatic relations in March 1938 Yiddish writers from Kaunas sought to initiate joint ventures with Jung Vilne, but this incipient cooperation was cut short by the war and Soviet occupation.[125]

Lithuanians and Jews in the Economy of the First Republic

Revolutionary structural changes in the country's urban demography impacted national politics. The republic's first census of 1923 showed that Kaunas and Šiauliai had Lithuanian-speaking majorities for the first time in history.[126] The

---

St. Petersburg in 1912; "the Joint" refers to the American Jewish Joint Distribution Committee.

123 Mordechai Zalkin, "Kultūrinės tarpukario Vilniaus žydų erdvės," in Sirutavičius, Staliūnas, and Šiaučiūnaitė-Verbickienė, *Lietuvos žydai: istorinė studija*, 416.

124 Jack Jacobs, "The Bund in Vilna, 1918-1939," *Polin* 25 (2013): 263–292.

125 See Atamukas, *Lietuvos žydų kelias*, 176–190; also, Akvilė Grigoravičiūtė, "Jidiš literatūra tarpukario Lietuvoje (1918–1940): savasties paieškos," *Colloquia* 29 (2012): 60.

126 The change was partly due to the forced evacuation of much of Lithuania's urban population to the Russian interior in 1915. The imperial Russian census of 1897 listed the following percentages of urban ethnic Lithuanians: in Kaunas, 6.6%; in Šiauliai, 27.7%; in Panevėžys,

unprecedented influx of ethnic Lithuanians into cities and towns during the early 1920s intensified competition in housing, commerce, industry, and the professions. In 1926 the Kaunas City Council debated allegations that Jewish landlords had manipulated the real estate market in favor of their coreligionists. Lithuanians migrating to Kaunas appealed to the president to help establish "Lithuanian neighborhoods" in the city and urged the government "to undertake a solution... since it is a question of ensuring the Lithuanian nation's status in Kaunas." The new urbanites complained about the unresponsiveness of local government, since "the dominant element in the City Council is composed of non-Lithuanians, who had, have, and will continue to have a negative attitude on the question of strengthening the Lithuanian element."[127] The petitioners eschewed antisemitic rhetoric, but they clearly assumed a political struggle along national lines.

Changes in the distribution of economic power led to interethnic tensions. Before independence, the nonagrarian economy had remained largely inaccessible to ethnic Lithuanians. In 1912 less than 7% of ethnic Lithuanians owned urban real estate, and only one of twenty-five were proprietors of commercial and industrial enterprises.[128] During the initial years of Lithuanian rule, change came slowly. In 1923, Jews still owned 83% of the country's commercial and retail establishments, but over the next decade Lithuanian-owned businesses expanded rapidly. In 1935 government statisticians estimated that ethnic Lithuanians made up half of traders (*prekybininkai*) in towns and 55% of persons defined as businessmen (*verslininkai*) (15% and 2% respectively, in 1923). By 1939–1940 Linas, the Lithuanian-owned flax producers' cooperative accounted for 58% of exports in a branch of the economy historically dominated by Jewish middlemen. Government policies tended to favor Lithuanian-owned corporations in which the state held substantial shares, such as the sugar concern Lietuvos Cukrus. Smetona's regime encouraged the expansion of ethnic

---

12.1%. See Vytautas Merkys, "Lietuvos miestų gyventojų tautybės XIX a. pabaigoje, XX a. pradžioje klausimu," *LTSR MA Darbai* A 2 (5) (1958): 85–98.

127 Petitions found in LCVA, f. 922, ap. 1, b. 13, l. 57–59, 72–73. A thorough investigation of the "Lithuanization" of Kaunas during the interwar period is in Mindaugas Balkus, *Kaip Kovno tapo Kaunu: miesto lituanizavimas 1918–1940 m.* (Kaunas: Vytauto Didžiojo universitetas, 2023).

128 On the differences between Lithuanian and Jewish economic development before the Great War see Abba Strazhas, "Die nationale Erwachen des litausches Volkes und die Judenheit," *Acta Universitatis Stockholmiensis-Studia Baltica Stockholmiensa* 2 (1985): 180–182.

Lithuanian business ownership, which Jews decried as favoritism but which the beneficiaries of the policy viewed as long overdue "affirmative action" on behalf of a previously sidelined community. However, the growing participation of Lithuanians in the economy by no means eliminated the economic role of the Jews. In 1936, despite considerable inroads by Lithuanian shopkeepers, Jews operated nearly half of the country's small retail outlets. In 1939 Jewish companies handled at least a fifth of Lithuania's exports and an estimated two-fifths of imports. Jews remained well-represented in the professions, comprising more than two-fifths of the country's doctors and lawyers on the eve of the Second World War.[129]

The Lithuanian Businessmen's Association (Lietuvių verslininkų sąjunga) founded in 1932 vigorously promoted what they regarded as ethnic Lithuanian interests. Popularly known as the *verslininkai*, they sought to limit "alien" economic influences and initially directed their antipathy towards Germans, "the most malevolent of our nation's enemies," urging well-to-do Lithuanians to hire Swiss or French rather than German nannies.[130] But the opposition to Germans was situational, no doubt influenced by Hitler's irredentist rhetoric and the danger of Nazi front groups in Klaipėda. In the end, the *verslininkai* came to identify Jewish economic "tyranny" as the major obstacle to ethnic Lithuanian prevalence in commerce, maintaining that the goal of the supposedly rightful share of 85% Lithuanian participation in business should be achieved by "natural evolution."[131] This benign posture was belied by vitriolic articles painting Jews as rootless profiteers with an inbred urge towards world hegemony. The Jewish press in Kaunas, especially *Di Yidishe Shtime* and *Apžvalga*, responded with their own scathing counterattacks, ridiculing crude antisemitic notions.[132]

Concerned by the agrarian unrest caused by the global depression of the 1930s and the Nazi threat in Klaipėda, the regime had little stomach for extremist rhetoric. The mayor of Kaunas, Antanas Merkys (1887–1955), and other

---

129 See Atamukas, *Lietuvos žydu kelias*, 140–150; Gediminas Vaskela, "Žydai Lietuvos ūkio struktūroje," in Sirutavičius, Staliūnas, and Šiaučiūnaitė-Verbickienė, *Lietuvos žydai: istorinė studija*, 338–339, 343; Vladas Sirutavičius, "Valdžios politika," 320.

130 As in "Vokietijos piliečių biznis Lietuvoje"; "Nekaskime sau duobės," *Verslas*, March 17, 1932, 1, and "Vokiečiai patys save plaka ir patys rėkia," *Verslas*, March 31, 1932, 1.

131 "Ko mes norime?" *Verslas*, February 24, 1932, 1–2.

132 For example, Nachmanas Lurje's comparison of "cultured" Polish antisemitism and the more primitive Lithuanian type, from *Yiddishe Shtime* as translated in, "Ką rašo žydai apie lietuvius," *Verslas* April 14, 1932, 5.

government ministers criticized the *verslininkai*, reaffirmed the regime's pledge to protect minorities, and cautioned business owners to observe the principles of "moral competition" and to reject "low-brow chauvinism."[133] The elder statesman Ernestas Galvanauskas (1882–1967) suggested that antisemitism among the younger Lithuanian generation resulted partly from failure to find employment in a saturated public sector and in professions previously dominated by non-Lithuanians. But he downplayed Jewish economic discrimination against Lithuanians, a favorite claim of antisemitic businessmen.[134] Chastened by the fact that they had been compelled to publish criticism of nationalist excesses in their own newspaper, the radicals briefly moderated their views and adopted a more professional stance. But there was no long-term change of colors. Emboldened by the growing right-wing opposition to Smetona during the late thirties, the *verslininkai* began to demand "laws that would regulate the Jewish question" and establish quotas in employment and business, "until such time as the majority percentage of Lithuanians is also reflected in commerce."[135] But the government never seriously considered such actions despite the pressure from the more radical wing of the Nationalist Union.

The economic consequences of majority rule, primarily readjustments towards a more equitable allocation of ownership and rewards within the economy as a whole, caused predictable rifts in Lithuanian-Jewish relations. It

IMAGE 1.2.
Jews in the provincial economy.
The Cheichelis (Cheichel, Haykhel) family inn and imported goods store, Skaudvilė, northwestern Lithuania, ca. early 1920s. (Courtesy of Skaudvilė Regional Museum.)

---

133 A B-is, "Į jūsų tikslus aš žiūriu teigiama prasme—sako burmistras Merkys," *Verslas*, December 19, 1935, 2.
134 "Rektorius E. Galvanauskas apie lietuvius ir žydus verslininkus," *Verslas*, February 6, 1936, 3.
135 "Ko mes norime," *Verslas*, December 16, 1938, 1.

1. Tradition, Accommodation, Conflict | 53

IMAGE 1.3. A lost relic of the modern Litvak economy.
Top: The Central Jewish Bank built in 1925, one of the first public buildings in the art deco style which came to characterize modern Kaunas.
Bottom: Restored in 1961 as the city's zoological museum but demolished in 1980.
(Courtesy of Kaunas City Museum.)

IMAGE 1.4. Group portrait of children from the Jewish kindergarten on 9 Mapų Street, Kaunas. 1932. (United States Holocaust Memorial Museum Photo Archives #60604. Courtesy of Association of Lithuanian Jews in Israel. Copyright of United States Holocaust Memorial Museum.)

IMAGE 1.5. Group portrait of the Gar family in Kruonis [Kron], 1921. (United States Holocaust Memorial Museum Photo Archives #21931. Courtesy of Libbey Sansanowicz. Copyright of United States Holocaust Memorial Museum.)

1. Tradition, Accommodation, Conflict | 55

IMAGE 1.6. Top: Group portrait of a Lithuanian military unit in front of a house owned by the Gar family in Kruonis [Kron], 1925. Jacob Gar, the photograph donor's uncle, served in the Lithuanian army in the early 1920s. (United States Holocaust Memorial Museum Photo Archives #21930. Courtesy of Libbey Sansanowicz. Copyright of United States Holocaust Memorial Museum.)
Bottom: Jewish soldiers from the 9th Battalion of the Lithuanian army, ca. 1920–1930. (United States Holocaust Memorial Museum Photo Archives #02186. Courtesy of Moshe Michles.
Copyright of United States Holocaust Memorial Museum.)

IMAGE 1.7. Jewish patriots of the Šeduva chapter of the Union for the Liberation of Vilnius at the town's Jewish elementary school, June 1937, with a sign reading: "Oh Vilnius, Jerusalem of the Jews, the Jews of Lithuania will fight for you forever!" Four people in the first row from right to left: principal Strolis Fišas (sitting), physician Julius Blumberg, shopkeeper Samuelis Nolis, a volunteer veteran of the independence wars, chairman Rabbi Mordechai Henkin. (Courtesy of Panevėžys Local Lore Museum, file No. PKM 3775 F1882.)

should be noted that precise statistics on interwar business ownership by nationality are subject to some variations because of the inconsistency of the different sources, but the general tendency as described above is clear enough. The nonagrarian economy more than doubled in size between 1924 and 1939, although this growth was less than in the agricultural sector. Considering the impact of Jewish emigration and the rapid demographic revolution in the cities and towns, it is not surprising that most of this expansion benefitted ethnic Lithuanians. The number of both Jewish businesses and Jews in the professions did not significantly change during this period. In most cases, the change in the relative Jewish-Lithuanian share of the economic pie was not a redistribution of already existing assets.[136]

---

136 See the detailed analysis in Gediminas Vaskela, "Žydu ir lietuvių santykiai visuomenės modernėjimo ir socialinės sferos politinio reguliavimo aspektais (XX a, pirmoji pusė)," in *Žydai Lietuvos ekonominėje-socialinėje struktūroje: tarp tarpininko ir konkurento*, ed. Vladas Sirutavičius and Darius Staliūnas (Vilnius: LII, 2006), 133–176. Redistribution is suggested in Götz Aly, *Europe against the Jews 1880–1945*, trans. Jefferson Chase (Metropolitan Books: New York, 2020), 184.

Cultural Reorientation: Tensions in a Modernizing Society

The struggle over the economy percolated within a broader landscape of political, cultural, and social problems. The depression of the early and mid-1930s provided the underground Lithuanian Communist Party (LCP) and its front organizations with useful propaganda against factory owners, many of whom were Jews. At times anti-capitalist complaints translated into antisemitic tropes, further amplified by long-standing cultural and religious irritants. In 1935, Lithuanian workers in Vilkaviškis petitioned to be released from Sunday work, claiming that the Jewish owners threatened to fire them for their impudence. The resentful workers found themselves, in their own words, "quietly observing [Saturdays] with the Jews." Gentile workers at the Tigras factory in Pilviškiai were scandalized because "the local owners and workers, mostly Jews, work on Sundays and even on national holidays."[137] But it was also the talk in the synagogues that "Jews are being increasingly persecuted in Lithuania. Various concessions to the farmers are impacting the Jews, who, at the same time, are burdened with [higher] taxes."[138]

There were examples of political cooperation on issues of mutual interest. Jews found they could support national goals that motivated Lithuanian society; for example, many adopted a pro-Lithuanian political stance during the conflict with Poland over Vilnius. As one Jewish leader explained, the Polish demand for, at the very least, "neutral" Jewish behavior on the issue would be a "sellout of our [Lithuanian] fatherland."[139] In 1933 the first Jewish chapter of the Union for the Liberation of Vilnius was established in Mažeikiai. On another front, as German-Lithuanian relations worsened in late 1935 because of Smetona's crackdown on Nazi front groups in Klaipėda, some Jews argued that rather than expending resources improving the city's port, the republic should use the money to buy up German land, settle it with Lithuanians, and "forbid the German language in schools and public institutions." The state security service noted "considerable interest in the economic and political situation [among Jews]."[140]

Official Lithuania negotiated accommodation to Jewish religious sensibilities. When Lithuania's rabbis asked the government to delay the drafting of

---

137 LCVA, f. 378, ap. 4, b. 240, l. 1, 29.
138 Ibid., l. 33.
139 Taken from *Unser Tag* as reprinted in LCVA, f. 1437, ap. 1, b. 100, l. 20.
140 LCVA, f. 378, ap. 4, b. 240, l. 33.

conscripts until after the Jewish New Year, the authorities approved the request.[141] In 1932, Kaunas rabbis asked the Ministry of Communication to release Jews from taxation on goods held over at railroad stations on Saturdays and in this case apply "Sunday" rules to Jewish businesses. Officials rejected the request on the grounds that "Saturday is a day of work for all state institutions."[142] The proposed Catholic University of Lithuania, which planned to open its doors during the early 1930s, announced its intention to treat both Saturdays and Sundays as holidays since it was expected that "Jews would form a large contingent of students," especially in the faculty of commerce.[143] Government subsidies for rabbinical salaries and cultural institutions continued throughout the interwar period, a contrast to the situation in Poland and other countries of the region.

The changing structure of the modernized higher education system in a country with limited white-collar employment prospects presented another arena of interethnic contention. Until 1930 Jews constituted an estimated 35–40% of medical students and at least a third of those enrolled in law. The government rejected demands for proportional national enrollment, the numerus clausus, but the introduction of compulsory Lithuanian-language entrance examinations reduced Jewish enrollment at the University of Kaunas. During 1935–1936 there were reportedly 486 Jews out of 3,223 students in Lithuania's higher education system, about twice the proportion of Jews in the total population but a two-fold decline in the percentage of Jewish students since the late 1920s.[144] Jews continued to participate in a significant way both on the faculty and among students. The 1931 elections to the University of Kaunas student assembly chose ten Jewish representatives, second only to the influential Catholic organization Ateitis (The future). The Communist front managed to elect only two representatives.[145]

The influx of ethnic Lithuanians into the educational system reflected the culmination of a change long in the making. The vernaculars of the largely

---

141 "Žydai per šventes prašo naujokų neimti," *Lietuvos žinios*, August 10, 1932, 5.
142 "Rabinų prašymas Susisiekimo ministerijai," *Lietuvos žinios*, August 5, 1932, 5.
143 "Katalikų universitetas švęs ir šeštadieniais," *Lietuvos žinios*, August 26, 1932, 5.
144 Royal Institute of International Affairs, *The Baltic States* (London: Oxford University Press, 1938), 31; cf. similar numbers in Atamukas, *Lietuvos žydų kelias*, 158. In 1930 the University was officially named the Vytautas Magnus University (Vytauto Didžiojo universitetas), a title restored in 1990.
145 "Kieno akademinis jaunimas?," *Aušra*, November 24, 1931, 1.

peasant nations living between the Polish and Russian heartlands (Lithuanians, Latvians, Estonians, Ukrainians) emerged as codified literary languages only in the late nineteenth century. Within the multinational empires, their use, unlike that of Russian and German, was geographically and socially limited and thus provided no obvious benefit in terms of cultural prestige or economic/professional advancement.[146] In 1918, for the first time in history, Lithuanian became the official language of a nation-state rather than the idiom of a social underclass. The widespread use of Lithuanian in government offices throughout the country became the norm only in the late 1920s, partly because of resistance from the national minorities who preferred the use of Russian, Polish, or German in public life.[147] Lithuanian-language official discourse in the First Republic confronted non-Lithuanians with an unfamiliar and vexing dilemma. In the words of historian Mordechai Zalkin, "The Jewish community . . . was watching this process with a mixture of wonder and skepticism. Due to its primitive image, Lithuanian cultural heritage was never considered worthy of serious interest by most local Jews."[148] Historically, most Yiddish-speaking educated Jews preferred Russian as their linguistic/cultural "second home."[149] The persistence of this pattern offended Lithuanians who were sensitive to the prerogatives of their native tongue.

In 1923–1924 nationalist youth carried out a cultural "Lithuanianization" of the country's major cities, demonstrating their patriotism by systematically defacing Yiddish- and Polish-language storefronts. The intellectual and political elite condemned the outbreak as hooliganism and called for respecting the rights of minorities, but the language issue festered and beginning in 1924 the government instituted rules regulating Lithuanian and minority-language displays.[150] Smetona wondered at the Jewish propensity for using Russian: like many Lithuanians, he preferred that the Jews preserve Yiddish or Hebrew among themselves but utilize Lithuanian when addressing persons outside

---

146 Verschik, "Lithuanian-Language Periodicals": 293–294.
147 Pranas Jankauskas, "Lietuviškasis lūžis: kalbų varžybos Kauno savivaldybėje 1918–1928 metais," *Darbai ir dienos* 34 (2003): 33–47.
148 Zalkin, "Sharunas, Prince of Dainava": 150.
149 See Darius Staliūnas, "Rusų kalba kaip lietuvių ir žydų komunikacijos priemonė: laikraštis Naš kraj (1914)," in Šiaučiūnaitė-Verbickienė, *Abipusis pažinimas*, 162–181.
150 Vladas Sirutavičius, "Antisemitism in Inter-War Lithuania: An Analysis of Two Cases," *Jahrbuch für Antisemitismusforschung* 12 (2012): 133–143.

the community.¹⁵¹ In 1937 Jewish organizations in Kaunas passed a resolution condemning the use of Russian in "public places," emphasizing that such behavior "really does intensely irritate Lithuanians," and urging understanding of Lithuanian feelings about past persecutions of their culture and language. The meeting was well received: even the *verslininkai* commented that "we can only welcome such an attitude on the part of Jewish society."¹⁵²

Life itself compelled the younger generation of Jews towards an accommodation to the newly dominant culture, although not without difficulty. The state budget supported 90% of Jewish primary schools and provided subsidies for Jewish cultural institutions. But even as they acknowledged progress in language competence among students, officials complained of the "woefully inadequate" knowledge of Lithuanian, particularly in provincial schools. Lithuanian educators pressed for more subjects to be taught in the state language, a demand that evoked protests over the diluting of "Jewishness" within the minority educational system.¹⁵³ Anecdotal and statistical evidence indicates that during the two interwar decades, Jews in the cities and larger towns acquired sufficient competence in Lithuanian, and at least some moved away from a Russian cultural orientation. Acculturation was less evident in the shtetls where the older generation had limited interest in acquiring a serious command of the "peasant tongue."¹⁵⁴ In any case, there is little evidence that ethnic Lithuanians desired Jewish assimilation into their world.¹⁵⁵ The centuries-old legacy of linguistically and/or territorially distinct national communities in the postwar successor states remained strong.

---

151 Antanas Smetona, *Pasakyta parašyta 1935–1940*, vol. 2 (Boston: Lithuanian Encyclopedia Press, 1974), 34. On relations between Smetona and the Jews see Liudas Truska, *Antanas Smetona ir jo laikai* (Vilnius: Valstybinis leidybos centras, 1996), 296–305.

152 "Pagaliau patys žydai pasmerkė rusų kalbos vartojimą," *Verslas*, November 4, 1937, 1.

153 See Benediktas Šetkus, "Valstybinės kalbos mokymas Lietuvos žydų gimnazijose ir progimnazijose 1919–1940 metais," *Istorija* 108, no. 4 (2017): 67–96.

154 Zalkin, "Sharunas": 149–153.

155 See Veronika Žukaitė, "Bandymai mokyti žydus lietuvių kalbos tarpukario Lietuvoje: mokomųjų priemonių tyrimas," in Šiaučiūnaitė-Verbickienė, *Abipusis pažinimas*, 312–331; Zalkin, "'Ant žodžių tilto': žydų susitikimas su lietuvių kultūra tarpukario Lietuvoje," in *Abipusis pažinimas*, 56–57; Jurgita Šiaučiūnaitė-Verbickienė, "Žydų ir lietuvių abipusio pažinimo ir kultūrinio bendradarbiavimo atspirtys tarpukario Lietuvoje: priemonės ir rezultatai," in Šiaučiūnaitė-Verbickienė, *Abipusis pažinimas*, 16–50.

One should not, however, ignore tendencies within the First Republic that held potential for positive developments.¹⁵⁶ The Litvak writer and journalist Uriah Katzenelenbogen (1885–1980) was one of the advocates of cultural collaboration between Lithuanian Jews and their fellow citizens. Jewish scholars published articles in the press concerning such cultural and historical issues as "Lithuanian influences on the Jews."¹⁵⁷ Lithuania's semi-official daily commented on a positive, albeit aspirational process:

> A few years ago, it was difficult to find a Jew who could speak fine Lithuanian and was acquainted with Lithuanian literature, but now we can see among the Jews young philologists who effortlessly compete with young Lithuanian linguists. This is a sign that Lithuanian Jews will go in the same direction as the Jews of other civilized countries, contributing their part to the cultural treasures of those nations in whose states they live.¹⁵⁸

Several prominent Lithuanian intellectuals took an interest in Jewish culture. In 1928 two of the country's leading literati, the writer Juozas Tumas-Vaižgantas (1869–1933) and the cultural historian Mykolas Biržiška (1862–1962), founded the Lithuania-Jewish Society for Cultural Cooperation (Lietuvių-žydų kultūrinio bendradarbiavimo draugija) which sponsored lectures and meetings. But the society failed to gain traction among a wider public and closed in 1937, its fate symptomatic of the reality that the promotion of interethnic cultural enrichment was limited to a relatively small segment of the Lithuanian and Jewish elites.¹⁵⁹ On the other hand, Lithuanian culture reached a part of the Jewish public that had not fully mastered the state language through a wide array of translations.¹⁶⁰

---

156 As in the case of the Olkinas family.
157 J. Livšinas, "Žydų įtaka lietuvių gyvenimui," *Lietuvos aidas*, August 2, 1929, 2–3; cf. Ch. Lemchenas, "Dėl lietuvių įtakos žydų gyvenimui," *Lietuvos aidas*, August 9, 1929, 5, and Livšinas's final response, "Dar dėl lietuvių įtakos žydams klausimo," *Lietuvos aidas*, August 27, 1929, 3.
158 "Būkime tikri patriotai," *Lietuvos aidas*, August 20, 1929, 1.
159 Jurgita Šiaučiūnaitė-Verbickienė, "Lietuvių ir žydų komunikacija viešojoje erdvėje: pažinimo paieškos," in Sirutavičius, Staliūnas, and Šiaučiūnaitė-Verbickienė, *Lietuvos žydai: istorinė studija*, 387–402.
160 See Zalkin, "Sharunas, Prince of Dainava," 152–162.

Anti-Jewish Rhetoric, Violence, and the "Iron Wall": The Struggle over Antisemitism from the Late 1920s to 1938

Anti-Jewish discourse ebbed and flowed, arising most noticeably during the early to mid-twenties during the crisis of democratic governance and then again during the late 1930s, when an exclusionary Lithuanian nationalism and antisemitic narratives gained currency among students, part of the intelligentsia, and Smetona's enemies on the right.[161] Two accusations common to modern antisemitism emerged among Lithuanians prone to antisemitic ideas: Jewish economic exploitation of non-Jews and the role of Jews in revolutionary movements. The secretive anti-Smetona Iron Wolf movement founded in 1927 proposed a program of humane antisemitism in order to "shake off Jewish mediation and Jewish exploitation":

> [T]he Wolves should not forget the Lithuanian struggle for liberation from Jewish economic slavery. The year 1929 should mark the beginning of a new antisemitic movement. Of course, excesses will not serve our final goal, but will only postpone its achievement. The anti-Jewish action initiated by us must flow into entirely different, cultural forms, which do not violate the principles of ethics and humanity.[162]

In 1933 the twenty-three-year-old army lieutenant Jonas Noreika amplified the Wolves' program and the *Verslas* propaganda on Jewish "economic tyranny" in a booklet titled *Lithuanian, Raise Your Head!* Stationed in Klaipėda where incipient local Nazi groups fought the territory's "Lithuanization," Noreika fired barbs at "the bloody life in Germany" and called for a "struggle against non-Lithuanians engaged in commerce." But the main target was unmistakable: "For once and for all: we never buy from the Jews. We can sell them butter, eggs, and cheese, but only if they do not profit from this, and only if they buy for [their own consumption]."[163] Despite calls for an anti-Jewish boycott, there is little evidence that Lithuanians ceased patronizing Jewish businesses on a significant scale. The anti-Jewish propaganda emanating from the Lithuanian Businessmen's Association, whose membership was never as robust as the *verslininkai*

---

161 Sirutavičius, "Antisemitizmo proveržiai," 403–416.

162 LCVA, f. 563, ap. 1, b. 1, l. 115; on the Iron Wolf's links to Italian fascism, see ibid., l. 18–21, 44–45.

163 Jonas Noreika, *Pakelk galvą lietuvi!!!* (Kaunas: V. Atkočiūno sp., 1933), 22, 24, 32. For Noreika's role during the German occupation, see Chapter 3.

claimed, had no appreciable effect on either the government's economic policies or successful Jewish businesses but did serve to "infect Lithuanian society with the bud of economic antisemitism."[164]

The Judeo-Bolshevik canard was to become a staple among extreme Lithuanian nationalists after 1940, but the idea had gained some influence in earlier years as well. In 1929 the writer Povilas Jakubėnas warned that the country's Yiddish-language schools, unlike the conservative and Zionist institutions, were "opening the door to internationalist and nihilist" thought and that without proper religious orientation, Jewish youth would become "victims of Communist propaganda." Dr. Mendel Sudarskis defended the Yiddish schools, while admitting that some of their graduates exhibited leftist tendencies. Conservative Jews shared the Smetona government's aversion to Communism.[165] In May 1929 the Central Committee of the Lithuanian Rabbinical Association directed a memorandum to the president opposing the Education Ministry's plan to integrate religious (Yavne) elementary schools with the general Jewish primary system, noting that devout parents desired that their children not be raised as "leftists" or come under other dangerous influences.[166] In this case, the position of the rabbis was not much different from that of the State Security Department that urged vigilance against antisemitic agitation but also warned of Communist influence among the Jews.[167]

International repercussions emerged from an incident on August 1, 1929 when, during the international Red Day protests organized by the Comintern,[168] authorities in Kaunas carried out an action against Communist activists. According to an initial report, "a few Jewish fellows who had tried to organize a protest against militarism" failed when "the police detained, with the help of workers, 81 persons, 16 women and 65 men, [among whom were] 76 Jews and five Catholics."[169] Ordinary citizens joined in suppressing the protesters.

---

164 As in Hektoras Vitkus, "Smulkiojo verslo lituanizacijs tarpukario Lietuvoje: ideologija ir praktika," in *Žydai Lietuvos ekonominėje-socialinėje struktūroje*, 177–216.

165 P. Jakubėnas, "Žydų mokyklos ir žydų jaunuomenė valstybingumo atžvilgiu," *Lietuvos aidas*, August 27, 1929, 5.; cf. M. Sudarskis, "Idišistiškų mokyklų ideologija ir uždaviniai" and P. Jakubėnas, "Atsakymas p. dr. Sudarskiui," *Lietuvos aidas*, September 5, 1929, 5.

166 LCVA, f. 922, ap. 1, b. 48, l. 1ff.

167 LCVA, f. 394, ap. 4, b. 273, l. 49–50.

168 The Communist International, also known as the Third International, was the global alliance of Communist parties from 1919 to 1943.

169 LCVA, f. 394, ap. 15, b. 138.

According to subsequent court proceedings, groups of armed men, some in civilian dress and others in Riflemen uniforms, had detained suspicious passers-by. The victims were "exclusively citizens of Jewish nationality," who were beaten, humiliated, and forced to perform "calisthenics." One of the victims avoided a beating when the anti-Communists found an issue of the "patriotic newspaper" *Lietuvos aidas* in the man's pocket.

Two years later judges in the case indicted seventeen persons who had "beaten citizens in the streets of Slabada [Vilijampolė neighborhood] because of hatred of the Jews." In relating the "reasons for the excesses," the daily *Lietuvos žinios* reported that they were the result of the "fact that the hooligans had for a long time been full of hatred for the Jewish nationality, since [according to the culprits] among the Jews there are many Communists, and that at least 95% of Lithuania's Communists are Jews."[170] But as the antisemitic character of the rioting became public, the Riflemen's Union (Šaulių sąjunga) issued a condemnation of antisemitism and pointed out that the union included Jewish members.[171] In his report to Smetona and in the order of the day, the interior minister announced the dismissal of policemen who had ignored the violence and reprimanded authorities for their initially irresolute response to the attacks on Jews.[172] While prosecutors demanded harsh prison sentences, the courts ultimately sentenced twelve men to terms of between three and nine months imprisonment and acquitted five of those accused. A civil case brought by some of the aggrieved Jews for damages inflicted during the riot was dismissed.[173]

The editors of *Lietuvos aidas* denounced the excesses, singling out the culprits as "yahoo patriots [*urapatriotai*]," and also "chauvinists," for whom "even the current nationally minded government is not patriotic enough." The daily regretted that some Jews of the older generation "still cannot get accustomed to the idea of an independent Lithuania," but stressed that the younger generation of Jews had demonstrated loyalty: "This means that Lithuanian Jews

---

170 "Slabados ekscesų byloj patraukta atsakomybėn 17 žmonių," *Lietuvos žinios*, October 1, 1931, 2.
171 V[pseud.], "Ar šauliai yra antisemitai?," *Trimitas* 35 (August 29, 1929): 583.
172 "Report on the Events in Slabada," LCVA, F. 922, ap. 1, b. 3, l. 3–8. An exhaustive investigation of the Slabada demonstrations and excesses is contained in the collection LCVA, f. 394, ap. 15, b. 138, l. 273–359. Cf. Vladas Sirutavičius, "Antisemitism in Inter-War Lithuania": 143–148. A useful review that includes Jewish sources is in Casper, "Strangers and Sojourners," 194–199.
173 "Slabados ekscesininkų motivuotas sprendimas paskelbtas," *Lietuvos žinios*, July 7, 1932, 6.

will also have to become good patriots of their country. But this depends partly on Lithuanian patriots as well, who must return the Jews' trust with their own." Since the summer of 1929 had also witnessed similar attacks on "Polish-speaking citizens," the paper generalized that violence against any non-Lithuanians deserved the "greatest condemnation."[174] Some Jews clearly wished to bury the incident. Iosifas Serebravičius, a teacher from Rokiškis active in local politics, warned Lithuanian Jews that "foreign interests" were exaggerating a local disturbance as a "pogrom" and questioned the wisdom of hiring foreign attorneys in the matter, as this would only aid Lithuania's enemies.[175]

The deadly 1931 pogroms in Polish-ruled Vilnius also provoked criticism of antisemitism, the indignation enhanced by the prospect of excoriating the "Polish occupation" of Lithuania's historic capital. *Lietuvos žinios* moralized that "a cultured person is always disgusted by the excesses of zoological nationalism and racism. . . Similar pogroms can never take place if the government is determined not to allow them."[176] On November 15, 1931, the Jews of Kaunas petitioned the government "to intervene and take steps to ensure the lives of our brothers in Lithuanian Vilnius, Lithuania's Jerusalem."[177] Four days later the Jewish-Lithuanian Association for Cultural Cooperation organized a demonstration, broadcast over radio, featuring prominent Lithuanian and Jewish public figures to protest that "the Poles have brought the pogrom tradition to Vilnius." Former foreign minister Juozas Purickis maintained that "until now Lithuanians had not been soiled with the blood of Jews," while Mykolas Biržiška, a proponent of Jewish-Lithuanian cooperation, invited people "to be vigilant that [our] beautiful toleration should never change in the future, and that our own instincts should not degenerate."[178] On November 20, 1931, the Presidium of the Central Committee of the Lithuanian Volunteers' Union, not known for liberal attitudes, issued a statement reminding readers of the 1919 Easter pogroms in Vilnius carried out by Polish legionnaires and expressing sympathy for the victims of the current attacks: "once again the cries of the Jews and the

---

174 "Būkime tikri patriotai," *Lietuvos aidas*, August 20, 1929, 1.
175 I. Serebravičius, "Į Lietuvos žydų visuomenę," *Lietuvos aidas*, September 9, 1929, 4.
176 "Dėl žydų studentų pogromo Vilniuje," *Lietuvos žinios*, November 18, 1931, 1.
177 "Kauno žydai prašo Lietuvos vyriausybės pagalbos Vilniaus žydams," *Lietuvos aidas*, November 16, 1931, 1.
178 "Didžiulis protesto mitingas Kaune," *Lietuvos aidas*, November 20, 1931, 1.

terrible suffering of the wounded have resonated within the walls of our [true] capital."[179]

The violence in Vilnius produced interesting commentary on antisemitism and racism from the editors of the nation's semi-official daily:

> It may seem to some that the Jewish nation has some unsympathetic characteristics (and what nation does not have them?). It may even be supposed that Poland's Jews have more such features than their co-nationals in other countries. But in no way and under no conditions can *pogroms* be justified. A pogrom is an inhuman, disorderly use of brutal force against other people, citizens of the same state of a different nationality. A pogrom is essentially an immoral and indecent method of struggle, the use of which contradicts the most elemental principles of human solidarity.... Independent Lithuania cannot forget that all inhabitants of the occupied Vilnius district, without regard to religious, national, or other differences, are her children. (Emphasis in original)

The editorial regretted that the Polish students who had been involved in the Vilnius pogroms had called themselves "National Democrats and carriers of Catholic ideas."[180]

The Catholic *Aušra* (Dawn) excoriated racism in a text that could have been written in any Western democracy of the 2000s:

> The European, an allegedly cultured person, has placed the heavy hand of slavery on people of a different color, destroyed the patriarchal structure of the New World, turning the free nations found there into blind instruments of labor... The essence of the pogrom is the attack on unarmed peaceful people, often old people, women, and children. If you put yourself in their shoes, what are they to do? They cannot become people of another nationality... they are also human beings. They have an equal right to be protected by the state from violence and destruction. ... Just as the slave trade, so the pogroms, no matter what slogans they utilize, are and remain the greatest shame of the civilized world.

After noting that racism and pogroms become possible when universal moral and religious values are undermined, the author warned that "To simply express condolences to the victims in banal words is not enough. All of us should

---

179 "Savanorių kūrėjų rezoliucija dėl žydų pogromų Vilniuje," *Lietuvos aidas*, November 21, 1931, 8.
180 "Pogromai Lenkijoj," *Lietuvos aidas*, November 14, 1931, 1–2.

exert more effort to protect the young people from the threatening danger so that, perhaps not understanding their actions, they follow the way of Poland's youth who try to create their country's greatness and progress through pogroms."[181] The same issue printed the more awkward response of the Union to Liberate Vilnius, which issued a "resolution of protest," albeit from a militantly anti-Polish stance, stating that "in these times the antiethnic actions are intolerable even against Africa's blackies."[182]

A more conservative pro-Jewish sentiment can be seen in the acceptance of Jews as "fellow nationalists," as imagined by *Lietuvos aidas* in a commentary on the upheavals in Palestine. In this view, the Arabs, an "ignorant and fanatical nation," were begrudging the Jews a slice of territory and tormenting "our Jewish citizens." "One's hair stands on end," wrote the editors, at the news on the persecution of the Jews:

> Every day terrible news flows from Palestine. Fired by religious and nationalistic fanaticism, the Arabs are attacking and murdering the unfortunate Jewish colonists. . . . The Zionist idea cannot be unattractive to any person who loves his own country. Formerly it was said that the Jews are a parasitic, purely cosmopolitan nation without any noble ideals and whose messiah is money. The Zionist movement has proven that this is not true.[183]

Aside from reflecting noble sentiments, expressions of philosemitism can function as a means of achieving practical, if not self-serving, goals, in this case arousing anti-Polish sentiment and scoring points with the international community. Instances of such "enlightened nationalism" in Lithuania thrived in an unusually nurturing political context of the late 1920s: the power struggle between Smetona and his charismatic right-wing rival, Augustinas Voldemaras (1883–1942), was in full spate and anti-Jewish excesses in Vilijampolė (Slabada) had resonated in the media and on the international stage.

The government's interest in maintaining law and order motivated the authorities to suppress mob violence, including anti-Jewish attacks and hooliganism, such as the student attacks on the country's multilingual heritage during the early 1920s. However, small-scale attacks on persons and property, duly

---

181 P. K., "Žydų pogromai," *Aušra*, November 17, 1931, 1.
182 "Protesto rezoliucija," *Aušra*, November 17, 1931, 3.
183 "Smūgis žydų tautai," *Lietuvos aidas*, September 3, 1929, 1.

chronicled in police reports and the press, continued throughout the interwar years. A typical incident, recorded near Kaunas, concerned three thugs who "smashed Jewish windows and tried to beat a Jewish woman." The detainees were hardly society's dregs: "the chief of the post office, his assistant and a representative of the Singer Co."[184] The authorities were not always consistent in punishing the culprits. In October 1931 prosecutors demanded the "severest punishment" for four youths who vandalized a Jewish cemetery in Klaipėda, arguing that the mandated three-year term was too lenient, but the judge sentenced one of the men to six months and the others to five, noting that the press had "overblown… the thoughtless work of drunken youngsters."[185] The Telšiai military commandant punished eighteen anti-Jewish "troublemakers" during the month of October 1935. As in tsarist times, outbreaks against Jews in the countryside sometimes resulted from blood libel rumors occasioned by the (usually short-lived) disappearance of village youth and routinely disproved by police investigations. State security recorded increasingly frequent anti-Jewish incidents during the late 1930s, although there are no fatalities documented in these reports.[186]

The greater threat to Jewish society were proposals intended to address the "Jewish problem," even when solutions appeared well-intentioned. In 1937 the theologian and sociologist Rev. Stasys Yla published a tract titled *Communism in Lithuania*, which cited materialist philosophy and social problems as factors in the ideology's appeal. Yla pointed out that a disproportionate element within the underground LCP consisted of national minorities, primarily Russians and Jews, speculating that the official Communist posture against ethnic discrimination provided a strong incentive for the latter to join the Party. He evoked the usual suspects: Jewish influence in the media; the collusion of Jewish capitalists with revolutionaries; Jews as influential cosmopolitans with global influence. Yla proposed confronting Communism by tackling the country's persistent poverty and embracing a tolerant multiculturalism, advocating patience in drawing minorities towards an acceptance of Lithuanian language and culture. The author admitted that Lithuanians "still need to learn cultured behavior with persons of

---

184 "Žydų mušimas Žąsliuose," *Lietuvos žinios*, November 28, 1931, 1.

185 "Nubaudė Klaipėdos žydų kapinių išniekintojus," *Lietuvos aidas*, October 3, 1931, 4.

186 Liudas Truska and Vygantas Vareikis, *Holokausto prielaidos. Antisemitizmas Lietuvoje XIX antroji pusė-1941 birželis. The Preconditions for the Holocaust: Antisemitism in Lithuania. Second Half of the Nineteenth Century–June 1941* (Vilnius: margi raštai, 2004), 58–61. See Linas Venclauskas, "Antisemitizmas Lietuvoje 1939–1940 metais: Valstybės saugumo departamento pranešimai," *Darbai ir dienos* 67 (2017): 293–332.

another national orientation," which, in his view, was supposedly practiced by the French, British, and other Western nations.[187]

Yla rejected overtly antisemitic action, which was in keeping with the Church's criticism of anti-Jewish violence, racial ideology, and eugenics,[188] but this did not prevent some Catholic clergy from seeking less inclusive solutions. "It remains a fact that the Jews never had any sympathy among Christian societies," wrote the Marian priest Dr. Juozas Vaišnora, who assumed this notion as a given because "virtually all experts on the Jewish question agree that, to a greater or lesser degree, Jews constitute a danger to society," citing the Catholic historian Hilaire Belloc as an authority. Since "elimination of the Jews is contrary to Christian charity and natural law," the author proposed a legal *numerus clausus* and a policy of separation, so that "the Jews, even as they enjoyed the same and equal rights as citizens, would not be in a privileged position," and thus Lithuania could avoid the dishonorable "domination of a minority."[189]

Overtly racist anti-Jewish theories appeared as well. In a 1934 scholarly article, the Kaunas University ethnologist Jonas Balys expounded on the essence of Ashkenazi Jewry, who were allegedly close to an "Asiatic character" alien to Lithuanians and were distinguished by "cunning, usury, fraud, [and] all kinds of exploitation and meddling." According to Balys, the "Jewish question" was a serious problem, since Jews had reached a commanding position among Europeans, intruding among a people of a "different spiritual composition." He cited German authors in concluding that "the Jewish question is neither a religious nor economic problem, but a national and racial one."[190] Racist notions found resonance outside academia. In 1935 the newspaper *Diena* (The day) reported that some villas at the Palanga resort segregated dining areas patronized by Lithuanians and Jews, thus ensuring that the "racial principle was fully

---

187 Juozas Daulius [pseud. Stasys Yla], *Komunizmas Lietuvoje* (Kaunas: Šviesa, 1937), 198–201, 232–235. Cf. the annotated edition: Stasys Yla, *Komunizmas Lietuvoje*, edited with an introduction by Nerijus Šepetys (Vilnius: aidai, 2012).

188 Even Soviet sources have admitted the opposition to racist doctrines among "bourgeois and reactionary" elements, as in Irmija Zaksas, *Rasizmas ir eugenika buržuazinėje Lietuvoje* (Vilnius: VPMLL, 1959), 138–157, 171ff.

189 Juozas Vaišnora, "Žydų klausimas," *Židinys* 11 (1937): 418–427.

190 Jonas Balys, "Antropologinė ir sociologinė žydijos problema," *Akademikas* 2 (1934): 40–42.

observed."[191] But in contrast to the boogeymen of Jewish economic tyranny and Judeo-Bolshevism, racial antisemitism in Lithuania was a marginal phenomenon. As with eugenics, it was inimical to Catholic teaching and discouraged by much of the elite, which was alarmed by the growing threat from the Third Reich.[192]

The dangers inherent in Europe's geopolitical crisis of the 1930s influenced the government's response to Nazi-style antisemitism. Three months after Hitler's appointment as chancellor, journalist Valentinas Gustainis, a close associate of Smetona, addressed the consequences of the Nazi rise to power in the monthly journal of the Nationalist Union. The article "Hitler's Foreign Policy" sprang from the author's acquaintance with Georg Gerullis (a.k.a. Jurgis Gerulis), an ethnic Lithuanian German citizen, academic, and Nazi activist who had provided the author with publications on National Socialism. Gustainis perused, in his words, "the entire boring *Mein Kampf*," from which he concluded that "the theory of race holds the most important place in Hitler's thinking." He predicted that if the Führer's theories were realized, "many nations would come under a threat not only to their freedom and independence, but to *their very existence in a purely biological sense*" (emphasis in original). Gustainis warned that "keeping in mind the modern, terrible methods of extermination... above all, the various horrible gases..., the rapid and complete annihilation of a weaker nation could easily become a reality."[193]

The journal's most important reader called Gustainis into the presidential office to consider this "hair-raising prognosis" and suggested that one should not take the Nazi leader's "ravings for the real thing," opining that Hitler was now "the responsible leader of a large state, so he will... obviously not be able to carry out what he had asserted as an irresponsible oppositionist."[194] And yet, in December 1933, Smetona addressed the Nazi threat in a gathering of

---

191 See Justas Stončius, "Žydų verslai Palangoje tarpukario laikotarpiu," in *Palangos žydai: išnykusi miesto bendruomenės dalis*, ed. Hektoras Vitkus (Klaipėda: DRUKA, 2017), 113–127.

192 The most recent and thorough survey of Lithuanian antisemitic discourse of the interwar period is in Venclauskas, *Tekstų byla*, 219–463.

193 Valentinas Gustainis, "Hitlerio užsienio politika," *Vairas* 4 (1933): 428, 433. Gerullis had joined the SA and during the war worked closely with the Abwehr in organizing Lithuanian, Belarusian, and Ukrainian nationalist support for the Germans. At war's end, he was arrested by Soviet security and executed in August 1945.

194 Valentinas Gustainis, *Nuo Griškabūdžio iki Paryžiaus* (Kaunas: Spindulys, 1991), 129–130. Smetona's view, as recalled by Gustainis in this memoir, was not uncommon at the time.

his Nationalist followers, describing the ongoing "movement against the Jews in Germany" as a "self-delusion." The president was troubled that "according to *Mein Kampf*..., all means are permissible in defending German interests" and warned: "everyone sees before them the *Ausrottungspolitik* (G. extermination policy)." Smetona extolled "the declaration of human rights of the French Revolution [which] will always shine as humanity's ideal."[195] In a January 1935 speech the president criticized H. Stuart Chamberlain's theories, arguing that it was impossible to "speak seriously about national or racial purity," while rejecting the "other extreme" of indiscriminate nation-mixing. Smetona stressed that there were no good or bad nations and referred favorably to the United States as an example of a "first-rate power," which had assimilated many peoples. He emphasized the rights of minorities who were, after all, "our citizens" and urged Lithuanians not to protest persecution of their ethnic brethren abroad [in Poland] by attacking minorities at home.[196]

The Jewish press extolled the president's speech of January 5, 1938, which emphasized that for the nationalist ideal to remain alive, it should include "a basis in universal human values." Smetona warned his audience about the dangers of extreme nationalism, pointing out that "wherever [this national idea] degenerates... wherever the leading people are blindly in love with themselves and their own, the national ideal cannot be pure and beautiful." The president also hopefully asserted that "in our country we do not have such antisemitism as in other states."[197] A few days later the mayor of Panevėžys, the president's brother-in-law Tadas Chodakauskas (1889–1959), told a meeting of Lithuanian Jewish veterans that "You [Jews] will always live here as equal and free citizens, because you share joys and sorrows with us, the Lithuanians."[198] A number of thought leaders shared Smetona's critical attitude towards Nazism and racial prattle. In 1934 the urbane diplomat and writer Ignas Jurkūnas (1889–1959) (pen name: Ignas Šeinius) published the satirical novel *Siegfried Immerselbe*

---

195 Quoted in *Tautos Vado Antano Smetonos kalba* (Kaunas: Savivaldybė. 1934), 14–20.
196 "Tautos Vado Antano Smetonos kalba," *Verslas*, January 10, 1935, 1–2 and "Tautos Vado Antano Smetonos Kalbar (tęsinys iš 2 nr.)," *Verslas*, January 10, 1935, 1–2.
197 "Valstybės prezidento Antano Smetonos kalba," *Apžvalga*, January 16, 1938, 1.
198 "Jūs visada čia gyvensite, kaip laisvi ir lygūs piliečiai! ," *Apžvalga*, January 23, 1938, 3.

atsijaunina (The rejuvenation of Siegfried Immerselbe), which mocked Nazi antisemitism, eugenics, and pseudo-scientific racial theories.[199]

Jews were not blind to the faults of the Nationalist regime as evidenced by their sympathetic contacts with the victims of rural protests during the depression of the 1930s. The VSD reported that a certain Manaškis Kopolovičius was spreading the word that local villagers wounded in clashes with the police should "seek out Dr. Freida in Šakiai, since he is the only one who will keep their injuries secret. Also, in Pilviškiai there is a certain Jewish doctor who helps the farmers."[200] At the same time, other Jews acknowledged the importance of the stability provided by the government. In April 1936 police spies reported that Jews "holding rightist opinions" were urging their community in Marijampolė to support the government against striking farmers in Suvalkija, since "we can never expect another President like Smetona, so one must fight for him." Local Jews reportedly referred to Smetona as "our father," while in nearby Šakiai the rabbi told local Jewish communities: "May God bless our President." Officials reported talk among Jews that Smetona and the government stand as "an iron wall against all sorts of persecutions."[201] On the occasion of the president's sixtieth birthday in 1934 several enthusiastic Jewish writers rather fancifully compared Antanas Smetona to Tomàš Masaryk.[202]

The Litvak diaspora reiterated pro-government sentiments. The newspaper *Di Yidishe Shtime* correspondent in Palestine reported that on February 16, 1938, Tel Aviv's Litvaks gathered at the San Remo Hall to celebrate two decades of Lithuania's independence. The city's mayor, Israel Rokach, welcomed the meeting, noting the "humane character" of the Lithuanian leader and expressing the hope that "the spirit of Smetona would long reign among future generations." Lithuania's general consul for Palestine read excerpts from Smetona's speeches that stressed "the principle of universal human morality," although one

---

199 Ignas Šeinius, *Siegfried Immerselbe atsijaunina* (Kaunas: Sakalas, 1934). There is an English version: Ignas Seinius, *The Rejuvenation of Siegfried Immerselbe*, trans. Albinas Baranauskas (New York: Manyland Books, 1965). Šeinius played on Siegfried's German surname ("always the same") to indicate the supposed inherent permanence of racial categories.

200 As noted in the 1936 VSD report in LCVA, f. 378, ap. 3, b. 4849, l. 4, 5, 8.

201 Quoted in Saulius Sužiedėlis, "The Historical Sources for Antisemitism in Lithuania and Jewish-Lithuanian Relations during the 1930s," in *The Vanished World of Lithuanian Jews*, ed. Alvydas Nikžentaitis, Stefan Schreiner, and Darius Staliūnas (Amsterdam–New York: Rodopi, 2004), 136.

202 Casper, "Strangers and Sojourners," 220–222.

could doubt the diplomat's concluding remark that the president's liberal attitude "corresponds to the opinion of all Lithuania." A similar gathering with the same sentiments took place in Cape Town where many Lithuanian Jews had gone to seek a better life. [203]

Ultimatums and War: Storm Clouds over Lithuania, March 1938–June 1940

Lithuanian historians have referred to the multiple crises that led to the demise of the First Republic as the "period of the three ultimatums." The Polish demarche of March 12, 1938, demanding the opening of diplomatic relations with Lithuania, and Germany's seizure of Klaipėda a year later, created a crisis for the Smetona government. The Kremlin's ultimatum of June 14, 1940, and the ensuing Soviet invasion dealt the final blow to the independent Lithuanian state. These multiple crises created anxiety among the populace and undermined the prestige of the Nationalist regime—developments that had ominous implications for Lithuania's Jews.

In 1938–1939 the democratic anti-Smetona political opposition joined right-wing forces in founding the semi-clandestine Lithuanian Activist Movement (Lietuvių aktyvistų sajūdis, LAS) in a coalition whose publications demonized Poles, compared Jews to rats, proposed a system of "authoritarian democracy," and advocated a pro-Axis realignment in foreign policy. The LAS chose Klaipėda as a base since under the provisions of the convention of 1924, the territory enjoyed considerable autonomy and therefore was less subject to censorship than the rest of Lithuania. However, according to Ernst Neumann, the leader of the Klaipėda Nazis, the Lithuanian radicals lacked a genuine antisemitic program since they were "too democratic and gentle in their behavior regarding the Jews."[204] (Within two years, a later reincarnation of Lithuanian

---

203 R. Ch., "Vasario 16-oji Tel Avive," *Apžvalga*, March 6, 1938, 3; Berelis Fadovičius, "Lietuvos žydai Pietų Afrikoje švenčia Lietuvos Nepriklausomybės 20 metu sukaktį," *Apžvalga*, March 20, 1938, 2.

204 See Gediminas Rudis, "Jungtinis antismetoninės opozicijos sąjūdis 1938-1939 metais," *Lietuvos istorijos metraštis* (1996): 185–215; cf. the LAS Proclamation, "Lietuviai" [undated], in LCVA, f. 378, ap. 7, b. 336a, 9; the January and February 1939 issues of *Bendras žygis*; the Pro Memoria from Algirdas Sliesoraitis, Juozas Pajaujis and J. Štaupas, to Prime Minister Mironas, March 16, 1939, LCVA, f. 378, ap. 7, b. 336, 2–3. See also the somewhat dated survey of Romuald J. Misiūnas, "Fascist Tendencies in Lithuania," *Slavonic and East European Review* 48, no. 110 (January 1970): 88–94.

antisemitic "activists" in Berlin would "correct" this deficiency.) The situation in Klaipėda was of particular interest to the Jews who comprised an estimated 12% of the port city's population. On the eve of the December 1938 elections to the territory's Diet (*seimelis*), pro-Lithuanian activists evoked the image of Kristallnacht in a desperate attempt to counter the popularity of Nazi front groups and appealed to Jews to vote against the German list:

> Jews! Citizens! In Germany they have destroyed 110 Jewish cemeteries. This did not happen in Lithuania. It is not Lithuanians who had drowned Jewish businessmen in blood. . . . Hitler's followers are the ones who want to drive out the Jews, not the Lithuanians. Jews are working in Lithuanian government institutions and as commandants in Klaipėda. [Walter] Rathenau, the Jewish minister in Germany was brutally murdered by Hitler's gang. So, Jews, open your eyes! Vote for the [Lithuanian] List No. 3.[205]

Nonetheless, a pragmatic orientation, which sought to realign Lithuania's foreign policy in order to maintain Lithuanian sovereignty over Klaipėda, became increasingly popular among the Christian Democrats and right-wing nationalists opposed to what they considered the listless leadership of Smetona and the older generation. In January 1939, security police spies reported that a prominent young historian, Zenonas Ivinskis, described to students the positive aspects of "German order and will."[206] In 1939, the Catholic philosopher Antanas Maceina proposed the creation of an "organic state" that would relegate non-Lithuanian nationals to second-class "guest" status in lieu of full citizenship.[207] Vytautas Alantas, a writer popular in radical *tautininkai* circles, urged the

---

205 See Ruth Leiserowitz, "Žydai tapukario Klaipėdos krašte," in Sirutavičius, Staliūnas, and Šiaučiūnaitė-Verbickienė, *Lietuvos žydai: istorinė studija*, 425–431. This appeal is quoted from Josef Rosin, *Preserving our Litvak Heritage* (League City, TX: JewishGen, Inc., 2005), 101.

206 As reported by the State Security Department on January 4, 1939, in LCVA, f. 378, ap. 10, b. 186, I t., l. 7–8, which also claimed that Ivinskis lauded Austria's post-Anschluss racial laws for "liberating the country from one parasitic minority . . . a positive aspect of racism." The historian denied the latter charge, asserting that he only wished to emphasize, as did many others, the need for planning, determination, and discipline in national policy, and is on record as referring to Nazis as "barbarous." The details of the incident are in Artūras Svarauskas, *Krikščioniškoji demokratija nepriklausomoje Lietuvoje (1918–1940: politinė galia ir jos ribos)* (Vilnius: LII, 2014), 321.

207 Antanas Maceina, "Tauta ir valstybė," *Naujoji Romuva* 11 (1939): 229–230. A discussion of Maceina's work is in Leonidas Donskis, "Antanas Maceina: doktrininis intelektualas XX amžiaus lietuvių kultūroj," *Akiračiai* 2 (1997): 4–6; *Akiračiai* 3 (1997): 4–7; *Akiračiai* 4 (1997): 4–7.

authorities to segregate beach facilities on the Baltic, citing the "dirty habits" of Jews and warning that those "who are constantly babbling in Russian" should understand that they cannot continue to ignore the wishes of the Lithuanians "without consequences."[208] In July 1939, the Anykščių šilelis resort, advertising itself as the "most modern place in Palanga," published a notice that Jewish guests were not welcome. The town council followed the suggestions of the local *verslininkai* and voted to prohibit kosher ritual slaughter, but the ban was overturned by the Kretinga district chief.[209] In the spring of 1940, Nationalist Union members in Šiauliai petitioned the government to address the "Jewish question" by establishing a reservation for Jews.[210]

In March 1938, there were disturbances at the University of Kaunas after some students posted a copy of the Nazis' antisemitic journal *Der Stürmer*. The rector, Prof. Mykolas Römeris, told the press that the "hooligan-like and uncultured outbreaks against the Jewish students were for me entirely unexpected" and vowed to punish the troublemakers. The Jewish *Apžvalga* worried that while the conservative *Lietuvos aidas* had named "leftist and Jewish" provocations as a cause of the troubles, only the more liberal *Lietuvos žinios* had exposed the "racist nature" of the outbreak.[211] In November 1939 the new rector of the University of Kaunas, Stasys Šalkauskis, addressed the issue of continuing conflict between Lithuanian and Jewish students. "The complex and convoluted problem of the Jews is a true test of our social and moral development," he announced, cautioning that "the wave of antisemitism that has inundated the whole world during recent years has found a certain resonance among us as well," especially in "the poorly developed part of society." Šalkauskis stressed that "aggressive antisemitism" was harmful, as shown by the consequences suffered by "a large state that has paid dearly for hatred and cruelty to Jews." The rector refused to consider demands for segregating the university's lecture halls as immoral and unjust.[212]

---

208 Vytautas Alantas, "Aktualieji paplūdimo klausimai," *Lietuvos aidas*, August 13, 1938, 6.
209 Stončius, "Žydų verslai," 125.
210 Liudas Truska, *Antanas Smetona*, 299–300.
211 Published from *Di Yidishe Shtime*, in "Kas įvyko V. D. un-te!," *Apžvalga*, March 20, 1938, 4.
212 "Prof. Šalkauskio pareiškimas spaudai," *Apžvalga*, November 3, 1939, 1. For a review of nationalist Catholic student attitudes to Jews and other minorities in the 1930s, see Svarauskas, *Krikščioniškoji demokratija*, 253–259.

Ethnic exclusion also infected the world of sport when issues were raised concerning participation in the World Lithuanian Olympics to be held in Kaunas in early 1938.[213] Initially, *Yiddishe Shtime* quoted reliable sources indicating that all athletes from Lithuania, regardless of nationality and religion, could participate in the event, while only ethnic Lithuanians would be included in the diaspora teams. However, soon afterward, the director of Kaunas's Physical Education Center told the Jewish *Folksblat* that the national olympiad was open only to ethnic Lithuanians, although the national team that would participate in the 1940 Olympics scheduled in Helsinki would be chosen without regard to ethnicity.[214]

Following an ultimatum from Berlin, Hitler rode into Klaipėda on March 23, 1939, under a banner proclaiming that "this land remains forever German," his last seizure of territory before the outbreak of World War II. The surrender of land by a government that had once sworn to defend every inch of sovereign soil was a political debacle for the Smetona regime and an existential crisis for the Lithuanian state.[215] Despite promises of "no more retreats" and calls for unity, political and social fissures widened. In April 1939, agitators appeared among Lithuanian refugees who had fled the seaport, urging the migrants to protest, "because the Jewish [exiles] have occupied most of the apartments, while the [ethnic] Lithuanian refugees are forced to live in schools," but according to police, this time "the refugees did not approve such an action."[216]

The residents of Leipalingis showed less restraint: in June 1939, the town witnessed the largest anti-Jewish disturbance of the interwar period. Trouble erupted after the town's annual religious holiday which was traditionally followed by large-sale trading. As a storm approached, some market goers crowded into merchant Perecas Kravecas's store to escape the rain. An altercation between

---

213 "Ar tautinėje olipmpiadoje galės dalyvauti ir Lietuvos žydų sportininkai?" *Apžvalga*, January 2, 1938, 8.

214 "Ir mažumos galės dalyvauti tautinėje olimpiadoje," *Apžvalga*, January 9, 1938, 7; "Žydai sportininkai negalės dalyvauti lietuvių tautinėje olimpiadoje," *Apžvalga*, January 23, 1938, 7. The 1940 Olympic Games were canceled because of the war.

215 A brief history of the Klaipėda issue is in Vytautas Žalys, *Kova dėl identiteto: kodėl Lietuvai nesisekė Klaipėdoje tarp 1923–1939. Ringen um Identität. warum Litauen zwischen 1923 und 1939 im Memelgebiet keinen Erfolg hatte* (Lüneburg: Verlag Nordostdeutsches Kulturwerk, 1993). A thorough and still valuable study of the history of Lithuanian East Prussia and the Klaipėda Territory is Rudolfas Valsonokas, *Klaipėdos problema* (Klaipėda: Rytas, 1932).

216 State Security Report of June 5, 1939, LCVA, f. 378, ap. 11, b. 214, l.1.

Kravecas and the Lithuanian customer Pranas Pilvelis resulted in broken glass. Raising his bleeding hand to a crowd in the street, Pilvelis implored the people to "look at what the Jews have done to me," and word soon spread that "the Jews had stabbed someone with a knife." The leader of a nearby reserve riflemen's unit then incited the crowd to "beat the Jews," upon which a window-smashing rampage ensued. The police, assisted by more disciplined riflemen called to the scene, prevented a lynching but were unable to halt the property damage. There were no serious injuries. The rioters, as well as Pilvelis, the store owner Kravecas, and his son, were given light sentences and fines. According to the extant police files, some of the ringleaders and the more active rioters were petty criminals.

A ranking official sent to investigate the troubles reported to the director of state security that "in the Leipalingis area a distinct antisemitic attitude is prevalent, created by general social, ethnic, and local factors" and identified economic rivalry as a main contributor to the violence: a Lithuanian cooperative had been competing with more established Jewish retailers. Ignoring warnings from the national Riflemen's Union office to desist, the local chapter of the *šauliai* (members of the Riflemen's Union) had staged an antisemitic play. Among the final comments in the report was a tragicomic description of delusions circulating among rural people:

> In order to illustrate the antisemitic mood in the Leipalingis area, it is characteristic that no one is condemning the excesses committed, but, on the contrary, everyone is praising the riot. It is said that severe punishments for the rioters will provoke even greater antisemitic excesses. Also, after the event, typical rumors were bandied about. It was said that, in return for smashing Jewish windows in Leipalingis, Hitler had presented to Lithuania, as a gift, some sort of expensive airplane. And if a few Jews had been finished off, then he would have returned the entire Klaipėda District to Lithuania. The farmers are spreading these tales in all seriousness.

The security police suggested that to stem dangerous rumors (for example, that Pilvelis had died), local officials should provide accurate information to the populace, utilizing local veterinarians and doctors whom the people trusted.[217] A study of the Leipalingis incident published in 2005 identified the social tensions and attitudes percolating among a considerable segment of both urban elites and village communities that may have contributed to the pogrom:

---

217 The extensive material on Leipalingis is in LCVA, f. 378, ap. 11, b. 206; see esp. the official report of June 30, 1939, l. 104ff.

IMAGE 1.8. Family and friends gather for a Jewish wedding celebration in Kaunas [Kovno], ca. 1938. (United States Holocaust Memorial Museum Photo Archives #01522, Courtesy of Henia Wisgardisky Lewin. Copyright of United States Holocaust Memorial Museum.)

intense Jewish-Lithuanian competition during worsening economic conditions; the frustration at the humiliations of the Polish ultimatum and the German seizure of Klaipėda; and the penchant for conspiracy theories, such as the conviction that the political elites were exploiting ordinary Lithuanians "in league with the Jews."[218]

Interior Minister Kazys Skučas (1894–1941) condemned "the recent outbreaks against Jewish citizens in several provincial towns inspired by irresponsible elements" and reiterated that it was the duty of the government as well as "broad segments of the Lithuanian nation and conscientious members of the intelligentsia" to counter such behavior. The minister hoped to curb the influence of "foreign winds, which carried the scourge of antisemitism" and warned the press "not to incite passions." For its part, *Apžvalga* praised both the local police and national authorities for their determined response to the disorders.[219]

---

218 Dangiras Mačiulis, "Žvilgsnis į vieno pogromo anatomiją tarpukario Lietuvoje," in Sirutavičius and Staliūnas, *Kai ksenofobija*, 181–196.

219 For Skučas's statement and commentary, see "Prie kurstymų bei ekscesų nebus prileista," *Apžvalga*, July 2, 1939, 1.

IMAGE 1.9. Jewish community leaders greet President Antanas Smetona in Molėtai, 1938. (Courtesy of Molėtai Regional Museum, Photo by Kazys Daugėla.)

The government's opposition to antisemitism had a political calculation as well as a moral message: concern for Lithuania's international reputation and the perception of Jews as useful allies, especially against the Poles. However, not all regime officials proved immune to the increasingly anti-Jewish popular mood. In 1938, the security chief Augustinas Povilaitis failed to persuade the interior minister to close *Apžvalga* and suppress its publisher, the Association of Jewish Soldiers, for their "divisive" attacks against Lithuanian antisemites.[220]

On August 23, 1939, Hitler and Stalin announced the German-Soviet Mutual Nonaggression Treaty, better known as the Molotov-Ribbentrop Pact, which cleared the way for Germany's attack on Poland on September 1. The catastrophe triggered regime changes, unleashing myriad social conflicts and nationalist movements. As Michael David-Fox notes, millions of people "suddenly faced fateful decisions about what to do and how to act." In this dangerous

---

220 Truska and Vareikis, *Holokausto prielaidos*, 55.

universe social behavior became "highly situational."²²¹ Lithuania chose neutrality in the conflict, but it was obvious that the destruction of the Polish state threatened the very existence of the First Republic. The war exacerbated the economic situation, already under stress because of the earlier loss of the country's seaport.²²² Public discontent with rising prices and unemployment mounted although it never approached the "revolutionary situation" described in Soviet historiography.

For the first time in a generation, the Red Army appeared on Lithuania's borders. Retreating Polish troops, seeking refuge from the Nazi and Soviet offensives, streamed into the republic, creating some fifteen thousand military internees by the end of September. Lithuanians were initially supportive of the traumatized officers and men who had fought bravely for their homeland,²²³ but there was less sympathy for the civilian refugees whose situation was less obviously tragic and who presented a more visible financial burden. More than thirty thousand civilian refugees were registered in Vilnius by the end of February 1940, of whom approximately ten thousand were Jews. Among the latter, a majority were men, mostly yeshiva students and Zionists from Soviet-occupied Poland, encouraged by the news that Vilnius would be attached to neutral Lithuania.²²⁴ Many of the Polish Jews could be better described as deportees: at times, both Nazi and Soviet authorities pressured them to cross into Lithuania.²²⁵ On October 27, 1939, the State Security Department forwarded to the government a report on the "Troubles of the Suwałki Jews":

> It has come to our attention that the German military government had ordered all the Jews to move from Vižainis and go to Lithuania. On the next day three hundred Jews appeared at the border and wanted to come over to our side, but our border security did not let them in. The Jews

---

221 Michael David-Fox, "The People's War: Ordinary People and Regime Strategies in a World of Extremes," *Slavic Review* 75, no. 3 (2016): 551.

222 Aldona Gaigalaitė, *Anglijos kapitalas ir Lietuva 1919–1940* (Vilnius: Mokslas, 1986), 65–66, 149–157. The loss of Klaipėda in March 1939 reduced agricultural exports, especially to Britain, which had been a mainstay of the country's foreign trade for most of the interwar period.

223 See the account in Piotr Łossowski, *Litwa a sprawy polskie 1939-1940* (Warsaw: PWN, 1982), 47–48.

224 Ibid., 193–194; Simonas Strelcovas, "Pabėgeliai, vizos, gelbėtojai," *Darbai ir dienos* 47 (2007): 63.

225 Simonas Strelcovas, *Antrojo Pasaulinio karo pabėgeliai Lietuvoje 1939-1940 metais* (Šiauliai: VšĮ Šiaulių universiteto leidykla, 2010), 127–129.

were determined to wait for another few days. If they are not admitted into Lithuania, they will trek along the border to Soviet Russia. Currently there are about one thousand such Jews on the move who are moaning and crying.[226]

Lithuanian government officials recorded several deaths among the desperate exiles. Hundreds of more fortunate Jews did manage to slip across the border into Lithuania and were registered as refugees. According to the Foreign Ministry, a mother tried to drown herself along with her two six-month-old twins, but the family was saved by the border patrol "and given refuge on our side." Lithuanian diplomatic protests in Berlin and to the German mission in Kaunas went unheeded.[227] For their part, in November 1939 Soviet authorities forced a number of Jewish refugees into the Lithuanian-controlled Vilnius region.[228] While the press viewed the Polish civilian refugees as a potential "fifth column," there was less written on the Jews. The daily *Lietuvos aidas* reported "that all Lithuanians are satisfied" that American Jewish relief organizations were busily arranging for refugees to leave Lithuania and thus lightening the burden for the country's taxpayers, although in one clueless passage, the paper announced that the Jews had no reason to "flee in panic from German-occupied Poland," since the Nazis were creating a "Jewish state with a capital in Lublin... thus realizing a dream of the Jews."[229] In fact, the latter referred not to a dream but rather a nightmare: in the fall of 1939 the Germans proposed a Jewish reservation (Reservat) in the Lublin region.

The refugee crisis pushed Jonas Šliūpas, the former mayor of the seaside resort of Palanga, to perform an about-face in his attitudes towards minorities. In July 1939 Šliūpas, perhaps the country's best-known atheist intellectual, had penned an anti-fascist essay for the biweekly *Laisvoji mintis* (Free thought). In "The Meaning of Antisemitism" he branded the "persecution of any group" as a form of "spiritual immaturity." In Palanga, Šliūpas had taken a pro-Lithuanian

---

226 VSD Bulletin No. 261 (November 2, 1939), LCVA, f. 378, ap. 10, b. 187, l. 354. The so-called "Suwałki Triangle" was a small but strategically located territory contiguous to Lithuania which separated the Soviet and German territories of occupied Poland.

227 According to the November 1939 report of Edvardas Turauskas (1896–1966), the head of the Foreign Ministry's political department, as quoted in Kasparavičius, "Lietuviai ir žydai katastrofos išvakarėse," in Sirutavičius and Staliūnas *Kai ksenofobija*, 148–149.

228 Simonas Strelcovas, *Geri, blogi, vagdieniai: Č Sugihara ir Antrojo pasaulinio karo pabėgeliai Lietuvoje* (Vilnius: Versus, 2018), 108–109.

229 A., "Žydų pabėgelių reikalas," *Lietuvos aidas*, November 21, 1939, 5.

stance during business disputes between the town's Jews and Lithuanians but, like Smetona, he publicly excoriated racism and warned against indulging stereotypes of rich urban Jews exploiting the poor. His article ended with a call for "every honest man ... to eradicate the awful poison of antisemitism as well as racial and ethnic hatred in general."[230] After the outbreak of war, some five thousand refugees from Poland arrived in Palanga, outnumbering the town's inhabitants. By December 1939, in letters to his daughter, Šliūpas portrayed the displaced people as an "unpleasant element" prone to theft and other misbehavior, affirming that "I am prejudiced against Jews and Poles, and do not want them to become citizens because, for us, both are parasites and enemies."[231] An American scholar who has studied Šliūpas's intellectual evolution was uncertain whether the doctor's "discourse about Jews represents a real change of heart or is yet another example of the difference between his public and private voices."[232]

On October 10, 1939, Stalin imposed on Lithuania the Treaty of Mutual Assistance, which provided for Red Army bases in the country and transferred Vilnius and its environs to Lithuanian jurisdiction. The nation celebrated the long-awaited return of Lithuania's "eternal capital," although the joy was diluted by the realization that the country had become a de facto Soviet protectorate which inspired the popular rhyming ditty: "Vilnius mūsų, Lietuva rusų" (Vilnius is ours, Lithuania is Russia's). A day later, an unruly pro-Soviet leftist demonstration with a large Jewish contingent clashed violently with police and anti-Communists.[233] Skučas once again exerted his moderating influence, announcing that "the excesses of certain Jewish young people cannot be allowed to harm and disturb good Lithuanian-Jewish mutual relations." *Lietuvos žinios* issued an editorial opposing racism and ethnic incitement, but the Catholic daily *XX Amžius* demanded that Jewish society "discipline its own." *Yidishe Shtime* retorted that it was time for some people to understand that Jews were not

---

230 Jonas Šliūpas, "Antisemitizmo reikšmė," *Laisvoji mintis*, July 15, 1939, 1–2.
231 As quoted in Charles Perrin, "Lithuanians in the Shadow of Three Eagles: Vincas Kudirka, Martynas Jankus, Jonas Šliūpas and the Making of Modern Lithuania" (PhD diss., Georgia State University, 2013), 240–241; also Charles Perrin, "From Philosemitism to Antisemitism: Jonas Šliūpas, Refugees and the Holocaust," Izb.It, accessed November 27, 2017, https://www.lzb.lt/wp-content/uploads/2017/11/Jonas-Sliupas-Refugees-and-the-Holocaust.pdf.
232 Perrin, "Lithuanians," 242.
233 Details are in the State Security Department Bulletins of October 12–15, 1939, LCVA, f. 378, ap. 10, b. 187, l. 232–246.

IMAGE 1.10. Searching for safe havens. Group portrait of members of an Akiva Zionist youth hachshara [agricultural collective] that had moved to Vilnius after the German occupation of Poland, March 1940. (United States Holocaust Memorial Museum Photo Archives #30332. Courtesy of Nava Schreiber. Copyright of United States Holocaust Memorial Museum.)

a "homogenous nation" and thus should not be held collectively responsible for the actions of the demonstrators.[234]

On October 31, 1939, within hours of the arrival of Lithuanian troops, trouble erupted in Vilnius. Amidst rumors that Jews were hoarding flour, Poles rioted against the "Lithuanian occupation," while disorderly pro-Soviet crowds also roamed the streets. The outnumbered Lithuanian forces initially faltered in controlling the situation, but eventually, reinforcements of mounted police, additional reserve constabulary and Red Army units managed to quell the unrest: sixty-six rioters, among whom the police listed forty-four Poles and twenty Jews, were arrested.[235] The initially tepid police response to the rioting created the impression that the Lithuanians had inspired the pogroms, a myth propagated by the Communist underground that had encouraged the pro-Soviet manifestations and a narrative which, unfortunately, has been accepted

---

234 Commentary published in "Supraskime momento rimtumą!," *Apžvalga*, October 22, 1939, 8.
235 State Security Department Report of November 2, 1939, in LCVA, f. 378, ap. 10, b. 187, l. 349ff.

by some authors.²³⁶ It made little sense for the Lithuanian authorities to antagonize the Jewish populace whom they hoped to court as a counterweight to the anticipated Polish hostility.²³⁷ Nor is there much to the idea that Soviet tanks were called out to "protect the Jews" against fascist pogromists. The Soviet action was directed against the Polish resistance movement in the spirit of the September 28, 1939, secret protocols to the German-Soviet Boundary and Friendship Treaty, which mandated a joint Nazi-Stalinist suppression of "Polish agitation." Nikolai Pozdnyakov, Moscow's envoy to Kaunas, criticized the Lithuanian government's policy towards the Vilnius Poles as "overly sentimental and too gentle," publicly suggesting that if the Lithuanians did not show sufficient resolve in combating "acts of [Polish] diversion and aggression," the Soviets would provide the muscle.²³⁸

As the rioting subsided, General Skučas blamed much of the violence on the fact that Polish-Jewish relations had been "abnormal and strained for some time" because of Polish antisemitism.²³⁹ Skučas criticized Jewish "malcontents" for contributing to the violence but affirmed the government's commitment to treat national minorities fairly and to eliminate the antisemitic discrimination which had been practiced by the previous Polish regime. Some of the ruffians who had participated in antisemitic rioting were imprisoned and one, Boris Filipow, was executed.²⁴⁰ The latter punishment was "greeted with satisfaction by the Jews," some of whom now appeared willing to explain the previously slow

---

236 For example, Knut Stang, *Kollaboration und Massenmord: die litauische Hilfspolizei, das Rollkommando Hamann und die Ermordung der litauischen Juden* (Frankfurt am Main: Peter Lang, 1996), 77; and Dov Levin, "Lithuania," in *The World Reacts to the Holocaust*, ed. David Wyman (Baltimore: Johns Hopkins, 1996), 329. Cf. Łossowski, *Litwa*, 65–66 and Regina Žepkaitė, *Vilniaus istorijos atkarpa: 1939 m. spalio 27 d.-1940 m. birželio 15 d.* (Vilnius: Mokslas, 1990), 66–69.

237 Šarūnas Liekis, "The Transfer of Vilna District into Lithuania, 1939," *Polin* 14 (2001): 213.

238 Foreign Minister Urbšys to Lithuanian Emissary in Moscow, Ladas Natkevičius, February 7, 1940, LCVA, f. 383, ap. 1, b. 3, l. 105.

239 It should be noted that many Poles were outraged by the perceived Jewish welcoming of the Red Army as it entered Vilnius on September 18–19, 1939, after a brief battle with the outnumbered Polish defenders. See Marek Wierzbicki, *Polacy i żydzi w zaborze sowieckim* (Warsaw: Fronda, 2007), 195–214.

240 Kazys Skučas, "Apie įvykius Vilniuje," *XX Amžius*, November 6, 1939, 10; cf. Žepkaitė, *Vilniaus*, 93.

response of the Lithuanian police by the fact that the newly arrived officers "did not sufficiently know their way around the city."[241]

The burial of Constable Ignas Blažys, killed in an altercation with Poles, led to further violence on May 14, 1940. The funeral entourage eventually grew into a crowd of some fifteen thousand angry Lithuanians, many of whom wandered the streets of Vilnius attacking Poles and Polish property. By evening the mounted police suppressed the disturbances, arresting fifty-six troublemakers, the majority Lithuanian youths. In a telling comment on ethnic politics in Vilnius, the police report noted that, recalling their past mistreatment under Polish rule, "some Jews expressed satisfaction that the Poles had suffered on this day."[242] The issue of antisemitism became a cudgel in the struggle over Vilnius. The press reported widely on Polish antisemitism, supposedly inflamed by jealousy of the aid Jewish refugees were receiving from abroad. The Lithuanian authorities hoped, unrealistically as it turned out, that Jews would strengthen their Yiddish roots and abandon a Polish orientation. Compared to the Polish response, the Jewish attitude to Lithuanian rule was not overtly hostile,[243] but entrenched Polish cultural influence among educated urban Jews of the Vilnius region remained strong, much to the annoyance of Lithuanian officials and commentators.[244]

The last year of independence saw an increase in street-level antisemitism, reflected in the police reports of vandalism against Jewish institutions, as well as the appearance of anti-Jewish leaflets distributed by shadowy groups of "patriots."[245] In view of these attacks and the uncertain mood within the country, Jewish circles responded to official Lithuania's reassurances with public declarations of loyalty and reminders of the state's multicultural traditions. In their 1940 Independence Day statement Jewish veterans stated: "The Association of Jewish Soldiers, who have participated in the restoration of Lithuania's

---

241 State Security Department Bulletin No. 268 (November 8, 1939), LCVA, f. 378, ap. 10, b. 187, l. 383.
242 LCVA, State Security Department Bulletin May 17, 1940, LCVA, f. 378, ap. 10, B. 225, 614.
243 An interesting account of a Lithuanian government minister's visit to a Jewish synagogue and their friendly reception is in Juozas Audėnas, *Paskutinis posėdis: atsiminimai* (New York: Ramovė, 1966), 158–159.
244 LCVA, State Security Department Bulletin, February 23, 1940, f. 383, ap. 7, b. 2234, l. 76.
245 State Security Department Report, December 13, 1939, Hoover Institution, Turauskas Collection, Box 7.

independence, greet the nation of Lithuania and the entire Lithuanian society."²⁴⁶ In May 1940 the veterans assembled in Vilnius where prominent leaders of the country's Jewish community, despite indications to the contrary, affirmed generally good Jewish-Lithuanian relations and urged avoidance of "misunderstandings." Captain Mošė Bregšteinas, the vice-chairman of the veterans' association, proudly reminded the audience of the thousands of Jewish soldiers who had fought in the wars of independence. The participants welcomed the speeches of Minister Kazys Bizauskas (1893–1941) and other high-ranking officials, citing their presence as proof that the "ruling strata of Lithuania, by participating in the proceedings of [our] Association, show all the people of Vilnius that Lithuanian statesmen value and cherish the loyal [Jewish] minority of Lithuania."²⁴⁷

Jews, Lithuanians, and the First Republic in Perspective

The challenges emanating from the intricate web of Jewish-Lithuanian relations, woven over the centuries, constituted only one of the many problems that confronted the Lithuanian state between the wars. Lithuanian and Jewish memoirs of the interwar period reflect a contradictory spectrum: from idyllic accounts of ethnic harmony to recriminations regarding systemic intolerance. As a result, generalizations concerning the mosaic of Jewish-Lithuanian relations of the interwar period based on the accounts of contemporaries must be evaluated with caution. The memories are indeed colorful and instructive but insufficient in understanding a contentious, complex history.

We can never know whether the creative potential of Matilda Olkinaitė's literary talent stood a chance of fulfillment had the First Republic survived, but there is no reason to reject the possibility outright. Like so many other developments, the process of Jewish integration into Lithuanian public life and acceptance of the independent state as the political home of the Litvaks was, in the end, not allowed to follow its course.²⁴⁸ While it is true that, in many ways, Jews

---

246 R. Polieskis, "Nepriklausomybė – brangiausias Lietuvos turtas," *Apžvalga*, February 15, 1940, 1. Interesting here is the use of the term "nation of Lithuania" (Lietuvos tauta) in place of the more common "Lithuanian nation" (lietuvių tauta), a subtle but important distinction, the former emphasizing citizenship rather than ethnicity.

247 "Reikšmingas aktas," *Apžvalga*, May 15, 1940, 1.

248 On the complex subject of Jewish attitudes to the interwar Lithuanian state and questions of "demonstrative loyalty" in the context of conditional and situational factors, see Saulius

and Lithuanians lived parallel lives that created tensions and occasional conflict, Jewish involvement in the life of the First Republic was considerably more robust than is sometimes appreciated. Despite the political dominance of the majority Lithuanians, there were many examples of significant Jewish contributions to the country's progress. The modern Jewish hospitals did not simply cater to Litvak patients: by the mid-1930s, more than fifty Jewish doctors' clinics operated in central Kaunas alone, and there were numerous others in most cities and towns in the country. Until 1940 Jews managed most of Lithuania's pharmacies. They did not operate a separate economy. The Jewish financial and credit institutions served the entire business sector and Jewish entrepreneurs owned many of the country's sawmills, tobacco and alcohol outlets, transportation companies, and leather works (the Frankel enterprise in Šiauliai was particularly noteworthy). The famous Ilgovski tycoons, the brothers Dovid and Gedal, built many of the important public spaces in Kaunas which still embellish the city's landscape, including the modernist Vytautas the Great Military Museum which opened in 1934.[249]

There were increasing contacts within the artistic and popular cultural worlds. The singer Danielius Dolskis (1890–1931) arrived in Kaunas in 1929, quickly learned the language, and became Lithuania's favorite crooner of contemporary versions of the "schlager" ballads long popular among the older generation. Jewish artists, who had worked within a restricted ethnic milieu during the 1920s, began to exhibit works in predominantly Lithuanian venues after the mid-1930s. These limited but real cultural shifts occurred at a time of rising antisemitic agitation in the country at large.[250] Jewish professionals in the academy and the press also made important contributions in fields outside the narrower concerns of their community. In 1932 the lawyer and editor Rudolfas Valsonokas (Rudolph Valsonok, 1889–1946), one of the foremost experts on the

---

Kaubrys, "Lietuvos žydų lojalumo raiška: apsisprendimo variacijos 1918–1939 metais," in Šiaučiūnaitė-Verbickienė, *Abipusis pažinimas*, 105–117; cf. Sirutavičius, "Valdžios politika," 297–320.

249 See Lukas Aluzas, "Stumbling Stones. Ilgovskis Brothers, the Developer Tycoons of Interwar Kaunas," Lrt.lt, June 13, 2020, https://www.lrt.lt/en/news-in-english/19/1187815/stumbling-stones-ilgovskis-brothers-the-developer-tycoons-of-interwar-kaunas.

250 See Evelina Bukauskaitė, *Žydų meninis gyvenimas Lietuvoje 1919-1940m.: tarp autonomijos ir integralumo. Jewish Artistic Life in Lithuania 1919–1940: Between Autonomy and Integrity* [abstract] (Vilnius: Vilniaus dailės akademija, 2021), 21, 43; see also Evelina Bukauskaitė, "Gatherings of Jewish Artists in Interwar Lithuania," *Art History and Criticism/Meno istorija ir kritika* 17 (2021): 17–30.

Klaipėda Territory, published what is still one of the most thorough studies of the history and politics of this demographically complex region from a markedly Lithuanian national perspective.[251]

The years of interwar independence were not a period of systemic persecution of Lithuania's Jewish community. Important factors mitigated the worst antisemitic tendencies, especially before the crises of the late 1930s. During its two decades of existence, the Lithuanian state passed not a single antisemitic statute and, in addition to funding Jewish education, continued to modestly subsidize Jewish religious and cultural life, sometimes to the annoyance of non-Jews.[252] The authoritarian constitution in 1938 provoked concern because of its lack of specific guarantees for minorities, but this did not result in antisemitic legislation.[253] Ethnic disturbances in independent Lithuania were localized, short-lived, and relatively infrequent. There is no record, as of this writing, of anyone having been killed in an antisemitic pogrom after the end of the independence wars in 1920, that is, during the two decades when the interwar government had effective control of the country. The First Republic also lacked a violence-prone antisemitic mass organization on the model of Romania's Iron Guard. In contrast to the coming period of foreign occupation, responsible leadership proved capable of checking the worst excesses even as the country underwent modernization, a process which, while sparking inevitable tensions, resulted in a society that reflected a far more equitable distribution of social and economic power than in centuries past. For all their problems, the nations of independent Lithuania were better educated, wealthier, and freer to pursue their cultural aspirations than they had been under the rule of the tsars. As historian Tomas Balkelis states: "By the late 1930s Lithuania hardly resembled the impoverished imperial Russian periphery of the early century."[254]

Recent studies of Lithuanian antisemitism conclude that the pious strictures of government, Church, and academia achieved limited success in stemming historically ingrained antisemitic attitudes among the people and that the

---

251 Valsonokas, *Klaipėdos*.
252 For example, the Ministry of Education's support for Jewish theater and choral music reported in the article "6000 litų žydu menui," *Verslas*, July 14, 1932, 1.
253 The Jewish press, nonetheless, reminded the regime of Lithuania's declaration to the League of Nations of May 12, 1922 and its obligation regarding minority rights not mentioned in the 1938 constitution, as in "Dėl pilietybės," *Apžvalga*, February 8, 1938, 2.
254 Balkelis, *War*, 158.

country's elite did not sufficiently counter radical nationalist tendencies.[255] Nonetheless, one should not dismiss the significance of the legal and administrative system that provided basic protection for the country's minorities and, when necessary, the physical barrier of police force against violent outbreaks. Invasion and war would sweep away this state structure at dreadful cost to the Lithuanian people at large and with genocidal consequences for Lithuania's Jews.[256] It is a counterintuitive irony that the allegedly "fascist" interwar dictatorship not only protected the country against the most egregious political extremes, but, by and large, suppressed antisemitic violence, accepted cultural diversity, disdained Nazi racism, and rejected legally sanctioned discrimination. For its part, the "people's power" imposed by the Kremlin, which in June 1940 destroyed the Nationalist regime and proclaimed the fraternity of all nations, intensified ethnic animosity, suppressed political and cultural expression, confiscated Lithuanian and Jewish enterprises, and inflicted state violence on a level that the restive subjects of Antanas Smetona could scarcely have imagined.

---

255 See Truska and Vareikis, Holokausto prielaidos, 58–61; see also Algimantas Kasparavičius, "Lietuviai ir žydai katastrofos išvakarėse," 134–135.

256 See Timothy Snyder's description of Hitler and Stalin as "state destroyers" in *Black Earth: The Holocaust as History and Warning* (New York: Tim Duggan books, 2015), 77–116.

2.

The Stalinist Cauldron: Lithuanians, Jews, and Soviet Power, June 1940–June 1941

Invasion: Images and Memories

At ten minutes before midnight on June 14, 1940, Juozas Urbšys, Lithuania's foreign minister, and Ladas Natkevičius, the head of the country's mission in Moscow, were ushered into the office of Vyacheslav Molotov, the commissar of foreign affairs, to receive, they were told, "a very important statement." As Urbšys recalled, Molotov picked up a paper from his desk and proceeded to read an ultimatum to the stunned diplomats. He accused their government of, among other sins, conspiring with Latvia and Estonia to create a military alliance against the Soviet Union, kidnapping Soviet soldiers, and maltreating personnel working at the Red Army bases stationed in Lithuania. To rectify matters, the USSR demanded the formation of a pro-Moscow government and the immediate admission of Soviet military forces sufficient in number "to ensure the effective execution of the mutual assistance treaty [of October 10, 1939]."[1] On the morning of June 15, 1940, the Lithuanian government accepted the ultimatum and ordered the border guards and military to allow the soldiers of a "friendly power" to enter the country. More than 150,000 Red Army troops streamed into Lithuania, part of a half-million-strong Soviet force that occupied the Baltic states over the next three days. Ignas Jurkūnas (pseudonym: Ignas Šeinius) witnessed the invasion as he returned to Kaunas after a business trip with the Red Cross in Vilnius: "As far as the eye could see . . . the dust rose like smoke from

---

1   Juozas Urbšys, *Lietuva lemtingaisiais 1939–1940 metais* (Vilnius: Mintis, 1988), 46–54; cf. Eidintas and Žalys, *Lithuania in European politics*, 175–186; the text of the ultimatum and Molotov's notes on the meeting are in Algimantas Kasparavičius, Česlovas Laurinavičius, and Natalia Lebedeva, eds., *SSSR i Litva v gody vtoroi mirovoi voiny*, vol. 1, *SSSR i Litovskaya Respublika (mart 1939–avgust 1940 gg.) Sbornik dokumentov* (Vilnius: LII, 2006), 595–599.

the road, choked with Bolsheviks and their vehicles. It was impossible to get around them, the dust infused with the unbearable smell of petrol and sweat." A mounted Red Army officer, "himself layered with dust, atop a dust-armored horse," helped the writer's official Mercedes-Benz through the log jam, the one bright moment in the depressing montage of the invasion that he captured in his memoir *The Red Deluge*.[2]

Unable to persuade his cabinet to authorize military resistance and unwilling to preside over the country's surrender, Smetona chose to flee. The leader of the nation left just in time. The presidential motorcade set out for the German border on the afternoon of June 15 just before a Soviet airplane carrying Molotov's deputy Vladimir Dekanozov, the Kremlin's viceroy for Lithuania, touched down at Kaunas airport. The circumstances surrounding the ignoble departure of Lithuania's head of state contributed mightily to the sense of national shame.[3] Augustinas Voldemaras, Smetona's archrival, unwisely chose to return from his enforced exile only to be arrested and sent to Russia.[4] The departure of interwar Lithuania's two most prominent politicians, one voluntary, the other forced, signaled the coming political and, in some cases, physical extinction of the leadership that had ruled the country for two decades. The inglorious demise of the First Republic did much to discredit the country's rulers and political culture which, despite its conservative authoritarianism, had provided a counterweight to extremism. This collapse of will was a powerful ingredient in the potion of rage and bitterness which poisoned social and interethnic relations during the ensuing years of foreign occupation.

Images of the "Red hordes" streaming into Lithuania were seared into the minds of an entire generation: Communists and Jews running to meet the Soviet troops with flowers; on the sidelines, the sullen and resentful majority. While Šeinius recalled the Red Army from the comfort of his car, the commander of the Lithuanian Sixth Infantry Regiment recorded his own memories, ironically titled *How They Showered Me with Flowers*. Colonel Jonas Andrašiūnas learned by telephone that plans to resist a foreign attack had been canceled; he was

---

2   Ignas Šeinius, *Raudonasis tvanas* (New York: Talka, 1953), 102–103.
3   See the account by Smetona's sister, Marija Valušienė, written on August 1, 1940, as published in *Lietuvos aneksija: 1940 metų dokumentai*, ed. Leonas Gudsitis (Vilnius: Periodika, 1990), 45–50.
4   See Augustinas Voldemaras, *Pastabos saulėlydžio valandą*, ed. Gediminas Rudis (Vilnius: Mintis, 1992).

ordered instead to guide a Soviet armored unit into the town of Plungė. He wrote with sadness about the "hitherto unknown passions and attitudes which suddenly appeared" on the day of the invasion:

> [My] car was in the lead followed by numerous Russian tanks. When we reached the outskirts of Plungė I saw that quite a few people had gathered, mostly the town's Jews. Since I was first in line, they assumed that I was the commander of the Soviet armored force and showered flowers both on my car and the tanks behind me. The blossoms were fresh, the shouts and greetings in Russian. True, not everyone did this, but such exalted enthusiasm was displayed particularly by young Jewish boys and girls. I watched as the excited young Jews leaped into the Lithuanian gardens, grabbed up the flowers and threw them on my car and the Soviet tanks which crept along behind me. A trifle? Perhaps, but the impression back then was dreadful, it burned in the mind. One part of Plungė's population exulted, the other wept. I saw how a young Lithuanian farm girl sobbed as the Jews tore up her flowers. It seemed as if two peoples had split up, separated, never to live in peace again. And these fleeting images are so ingrained in my memory that I can still see them today.[5]

The historian Zenonas Ivinskis walked along the main thoroughfare in Kaunas as the tanks entered the city, noting that the streets were "full of people... especially Jews, crowding around the tanks and ingratiating themselves [with the soldiers]." He noted that "the scattered gaggles of Jewish boys and girls, no older than 15–18, who greeted every passing [Soviet] vehicle, made a very bad impression on me.... But it was only the young Jews who were happy; the older Jews disapproved. They just looked on." Ivinskis left Kaunas a few days later, depressed at the sight of the "seemingly endless columns of the Bolshevik army, surging into Lithuania."[6] For his part, the then fifteen-year-old future president of Lithuania, Valdas Adamkus, was more circumspect regarding the identity of the greeters but remembers finding the reception of the Soviet soldiers odd:

> I was even more surprised when small groups of people appeared carrying bouquets of flowers. I could not understand who they were, why they were rushing to hug these reeking soldiers of a foreign army. At the time

---

5   Jonas Andrašiūnas, "Kaip mane apmėtė gėlėmis," *Akiračiai*, 10 (1984): 13, 15.
6   Zenonas Ivinskis diary, entries for June 1940, in LYA, f. 3377, ap. 55, b. 240. The reservation of the older generation of Jews is noted in Yehuda Bauer, *The Death of the Shtetl* (New Haven: Yale University Press, 2009), 38.

I did not quite understand the concept of "occupation," but I grasped that Lithuania had suffered a great misfortune. I did not condemn these people, but only wondered: they were nicely dressed, clearly Kaunas people, but for some reason they were handing flowers to the Russians.[7]

Jewish memories of the foreign troops are nearly identical, albeit with a different perspective. Frieda Frome's childhood memories of Lithuania under Smetona were idyllic.[8] But during the last year of independence she had, along with some other young people, turned to Communist agitation, much to the disapproval of her anti-Soviet parents. She recalls the day of the occupation:

> I was at home on the afternoon of June 15, 1940, when I heard singing outside in the street. . . . People were hurrying along the street, shouting, singing and clapping their hands. They were joined every few yards along their march by other excited men, women, and children. I rushed out of the house and into the street. . . . "Our liberators are coming," they shouted joyously. "The Russians will make us free. Down with Smetona and the Fascists!" Looking in the direction they were headed, I saw great hordes of Russian soldiers in olive drab uniforms coming down from the hills.[9]

Harry Gordon records that the sudden appearance of tanks generated fears of a German invasion, but as the red stars came into sight:

> [O]ur mood changed. Instead of panic we felt an unnatural joy. Everyone started hugging and kissing each other, family and neighbors, as if the Messiah had just arrived. Those who had been hiding ran out of their houses and began throwing bouquets of flowers at the approaching army. It took a week of marching day and night for the army to move through the town. During this time the young Communists, some of them Jewish, had quite a celebration.

Gordon described how "young Jews insulted the Lithuanian police, laughed about the president, Antanas Smetona, who had run to Germany, and told

---

7   Valdas Adamkus, *Likimo vardas – Lietuva; apie laiką, įvykius, žmones* (Kaunas: Santara, 1997), 9–10.
8   See above, Chapter 1.
9   Frome, *Some Dare*, 7–10.

exaggerated stories about the Lithuanian police beating up Jews. This antagonized the whole Lithuanian population."¹⁰

The Šiauliai police reported on the hubris of the young: "The irresponsible Jewish element, especially youths, walk in the streets of the towns and do not even allow Lithuanians to pass by on the pavement. . . . Lithuanians complain that the Jews are bragging in a threatening way: 'We are now the masters.'"¹¹ A month later, the American mission in Kaunas informed Washington that "Jews had hastened to wave the Red flags of welcome" to the invading force and that "there seems to be a great deal of friction between the Gentile and the Jew even when both seek to embrace the Red tenets."¹² At the time, and in later years, observers who noted the Jewish reaction to the occupation failed to recognize that while there was a significant Jewish component within the LCP, it constituted but a small segment of the largely Zionist and Orthodox Litvaks in 1940 Lithuania. By then, the Nazis' treatment of Jews was already an open secret, so that the reactions of many Jews to the Red Army did not necessarily stem from any sympathy for Communist ideas.¹³

Bitter fault lines separate Lithuanian and Jewish wartime memories, but the contrasting reaction of the communities to the arrival of the Soviet troops, recorded in numerous contemporary accounts, is not one of them. Even when the clichés of flower-throwing Jews who welcomed the Bolsheviks and of effusive Lithuanians who greeted the Nazis a year later are noted without rancor, they reproduce archetypes which have survived to this day. Among the greeters of the Red Army were ethnic Lithuanian leftists who detested Smetona and rejoiced in the dictator's downfall, but they do not stand out in the diaries and memoirs. Historians can impose some clarity on processes that, at the time, must have

---

10 Harry Gordon, *The Shadow of Death: The Holocaust in Lithuania* (Lexington, KY: University Press of Kentucky), 8–9, 11. See also Gediminas Bašinskas, "Lietuvių-žydų konfliktai sovietinės okupacijos pradžioje 1940 metų vasarą: tęstinumai ar lūžiai," in Sirutavičius and Staliūnas, *Kai ksenofobija*, 210–211.

11 Šiauliai District Security and Criminal Police Bulletin, June 24, 1940, LCVA, f. 378, ap. 12, b. 296, l. 47.

12 Norem to State, July 17, 1940, National Archives, College Park, Maryland (hereafter NARA), M1178, Roll 19, 860.00/464.

13 See the summary of Jewish first reactions to the invasion in Dov Levin, *The Lesser of Two Evils: Eastern European Jewry under Soviet Rule, 1939–1941*, trans. Naftali Greenwood (Philadelphia: Jewish Publication Society, 1995), 35–37.

presented a kaleidoscope of conflicting images; nevertheless, the selective initial impressions are revealing and signal the conflicts to come.

The anxiety of prosperous Baltic urbanites, including Jews, was intensified by their first impressions of the Soviet infantry. To some, the invaders contrasted shockingly with the "cultured" West. Bernhard Press recounted his "alienating impression" of the "Mongolian" Soviet soldiers as "Huns storming Europe," whose singing, at least to his ears, sounded like the "howling of wolves."[14] Stories of officers' wives appearing on the streets in newly purchased nightshirts they mistook for evening gowns elicited snickering. Many of the tales of simple Soviet soldiers confused by indoor plumbing and entranced by consumer goods were probably apocryphal, but at least a few were based on first-hand observations.[15] While there was no systemic violence against civilians on the part of the Soviet forces during the first months of the occupation, numerous incidents involving undisciplined elements of the Red Army did little to endear the foreign soldiers to the locals. Before the invasion, the Smetona regime, fearful of antagonizing the Kremlin, had suppressed publicity involving the misbehavior of the Soviet personnel based in the country, including reports of robberies, rapes, and even several killings.[16] In mid-July 1940 Colonel Vincas Kiršinas translated and summarized a report by the Telšiai police on its investigation into the robberies and rapes of young women carried out by an unidentified Soviet sergeant and enlisted men in a two-day crime spree in the countryside.[17] Some Red Army officers seized the apartments of detained citizens sealed by the NKVD, ignoring the protests of Lithuanian "comrades" whom they "treated rudely." Piotr Gladkov, the deputy commissar of internal affairs of the Lithuanian SSR and the de facto head of the republic's Soviet security police, was driven to plead to the top brass of the Eleventh Army of the Baltic Military District to warn all officers against "tearing down the seals of the NKVD."[18] These and other reports

---

14 Bernhard Press, *The Murder of the Jews of Latvia 1941–1945*, trans. L. Mazzarins (Evanston, IL: Northwestern University Press, 2000), 32.

15 See the racial musings in Šeinius, *Raudonasis*, 104–108. The nightgown episode and similar incidents are also repeated in Jewish memoirs, as in Gordon, *The Shadow*, 14 and Frome, *Some Dare*, 13.

16 Norbertas Černiauskas, *1940. Paskutinė Lietuvos vasara* (Vilnius: Aukso žuvys, 2022), 167–170.

17 Report of Vincas Kiršinas, "Svodka doznanii," July 1940, LCVA, F. 384, ap. 4, b. 20, l.115–117.

18 Gladkov to Eleventh Army Headquarters, September 1940, LCVA, f. R-756, ap. 2, b. 63, l. 40–41.

portray Soviet military personnel behaving with impunity and a sense of entitlement. The perception of Soviet power as representative of primitive "Asiatic" values aroused contempt among those already predisposed to reject Communism. The security police reported that rumors of annexation "truly frighten many people, who say that they fear destitution, which might result from the loss of Lithuania's independence."[19] In time, throughout the regions occupied by the USSR in 1939–1940 the living standards of middle-class and prosperous farmers declined sharply, and it became evident that the political repressions of the former authoritarian regimes paled in comparison to those of the Soviet occupiers.

The People's Government and Its Discontents: Bringing "Stalin's Sun" to Lithuania

Smetona's principled but unsuccessful argument in favor of rejecting the Kremlin's ultimatum might have brought clarity to the tragedy: armed resistance, however futile, would have exposed an act of aggression to the outside world and provided a model of national heroism for future generations. Instead, the confusing and farcical political machinations surrounding the occupation baffled even seasoned observers and politicians.[20] The Soviet mission in Kaunas ignored attempts to pass power to a legitimate successor of the departed president and installed the People's Government (Liaudies vyriausybė) with leftist journalist Justas Paleckis (1899–1980) as head of state with a cabinet headed by Vincas Krėvė-Mickevičius, a celebrated writer known for his pro-Soviet views, all of whom swore to uphold the constitution of 1938. The ministers included one Communist, Interior Minister Mečislovas Gedvilas (1901–1981), a member of the International Red Aid (Mezhdunarodnaya organizatsiya pomoshchi revoliutsioneram, MOPR), Moisiejus Leonas Koganas (1894–1956), and left-leaning intellectuals, as well as public figures who had no obvious connection to the LCP. The presence of former prime minister Ernestas Galvanauskas as head of finance provided the government with a veneer of respectability and a perceived (but false) connection to the First Republic. Engineered by the Soviets as a political Trojan horse, the new

---

19 Vilnius District Security Police Bulletin, June 25, 1940, LCVA, f. 378, ap. 10, b. 699, l. 584.
20 Gediminas Rudis, "Rašytojo atsiminimai apie pirmąjį sovietmetį," 1–3. Unpublished manuscript provided to author.

regime was rudderless, befuddled by the rapid pace of events. On June 19 Antanas Sniečkus (1903–1974),[21] the leader of the interwar underground LCP, seized control of Smetona's State Security Department. By mid-July, the security police, now under the tutelage of the NKVD,[22] arrested more than five hundred prominent citizens and political leaders, a number of whom were later executed.[23] Gedvilas and Sniečkus took their instructions from the Soviet mission and openly ignored Krėvė's ineffectual government. The pent-up resentment of the Nationalists' monopolization of power meant that much of the orchestrated celebration of Smetona's downfall was shared by at least a part of the Lithuanian public. The promise of social reforms appealed to economically marginal groups, while many Jews celebrated the prospect of the newly proclaimed "equal treatment for all nationalities." But the urban middle class and landed peasantry had little desire for social revolution; during the first days of the occupation, then, the authorities reiterated promises to safeguard private property and the country's sovereignty. Only a minority expressed any desire to join the "Soviet family of nations."

The politics of the summer of 1940 have evoked inconsistent, even contradictory, interpretations, the least convincing of which is the Soviet portrayal of the occupation as a popular revolution. Since the late 1990s the Russian explanation of the ultimatums and military deployments in the Baltics as consistent with international legal norms has become an official stance.[24] There is little doubt about who wielded real power once the Red Army had secured the country. The Soviet military conducted itself as a conquering force, frequently directing and providing personnel for demonstrations glorifying Stalin and the Soviet Union. At the apex of the new system was a working group of Soviet officials and operatives of the LCP which coordinated the activity of the People's

---

21 With brief interruptions, Sniečkus headed the LCP from 1936 until his death in 1974, one of the longest-serving Party bosses on record.

22 The People's Commissariat of Internal Affairs (Narodnyi kommissariat vnutrennikh del).

23 Beria's report to Stalin and Molotov, undated, LYA, f. K-1, ap. 49, b. 828, l. 85. Among the detainees who were deported to the USSR were Antanas Merkys and Juozas Urbšys, the last prime minister and foreign minister, respectively, of the independent state.

24 On Soviet preparations in the event of a "Finnish variant" of resistance by Baltic armies, see Natalia Lebedeva's introduction to Kasparavičius, Laurinavičius, and Lebedeva, *SSSR i Litva*, 51–53. As an analogy, the Czech president Emil Hácha formally agreed to Hitler's "protection" in March 1939, but no German scholar would argue that the Nazi occupation of the Czech lands under threat of force was anything other than aggression against an independent state.

Government through the Soviet mission in Kaunas led by the urbane Nikolai Pozdnyakov, who played the "good cop" to Dekanozov's "bad cop."[25]

The days following the Soviet invasion presented a counterintuitive postscript to Jewish-Lithuanian relations of the interwar period. Smetona, the erstwhile critic of narrow-minded nationalism, was vilified as an antisemite. General Skučas, who had suppressed anti-Jewish disturbances and called society to heel, and the state security chief Povilaitis, who had chronicled the deeds of the culprits, were derided as "fascists." On the evening of June 18, 1940, Paleckis addressed the nation on radio: "The plutocratic [Smetona] regime was rotten at its core . . . , [its] tragic end crowned by the former president's and his sycophants' shameful flight from their nation." Paleckis solemnly declared that the new People's Government would make every effort "to realize the principle of the equality of nationalities, and to resolutely eradicate chauvinism."[26] In its issue of June 25, 1940, the Sovietized *Apžvalga* determined that "the provocateurs from Kaunas had contributed to the anti-Jewish excesses which had occurred when Lithuania took Vilnius," announcing that a veritable St. Bartholomew's Night for the Jews had been prevented only by the supposed "healthy instincts of Lithuania's masses."[27] Within days, its function as the oracle of Jewish Lithuanian patriotism no longer of use in the new order, the country's sole Lithuanian-language Jewish newspaper ceased publication along with most of the mainstream press.

The new government's masquerade as a democratic alternative to Smetona, as well as the delusions of some of its non-Communist members, were short-lived. Despite the occupation, Paleckis's regime had promised political changes based on the "constitutional order" and respect for private property. On June 26, 1940, Krėvė instructed the country's diplomats to inform the outside world that Lithuania would continue observing its international obligations as a sovereign, independent state, a message duly reaching Washington and European capitals.[28] On the same day the acting premier met Pozdnyakov and told a different story to

---

25 See Alfred E. Senn, *Lithuania 1940: Revolution from Above* (Amsterdam: Rodopi, 2007), 119ff.

26 "Respublikos prezidentas J. Paleckis apie svarbiausius naujosios vyriausybės uždavinius," *Lietuvos aidas*, June 19, 1940 (morning ed.), 1.

27 "Žydų visuomenė sveikina naująją vyriausybę," *Apžvalga*, June 25, 1940, 1.

28 Laurynas Jonušaukas, *Likimo vedami: Lietuvos diplomatinės tarnybos egzilyje veikla 1940–1991* (Vilnius: LGGRTC, 2003), 54–55.

the Kremlin's envoy, speaking to him as a "good friend" rather than as an official. Krėvė complained that the rapid "methods and tempo" of Sovietization were leading to social disorder and economic collapse and expressed resentment at his powerless role as, in his words, "an executor of the directives of the [Soviet] Mission," warning that he could not be held responsible for the people's hostile reaction. Krėvė alleged that the legalization of the Communist Party was a political mistake, "because its slogans had aroused panic among a population which was also perturbed by the behavior of the Jews, who have disdain for Lithuanian statehood."[29] Well-known for his pro-Soviet leanings and one of the country's few public figures with a Jewish wife, Krėvė was no antisemite, but his perception of "Jewish behavior" at the onset of the occupation was widely shared.

Colonel Kazys Škirpa (1895–1979), the Lithuanian envoy to Germany, was lucky enough to avoid arrest when he visited Kaunas a few days after the occupation. Upon returning to Berlin, Škirpa sent his impressions to fellow diplomats in the West, reporting an altercation between a Lithuanian soldier and a Jewish worker that escalated into a window-smashing melee in Marijampolė, and then expressing his disgust at the Jews:

> The only ones who still feel good [in the current situation] are the Jews. It goes without saying that, just as there were Communists among them before, very many new ones have now appeared. Also, fearing the Reich, many Jews, who basically do not hold Communist convictions, are more inclined to think that it is better to align with Soviet Russia and submit to Communism. For this reason, in the various street demonstrations it is the Jews who above all express sympathy for Soviet Russia, completely forgetting that only yesterday they were licking the Lithuanians' soles, expressing loyalty to Lithuania for its liberalism towards the Jews. Lithuanian society, of course, is indignant at this Jewish fawning over the Russians and thus each day is more infected with antisemitism, especially since the Jews, in emphasizing their loyalty to the Soviets, often publicly insult Lithuanians, particularly former government officials. . . . The Russian language, as in tsarist times, has once again become for the Jews an expression of Russian patriotism.[30]

---

29   Details of the conversation are in the telephone transcript [Telefonograma] June 27, 1940, Makarov to NKVD (Moscow), LYA, f. K-1, ap. 49, b. 828, l. 45–46. Makarov described Krėvė as "vice-premier."
30   Škirpa to Jurgis Šaulys (Bern), Bronius Balutis (London), and Petras Klimas (Paris), Hoover Institution, Turauskas Collection, Box 3, July 1, 1940, 10. The Marijampolė riot appears in several police reports.

Škirpa's pro-German orientation might make his observations of Lithuanians' social attitudes suspect if it were not for numerous police and Party documents, which describe the groundswell of popular antisemitism.

In order to legitimize the rule of the now exalted "toiling masses," on July 1, 1940, Paleckis's government announced that it would call elections for a new legislature that would lay the basis for a socially just order. The vote for the People's Diet (Liaudies Seimas) was an efficiently managed electoral charade. The hitherto unknown Lithuanian Union of Working People (Lietuvos Darbo liaudies sąjunga) appeared as if by magic on July 6. The balloting then followed a week of "campaigning" for the only permitted list of seventy-nine union candidates all chosen by the LCP, one for each seat in the proposed Diet. Half of the future legislators were center-left candidates selected to appeal to a wide audience. In order to maintain the fiction of state sovereignty, slogans of a Communist future were discouraged (although not always successfully). The balloting procedure lent itself to confusion and manipulation. There was no registration. Officials simply handed voters an envelope containing the ballots, one for each candidate. It was expected that the voter would "choose" all the candidates by simply depositing the envelope into the ballot box. However, this made it easy to "select out" unpopular candidates by simply tossing their individual ballots aside. Of course, this would in no way change the outcome, since everyone on the published Working People list was guaranteed a place in the assembly, regardless of the "votes" they received. There were other bizarre aspects to the election: at least two candidates later claimed to have learned that they were on the ballot only after reading their names in the media. There was a phantom candidate, one Jonas Abakonis, who reportedly found a place on the list of deputies at the suggestion of a comrade who vaguely remembered the peasant as a once stolid underground Party member. Apparently, no one bothered to check whether the man was available. When the duly elected Abakonis failed to turn up at the first session of the People's Diet, his place was taken by Paleckis.[31]

How many voters supported a radiant socialist future may never be known. Some citizens stayed home, fearful of being held to account should the new order not prevail. Others, less sure about Soviet prospects but in a show of

---

31 Liudas Dovydėnas, *Mes valdysim pasaulį: atsiminimai*, 2 vols (Woodhaven, NY: Romuva, 1970), 1:193–194; Antanas Garmus, "Lietuvos įjungimas į SSSR-Maskvos diktatas," in *Lietuvių archyvas: Bolševizmo metai*, vol. 3, ed. Juozas Balčiūnas (Kaunas: n.p., 1942), 36–37; Juozas Bulavas, "Žaidimas seimu," *Vilniaus balsas* 2/3 (Oct. 1989); Rudis, "Rašytojo atsiminimai," 13–14.

conformity, went to the precincts but, as insurance, "forgot" to bring their identifying documents, thus avoiding the incriminating stamp signifying that they had cast their ballots.[32] Yet despite the lack of reliable voter registration and turnout records, abundant circumstantial evidence indicates that a majority participated in the sham election. Reassured by the presence of prominent non-Party candidates, some hoped that the leftist pro-Soviet government would manage to preserve some form of Lithuanian statehood, perhaps as a subservient satellite (the example of Mongolia was one option discussed among the intelligentsia). Another motive for participation in the election was growing antisemitism and the desire to "elect one's own," as indicated by the poor showing of Jewish candidates and the strong preference for non-Communists who had been placed on the union's list.[33]

In order to present the People's Diet as the authentic voice of Lithuanians, officials from the Soviet mission in Kaunas, who had the last word in organizing the electoral charade, insisted that ethnic Lithuanians should dominate the assembly. As a result, despite the large share of Jews and Russians within the LCP, especially in Kaunas, ethnic Lithuanian representation in the Diet was overwhelming: of the seventy-eight delegates, there were but four Jews, three Poles, two Belarusians, one Latvian, and one Russian.[34] On July 16, 1940, the electoral commission announced that 1,386,569 voters, or 95.5% of the total, had cast 99.2% of their votes for the Lithuanian Union of Working People. Some locales claimed 100% participation; in other places, the vote totals surpassed the number of possible adult participants. In the Kalnuotė district near Vilnius voter participation was reported as 133%.[35] On July 21–23, in a circus atmosphere

---

32 Report of Tauragė District Chief Baldušis, July 21, 1940, in Laimutė Breslavskienė, Alfonsas Eidintas, Ramutė Jermalavičienė, Leonora Kalasauskienė, Stasė Marcikonienė, et al., eds. *Lietuvos okupacija ir aneksija, 1939–1940: dokumentų rinkinys* (Vilnius: Mintis, 1993), 385.

33 Artūras Svarauskas, "Kodėl dalyvauta ir už ką balsuota rinkimuose į Liaudies seimą 1940 metais?," *Lietuvos istorijos metraštis* 2 (2018): 101–128.

34 Nijolė Maslauskienė, "Valdininkijos šalinimas iš okupuotosios Lietuvos administracijos ir jos keitimas okupantų talkininkais 1940m. birželio-gruodžio mėn.," *Genocidas ir rezistencija* 2, no. 8 (2000): 19.

35 "Kaip rinko Seimą Vilniaus miestas ir kraštas," *Darbo Lietuva*, July 17, 1940, 2; Konstantinas Surblys, ed., *Lietuvos Liaudies Seimas: Stenogramos ir medžiaga* (Mintis: Vilnius 1985), 31. See Marijampolė District Security and Criminal Police Report, July 18, 1940 and Panevėžys District Security and Criminal Police Report, July 18, 1940, in Breslavskienė, Eidintas, Jermalavičienė, Kalasauskienė, Marcikonienė, et al., *Lietuvos okupacija ir aneksija*, 366, 375–377; also, LYA, f. 1771, ap. 1, b. 110, l. 2–5; LKP Central Committee Directive, July 14, 1940, LYA,

IMAGE 2.1. Russian tanks roll through the streets of Kaunas during the Soviet occupation of Lithuania, June 15, 1940. These photos were taken through a hole in a piece of paper that was used to cover a window. (United States Holocaust Memorial Museum Photo Archives, Top: #12035, Bottom: #12036. Courtesy of George Birman. Copyright of United States Holocaust Memorial Museum.)

IMAGE 2.2. The People's Government, June 17, 1940: Acting Premier and Foreign Minister, Vincas Krėvė-Mickevičius (second from left); Acting President Justas Paleckis (fourth from left). (Source—public domain.)

of organized enthusiasm, the Diet met in Kaunas to declare Soviet power and choose a delegation of "progressive" literati and fellow travelers to journey to Moscow and, in the parlance of the time, "bring back Stalin's sun." They succeeded: on August 3, 1941, the USSR Supreme Soviet accepted Lithuania into the Soviet Union.[36]

The Changing Face of the LCP: Lithuanians, Jews, Russians

The history of the country's Sovietization became the subject of obfuscation at the hands of Marxist historians who understood that the legitimizing rationale for the existence of the Lithuanian SSR depended on evading any genuine

---

f. 1771, ap. 1, b. 108. Cf. the reports by the head of the American mission in Kaunas, Norem to State, July 15, 1940: NARA, M1178, roll 19, 860M.00/450; Norem to State, July 19, 1940, NARA, M1178, roll 19, 860M.00/452.

36 Senn, *Lithuania 1940*, 238–241.

IMAGE 2.3. July 1940. Top: Lithuanian People's Army soldiers attending a session of the People's Diet. Bottom: Soldiers marching in an election rally. A year later many of the men would mutiny when the Wehrmacht invaded Lithuania.

investigation into the events of 1940, including the dynamics of interethnic relations, or in Soviet verbiage, the "friendship of peoples." To what extent did the conflicting perceptions, stereotypes, and myths that swirled around the politics of the first year of the Soviet occupation correspond to the realities of power? Since the pernicious charge that "Jews and Bolsheviks are one and the same" constituted the most successful theme in Nazi propaganda during the German occupation, there is clearly a need to examine the distribution of power in Soviet Lithuania. The subject is laden with potentially ugly connotations and thus caution is in order. One can reject outright the accusation that "most NKVD torturers were Jews" and similar canards in the antisemitic arsenal. But the archival evidence is easily manipulated and can produce contradictory images. The social and ethnic face of Lithuanian Communism throughout the entire Stalinist period represents a shifting mosaic, so selective statistical snapshots are of little help and can mislead casual readers of the data.

The successful imposition of the Stalinist system in Lithuania depended on forging the LCP into a dependable instrument of Moscow's rule. In the Baltic states, the Kremlin faced, for the first time since the establishment of the Comintern, the task of integrating foreign comrades into the All-Union Communist Party (Bolsheviks), the AUCP (B).[37] On the eve of the Soviet invasion the LCP numbered between sixteen hundred and two thousand members, the majority in the underground. Native-born Jews and Russians constituted nearly half of the membership. Upon the arrival of the Soviets, the prisons disgorged hundreds of comrades, but the Party also took in a flood of new recruits. Many who joined turned out to be opportunists of questionable "ideological maturity": merchants, tradesmen, office employees, and uneducated proletarians. By mid-July, Jews, albeit briefly, made up three-fourths of Communists registered in Kaunas city, as well as 40–50% of new candidates in the small towns. A significant number of ethnic Lithuanians also signed up, including former Riflemen's Union members. By October 8, 1940, when Lithuanian Communists were formally enrolled as constituent members of the All-Union Party, the republic's Communist membership had tripled to more than five thousand.[38]

---

37 In Russian: *Vsesoyuznaya Kommunisticheskaya partiya (bol'shevikov)*, the VKP(b). This was the official designation of the Communist Party of the Soviet Union from 1925 to 1952.

38 Following the Soviet example, the LCP was rechristened the Lithuanian Communist Party (Bolsheviks), L. Lietuvos Komunistų partija (bolševikų).

Moscow mistrusted the newly baptized but ideologically polluted LCP.[39] A review completed on December 1, 1940, concluded that of 5,388 Communists who had been registered by the regional Party committees only 1,507 had the experience (R *stazh*) of "service in the underground."[40] In the autumn of 1940 the Party began the expulsion of unreliable recent members, a housecleaning accompanied by an influx of Communists from outside the Lithuanian SSR, primarily Russophone "experienced cadres." Russian became the language of the LCP Central Committee. By the end of the year about half of Lithuania's Communists had been drummed out of the Party.[41]

Official orthodoxy mandated the LCP to work in a spirit of "internationalism," that is, ethnic solidarity, but the Party politics of Soviet Lithuania were rife with tensions. Native Jewish and Lithuanian Communists, whatever their differences, resented the tutelage of the Russophone arrivals who saw their new positions in the Baltic as launchpads for career advancement and were quick to realize that charges of Zionism and/or Lithuanian nationalism provided ammunition against local rivals. In Kaunas, recent arrivals Shupikov and Parashchenka launched a hunt for Zionists and Jewish Mensheviks, but Jews on the city's Party committee and within the LCP Central Committee resisted the inquisition.[42] By early October ethnic Lithuanians temporarily achieved a majority in the Kaunas Party organization, making up 60% of the Communists in the city, mainly owing to the arrival of replacements for "bourgeois" officials.[43] But nothing illustrates better the transitory nature of Party membership data during this period than the fact that this supposed Lithuanian dominance lasted but a few weeks, after which Russophone comrades more or less owned the Kaunas organization until the early 1950s.

---

39 Nijolė Maslauskienė, "Lietuvos komunistų tautinė ir socialinė sudėtis, 1939 m. pabaigoje-1940 m. rugsėjo men.," *Genocidas ir rezistencija* 1, no. 5 (1999): 95–99.

40 LYA, f. 1771, ap. 1, b. 139, l. 2–4. By another estimate, by October 1940 the percentage of Lithuania's Communists who had been in the Party for at least one year had plummeted from 82% to 19%.

41 Nijolė Maslauskienė, "Lietuvos komunistų sudėtis 1940 spalio-1941 birželio men.," *Genocidas ir rezistencija* 2, no. 6 (1999): 28–29. On Lithuanian-Jewish rivalry within the LCP and Soviet Lithuanian government, see Nijolė Maslauskienė, "Lietuvos tautinių mažumų įtraukimas į LSSR administraciją ir sovietinės biurokratijos tautiniai santykiai 1940–1941 m.," *Genocidas ir rezistencija* 1, no. 9 (2001): 35–39.

42 Maslauskienė, "Lietuvos komunistų tautinė ir socialinė sudėtis, 1939 m. pabaigoje-1940 m. rugsėjo men," *Genocidas ir rezistencija* 5, no. 1 (1999): 28–36.

43 Ibid., 99.

An important instrument of foreign power within the Party was the system of control by which imported second secretaries supervised the work of native figureheads. Lithuanians constituted three-fourths of first secretaries, while Russians and Belarusians made up 84% of their deputies. As the Party explained, the latter constituted "the better-trained and selected Communists . . . assigned by the Central Committee of the All-Union CP."[44] By December 1940 there was not a single case where both the first and second secretaries of any city or district Party committee were of the same nationality.[45] On another front, Lithuanians continued to lose ground among the regional Party committees: in January 1941, exclusive of the first and second secretaries, they made up but 55% of committee members, with Jews (22%) and Russians (21%) providing most of the remainder.[46] According to the membership rolls of the LCP of January 1, 1941, ethnic Lithuanians made up two-thirds of the 2,486 listed Party members and candidates. These figures supposedly demonstrated the predominance of native cadres,[47] but they are of little use in understanding who ruled the Lithuanian SSR.

The Fifth Congress of the LCP, which took place in Kaunas on February 5–9, 1941, decisively accelerated the republic's Sovietization. The opening speeches included the requisite expansive militant incantations about exporting revolution as articulated by the delegate Shuvalov who declared that the war ignited by the capitalist powers would inevitably involve the world proletariat; thus, the Communist cause required not peace, but the conclusion of "a just war, *a war for socialism, for the liberation of other nations from the bourgeoisie*" [emphasis in the original].[48] The usual odes to Stalin played to a receptive audience: a third of the 277 voting delegates to the Congress were listed as "workers of the Red Army and NKVD," mostly recent Russian, Ukrainian, and Belarusian arrivals.[49] Of the 342 delegates in attendance (sixty-five were nonvoting participants) less than a quarter were veterans of Lithuania's prewar underground

---

44 LYA, f. 1771, ap. 2, b. 457, l. 10.
45 LYA, f. 1771, ap. 1, b. 282, l. 174, also l. 7–11, 53, 75, 124; cf. the list of first and second secretaries of the Lithuanian SSR's city and district Party committees in December 1940. LYA, f. 1771, ap. 1, b. 283; also, the documents in LYA, f. 1771, ap. 1, b. 281, l. 7–8, 27.
46 The data are based on LYA, f. 1771, ap. 2, b. 457, l. 10–13.
47 See for example, Konstantinas Surblys, ed., *Lietuvos Komunistų partija skaičiais 1918–1975* (Mintis: Vilnius, 1976), 45ff.
48 LYA, f. 1771, ap. 2, b. 4, l. 139.
49 LYA, f. 1771, ap. 2, b. 4, l. 197–198.

TABLE 1. Delegates to the Fifth Congress of the LCP by nationality, February 1941

National Group	Voting Delegates		Non-voting Delegates	
	N	(%)	N	(%)
Lithuanians	107	(38.6)	30	(46.2)
Russophones	128	(46.2)	24	(36.9)
Jews	33	(11.9)	9	(13.8)
Other	9	(3.3)	2	(3.1)
Total	**277**	**(100)**	**65**	**(100)**

Sources: LYA, f. 1771, ap. 2, b. 12, l. 1; LYA, f. 1771, ap. 2, b. 4, l. 200.

Note: The numbers of delegates to the congress in the Party records show slight variations, but since they amount to less than 1%, the inconsistencies are not statistically significant. See Konstantinas Surblys, ed., *Lietuvos Komunistų partija skaičiais 1918–1975* (Mintis: Vilnius, 1976), 61 and Romas Šarmaitis, "LKP(b) Penktasis suvažiavimas," in *Revoliucinis judėimas Lietuvoje: straipsniu rinkinys*, ed. Romas Šarmaitis (VPMLL: Vilnius, 1957), 576.

Communist Party who had "suffered repression during bourgeois times." The proceedings were held in Russian.

After the triumphal opening ceremonies, the Congress confronted the major obstacles to Lithuania's Sovietization: the anti-Communism of the Catholic population, "reactionary" Lithuanian nationalism, and the hostility to Soviet power in general.[50] The discussions concerning the Party's cadres exposed the prevailing national tensions. There were persistent complaints that ethnic Lithuanians favored "their own" in staffing administrative and economic institutions,[51] as did the other nationalities. The Vilnius Party boss Povilas Baltruška (Pavel Baltrushka), an ethnic Lithuanian from Russia, reported that among 180 recent applications for membership within his Party section, 157 were non-Lithuanians, primarily Jews, Russians, and Belarusians.[52] As first

---

50 Speeches of Damulevich and Alekna, LYA, f. 1771, ap. 2, b. 4, l. 248, 322.

51 According to the veteran Communist Bronius Pušinis, the Commissariat of Agriculture was a bastion of anti-Soviet Lithuanian nationalism. Delegate Lukoševičius complained of Lithuanian chauvinism against Jews and Poles in the Lietūkis and Maistas companies. LYA, f. 1771, ap. 2, b. 4, l. 31, 124.

52 Ibid., l. 211.

secretary, Baltruška presided over a Vilnius city committee consisting of four Jews and four Russians. The Vilnius district committee of thirteen members employed a majority of Russian and Ukrainian immigrants and only two Lithuanians.[53] At the same time, Feliksas Bieliauskas, the head of the Komsomol, who had replaced a Jewish chief, complained that only 57% of the Party's youth wing consisted of ethnic Lithuanians, which, he insisted, was clearly insufficient, considering that Lithuanians constituted 80% of the republic's population.[54]

Justas Paleckis, Soviet Lithuania's nominal head of state, provoked a sharp exchange at the meeting. He criticized overly enthusiastic ideologues who saw it as "their chief duty to hang a sword of Damocles over every office employee ... because of some lapse in his résumé, regardless of the quality of the work." Paleckis appealed for a more balanced approach to the problem of nationalism in economic and social life, claiming, albeit in typically obsequious fashion, that it was not only the Lithuanians who were at fault:

> On the national question, it must be said we do not yet have that healthy, authentic internationalism which has already developed in the other [Soviet] republics. We must take this fact into account. We often observe the phenomenon of people usually supporting "their own." And so, a Lithuanian will above all support a Lithuanian, a Jew will trust only another Jew, a Pole will promote a Pole, a Russian will try to attract more Russians.[55]

Newly arrived "fraternal" members of the Party took Paleckis to the shed, rebuking his comments about Russians as "an evil jest" and "strange theory."[56] Pozdnyakov, the Kremlin's de facto viceroy at the meeting, played the role of peacemaker, acknowledging that Paleckis's critics were doctrinally correct but tactfully refusing to take sides, reminding the Congress that, from a Marxist point of view, nationality held only "secondary importance."[57] Whatever the rhetoric, the actual redistribution of power was formalized when the Congress

---

53   LYA, f. 1771, ap. 1, b. 283.
54   Ibid., l. 223–228.
55   Ibid., l. 242–243.
56   Ibid., l. 251–252, 282, 293–294, 312.
57   Ibid., l. 335–350. Pozdnyakov was particularly keen to avoid exacerbating Polish-Lithuanian tensions in Vilnius. Cf. Vytautas Tininis, *Sovietinė Lietuva ir jos veikėjai* (Vilnius: Enciklpedija, 1994), 299–230.

approved the makeup of the Party's leading organs on February 9, 1941. The new Central Committee (CC) of the LCP contained forty-eight full members, of whom scarcely half were ethnic Lithuanians; of sixteen candidate members only three can clearly be identified as Lithuanians, who also constituted less than half of the important control commission attached to the CC.[58]

Lithuania's Communists desperately needed fraternal guidance from more experienced cadres. The demographic breakdown of the republic's Communists of January 1, 1941, indicated that only twenty-nine comrades (1.2%) had completed higher education and only seventy-eight (3.1%) could boast secondary school certificates. Only a tenth of the members and candidates had ever attended secondary school. The majority (1,296, or 52%) had completed a primary education, which in Lithuania consisted of the first four grades. More than a third (36%) of Party members and candidates were described as "literate but without primary schooling."[59] The educational profile of the most ignorant political body in the history of Lithuania is revealing: a minimally educated mass in no position to debate, let alone decide, anything. The image of uncomprehending faces, hands raised during votes, captures the reality.

The Russification of Soviet Lithuania's power structure accelerated swiftly during the early months of 1941.

TABLE 2. The ethnic composition of the LCP, 1940–1941 (%)

Nationality	October 1, 1940 (N = 5,365)	January 1, 1941 (N = 2,486)	June 22, 1941 (N = 4,703)
Lithuanians	68.5	67.0	46.4
Jews	16.2	16.6	12.6
Russophones*	15.3	16.4	41.0

* Mainly Russians, Ukrainians, and Belarusians. Non-Slavic "others" are statistically insignificant.

---

58   LYA., f. 1771, ap. 1, b. 283, l. 361, 390–391, 408, 412–445.
59   LYA, f. 1771, ap. 2, b. 250, l. 21.

Sources: LYA, f. 1771, ap. 1, b. 162, l. 4; LYA, f. 1771, ap. 1, b. 170, l.27–129; Maslauskienė, "Lietuvos komunistų, tautinė ir socialinė sudėtis," 99, and "Lietuvos komunistų sudėtis," 38; Liudas Truska,"Lietuvos valdžios įstaigų rusifikavimas 1940–1941 m.," *Lietuvos gyventojų genocido ir rezistencijos tyrimo institutas: Darbai*, 1 (1996): 16.

Note: The figures for membership on January 1, 1941, differ slightly from those presented here if one includes data from the Švenčioniai district incorporated into the Lithuanian SSR and formerly within the jurisdiction of the Belarusian Communist Party. I have excluded these figures, which hardly affect the overall statistics, because they were not included in the LCP's own reports of January 1, 1941.

And yet Table 2 understates the Russian grip on power. A better indication of relative influence is revealed by the situation in the country's two largest cities. In Vilnius the LCP's list of January 1, 1941, recorded a majority of Russians (45%) and Jews (26%). Ethnic Poles, a plurality in Lithuania's historic capital at the time, were largely left out of the Party. The scale and timing of Russian assumption of control in Kaunas, where Lithuanians made up three-quarters of the population and which was the republic's de facto administrative center during 1940–1941, is revealing of the real dynamic of interethnic power as indicated:

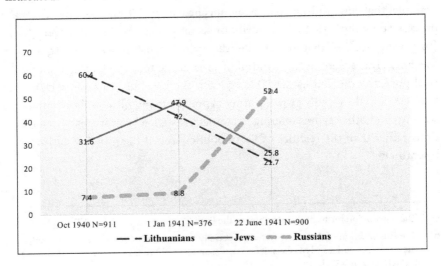

CHART 1. National Composition of the Kaunas City LCP October 1940 — June 1941.

Note: The June 1941 percentage of Lithuanians in this chart, approximately one-fifth of Party members, reflected the reality in the entire country until the early 1950s.

Sources: Based on party lists as found in LYA, f. 1771, ap. 1, b. 165; LYA, f. 1771, ap.1, b. 170, l. 20; Maslauskienė, "Lietuvos komunistų tautinė ir socialinė sudėtis," 99 and her "Lietuvos komunistų sudėtis," 27; Truska, "Lietuvos valdžios įstaigų rusifikavimas," 16.

The same pattern can be seen among the sixty-seven Kaunas city delegates to the Fifth Congress: only seventeen were Lithuanians (25%); twenty were Jews (30%), while the largest number (45%) were Russophones, mostly newcomers from other republics.[60] Among all Communists of the Kaunas district, Russophones (42%) outnumbered both Lithuanians (41%) and Jews (14%). Aside from the large urban Party organizations, the influx of Russians was noticeable among the cadres in the LCP Central Committee, in mid-level administrative posts, and in the upper echelons of the security services.[61] In the latter case, the records make clear that the antisemitic chimera of "Jewish dominance" in the NKVD was false: the majority of the department chiefs were ethnic Lithuanians with either a grade school education or "self-taught." Decision-making rested with Russians who constituted most of the deputy chiefs and other "assisting personnel."[62] The numerical prominence of rank-and-file ethnic Lithuanians in the Party and part of the administrative apparatus obscured the real prop of Soviet control throughout the Lithuanian SSR: "Russian power."

The opening of the archives since the late 1980s has undermined the politicized stereotypes embedded in memoirs and other anecdotal accounts: for example, that Jews did not play a significant part in Lithuania's Sovietization process (they did); that the majority of secret police interrogators were Jews (they were not); or that Soviet rule was really "Jewish power" in disguise (it was not). There were only a handful of Jews in the top echelons of the LCP.[63] Real power in the Lithuanian SSR lay with the handful of native doctrinaire Stalinists and the rapidly growing army of predominantly Russophone military, security, and other cadres offering "fraternal assistance." Unfortunately, perceptions rather than the realities of Party politics stoked the growing anti-Jewish resentment.[64]

---

60 The registration forms of the delegates to the Fifth Congress are in LYA, f. 1771, ap. 2, b. 19.
61 The Russification of the entire system, especially the security police, is well documented in the works of Truska and Maslauskienė. Also, examples in LYA, f. 1771, ap. 1, b. 170, l. 6; LYA, f. 1771, ap. 2, b. 457, l. 10.
62 See the detailed analysis in Liudas Truska, Arvydas Anušauskas, and Inga Petravičiūtė, *Sovietinis saugumas Lietuvoje 1940–1953* (Vilnius: LGGRTC, 1999), 90–102.
63 Valentinas Brandišauskas, "Lietuvių ir žydų santykiai 1940–1941 metais," *Darbai ir dienos* 2 (1996): 50–51.
64 A useful overview of the issues is in Joachim Tauber, "Hitler, Stalin und der Antisemitismus in Litauen 1939–1941," *Jahrbuch für Antisemitismusforschung* 21 (2012): 166–182.

"We Are Ruled by the Jews": Nationalism, Class Warfare, and Antisemitism in the Streets

Despite the massive support of the All-Union Party, the NKVD, and the Red Army, the LCP faced considerable problems on the domestic front. The sham elections that created the Lithuanian SSR had proceeded relatively smoothly. The pro-Stalin demonstrations produced impressive street theater, while the problems of interethnic friction within the governmental and Party bureaucracies were largely hidden from public view. But achieving the acceptance of Soviet power in Lithuania and thus cementing the legitimacy of the Party was a more difficult challenge. The official veneer of "friendship among Soviet peoples" could not mask the resentment of foreign rule, the social polarization, and the deepening rifts among the nationalities, the most striking aspect of which was the upsurge in popular antisemitism.

The citizens who had benefited from the first modern polity dominated by ethnic Lithuanians had come to accept independence as the sole legitimate form of state governance. Lithuania's strong identification with the Catholic Church ensured that attacks on religion would rouse opposition, as did denigration of the national army, another institution held in high esteem. Formerly prosperous farmers were angered by the onerous taxes and the redistribution of part of their holdings to the landless. A destabilizing factor was the widespread conviction that Soviet power was transitory: after the Red Army marched into Vilnius, rumors of an imminent Russo-German war emptied the shops as panicked buyers bought up supplies in anticipation.[65] Unsurprisingly, as anti-Soviet attitudes festered, the Germans increasingly came to be seen as potential liberators, especially among "the wealthy bourgeois."[66] But this Marxist notion was wishful thinking, since it was not only the well-to-do who came to see their salvation in the West. The anticipated German invasion (and, later, during 1945–1950, the hope of a United States-led intervention) raised hopes of foreign assistance in the face of overwhelming force. But such dreams were confined primarily to ethnic Lithuanians, many of whom came to believe that their grief and shame at the loss of independence was not shared by Jews.

---

65 Vilnius District Security Police Bulletin, June 25, 1940, LCVA, f. 378, ap. 10, b. 699, l. 582. Cf. Šiauliai District Security and Criminal Police Bulletin June 1940, LCVA, f. 378, ap. 12, b. 296, l. 40–41.

66 Vilnius District Security Police Bulletin, July 17, 1949, LCVA, f. 378, ap. 10, b. 699, l. 640.

Aside from committed Communists and fellow travelers who welcomed the new order on ideological grounds, much of Lithuania's Jewish community had reasons to see some aspects of the Party's rule as beneficial. From the perspective of many years later, some may find it perplexing to read a memoir of a Holocaust survivor on the reaction of young Jews in Plungė to their Stalinist liberation: "Therefore it is no wonder that [in response to antisemitism] a large number of the Jewish youth happily greeted the Red Army when it entered town in the summer of 1940. A large number of the Jewish youth felt like equal, free citizens [sic] and took part in the economic and political life of Plungė."[67] Soviet power provided protection from Nazi Germany so that even anti-Communist Jews could argue that "under Germany we were doomed, under Russia we were free"—a peculiar formulation, but understandable in context.[68]

In some cases, the new regime promised career opportunities to Jews in fields where their participation had been limited. For example, during the 1940–1941 academic year, the number of Jewish students at the University of Vilnius doubled as the restrictions imposed by the previous Polish government were lifted.[69] Harry Gordon remembers that "At this time, they began hiring Jews at the NKVD, the Russian FBI [sic], and many Jews became food distributors to the Russian army."[70] William Mishell recalls that "as citizens with equal rights [sic]" his brother-in-law, sister, and father all found employment in the new order. At his own job in Kaunas, he wrote, "I progressed very nicely and my prospects for the future were extremely bright." But he also lamented: "With their economic base totally destroyed, the Jews reached out to whatever was offered to them." Noting that this "contributed to the strained relations between the two nations," Mishell remarked that "although there were relatively few Jews who got these new jobs, to the Lithuanians it looked like an invasion."[71] Some Jews found their niche in highly visible economic positions as the pace of nationalization accelerated. Jews made up nearly 40% of the workers in the newly formed People's

---

67 According to Mashe Rikhman's testimony in David Solly Sandler, comp. and Jonathan Boyarin, trans., *The Lithuanian Slaughter of Its Jews: The Testimonies of 121 Jewish Survivors of the Holocaust in Lithuania Recorded by Leyb Koniuchowsky, in Displaced Persons Camps (1946–1948)* (self-pub., 2020), 66.

68 William W. Mishell, *Kaddish for Kovno: Life and Death in a Lithuanian Ghetto, 1941–1945* (Chicago: Chicago Review Press, 1988), 8–9.

69 Wierzbicki, *Polacy i żydzi*, 217.

70 Gordon, *Shadow of Death*, 12.

71 Mishell, *Kaddish for Kovno*, 8.

Commissariat of Industry.⁷² At times, Lithuanian officials served as figureheads, in whose name more experienced Jewish assistants administered the nationalized companies. One such newly minted Lithuanian factory chief's child-like scribbles can be found on his delegate form submitted to the Fifth Congress. Silvestras Runča listed himself as a "self-educated former worker of the Neris factory," misspelling the name of the enterprise, his own title of "director," and the word "factory."⁷³

In his memoir of the occupation, Krėvė claimed that Minister of Health Koganas had, within days of his appointment, purged Lithuanian doctors, characterizing them as "reactionaries and pillars of the old Smetona regime." Following Krėvė's protests, most of the fired physicians were reinstated.⁷⁴ In March 1941, one M. Vasiljevas complained to the Kaunas Municipal Personnel Office that Jews in the city's hospitals were working in a nationalistic spirit, including Dr. M. Bermanas, the former physician to Smetona's household, who allegedly assigned the "menial work" to other nationalities. The Jews, he said, "accuse others of antisemitism and reaction, but then, hiding behind the veil of Communism, carry out chauvinistic and reactionary work." Society is losing patience, warned Vasiljevas, and "if the Health Department does not solve this problem in due course, the working class itself will have to settle the issue. After all, working people would occasionally like to see a non-Jewish doctor in the clinics."⁷⁵

The grousing about Jewish business and professional influence was reminiscent of the "Jewish economic tyranny" propaganda that the *verslininkai* had invoked in the 1930s, but the visible involvement of Jews in the Soviet administration and their alleged betrayal of the fatherland raised animosity to hitherto unseen levels. The perception of "Jewish power" in the new order spurred grassroots protests: according to the Interior Ministry, this trope constituted "the most important reason for the unpopularity of the Communist Party."⁷⁶

---

72 Dov Levin, "The Jews and the Socio-Economic Sovietization of Lithuania, 1940–1941 (Part I)," *Soviet Jewish Affairs* 17, no. 2 (1987): 27; cf. Linas Tatarūnas, "Žydai Lietuvoje pirmosios sovietų okupacijos metais (1940–1941 m.)," *Istorija* 73, no. 1 (2009): 41.

73 List of Delegates to the Fifth Congress of the LKP(b), Feb. 1941, LYA, f. 1771, ap. 2, b. 19, l. 344.

74 Vincas Krėvė, *Bolševikų invazija ir liaudies vyriausybė*, ed. Albertas Zalatorius (Vilnius: Mintis, 1992), 29–30.

75 LYA, f. 1771, ap. 1, b. 341, l. 153–155.

76 Ministry of the Interior Information Bulletin, August 7, 1940, LCVA, f. R-754, ap. 3, b. 314, l. 77.

116 | Part One. Before the Shoah

On July 6, 1940, Jonas Bumblauskas, a self-described "idealist," applied to join the Party, noting in his application that "one hears that the Jews have numerous organizations, arrange meetings and various assemblies, even though they are a minority. Meanwhile, we Lithuanians, who are in the majority, are still unorganized in the provincial towns." Not surprisingly, Comrade Grinfeldas recommended that Bumblauskas's application be rejected.[77] In early July, a group of villagers from Taurai petitioned their district chief to request a permit for an "anti-Jewish rally" to counter the "Jewish intrusion into all government agencies."[78] In Šakiai, the police reported, "many farmers and Lithuanians" were angered at the inclusion of "citizens of Jewish nationality" in the militia.[79] At the same time, the security police in Vilnius noted the widespread resentment against Jews, "who have become very insolent and dare to brag that they are now in power; consequently, there is talk among Lithuanians and Poles that, if the Germans were to come, the Jews would suffer greatly."[80] The police noticed that antisemitic feelings united unlikely allies: "Recently there has emerged a strange cooperation of Lithuanian and Polish nationalists."[81] Clashes became commonplace: the authorities reported "incidents of fisticuffs in the streets, Poles and Lithuanians against the Jews."[82] Such a Polish-Lithuanian coalition was unimaginable under the Smetona regime, and certainly not the type of bond between "fraternal peoples" envisioned in Soviet propaganda.[83]

The plethora of demonstrations and rallies during the campaign for the People's Diet was intended to unify the working class but often served only to expose ethnic divisions. On July 11, 1940, an election rally attracted a predominantly Polish crowd in Trakai. As a Jewish agitator began to speak, "the crowd began to ridicule him . . . , from all sides it was proclaimed that the Jews promise the people all sorts of wonderful things" only for the purpose of gaining power.

---

77   LYA, f. 1771, ap. 1, b. 341, l. 3–4.
78   Šiauliai District Secuirity and Criminal Police Bulletin, July 3, 1940, LCVA, f. 378, ap. 12, b. 296, l. 27.
79   State Security Department Bulletin, July 16, 1940, LCVA, f. 378, ap. 10, b. 225, l. 758.
80   Vilnius District Security Police Bulletin, July 9, 1940, LCVA, f. 378, ap. 10, b. 699, l. 619.
81   State Security Department Bulletin, July 23, 1940, LCVA, f. 378, ap. 10, b. 225, l. 767.
82   See Vilnius District Security Police Bulletin, July 12, 1940, LCVA, f. 378, ap. 10, b. 699.
83   Vilnius District Security Police Bulletins, July 9, 1940, LCVA, f. 378, ap. 10, b. 699, l. 619. For more on this, see Bašinskas, "Lietuvių-žydų konfliktai sovietinės okupacijos pradžioje 1940 metų vasarą: tęstinumai ar lūžiai," 205–207.

"Otherwise," the report noted laconically, "the rally went off without incident."[84] On the same day another campaign event took place in nearby Lentvaris. As the police reported:

> A bus arrived . . . from Vilnius bedecked with election campaign placards in Yiddish. Only Jews singing Russian songs were riding on the bus. When the bus stopped near the railway station and the newcomers began speaking in Yiddish and Russian, the Poles and Lithuanians who had gathered to listen to the speeches immediately dispersed, expressing their dissatisfaction with the Jews. Only about eighty local Jews, of whom the majority were underage youths, listened to the speeches. The Lithuanians and Poles were determined to beat up these Jews, but the police officials, who arrived just in time, did not allow disorder.[85]

On the eve of the balloting, the NKVD chief in Kaunas reported to Moscow that leaflets had appeared in Alytus district urging a boycott of Jewish businesses and a "quiet struggle" against the Jews to prevent the establishment of a "second Palestine" in Lithuania.[86] Even the poorer Lithuanians and Poles, while approving of the new, ostensibly more socially equitable political system, expressed resentment towards Jews' alleged "leading role in political and social life." The Šiauliai police reported in typical bureaucratese: "It is characteristic that in the various election district precincts, the rejected ballot cards were mainly of Candidate No. 5, Noachas Mackevičius. Most people of Jewish nationality placed only ballot No. 5 into the envelopes, while the villagers and other voters of non-Jewish nationality would throw it out." The same phenomenon was noted elsewhere.[87] Officers observing the electoral behavior of the Fifth Infantry Regiment recounted: "Many soldiers, without being subject to outside influence,

---

84 Vilnius District Security Police Bulletin, July 11, 1940, LCVA, f. 378, ap. 10, b. 699, l. 622–623.
85 Vilnius District Security Police Bulletin, July 12, 1940, LCVA, f. 378, ap. 10, b. 699, l. 631. For an account of Jewish participation in the July 1940 elections based on Yiddish sources, see Dov Levin, "The Jews and the Election Campaigns in Lithuania, 1940–1941," *Soviet Jewish Affairs* 10, no. 1 (1980): 39–45.
86 Makarov report, July 10, 1940, LYA, f. K-1, ap. 49, b. 828, l. 72.
87 Šiauliai District Security and Criminal Police Bulletin, July 18, 1940, LCVA, f. 378, ap. 12, b. 296, l. 13; cf. State Security Department Bulletin, July 20, 1940, LCVA, f. 378, ap. 10, b. 225; and Vildžiūnas report, in Breslavskienė, Eidintas, Jermalavičienė, Kalasauskienė, Marcikonienė, et al., *Lietuvos okupacija ir aneksija*, 375.

tore out the ballot of the only candidate of Jewish nationality, putting it in their pocket or just throwing it on the floor. Most of the ballots scattered on the floor belonged to the Jewish candidate."[88] Offended soldiers complained about the overwhelming presence of red flags and grumbled at the conspicuous lack of the national tricolor, which reflected the collapse, in their words, of "a general national and civic consciousness." One lieutenant carped that "now there is no place for chauvinism, but the Jews demonstratively denigrate Lithuanians, their language and songs," reporting that when his regiment appeared in a demonstration and broke into song, "Jews who had gathered on the pavement began to jeer."[89] Rumors that pro-Communist voters would be "dealt with when the Germans come" reflected the sense of impermanence surrounding the new order.

Rather than choosing candidates on the lists, some voters deposited anti-Communist scraps of paper and assorted clippings into the ballot envelopes. The archive of Justas Paleckis contains a representative sample of thirty such enclosures left at precincts in Kaunas. Fourteen of the messages are antisemitic; some are ungrammatical, indicating lower-class origins. A few proclaim dire threats and bloody vengeance against "Jews and degenerate Communists." Even some protesters of a leftist orientation showed impatience, demanding a "true Lithuanian socialism" free of Jews. "Adolf Hitler, the liberator from the Jews" was one of the impromptu votes. Another scrap dropped in the ballot box read: "The entire battalion for Adolf Hitler. Signed: A soldier." There were other write-in candidates to the Diet: Smetona, former army commander General Stasys Raštikis, Marshal Mannerheim of Finland, Mussolini, Voldemaras, and Mickey Mouse.[90]

In 1940 Lithuania became the only predominantly Roman Catholic republic of the Soviet Union. The secularizing policies of the People's Government, such as the introduction of civil registry, welcomed as a long overdue modernization, were, however, soon supplanted by much-resented attacks on the Church. As early as June 27–28, 1940, leaflets appeared in Šiauliai city directed

---

88 Report on the Second Infantry Regiment, Army Staff Second Section, July 16, 1940, in ibid., 367.
89 Ibid.
90 "Antitarybiškai nusiteikusių piliečių biuleteniai, paduoti Kaune renkant Liaudies Seimą," July 14–15, 1940, LYA, f. 3377, ap. 58, b. 593, l. 6–83. For more on anti-Jewish electoral attitudes, see Svarauskas, "Kodėl dalyvauta": 113–117.

against Communists and Jews, proclaiming "Long live Catholic Lithuania!"[91] On July 10, Kaunas Party workers arrived in Trakai in a truck adorned with portraits of Soviet leaders to conduct a rally attended by hundreds of locals, mostly Poles and Lithuanians. As one speaker shouted "down with the priests, down with the Church," the crowd countered with "give us bread and work, but don't touch the priests!" In the end, the campaign lorry barely escaped; as the police noted, the agitators "would have come to harm from the enraged crowd."[92] Some local Communists were unhappy with such heavy-handed agitation by outsiders, which only made their work more difficult.

In early August 1940 the Health Ministry reportedly planned to seize the Theological Seminary in Kaunas, the republic's last remaining Catholic institution of higher learning, in order to expand the city's Jewish hospital. Lithuanian Communists recognized the move as a foolish provocation, and Interior Minister Gedvilas quashed the idea. By the end of the year, the seminary buildings had instead been transferred to the Red Army.[93] In August the security police reported that a Jewish official named Kleinas had been appointed as liquidator of the bookshop of the St. Casimir Society in Kaunas. Since the society had assisted poorly educated villagers, maidservants, and devout older women (commonly known as *davatkos*), its demise caused "widespread disgruntled talk among the people about the fact that the society has been seized by the Jews."[94] Atheist activism involving supporters of the new regime angered a Catholic population already suffused with antisemitic sentiment. Many incidents were likely apocryphal. The following secondhand memoir is suspiciously reminiscent of the anticlerical desecration stories which circulated among Catholics during the Spanish Civil War:

> The worker from Vilkija, Petrauskas, told me that the former notary public, the young Jewish Communist Dov Tam, who had become a famous

---

91 Šiauliai District Security and Criminal Police Bulletin June 1940, LCVA, f. 378, ap. 12, b. 296, l. 35.

92 Vilnius District Security Police Bulletin, July 11, 1940, LCVA, f. 378, ap. 10, b. 699, l. 621.

93 See Vincentas Brizgys, *Katalikų Bažnyčia Lietuvoje: pirmoje rusų okupacijoje 1940–1941 m., vokiečių okupacijoje 1941–1944 m.* (Draugas: Chicago, 1977), 25–26 and his "Kunigų seminarija Kaune bolševizmo metais," in *Lietuvių archyvas*, vol. 1, ed. Juozas Balčiūnas (Kaunas: Studijų Biuras, 1942), 56–58.

94 State Security Department Bulletin, August 5, 1940, LCVA, f. 378, ap. 10, b. 225, l. 788; cf. the account in Mykolas Vaitkus, *Atsiminimai*, vol. 8, *Milžinų rungtynese, 1940–1944* (Nida: London, 1972), 46–47.

Communist official, on one Sunday, invited all officials and other people into the Riflemen's Union Hall. He placed a small cross on a table and ordered everyone to make a disrespectful gesture in poking at the Christ-figure in order to show their loyalty to the Communist Party. Then the worker Čiapas shouted: "Jew! It's not your business to handle the priests, it's better that you deal with your rabbis! And if there is nothing there, then what's this business with poking?" The others were also appalled but remained silent out of fear.[95]

The impression that Jews sought to destroy Christianity was based on the behavior of a relatively small number of Party members and supporters,[96] but the distorted logic, however faulty, gained influence among the faithful. On August 19, 1940, Jonas Malašauskas, a bookbinder, appealed to the LCP Central Committee to open businesses on Saturdays and reported the following conversation among "a group of pious old women and a neighbor's son":

> Listen, the Jews are ruling us now. Look: they seized the salaries of our priests, drove them out of the schools, and now they want to discontinue religious services over the radio. But they don't do anything to the Jews: *just as they celebrated their sabbath before, so they do it now, just as they closed their stores, so they have the shabas now.* And you can see that nearly all government employees are Jews. So, isn't it obvious that we are ruled by the Jews?[97] (Emphasis in original)

Shared socialist values failed to bridge the animosities among the lower ranks of comrades. National tensions were particularly intense within the Komsomol, where Jewish influence was historically strong. A Communist official in Panevėžys observed a local Komsomol meeting:

> Sitting by a table in the Komsomol club is a Jewish committee member and around him are Jewish comrades speaking Yiddish loudly, while on the other side of the club sits a Lithuanian committee member and around him are Lithuanian members speaking Lithuanian. The Jewish

---

95 From the account by Bruno Ignatavičius, written down in Ottawa, August 22, 1974, and provided to the author by Klemensas Jūra.
96 Dov Levin cites instances in which "Jews were involved in desecration of Christian religious artifacts" (Levin, *The Lesser*, 63).
97 LYA, f. 1771, ap. 1, b. 280, l. 153–154.

Komsomol members explained the phenomenon by saying that it is impossible to become friends with them [the Lithuanians] there.[98]

A flyer left at a police precinct by the self-described Lithuanian Anti-Jewish Committee on July 8, 1940, hailed the achievement of "freedom and equality," which was endangered by "a new exploiter climbing onto the ungainly Lithuanian's neck, the Jew." The same Jews, it was said, who once shouted "Long live Antanas Smetona!" and who had "purchased a plantation in Palestine for their friend Smetona" now supported the new regime. The leaflet explained further that:

> We do not say that we must beat the Jews, for the Jews never beat us either. We will declare a quiet war against them. We will not buy their goods, but, most important, we will not allow them into our organizations. We will create our own communism.... As for the Jews, let them build their own if they wish. We want to see those truly rich Jews next to us doing manual labor, which they have avoided and feared all their lives. We want them to get only that which they conscientiously earn.[99]

The contempt for Soviet power and hopes for its demise were widespread in the Lithuanian People's Army (Lietuvos liaudies kariuomenė), so christened on July 3, 1940, whose personnel represented a cross-section of society. The notoriously insubordinate Ninth Infantry Regiment was an especially hard nut to crack. The men refused to behave during political indoctrination meetings, chanted anti-Soviet and antisemitic slogans, harassed their Communist instructors (*politruks*), and clashed repeatedly with local Jews. On July 24, 1940, Soviet tanks surrounded two of the regiment's most rebellious battalions and the security police arrested thirty-one soldiers.[100] On August 30, 1940, the armed forces were formally reconstituted as the Twenty-Ninth Territorial Riflemen's Corps of the Red Army, but from the very beginning the integration of

---

98 As cited in Dov Levin, "The Jews in the Soviet Lithuanian Establishment, 1940–1941," *Soviet Jewish Affairs* 10, no. 2 (1980): 33.

99 State Security Bulletin, July 8, 1940, LCVA, f. R-754, ap. 3, b. 311, l. 38–40. More examples of police information on antisemitic agitation during the summer of 1940 are in Venclauskas, "Antisemitizmas Lietuvoje": 326–332.

100 As recounted by a junior officer in Trečiokas, "Atsiminimai iš 9 P.L.D.K. Vytenio pulko gyvenimo," in *Lietuviu archyvas: bolševizmo metai*, ed. J. Balčiųnas, vol. 2 (Kaunas: Studijų Biuras, 1942), 229–242.

Lithuanian personnel into the Soviet military exposed national tensions. On September 4, 1940, the Soviet security's secret agent "Jurgėnas" reported on "clashes between the Eighth [Lithuanian] Regiment in Gruzdžiai and Russian units." Lithuanian solders refused to sing "The Internationale," insisted on their own national anthem, announced that they would not join the parade for the Great October Revolution, and attended church.[101] As the NKVD continued to spy on the soldiers, it became clear that this was not an isolated case.

Experienced cadres, mostly from outside Lithuania, began replacing those officers and political instructors deemed insufficiently committed to the new order. An NKVD secret report on the political atmosphere within the corps, compiled over several months and presented to the LCP Central Committee in January 1941, revealed that the change had done little to mitigate the anti-Soviet mood among the troops. One Lithuanian soldier consoled himself with the hope that "we'll survive somehow: soon the Germans will come, and we'll get back what is ours and be free." A junior officer opined: "Hitler has proposed to clean out the Baltics, the Soviet Army will be gone, and our Lithuania will be free." One lieutenant thought that "Germany is much more cultured than the USSR, and Lithuanians are more cultured than Russians. If Germany seizes Lithuania, we will save culture." The NKVD acknowledged the growing ideological radicalization, stating that "Formerly the Nazi territorial-racial theory did not attract [the men], but now very often there is talk among the officers that only German culture can save Lithuania." Another cited opinion was that "barely literate Asians [*aziyaty*] have come here and have destroyed our national culture. Only Hitler can save us." As an alternative, the men pointed to Germany's ally Slovakia, where "life is splendid."

Attempts to change the mood among the soldiers by intensifying their indoctrination proved counterproductive: "The replacement of the Lithuanian political officers by Russians and other nationalities has tremendously worsened the national problem in ... the Territorial [Corps]." As an example, the NKVD noted that in the Twenty-Sixth Cavalry Regiment "there is a Jewish political officer [*politruk*] who, because of his ignorance of the Lithuanian language, is openly ridiculed by the officers in front of the Red Army men." The Soviet secret police remarked that the majority of the Lithuanian officers and a significant number of the twelve thousand enlisted men were "completely unreliable" and predicted, with a reference to the events of 1918–1921, that "given the

---

101 "Agenturnoye doneseniye," September 4, 1940, LCVA, f. R-756, ap. 2, b. 63, l. 42.

opportunity, the officers would go across to the Germans by the hundreds, just as, in their time, tsarist officers crossed the Don to [join] the Cossacks."[102]

In March 1941 John Mazionis, a foreign service officer assigned to the U.S. embassy in Moscow, visited Lithuania and reported to the State Department on his return. A London-born Lithuanian who had previously worked for the American mission in Kaunas, Mazionis had obtained a rare permit to visit his ailing parents but also found time to gather information about the mood in the country. His account contained several questionable generalizations as well as antisemitic notions, but this document on the volatile and toxic atmosphere in the country complements numerous other sources. The diplomat noted the dangerous confluence of internal ethnic divisions with the geopolitical hopes of much of the populace, observing that the "hatred of the Reds" went hand-in-hand with resentment of what many Lithuanians described as the "Jewish Government." Mazionis wrote that a conversation "with any Lithuanian in Kaunas" usually began with the question: "When do you think the war will begin and what is being said in Moscow?"[103] Mazionis described the Lithuanian "eagerness for a war between the Soviets and Nazis" and wrote that "the people desire to see the Germans in Lithuania instead of the Reds." But the support for a German attack was not without a caveat since, according to the author, "people hope that Germany will lose the war with Great Britain in order that Lithuania may again arise as an independent state."[104] This latter qualification was not uncommon among the intelligentsia as they awaited the progress of the war in the West.

Much of the popular resentment against Soviet power that simmered under the surface in 1940–1941 can be explained by the fact that the Lithuanian SSR in 1940–1941 embodied a paradox. The Stalinists' impressive police power masked a political weakness, that is, the regime's failure to achieve legitimacy in the eyes of the republic's majority nation. Most of the educated generation

---

102 As quoted in the report of Major Aleksandras Gudaitis-Guzevičius, the head of the NKVD of the Lithuanian SSR, "Dokladnye zapiski NKVD o politiko-moral'noi sostoyanii 29-go territorial;nogo korpusa," January 1941, LYA, f. 1771, ap. 2, b. 531.

103 As cited in Alfred E. Senn, "Lithuania in March 1941: An American Diplomat's Report," *Journal of Baltic Studies*, no. 26 (1995): 153–154. More details on the Mazionis's trip are in Mallory Needleman, "Lithuania under the Soviet Occupation, 1940–41: Observations and Operations by the United States," *MCU Journal* 9, no. 2 (2018): 62–75.

104 Senn, "Lithuania in March 1941": 155. On the later illusory hopes for liberation based on a repetition of the World War I scenario of a Russian defeat or at least military stalemate in the East and a German capitulation to the Anglo-American forces in the West, see below, Chapter 7.

which had come of age during the interwar period, ethnic Lithuanians in particular, had come to consider independence as the only acceptable form of national existence and thus perceived Soviet power as a foreign imposition. These sentiments grew stronger with the abandonment in August 1940 of the sham state sovereignty represented by the People's Government. Anecdotal accounts, as well as police reports, recount growing resentment as the process of Sovietization accelerated. As an example, Gladkov reported that a twenty-two-year-old Kaunas University student explained, when questioned, that he had participated with like-minded classmates in an anti-Soviet demonstration on Lithuanian independence day (February 16) because he detested Russification and had been indoctrinated in school with the idea that "Lithuania can only be free as a separate, independent state."[105]

Soviet Reality and the Myth of "Jewish Power"

Jews were hardly a monolith in their attitude to the new regime. The warm welcome given to the Soviet troops in Kaunas did not reflect the attitude of the older and more conservative elements in the community. Days before the invasion, the rabbis of the Vilnius region had gathered to pray "that the Soviets do not seize Lithuania."[106] Sniečkus reported that "two opinions were noticeable among Jewish society": wealthier Jews tended to oppose annexation by the Soviet Union and "preferred the current government since it guarantees democracy and private property." The Jewish poor, however, held the opposite view, supporting the "complete absorption of Lithuania by Russia."[107] The Jews of Eišiškes were disturbed that "in Vilnius many rich Jews have been arrested who have nothing to do with politics."[108] Frieda Frome, who, in her own words, had initially succumbed to the "Russian way of thinking," became increasingly disenchanted: Juozas, a "very ignorant" Lithuanian commissar,

---

105 Quoted from Gladkov's report of April 4, 1941, as published in A. R. Dyukov, ed., *Nakanune Kholokosta: Front litovskikh aktivistov i sovetskiye represii v Litve 1940–1941 gg.: Sbornki dokumentov* (Moscow: Fond "Istoricheskaya pamyat'," 2012), 165.

106 State Security Department Bulletin, June 12, 1940, LCVA, f. 378, ap. 10, b. 225, l. 695.

107 State Security Department Bulletin, June 27, 1940, Ibid., l. 712; cf. Šiauliai District Security and Criminal Police Bulletin, July 1, 1940, LCVA, f. 378, ap. 12, b. 296, l. 33.

108 Vilnius District Security Police Bulletin, July 20, 1940, LCVA, f. 378, ap. 10, b. 699, l. 650.

was put in charge of her father's shop and the family began to bear the brunt of the regime's anti-bourgeois policies.[109] At the end of July an army report stated that "it is interesting that dissatisfaction with the present order has been observed among soldiers of Jewish nationality. Previously there were never such cases."[110]

The Soviet government nationalized manufacturing and commercial enterprises during its first year, many of which were Jewish-owned, and eliminated middlemen as "the great exploiters of the working class."[111] At the same time, however, some previous owners reinvented themselves as socialist directors of their now state-owned enterprises. To antisemitic minds this reaffirmed both the conviction that Jews were behind the big money in any social system and the simplistic axiom that Jews, more favorably inclined towards Soviet rule, suffered less than Lithuanians. In economic terms this was a glaring falsehood: Jews had once owned most of the newly nationalized industries and commercial companies.[112]

The employment of Jews as managers of Lithuania's socialist economy and their role as officials in the Soviet administration, real but limited in scope, obscured the suppression of independent Jewish religious and cultural life. Hebrew-language schools in the republic were closed after the Soviet invasion, although a smaller number of Yiddish institutions remained open. Only twelve of the twenty-three Jewish secondary schools that had functioned in the spring of 1940 were still open a year later. The diverse and lively Jewish political, social, and cultural life of the interwar period was severely curtailed. Seventy-nine of the 217 Soviet-banned public organizations were Jewish. Most Yiddish and Hebrew periodicals ceased publication. By August 1940 only two Yiddish-language newspapers remained: *Volskblatt* in Kaunas and *Vilner Emes* in Vilnius. In March 1941, the authorities consolidated the Jewish press into *Der Emes* (The Truth)

---

109 See Frome, *Some Dare*, 11–18. For a useful overview, see Dov Levin, "The Jews and the Socio-Economic Sovietization of Lithuania, 1940–1941 (Part 1)," *Soviet Jewish Affairs* 17, no. 2 (1987): 18–30 and his "The Jews and the Socio-Economic Sovietization of Lithuania, 1940–1941 (Part 2)," *Soviet Jewish Affairs* 17, no. 3 (1987): 26–38.

110 Army Staff Second Section Bulletin, July 29, 1940, in Breslavskienė, Eidintas, Jermalavičienė, Kalasauskienė, Marcikonienė, et al., *Lietuvos okupacija ir aneksija*, 392.

111 "Dėl darbininkų ir tarnautojų žydų darbo šventadieniais," *Tarybų Lietuva*, October 2, 1940, 10.

112 Vitkus, "Smulkiojo verslo lituanizacija," 210.

which remained the official, Sovietized public voice of Lithuanian Jewry until the outbreak of the war.[113]

Lithuania's world-famous yeshivas were closed and Jewish religious holidays, which had official status under the First Republic, were declared workdays. On October 1, 1940, a gathering of "Jewish workers and white-collar employees" demanded that Jews work during religious holidays; otherwise, since many enterprises contained a majority Jewish work force, offices and factories would close. In view of the "imperialist war" and the grave economic situation, declared these selfless Soviet patriots, "we have no right to aggravate our economic situation and harm the cause of our nation and country."[114] It is difficult to imagine such anti-Jewish cultural policies and enforced self-flagellation under Smetona's regime. The suppression of Jewish cultural and religious life fed the growing disappointment with Soviet power among Lithuania's Jews.

The Soviet authorities knew better than to assume Jewish support for a Communist future. On March 29, 1941, Major Gladkov, who had been promoted to People's Commissar of State Security (NKGB) of the Lithuanian SSR, penned the report *On the Counter-Revolutionary Activity of Jewish Nationalist Organizations*, in which he related his concern about the "Zionist, bourgeois, revisionist, Betarist, and other formations" which had flooded the republic, particularly the Vilnius area. The resistance of religious Jews, and the contacts that Jewish organizations maintained with the "imperialist powers," Britain and the United States, were a supposed danger to the Soviet state. Gladkov assumed that the American Joint Committee was a major force behind anti-Soviet activity. Even worse, Soviet security observed that "at the present time Jewish counter-revolutionary elements have begun to ally themselves with other anti-Soviet elements regardless of nationality." The main purpose of the Jewish organizations, according to the NKGB, was to facilitate emigration to America and Palestine, and they were not above cooperating with Polish nationalists in forging travel documents. The heart of the "Jewish nationalist counter-revolutionary element" consisted of the remaining synagogues and rabbinical schools. Gladkov singled out Rabbi Zhukovich, who "educates the Jewish people in a spirit of hatred of Communism." The security police arrested eighty-nine Jewish counterrevolutionaries at the end of 1940. In the spring of 1941, Soviet security uncovered

---

113 Dov Levin, *Baltic Jews under the Soviets 1940–1946* (Jerusalem: The Hebrew University of Jerusalem, 1994), 9–10.

114 "Dėl darbininkų ir tarnautojų žydų," 10.

dozens of Bundist, Betarist, and Zionist circles in Kaunas, Vilnius, Ukmergė, Kėdainiai, and other Lithuanian towns with large Jewish communities.[115] By early June 1941 another 334 Jews had been arrested by Soviet security forces. A total of 2,613 Jews has been listed by researchers as "having suffered repression during the first year of the Soviet occupation."[116]

Jews were acutely aware of their vulnerability in the increasingly hostile atmosphere. "This is not the time of the Smetona government, we are now living as if on a volcano," a member of the Betar Central Committee named Khrust confided to a police informer.[117] Some Jews claimed that they had not experienced Khrust's "volcano" and had been on good terms with Lithuanians, but such narratives are outliers. For example, in a 2015 interview deportee Liuba Segala recalled: "We had always been friends with Lithuanians. My best friend was a Lithuanian girl . . . we did not feel any kind of antisemitism coming. There were no signs of anything, really."[118] The successful exodus of many Jews from Lithuania via the USSR during the summer of 1940 with the assistance of the famed Japanese consul in Kaunas, Chiune Sugihara, and the Dutch businessman-consul, Jan Zwartendijk, provided an avenue of escape from the Stalinist cauldron. The well-known "Visas for Life" episode is usually associated with rescue from Nazism, but for many yeshiva students who boarded the trains to the Far East and other destinations, freedom from Soviet religious persecution seems to have been the primary motivation.[119]

Matilda Olkinaitė: Prospects and Forebodings, 1940–1941[120]

We know little of Matilda's activities during the summer months of political turmoil. The Lithuanian SSR was already in existence by the time of the first entry

---

115 Gladkov's report is in LYA, f. K-1, ap. 10, b. 4, l. 179–198. "Betarist" refers to Betar, the radical Zionist youth organization.
116 Cf. Maslauskienė, "Lietuvos tautinių mažumų": 27. This number does not include the deportees of June 14–17, 1941.
117 As cited in the Gladkov report.
118 Quoted in Violeta Davoliūtė, "Multidirectional Memory and the Deportation of Lithuanian Jews," *Ethnicity Studies* 2 (2015): 143. Cf., the Matilda Olkinaitės story above, Chapter 1.
119 For more on this history, see below, Chapter 6.
120 The diary as published in Olkinaitė, *Atrakintas dienoraštis* is unpaginated and will be referenced in the text by date. See above, Chapter 1 about the Olkinas family before the Soviet occupation.

in her diary (August 15, 1940). We can follow Matilda, in her own words, until February 28, 1941. The writings reveal a sensitive young woman in the middle of an insoluble, yet familiar, conundrum. Matilda's family was keen to tie her romantic interests, if not her marital future, to Eliezeris Šėras (Eliezir Sher), the son of an apothecary owner in Rokiškis. Matilda respected the studious and serious Eliezeris who, like her, had also enrolled at the University of Kaunas, but she found little comfort in his bossiness and lack of emotional depth. He criticized Matilda's flights of poetic fancy, her lack of concern for real-life prospects and disapproved of her choice to write in Lithuanian rather than Yiddish (the language in which he wrote his letters).[121] Eliezeris laid down conditions for their relationship: "If you will be capable of action and going forward, filled with courage and enthusiasm, only then will I love you."[122] Matilda's life grew complicated when she encountered a soulmate from Kaunas who presented her with an expensive hardcover notebook in which she poured out her longings and frustrations during what became a difficult love affair. A single passage in the diary mentions one "Arūnas," but, despite interviews with Matilda's surviving friends, her true love has never been identified. Matilda described the stark difference between the two young men: "He (not Šėras) is dear and lovable, whom I alone understand and treasure. Šėras is but a student pharmacist who knows how to speak at meetings, is arrogant and is prone to dismiss much of what is around him" (October 31, 1940).

Leaving aside the personal turmoil of a passion that occupies most of her diary, Matilda's account of her social and family life provides insight into the anxieties of the period. Her brother was an early convert to the worldview of the Soviet regime: he joined the Komsomol, and, in his sister's words, was "up to his neck in Party matters" (October 22, 1940). She described his idealism: "Today we received a letter from Ilyushka [her affectionate name for Elijas]. Very patriotic about our socialist fatherland. Ilyushka belongs to those enlightened people who believe" (September 29, 1940). According to Elijas's fiancée Liza Abramson, a medical student and daughter of a prosperous brewery manager in Šiauliai, Matilda's brother became the head of the Komsomol branch at the

---

121 Matilda's diary contains only one entry in Yiddish: Olkinaitė, *Atrakintas dienoraštis*, November 12, 1940.

122 Quoted from a surviving copy of Šėras's letter to Matilda, March 25, 1941, as described by Mindaugas Kvietkauskas, "Mėlynas Matildos talento paukštis," in Olkinaitė, *Atrakintas dienoraštis*, 30.

University of Vilnius. Matilda looked down upon Liza as an unimaginative and shallow representative of the commercial class.

While immersed in her personal struggles, studies, and hopes for a literary career, Matilda nonetheless understood the realities of regimented Stalinism, aware that her writing style did not match the demands of the time. Even as she prepared her poems for publication, she was despondent: "Oh well, there's my collection of verse! . . . I know no one's going to publish it. I'm writing about the sufferings of centuries, while they are demanding songs about the joys of today" (September 4, 1940). Matilda was contemptuous of the constraints imposed by the Soviet literary canon of the time:

> I'm reading the newspapers. There's nothing there. People are writing things that they don't believe themselves. Šeinas (can it be the person I know?) writes about the new literature, which now can grow and flourish, as if freely . . . To grow and flourish, and, at the same time, they have assigned it such narrow boundaries. The path of socialist realism is so clear and simple, and I would say, uncreative. . . . To picture a priest who must always be obese and a lover of card games, to depict the landowner, who must always be stupid and rotten, and to picture the worker, inevitably ill and unhappy . . . Literature can grow and flourish! Sad and yet laughable. (September 23, 1940)

Matilda's references to the politics of the moment show disdain for the enforced public spectacles of class solidarity. She berated the fawning displays of one of her favorite women poets:

> What horrible times. The world has gone out to the street, has put a red kerchief in the pocket, and then goes around shouting. The poems of Salomėja Nėris and Liudas Gira—I don't know how normal people can write like that. [Propaganda] billboards everywhere, nothing more. The most dedicated Communist, if he were a cultured person, could never tolerate such a thing. I often think how much culture is lacking among the people. Sad. Why must Communism and its ideas be governed by expressions of destruction and hatred, rather than creativity and love? (August 29, 1940)[123]

---

123 Salomėja Nėris (1904–1945) and Liudas Gira (1884–1946) were prominent leftist literati of the interwar republic who were among the dignitaries in attendance during the Supreme Soviet's announcement of the formal incorporation of Lithuania into the Soviet Union in Moscow on August 3, 1940. During this session, Nėris read her laudatory "Poem about Stalin."

Like most of the populace, Matilda adapted, recording that she had learned how to "march in parades." A product of the well-read intelligentsia, she was not above falling back on some unpleasant stereotypes about low-class Soviet newcomers. In November 1940 Matilda was tasked with registering the families of Red Army soldiers for the upcoming elections to the Supreme Soviet: "Yesterday I was signing up Red Army families for the voting," she wrote. "All day their scent persecuted me, as did the stench which I often encountered. The ugly big-breasted women, the babies, and the little old grandmothers who, when asked about their nationality, answered that they were Eastern Orthodox" (November 29, 1940).[124]

The Olkinas family suffered the indignities and hardships of small businesses squeezed by the new system. Noachas was constantly away, begging friends and banks for loans to keep his pharmacy afloat. "The economic situation of our household has collapsed completely," wrote Matilda (August 19, 1940). A few days later she added: "Papa returned from Panevėžys, worried and nervous. Complete disintegration threatens our home, it's starvation. No. I will work. Everything must turn out right" (August 28, 1940). The family took in boarders and there was talk of selling the house. People close to her had suffered expropriation. Matilda worried about continued funding for her studies: because of her bourgeois origins, she must have feared that children of the proletariat might take her place on the scholarship list. In the fall of 1940 Noachas's apothecary was nationalized, although he continued to run it, now as an employee of the Soviet state. On January 19, 1941, Olkinas submitted a statement to the Soviet authorities, describing his social origins as a class-conscious child of "working class intelligentsia" who had "always suffered poverty."[125]

Matilda's distaste for the Soviet order should not be confused with an apolitical lack of interest in the world around her. She read widely and shared the anxieties of her contemporaries. She could be self-critical about her romantic preoccupations: "People in the world are dying by the millions," she wrote, "they are starving, the war is coming ever closer. I may not get a scholarship—everything is hazy and unclear, while I sit on the edge of the precipice and pick the petals of a daisy flower—he loves me, he loves me not. It's stupid and naïve"

---

124 Providing religious affiliation on the questionnaires would strike an educated person as strange, since in conducting official business Soviet citizens were required to indicate their membership in one of the officially approved nationalities of the USSR.

125 N. Olkinas, "Curriculum vitae," as published in Kvietkauskas, "Mėlynas," 21.

(September 24, 1940). Matilda longed to start a family and at times addressed a future child as an embodiment of her love, hopes, and fears. Researchers who have examined her writings and drafts of poetry during her student days note a sense of pessimism and apprehension.[126] In November 1940, despite some pleasant memories during her previous vacation, she admitted that "this [past] summer was not like the others, not quite right, many traditions have unraveled; I lived in a constant state of unhappy foreboding" (November 18, 1940). A few days earlier she had written a poem: "Oh, many guests are gathering this night / To the house of my mourning / I hold an infant in my arms / And my infant is Death" (November 14, 1940).

Did Matilda profess a premonition of coming tragedies? Or did her fluctuating moods of joy and despair reflect the inner turmoil of a young woman in love? One can speculate, although considering her openness to the world around her, she must have been aware of the fears pervading society at large. "War in the spring. That's what Papa says," she had written in September before returning to the university, an expectation that we know was widespread. The increasingly strident Sovietization of the country following the Fifth LCP Congress in February 1941 could not have lightened the mood of someone who viewed the regime with guarded suspicion. Her diary ends soon after, so to understand the fate of the Olkinas family in the coming apocalypse, we must rely largely on the accounts of their neighbors.[127]

Fear and Exile on the Eve: June 1941

The most traumatic event of the Soviet occupation in Lithuania occurred on June 14–17, 1941, as nearly eighteen thousand men, women, and children were loaded onto cattle cars, most bound for Siberia and the Soviet far north. The impact was shattering: "The mood in the country was as before an explosion," remarked William Mishell when describing the days leading up to the Nazi invasion.[128] Grigory Shur, a chronicler of the Vilna Ghetto, described the effect of the operation on the people:

---

126 Best described by Matilda's translator Laima Vincė in "Nutildyta mūza," in Olkinaitė, *Atrakintas dienoraštis*, 80–81.
127 See below, Chapter 3.
128 Mishell, *Kaddish for Kovno*, 9.

When the war broke out, this deportation created a lot of difficulty for the Red Army and, also, affected the behavior of the local inhabitants when the Germans arrived. Many locals considered the Germans their real or potential saviors from the inescapable deportations. Thus, the [German] occupiers found many new people who sympathized with them, and soon even found helpers who diligently carried out actions planned by them.[129]

Some Jewish historians, émigré authors and Western scholars have misstated the number, social backgrounds, and ethnic/national make-up of the deportees. The figures of as many as thirty to forty thousand victims and more, including a disproportionately large number of Jews, were regurgitated by authors unaware of the research conducted since the late 1980s (for example, the claim by Dov Levin that Jews constituted nearly a quarter of the thirty thousand deportees).[130] Lithuanian historians of the post-Soviet period have accessed hitherto closed archival files and have corrected the record. By nationality, Lithuanians (70%) made up the lion's share of deportees, while Poles (17.7%) constituted a disproportionately large minority. The percentage of Jewish deportees (9.2%) was roughly proportionate to the ratio of the Jewish population in the republic, although this statistic may hide some deportees who, like the future Israeli prime minister Menachem Begin, may have been classified as Poles.[131] It should be noted that the numbers of exiled people cited for June 14–17, 1941, in the newer studies usually exclude people exiled before the mass deportations as well as the political prisoners evacuated at the outbreak of the Nazi-Soviet war.

---

129 Grigorijus Šuras, *Užrašai: Vilniaus geto kronika 1941–1944*, trans. Nijolė Kvaraciejūtė and Algimantas Antanavičius (Vilnius: ERA, 1997), 23.

130 Levin, *The Lesser*, 273; also, Levin, *Baltic Jews*, 127; Azriel Shochat, "Jews, Lithuanians and Russians, 1939–1941," in *Jews and Non-Jews in Eastern Europe, 1918–1945*, ed. Bela Vago and George L. Mosse (New York: Wiley and Israel Universities Press, 1974), 310; and many other works.

131 See Eugenijus Grunskis, *Lietuvos gyventojų trėmimai 1940–1941, 1945–1953 metais* (Vilnius: LII, 1996), 38–53. An extensive analysis is in Violeta Davoliūtė, "A 'Forgotten' History of Soviet Deportation: The Case of Lithuanian Jews," in *Population Displacement in Lithuania in the Twentieth Century Experiences, Identities and Legacies*, ed. Tomas Balkelis and Violeta Davoliūtė (Brill: Leiden, 2016), 179–210. Cf. the dissenting view of Atamukas, *Lietuvos žydų kelias*, 230–231; also, Eliyana R. Adler, "Exile and Survival: Lithuanian Jewish Deportees in the Soviet Union," in *That Terrible Summer: 70 Years since the Destruction of the Jewish Communities in Lithuania* [Hebrew], ed. Michael Ben Ya'akov, Gershon Greenberg, and Sigalit Rosmarin (Jerusalem: Efrata College, 2013), 31.

IMAGE 2.4. Deportations, June 14–17, 1941: Cattle cars on display near Vilnius. Inset: Child deportees. (Source—public domain.)

The Jewish victims reflected the Soviet policy of targeting the propertied, educated, and patriotic elements (for example, the construction tycoon Gedal Ilgovski), but the deportees included working-class people and ordinary citizens. Seven members of the Lithuanian Jewish veterans' society (LŽKS) and their families from Zarasai were among the prisoners.[132] In 1942 the Šiauliai *Judenrat*, on the order of the mayor, compiled a list of the deported "citizens of Jewish nationality" in preparation for the disposal of the victims' property.[133] These sources contradict the Nazi-era propaganda that Jews were the primary organizers of the Kremlin's operation and had not suffered exile. But even in this case Jews had reason to consider the Kremlin's rule the lesser of two evils, con-

---

132 Listed in Zarasų krašto žydų istorija, accessed March 8, 2019, www.zarasu-zydai.lt/index.php/project/zydu-kariu-dalyvavusiu-lietuvos-atvadavime-sajungos-zarasu-skyriaus-valdybos-nariai-1934–m/.
133 LMAVB RS, Vilnius, f. 76–190, Šiauliai City Archive-Jewish Ghetto Affairs, April 2, 1942, l. 19–23.

sidering the chances of survival: the majority outlived the Soviet deportation.[134] Thus, a number of Lithuanian Jews escaped the Holocaust by enduring a police operation aimed at an imagined security threat in the Baltic republics from civilians who, in reality, posed no threat to the Kremlin.

Among ethnic Lithuanians the deportations of the "June days," rather than the Holocaust, came to signify *the* commemorative tragedy of the war and are today officially marked as the Days of Mourning and Hope. But even many non-Lithuanian contemporaries saw the Kremlin's deportations as an unprecedented disaster. It must have been difficult to imagine that worse was yet to come, to foresee the murderous rampage that would soon eclipse this exile.

The Witches' Brew of Radicalism: Geopolitics, the LAF, and the New Antisemitism

The turmoil that followed the collapse of independent Lithuania played out against the setting of the wider European crisis which ensnared Lithuania's nationalities in a zero-sum trap. In 1918–1920, thousands of Jews and other national minorities had joined Lithuanians in the struggle to create an independent state even as they entertained differing visions of the emerging polity. But the country's nationalities turned inward as their geopolitical orientations became incompatible after the German-Soviet assault on Poland and the outbreak of the broader European war. Most of the Germans (and some Lithuanians who could "pass" by claiming German ancestry) happily repatriated to the Reich during the spring of 1941. The Poles were in an impossible situation: most detested Soviet rule, but they also resented Lithuanians as the "occupiers" of Vilnius, while the Germans hardly figured as potential liberators. In short, Jews, Lithuanians, Russians, and Poles viewed Nazi Germany and Stalinist Russia through the prisms of their own fears and expectations.[135] The other nationalities had reason to chafe at Soviet rule, but none saw their situation in quite the same way as those

---

134 For example, four of the seven Zarasai Jewish veteran families noted above survived the deportation. See more stories in Adler, "Exile and Survival," 27–49.

135 The predicament of communities caught in diametrically opposite and often illusory geopolitical solutions to their distress was not unique to Lithuania. See Bauer, *Death of the Shtetl*, 32ff.; cf. Elazar Barkan, Elizabeth A. Cole, and Kai Struve, eds., *Shared History-Divided Memory: Jews and Others in Soviet-Occupied Poland, 1939–1941* (Leipzig: Leipziger Universitätsverlag GMBH, 2007).

ethnic Lithuanians who mourned the loss of independence and were committed to its restoration. For many patriots, Smetona's relatively moderate political discourse and his commitment to neutrality in the war now appeared outmoded, if not irrelevant. Unless one were incurably naive, it was obvious that the only avenue of liberation lay in a violent breakdown of the partnership established in August 1939 between the Soviet occupiers and the Reich.

Lithuanians and Jews in particular found themselves in a predicament that led them towards illusory and diametrically opposed geopolitical solutions to what they saw as existential threats. Looking to the West, Lithuanians increasingly saw the German option as the only realistic alternative to a Stalinist future. It seemed that the British were losing the war, while the Americans were carrying out diplomacy from across the ocean. These circumstances, of course, meant disaster for Jews. The belief of many Jews that Soviet rule offered them safety, a chance at power-sharing, and protection against violent antisemitism was, in hindsight, a chimera. The idea that the Red Army's arrival in June 1940 brought a protection which would defer the Holocaust in Lithuania is implausible.[136] It is closer to the truth to say that Soviet power intensified already inflamed ethnic passions while destroying the political leadership which had in the past suppressed antisemitic outbreaks.[137]

Lithuanian authors were not the only ones who pointed to the political and geopolitical dynamics of 1940–1941 as factors in the rising antisemitism of the period. Dov Levin describes the essential divide which afflicted the "relations between the Jewish minority and local peoples" in the regions annexed by the Kremlin in 1939–1941:

> The indigenous [Gentile] peoples of the area regarded the Soviet regime as an enemy, and the Red Army as an intruder who had come to stamp out Baltic independence and conspire to dismember Poland in the east. In the eyes of these peoples, the Soviet annexation was both a political

---

136 See Dov Levin, *Fighting Back: Lithuanian Jewry's Armed Resistance to the Nazis, 1941–1945* (New York: Holmes & Meier, 1984), 21, 23. The author's argument that "Soviet rule in Lithuania deferred the Holocaust there for twelve months and seven days" (that is, from June 15, 1940 to June 22, 1941) is difficult to understand: it would only make sense if the Germans had attacked the USSR in the fall of 1939 or if the Lithuanians had initiated the Holocaust on June 14, 1940.

137 On the dynamics of antisemitism on the eve of the war, see Kęstutis Girnius, "Lemtingieji 1941-ji metai: Holokausto Lietuvoje prielaidų klausimu," *Naujasis Židinys-Aidai* 2 (2011): 85–100.

and social disaster. The Jews, in contrast—although they were loyal citizens of their respective countries—hardly shared these sentiments. Their alternative was a regime of Nazi terror; the Soviet occupation was decidedly the lesser of two evils. The relations between the Jews and the local non-Jewish peoples [were] determined by these utterly contradictory basic attitudes. There was, however, a "third party" in these relations: the Soviet establishment and its attitudes towards the Jews and the national groups in the area under its control.[138]

Azriel Shochat generalizes even more: "the special ferocity which the population demonstrated toward Lithuanian Jews during the Holocaust was undoubtedly the outcome of the very complex political situation created by the Soviet occupation in 1940 and 1941."[139] The noted economist and survivor of the Kovno Ghetto Samuel Gringauz (1900–1975) remarked that "during the time of Soviet rule, in 1940, a black cat ran between the Lithuanian Jews and the Lithuanian intelligentsia." Gringauz argued that the "fundamental difference of psychological orientation" which emerged as a result of clashing geopolitical visions that is, "fear of war and reliance on the Soviets on one side, and desire for war and reliance on Hitler's Germany on the other," constituted the "objective cause of Jewish-Lithuanian tension during the least year of Jewish life in Lithuania . . . and the root cause of the extreme anti-Semitism in evidence among certain Lithuanian sectors in the years 1940–1941."[140] In other words, hatred of Jews gained new strength during the wrenching political and social crisis of the first Soviet occupation.

Evidence of this phenomenon is abundant, and there is no reason to doubt the importance of the geopolitical divide on people's attitudes, but the explanation is incomplete, minimizing the antisemitism that preceded June 1940. Some unscrupulous authors have zeroed into the 1940–1941 period as a causal factor in rationalizing antisemitism by embracing the "theory of two genocides," according to which Lithuanian collaboration in the Holocaust was simply revenge for the atrocities committed by Jewish supporters of the Soviets.[141] (This theme is evident in other tendentious accounts in post-Communist Eastern Europe.) Hopefully, the recent scholarly interest in the issue of "Jews and Others"

---

138 Levin, *The Lesser*, 59–60.
139 Shochat, "Jews, Lithuanians, and Russians," 310.
140 As cited from Gringauz's text in *The Lithuanian Slaughter of Its Jews*, 20.
141 See below, Chapter 7.

in the Soviet-occupied territories will help us better understand the dynamics of communal conflict and avoid politicized narratives.[142]

The emerging resistance to Soviet rule and the movement to restore Lithuania's independence were made up of a diverse coalition. Within weeks of the occupation, the First Republic's diplomatic corps, which still functioned in Western capitals, grew alarmed at Soviet intentions and lobbied governments not to recognize the Kremlin's annexation. Hundreds of disaffected military officers, politicians, and intellectuals fled the country in the wake of the invasion, mostly to Germany. These refugees proved decisive in articulating a response to the crisis back home.[143] On November 17, 1940, a group of émigrés who had gathered in Berlin founded the Lithuanian Activist Front (Lietuvių aktyvistų frontas, or LAF). The group represented a spectrum of non-Communist political factions, but its more radical members embraced a politics reflecting a radical departure from interwar political norms, including a geopolitical tilt towards Germany, extreme nationalism, an embrace of authoritarian rule, and a newly virulent antisemitic ideology.

The LAF's leader, Kazys Škirpa, was convinced that exploiting the German connection during Hitler's inevitable clash with Stalin was the only path to Lithuania's restoration. Although the colonel was stripped of his diplomatic credentials in July 1940, he pursued meetings with German officials, arguing that it was in their interest to sponsor a national liberation movement in Lithuania, which, freed from Bolshevism, would become Germany's ally in the crusade for a "New Europe."[144] Škirpa's close relationships with Nazi officials were to prove morally and politically ruinous, but his arguments were persuasive to many who were cognizant of the military situation at the time. Britain was uninterested in the issue of the Baltic states' independence and seemingly on the verge of defeat. Smetona, the veteran pro-Western diplomat Jurgis Šaulys, and others of the older generation of Lithuanian politicians saw it differently. Suspicious

---

142 See especially Elazar Barkan et al., *Shared History-Divided Memory*, as well as the works of Liudas Truska and Nijolė Maslauskienė cited above.

143 Saulius Sužiedėlis, "Foreign Saviors, Native Disciples: Perspectives on Collaboration in Lithuania, 1940–1945," in *Collaboration and Resistance during the Holocaust: Belarus, Estonia, Latvia and Lithuania*, ed. David Gaunt, Paul A. Levine, and Laura Palosuo (Frankfurt am Main: Peter Lang, 2004), 318–320, 333–334.

144 These activities are detailed in Kazys Škirpa, *Sukilimas* (Brooklyn: Franciscan Fathers Press, 1973). The memoir contains many useful documents but is marked by apologia and deletions intended to conceal the antisemitism in the LAF program.

IMAGE 2.5. Colonel Kazys Škirpa, Lithuania's envoy to Germany and founder of the LAF. (Source—public domain.)

of Nazi intentions towards a future Lithuania, they were also unconvinced of Hitler's ultimate success against the Western allies. Smetona's public criticism of Hitler and Nazism after his arrival in the United States in March 1941 annoyed Škirpa. Col. Kazys Grinius, Jr., the former military attaché in Berlin, had advised Škirpa that, given the likelihood of a victory by the Western allies, an alliance with the Reich was imprudent. After the fall of France, Grinius reluctantly admitted that German power was the only force capable of ending Soviet rule in Lithuania and then wisely left for America. Inevitably, those who favored ties to Germany held the upper hand within the LAF.[145]

The LAF's political philosophy and program rejected the mainstream Lithuanian nationalism of the First Republic that had officially tolerated ethnic, religious, and cultural diversity. The philosopher Antanas Maceina, who had once suggested the institution of second-class citizenship for Lithuania's minorities based on racial criteria, headed the LAF's "ideological commission." The draft outline of the LAF platform for the future of the country emphasized corporatist economics and the overarching importance of the national will exemplified by solidarity, discipline, and authoritarian leadership, which would offset the degenerate and corrupt liberalism which had characterized the older generation's interwar leadership. The LAF's proposal for Lithuania's future economy was telling: "Simple justice demands that Lithuanians must take the

---

145 On Škirpa's pro-German thinking see Arūnas Bubnys, "Provokiška Lietuvos valstybės atkūrimo vizija (1940–1944)," in *Lietuvos diplomatija XX amžiuje*, ed. Vytautas Žalys, Raimundas Lopata, and Česlovas Laurinavičius (Vilnius: Vaga, 1999), 132–146; cf. the memorandum of Edvardas Turauskas summarizing the discussion of Lithuanian diplomats in Bern on September 9–11, 1940, as published in Jonušauskas, *Likimo vedami*, 88, 333–334; also, Truska, *Antanas Smetona*, 391, Škirpa, *Sukilimas*, 268–270; Škirpa to Smetona, May 30, 1941, Hoover Institution, Turauskas Collection, Box 3; Škirpa to Lozoraitis, October 1940, in LMAVB RS, f. 9–3105, l. 2–5.

place of the Jews in commerce. The Jews, who for centuries utilized the hard work of our nation, often colluded with the nation's enemies during difficult times.... The recent occupation of Lithuania makes this clear."[146]

In March 1941, the LAF issued "Instructions for the Liberation of Lithuania," which addressed the international situation, concluding that Britain would be of no help in liberating the homeland. The directives, which resisters were under strict orders to distribute to reliable activists only by word of mouth, urged patriotic Lithuanians to organize an anti-Soviet insurrection, which was to coincide with the onset of the inevitable German-Soviet war, with or without prior agreement with Berlin. According to Škirpa, a successful revolt would force the invading Germans to accept a fait accompli and deal with a resolute Lithuanian people who had expressed their desire for independence. At the appropriate hour of liberation, the LAF urged rebels to "determine the fate of Lithuania," and then addressed the "Jewish question":

> It is very important on this occasion to get rid of the Jews. For this reason, it is necessary to create within the country such a stifling atmosphere against them that not a single Jew would dare to allow himself even the thought that he would have minimal rights or, in general, any possibility to earn a living in the new Lithuania. The goal: to force all the Jews to flee Lithuania together with the Red Russians. The more of them who leave Lithuania at this time, the easier it will be to ultimately free ourselves from the Jews. The hospitality granted the Jews during the reign of Vytautas the Great is hereby revoked for all time on account of their repeated betrayal of the Lithuanian nation to its oppressors.

The proposed revolution would restore independent Lithuania "on a new basis" under LAF leadership (meaning Škirpa), which would then guide the people with a nationalist program "based on principles of Christian [sic] morality." This lofty goal required the "ripping up by the roots of corruption, injustice, Communist degeneracy and Jewish exploitation."[147]

---

146 "Lietuvos aktyvistų platformos metmenys: projektas," Hoover Institution, Turauskas Collection, Box 5, 3–4, 20.
147 From the text of "Lietuvai išlaisvinti nurodymai," March 24, 1941, Hoover Institution, Turauskas Collection, Box 5, 11. In his *Sukilimas*, Škirpa published this and other documents but omitted references to Jews. The entire text is published by the IHC, along with other documents on antisemitism and anti-Jewish agitation in the period before June 1941 in Truska and Vareikis, *Holokausto prielaidos*, 211–332.

Along with plans for an insurrection, the LAF leadership drafted proclamations to be dropped by the Luftwaffe after an agreement with the Germans for the establishment of a Lithuanian government. The arrangement never materialized and only a few of these leaflets were ever distributed, but the texts have survived as proof of the intended ethnic cleansing, including a historic indictment of Lithuania's Jews in formal idiom, adding the accusation of treason to the long-familiar complaint about Jewish economic exploitation:

> Lithuanian Jews! Five hundred years ago the prince Vytautas the Great invited you to our land hoping that You would help create with us a benefit for the state. In Lithuania You took advantage ... of our state's protection, security, material resources as well as political, cultural, and social rights.... [A]s a nation of nomads You were able to preserve Your nationality, religion, and customs, but in creating this prosperity You harmed and viciously exploited the Lithuanians, the rightful masters of the land....
>
> [As in the past], so in independent Lithuania, You did not go together with the Lithuanian nation. You stubbornly persisted with the Russian language, ridiculed all that was Lithuanian and exploited our country for Your egotistical purpose of enrichment.... Your nation organized in Lithuania the illegal Communist Party in which 90% of the active members were of Your nationality.... Moreover, Your disloyalty reached an unbelievable degree when Soviet Russia occupied our lands. You were the first to welcome the invading gangs of the Russian army with ovations and gifts of flowers.
>
> Jews! Your five-hundred-year history in the Lithuanian lands is at an end. Have no hopes or illusions that You will have a place in Lithuania. There is no place for You in Lithuania! The Lithuanian nation, rising for a new life and a new history, considers You traitors and will behave as necessary when handling such dregs.

In this antisemitic screed, the new Lithuania would offer Jews only two choices if they failed to leave with the Soviets: for those who had maltreated Lithuanians, "arrest and trial before a military court"; for the rest, forcible expulsion and transfer of property "for the general needs of the Lithuanian nation and state."[148] On the eve of the war, paragraph 16 of the proposed "LAF Program" affirmed that "the Lithuanian Activist Front rescinds hospitality

---

148 "Svetingumo atšaukimas žydams," Hoover Institution, Turauskas Collection, Box 5.

towards the Jewish national minority in Lithuania."[149] It is noteworthy that the proclamation addressing ethnic Lithuanian Communists "Urging the Nation's Strays to Reconsider" offered redemption if the culprits returned "to the ranks of their Lithuanian brothers and patriots."[150] Nearly all the proclamations, directed towards different strata of Lithuanian society and even to the Red Army, contained antisemitic messages.

A prime example of the new ideological radicalism was the fascistic and racist thirty-eight-page draft brochure *What the Activists Are Fighting For*, penned by Bronys Raila, the head of the LAF propaganda commission, and presented to the organization's leadership in May 1941. Raila first addressed what he viewed as the nation's geopolitical dilemmas. In his view, the effete and "criminally negligent" Smetona regime had committed three unpardonable sins: it had failed to defend the country against Jewish power and Communism; it had proved irresolute in confronting Poland over Vilnius; and it had pursued the useless policy of neutrality. To undo the ineffective foreign policy of the past, Raila proposed, despite the nation's difficult past with its Teutonic neighbor, a staunch pro-German alignment based on Lithuania's national self-interest. Some goals, such as achieving the borders delineated in 1918–1920, a revised relationship with a future (and much diminished) Poland, and vigilance with regard to Russia, were causes which many Lithuanians of various political persuasions could support. But how all this would square with the racial Nazi empire envisioned by Hitler about which Smetona had warned, Raila did not say.

Raila emphasized that, while Germans, Russians, and Poles had all contributed to the historic weakening of the Lithuanian state and nation, Jews had done the most harm. The "pack composed of the Caucasian Dzhugashvili-Stalin and his innumerable Israelite leeches," he wrote, had allegedly concocted the Russian imperialism of the Bolshevik type. If Lithuania surrendered to Asiatic Judeo-Communism, the nation would be cut off from "Western culture, and most important, from the orbit of National Socialist Germany's politics and civilization." In a curious version of pseudo-Marxist dialectics, Raila argued that the bourgeois and proletarian democracies had exhausted their roles as vehicles of progress: "their main objective as the liberator of new political, economic, and social forces accomplished, they have inevitably become regressive factors."

---

149 "Projektas: Lietuvių aktyvistų fronto programa," in "Priedai," LCVA, f. 648, ap. 2, b. 582, l. 141.

150 "Raginimas tautos paklydėliams susiprasti," Hoover Institution, Turauskas Collection, Box 5.

In Raila's view, what he called "democratism," which preached "the equality of all races," was essentially "incapable of expressing the national will," which was more than simply "the sum of persons speaking the same language and united by a common historical consciousness." Raila was convinced that the nation constituted "*an idea and indivisible organism... created by blood, land, historical fate and a struggle for a common future*" (emphasis in original). He urged Lithuanians to unite with the racially akin Latvians and create a "unified Aestian ideal."[151]

Raila alleged that the countless "Jewish breed," coddled by Smetona, had made Lithuania one of the "most Jewish states in Europe." The Jew could never be assimilated, he wrote, because "his peculiar Semitic race, the nature of this vagabond nation, seeks only a parasite's life." The false socialism of "the Jew Marx and other apologists of class struggle, had distorted, wounded and tarnished the true socialism" of the national variety. A future Lithuanian state, purified of "Jews, parasites and traitors," could only develop fruitfully if it were welded into a single national body, "an ethnic... racial, political, economic and spiritual unit." Raila made clear that the Jews had no place in such an exalted society:

> *The LAF, acting in accordance with the Aryan spirit of Europe reborn, is determined to totally separate the Jews from the Lithuanian state and national body and to progressively accomplish the general expulsion of the Jews from Lithuanian land. All the property accumulated by Jewish exploitation and deceit will have to be returned to the Lithuanian nation through legal means and justly distributed for Lithuanian use and possession.* (Emphasis in original)

Absent Jews and traitors, the weak and inactive elements of society would eventually join the "clean and healthy" national body. The LAF would then become "the sole expression, leader and executor of the will of the national community" and construct a new Lithuania on the basis of "the national state, nationalism, Christian ethics and socialism." According to Raila, the Lithuanian nation, having uprooted the "remnants of Eastern nihilism," would gather strength from "the depths of the Lithuanian soul and its Aestian land." At a future point, "the creative will of the Lithuanian nation would harmoniously join the healthy current of Western European culture." Rhetorical excess reached a peak in Raila's vision of Lithuanian supermen. He maintained that "the [LAF] activist is a new

---

151 "Aestians" (aisčiai): Roman historian Tacitus's reference to the tribes of the eastern Baltic, which some scholars considered the ancestral community of the Baltic peoples.

ethical Aestian type," whose commitment to the struggle "has permeated his entire being, bursting with the desire to set out on new campaigns, ever more determined actions, and greater victories." Like most fanatics, impervious to paradox or irony, the long-winded Raila maintained that the actions of LAF members "were more expressive than their words."[152] Such histrionics proved too much for some in the Berlin LAF who had not yet lost their senses. Stalwarts of the interwar establishment, Dr. Petras Karvelis, a former diplomat, and General Stasys Raštikis, the former commander of the army, protested, offended by Raila's scathing criticism of the First Republic. Škirpa was forced to admit that the action program, "written in a militant spirit..., was, perhaps, a bit too sharp." Publication of Raila's manifesto was abandoned.[153]

Raila's polemic reveals the extent to which otherwise intelligent people could embrace racial language and geopolitical illusions, but an important minority within the LAF proved even more extreme and eventually separated from the group: the supporters of Smetona's former rival Augustinas Voldemaras (the Voldemarists or *voldemarininkai*), among whom young military officers took the lead. A week before the outbreak of the German-Soviet war, thirty-two self-described "remnants of the Voldemarists" coalesced into the Lithuanian National Socialist Iron Wolf Front which outlined a program for a "Third Lithuania," on behalf of the "young Lithuanian generation . . . which has come to honor the new racial ideals of fascism and National Socialism." Their political program listed as its second point: "Jews are stricken from life." Lithuania's educational system was to be imbued with the "National Socialist spirit." The leader of the Iron Wolf Front was to head the state, while, in foreign policy, this Third Lithuania would establish the "closest cooperation with the Great Third Reich and normal relations with other nations in the new European order."[154] The Voldemarists formed the core of the Lithuanian Nationalist Party (Lietuvių nacionalistų partija, the LNP) which would carry out a coup against the LAF's Provisional Government in mid-July 1941.

---

152 All citations are from Bronys Raila, "Už ką kovoja aktyvistai," Škirpa papers, LMAVB RS, f. 9–3105, l. 10–48. It is published in, among other venues, Truska and Vareikis, *Holokausto prielaidos*, 270–308.

153 In Škirpa's account, LMAVB RS, f. 9–3105, l. 102–103.

154 The document is cited in the diary of Zenonas Blynas, *Karo metų dienoraštis 1941–1944*, ed. Gediminas Rudis (Vilnius: LII, 2007), 123–124. Cf. Truska and Vareikis, *Holokausto prielaidos*, 86–94.

Without opinion polls, there is no way to measure the impact of the LAF's propaganda in stoking the radical mood in Lithuania, but there is good reason to doubt that the rising tide of antisemitism within Lithuania needed much outside prodding. Škirpa noted as much at the time:

> In planning for the liberation of Lithuania . . . we decided to develop a wider, secret propaganda operation in occupied Lithuania in order to prepare the spirit of the nation for the decisive campaign. But . . . it soon became clear that this was totally unnecessary: The Soviet system itself, the inhuman terror of the occupiers and their Jewish helpers, had already prepared our nation for the insurrection. On the contrary, the LAF leadership received from Lithuania a request not to send any secret [propaganda] literature to the country. So, on behalf of the LAF leadership, only the bulletin "From Bolshevik Slavery to a New Lithuania" was sent out, which contained the [anti-Soviet] protests of Lithuanian diplomats. In addition, a few weeks before the onset of the Russian-German war, a proclamation specifically directed against the Jews was put out. This was done to warn them in advance that there would be no life for them in the New Lithuania. In that way the Jews would be cautioned that, for the purpose of saving their own lives, they should abandon Lithuania in advance of [the war], or at least flee along with the Red Army. Five hundred copies of this proclamation were distributed, but only along the border region.[155]

It is noteworthy that even otherwise level-headed diplomats who were skeptical of Škirpa's belief that Germany was the key to restoring Lithuania, and who had never been known to traffic in antisemitism, were swept up in the emotions and expressed anti-Jewish views. On May 10, 1940, as the crisis with the USSR loomed over Lithuania, the former foreign minister and ambassador to Italy, Stasys Lozoraitis (1898–1983), wrote to Edvardas Turauskas, the country's envoy to the League of Nations, that the "suffering of some innocent Jews" was not something the world would care about compared to the fate of three million Lithuanians. A year later, Petras Klimas, the veteran diplomat stationed in Paris, adopted the LAF position, arguing that Jews had no place in a future Lithuania

---

155 The excerpts cited are from Kazys Škirpa's manuscript "Kovok! Pastangos gelbėti Lietuvą, 1939–1941 m.," LCVA, f. 648, ap. 2, b. 581, l. 136–137. The antisemitic appeal in question, addressed to "Lithuanian brothers and sisters" and titled "Amžiams išvaduokime Lietuvą nuo žydijos jungo" (Let us forever liberate Lithuania from Jewry's yoke), is in LCVA, f. 648, ap. 2, b. 582, "Priedai," l. 213–215.

"because they declared their war against us, instead of being in [solidarity] during this unfortunate hour [that is, the Soviet occupation]."[156]

The LAF's proclamation of March 19, 1941, addressed to "Our Dear Enslaved Brothers," suggests the extent of domestic radicalization. Ostensibly issued by the LAF's information bureau in Berlin, it called on the populace to rise up "once the [German] march from the west" had begun. The second point urged the future rebels to "immediately arrest all the local Communists and other kinds of Lithuania's traitors, so that not one would avoid retribution for their actions." Another version of the March 19 message, identical except for minor misspellings, adds a telling caveat in parentheses: "(Traitors will be forgiven only if they cannot really prove that they had liquidated at least one Jew.)."[157] One reasonable explanation for this discrepancy is that the call to kill, unique among the extant LAF documents, was added to the original message from Berlin as it changed hands numerous times during distribution in Lithuania; another is that Voldemarists had already authored the document before it was smuggled across the border.[158] More than a dozen copies of the appeal have been discovered in the archives, seized by security forces in various locales, indicating that anti-Soviet resisters copied and surreptitiously passed along the instructions.[159] According to Škirpa, this and other "inciting leaflets," which included detailed instructions on liberating prisoners, attacking the Soviet forces, and seizing control of local offices at the outbreak of the war "brought more harm than good," since the Soviets responded by increasing roundups of local activists. The Germans were also unhappy about such spontaneous activities because they ran the danger of provoking Soviet countermeasures. The LAF instructed its people not to take any "thoughtless actions" and thus endanger the Front's people within Lithuania.[160]

---

156 As cited in Stanislovas Stasiulis, "The Holocaust in Lithuania: The Key Characteristics of Its History, and the Key Issues in Historiography and Cultural Memory," *East European Politics and Societies: and Cultures* 34, no. 1 (February 2020): 264–265.

157 "Brangūs vergaujantys broliai." The facsimiles of the two documents are published in Truska and Vareikis, *Holokausto prielaidos*, 264–265.

158 The most detailed analysis of the path taken by this anti-Jewish appeal from Berlin to Lithuania is in Stanislovas Staniulis, "1941 m. kovo 19 d. LAF atsišaukimas: provokacija, falsifikatas ar tikras dokumentas?," *Lietuvos istorijos studijos* 38 (2016): 72–83.

159 Valentinas Brandišauskas, *Siekiai atkurti Lietuvos valstybingumą (1940 06 – 1941 09)* (Vilnius: Valstybinis leidybos centras, 1996), 60.

160 Škirpa, "Kovok!" l. 137.

Whatever the direct impact of LAF propaganda, there can be little doubt about the extent of rising anti-Jewish hatred during the Soviet occupation of 1940–1941. Liudas Truska, one of the first Lithuanian historians to write extensively on antisemitism, offered this blunt assessment of the trajectory of hateful messaging:

> Lithuanian-Jewish relations entered a new level, dangerous to the Jews. Next to the earlier images of the Jews, that is, as killers of Christ, exploiters of Lithuanians, swindlers, spongers, Communists, there now arose new ones which drowned out these earlier ones, namely: gravediggers of Lithuania's independence, eager helpers of the occupiers, informers, cruel NKVD interrogators, torturers and those who deported Lithuanians.[161]

In an insightful essay, historian Gediminas Bašinskas concludes that the notion of Jewish support for the Soviet regime had, for many people, become self-explanatory and obvious, "a traditional mode of thinking and speaking about the behavior of the Jews . . . , and the fact that they were integrated into the [Soviet] political structures was understood as the regime's favoring the Jews." He further notes: "The construction of the Jewish-Communist image was also *functional*: it was a way to remove collective responsibility from those Lithuanians who had themselves helped consolidate the Communist regime, and to assist in mobilizing potential [anti-Soviet] supporters against a common enemy, which some of the people understood as Jewish power" (my emphasis).[162] While the desire for pro-Soviet Lithuanians to expiate their sins by invoking the Judeo-Bolshevik myth inspired some perpetrators, it is not certain that this sense of guilt motivated most of those who killed Jews in the summer and fall of 1941.

No monocausal narrative can easily clarify the quantum leap from Smetona's pre-1940 moralizing lessons on national tolerance to the LAF's program, which elevated antisemitism to one of the core principles by which the organization expected to govern the new Lithuania. The antisemitism that stirred anti-Jewish hatred under the Kremlin's rule had a long history, beginning with the tensions which afflicted the social hierarchies of premodern society, for

---

161 Liudas Truska, "Tikros ir primestos kaltės: žydai ir lietuviai pirmuoju sovietmečiu," *Darbai ir dienos* 34 (2003): 285.

162 Bašinskas, "Lietuvių-žydų konfliktai sovietinės okupacijos pradžioje 1940 metų vasarą: tęstinumai ar lūžiai," 207–208.

example, the conflicts between Christian peasants and Jewish townspeople. The religious, anti-Judaic mythologies, village superstitions, and fights over market tolls of that age did not in themselves constitute an ideological program. The first traces of antisemitic thought emerged in the late nineteenth century, but there was no broad political consensus on relationships with the Jews among the nationalist intelligentsia. The revolution in national/ethnic relations which followed the restoration of a Lithuanian state after World War I injected new economic and political anti-Jewish themes into the national narrative. Right-wing students and intellectuals adopted elements of racial antisemitism based on pseudoscientific constructs which, however, did not resonate among the majority of Lithuanians as a worldview.

The development of antisemitism in Lithuania was dynamic, waxing and waning over time, combining new forms with older, traditional anti-Jewish feelings, a phenomenon analyzed extensively in recent scholarship. But there is no question that it was also intensified by the clash of very real political/economic interests and incompatible geopolitical orientations, in effect, a distorted response to a genuine calamity. There is no evidence that Škirpa and his circle intended the physical extermination of Lithuania's Jewish population, but the calls for expropriation and expulsion injected a radical antisemitic component into the political rhetoric in the struggle for Lithuania's independence. The crisis of 1940–1941 thus provided fertile soil for the emergence of a newly toxic and more coherent antisemitism emanating from the Berlin LAF built on previous anti-Jewish narratives, articulated in the various writing emanating from Berlin and developed further in the official Lithuanian press during the German occupation. Despite the unhappiness of some in the LAF with Raila's "sharp" agenda, the antisemitic consensus is clear in Maceina's LAF program outline and repeated in more crude and activist language in the Front's proclamations to the people. The LAF joined the ranks, then, of extreme right-wing antisemitic movements, even as its radical fascist wing eventually broke away, reorganized itself as the LNP, and turned against their former comrades.

Preparing for War: The LAF, Geopolitics, and the Contradictions of National Restoration

The LAF's ambitious plans for a mass uprising to create a government to replace Soviet power required the willingness of thousands of potential fighters within Lithuania to take up arms concurrent with a German attack on the Red Army. The LAF envisioned a disciplined underground network which would lead the projected insurrection, but this grand project collided with realities back in the homeland. The Front's influence was real but limited given the infrequent and dangerous cross-border contacts between its couriers from Germany and the resistance in Lithuania. The Soviet secret police eventually penetrated most of the anti-Soviet groups. One well-documented study concluded that "it is somewhat problematic to speak of organized resistance."[163] Nonetheless, the Berlin LAF did maintain contacts with two significant opposition centers. In Kaunas, a group of activist intelligentsia organized an underground network in December 1940 which received news from Berlin and encouraged like-minded resistance groups in the provinces. In Vilnius, Major Vytautas Bulvičius led a clandestine band of officers in the Lithuanian 179th Division of the Red Army who hatched plans to promote an uprising among the troops at the outset of a German-Soviet war and maintained contact with the Front's leaders who mistakenly informed them that war would break out in May. The conspiring soldiers had also contacted German intelligence operatives on the issue of Lithuanian statehood and had received (false) assurances that Lithuania's independence would follow if the soldiers mutinied and assisted the German army. In early June 1941 Soviet counterintelligence discovered the officers' network and arrested the ringleaders.[164] The USSR Commissariat for Defense reported that 908 "anti-Soviet" officers from the three Baltic Red Army formations had been arrested, including 285 Lithuanians, but this did not prevent widespread desertion and mutiny among Baltic Red Army men when the Germans invaded.[165]

It was, however, in the interest of émigré Lithuanian writers sympathetic to the LAF, as well as revisionist Russian historians, such as Aleksandr Dyukov, to exaggerate the extent and effectiveness of the anti-Communist underground: the former to magnify the scale of patriotic resistance, the latter to justify Stalinist repression. It is doubtful that the underground activists constituted a serious threat to the Kremlin's control. Soviet mass deportation plans make

---

163 Brandišauskas, *Siekiai*, 47–58.

164 Juozas Jankauskas, *1941 m. birželio sukilimas Lietuvoje* (Vilnius: LGGRTC, 2010), 266–287; Arūnas Bubnys, *Vokiečių okupuota Lietuva (1941–1944)* (Vilnius: LGGRTC, 1998), 27–29; Alexander Statiev, "Motivations and Goals of Soviet Deportations in the Western Borderlands," *Journal of Strategic Studies*, 28, no. 6 (2005): 980.

165 From the Central Archive of the Russian Federal Security Service (FSB) as published in Dyukov, *Nakanune*, 427, 430.

no mention of the LAF or any other anti-Soviet underground network. Nazi spying operations in Lithuania throughout 1940–1941 were not extensive, hampered as they were by the mass repatriation of citizens of German ancestry to the Reich during the early months of 1941. The more immediate concern of Soviet security was the problematic attitude of the populace at large. The NKGB instructions from Moscow of June 1941 stressed that "the deportation of the anti-Soviet element from the Baltic republics constitutes a task of great political importance," which must be accomplished in a manner not to antagonize "the part of the surrounding population known to be hostile to Soviet power."[166] It should be noted that membership alone in certain occupations, political groups, and social classes made one a "counterrevolutionary." Even certain hobbies were condemned. In 1941 such groups included Trotskyists, Zionists, Catholic youth leaders, non-Communist political activists, landowners, stamp collectors, Esperanto enthusiasts, and people corresponding with relatives abroad. The Soviets listed seventy Germans among the thousands targeted for deportation, mainly persons who had "registered for repatriation but had chosen to remain."

While German intelligence services were not a significant factor in the anti-Soviet resistance within Lithuania, this connection was crucial to the LAF members in Berlin as they prepared to exploit the coming war for their goal of national liberation. Škirpa counted on the Reich accepting an LAF government, albeit as a junior ally in the campaign against Bolshevism, but relations with the Germans entangled the colonel in a web of contradictions. Škirpa's constant pleas for Lithuanian statehood forced him into an obsequious if not humiliating posture vis-à-vis German officials who studiously avoided any commitment to the country's restoration, even as a client state on the Slovak model. German promises never went beyond vague assurances that the conquered peoples of Eastern Europe would find their proper place in the "New Europe" after the campaign against Bolshevism was concluded and the said nations' contributions to this goal had been suitably evaluated.

In January 1941, the authorities initiated a policy of Germanization in the Suwałki region which had been annexed to the Reich, pressuring Lithuanian farmers there to abandon their lands and resettle on the Soviet side of the border, ignoring Škirpa's pleas to leave the affected villagers in place. The German

---

166 Russian text is in the IHC publication, Nijolė Maslauskienė and Inga Petravičiūtė, *Okupantai ir kolaborantai: Pirmoji sovietinė okupacija (1940–1941)* (Vilnius: Margi raštai, 2007), 291–299.

commissar for the region threatened the area's Lithuanians with "the fate of the Poles" if they did not submit. On February 20, 1941, the LAF leadership met to consider the situation. Some members doubted whether it still made sense to seek Lithuanian independence through an alliance with Berlin. Would it not be better, they asked, "to abandon the idea and just break off the political arrangement with the Germans"? The Vilnius LAF group of officers had their own doubts. In the end, the LAF concluded that preparations for the insurrection were too far advanced and that there was no realistic alternative to the German connection. It was decided not to "succumb to emotions," especially in view of the "greater threat to the national body posed by the Red terror." For their part, German officials continued to pressure Škirpa to scrap plans for the reestablishment of a Lithuanian government both directly and through their Lithuanian agents in Berlin. Škirpa was aware of Nazi perceptions of the Baltic nations as unsophisticated farmers, noting in his memoir an article by Goebbels which seemed to leave no opening for the political aspirations of the Eastern peoples. But he chose to grasp at every straw, assigning importance, for example, to Ribbentrop's statement of March 1, 1941 on Bulgaria's accession to the Tripartite Pact in which the German minister claimed that in the "blossoming Europe of the future" each nation would be free to develop its own political and cultural life to "unprecedented heights." [167]

Škirpa also faced difficulties on the Lithuanian front. He was wary of the Voldemarist faction among whom, he claimed, were Nazi puppets engaged in intrigues against his leadership, accusing one of the most radical members of the group, Jonas Pyragius, of attempting to promote "German Nazi ideology" in the LAF and of an "inability to separate Lithuania's interests from German designs on our country." On the other end of the political spectrum were the diplomatic corps and the Lithuanian diaspora in the West, some of whom were skeptical of the LAF's ties to Berlin. In August 1940, three of the country's veteran diplomats, Jurgis Šaulys, Petras Klimas, and Edvardas Turauskas, met at the Lithuanian mission in Bern. They understood the geopolitical reality of German power as the only force capable of expelling the Soviet occupiers but were unwilling to place all their bets on the Reich. The diplomats were wary of Škirpa's suggestion that a future Lithuania should be based on "the principles of

---

[167] Described in Škirpa's partial memoir, LMAVB RS, f. 9–3105, l. 116–130.

a [specifically] Lithuanian National Socialism."[168] Between September 17–25, 1940, a wider gathering of diplomats, including Škirpa and hosted in Rome by Lozoraitis founded the Lithuanian National Committee (Tautinis Lietuvos komitetas).[169] The Committee elected Ernestas Galvanauskas chairman, but the group was actually led by Lozoraitis, with Turauskas and Škirpa as members. From the beginning, the committee foundered on the rocks of its inherent contradictions. The group sought to establish continuity with the First Republic by requesting Smetona's imprimatur as a kind of government-in-exile but could not find a country than would host it. There were personal clashes, as Turauskas and, in particular, Šaulys resisted any attempt to give Škirpa a leading role. In the end, as the members later admitted, the committee achieved nothing. Perhaps the ultimate exemplar of its ineffectiveness was the sole official act of the "chair" Galvanauskas who, on June 22, 1941, wrote a letter inviting Škirpa to form a Lithuanian government "on the basis of the Lithuanian Constitution of February 11, 1938,"[170] seemingly unaware that such a political structure was unworkable under the circumstances.

Škirpa tended to adjust his communications depending on what he thought would resonate with whomever he was addressing when promoting his plans. He played down, when necessary, the LAF's ideological radicalism. In April 1941, he wrote to Lozoraitis, in effect the senior Lithuanian diplomat-in-exile, arguing that his LAF was not to be confused with the anti-Smetona extremists of the 1930s:

> Sir, as for the Activist Movement, you imagine it wrongly. That which I have created has nothing to do with those activists [the former LAS] which you have in mind. The current Lithuanian activist movement [LAF] is not some narrow gathering of fanatics and hotheads, but a real expression of national unity, shaped by the misfortune which has befallen our county. The only thing this movement has in common with the activists of old is that it has taken the activist name. This was done

---

168 Jonušauskas, *Likimo vedami*, 85. Based on a quote from the archive of Stasys Bačkis, head of the Lithuanian Mission in Paris.

169 Galvanauskas was elected chair but was interned in Germany and was never able to assume any meaningful duties.

170 The various machinations among the committee members are detailed in Jonušauskas, *Likimo vedami*, 88–98.

to stress that fact that only the active forces of our nation can restore Lithuania's independence.[171]

Škirpa was aware that his pro-German stance was "difficult for our countrymen across the ocean [in America] to understand."[172] The Front's leader sought to convince doubters by insisting that an LAF-led Lithuania would not be a carbon copy of the German Reich. Notwithstanding evidence to the contrary, in January 1941 Škirpa wrote to the Lithuanian American leader, Leonardas Šimutis, that there was "no doubt that Germany is interested in Lithuania becoming once again an independent state." Even if Britain were to win the war with American backing, he argued, the Western powers would be unwilling to support Lithuania's cause in postwar Europe. Škirpa described the political philosophy of the LAF as "nationally minded, Christian-oriented, partially socialist" with an emphasis on a "disciplined society," which would "emancipate the Lithuanian nation from exploitation by non-Lithuanians, especially the Jews." Škirpa maintained that the LAF was "no coalition of previous political parties" and that it embraced "neither fascism nor national socialism, but a purely Lithuanian activism" (whatever that meant)—in other words, a movement based on a home-grown philosophy, rather than on imported ideas.[173] Elsewhere, he described the LAF ideology as a fusion of "Lithuanian nationalism, Christian morality and social justice."

In his lengthy memorandum (*Denkschrift*) to the Japanese ambassador in Berlin General Hiroshi Oshima (May 21, 1941) and a similar version to Ribbentrop (June 12, 1941), Škirpa, speaking in the name of the Lithuanian diplomats' defunct committee, described Europe's ostensibly "oldest Aryans" (that is, Lithuanians) as a historic "guard [*Wacht*] against the incursion of the various peoples from Russia's plains into the West." Škirpa explained that "in the case of Lithuania, we are not dealing with the building of a new state," but with the restoration of an independent country which had less than a year before been recognized by the world as an "equal, rightful [*gleichberechtigt*] member of the family of nations." But the restored Lithuanian state would not

---

171 Škirpa to Lozoraitis, April 7, 1941, Hoover Institution, Turauskas Collection, Box 3, 6. On the LAS, see Chapter 1.
172 See Škirpa's manuscript in LMAVB RS, f. 9–3105, l. 101–130.
173 Škirpa to Šimutis, January 21, 1941, Hoover Institution, Turauskas Collection, Box 3; also see the copy in LMAVB RS, f. 9–3105, l. 49–66.

be Smetona's neutral polity; it would be an ally of Germany in the New Europe. In these messages Škirpa avoided any mention of Jews, describing the LAF as "a people's national and socialist, but strictly anti-Communist" movement under unified leadership.[174]

In his thirty-six-page tract *From Bolshevik Slavery to a New Lithuania*, intended for distribution in Lithuania, Škirpa attempted to satisfy both his LAF activists and the Lithuanian diplomat colleagues in Western capitals who doubted his faith in the German connection. The text published the dispatches of Lithuania's foreign missions to their host governments protesting the Soviet annexation without any mention of the LAF's antisemitism or its pro-Axis geopolitical stance. However, the official documents of the First Republic's diplomats were sandwiched between two discordant polemics authored by Škirpa: a denunciation of Smetona's foreign policy ("Neutrality—the Fatal Mistake") and a proposal for a new state under LAF leadership ("Assistance in Restoring Lithuania"). The latter text accused the governments of interwar Lithuania of failure "to compel the national minorities towards positive, creative work for the benefit of the Lithuanian State and Lithuanian nation, . . . [and failure] to curb the Jews and similar elements, who had cruelly exploited the Lithuanians." In this view, "the creator of any State . . . must be a unified organized national community in all respects, not a mixture of various nations." At present, it was noted, "the Bolshevik regime in Lithuania is but slavery imposed by a caste of Jews and their associates." The LAF leader sidestepped the embarrassing reality that the Western powers, notably Britain and the United States, had refused to recognize the Soviet incorporation of the Baltic states and continued to recognize their diplomats, whereas the Germans had promptly handed the keys of the Lithuanian mission in Berlin to the Soviets. In a convoluted passage, Škirpa explained that "the European states, which have more practical relations with the USSR, for example, Germany and Italy, have acknowledged the fact of the incorporation of Lithuania into Soviet Russia, but as far as is known, have not tied their hands for future possibilities by any formal act." He added, again without any evidence, that the Axis powers supported Lithuania's cause and that the

---

174 That is, "völkisch national und sozialistisch, aber scharf anti-kommunistisch," as quoted in a memo to Oshima, May 21, 1941, "Denkschrift betreffend die Wiederherstellung der staatlichen Unabhängigkeit Litauens," Hoover Institution, Turauskas Collection, Box 8. The same formula is repeated in a slightly different version of the memorandum to Ribbentrop.

now uncredentialed diplomats of the closed missions could "work unofficially" for the nation.[175]

Despite the loss of his diplomatic status after the Soviet occupation, Škirpa held numerous conversations with German officials on the role of the Lithuanian anti-Soviet resistance in the coming war with the Soviet Union. His contacts included Dr. Kurt Gräbe of the Second Section of the Abwehr (German military intelligence), officers of the Sixth Section (foreign intelligence and sabotage) of the RSHA [Reichssicherheitshauptamt, or the Main Office of Reich Security], and Dr. Heinz Gräfe of the Tilsit Gestapo. In the spring of 1941, the Abwehr intensified preparations to support "insurrection movements among the ethnic minorities of the Soviet Union" and coopted Baltic refugees to support its efforts. German training centers in East Prussia housed several hundred Lithuanian exiles, mainly former military and police officers, along with several ethnic Germans from Lithuania [*Volksdeutsche*], such as Richard Schweizer, a junior SS officer from Kybartai, who helped instigate the anti-Jewish pogroms of late June 1941 in Kaunas.[176]

A sizable cohort of the Lithuanians tasked with accompanying the German forces into Lithuania included extremist pro-Nazi Voldemarist elements, some of whom were to become foot soldiers of the Holocaust. Major Stasys Puodžius became the de facto head of the LNP during the initial period of the German occupation. Among others were Major Pyragius, Captain Bronius Aušrotas, and the linguist Pranas Germantas-Meškauskas,[177] all known spies for the Abwehr. The latter, along with the ideologue and writer Vytautas Alantas (pen name: Vytautas Benjaminas Jakševičius), advocated for the union of a National Socialist Lithuania with the Reich. Major Kazys Šimkus headed the first TDA battalion involved in the murders of Jews, while Aušrotas and Captain Ignas Vylius-Vėlavičius commanded, at different times, the German occupation's penal system, including the infamous Ninth Fort prison. Perhaps the most egregious collaborator of this group was Colonel Vytautas Reivytis (1901–1988), the future chief of the Lithuanian Police Department, who was to play a significant

---

175 Cited from the text in Attachment XLIII, "Iš bolševistinės vergijos į Naują Lietuvą," LCVA, f. 648, ap. 2, b. 582, l. 156–192 [1–36].

176 Christoph Dieckmann, *Deutsche Besatzungspolitik in Litauen 1941–1944*, 2 vols. (Göttingen: Wallstein Verlag, 2011), 1:258–265; see below, Chapter 3.

177 Germantas-Meškauskas had been a student of the German Lithuanian Nazi philologist Jurgis Gerulis (Georg Gerullis). See above, Chapter 1.

role in the extermination of the country's provincial Jews in the summer and fall of 1941.[178]

Škirpa could not have known that on March 3, 1941, Hitler had ordered that emigrants from the USSR be excluded from plans for the political reorganization of future German-occupied areas, "especially from the former Baltic States," since he considered these countries nationalistic and thus potentially hostile to Germans (*deutschfeindlich*).[179] Despite the ultimately incompatible political goals of the Reich and the LAF, Škirpa continued to advocate for an alliance with Germany, even as Nazi contempt for Lithuanian national aspirations remained all too obvious. Desperate to secure support for their political aspirations, LAF ideologues hoped to gain support for a Lithuanian protectorate through fawning endorsements of Hitler's leadership and cringeworthy enthusiasm for the dawn of a racist "New Europe," which grew even more strident after the German invasion.[180] All this belied Škirpa's assurances to Lozoraitis, the American diaspora, and foreign ambassadors about a distinct "Lithuanian path" to the future. His attempts to portray geopolitical maneuvers as a shrewd gambit for power rather than slavish submission to the Germans, as well as the notion of a Lithuanian road to a political system distinct from a foreign fascist model, were disingenuous. In the end, the LAF's political ideology and its close ties to the Germans were to prove morally and politically catastrophic, their ambitious plans and hopes laid waste by the war and what followed in its aftermath.

---

178 See below, Chapter 4.
179 Dieckmann, *Besatzungspolitik*, 1:257.
180 On the glowing praise for the German invaders, see below, Chapter 3 and Chapter 6.

PART TWO

DESTRUCTION

3.

The Specter of Genocide: Invasion, Insurrection, and the Assault on the Jews, June 22–July 31, 1941

The annihilation of most of Lithuania's Jewish community during the summer and fall of 1941 constitutes the greatest eruption of violence in the country's modern history. The initial massacres of Jews occurred in western Lithuanian border towns and in Kaunas under conditions which were also, to some extent, characteristic of the early stages of Operation Barbarossa along the Eastern Front, particularly in Latvia and Western Ukraine. A concurrent uprising contributed to a rapid collapse of Soviet power amidst widespread chaos. A pervasive atmosphere of vengeance was amplified by the people's rage at the Kremlin's deportations carried out in the days before the war. Even more significant were the Lithuanian administrative and police structures created on the heels of the Soviet retreat, which were to become instruments in the Nazi-led campaign against Lithuanian Jewry. A closer examination of this history is essential for understanding the first steps on the road to destruction.

Vernichtungskrieg: Military Operations and Collateral Damage

There is reason to doubt the accepted uncritically accepted narrative that the annexation and Sovietization of Lithuania in 1940–1941 enhanced the security of the USSR by moving its borders westward, thus providing a supposed military bulwark against a German invasion. Stalin's decision to abandon the October 1939 mutual assistance treaties with the Baltic states and proceed with a military occupation of the region failed to protect the Soviet northern flank against a threat from the west. As some scholars have suggested, the military pacts, rather than outright annexation of their lands, might have provided a better Soviet strategy against Germany, acting as an early warning tripwire against an attack that would have prevented the enormous losses of men and equipment suffered during the first days of Operation Barbarossa.[1]

On June 22, 1941, the Wehrmacht's Army Group North, consisting of nearly 630,000 troops, attacked Soviet forces in northern and central Lithuania. The German forces broke through the Red Army border defenses, trapped and encircled many of the frontline units, and then pushed through the country in the first week of the invasion. Although there were instances of determined resistance, the Soviets fell back in retreat. The first detachments of the Sixteenth Army entered Kaunas on June 24. Meanwhile, southern Lithuania fell under the sector assigned to Army Group Center; here, units of the Ninth Army seized Alytus on the first day of the invasion and reached the outskirts of Vilnius by the evening of June 23. German soldiers entered the city at dawn on the next day. A battalion commander of the Seventh Panzer Division reported that his men found the historic capital "decorated with Lithuanian flags" and that the troops were "greeted with jubilation."[2] The Soviets had lost control of the country's two largest cities within forty-eight hours of the invasion. On June 27, German forces reached Daugavpils in Latvia. The Soviet military in Lithuania had been effectively routed in less than a week, although sporadic skirmishes with Red Army stragglers and armed Communist groups persisted in the aftermath. The speed of the German advance and the capture of thousands of Soviet troops encouraged a widespread belief that the destruction of Bolshevism was imminent.

This public confidence was in fact unwarranted. At the strategic level, the success of Barbarossa depended on a Blitzkrieg strategy which anticipated the rapid encirclement and destruction of Red Army divisions along the Soviet-German border. The risk of such a gamble was evident to the Nazi planners who understood that failure to achieve a quick victory would force Germany into a long and grueling war that would, in turn, drain the Reich's human and material resources. On June 27, Goebbels confided to his diary the fear that the Red Army would retreat prematurely (*vorzeitig*) and escape wholesale destruction. As it turned out, despite devastating losses, the greater part of the Soviet forces

---

1   See the argument in Romuald J. Misiunas and Rein Taagepera, *The Baltic States: Years of Dependence* (Berkeley: University of California Press, 1983), 44. As the authors point out: "The unusual speed of the German thrust is at least partially explained by the Stalinist feat of making the Baltic populations friendly towards the Germans."

2   As quoted in Prit Buttar, *Between Giants: The Battle for the Baltics in World War II* (Oxford: Osprey Publishing, 2013), 87.

on the northern and central sections of the Eastern Front escaped encirclement. By mid-July Wehrmacht commanders acknowledged that the Red Army had survived the offensive, conveying their disappointment in private messages and reports from the field. Writing weeks later, Goebbels admitted that the military predicament was "a difficult time for all of us," noting that between mid-July and mid-August Hitler had become increasingly "irritable." The Führer directed his anger at Jews. On August 19, Hitler spoke with Goebbels and reiterated his notorious prophecy that Jewish provocation of a global conflict would signal the annihilation of European Jewry.[3] "In the East," the Führer declared, "the Jews must pay the price."[4]

Whatever their operational miscalculations, the commanders were correct in their expectation that much of the populace in the western borderlands of the USSR would greet the Wehrmacht as a liberating army. The first German warplanes appeared in the skies only hours after the last trains of deportees had left Lithuania. The sounds of the guns must have come as relief to those who had anxiously watched the crowded cattle cars as they left the stations. The joyful reaction of thousands to the outbreak of war may seem bizarre, but only to those who had not undergone the experience. The Wehrmacht sought to reassure civilians of its intentions. The "Supreme Commander of the German Army" announced to the Lithuanian people that his soldiers were "friends and saviors from the Bolshevik yoke..., bringing freedom and restoring decent conditions of life." In the same announcement of German benevolence, the army warned that the invading troops would severely punish assistance to the enemy, including failure to reveal the whereabouts of Communist officials and Red Army personnel.[5]

Combat operations and military responses to perceived threats inflicted significant losses. The German air force bombed and strafed Lithuania's roads

---

3   In Hitler's speech to the Reichstag, January 30, 1939: "If international finance Jewry inside and outside Europe should succeed in plunging the nations once more into a world war, the result will be not the Bolshevization of the earth and thereby the victory of Jewry, but the annihilation of the Jewish race in Europe."

4   The relevant citations are in Dieckmann, *Besatzungspolitik*, 1:267–274, also see, ibid., 2:924.-925. On the consequences of German miscalculations, see David Stahel, "Radicalizing Warfare: The German Command and the Failure of Operation Barbarossa," in *Nazi Policy on the Eastern Front, 1941*, ed. Alex J. Kay, Jeff Rutherford, and David Stahel (Rochester, NY: University of Rochester Press, 2012), 19–44.

5   The text was published in provincial newspapers, as in *Naujosios Biržų žinios*, no. 1, July 19, 1941, 4.

which were clogged with refugees, including many Jews, as well as retreating Soviet soldiers. Many civilians were caught in the line of fire, while others perished at the hands of German troops who were intent on suppressing any perceived threats. On June 23, the commander of the hastily formed anti-Soviet rebel unit in Kazlų Rūda made an entry in his journal: "No shooting [today]. Overnight the casualties of the Red Army: 71 killed. Four Jews (local inhabitants) have also been killed."[6] After Soviet troops ambushed two German cyclists, soldiers of the Wehrmacht's 291st Infantry Division retaliated, massacring forty-two Lithuanian villagers in the hamlets of Ablinga and Žvaginiai and burning their homes. German soldiers also executed eleven men in the village of Švendūna as retribution for casualties inflicted by Soviet forces.[7]

In Alytus former members of the town's Riflemen's Union had assembled to fight the Soviets. The local Lithuanian police precinct, now controlled by insurgents, assigned groups of men to guard duty at various locations. The situation was chaotic: the precinct chief reported that "during the night of June 24 and 25 there was shooting between German sentries and local Communists." Five of the Alytus city Lithuanian policemen, all with German-language armbands issued by the city committee, were mistakenly detained and shot by the invaders.[8] When Soviet rearguard troops killed several Germans, Nazi soldiers shot two priests and several local policemen, then rounded up and executed scores of male suspects between the ages of fifteen and fifty. A police report of August 1941 counted "271 Germans, 247 Russians and 319 Lithuanians" among the wartime casualties in the district.[9] A study of the first three days of the war listed by name 154 men killed in "punitive German operations" in Alytus among whom were thirty-two Jews. In rural areas around Alytus, seventy-nine local people with mostly Lithuanian surnames were reported as "shot by Germans." Another estimated eighty civilians are thought to have been killed in bombings and "acts of war" in the city itself.[10] On June 25 in Židikai, a town on the Lithuanian-Latvian border, a unit of anti-Soviet insurgents, after an engagement with the retreating Red Army, were ferrying their wounded comrades in a lor-

---

6   Malakauskas report, LCVA, f. R-635, ap. 1, b.1, l. 25.
7   Dieckmann, *Besatzungspolitik* 1: 299.
8   LCVA, f. R-1436, "Raportas Alytaus apskr. viršininkui," July 1, 1941, ap. 1, b. 27, l. 58a.
9   Report on casualties in Alytus district, August 25, 1941, LCVA, f. R-1436, ap. 1, b. 48, l. 1.
10 Gintaras Lučinskas, *Vermachto nusikaltimai Dzūkijoje 1941 m. birželį* (Alytus: Gintarinė svajonė, 2011), 222–249.

ry flying the Lithuanian tricolor. An approaching Wehrmacht unit fired on the vehicle, killing everyone inside.[11]

Overt expressions of friendliness to the invaders did not guarantee safety. The fourteen-year-old Laimonas Noreika, who was to become one of Lithuania's premier actors, remembers what happened to an overly enthusiastic local as the Germans entered the working-class Kaunas suburb of Julijanava: "Our neighbor saw the Germans arriving on their motorcycles, and immediately ran through the rye fields, waving his arms in cheerful greeting. The [soldiers] began shouting something at him, but he couldn't understand and joyfully raced toward the men, so the Germans opened fire. Soon the man's wife came running to us for help, shrieking that they had killed her husband."[12] On the basis of German and Lithuanian materials, historian Christoph Dieckmann has concluded that these killings and other German punitive actions related to the exigencies of the military campaign resulted in about three hundred civilian deaths in the country, although the Alytus police report cited above indicates that the toll may have been higher.

"All necessary actions": The German Security Police and Mass Killings in the Border Zone

In the words of historian Alex J. Kay, while mass shootings of male Jews had been a mark of German military operations in Serbia in the spring of 1941, Operation Barbarossa "was the first campaign in which the systemic mass murder of Jews and other racial opponents was the order of the day from the very outset."[13] During the Polish campaign of 1939, the German military and the SS had difficulty in agreeing on the treatment of the civilian population, but by spring of 1941 the Wehrmacht and the Nazi security police had adopted a more coordinated approach in planning for the invasion of the USSR. All laws of war were to be ignored and the army was to take "ruthless and decisive actions against the Bolshevik rabble-rousers, partisans, Jews, and totally destroy any active or

---

11 Dieckmann, *Bezatzungspolitik*, 1:421.
12 Laimonas Noreika, "Mano 1941–1942 metai," *Metai* 5–6 (2001): 153.
13 Alex J. Kay, *Empire of Destruction: A History of Nazi Mass Killing* (New Haven: Yale University Press, 2021), 67.

passive resistance."[14] The German high command's infamous Commissar Order (Kommissarbefehl) issued on June 6, 1941, authorized the killing on the spot of Red Army political instructors (*politruki*).[15]

During the spring of 1941 four battalion-size Einsatzgruppen or "special action groups" (EG), totaling some three thousand men, came under the direction of Reinhard Heydrich, the head of the RSHA. In preparation for Barbarossa, the EG groups, denoted by the letters A to D, were deployed along the border with the USSR from the Baltic to the Black Sea. They were further subdivided into "action commandos" (Einsatzkommando, EK). These special operation units of the German Security Police were to follow the Wehrmacht into the Soviet Union and eliminate security threats in the areas behind the frontlines. In terms of the latter task, RSHA chief Heydrich provided guidance on the question of Jews and the actions of potential anti-Soviet elements to the German Security Police whose special forces had assembled to join the invasion of the USSR:

> The self-cleansing attempts of the local anti-Communist and anti-Jewish minded inhabitants in the newly occupied countries should not be hindered. On the contrary, they must be encouraged, of course, without a trace [back to us], and motivated, and when necessary, directed to the right path, but in such a way, that the local "self-defense units" could not later refer to the orders or the proclaimed political goals. . . . At the beginning, the formation of standing self-defense units controlled from the center must be avoided; instead, it is advisable to encourage local pogroms organized by the public, as noted before.[16]

---

14   From the Wehrmacht's guidelines "on the behavior of troops in Russia" issued on May 19, 1941, as quoted in Christoph Dieckmann and Saulius Sužiedėlis, Lietuvos žydų persekiojimas ir masinės žudynės 1941 m. vasarą ir rudenį: šaltiniai ir analizė / The Persecution and Mass Murder of Lithuanian Jews During Summer and Fall of 1941: Sources and Analysis (Vilnius: margi raštai, 2006), 111.

15   An English version of the Commissar Order is here: "Directives for the Treatment of Political Commissars ('Commissar Order') (June 6, 1941)," German History in Documents and Images 7, accessed July 27, 2023, https://germanhistorydocs.ghi-dc.org/pdf/eng/English58.pdf.

16   From Heydrich's June 29, 1941, telegram reaffirming the instructions given orally to the EG commanders "as far back as June 17," as quoted in Dieckmann, Bezatzungspolitik, 1:301. On July 1, 1941, in an order to the highest German Security Police officials Heydrich included virtually all captured Soviet officials, including "Jews in Party and state institutions," as subject to immediate execution (see text in ibid., 393).

The German Security Police interpreted the guidelines broadly and increasingly began to view all male Jews of military service age (usually between fifteen and sixty) as fitting the category of "potential resisters" and "carriers of Bolshevism," who needed to be neutralized as the front moved eastward.[17] EG A, under SS General Walter Stahlecker, which was to operate in the Baltic states, was the largest of the action groups. On June 24 Stahlecker met with SS Major Hans-Joachim Böhme, the head of the Tilsit police (*Polizeistelle*), and the town's chief of the SD. Böhme proposed "cleansing operations" (*Reinigungsaktionen*, or *Säuberungsaktionen*) against Communists and Jews to clear a twenty-five kilometer border zone in western Lithuania of allegedly dangerous and subversive elements, an operation which would allow other EG units to move more quickly eastward to take up the territory left behind by the rapidly retreating Soviet forces. Stahlecker agreed, and Böhme now headed a force which undertook "all necessary actions."[18] This decision resulted in the first mass murders of Jews in modern Lithuanian history.

The border town of Gargždai held a population of about three thousand, including seven hundred Jews among whom were refugees who had fled the German seizure of Klaipėda in March 1939. The Wehrmacht captured the town on the first day of the war but managed to secure the area only after intense combat, suffering more than a hundred casualties. Following the ambush of two German dispatchers, one of the officers complained about "treacherous civilians." To deal with this supposed security threat, the Tilsit commando reinforced their group with men from the Klaipėda/Memel city police (*Schutzpolizei*). This augmented German security force immediately began the arrests of alleged subversives. Böhme's men drove the male suspects to a field near the border, detaining the Jewish women and children in a nearby barn. On the morning of June 24, the Klaipėda Schutzpolizei arrived at the killing site. The Germans first forced the condemned men to bury the bodies of Red Army soldiers, and then to dig a huge pit for themselves. The director of the Klaipėda police, Bernhard Fischer-Schweder, gave a speech to the assembled policemen, alleging that civilians had fired on the German forces. The records indicate that the police killed two

---

17 See Dieckmann and Sužiedėlis, *Mass Murder*, 106–120, and in greater detail, Dieckmann, *Besatzungspolitik*, 1:178ff.; cf. Kay, *Empire*, 67–71.

18 Böhme's claim during his postwar trial (the *Ulmer Einsatzgruppenprozess* of the late 1950s) that the RSHA office in Berlin had ordered the killings has now been questioned in the face of new research. See Dieckmann, *Besatzungspolitik*, 1:380–382.

hundred men and a Soviet commissar's Russian wife. Most of the victims were Jews. The Germans, including Wehrmacht personnel, reportedly carried out this first mass shooting without local assistance, an unusual circumstance in the history of the Holocaust in Lithuania.[19]

The Gargždai massacre provided a template for further "cleansing" in the designated border zone. Kretinga, a historic border town of some eight thousand inhabitants twenty kilometers north of Klaipėda, was next. According to Soviet estimates, nearly four thousand Jews lived in the Kretinga district on the eve of the war. The Germans had met little resistance as they swept into town during the first hours of the invasion. Böhme appointed Pranas Jakys,[20] the former Kretinga security chief who had fled to Germany in 1940 and had joined the SD, to head the local police. The anti-Soviet partisans quickly established an LAF unit and with Jakys's encouragement began to compile lists of local Communists. On June 24, the German military commandant ordered all Kretinga men between the ages of fourteen and sixty to gather in the market square. German troops and the hastily organized Lithuanian auxiliary force rounded up hundreds of men (according to one source, as many as two thousand) in the center of town and ordered all Jews, Communists, Komsomol members, and "Soviet activists" to step forward. Since few wished to identify themselves as the enemy, the auxiliary police charged into the crowd and began to seize Jews and alleged Soviet collaborators, beating, abusing, and humiliating the men, reportedly settling personal scores as well. The suspects were corralled into a collective farm overnight and on the following day were escorted out to repair bridges and roads.

On June 25, Böhme's task force herded both the Jewish men and alleged Lithuanian Soviet activists to woods located five kilometers from Kretinga. The German police, along with Jakys and his Lithuanian deputy, called out the men and demanded that they account for their activities during Soviet rule, releasing

---

19 Fischer-Schweder case records (author's archive), deposition of Emil Thomsen, March 15, 1958, Ulm. For a detailed account of the Gargždai massacre, see Joachim Tauber, "Garsden, 24 Juni 1941," *Annaberger Annalen* 5 (1997): 117–134. More information on Gargždai, including accounts of Lithuanian witnesses, is in research collected by the students of the town's secondary school, "Holokaustas prasidėjo Gargžduose," in *Mūsų senelių ir prosenelių kaimynai žydai*, ed. Linas Vildžiūnas (Vilnius: Atminties namai, 2007), 138–154.

20 During the Ulm trial, Jakys is listed as "Pranas Lukys." He explained that his Jakys surname came about because of a transliteration error on his tsarist Russian birth certificate. Fischer-Schweder case records (author's archive), preliminary interrogation of Pranas Lukys, February 22, 1957.

about thirty to thirty-five of the detained ethnic Lithuanians. None of the Jews were given a reprieve except for one man who claimed to have served in the German army during the Great War. Fischer-Schweder commanded the operation which killed 214 men and one woman; an estimated 180 of the victims were Jews. Most of the Jewish women and children were confined to a local school and later transferred to a camp outside the town. The police jailed another group of Jewish men in the Kretinga synagogue, which was later set ablaze under suspicious circumstances. The fire spread through the town, triggering a wave of looting by German troops, local police, and criminals, after which fifteen Jewish men were executed. In Kretinga, smaller scale killings of Jews and suspected Communists continued until the annihilation of the Jewish community in September 1941.

The Germans now turned their attention to Palanga, a resort town on Lithuania's Baltic coast with a population of some seven hundred Jews that had fallen to the Germans during the first hours of the invasion. After the Soviets fled, a provisional Lithuanian municipal committee had quickly established a rudimentary local administration and police force. Following Böhme's instructions, the local Lithuanian police rounded up Palanga's Jews and jailed them in the local synagogue on June 26. On the next day officials of the SD and police convoyed the detained Jewish men to the sand dunes on the Baltic coast where they were shot in an operation commanded by Edwin Sakuth and the Klaipėda police adjutant Werner Schmidt-Hammer. According to postwar German testimony, the Tilsit men, assisted by twenty Wehrmacht soldiers, were thorough in their work, even hunting down a Jewish pediatrician who had been treating wounded German soldiers, the last of the 111 victims killed that day. The police transferred the Jewish women and children to a camp at the village of Valteriškė where most of them survived until the mass murder campaign of the late summer and fall of 1941.

When the Nazi forces entered Darbėnai, they found eight hundred Jews, about 40% of the town's population. The invaders mobilized Jews to clean toilets, sweep streets, and perform other humiliating menial tasks. On June 24, the Germans set the town on fire and blamed Jews, whereupon the military commandant ordered them to wear yellow patches. German soldiers killed the town's rabbi and several other Jewish men accused of Communist activity. On June 28, the local Lithuanian partisans rounded up the town's Jews for transfer to Kretinga, but for some reason, convoyed the victims back to Darbėnai on the same day. The ordeal exhausted the Jews, who were refused food and water. On the next day, a group of officers arrived in Darbėnai, selected the Jewish men, and escorted them to a wooded area outside of the town. The Germans then shot nearly 150 Jewish men and four Soviet prisoners of war with automatic weapons. The Lithuanian partisans confined the Jewish women and children in the town's synagogue for several weeks and forced some of the adults to work for the local farmers. Sources report that the guards kept their charges on starvation rations, while tormenting the inmates, especially the women.[21] Killings in other towns along the border zone in western Lithuania continued into the first week of July. The German Security Police and the Wehrmacht rationalized their actions of the first week as security operations in support of the military campaign.

The Tilsit killing unit continued their work into July and, along with their helpers among the Lithuanian auxiliary police, massacred at least 5,500 mostly civilian Jewish men in the designated border zone.[22]

The June Insurrection, Imagined Liberation, and "Vengeance on the Run"

The Wehrmacht's campaign and the first killing operations of the German Security Police were carried out against a backdrop of concurrent social violence and political revolution. War had come to a country which in the previous year had undergone wrenching transformations within a cauldron of social, ethnic, economic, and political tensions.[23] Numerous accounts relate the relief and exaltation at the news of the long-awaited war. On the morning of June 22, the young Noreika ran outside to investigate the explosions. He recalled that soon "a neighbor came running, reporting happily that Kaunas was already liberated, and that the city's people are attacking the fleeing Russians. Only a week before people were being jammed into cattle cars and shipped towards Belarus. At that time, a terrible fear and uncertainty had suffused the city, so the happiness that

---

21 Dieckmann, *Besatzungspolitik*, 1:380–386; cf. the entries for Gargždai, Kretinga, Palanga, and Darbėnai in Arūnas Bubnys, *Holokaustas Lietuvos provincijoje 1941 metais* (Vilnius: margi raštai, 2021), 153–166, 178–181, 185–192.

22 As in the towns of Tauragė, Švėkšna, and other communities in the regions, see below, Chapter 4.

23 See above, Chapter 2; cf. Saulius Sužiedėlis, "'Listen, the Jews Are Ruling Us Now': Antisemitism and National Conflict During the First Year of Soviet Occupation," *Polin* 25 (2013): 305–333.

the Russians were fleeing was understandable. On that day or the next, the Germans appeared."[24] (As related above, this same neighbor was shortly to die at the hands of the presumed liberators.) In contrast to such enthusiasm, most Jews reacted in panic. One of the few Lithuanian observers who saw a different picture described the cruel and impossible situation of Jews during the first hours of the invasion. Elena Kutorgienė-Buivydaitė wrote in her journal on the second day of the invasion:

> The condition of the Jews is shocking.... The son of my Jewish neighbor, a good fellow, escaped from home with his backpack. The father will also leave soon. He came to me and asked to help his family. He said that maybe the Germans would not kill women and children.... They started packing up, but later the husband and the wife just left as they stood, the latter only with her handbag. The Jews were fleeing with bags, prams, trunks, bundles, and some just empty-handed... with anxious and pale faces.[25]

It is notable that such tragic accounts are, for the most part, characteristic of Jewish accounts of the invasion. Many Lithuanians observed fleeing Jews with satisfaction, even contempt.

In his diary journalist Rapolas Mackonis waxed poetic in describing Vilnius on June 24: "At about six o'clock I heard cars and the roar of engines. Bolsheviks or Germans? I questioned a fellow walking near the bridge about what was happening in the city. 'They're ours [mūsiškiai],' he answered, elated. 'What do you mean "ours?"' I ask. 'Germans.' I couldn't contain my joy. 'Germans,' the word, as if voiced by the clear blue sky, the radiant sun, the soft, gentle summer wind. 'Germans!' The word resounded throughout liberated Lithuania. Throngs of people poured into the streets, embracing and kissing, some weeping with joy."[26]

The renowned feminist archeologist and UCLA professor Marija Gimbutas (1921–1994) shared in the joy. She was in Kaunas as the bombs fell on the Sunday morning of the attack. The twenty-year-old student expressed her hatred for the Soviet occupiers:

---

24 Noreika, "Mano": 153.
25 Selection taken from the June 23, 1941 entry in the diary of Elena Kutorgienė-Buivydaitė, in Dieckmann and Sužiedėlis, *Lietuvos žydų persekiojimas*, 104.
26 The excerpts are from the diary attached to the Soviet police interrogation file of Rapolas Mackonis, LYA, f. K-1, ap. 58, b. 20317/3, l. 18—henceforth, Mackonis diary.

> War today! For life or death. For freedom, for dearest Lithuania. Against the murderers, against the damned barbarians..., oh, my rage is burning. One can almost hear something prophetic in the sounds coming from the symphony of the warplanes. A happier morning will now dawn. The sirens are shrieking. In any case, the beasts will flee and perish. In this past year, they have tortured, murdered, and looted enough.

On the following day, as the Soviet troops abandoned Kaunas, Gimbutas's mood changed from rage and contempt for the retreating Stalinists to euphoria about the pending restoration of the country:

> The beasts are already in retreat. Exhausted, hungry soldiers are dragging themselves along the streets of Kaunas; soldiers who didn't understand what they were fighting for. Meanwhile, the hangmen, the dogs, were the first to flee.... A free independent Lithuania.... I'm hearing the national anthem on the radio. A new government, they are golden people. The tricolor is once again shimmering above Freedom Boulevard. It's like a dream, and my heart is less heavy. Perhaps, this slavery will collapse entirely, that gang of animals, of the most carnivorous beasts! Perhaps, people will now breathe a sigh of relief.[27]

The newsreels of Lithuanian girls greeting German soldiers with flowers are a well-known image, but it is one which, for many at the time, reflected a genuine sense of deliverance.

Gimbutas was initially frustrated at her inability to join the rebels: "the barbarians are shooting at people on the streets, I can't reach the activist ranks." Her fiancée Jurgis and some friends joined the fighters for a two-day battle with the Soviets, while Marija worked at the insurgents' headquarters. She found her duties heartbreaking: running errands for the Red Cross, and worst of all, tasked with the work of registering dead partisans, "our youngest and bravest."[28]

Marija and Jurgis joined thousands of mostly young people in the uprising that erupted upon news of the German attack. As Lithuania's Soviet leaders fled in the face of the German onslaught, jailers abandoned their posts and many inmates broke out of their cells, thus evading evacuation to the Russian

---

27 Marija Gimbutienė, *Dienoraštis ir prisiminimai*, ed. Živilė Gimbutaitė (Kaunas: Naujasis lankas, 2015), 97 (diary entry for June 22–23, 1941).

28 Ibid., 97–98 (entry for June 28, 1941); cf. Gimbutas's reminiscences written in April 1945 below, Chapter 6.

interior, or worse. In the confusion, insurgents broke into abandoned armories or simply wrested weapons from retreating Red Army men. Fighting between Soviet troops and the rebels broke out in Kaunas, mainly at the strategic bridges across the Nemunas River and at the Metalas factory, where the Lithuanians had managed to assemble a substantial force. In general, however, the speed of the German advance meant that only some of the anti-Soviet irregulars engaged in significant battles with the Soviet forces. Nonetheless, the rebels' disruption of communications and seizure of radio stations hampered the Red Army's attempts to organize a coordinated defense and contributed to the panic among top Soviet officials and their staff. In some places, rebels captured local government offices without resistance, but elsewhere skirmishes erupted between the rebels and local pro-Soviet groups, such as the Komsomol.

The LAF, despite its claim as the undisputed leader of the anti-Soviet movement, was a political coalition not widely known in Lithuania before the invasion. Some insurgents came from the remnants of the anti-Soviet underground within Lithuania which had escaped detection by the NKVD, but many others joined the uprising on the spot, particularly in the countryside. Most were young. In the days before the German attack, some men had hidden in the forests to avoid the deportations and now emerged to join the fight. In the words of Juozas Vėbra, a former colonel who had been working as a chemistry professor after the Soviet reorganization of the Lithuanian army: "I first heard about the Lithuanian Activist Front from Mr. L. Prapuolenis at the beginning of the uprising. Earlier I had not participated in this organization." Vėbra quickly joined the "activists" and accompanied Prapuolenis with several other LAF underground leaders to the Kaunas radio station on the morning of June 23, 1941, where, according to his account, they found sentries "composed of local Communists (at the gate we found one of my former students standing guard, a Jewish fellow, of course)." The men quickly brushed past the Communists, who offered no resistance, and went on to broadcast the restoration of Lithuania's independence. As an experienced officer, Vėbra was then assigned to the rebels' headquarters.[29] There were also scores of Lithuanians who had trained in East Prussia and had slipped back into the country before the German attack or had arrived with the

---

29   From Vėbra's letter to A. Gražiūnas as quoted in Jankauskas, *1941 m. birželio sukilimas*, 11, also 109–110, 138–147. Leonas Prapuolenis, one of the founders of the LAF underground, made the announcement on the radio in Lithuanian, followed by the reading in German (by Adolfas Damušis), and in French by Vėbra who had studied in France during the 1930s.

Wehrmacht and Nazi Security Police during the invasion. Some were closely tied to the LAF, while others, for example, Pranas Jakys in Kretinga and Stasys Čenkus, the future head of the collaborationist Lithuanian Security Police (L. Lietuviu Saugumo policija, LSP), were German agents posing as "activists." Another anti-Soviet cohort emerged from the Voldemarists.[30]

The soldiers of the Red Army's Lithuanian Twenty-Ninth Territorial Riflemen's Corps provided another source of recruits, both for the uprising and, later, for the militarized police units under the Germans. Just as Soviet security had feared, most Lithuanian Red Army men showed no interest in dying for Stalin. At the outbreak of the war, the majority of the 184th Division of the Corps deserted, and, in some cases, troops mutinied against orders to withdraw to the Russian interior. In Vilnius rebellious Lithuanian officers and soldiers ambushed Soviet convoys and assisted the insurgents in seizing the radio station. The troops of the 179th Division were stationed further east and thus were less able to abandon their posts but even here some of the men succeeded in slipping away. It is estimated that no more than a fifth of the nearly twelve thousand men of the Twenty-Ninth Corps remained with their units and retreated eastward. Unlike in Kaunas where the rebels had engaged the Red Army in pitch battles, Soviet resistance in Vilnius was minimal and the rebels suffered, at most, a few dozen casualties. It should be noted that unlike the Russian Soviet POWs, most Lithuanian Red Army men who surrendered to the Germans were soon freed.[31]

The nomenclature attributed in the sources to the participants of the 1941 June uprising can be confusing. As in Vėbra's case, many of the rebels who attacked the retreating Soviet forces had little or no previous connection to the LAF. German and Lithuanian officials, who registered local men joining the police groups, labeled former rebels variously as "activists," "partisans," or "insurgents" (L. *sukilėliai, partizanai*, G.. *Aufständische, Partisanen*). People dubbed the men with guns the "white armbands" (L. *baltaraiščiai*). These designations for the emerging Lithuanian auxiliary police, many of whom had joined their units after the uprising, continued for weeks after the insurrection had ended when these terms no longer described their role within the emerging

---

30 See above, Chapter 2.
31 See pages 26–32 in Stasys Knezys, "Nusikalstamos okupacinės politikos sistema—karinių struktūrų vaidmuo ir kolaboravimas su jomis," Komisija.It, accessed May 19, 2019, https://www.komisija.lt/wp-content/uploads/2016/06/S.-Knezio-mokslinis-darbas-%E2%80%9ENusikalst...%E2%80%9C-lietuvi%C5%B3-k..pdf.

administrative structures of the German occupation.³² These terms of the earlier period are even less useful when describing the perpetrators of the killings in September and October 1941, the majority of which were carried out by uniformed police and police battalion members under a recognizable command-and-control system with the Germans at the head.

Despite the chaos and confusion of the first days, LAF leaders did not lose sight of their political goals. On June 23, 1941, the hastily assembled group of activists proclaimed the restoration of Lithuania's independence, announcing the formation of the Lithuanian Provisional Government (Lietuvos laikinoji vyriausybė, PG). In place of Škirpa, whom the Germans had detained in Berlin, the LAF chose Juozas Ambrazevičius (1903–1974), a Catholic literary scholar, as acting prime minister. The announcement of the formation of the new cabinet on the radio, accompanied by the playing of the national anthem, captured the patriotic emotions of much of the populace. Despite the euphoria at the expulsion of the Soviets and widespread public support, the PG found itself in an untenable position from the very beginning. The government, such as it was, claimed the high ground of popular sovereignty, but its decision-making ability was severely restricted, first by the Wehrmacht's commandants and then, in its final days, by the German Civil Administration (Zivilverwaltung, ZV). Furthermore, as an LAF-dominated body it reflected the ideological and geopolitical position of Škirpa and his Berlin associates. The June 23 radio proclamation issued by the LAF Staff in Kaunas announced that "the constitution of the Republic of Lithuania suspended by the Bolshevik occupation on June 15, 1940 is now again in force" and that the appointed ministers would rule accordingly.³³ The PG called on former officials to replace the Communist bureaucracy and instructed them, until informed otherwise, to resume their duties "on the basis of the laws of the independent Republic of Lithuania which had been in effect [before the Soviet occupation]."³⁴ Thus, the new Lithuania proclaimed on June 23, 1941, was rhetorically a restoration of the First Republic; but in both spirit

---

32 For example, the Jäger Report refers to the Lithuanian auxiliary police who participated in the roundup of the victims in Rokiškis in August 1941 as "partisans." This study utilizes terminology appropriate to the given functions of the security services after the end of the uprising, thus "police" or "auxiliary police." The term "soldiers" is sometimes appropriate in describing the men of the Lithuanian police battalions (see below, Chapter 6).

33 The document is published in Jankauskas, *1941 m. birželio sukilimas*, 110.

34 For example, as stated in Order No. 1 of Kostas Kalendra, the director of Internal Affairs of the District of Vilnius [undated], author's archive.

and letter, the PG departed from the legacy of the state created in 1918. The PG's decrees segregating and expropriating Jews violated the Lithuanian constitution of 1938 that had affirmed citizens' equality under the law without regard to nationality or religion. The cabinet of ministers acknowledged as much during a discussion on the disposition of nationalized property in July. Simply put, the authoritarian and antisemitic elements of LAF ideology broke with the civic norms and legal standards of the First Republic.

Before the collapse of the USSR, most historians outside Lithuania had either ignored or minimized the June insurrection, while Soviet historiography denigrated the rebel movement as a traitorous fifth column. Despite the hopes of LAF leaders, the PG failed to extend effective control over much of the country, let alone restore a Lithuanian state. Yet studying the uprising is important in making sense of the history which followed, as well as in understanding the myth-making and selective remembrance which has since surrounded the event. The "days of June" became the centerpiece of a national narrative emphasizing martyrdom (the deportations of June 14–17, 1941), heroic resistance (the anti-Soviet uprising), and political legitimacy (the proclamation of independence). On July 9, 1941, the newspaper *Žemaičių žemė* (The Land of Samogitia) published "An Outline of the Activity of the Lithuanian Activist Front," which claimed that thirty-six thousand had participated in the uprising, some four thousand fighters had given their lives to liberate the homeland, and one hundred thousand men had joined the ranks of the LAF.[35] Lithuanians often cited such inflated numbers to impress the Germans, and years after the war, apologists for the Front also offered the exaggerated statistics as proof of patriotism. At least one Jewish author accepted the same unreal data as evidence of massive pro-Nazi collaboration.[36] Research conducted since 1990 has vanquished the hyperbole. An LAF document of late June 1941 listed nearly 3,500 members of "temporary partisan groups" in Kaunas and environs. This and other records of rebel units point to a sensible nationwide estimate of about sixteen to twenty thousand participants in the uprising. Newspapers reported that sixty-four insurgents were solemnly buried in Kaunas on June 26 and subsequent claims of

---

35 "Lietuvių Aktyvistų Fronto metmenys," *Žemaičių žemė*, July 9, 1941, as published in Truska and Vareikis, Holokausto prielaidos, 319.

36 Sara Shner-Neshamit, "Lithuanian-Jewish Relations during World War II: History and Rhetoric," in *Bitter Legacy: Confronting the Holocaust in the USSR*, ed. Zvi Gitelman (Bloomington: Indiana University Press, 1997), 170.

some two hundred rebel casualties in the city seem credible enough. Documentation from other regions suggests that it is unlikely that total casualties among the anti-Soviet fighters in Lithuania exceeded five to six hundred persons.[37]

As the rebels acquired firepower, pitched battles erupted between opponents and backers of Soviet rule. In some cases, the rebels invoked the assistance of the German invaders, while pro-Soviet elements looked for help from Red Army and NKVD units still in the area. In 1942 the Lithuanian Communist leadership in Moscow collected statements of evacuated Party activists on their "defense of Soviet power" which painted a mosaic of the social violence that gripped Lithuania's towns and villages during the military campaign and insurrection.[38] Youths discovered with Komsomol identification cards were sometimes shot on the spot by the insurgents, while, for their part, Party activists gunned down alleged "fascists" and "bandits." Smallholders who had received Soviet-requisitioned land from their "bourgeois" neighbors cowered in fear of retribution. Years later, Petras Šmila from Kvetkai village recalled how a group of Soviet activists from the Zarasai and Raseiniai districts headed east but failed to reach safety:

> Here [in Kvetkai] the Germans shot Communists from the Zarasai and Raseiniai districts who were caught as they escaped eastward in June 1941. The women were traveling in wagons, while the men walked alongside. It was a long column of about fifty people, armed with guns. They entered Kvetkai and came into a shop for something to eat, just as a column of Germans arrived in their tankettes. Near the old school, today's post office, Lithuanian partisans had gathered, probably the "white armbands." A shoot-out broke out. After it ended, we found 32 dead. The Germans brought by lorry those who had been hiding in the basement of the post office, they [prisoners] had their hands up. They took them behind the cemetery and shot them. Pranciškus Šiaučiūnas (now deceased) brought them there. The headman told me to bury them. We dug a large pit and interred them, laying them down in two rows, One Jew happened by who said that he had been traveling [with the Soviet activists], so they shot him as well. He lies there as the 33rd one. They called him Zrolya. At the same time, they shot the day laborer Marcinkevičius, his pregnant wife, and their young daughter. They buried the family in a common grave without a coffin and no marker. They put me against the wall

---

37   Brandišauskas, *Siekiai*, 79–88.
38   Valentinas Brandišauskas, ed. *1941 m. birželio sukilimas: dokumentų rinkinys* (Vilnius: LGGRTC, 2000), 296–347.

as well, thinking that I'm a Communist and wanted to shoot me along with the others, but their commander released me, because I could speak a little German (my mother spoke it well, as we had been servants to a homeowner in Riga). I had a medal and showed it to him as proof that I was a Catholic, so they released me.[39]

There are no reliable estimates of the toll exacted by similar clashes, but it is reasonable to assume that these internecine firefights and killings resulted in hundreds of deaths. As the fighting subsided, the hunt for Soviet collaborators continued. According to the final June report of the German 281st Security Division, partisans operating in Pilviškiai quickly arrested thirty suspects, "unmasking" fifteen of these detainees as "arch-Communists" and sympathizers of the Red Army who had snitched on German-friendly locals and had even "shot a few Lithuanians." The division's officers found charges against twelve of the alleged traitors to be groundless, but three suspects were turned over to the newly formed Lithuanian police.[40] In nearby Kudirkos Naumiestis the local partisans shot nine suspected Lithuanian Soviet collaborators, including a fifteen-year-old boy whose crime was leading a chapter of the Soviet Pioneers youth organization. There are reports of rebels killing Communists on the first days of the war in Alytus and instances of such murders in eastern Lithuania before the Germans had arrived in the region. Sources describe the humiliation, torture, and even mutilation of real and alleged Soviet collaborators. A detailed study published in 2005 calculated the probable number of politically motivated executions of ethnic Lithuanian Communists and alleged Soviet collaborators during the German occupation at about two thousand, the majority killed in 1941.[41]

The former deputy of the People's Diet, Liudas Dovydėnas, was arrested by insurgents and detained along with a group of Jews. Describing the atmosphere,

---

39 Excerpted from a March 11, 1978, interview published in I. Kopchenova et al., eds. *Evrei na karte Litvy. Birzhai: Problemy sokhraneniiya͞ evreiskogo naslediiya͞i istoricheskoii pamyati* (Moscow: Sefer, 2015), 203.

40 Dieckmann, *Besatzungspolitik*, 1:309–310.

41 Julija Šukys *Siberian Exile: Blood, War and a Granddaughter's Reckoning* (Lincoln: University of Nebraska Press, 2017), 37; cf. Christoph Dieckmann, Vytautas Toleikis, and Rimantas Zizas, *Karo belaisvių ir civilių gyventojų žudynės Lietuvoje, 1941–1944. Murders of Prisoners of War and of Civilian Population in Lithuania, 1941–1944, Totalitarinių režimų nusikaltimai Lietuvoje* (Vilnius: Margi rastai, 2005); see also Michael MacQueen, "Jews in the Reichskommissariat Ostland, June–December 1941: From White Terror to Holocaust in Lithuania," in Gitelman, *Bitter Legacy*, 91–103.

he wrote that "when the German-Russian war broke out, some were seized by a kind of rage and a passion for revenge.... Watching the participation of previously innocent youth in this was especially distressing."[42] The disorder provided cover for criminal lawlessness, numerous robberies, public beatings, rapes, and even murders, a crime wave chronicled by the insurgents themselves. A month after the uprising the partisan Gracius Remesa reported that "One could see that there were two kinds of our soldiers [that is, rebels—S. S.]: some grabbed a rifle and went to fight for the fatherland, others broke into the stores, the apartments of the refugees and other private citizens, and wherever they could, they stole, they plundered, burying their loot."[43] Some of the rebels sought to restrain the criminal elements: when Elena Nikolayevna, a Russian officer's wife, came to the partisans' headquarters to complain that she had been robbed, two rebels returned her property and detained the culprit, stating that "such a person does not deserve to be a partisan."[44]

On June 24 the PG warned that partisans were firing their weapons "needlessly and too often" and admonished fighters who were "settling accounts with persons whom they detest," insisting that "all the scum who have transgressed against the Lithuanian nation will receive their punishment in the courts."[45] On the same day the newly appointed Lithuanian commandant of Kaunas, Colonel Jurgis Bobelis, issued Order No. 6: "It has been observed that some elements are trying to commit break-ins, robberies and other crimes. I warn them: these types of criminals, thieves, robbers, and the like will be executed on the spot."[46] During their cabinet meeting of June 25 the PG ministers noted "the heroic campaigns" of the insurgents, approved the organization of a police force in Kaunas, and encouraged "the expansion of partisan activities in the provinces where there are still residual gangs of Bolsheviks, Communists and Jews." At the same time the government urged local leaders "to dismiss as quickly as possible

---

42 Liudas Dovydėnas, *Mes valdysime pasaulį*, 2:466.
43 Quoted in Brandišauskas, *1941 m. birželio sukilimas*, 55.
44 Ibid., 51. It is telling that in 1942 former rebels became eligible for social benefits as "partisans" only if they had joined the ranks before the arrival of the German forces, had not "besmirched their name by stealing property," and had not acted against the "interests of the nation" during the Soviet period. As related in Valentinas Brandišauskas, "Sukilimo faktografiniai aspektai," 7 (unpublished ms).
45 "Šaulių ir partizanų žiniai," *Į laisvę*, June 24, 1941, 1.
46 Bobelis Order No. 6, June 24, 1941, LCVA, f. R-1444, ap. 1, b. 8, l.11.

the undesirable element which has opportunistically infiltrated the partisans."⁴⁷ But the mayhem was not easily suppressed. Two weeks later Bobelis was forced to warn the public that "people of ill will" were committing "unauthorized searches and assaults."⁴⁸

IMAGE 3.1. Meeting of the Provisional Government's cabinet chaired by Acting Prime Minister Juozas Ambrazevičius. (Undated; public domain.)

The retreating Red Army, the NKVD, and Communist activists took action against real and imagined enemies of Soviet power, a series of killings later characterized in Lithuanian documents as "vengeance on the run." On the night of June 24, Soviet prison guards and NKVD men murdered seventy-three political prisoners in the Rainiai woods near the town of Telšiai. On the next day, a Soviet armored unit massacred an estimated 230 inmates and their guards at the Pravieniškės labor camp located twelve kilometers from Kaunas. Nearly a hundred other Lithuanian prisoners were evacuated from the city eastward and some of them were killed by the NKVD in Minsk; then, as the German army closed in, more were shot near the Belarusian town of Chervene on June 27, 1941. Smaller-scale punitive actions took place in Panevėžys and other locales: in total, it is

---

47 Arvydas Anušauskas, ed. *Lietuvos laikinoji vyriausybė: posėdžių protokolai* (Vilnius: LGGRTC, 2001), 11 (henceforth, *LLV*).
48 Bobelis Order No. 14, July 8, 1941, LCVA, f. R-1444, ap. 1, b.8, l. 39.

3. The Specter of Genocide 177

IMAGE 3.2. Mutiny and Insurrection, late June 1941. Above: Lithuanian officers and enlisted men of the Twenty-Ninth Soviet Riflemen's Corps gathered in Cathedral Square in Vilnius after their desertion from the Red Army. Below: Insurgents ("white armbands") escorting Soviet POWs in Kaunas. (Source—public domain.)

IMAGE 3.3. Red Army massacre of prisoners and staff at the Pravieniškės labor camp, June 26, 1941. (Source—public domain.)

estimated that Communist forces murdered nearly one thousand unarmed civilians within the first five days of the war.[49] The Soviets carried out similar massacres in the other Baltic states and, on a much larger scale, in western Ukraine.

It would be unprincipled to equate these Soviet killings to the immeasurably greater scale of the atrocities carried out under German leadership during the summer and fall of 1941. Nonetheless, the Soviet massacres provided a propaganda windfall for the Nazis and their collaborators. The photographic record of the aftermath of the violence provided graphic evidence of the evils of Bolshevism, adding impetus to the LAF's dire warnings against "traitors" among the population. In the wake of the invasion the anti-Soviet media urged the people to join the battle against Bolshevism. On June 29, 1941, the Vilnius daily newspaper *Naujoji Lietuva* (New Lithuania) exhorted the citizens of the city and region to act "in a radical fashion" to assist security forces in liquidating "the hostile element left behind,"[50] that is, Soviet activists and sympathizers. The incendiary rhetoric undercut the PG's published appeals to observe judicial norms.

---

49 Details are in Arvydas Anusauskas, *Lietuvių tautos sovietinis naikinima: 1940–1958 metais* (Vilnius: Mintis, 1996).

50 Dieckmann, Toleikis, Zizas, *Karo belaisvių*, 98.

The publicity surrounding Stalinist crimes reinforced the already prevalent Judeo-Bolshevik mythology and intensified hatred of the Jews who, as alleged Bolshevik allies, could now be blamed not only for the deportations of June 14–17 but for complicity in murder as well. The gruesome details of the torture of the political prisoners at the Rainiai woods were tailor-made for anti-Jewish incitement. After the victims were discovered, anti-Soviet activists drove the Jews of Rainiai to the killing site, forcing them to bury the dead in a humiliating ritual justified as atonement for the community's alleged treason.[51] Coercing Jews into burial work is described in other sources as well. The partisan Kęstutis Miklaševičius wrote the following about the aftermath of a battle on the Aukštieji Šančiai neighborhood in Kaunas on June 25: "The Jews who have been rounded up are now digging graves for their Red 'comrades.'"[52] Laimonas Noreika recalled an encounter at the Aleksotas bridge in Kaunas: "One man warns us not to go further, they're grabbing people to collect the bodies from the bridge, but another fellow says to go on: they're only taking Jews. Here we see eight, maybe ten Jewish women, surrounded by a few men."[53] While everyone connected to the Soviet regime was in peril, the breakdown of authority and the sense of impunity which facilitated violence proved particularly lethal for Lithuania's Jews.

Judeo-Bolshevik Propaganda and Pogroms: The First Days

From the very beginning of the anti-Soviet insurrection, Lithuanian print and radio media trumpeted the Judeo-Bolshevik nexus. The first issue of the LAF's daily *Į laisvę* (Towards Freedom), which appeared in Kaunas on June 24, exulted in the defeat of the Communist enemy: "We are witnessing how those who had tortured, suppressed, and enslaved us . . . are now fleeing Lithuania. The Russian army units are retreating from Kaunas." In the same breath, the editors emphasized, in capitalized text: "THE BOLSHEVIK ACCOMPLICES, THE JEWS, ARE ALSO FLEEING AT BREAKNECK SPEED. FOR THEM, COMMUNISM WAS THE BEST MEANS BY WHICH TO EXPLOIT OTHERS AND TO RULE, BECAUSE

---

51 The practice of Jews exhuming and reburying bodies of the victims of Soviet massacres as "penance" was widespread in western Ukraine as well.
52 Brandišauskas, *1941 m.*, 50.
53 Noreika, "Mano": 153.

Bolshevism and the Jews are one and the same, inseparable." The image of Jews escaping east together with the Russian enemy reinforced the widely assumed Jewish connection to the Soviet occupiers. *Į laisvę* also made certain that its readers understood the difference between Jews, on the one hand, and "Lithuanian mercenaries who served Russian Bolshevism," on the other. Jews, the paper claimed, had "grown horns" while cynically adapting to Soviet power, happily directing socialist institutions as easily as they had once dominated "stores, factories and banks" under capitalism. They were beyond redemption. But the Lithuanian traitors warranted understanding: "These are pathetic people, *deserving of pity*, who have been deceived and disappointed. They thought that they were working for the good of the people and common folk, but actually, they served Russian imperialism" (emphasis added).[54]

On July 4, 1941, *Naujoji Lietuva* [New Lithuania], the daily that was the mouthpiece of the rebels' Vilnius City Committee, published an even more vicious lead editorial. Amidst the usual gratitude to Greater Germany for the liberation from Soviet oppression and the importance of a "common front" against

IMAGE 3.4.
Antisemitic Propaganda.
Top: The front page of the LAF newspaper *Į laisvę*, June 24, 1941, celebrating the restoration of a "free Lithuania," the retreat of the Russian army and "the headlong flight of the Bolsheviks' Jewish accomplices." Bottom: The Vilnius daily, *Naujoji Lietuva*, July 4, 1941, advocating a "Lithuania without Jews." (Courtesy of Martynas Mažvydas National Library of Lithuania.)

---

54 K. P., "Priespaudą numetant," *Į laisvę*, June 24, 1941, 1.

Bolshevism, the editors declared that "the New Lithuania, having joined Adolf Hitler's New Europe, must be clean from the mud of Jewish Communism.... To annihilate Jewry, and also Communism, is the first task of the New Lithuania."[55]

The official announcements of the authorities connected Jews to the Communist enemy. The Lithuanian military commandant in Kaunas declared on the radio that Jews had fired upon the Wehrmacht from their homes, and, as a result, a hundred Jews would be shot for every dead German. On June 28, Bobelis cited the crimes of the "Bolshevik gangs" at Pravieniškės and then urged the people to be vigilant: "Lithuanians! Beware of the scattered groups of Russian soldiers and Jewish Communists!" The PG's interior ministry instructed local officials to collect materials on the June deportations, the Soviet atrocities during the retreat, and the activities of partisans who had engaged in an "energetic struggle against the Bolshevik terror, Communist-Jewish violence, and the shootings of defenseless inhabitants."[56]

The insurgent rank and file often described the war against Soviet power and the battle against Jewry in the same breath. On June 24, the partisans at the Metalas factory reported that "to eliminate hostile elements from Šančiai [district], we sent various shock/attack [*smogiamosios*] groups which liquidated many Jews and Communists." The fighters were desperate to prevent the retreating Soviets from crossing the bridge across the Nemunas fearing that "the Russians, encouraged by the Jews, would cross the river and massacre not only the partisans, but the people of Kaunas as well."[57] Some rebels claimed that the insurgents were taking fire from "Jewish houses." Kaunas fighters routinely identified arrestees turned over to the security police as "Communists and Jews." Jonas Ženauskas, one of the local partisan leaders, noted that "from June 27, I began to organize the State Security Department. Until the current directors and heads arrived from Germany, I, along with Captain Kirkila, that is, with his group, liquidated the remaining Communist Jews and other Communist lackeys."[58] (This latter action likely refers to the executions which commenced at the Seventh Fort on June 29–30.)

---

55 P. L., "Lietuva be žydų," *Naujoji Lietuva*, July 4, 1941, 1.
56 Circular from Colonel Jonas Šlepetys, July 14, 1941, in Brandišauskas, *1941 m. birželio sukilimas*, 28.
57 Ibid., 38.
58 Ibid., 79.

One notable example of how Judeo-Bolshevik themes had penetrated the elite is the elderly Metropolitan of Lithuania, Archbishop Juozapas Skvireckas (1873–1959), who lived in semi-retirement at the Linkuva estate on the outskirts of Kaunas. His diary entries for the first days of the war are a revealing mix of secondhand reportage filtered through an antisemitic prism. On June 26, Skvireckas recorded rumors that "the Jews were attacking relentlessly and shooting from their homes, seeking to kill as many as possible," adding that "many partisans have already fallen while battling the Jews." On the following day he wrote that "the battles against the Jews are continuing, and the Jews are not ceasing their attacks." The archbishop also related the "news" from Kaunas that "bullets and grenades had been found in the possession of a Jewish nurse who had been shot," adding that "three or four Jewish women in Šilainiai, dressed up as nuns to avoid detection, had also been found carrying ammunition." Skvireckas acknowledged that the scenes of executions in Kaunas described to him were "extremely painful and unbearable for our people, the partisans. All members of the family are shot, the young and the grown-ups. But the crimes [of these people] are inhuman: there were lists discovered of Lithuanians who were to be shot or otherwise murdered by them. There is a great deal of sadism among the Jews." After reading an excerpt of Hitler's writings published in Į laisvę, Skvireckas confessed in his diary entry of June 30 that "the thoughts of *Mein Kampf* about the Jews are really interesting. . . . In any case, they show that Hitler is not only an enemy of the Jews, but also a man who very much thinks in the correct way."[59]

Leaders wary of anti-Jewish violence hesitated to intervene in the face of the rage which, as they saw it, had gripped the masses. Skvireckas acknowledged that "obviously, not all Jews are guilty, but the guilty ones have brought on the hatred of Lithuanian society against all Jews." His journal also relates an interaction between Jewish elders and the auxiliary bishop of Kaunas who often acted on behalf of the aging metropolitan. Vincentas Brizgys told Jewish elders who had appealed for help that the Church disapproved of violence, but if the clergy, in his words, "were to support the Jews publicly at this time, they would be lynched themselves."[60] In early July, Jakov Goldberg, a leader of Kaunas's Jewish community, visited Jonas Matulionis (1898–1980), the PG's finance minister, seeking the latter's intervention in halting attacks on the Jews. According to

---

59   Skvireckas diary entries of June 25–30, 1941, as in Brandišauskas, *1941 m. birželio sukilimas*, 270–273.

60   Skvireckas diary entry July 11, 1941, in ibid., 282.

Goldberg, Matulionis answered that "the wrath of the people" was too great to halt the violence, but that things would "quiet down" once a ghetto was established and the two nations were physically separated.[61] Justinas Staugaitis, the bishop of Telšiai, was the sole member of the hierarchy to publicly condemn, as he said, "revenge and licentious violence against the Other [non-Lithuanians]."[62]

The LAF press and the PG criticized unsanctioned violence and criminality in general but never publicly censured anti-Jewish attacks. Roving bands of armed men, often wearing the notorious "white armbands," spread throughout Kaunas, invading Jewish homes and terrorizing the inhabitants. Rebels accosted and detained Jewish passerbys and suspected Soviet sympathizers, often transferring the detainees from various stations to the central prison or the notorious Seventh Fort, located north of the city. The level of vulnerability of the city's Jews often depended on the behavior of Lithuanian janitors and landlords. Some Lithuanian homeowners and employees of Jewish residents avoided trouble by claiming that their occupants had fled or had already been arrested. Fanny Pitum considered it a real "stroke of luck" that she had enjoyed "good relations with the owner of the house who therefore did not let in the partisans." But she was also aware of cases when the Lithuanian landlords denounced their tenants.[63] There are accounts of murders during the arrests and robberies of Jews although even an approximate estimate of the number of victims of this kind of criminal activity is difficult to ascertain.

The bloodiest outbreak of antisemitic mob violence in the country's history was the pogrom in the Vilijampolė (Slobodka) neighborhood of Kaunas that commenced on the night of June 25, 1941.[64] An entry in the diary of the finance minister Matulionis refers to the killings. Having learned of his appointment to the PG on the radio, Matulionis made his way to Kaunas in time for

---

61 Recounted in Avraham Tory, *Surviving the Holocaust: The Kovno Ghetto Diary*, ed. Martin Gilbert and Dina Porat (Cambridge, MA: Harvard University Press, 1990), 13.

62 Justinas Staugaitis pastoral letter of July 12, 1941, Lietuvos valstybės istorijos archyvas [Lithuanian State Archive of History, LVIA], f. 1671, ap. 5, b. 63, l. 16; cf. below, Chapter 6.

63 Dieckmann, *Besatzungspolitik*, 1:314.

64 In explaining the nature and scale of the anti-Jewish violence of the first week of the war, it is essential to understand what we mean by "pogrom." Historians generally understand the term to mean what the Russian verbal root of the term conveys: *gromit'*, "to smash, destroy." A pogrom is thus a *riot* with the aim of massacring or expelling an ethnic or religious group. It is best understood as the action of a mob denoting a level of spontaneity and is not to be conflated with the mass executions carried out by militarized police formations, such as at the Seventh and Ninth Forts in Kaunas described below.

the second meeting of the cabinet. He recalled that as the session broke up, the ministers asked him to remain overnight and keep watch in the office:

> Just as everyone was going out the door a certain boss of the partisans, or at least he described himself as such, barged into the room and reported to the interior minister that the Germans had ordered them to shoot Jews, the more, the better. I couldn't make out what sort of leader he was, or what kind of partisans he represented. I couldn't hear what [Interior Minister] Colonel [Jonas] Šlepetys answered. So much for keeping watch! About twelve o'clock, at midnight, after everyone had left, a woman next door began to scream in an ungodly voice. I assumed that she was a Jew since this was mostly a Jewish neighborhood. I never learned why she was screaming but for some reason that report by the "partisan leader" stuck in the back of my mind. The rest of the night was uneventful.[65]

Matulionis did not see the attackers who broke into Jewish homes and assaulted the inhabitants during a two-day rampage. Stahlecker, the head of EG A. who had just arrived in Kaunas, later reported that he encouraged the organization of a killer squad under the leadership of the journalist Algirdas Klimaitis whose men were drawn from what the Nazi commander described as "reliable elements of the undisciplined partisan groups," and noted that the pogromist leader acted "according to the orders given him by [our] small advance unit."[66] It would seem reasonable to assume that the "partisan leader" described in Matulionis's journal refers to the Klimaitis of the Stahlecker report published in the Nuremberg Trial proceedings.

At least one account asserts that rioters decapitated Rabbi Zalman Osovsky and that Germans shot at Jews who tried to escape the attackers by leaping off a bridge into the Neris River. But while several sources implicate Stahlecker's advance group in helping instigate the attack, there is no evidence of direct German participation in the rampage. Estimates of the number of victims differ considerably, ranging from six hundred to several thousand. It is likely that the higher figures include persons murdered days later in shootings at the Seventh Fort. There are reports of a third mass killing during the same period on Jonava Street,

---

65 Jonas Matulionis, *Neramios dienos* (Toronto: Litho-Art, 1975), 18. On the afternoon of the following day, the PG disassociated itself from Klimaitis.

66 See L-180 Stahlecker Report (Einsatzgruppe A: Gesamtbericht bis zum 15. Oktober 1941), in *Trial of the Major War Criminals before the International Military Tribunal* [IMT], vol. 37 (Nuremberg: International Military Tribunal, 1949), 677–682. Cf. Algirdas Budreckis, *The Lithuanian National Revolt of 1941* (Boston: Lithuanian Encyclopedia Press, 1968), 62.

IMAGE 3.5. Aftermath of a pogrom. Civilians and German soldiers look on at the bodies of Jewish men murdered at the Lietūkis garage, June 27, 1941. (Dokumentationsarchiv des österreichischen Widerstandes.)

near the Neris (Vilija) River bridge to Vilijampolė. According to several sources about twenty-five to thirty Jewish men were forced to dance, recite prayers, sing Russian songs, and perform "calisthenics." After this collective humiliation, a practice repeated elsewhere as a form of demeaning the Jews, Lithuanian "white armbands" forced the men to their knees and shot them. Some of the victims of the pogrom were buried in the Jewish cemetery, while others were interred in a mass grave on the riverbank.[67]

On the day after the Vilijampolė killings, the PG cabinet met twice. The minutes of the second session record the first item on the agenda:

> 1. Discussion on the present situation:
> The [acting] Prime Minister Mr. Ambrazevičius complained that the security forces [*saugumas*] are working poorly as there are arrests and searches of people who are entirely innocent. It is stated that the Klimaitis partisan group is not working together with the Staff of the Lithuanian Armed Forces. The partisans of Lithuania are operating in contact

---

67 See statement of Efraim Oshry, May 18, 1945 (Kaunas), LMAVB RS, f. 159–25, l. 18–19. Cf. Dieckmann, *Besatzungspolitik*, 1:314–315.

with the Lithuanian Activist Front and the Lithuanian Provisional Government. Where military operations have ended, partisan activity must take up the functions of the police and the *šauliai* [Riflemen].[68]

While lesser in scale than the slaughter in Vilijampolė, the most notorious anti-Jewish atrocity of the first week of the war was the torture and murder in broad daylight of some fifty to sixty men at the Lietūkis garage in Kaunas on June 27, an outrage which took place some two hundred meters from the Sixteenth Army's headquarters, in full view of German soldiers and civilian onlookers. Unlike other pogroms, the Lietūkis killings produced abundant eyewitness testimony and photographic evidence. Among the dead were a soap factory worker, Yitzhak Grin, musician Shlomo Goldstein, water works employee I. Kurliancikas, merchants B. Komasas and Ch. Cukermanas, the students Pessach and Goldberg, as well as Moshe Shtrom, the father of the Soviet dissident and émigré academic, Aleksandras Štromas (1931–1999). German Army photographer Wilhelm Gunsilius recorded the scene. The pictures show about a dozen perpetrators—some in uniform, some with armbands—as well as civilians who, according to some sources, had just been released from prison. The photos also show bystanders, both German soldiers and Kaunas people, including women. Several eyewitnesses have identified Germans as active participants in the humiliation and beating, but not the murder, of the Jews at the site. Some reports speak of onlookers egging on the killers to "beat the Jews."

The conflicting accounts of the details of the massacre, including postwar testimony by men of the Wehrmacht's 562nd Bakers' Company, have led some historians to conclude that the killing underwent several stages or took place in two different nearby sites. Most accounts center on the Lithuanian killers, especially an unidentified young man who murdered people with an iron bar. Witnesses related that, at first, the Jews were forced to clean the horse manure from the ground, then wash down the yard. At that point, the torture began: the perpetrators beat and choked the victims, spraying them with water hoses. The bodies were buried in a mass grave. Contemporary accounts recount dismay at the barbaric spectacle. Some of the more sensational details, such as the claim that women hoisted up their children to better view the atrocity, or that one perpetrator played an accordion while the crowd joined in the singing of the

---

68 Minutes of June 26, 1941, *LLV*, 15. The "Staff of the Lithuanian Armed Forces" and the PG's Ministry of Defense were in fact hollow structures with no real impact on the events.

national anthem, have been contradicted by some of the witnesses and questioned by historians.[69]

The minutes of the PG's cabinet meeting of the same day record that the minister of economy, Vytautas Landsbergis-Žemkalnis (1893–1993), informed members about "the extremely cruel torture of the Jews at the Lietūkis garage." In response, the ministers entered a peculiar, morally equivocal resolution: "*Decided* [emphasis in the original]: Regardless of all the actions which must be taken against the Jews for their Communist activity and harm to the German Army, partisans and individuals *should avoid public executions of Jews* [emphasis added]. It has been learned that such actions are carried out by people who have nothing in common with the Activist Staff, the Partisans' Staff, or the Lithuanian Provisional Government."[70] On the day after the massacre the military doctor Colonel Balys Matulionis and urged the Rev. Simonas Morkūnas drove to the residence of Archbishop Skvireckas urging him to intercede with Bobelis and the partisans' headquarters to prevent further attacks. On July 1 Skvireckas noted in his diary that "intervention in the matter of the mass murder of the Jews" had found little support and remarked that, given the situation, he had done "everything that was required by considerations of humanity."[71]

In terms of scale and ferocity the Vilijampolė and Lietūkis massacres in Kaunas marked the most egregious pogroms of the first week of the war. In Vilnius, as anti-Communist rebels and mutinous soldiers of the Twenty-Ninth Corps attacked the retreating Soviet troops, insurgents carried out a massacre of at least several dozen captured Red Army men, suspected Communists, and

---

69 Tomasz Szarota, *U progu zagłady: zajęcia antyżydowskie i pogromy w okupowanej Europie: Warszawa, Paryż, Amsterdam, Antwerpia, Kowno* (Warsaw: Sic!, 2000), 243–257; Algirdas Mošinskis, "Liūdininko pasisakymas – I," *Akiračiai* 9 (October 1984): 1, 14; the depositions of J. Vainilavičius (1959) and L. Survila (1961), in *Masinės žudynės Lietuvoje dokumentų rinkinys, 1941–1944*, ed. Boleslovas Baranauskas and Evsiejus Rozauskas, vol. 1 (Vilnius: Mintis, 1965), 231–232; Ernst Klee, Willi Dressen, and Volker Riess, eds., *"The Good Old Days": The Holocaust as Seen by Its Perpetrators and Bystanders* (Old Saybrook, CT: Konecky and Konecky, 1991), 24–35. According to Christoph Dieckmann, German observers sought to put their own actions "in a better light" by contrasting them to Lithuanian barbarism, and he notes that, according to numerous postwar depositions of members of the 562nd Bakers' Company, "most of the spectators [of the atrocity—S. S.] were German soldiers." See Dieckmann, *Besatzungspolitik*, 1:322–323. Cf. Alex Faitelson, *The Truth and Nothing but the Truth: Jewish Resistance in Lithuania* (Jerusalem: Gefen, 2006), 27–38.

70 *LLV*, 18.

71 Skvireckas diary entry July 1, 1941, in Brandišauskas, *1941 m. birželio sukilimas*, 274; also, see below, Chapter 6.

Jews at the garden of the St. Francis Church on Trakų Street on June 24–25. On June 25 the German military commandant, Eberhard von Ostman, and the leader of the Lithuanian rebels' Citizens' Committee, which claimed civilian authority in the city, ordered the detention of sixty Jews and twenty Poles as hostages in order to assure the population's compliance with the directives of the new order. Three weeks later, most of the Jewish hostages were murdered. On June 27 Germans and Lithuanian partisans commenced a wave of kidnappings of Jewish men and suspected Communists which continued into mid-July. Jews derided the Lithuanian and Polish kidnappers and looters as the *khapuny*, the "grabbers." Most of the arrestees were incarcerated in the Lukiškės prison where many of the victims were executed or vanished without a trace. On June 29 the authorities severely limited Jewish access to the food shops. However, the commander of EG B, Arthur Nebe, was unable to duplicate Stahlecker's success in inciting a large-scale pogrom, perhaps because, as Yitzhak Arad has suggested, the Lithuanian authorities were preoccupied with consolidating their control in the face of resistance from the Poles who made up a plurality of the city's population.[72]

Smaller scale attacks, individual murders, and persecution of Jews occurred elsewhere in the country as well. Jewish survivors remember well the mistreatment and harassment that followed the invasion. In Vilkaviškis, a synagogue dating from the seventeenth century was burned on the first day of the war. Several Jews were reportedly killed in nearby Pilviškiai after the Germans seized the town on June 23, but the details are sketchy. Here the anti-Soviet partisans set upon suspected Communists and Jews, with particular attention to Jewish men who were imprisoned in the local seminary where they were routinely abused by the guards. Two weeks later, the men were transferred to barracks and employed as forced labor. Within a week of the occupation the local German military commandant, encouraged by the SD, had issued restrictive ordinances, including the wearing of yellow patches, which were enforced by the newly reorganized Lithuanian police. Survivors report the widespread looting of Jewish property.[73]

---

72 Yitzhak Arad, *Ghetto in Flames: The Struggle and Destruction of the Jews in Vilna in the Holocaust* (New York: Holocaust Library, 1982), 47–49.

73 David Bankier, *Expulsion and Extermination: Holocaust Testimonials from Provincial Lithuania* (Jerusalem: Yad Vashem, 2011), 63–64, 77; Bubnys, *Holokaustas Lietuvos provincijoje*, 544, 549–551.

Insurgents seized control of the northeastern town of Anykščiai even before German troops arrived and quickly proceeded to round up Communists, Komsomol activists, and Jews. The rebels imprisoned Jewish refugees in the town's four synagogues and detained at least a hundred suspected Communists. The "white armbands" reportedly executed ten Jews outside one of the synagogues on June 27–28. Fearing for their lives, thousands of Jews fled eastwards joining Soviet troops in retreat. In the eyes of Lithuanian rebels this constituted further proof that traitorous Jews were fleeing with their alleged masters. As survivor Motl Kuritsky recounted:

> All the roads were clogged with refugees and retreating Red Army vehicles, a mingling of humanity, with horses and vehicles. Everyone was trying to move as quickly as possible. Suddenly, as they were going through Svėdasas forest, gunshots were heard all around. Armed Lithuanians were shooting at the Jewish refugees and many were killed. The forest shook in uproar with continuous shooting from all sides and with terrible crying from the women and children, the wounded and the dying.

The Kuritsky family reached Rokiškis only to find that the Germans had already passed through the town, now controlled by partisans who forced the refugees to turn back. During the return trek to Anykščiai the insurgents robbed and detained some of the refugees. On June 30 Lithuanian police "went through all the Jewish houses and announced that the women and children were required to wear the Star of David."[74] In another case, Jews who fled from Krekenava managed to reach Panevėžys but were forced to return home only to discover that the Germans had seized their town. Lithuanian rebels took charge and imprisoned the young men, some of whom were shot a few days later. Several of the town's Jewish women were raped.[75]

Many more Jews attempted to flee than succeeded in making it to safety. Luck failed even those who found a place on the last crowded trains leaving Vilnius. Soviet security feared Lithuanian saboteurs and screened people before they crossed the old Soviet-Lithuanian frontier, turning back many refugees, even Party members with valid Soviet-issued identity papers. At the Radoshkovichi border post the police permitted only persons with post-1939 Soviet passports to continue their journey, forcing the others, including Jews, to dis-

---

74 As related by Motl Kuritsky in Bankier, *Expulsion and Extermination*, 45–47.
75 Dieckmann, *Besatzungspolitik* 1:308.

embark from the train.⁷⁶ Many of these unfortunates were to fall victim to the Nazi execution squads in Vilnius. According to Soviet sources, by the end of 1941 more than ten million people were evacuated to the interior of the USSR, including some 42,500 people from Lithuania, but this estimate is not useful in precisely establishing the number of Jews who successfully escaped during the early days of the war. Dov Levin assumes that about fifteen thousand Jews managed to flee Lithuania in time, while Yitzhak Arad estimates that number at only about four thousand to six thousand persons, a figure that seems low. According to a 1970 assessment by Lithuanian historian Kazys Varašinskas some 8,500 Jews were among the approximately twenty thousand Lithuanians who were successfully evacuated.⁷⁷

As with attempts to quantify the successful flight of Jewish refugees before the end of June, historians find themselves in a similar quandary regarding the victims of individual criminal attacks, mob violence, and pogroms. A reasonable assumption is that the pogroms in Kaunas resulted in about one thousand deaths, the majority during the slaughter in Vilijampolė-Slobodka, a figure close to the number estimated by the Kovno Ghetto Jewish council in 1942. Anti-Jewish attacks in Vilnius were smaller in scale. It is difficult to gauge the magnitude of anti-Jewish assaults in the smaller towns and countryside. Aside from the special operations of the SD in the border zones, a realistic account suggests that local perpetrators killed approximately two thousand Lithuanian Jews in pogroms, summary executions, and individual murders before the onset of the shootings at the Seventh Fort which culminated in the mass killings of July 4 and 6, 1941. Evidence gleaned from postwar depositions reveals that Stahlecker's EG A was active in efforts to direct rebel groups against the Jews and that elements of the German Security Police and Wehrmacht participated directly in purportedly "unsanctioned" anti-Jewish violence, but the majority of Jews who perished in pogroms and individual attacks during the first week of the war died at the hands of the "white armbands" and other armed groups.⁷⁸

---

76   Ibid., 1:305; cf. Levin, *Baltic Jews*, 173.
77   Zizas et al., *Karo belaisvių*, 96.
78   A report from the Sixteenth Army headquarters claimed between 2,500 and three thousand Jewish deaths in Kaunas between June 24 and 26 resulting from the fury of the people ("Wut der Bevölkerung"), but this number does not correspond to other accounts; see Dieckmann, *Besatzungspolitik*, 1:315, 331.

The numerous survivor testimonies and bystander accounts, such as the Kuritsky memoir, vividly recount the appalling brutality, chaotic violence, and hatred directed at the victims who bore the initial impact of the terror, but these narratives are less reliable in providing meaningful statistics and have limits as historical explanations of the process of destruction. Communal violence, summary executions, and "cleansing" operations to safeguard the rear areas of an ostensibly vulnerable Wehrmacht were egregious atrocities but were insufficient as a "solution" to the Jewish question. The final objective of creating an occupied region "free of Jews" (*Judenfrei*) required more radical decisions and greater operational capability.

Anti-Jewish Persecution as the Norm: the Wehrmacht, the PG, and the Civil Administration

In his seminal work on the destruction of European Jewry, Raul Hilberg discussed genocide as a process of progressive escalation with its own inherent logic. He proposed, in sequence, that the identification, expropriation, and concentration (ghettoization) of the victims are the essential operational stages preceding physical annihilation. In Germany, the state's attack on Jews began with the Nuremberg Laws of the 1930s and then inexorably intensified over time.[79] At first glance, Hilberg's stages of the Holocaust are not easily applied to the Lithuanian case. Before the Nazi occupation, there were no antisemitic laws in the Baltic states. And yet, the Hilberg model can still illuminate the progression of the Holocaust in Lithuania although some caveats are in order.

The Nazi policy of creating a legal structure which would racially identify and separate Germany's assimilated Jewish citizenry from the rest of the populace took years to accomplish. The reality in Lithuania or, for that matter, in most of Eastern Europe was fundamentally different. In general, aside from middle-class urban people, the national minorities, including the Jewish communities, tended to live as separate social entities, often in ethnic enclaves. In many cases, they were recognizable by appearance (for example, traditional dress) but also easily identifiable by religious affiliation and/or language. Jewish intermarriages with Gentiles were rare. Thus, with some exceptions, even

---

79 Raul Hilberg, *The Destruction of the European Jews* (New York: Harper Torchbooks, 1961), 43–174.

outsiders, such as the German invaders, had little trouble with the question of "who is a Jew?" Identification was thus relatively simple, leading, in turn, to rapid expropriation and concentration (ghettoization). The implementation of these stages of persecution was at times haphazard but the archives indicate a pattern. The segregation of provincial Jews was underway even before the ZV announced its rule over the Baltic states in late July 1941. By this time the Nazis and a growing number of local collaborators had already carried out mass executions in the cities and the countryside. These shooting operations, a veritable praxis of murder, coincided with the three stages of persecution noted above, but the full force of annihilation was not unleashed until they were completed, or at least well underway, by August 1941.

Several of the Wehrmacht's commandants implemented and then formalized the physical identification of the country's Jews during the first days of the invasion (as in Pilviškiai and Vilkaviškis). In Vilnius, the police chief Antanas Iškauskas and the head of the Vilnius Citizens' Committee, Stasys Žakevičius, posted notices that informed the people of the city that "according to the German Military Commandant's Order of July 3, 1941..., all Jews of male and female gender, regardless of age, are to wear, in a visible place on the chest and the back a sign 10 cm. in width, a sample of which is posted in all the police precincts." A curfew between 6:00 p.m. and 6:00 a.m. was imposed, the measures to go into effect by July 8.[80] At the same time, the German commandant also ordered the creation of a Jewish ghetto,[81] but the actual implementation did not take place for another two months. Officials outside the major cities soon adopted the spirit of the new racial order. On July 14, 1941, the police chief of the resort town of Druskininkai noted that a German military unit had arrived in the town and established their headquarters after "abolishing the Lithuanian commandant's office." He reported that in accordance with German orders "the Jews will place on their right arm a white band with a star of David, and in two days' time, they will be settled in a Jewish quarter. The Jews are forced to work."[82] The authorities in Alytus announced a hierarchy of the region's citizens: only Germans and Lithuanians would occupy the highest Aryan "first class" designation. On July 12 and 14, 1941, they issued detailed anti-Jewish regulations,

---

80 "Skelbimas," copy in author's archive.
81 Arūnas Bubnys, *Vokiečių okupuota Lietuva*, 189.
82 "Druskininkų policijos vado raportas," LCVA, f. R-1436, ap. 1, b. 27, July 14, 1941, l. 122.

including strict limitations on food rations, which were to be half those allowed non-Jews, as well as a ban on Jewish consumption of sugar and meats.[83]

The "Announcement to an Occupied Land" proclaimed by the German military in July 1941 represented the first official racial edict in Lithuanian history, corresponding in letter and spirit to the laws enacted years earlier in the Reich: 1. "A Jew is a person who has at least three grandparents who were pure-blooded Jews and, in addition; 2. One is considered a Jew whose two grandparents are pure-blooded Jews if, a. on June 22, 1941 [the person] belonged to the Jewish faith; b. [and] as of this announcement was married to a Jew." The text also stipulated that "Jews and Jewesses are forbidden to greet persons of non-Jewish nationality." The order went on to prohibit ritual kosher slaughter of animals and warned that local military commandants would punish by death anyone who infected a German through sexual relations.[84] In the following weeks, the ZV expanded and codified anti-Jewish regulations throughout the country.

For its part, the PG in Kaunas issued decrees stripping minorities of property rights and imposing other restrictions albeit without the racialized terminology of the Reich's officials but in accordance with the LAF platform developed in Berlin. On June 30, 1941, the cabinet mandated the return of nationalized land and properties to "their previous owners," except for assets "belonging to Jews and Russians, which remain the uncontested property of the Lithuanian state," or those owned by "persons who had acted against the interest of the Lithuanian nation." The legal disposition of properties of persons killed, deported, and missing, as well as assistance to former political prisoners and those who had "suffered from the war," was restricted to "citizens of Lithuanian nationality."[85] The PG's Law on the Denationalization of Land of July 17 proclaimed that the farms of "Jews and non-citizens are not to be returned to their previous owners but are to be transferred to [the publicly owned] Land Trust." During the cabinet meeting of July 18, the minister of communications Antanas Novickis endorsed the law, noting that it would be impossible "to announce the return of land based on the situation as existed before [the Soviet invasion of] June 15, 1940, since this would rebound to the benefit of the non-Lithuanian element."[86]

---

83   Brandišauskas, "Lietuvių ir žydų santykiai": 55–57.
84   As cited in ibid., 57. Full text published in "Krašto vado skelbimas užimtam kraštui," *Naujoji Lietuva*, July 23, 1941, 5; archival copy is in LCVA, f. R- 1436, ap. 1, b. 38, l. 32.
85   The relevant decrees are in *LLV*, 23, 37, 50–51.
86   Minutes of July 18, 1941, *LLV*, 93.

On July 19, a new law approved the restoration of nationalized homes and other real estate, once again excluding "Jews and foreigners" from the process. The same discriminatory expropriations were applied to the remaining sectors of the economy in a subsequent series of decrees.[87] On July 28, the PG's interior minister Šlepetys led a discussion on proposed "statutes for the regulation of the Jewish question," which were intended to institute a nationwide policy regarding Lithuanian Jewry. The minutes record that "the ministers' cabinet recognized the statutes as acceptable in principle but decided to hand them over to a commission of jurists for final rendition."[88]

On July 30, 1941, Lithuanian newspapers published a proclamation by the Reich Commissar (Reichskommissar) Hinrich Lohse, the head of the newly created occupation authority of the Baltic states and Belarus (Reichskommissariat Ostland, RO), to the Lithuanian people informing them that Hitler's decree of July 17 had appointed Adrian von Renteln the General Commissar (Generalkommissar) for the "territory of the formerly independent Lithuanian state," now designated as the Lithuanian General Commissariat (Generalkommissariat Litauen). Lohse demanded "unconditional obedience" to all orders of the new administration. In an appended announcement, von Renteln cautioned that the "previously issued directives of the military administration concerning the civilian sector remain in force."[89] Presumably, this included the antisemitic orders imposed by the Wehrmacht, such as curfews, segregation, and the wearing of identifying patches.

On the same day, the worried PG ministers discussed the news and decided to seek a meeting with von Renteln, in order to "explain the view of the Lithuanian government on the situation," and then to prepare an appropriate memorandum to be delivered to the "governing organs of the Great German Reich."[90] But the PG had already suffered severe constraints in its attempts to continue governmental operations. To add insult to injury, on the night of July 23–24, 1941, radical officers of the Iron Wolf group of the LNP seized the Lithuanian commandant's office in Kaunas with the encouragement of the

---

87 *LVV*, 99; for examples of the exclusionary statutes, see ibid., 101, 107, 115, 117, 130, 132.
88 Ibid., 123.
89 Quoted from the announcement dated July 28, 1941, in "Aufruf/Atsišaukimas," *Į laisvę*, July 30, 1941, 1. The term "Generalbezirk Litauen" (Lithuanian General District) is often found in German archival sources when referring to the ZV authorities in Lithuania.
90 *LVV*, 134.

Gestapo and dismissed Colonel Bobelis, but stopped short of an outright coup against the PG itself. Captain Stasys Kviecinskas took over Bobelis's post, while the LNP, composed in part of former Voldemarist officers from Berlin (notably Colonel Vytautas Reivytis and Pyragius), increasingly gained control over the Lithuanian police. Fruitless power-sharing negotiations then ensued in order to deescalate the conflict, but it was clear that the factions were arguing over a doomed political structure.[91]

Even as they recognized the approaching end of any semblance of an independent government, on August 1, 1941, the ministers attached to their meeting the "Statutes on the Jewish Situation," the preamble of which stated that "the Jews had for centuries exploited the Lithuanian nation economically, caused its moral degradation, and, in recent years, had carried out a wide-ranging campaign against the Lithuanian nation and the independence of Lithuania." It was thus necessary "to put an end to their [Jews'] pernicious influence and protect the Lithuanian nation." The proposed measures created two categories of Lithuanian Jewry: first, members of Communist organizations and Bolshevik sympathizers; second, all remaining Jews. The first group would be arrested and tried for their crimes, while "all other persons[92] of Jewish nationality will be settled in special designated areas and must wear on the left part of their chest a yellow patch of eight centimeters in size, in the center of which there shall be the letter 'J.'" Jews would be allowed to own real estate only in designated areas and would be prohibited from possessing automobiles, motorcycles, and "other mechanized means of transport," as well as bicycles, pianos, and cameras. Jews who had volunteered to fight in the wars of independence or had been awarded medals for valor were exempt from the statutes "if they had not since then acted against the interest of the Lithuanian nation."[93] The proposed measures indicated that the PG was willing to adopt the LAF's stance on the Jews, albeit short of wholesale expulsion. As it turned out, the cabinet did not get the opportunity to implement the project.

On August 5, 1941, von Renteln received the ministers in a formal setting. Ambrazevičius addressed "His Excellency" in a deferential appeal, asserting

---

91 See Budreckis, *The Lithuanian National Revolt*, 117–118; Jakubėnas, *1941 m.*, 48, 79. More details are in the wartime diary of the general secretary of the LNP, Blynas, *Karo metų*, 78ff.

92 The departure here from the legal verbiage of the First Republic ("*citizens* of Jewish nationality") is noteworthy.

93 *LVV*, 135–137.

the PG's "honor in meeting, in your person, such a high representative of the Great Reich." The premier asked the general commissar to "convey to Adolf Hitler, the Leader of the Great Reich, and his courageous army the gratitude of the Lithuanian nation, which had liberated Lithuania from the Bolshevik occupation." He pointed out that the PG had publicly "expressed its desire to maintain an independent state in close union with Greater Germany" and to join in the military campaign in the East. Ambrazevičius presented von Renteln with a memorandum explaining in more detail the rationale for an independent Lithuania and concluded: "In requesting you to accept this statement of our position, we reiterate the determination of the Lithuanian nation to continue cooperation with Greater Germany and await your authoritative word regarding the manner of such cooperation."[94]

Von Renteln's reply was unequivocal. After thanking the PG for its expressed cooperation, he declared that "as general commissar he has taken over civilian authority in the formerly independent Lithuanian state..., and [thus] your work as ministers must be considered finished." Von Renteln agreed to transfer the memorandum to the Reich's government but pointed out that the future disposition of the occupied countries within a New Europe was solely at the discretion of the Führer who would make his decisions at war's end. He announced the appointment of General Petras Kubiliūnas as first counselor to head a group of subordinate Lithuanian "general counselors," each of whom would manage the former ministries of the PG as "departments" subject to the instructions of von Renteln's office.[95]

Recognizing the futility of pretended independence under von Renteln, the ministers returned to their office for their final meeting, during which the acting premier delivered a report on the PG's six-week tenure. Ambrazevičius explained that the LAF, as the leader of the nation, "had been determined to restore a free and independent Lithuania, and thus had declared the Provisional Government, which would emphasize friendly relations with Germany and a willing desire to join a Europe managed by Adolf Hitler on a new foundation." Ambrazevičius complained that from its very inception the government had confronted obstruction from German military and police authorities and had been virtually

---

94 A draft of the speech is in Blynas, *Karo metų*, 135–136.

95 Lithuanian translation is in ibid., 115–117; Bubnys, *Vokiecčiu okupuota Lietuva*, 162–165. In March 1942 Alfred Rosenberg, the Reich Minister of the Occupied Eastern Territories, formalized the roles of the counselors under strict German supervision.

IMAGE 3.6.
Left: General Commissar Adrian von Renteln, head of the German Civil Administration (ZV). Right: General Petras Kubiliūnas, first counselor and head of the Lithuanian Advisory Council under the ZV.

ignored by Berlin. After mid-July, he said, the Germans had essentially removed the PG's access to communications and transport (although censored print media still proliferated). In referring to the widespread violence which followed the invasion and insurrection, the premier simply noted that his government had lacked the means "to effect in a positive way, any of the excesses, for example, the execution of Jews taking place in Kaunas and the provinces."[96] But the fact remains that the PG's rhetoric and intentions regarding the segregation of Jews had been made clear, and, despite calls for an end to unsanctioned violence and private inquiries with German authorities,[97] responsible leaders had failed to publicly and unambiguously protest the ongoing massacres and had provided funds for setting up the camp at the Seventh Fort. The PG's ministers concluded the meeting by asserting that it was disbanding "against its will" and then visited the Tomb of the Unknown Soldier to lay a wreath.

Although the end of the PG had little perceptible impact on the policies of the Nazi occupation authorities, the difference between the incoming General Council of native advisors and the PG was significant and became more obvious over time. For many, if not most, of the country's ethnic Lithuanian majority, the latter had represented hopes for a restoration of sovereignty, albeit within a vaguely defined German-led "New Europe." In this sense the PG, however brief

---

96 There are several versions of the speech. One is in LYA, ap. 58, b. 265, l. 2–5, from which a redacted Soviet version is published in Boleslovas Baranauskas, Evsiejus Rozauskas, and Kazys Rukšėnas, eds., *Nacionalistų talka hitlerininkams* (Vilnius: Mintis, 1970), 35–41. Another edited version appeared among the diaspora in the United States in Juozas Brazaitis, *Vienų vieni, rezistencija*, vol. 6, *Raštai*, ed. Alina Skrupskelienė and Česlovas Grincevičius (Chicago: Į laisvė fondas, 1985), 419–427.

97 See below on the stance of procurator Matas Krygeris and the memoir of General Raštikis concerning his visit to German headquarters in July 1941, Chapter 6.

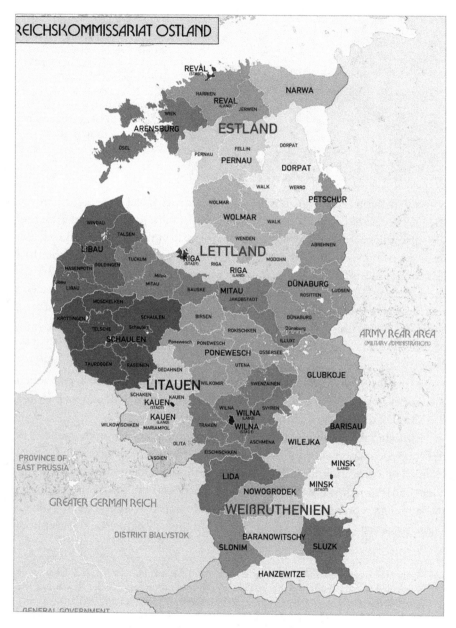

MAP 6. Reichskommissariat Ostland:
The Baltic States and Belarus under German Civil Administration, 1941–1944.
Public domain.

and ephemeral its power, represented legitimacy which carried with it an aura of moral authority. Initially, General Kubiliūnas's bureaucrats represented a sense of continuity: four ministers, including Matulionis, joined his advisors in their respective fields of expertise. However, the collaborating "general counselors" became increasingly unpopular over the next three years of Nazi rule, particularly after the fiasco of the SS mobilization campaign in the spring of 1943.[98] The men projected no vision for the country's future: at best, they could only engage in petitions and pragmatic maneuvering in attempts to alleviate the effects of the most exploitative German policies affecting ethnic Lithuanians.

Selective Killing Operations in the Cities, June–July 1941

After the first week of the invasion, observers in Kaunas noted a decline in violence against civilians, primarily Jewish men and suspected Communists, the ferocity of which had unsettled at least some of the men in the PG and the Wehrmacht. As Stahlecker admitted in his oft-quoted report, the Nazi-inspired initial pogroms could not easily be restarted and, in any case, were possible "only during the first days after the occupation."[99] One German officer reported that by the evening of June 29 the city was "gradually becoming quiet." The civil and military authorities suppressed much of the criminal outbreaks in the streets, but if the Jews of Kaunas had any illusions that this lull would bring safety, they were to be disappointed. Years later the Jewish survivor Meir Yellin caustically summarized the situation: "After the 'spontaneous' pogroms, the Germans brought 'order' and 'system' to the extermination campaign against the Jews."[100] While some German officials played their role as "protectors" of the Jews against their vengeful Lithuanian neighbors, the killing operations under a system of Nazi command and control now replaced the pogroms.

The harbinger of a more organized phase of destruction was SS Lt. Colonel Erich Ehrlinger who arrived in Kaunas on June 28 with his Sonderkommando (SK) 1b, a small unit attached to Stahlecker's command. On the same day Colonel Bobelis and the German commandant in Kaunas ordered the disarming of the Lithuanian insurgents and issued an appeal for volunteers to join a force euphemistically named Defenders of National Work (Tautino darbo apsauga,

---

98   See below, Chapter 6.
99   *IMT*, Nuremberg Document 180–L, 683.
100 As related in Dieckmann, *Besatzungspolitik*, 1:324–325.

TDA). On July 1 Ehrlinger notified the RSHA that his detachment had "created five companies of auxiliary police [Hilfspolizeitruppe] from the ranks of reliable partisans." According to his report, "Two of these [TDA] companies are subordinate to the Einsatzkommando [EK 3]. One of them is guarding the inmates of the Jewish concentration camp established at the Seventh Fort and carries out executions, while the other has been directed to ordinary police tasks by the EK in agreement with the military commandants (Feldkommandanten)."[101]

The Seventh Fort was one of twelve military installations encircling Kaunas which were constructed at the turn of the twentieth century to guard the western borders of the tsarist empire. Until August 1941 officials referred to the Fort as a "concentration camp," but the term should not evoke images of the better-known institutions in the Reich and General Government. The Germans and their collaborators utilized some of the Kaunas forts as temporary detention centers and killing sites primarily for Jews, Communists, and Soviet prisoners of war. Nazi officials negotiated the logistical arrangements for the "concentration camp" (and the future Jewish ghetto) with Bobelis and General Robert von Pohl, the Wehrmacht's commandant in Kaunas. On June 30, 1941, the PG ministers voted for a ten-day financial advance for the upkeep of the TDA battalion and, as recorded in the minutes, "approved the establishment of a Jewish concentration camp, [the matter] to be handled by the vice-minister of the communal economy Mister Švipas in consultation with Colonel Bobelis."[102] German documents indicate that EK 3, under the command of SS Colonel Karl Jäger (1888–1959), the infamous chronicler of genocide,[103] intended to establish two sections of a proposed Jewish concentration camp: one for Jewish men, the other, for women and children. The Seventh Fort held approximately 1,500 Jews, while the Kaunas central prison listed 1,869 Jews, 214 Lithuanians, 134 Russians, one Latvian, and sixteen Poles at the beginning of July. By the beginning of July more than 3,200 people had been arrested in Kaunas.[104] According to Bobelis's Office, on July 5, the TDA consisted of fifty-five officers and 774

---

101 Ehrlinger Report to RSHA, July 1, 1941 (author's archive).
102 *LLV*, 19–20; cf. Dieckmann, *Besatzungspolitik*, 1:326.
103 A detailed biography is in Wolfram Wette, *Karl Jäger: Mörder der litauischen Juden* (Frankfurt am Main: Fischer Taschenbuch Verlag, 2011).
104 See details in Dieckmann and Sužiedėlis, *Mass Murder*, 137–138.

non-coms and enlisted men; 163 men were attached to the Commandant's HQ and 21 TDA-men were stationed at the Seventh Fort.[105]

Mass killings at the Fort commenced on June 29–30, 1941. The German perpetrators included Ehrlinger's SK 1b squad and Gestapo officers under SS Second Lieutenant Kurt Burkhardt as well as men from the Ninth Police Battalion who served as part of EK 3. A German medical orderly stationed near the Seventh Fort who "heard shots during the night" went to investigate and found "a crowd of people below us guarded by SS or SD men." He observed that the guards "were all Germans; there were no Lithuanians" and attempted to help a wounded Jewish woman only to be sternly rebuked by a German SS or SD man who dragged the victim away.[106] But this memoir reflects only one aspect of the operation.

Jewish witnesses remember the horrors at the fort differently, noting with bitterness the role of the Lithuanians, especially the First and Third Companies of the TDA men, who took part in the killings and, as survivors recall, behaved with great cruelty. In the summer heat the inmates were denied water from the nearby well; the guards shot at the prisoners who crawled to the water to quench their thirst. On July 3 the people who had been starving received some moldy bread from the German supplies. Survivor Yitzhak Nemenchuk remembered a Lithuanian officer in a blue air force uniform who commanded the selected Jewish men to lay down in rows, "pressed together as if herring in a barrel." Anyone who dared to move was dispatched "with a bullet to the head." After the officer left, the guards standing on the raised hillocks surrounding the yard opened fire at the crowd below as the screams of the dying reverberated throughout the night and the next day. Groups of Jews wearing glasses, suspected as doctors, lawyers, and engineers, were selected and shot separately away from the site. Nemenchuk described the constant terror: "The night from Thursday to Friday and the whole of Friday were terribly bloody. The shootings would not stop. New groups of people were taken behind the bulwarks." The TDA men forced the women and children into the fort's underground barracks where some of the women were raped, others murdered by drunken guards.

EK 3 registered the shooting of 416 men and forty-seven women on July 4, 1941. On Sunday, July 6, the Seventh Fort killers perpetrated the largest single massacre of Jews to date: Jäger reported that 2,514 Jews were slain by

---

105 *LLV*, 45.
106 The report is published in Klee, Dressen, and Riess, *"The Good Old Days,"* 35–37.

IMAGE 3.7.
Seventh Fort, July 1941.
Top: German and Lithuanian police guard Jewish men as civilians look on.
Middle: Murders in progress. Some of the dead and their belongings can be seen in the background.
Bottom: Aftermath.
(Imperial War Museums, © Crown Copyright.)

"machine-gun fire."[107] People testified that the killings carried out at the fort during the first week of July could be heard throughout the city. A Catholic priest at the nearby Wehrmacht military hospital confided to his diary on July 4 that "the shootings in the Fort lasted until late in the evening." On the night of

---

107 Jäger to RSHA, September 10, 1941 (author's archive).

July 6–7, he again noted "wild shooting of the Jews."[108] Some people appealed to Lithuanian officials to save their loved ones. The German Helene Holzman sought to free her Jewish husband Max by utilizing her connections with prominent Lithuanians, but failed, despite promises of help.[109] A lucky few managed to escape the massacre either through bribery or as a result of special circumstances. Commandant Bobelis who visited the fort ordered the release of seventy men who had been volunteers in the Lithuanian independence wars of 1918–1920, but it can be assumed that most of them eventually perished.[110]

The situation at the fort concerned the Wehrmacht, which generally approved of anti-Jewish actions in principle but were disturbed by the "uncivilized" and disorganized killings. Stahlecker, who had previously agreed with the Sixteenth Army that "executions would be carried out only under the supervision of the SS commander in Kaunas," returned to the city from Riga to explain the debacle to the Wehrmacht, blaming "nervous Lithuanians who have simply overdone it." But the German commandant in Kaunas doubted Stahlecker's explanation that the "Lithuanians had done this on their own." In his July 8, 1941, diary, Wilhelm von Leeb, the commander of Army Group North, noted a message from Kaunas:

> General von Rocques, Commander of the Army Rear Area, complained about the mass shooting of the of the Jews in Kaunas (thousands!) carried out by the Lithuanian security units [Schutzverbände] at the instigation of the German police authorities. We have no influence on these measures. All that is left for us is to remain aloof. Rocques reckoned correctly that the Jewish question cannot be solved in this manner. The sterilization of all male Jews would be the surest way to solve this [problem].[111]

---

108 The exact figures of the July 4–6 killings at the Seventh Fort are in Jäger's better-known December 1, 1941 report, often cited as the Jäger Report by scholars (see Appendix 1). See also the accounts of survivors Yitzhak Nemenchuk and Fritz Gernhardt; also, testimonies in the Koniuchowsky archive; the report by Yosif Gar in 1948; excerpts from the diary and testimony of Georg Handrick; as well as the numerous depositions of SK 1b members, as outlined in Dieckmann and Sužiedėlis, *Mass Murder*, 138–142.

109 Helene Holzman, *Dies Kind soll leben. Die Aufzeichnungen der Helene Holzman*, ed. Margarete Holzman and Reinhard Kaiser (Frankfurt: Schöffling, 2000), 19–26.

110 Sara Ginaitė, *Žydų tautos tragedijos Lietuvoje pradžia* (Vilnius: Miša, 1994), 11–12.

111 As cited in Helmut Krausnick and Hans-Heinrich Wilhelm, *Die Truppe des Weltanschauungskrieges: die Einsatzgruppen der Sicherheitspolizei und des SD 1938–1942* (Stuttgart: Deutsche Verlags-Anstalt, 1981), 207–208.

SS Colonel Karl Jäger testified after the war that TDA Lieutenant Bronius Norkus had killed about three thousand Jews at the Seventh Fort without a direct order and claimed that he then commanded the TDA men "to discontinue such self-initiated shootings" without explicit authorization from EK 3.[112] Two documents undermine this disingenuous excuse: Ehrlinger's July 1, 1941, report that the TDA had been placed under the command of SK 1b, and Jäger's report of December 1, 1941, in which the killings of July 4 and 6 were recorded as "executions carried out by Lithuanian partisans under my direction and orders."[113] During the afternoon session of the July 7 PG cabinet meeting Colonel Bobelis gave a detailed report to ministers concerning police matters. The penultimate paragraph in the minutes included the following bureaucratic summary: "The Commandant [Bobelis] also informed us about the Jews. According to a statement from the German general Stahlecke [sic], the massive liquidation of the Jews will no longer be carried out. According to German orders a ghetto for the Jews is being established in Vilijampolė to which all the Jews of Kaunas must be moved within four weeks."[114]

Aside from the massacres at the Seventh Fort, SK 1b troops and members of the German Sixty-Fifth Police Battalions shot hundreds of people in fields near Kaunas, but it is difficult to determine the number and identity of these victims. The postwar interrogations of the German members of the two units provide considerable evidence for both extensive Lithuanian participation and German initiative in the massacres. The mass killings between June 30 and July 7 resulted in approximately five to six thousand victims in Kaunas, mostly Jews. Considering that at least one thousand Jews perished during the period of the pogroms (notably at Vilijampolė and Lietūkis) as well as in smaller scale shootings prior to the Seventh Fort actions, it can be estimated that nearly seven thousand Jews were murdered in Lithuania's second city during the first two weeks of the war.

To avoid any future conflicts with the Wehrmacht regarding such "utterly disorganized mass shootings," the German Security Policy decided to create special death squads. In the parlance of EG A Commander Stahlecker, due to the previous unfortunate "occurrences" it "became necessary" to form a mobile unit (the Rollkommando) of Germans and Lithuanians to exert more control during killing operations, a decision with fateful consequences for Lithuania's

---

112 As described in Dieckmann and Sužiedėlis, *Mass Murder*, 140.
113 Jäger Report, December 1, 1941, 1.
114 *LLV*, Minutes of July 7, 1941, 50–51.

provincial Jews in the following months. In another attempt to establish greater discipline, on July 11, 1941, the TDA battalion's commander Colonel Andrius Butkūnas prohibited members of the unit, under penalty of death, to arrest people and search private homes without an explicit order from senior officers, the Lithuanian military commandant, or the chief of the Lithuanian Security Police. Apparently, such attempts failed to stem the lawlessness entirely and the Lithuanian police were forced to repeat a similar warning in November 1941.[115]

Smaller scale executions at the Fort continued however: on July 9 EK 3 recorded the killing of "21 Jewish men and 3 Jewish women", and on July 19, the commando listed as its victims "17 Jewish men, two Jewish women, four Lithuanian Communist men, two Lithuanian Communist women, and one German Communist."[116]

The aftermath of mass murder posed public health concerns. Horst Schweinberger of the Ninth Police Battalion testified that he ordered three hundred

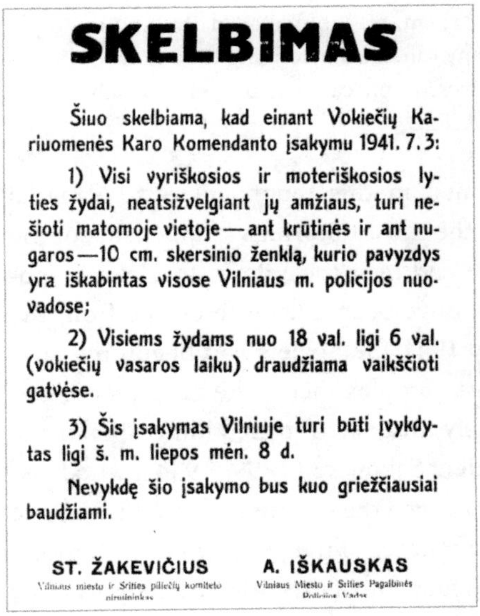

SKELBIMAS

Šiuo skelbiama, kad einant Vokiečių Kariuomenės Karo Komendanto įsakymu 1941. 7. 3:

1) Visi vyriškosios ir moteriškosios lyties žydai, neatsižvelgiant jų amžiaus, turi nešioti matomoje vietoje — ant krūtinės ir ant nugaros — 10 cm. skersinio ženklą, kurio pavyzdys yra iškabintas visose Vilniaus m. policijos nuovadose;

2) Visiems žydams nuo 18 val. ligi 6 val. (vokiečių vasaros laiku) draudžiama vaikščioti gatvėse.

3) Šis įsakymas Vilniuje turi būti įvykdytas ligi š. m. liepos mėn. 8 d.

Nevykdę šio įsakymo bus kuo griežčiausiai baudžiami.

ST. ŽAKEVIČIUS
Vilniaus miesto ir Srities piliečių komiteto

A. IŠKAUSKAS
Vilniaus Miesto ir Srities Pagalbinės

IMAGE 3.8.
Lithuanian civil and police authorities in Vilnius announcing the enforcement of the German Military Commandant Colonel Georg Neyman's Order of July 3, 1941, instructing Jews to wear identifying patches and declaring a curfew. (Author's archive.)

Soviet prisoners of war to bury bodies in nearby bomb craters. The commander of the EK 3 criminal section, Johannes Schafer, who photographed the bodies, stated that "the threat of an epidemic, the use of quicklime and the like were

115 Dieckmann and Sužiedėlis, *Mass Murder*, 140–142.

116 Jäger Report, December 1, 1941, 1.

causing problems." Soon after the killings, local people complained about the unbearable stench to the chief of the Kaunas commandant's sanitation section. In the second part of July 1941, the authorities continued a ban on bathing in the Nemunas and Neris Rivers which had been "poisoned by the corpses."[117]

In Vilnius, the persecution of Jews, as well as selective shootings, became a fact of daily life from the very beginning. On July 4–5 Alfred Filbert's EK 9, which had just arrived in Vilnius, shot 147 Jews.[118] The EG Report No. 21 of July 13, 1941, noted:

> In Vilnius, by July 8th the local Einsatzkommando liquidated 321 Jews. The Lithuanian Ordnungsdienst [order police] which was placed under the Einsatzkommando after the dissolution of the Lithuanian political police was instructed to take part in the liquidation of the Jews. 150 Lithuanian officials were assigned to this task. They arrested the Jews and put them into the concentration camp where they were subjected the same day to Special Treatment. This work has now begun, and thus about 500 Jews, saboteurs amongst them, are liquidated daily. About 460,000 rubles in cash, as well as many valuables belonging to Jews who were subject to Special Treatment, were confiscated as property which had belonged to the enemies of the Reich.[119]

The "concentration camp" mentioned in this report refers to Paneriai (Ponary, Ponar), which became one of the most notorious killing fields of the Holocaust. Located on a major rail line and near the Vilnius to Grodno motorway, the groves around Paneriai had once been a favorite escape from the summer heat for city residents. In early 1941 the Soviets had begun the construction of an underground fuel storage complex there. The deep pits of this unfinished project provided a gruesomely ideal site for the killing operations. In his diary, the Polish journalist Kazimierz Sakowicz (1899–1944), who lived on the edge of the Paneriai woods and observed the shootings from this vantage point, related the accelerated pace of the murder of the Jews. On the afternoon of July 11 Sakowicz wrote: "This was the first day of executions. An oppressive,

---

117 Dieckmann and Sužiedėlis, *Mass Murder*, 142.
118 Details are in Arūnas Bubnys, *Vokiečių saugumo policijos ir SD Vilniaus Ypatingasis būrys 1941–1944* (Vilnius: LGGRTC, 2019), 8.
119 "Ereignismeldung 21 v. 13.7.1941," in *Die 'Ereignismeldungen UdSSR' 1941: fur Konrad Kwiet zum 70. Geburtstag*, ed. Klaus-Michael Mallman et al. (Darmstadt: WBG, 2011), 114—henceforth, *Ereignismeldungen*.

overwhelming impression. The shots quiet down after 8 in the evening." He kept watch: "By the second day, July 12, a Saturday, we already knew what was going on, because at about 3 P. M. a large group of Jews was taken to the forest, about 300 people, mainly intelligentsia with suitcases, beautifully dressed.... An hour later the volleys began. Ten people were shot at a time. They took off their overcoats, caps, and shoes (but not their trousers!). Executions continue on the following days: July 13, 14, 15, 16, 17, 18 and 19, a Saturday." Sakowicz confirmed that further shootings took place on July 23–26, and July 28–31. He estimated that nearly five thousand people were shot in these operations during the month of July 1941, mostly Jews, along with a smaller number of alleged Communists and Polish activists.[120]

The German and Lithuanian Security Police as well as the "white armbands" participated in the roundups of the victims. To carry out the mass shootings themselves the German SD founded a special unit composed of mostly Lithuanian volunteers, known in German as the Sonderkommando (in Lithuanian, Ypatingasis būrys, literally, the "Special Platoon," YB). In contrast to the TDA killers at the Seventh Fort, the YB constituted a smaller but more efficient and permanent execution force. The documents indicating the existence of the unit from July 15, 1941, but according to postwar testimony, the Germans put together the core of the YB within a few days after seizing Vilnius. Initially the platoon consisted of about a hundred men in civilian apparel, later supplied with Lithuanian army uniforms. In 1942 the YB were equipped with the uniforms of the German SD to whom they reported. For most of its existence this force consisted of about forty to fifty killers but was at times supplemented by personnel from other police units. Periodic rotations suggest that the number of men who served in the platoon must have numbered several hundred. As in the situation of the TDA in Kaunas, some of the YB men did not wish to continue participating in the killing and left the unit. The detailed accounts of their activities in postwar trials suggest that those who remained came to see their job as routine and, further, as an opportunity for plunder. The "Ypatingai," as they came to be known by Jews, developed a fearsome, brutal reputation.

---

120 Kazimierz Sakowicz, *Ponary Diary, 1941–1943: A Bystander's Account of a Mass Murder*, trans. Laurence Weinbaum, ed. Yitzhak Arad (New Haven: Yale University Press, 2005), 11–14.

German police, who oversaw the murders, were present at most of the killing operations.[121]

Šiauliai, Lithuania's third city, experienced less anti-Jewish mob violence before the arrival of the Wehrmacht commandants who quickly issued a series of decrees, such as banning Jewish possession of radios and confining Jews to their homes. On June 27 Lithuanian "activists" invaded Jewish homes and arrested hundreds of Jewish men as "security risks," publicly humiliating and tormenting the detainees. On the night of June 28–29, the Germans shot an undetermined number of the men at Kužiai forest some fifteen kilometers outside of the city. In later weeks, the site was utilized for further executions. New waves of arrests targeting Jewish men intensified during the first week of July. As Šiauliai survivor Aron Abramson recalls: "The captives were primarily the intelligentsia, such as lawyers and clergy as well as suspected Communists. Also, many of those who rounded up the people had personal scores to settle with the victims. The arrests went on for an entire week. . . . Only men were arrested, but not the women and children." Surviving witness Sonja Greene recalls that her father was taken during the manhunt never to be seen again. Her mother turned gray overnight.[122]

The city had strategic value for Operation Barbarossa as an industrial center and transport link with Riga and Daugavpils, thus necessitating a larger than usual German presence, whose security forces participated extensively in the killing operations of Jewish men and accused Soviet collaborators. The main strike force was led by a special unit (Teilkommando) of EK 2, consisting of a platoon of the German Eleventh Reserve Police Battalion and Lithuanian auxiliaries, reportedly numbering as many as sixty men. German trial testimony also implicated personnel from the German Sixty-Fifth Reserve Police Battalion, field gendarmerie (FK 819), officers and men of the Wehrmacht's security divisions, and even "young members of the Reich Labor Service (RAD)."[123] The execution squads convoyed the victims by lorry from Šiauliai to the village of

---

121 Arūnas Bubnys, *Vokiečių saugumo policijos ir SD*, 9ff. The role of individual perpetrators based on postwar interrogations and archival documents is described in Mantas Šikšnianas, "Tarp masės ir individo: Vilniaus Ypatingasis būrys 1941–1945 m.," *Genocidas ir rezistencija* 1, no. 39 (2016): 93–110; cf. the revised and updated Mantas Šikšnianas, "Ypatingasis būrys ir masinės žudynės Paneriuose," in *Nusikaltimų pėdsakai neišnyksta: Masinės žudynės Panerių miške 1941–1944 metais*, comp. Saulius Sarevičius, ed. Stanislovas Stasiulis and Nerijus Šepetys (Vilnius: LII, 2021): 24–45.

122 Survivor testimony quoted in Dieckmann, *Beatzungspolitik*, 2:824.

123 See ibid., 820ff.

Pročiūnai seven kilometers outside the city. The investigators of the Soviet Extraordinary Commission reported excavating eight pits containing the remains of 772 victims. The July statistics of death for Šiauliai city are less reliable than those compiled in Kaunas and Vilnius, but the sources available suggest that Nazis and their collaborators may have murdered as many as one thousand of the city's Jews before the establishment of the Šiauliai Ghetto in August 1941.[124]

The Joniškis Paradigm: Expropriation and Ghettoization of Provincial Jews

Even before the administrative restructuring of the occupation under German civilian rule, the Wehrmacht commandants and the German Security Police had begun to implement measures to identify, expropriate, and ghettoize Lithuanian Jewry. In the major urban centers (Vilnius, Kaunas, and Šiauliai), Nazi policy created ghettos under a system of Jewish labor administered for the longer term, a protracted course of persecution and selective mass murders which continued until the end of the German occupation. In the provinces, Lithuania's historic shtetls experienced the processes of destruction differently. During the first month of the occupation, local initiative during the stages of concentration/ghettoization was often instrumental.

One of the earliest examples is the town of Joniškis in the Šiauliai district, a case in which the documents speak for themselves. At the outbreak of the war, the town's anti-Soviet insurgents had, according to their initial reports, "participated in partisan battles against the Russians and Jews." On June 28, 1941, local LAF activists convened a meeting in order "to create a provisional committee to protect the town and maintain order." The group appointed a mayor and police chief on the spot and asked the former head of the local chapter of the Riflemen's Union to organize security in the town. Among the list of initial goals was the fourth point: "To concentrate the Jews in one place and utilize them for labor in the fields and public works."[125] Within days the leaders of the group declared

---

124 Arūnas Bubnys, "Šiaulių miesto ir Šiaulių apskrities žydų likimas," in *Šiaulių getas kalinių sąrašai: 1942*, ed. Irina Guzenberg and Jevgenija Sedova (Vilnius: Valstybinis Vilniaus Gaono žydų muziejus, 2002), 44.

125 "Protokolas Nr. 1," June 28, 1941, l. 1, and "Joniškio aktivistų [sic] veikla," undated, LCVA, f. R-739, ap. 1, b. 4, l. 3.

themselves the "Staff of the Joniškis section of the Lithuanian Activist Front" under a new leader, Kazys Ralys, who maintained contact with the LAF center in Šiauliai. The minutes of the Joniškis LAF Staff's meeting of July 11 identify a "commission for Jewish matters."[126] Two days later, the former riflemen and partisans banded together into a regional auxiliary police force under the command of Petras Butkus who extended their reach into the countryside in order to protect villagers from "the remnants of the Red Army, as well as other Red bandits and Jews hiding in the forests." The unit was well armed, listing "44 rifles, eight machine guns, three to four thousand rounds of ammunition, ten grenades. . ., all weapons taken from the Red Army." The police laid out their accomplishments and ongoing tasks in the protocol of their organizational meeting:

> On the matter of Jews and Communist traitors:
> 1. The arrest of more prominent Communists and Jews.
> 2. An order of the Commission on Management of the Jews has been issued.
> 3. Planning to settle the remaining Jews in a separate part of the town.
> 4. The Jews have been and are continuing to be employed in public works.
> 5. A former activist [Communist] Jew has been shot; the other ones have escaped.
> 6. There are efforts to utilize Jews for work in the fields.[127]

In mid-July 1941, a discussion was recorded in the minutes of "The Meeting of the Joniškis Activists' Staff on the Question of Handling the Jews." The town's mayor raised the issue of coordination between the activists (LAF) and local authorities, since it was not entirely clear who was in charge of Jews. Ralys noted that the collapse of Communism was imminent and that there was no doubt that "we will arrive at National Socialism." It was decided that local governments would "work in contact with the [LAF] activists' staff and the commission on Jewish matters." The participants unanimously endorsed the relocation of the estimated 1,200 Jews of Joniškis and then discussed alternatives for an exchange of populations. Some argued for the housing of Jews in synagogues and in homes adjacent to the market since "no Lithuanians live there," but there was disagreement as to the exact location. All present agreed to impose a "Jewish

---

126 "LAF Joniškio skyriaus štabo protokolas," July 11, 1941, ibid., l. 2.
127 "Joniškio pagalbinės policijos įkūrimas," July 14, 1941, ibid., l. 29.

contribution" of twenty thousand rubles: twelve of the town's "more influential Jews" were to be held hostage until they signed for the money. The meeting decided to appropriate furniture from "well-to-do Jews and those who had fled," in order to satisfy the needs of the "Activists' Staff, the police and citizens who had suffered on account of the war." The police chief announced the immediate imposition of the Star of David on outer garments in a way that was consistent with the practice in other towns.[128] The Jewish commission ordered "all Jews who were living among the farmers of the rural county [*valsčius*] to return to Joniškis and register at the Municipality by July 15 at 1400 hours," threatening punishment for those who failed to appear, and obligated "all persons to whom Jews had entrusted or hidden any kind of property to report this to the heads of the rural county as quickly as possible."[129]

According to the records, implementation of the new regulations was not without difficulty. On July 18 the Joniškis LAF Staff noted that:

> [T]he Lithuanian Activist Front's Commission for Jewish Affairs had on July 11 publicly issued nine orders to the Jews which many of them did not carry out. For example, not all Jews had returned to the town from the villages, and not a single Jew is wearing the Star of David on the chest. Some Jews are still using sidewalks, other Jews are still employing the services of Aryans, etc. The Staff of the Activist Front, observing that the Jews are not obeying the orders, has decided to impose a 20,000 rubles contribution, which must be paid to the Activist Staff on July 19 between 1200 and 1500 hours.[130]

The July 20 meeting of the Joniškis leadership asserted that "the Jews who were moving into their district [ghetto] can take all movable property," but also decided that "Jews who are working in the fields can stay in place."[131] Despite delays, the ghettoization of the Jews proceeded apace.

The anti-Jewish measures of the Joniškis LAF were embedded in a wider upsurge of repression and persecution, fueled by fears of conspiracies, which included non-Jewish Communist suspects and alleged saboteurs. A sense of the paranoia is reflected in the following passage of the police report of mid-July:

---

128 "Joniškio aktyvistų štabo, žydų tvarkymo klausimu susirinkimo protokolas" [undated], ibid., l. 10.
129 "Aktyvistų fronto štabo žydų tvarkymo komisijos įsakymai" [undated], ibid., l. 11–12.
130 "LAF Joniškio skyriaus žydų tvarkymo komisijos įsakymas," July 18, 1941, ibid., l. 13.
131 "LAF Joniškio protokolas," July 20, 1941, ibid., l. 8.

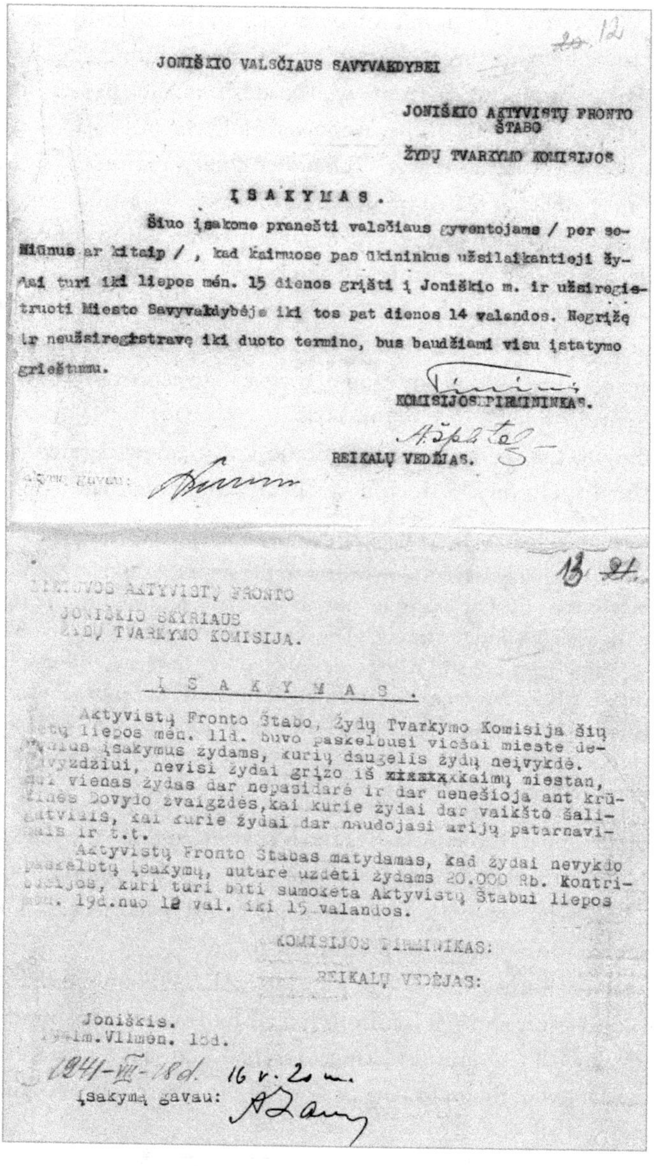

JONIŠKIO VALSČIAUS SAVYVALDYBEI

JONIŠKIO AKTYVISTŲ FRONTO ŠTABO

ŽYDŲ TVARKYMO KOMISIJOS

ĮSAKYMAS.

Šiuo įsakome pranešti valsčiaus gyventojams / per seniūnus ar kitaip /, kad kaimuose pas ūkininkus užsilaikantieji žydai turi iki liepos mėn. 15 dienos grįšti į Joniškio m. ir užsiregistruoti Miesto Savyvaldybėje iki tos pat dienos 14 valandos. Negrįžę ir neužsiregistravę iki duoto termino, bus baudžiami visu įstatymo griežtumu.

KOMISIJOS PIRMININKAS.

REIKALŲ VEDĖJAS.

LIETUVOS AKTYVISTŲ FRONTO
JONIŠKIO SKYRIAUS
ŽYDŲ TVARKYMO KOMISIJA.

ĮSAKYMAS.

Aktyvistų Fronto Štabo, Žydų Tvarkymo Komisija šių metų liepos mėn. 11d. buvo paskelbusi viešai mieste devynius įsakymus žydams, kurių daugelis žydų neįvykdė. Pavyzdžiui, nevisi žydai grįžo iš ~~xxxxx~~ kaimų miestan, nei vienas žydas dar nepasidarė ir dar nenešioja ant krūtinės Dovydo žvaigždės, kai kurie žydai dar vaikšto šaligatviais, kai kurie žydai dar naudojasi arijų patarnavimais ir t.t.

Aktyvistų Fronto Štabas matydamas, kad žydai nevykdo paskelbtų įsakymų, nutarė uždėti žydams 20.000 Rb. kontribucijos, kuri turi būti sumokėta Aktyvistų Štabui liepos mėn. 19d. nuo 12 val. iki 15 valandos.

KOMISIJOS PIRMININKAS:

REIKALŲ VEDĖJAS:

Joniškis.
1941m. VIImėn. 18d.

1941-VII-18d. 16 v. 20 m.

Įsakymą gavau:

IMAGE 3.9. Ghettoization in the provinces.
Top: The Joniškis LAF chapter's Jewish Affairs Commission orders Jews who are "staying [as workers] among farmers" to return from the countryside to the town (undated).
Below: The town's Jewish Affairs Commission reiterates the order citing the reluctance of Jews to wear the Star of David, observe the curfew, and other restrictions, July 18, 1941.
(Courtesy of Lithuanian Central State Archive.)

Rumors are spreading in Joniškis:
1. Jewish women are spreading gossip that Russians will come here in two weeks, and they will take revenge on the Lithuanians.
2. There is a rumor that a class of rich people will emerge and enslave the working class. ...
3. The [Lithuanian] nation's undesirable element is broadcasting the rumor that in the future workers will be arrested.[132]

On July 16, the local LAF decided to organize "a parade of Komsomol members with the appropriate banners and pictures on July 26 (during St. Ann's festival)," intended as a "moral punishment" to the former Communist youth. Milder penance was planned for "the children of workers," with harsher measures against the offspring of "farmers, or otherwise well-to-do parents." The activists compiled a list of 104 Komsomol members for the exercise, about a third of whom were Jews.[133] There are numerous other reports of the public humiliation of the Jews in the shtetls which took the form of coerced processions singing the praises of Lenin and Stalin amidst much mockery and abuse, a well-known ritual throughout the German-occupied USSR during the first month of the war, also noted by Jan T. Gross in his study of the Polish town of Jedwabne.[134]

The establishment of the "small ghettos," as in the example of Joniškis, resulted in the community's descent into a zone of "otherness" unprecedented in the country's history. Whatever the initial aims of the local authorities in segregating the Jews of the shtetls, the isolation of the victims considerably facilitated their rapid destruction once the Nazi officials in Berlin and Kaunas decided to proceed with the systemic annihilation of Lithuania's provincial Jewry.

Pacification, Terror, and Anti-Jewish Violence: "Bloody July" across the Provinces

During the first month of the occupation, anti-Jewish actions took place within the context of a wider pacification campaign, as German security forces and

---

132 "Joniškio pagalbinės poicijos įkūrimas," July 13, 1941, ibid., l. 29.
133 "LAF Joniškio skyriaus, susirinkimo protokolas," July 16, 1941, ibid., l. 4; also, "Buvusiųjų komjaunuolių registracijos sąrašas," July 26, 1941, ibid., l. 5–6 a.p.
134 Jan T. Gross, *Neighbors: The Destruction of the Jewish Community in Jedwabne, Poland* (Princeton University Press: Princeton, 2001), 88–89, 98–99.

their auxiliaries tightened their control. Lithuanian police reports described the mopping up campaign as protecting the population from internal enemies, traitors, and saboteurs. References to the specific targets, "gangs of Red Army stragglers, Russian vagabonds, Soviet activists and Jews hiding in the forests," appear frequently in the documents.[135] On July 6, 1941, the Alytus police created a list of fifty-one persons subject to arrest. The majority were ethnic Lithuanians, but several Jews were also named, including a "security agent," Chaimas Zingeris. On July 17 the Alytus district chief Antanas Audronis reported to the PG's interior minister that "the police are carrying out arrests and searches, and are investigating cases of Communists, robbers, and rumor mongers, which are then brought to the local German military leaders. According to German orders, 82 Communists have been executed. There are 389 people under arrest, and another 345 Communists should be detained."[136]

By mid-July the Alytus partisans had created a TDA company whose avowed purpose was "to cooperate closely with the security and police, as well as the society-at-large in Alytus and the surrounding area, and to complete the liquidation of the lingering traitors to the nation and the Bolshevik-Communists who have inundated our country, thus insuring the serenity and security of the region's inhabitants." The company included a special unit composed of "volunteers, mostly active partisans," who led the hunt. As they combed the forests, the TDA men invoked the help of local villagers and informers. On July 28, 1941, the company received a report that "Communist Party instructor Videikas is hiding in Vabaliai forest in the Alovė rural county with several other Communists and Jews, and they are threatening the local inhabitants." The unit's commander kept a journal of his successes and concluded:

> Until now, in the space of a month and a half, we have received more than fifty reports requiring active measures. In response to citizens' complaints 36 Communists, nine Red Army men and a larger number of Jews were detained and arrested. It should be noted that among the reports received, several came directly from the local German commandant's office. In carrying out various tasks the platoon suffered no injuries or combat fatalities. The platoon operated quickly and decisively,

---

135 For example, in "Alytaus šaulių rinktinė," LCVA, f. R-660, ap. 2, b. 131; also "Alytaus apskrities viršininkas," f. R-1436, ap. 1, b. 29.

136 Cited in Bubnys, *Holokaustas Lietuvos provincijoje*, 29.

which created a huge impression on those in hiding, [as well as among] the plundering element, and their lackeys.¹³⁷

Contemporary reports make clear that much of the population, energized by the euphoria of liberation from Communist rule, strongly supported the "cleansing" efforts. Many informers were motivated by a desire to settle scores, often based on grievances accumulated during the Soviet occupation. Others were enraged by the attempts of Soviet sympathizers to return to positions of authority and even enroll in the TDA. As an example, on July 12, 1941, residents of Butrimonys filed a complaint, utilizing antisemitic arguments, alleging that former Communist activists had been released from detention and had wormed their way into positions of authority. The chief of police, Kazys Pilionis, had announced to his force that "from now on there is no difference between the Jews and other people." According to the petitioners, local Jews "began to feel as if they were masters of the town again, that is, not only were they hanging out by the windows or on doorsteps, but now they dare to stroll on the sidewalks." The specter of the threat posed by armed Jewish activists was raised: "it is becoming unsafe for us, the town's residents, since then it might happen as it did in Alytus, Varėna and elsewhere, where German soldiers died at the hands of the Jews, and then innocent townspeople were killed [in reprisal]." In July the local forest ranger Kazys Rėklaitis visited Butrimonys and wrote a report indicting the police chief as a "very great friend of the Jews" and accused him of releasing the "Communist and Jewish activists" who had been arrested by the local chapter of the former Riflemen. As a sign of their impudence, he wrote, the Jews had erased the signs identifying their homes and spread rumors of imminent revenge against Lithuanians, all of this without any response from Pilionis.¹³⁸

Some of the arrest records of suspected Soviet collaborators and Komsomol members combined ethnic Lithuanians and Jews in a single list, but more often, the authorities registered them separately. Most important, from the point of view of the victims, was the disposition of their cases. Two pages from the correspondence of the Veliuona police precinct in western Lithuania are instructive.

---

137 "Trumpa TDA (Alytaus kuopos) veikimo apžvalga," LCVA, R-660, ap. 2, b. 231, 1–1 ap., and "Šaulių-partizanų kuopos vykusių darbų dienynas," ibid., l. 3–13 ap.

138 "Raportas-skundas," July 12, 1941, LCVA, f. R-1436, ap. 1, b. 27, l. 33–35, and "Piliečio Kazio Rėklaičio pranešimas," July 17, 1941, ibid., l. 32. The "reprisal" noted here probably refers to the incident in Alytus on the night of June 24–25, 1941.

On July 11, 1941, the police chief, the "leader of the partisans," and two "activists" reported the transfer of alleged Communist detainees to Kaunas. One document, addressed to the Chief of the Prison of Hard Labor, that is, the Seventh Fort,[139] recorded fifteen "detained Jewish Communists of Veliuona, who had persecuted and terrorized Lithuanians, and mercilessly sent them to the depths of Russia. Through their efforts, more than one nationally conscious Lithuanian was martyred." The second list included eleven ethnic Lithuanians sent to the chief of the Security Police of Kaunas district, the men described as "the fiercest Communists, the most active propagators of Communist ideas and persecutors of the people, who mercilessly tortured the nationally conscious Lithuanians of the Veliuona region."[140] The destinations of the detainees are revealing: the Jews are headed to the Seventh Fort, almost certainly to their deaths. But the Lithuanian collaborators were sent to the security police in Kaunas where they had a chance of a better outcome.

An atmosphere of vengeance, score-settling, and a sense of impunity marked the witch hunts. On July 24 the Šiauliai district LAF sent out a circular noting that "the leadership of the LAF sections are not coordinating their activity with the local administrative organs and the police ... [and] arbitrarily assume rights which are not assigned by the LAF Staff and do not fall under their jurisdiction." The staff complained that "seized by their mood, people have committed untactful acts which besmirch the name of our organization and hamper creative work." All local LAF chapters were ordered to "cease interfering in the work of the police ... who have sole jurisdiction in maintaining order."[141] A few days later, the Šiauliai district procurator Matas Krygeris cautioned local administraetions about abuses directed against alleged Communists and fellow travelers, noting that many people "had expressed concern about the arrests and *elimination of Lithuanians* in many districts" (emphasis in original). Krygeris wrote:

> In some places the arrests are equivalent to shooting [of the suspects]. *There is not a single city, town or rural county where Lithuanians themselves*

---

139 In other documents, the fort was designated as a "concentration camp."

140 LCVA, f. 378, ap. 5, b. 3720, l. 13–14. While the document listing Jewish detainees refers to the destination as "Fort Seven," the words are struck out and replaced with "hard labor." At that point in mid-July the Seventh Fort's official designation was that of a concentration camp, but the facility was utilized primarily as an execution site.

141 "Lietuvių Aktyvistų Fronto Šiaulių Apskr. Štabo įsakymas Nr. 2," July 24, 1941, LCVA, f. R-739, ap. 1, b. 4, l. 17.

are not arresting other Lithuanians. Among the arrested Lithuanians are public employees, farmers, craftsmen, workers, women, minors and even children 15–16 years of age. In many places, *the death penalty has been carried out* against the detained without any investigation. I have confirmed the very sad fact that entirely innocent Lithuanians have been among those arrested. The baseless elimination of Lithuanians who worked in Bolshevik offices constitutes a destruction of the Lithuanian nation itself and such a full sweep of revenge deserves the sternest rejection. (Emphasis in original)

The procurator demanded that all cases of Soviet collaborators, except those investigated by the German Security Police, be turned over to the relevant local Lithuanian police authorities and that the excesses of what he termed unauthorized "outsiders" be severely punished.[142] Krygeris made no mention of the detained Jews.

Nazi control was more evident in the cities and larger towns where the German military commandants had announced anti-Jewish measures early in the occupation. In the provinces, as in the Joniškis case, Lithuanian administrators and police leaders at times implemented their own anti-Jewish policies with little or no German encouragement. For Lithuanian Jews, more deadly than the ghettoization and the gratuitous humiliation at the hands of "activists" were the concurrent "selective cleansing" operations: the roundups and executions of Jews, mostly young and adult males, as well as a smaller number of accused "women Communists." These killing operations were generally similar but varied in terms of organization and scale depending on the locale. An important feature of these actions as they progressed into July was the increasing participation of local police and paramilitary units.

In the border zone, the killings in July 1941 followed the pattern laid out in the actions of the first week in Gargždai, Kretinga, and other towns. On the eve of the war Jews made up about one third of the ten thousand residents in Tauragė, the largest community close to the German border, which was captured by the Wehrmacht on the first day of the invasion after a fierce battle which destroyed much of the town. Following their victory, German soldiers murdered Rabbi Levin Shpitz. As elsewhere, anti-Soviet partisans quickly established Lithuanian control and appointed former officials to head the district offices and the police. Lieutenant Paul Schwarz, the head of the Lauksargiai (Laukszargen)

---

142 Krygeris to Tauragė district chief, July 29, 1941 (copy provided to author).

border post, induced the mayor Jonas Jurgilas and the leader of the 150–man insurgents group to provide a list of the town's Communists as well as Jewish men between fourteen and sixty years of age. The police arrested about three hundred Jewish men and twenty-five Lithuanian Communists, although some of the latter detainees were quickly released. On July 2 about twenty SD men from Tilsit, a second group led by Schwarz, and a unit of Lithuanian policemen escorted the selected men, mostly Jews and several alleged Lithuanian Communists, out of the prison and robbed the victims of their valuables. The SD men and the Lauksargiai border guards then reportedly shot 133 victims in a pit outside of the town. The physician Joffe and the dentist Möst were among the Jewish victims. Between July 3 and July 10 Schwarz commanded a group of German and Lithuanian police in the execution of another 122 men in woods about two kilometers outside of Tauragė, and later led some of the Lithuanian "white armbands" in the killing of twelve Jewish men and three Lithuanian Communists in the village of Visbutai.[143]

At the end of June, anti-Soviet insurgents at Švėkšna (Tauragė district) arrested suspected Lithuanian and Jewish Communists, eleven of whom were later shot at the Jewish cemetery.[144] In nearby Šilalė, the partisans and police corralled the local men in the synagogue in early July, while women and children were housed in several blocks of an improvised ghetto. During an alleged escape attempt from the synagogue, the Lithuanian guards reportedly killed some of the men with grenades and gunfire. Soon after the incident a carload of SD officers arrived and supervised the shooting of the remaining 135 men at the Jewish cemetery outside of the town. On July 24 the local auxiliary police organized the killing of some fifty-five men at the nearby hamlet of Pajūris. In Skaudvilė the one thousand Jewish inhabitants made up nearly half of the town's population. On July 17, 1941, the town's mayor instructed Jewish men to gather in the town square where, according to postwar testimony, a "uniformed German" told the gathering that they would be taken to work. The number of victims has not been established although at least several hundred men were reportedly detained at the nearby Pužai village post office. On the following day Germans shot the Jewish men in nearby woods as Lithuanian auxiliary police guarded the perimeter of the execution site. A few days, later German and Lithuanian police executed

---

143 Bubnys, *Holokaustas Lietuvos provincijoje*, 435–439.
144 Bubnys, *Holokaustas Lietuvos provincijoje*, 449.

more than a hundred of Skaudvilė's older men at the Jewish cemetery in Upyna village some twelve kilometers from the town.[145]

Further to the south, the seven hundred Jewish residents who lived in the border town of Kudirkos Naumiestis were trapped when the town fell on the morning of June 22. On the same afternoon, the German military commandant initiated the organization of a local Lithuanian committee, one of whose members, Jurgis Krasauskas, later reported: "During the first days the organized police and partisans cleansed the surrounding areas of Jews, Communists, and gangs of Soviet soldiers. Currently life in Kudirkos Naumiestis proceeds normally, as if the war had never happened, except that very few Jews are to be seen."[146] Postwar court records indicate that on June 28, 1941, a German police unit executed seventeen accused Lithuanian Communists and Soviet activists. Other reports cite the killings of pro-Soviet elements in the town's Jewish cemetery. During the first week of July, the Tilsit SD led a squad of German police and Lithuanian auxiliaries in the shootings of 192 Jewish men. The town's leaders invited the killers to a dinner after the executions. The remaining Jews were incarcerated until mid-September. Yosef Gertner recounts a killing action in the nearby hamlet of Kriūkai: "On July 2 the local police and partisans assembled all the men over the age of 14, including the very old, and took them to Šakiai, the nearest large town... They were herded into a barn on the edge of town and put to work digging pits. On Wednesday July 9, 1941, they were all shot."[147] German-Lithuanian units led by the Tilsit SD and other police agencies shot nearly two hundred "dangerous Soviet elements," the majority of whom were Jews, in the border towns of Kybartai and Virbalis in mid-July, although the sources are not consistent as to the exact number of victims or the dates of these particular killings.[148]

On the eve of the war, the 2,900 Jews who lived in Marijampolė, the largest town in the southwestern Suvalkija region of Lithuania, constituted about a fifth of the population. The Germans captured Marijampolė on the second day of the war amidst fighting which severely damaged the town, destroying at least two hundred homes. Lithuanian authorities quickly organized a municipal authority

---

145 Ibid., 443–448.
146 Quoted in Brandišauskas, *1941 m. birželio sukilimas*, 145.
147 Testimony of Yosef Gertner in Bankier, *Expulsion*, 124.
148 Dieckmann, *Besatzungspolitik*, 1:389–390; cf. the more detailed account in Bubnys, *Holokaustas Lietuvos provincijoje*, 546–548.

and a police force largely recruited from men who had previously served in the army. A special unit of about twenty policemen were directed against perceived enemies. On July 9, Vaclovas Goštautas, the chief of the district, ordered the confiscation of means of transport owned by Jews, transferring expropriated horses to farmers in need. Further anti-Jewish decrees followed: forced labor, a curfew, the wearing of the yellow Star of David. A six-man Jewish council headed by Rabbi Abromas Geleris was appointed as the community's liaison to the authorities. By the end of July police reports counted at least five shootings of Jews and suspected Communists totaling more than two hundred victims. According to postwar interrogations, the initial killings were carried out by German security forces while auxiliaries guarded the sites and buried the victims but in time, the Lithuanian force took an active part in the shootings. On August 5, 1941, the mayor wrote to the district commandant that his accounting of the townspeople listed 2,425 Jews out of a population of 13,266,[149] the decline in the Jewish population due to escapes eastward and the first wave of shootings.

German troops occupied Lazdijai, some thirty-five kilometers south of Marijampolė, on the first day of the war after a heavy bombardment which destroyed much of the town's center. About forty Jews managed to escape eastward with the retreating Soviet troops, while hundreds more fled the town and sought to find safety in the surrounding villages and forests. On June 23 a group that described itself as "the entire intelligentsia community of Lazdijai town, with the exception of the Jews as well as Lithuanians who had been polluted with the Communist spirit," called a meeting and elected a provisional district committee. It is recorded that "the gathering concluded with the Lithuanian national anthem and powerful hurrahs for the German army and its Commander-in-Chief Adolf Hitler."[150] On the next day the Lazdijai committee received German permission to establish an auxiliary police force. On June 25, the group's first item on the agenda reads: "The Jewish question. At the request of the German military commandant, it has been decided to settle those Jews who are most dangerous to the public order in barracks on Vytautas Street." On July 2, the committee received a formal mandate to establish civilian rule in the Lazdijai district and on the same day adopted two decisions concerning the

---

149 The archival sources for the Marijampolė population statistics are listed in Arūnas Bubnys, *Holokaustas Lietuvos provincijoje*, 243–244..

150 Protocol of the Meeting of the Intelligentsia of Lazdijai Town, June 23, 1941, in Brandišauskas, *1941 m. birželio sukilimas*, 239.

Jews: "1. All [Soviet-]confiscated farms, homes, and other properties are to be transferred to the legal owners for their use. This decision does not pertain to the Jews who are only permitted as residents in their farms or homes . . . ; 6. Jews are not permitted to engage in commerce and industry."[151] On July 15, the Lazdijai Lithuanian Security Police chief reported that he had arrested local Communists: eleven Lithuanians, four Jews and a Russian who were subsequently executed in Marijampolė.[152]

The well-documented case of Jurbarkas is instructive on the manner in which German and Lithuanian perpetrators interacted during the early anti-Jewish operations in the western borderlands. Jews numbered almost a third of the 4,400 citizens in this historic town on the Nemunas River located within five kilometers of the Lithuanian-German border which the Wehrmacht captured in the first hours of the invasion. The German commandant ordered everyone to obey Jurgis Gepneris, the Lithuanian mayor, and announced that sabotage and plunder would be punished by death. (Unbeknownst to the Germans, Gepneris, who Germanized his surname to Hopfner in 1942, had supported the Communists during the Soviet occupation.) The Lithuanian insurgents quickly reconstituted the police force under the command of Mykolas Levickas, a thirty-two-year-old secondary school teacher who also served as the Germans' translator and informer. On June 23 SS Squad Leader Gerhard Carsten, the chief of the German border police station in Smalininkai (German: Schmalleningken), arrived in Jurbarkas and met with Levickas and another ten Lithuanians at the home of a local priest. Carsten ordered the townspeople to compile lists of Communists and Jewish men and then inspected the Jewish cemetery as a place for future executions. The Lithuanian police used the lists to arrest the victims and steal their valuables. The Germans and the local police forced the Jews of the town to wear an identifying badge, banned them from the sidewalks, and ordered them to give up their radios. The persecutors publicly humiliated the victims, forcing Jews to destroy, with their own hands, the town's wooden synagogue and the small Jewish slaughterhouse, then to burn the Torah. Germans reportedly photographed an incident in which Jews were ordered to sing and dance before the portraits of Stalin and Lenin and then compelled to wash up in the Nemunas River in a mock "baptism."

---

151 As in the committee's protocols of June 25 and July 2, 1941, as published in ibid., 242, 247.
152 Bubnys, *Holokaustas Lietuvos provinciojoje*, 221.

On July 3, 1941, SS Major Böhme led a squad of the Tilsit Gestapo office police in the shooting of the detainees: two hundred fifty Jewish men and seventy Lithuanians (five women were also reported among the victims). Böhme then ordered the arrest of sixty more Jewish men who were brought to the execution site. During the shootings, some Jews resisted: Emil Max, who had fled Klaipėda in 1939 and was a recipient of the Iron Cross from World War I, attacked the SS officers and injured one of them in the leg before he was killed. SS Second Lieutenant Wiechert who was in charge of the grave-digging detail forced Jews to beat each other before they were murdered. Two men succeeded in crawling out of the killing pit after the executions, one of whom, Antanas Leonavičius, later testified about the massacre. The victims represented a part of the local elite. The Lithuanian dead were mostly people who had worked for the Soviet authorities or had been accused of pro-Communist leanings, notably Vincas Grybas, Lithuania's best-known sculptor. The valuables stolen from the Jews served to buy food and drinks for the Jurbarkas killers who celebrated the atrocity; later, the German police used the victims' money to pay for a week-long vacation at the Palanga resort.[153]

Attacks on Jews at the outbreak of the war also occurred in the central and eastern regions of the country which were beyond the reach of the German police units from East Prussia who had commanded the early killings along the western border areas. The Jews of Kėdainiai and its environs had maintained a flourishing community with roots dating to the sixteenth century. The Soviet population estimate of January 1941 counted 4,682 Jews living in the district, mostly in Kėdainiai, Ariogala, and Krakės. During the invasion and concurrent insurrection, a unit of Lithuanian partisans took over the town and established a rudimentary administration. As elsewhere, the German commandant issued antisemitic discriminatory decrees including one about the wearing of yellow stars. The "white armbands" reportedly beat to death Mayke Berger, the owner of the Kėdainiai cinema, and shot to death the tailor Reubin Chessler. On July 23, 1941, German and Lithuanian police carried out a mass execution of alleged Communists in the nearby village of Babėnai: eighty-three Jewish men, twelve Jewish women, fifteen Lithuanians, fourteen Russians, and a "Russian political officer."[154]

---

153 Account based on the documentation in Dieckmann and Sužiedėlis, *Mass Murder*, 156–164; cf. Bubnys, *Holokaustas Lietuvos provincijoje*, 308–311.
154 Jäger Report, December 1, 1941, 1.

On the eve of the invasion an estimated eight hundred Jews constituted a fifth of the populace in Mažeikiai, had maintained a vibrant cultural and economic life, including a Hebrew-language school, and owned most of the city's retail outlets. The Wehrmacht arrived there on June 26, but the main job of securing the town was left to a band of insurgents who overcame resistance from Soviet supporters and then seized control. By July 1, the "white armbands" felt confident enough, as they later reported, "to begin visiting the Jews who were hiding behind closed doors and shutters," with the purpose of disarming supposedly dangerous elements. Some of the Jews, they claimed, "did not want to let the partisans into their homes (such as Girša Geimanas and others) and intended to fight back with automatic pistols." A more permanent Nazi presence, "seven German soldiers," arrived on July 3 and ordered the segregation of the Mažeikiai Jews, some of whom were imprisoned in the town's synagogue. The partisans arrested nearly a hundred accused Soviet collaborators of different nationalities and shot the dentist Pnina Lamp and her daughter who were slow to obey orders. One report confirms that a twenty-man German unit armed with automatic weapons carried out two actions in mid-July: the execution of some forty-five Soviet activists and the shooting of Jewish men held in the Mažeikiai synagogue. Soon after, the "white armbands" and police gathered the old men, women, and children of the town, as well as Jews from Akmenė, Viekšniai, Seda, Židikai, Laižuva, and other shtetls of the region, and imprisoned them in a large compound owned by the local German miller Latsch.[155]

Located thirty-five kilometers northeast of Kaunas, Jonava was home to one of the largest Jewish communities in central Lithuania comprising, on the eve of the invasion, roughly 60% of the municipality's estimated five thousand citizens. Between the wars, the shtetl had supported seven synagogues, a large Jewish bank, and numerous cultural, political, and sports organizations. Jonava had been the site of a fierce battle between the Red Army and the Wehrmacht before the Germans finally captured the town on June 25, 1941. Anti-Soviet insurgents attacked Soviet troop convoys as well as Jews and Communist activists as they fled eastward. Some refugees escaped, but most were forced to turn back. Other Jews who tried to seek safety in Kaunas were reportedly among the victims shot at the Seventh Fort during the first week of July. At first the insurgents limited themselves to maintaining order and securing bridges and the rail station but

---

155 As reported in Brandišauskas, *1941 m. birželio sukilimas*, 111; more in Bubnys, *Holokaustas Lietuvos provincijoje*, 257–259.

within a few weeks, dozens of fighters were issued Lithuanian uniforms and renamed a "self-defense" unit under the command of Vladas Kulvicas, a former officer in the Lithuanian army reserve. These militarized policemen came under the authority of the German commandant and thus resembled the command structure of the TDA. By all accounts they became increasingly more involved in systematic persecution of the area's Jews and suspected Communists.

On July 8, 1941, Lithuanian auxiliary police corralled the more than one thousand Jews of the north-central town of Radviliškis, about twenty kilometers from Šiauliai, and confined them to an army barracks near the local railroad depot where the men were put to work. Four days later German police and Lithuanian auxiliaries separated about three hundred males over the age of sixteen from the other inmates and massacred them in a forest not far from the Jewish cemetery. About a hundred of the women and children were transferred to the Šiauliai ghetto, while the remaining Jews were imprisoned in a walled barracks outside the town until late August 1941 when they were escorted to the ghetto in Žagarė.[156] In Linkuva, further east of Šiauliai city, the arrests of suspected Soviet collaborators and Jews intensified after the first week of the war. The Soviet commission which investigated the atrocities exhumed seventy-one Soviet activists murdered during this initial period of whom only half were ever identified. Witnesses related that on July 25 or 26, a squad of Lithuanian policemen rounded up the Jewish men of Linkuva. Several German Security Police officers arrived after the detention and supervised the convoy of the nearly two hundred doomed men to the outskirts of Dvariūkai village where the local police carried out the shootings.[157]

According to the Soviet population survey of January 1, 1941, the 6,723 Jews of Panevėžys, Lithuania's fourth largest city, made up nearly a fourth of the population; another 5,231 Jews lived in the surrounding rural counties. The Germans entered the city on June 26 and found anti-Soviet rebels already in control of much of the city. On July 11, the Wehrmacht ordered the creation of what was termed a "Jewish quarter" in a four-street block. On July 17, the enclosure was surrounded by barbed wire and guarded by armed police. Non-Jews forced to leave the neighborhood that had become the ghetto were transferred to other properties. On July 28, the "Committee of the Jewish Quarter"

---

156 Ibid., 394–395; cf. the testimony of Reyne Kaplan in Bankier, *Expulsion*, 89–90. On the fate of the Jews of the Žagarė Ghetto see below, Chapter 4.

157 Bubnys, *Holokaustas Lietuvos provincijoje*, 386–388.

reported that their charges included 4,423 Jews, of whom only 3,207 lived in houses, the remainder in makeshift arrangements outdoors.[158] The overcrowding was extreme: survivor Y. Molk reported that "After the ghetto was totally filled all the men were taken to the local prison. Several hundred men were kept in one small room, which was so crowded there was hardly room to stand. They were not given any food or water."[159] The unsanitary conditions led to the outbreak of disease. The police routinely escorted the men to hard labor outside the ghetto.

The northeastern town of Utena counted some seven thousand residents in the summer of 1941, including more than two thousand Jews. Witnesses report that a young Jewish woman was raped and murdered in Utena on the very first day of the war. The ranks of anti-Soviet insurgents swelled as men who had fled into the forests during the deportations of June 14–17 came out of hiding. The rebels engaged both the Red Army and Soviet activists in pitched battles, liberated hundreds of prisoners, and gained control of Utena before the arrival of the Wehrmacht. On June 25, the Voldemarist and Gestapo agent Malinauskas was appointed the chief of police. On the following day, the Fifty-Sixth Army Corps of the Fourth Panzer Group passed Utena on the way to Daugavpils. At this time, nearly five hundred men had already joined the insurrection.

The partisans searched and plundered Jewish homes while abusing the residents, singling out the Jewish intelligentsia, Communists, Komsomol members, and other suspected enemies found on lists captured from abandoned Soviet offices. Throughout July of 1941 personnel from the 691st Military Gendarmerie headed the administration in Utena. The Germans made clear that attacks on Jews carried no punishment and encouraged the channeling of anti-Jewish violence into a more systematic policy of persecution. The authorities forced the Jews to perform humiliating labor such as searching for mines, which resulted in several deaths. Lithuanian police turned the town's four synagogues into prisons for Jews, refugees, and persons accused of pro-Soviet collaboration. Rabbis who refused to burn the Torah were publicly tortured. On the morning of July 14, 1941, the Lithuanian municipal authorities ordered Jews to leave Utena by noon: anyone discovered in town after the expulsion would be shot. The police assembled Jews in the Šilinė forest in the outskirts of town, registered

---

158 Arūnas Bubnys, "Lietuvių policijos Šiaulių (14–asis) ir Panevėžio (10–asis) batalionai (1941–1944)," *Genocidas ir rezistencija* 2, no. 27 (2010): 85.

159 Bankier, *Expulsion and Extermination*, 154.

the captives, and seized their valuables. The press and radio announced that Utena was the first town in Lithuania to be "free of the Jews." For more than two weeks, nearly two thousand Jews from Utena were confined in the forest, suffering unsanitary conditions, adverse weather, and the taunts of their guards. There was little to eat. The younger people were taken to forced labor during the day. Periodically, the guards executed groups of young Jewish men.[160]

Nearby Rokiškis underwent a similar trajectory of violence. Despite emigration during the 1930s, it is estimated that approximately 4,500 Jews lived in this district on the eve of the war, of whom more than a third resided in the town. When news of the invasion broke, well-armed insurgents attacked the Red Army and local Communist militias. Soviet atrocities against dozens of civilians during the Red Army's retreat were well publicized, contributing to an atmosphere of rage and calls for vengeance. German troops entered Rokiškis on June 27 and found the insurgents in charge; the invaders reportedly killed two Jewish men during the first hours of the occupation. Most Rokiškis Jews who attempted to flee were turned back at the old Soviet-Lithuanian border. The anti-Soviet rebels, their ranks swelled by Red Army deserters, established a company-sized Lithuanian paramilitary unit which carried out the first large-scale arrests of Jewish men and alleged Communists on June 29, under the leadership of Lieutenant Jonas Žukas, the town's self-appointed commandant. Some of the detainees were executed in a forest near the Steponiai village about five kilometers north of the town. According to postwar Soviet investigations, on about July 8, "white armbands" seized over a hundred young Jews between the ages of fourteen and thirty ostensibly for a work detail, but then shot them during the night. On July 22, the commandant's soldiers executed thirty mainly Russian and Lithuanian Soviet activists. A monument erected in 1958 listed 981 "victims of fascist terror," a number corresponding precisely to the Jäger report, which counted "493 Jews, 432 Russians and 56 Lithuanians (all active Communists)" executed between June 27 and August 14, 1941.[161]

Over the next weeks hundreds of Jews from surrounding villages and shtetls were also brought into the Rokiškis Ghetto, among whom were some of Matilda

---

160 Bubnys, *Holokaustas Lietuvos provincijoje*, 523–524; Dieckmann and Sužiedėlis, *Mass Murder*, 70–76.

161 Ibid., 349–358; cf. Jäger reports of September 10 and December 1, 1941. The large number of Russians reflects the sizeable Old Believer community which arrived in northeast Lithuania during the tsarist period.

Olkinaitė's friends and acquaintances from Panemunėlis. The men were taken to stables outside of the town, while the young children and women were incarcerated for a time in the Antanašė estate located near Obeliai. Extant documents indicate that the detention centers, designated as a Jewish "concentration camp," were guarded by twenty-four men under the command of Lieutenant Vladas Baltrušaitis. On August 4 Žukas ordered the Jews to surrender their furniture and other valuable items and conscripted able-bodied Jews for work to benefit the Lithuanian community, but this latter plan does not appear to have gone smoothly. On August 8, Žukas publicly criticized people who had received the appointed "persons of Jewish nationality" for labor but had been lax in supervision, or had not compelled them to work at all, warning that such soft-hearted types would be punished as saboteurs and placed on a shaming list of "those who honor the Jews."[162]

Located on the border of Belarus, Švenčionys was home to a large Jewish community whose roots can be traced to the eighteenth century. Under the Polish rule of the interwar years, the town contained five synagogues, Hebrew and Yiddish schools, as well as a plethora of social, religious, and political organizations. It was the birthplace of noted Yiddish poet Menke Katz (1906–1991), the founder of Reformist Judaism Mordecai Kaplan (1881–1983), and renowned Holocaust historian Yitzhak Arad (1926–2021). Before the war the town's three thousand Jews made up about a third of the population. The area underwent an unusual and traumatic series of changes in government in 1939. Following the outbreak of war in 1939, the region came under the control of the Soviets after the Red Army's invasion of Poland on September 17; soon after, Švenčionys was annexed by the Soviet Union and became part of the Belarusian SSR. In August 1940 as part of the Supreme Soviet's decree formalizing the Kremlin's incorporation of Lithuania into the Soviet Union, the town and its environs were transferred to the Lithuanian SSR, resulting, for the first time, in a significant ethnic Lithuanian presence in the local administration.

The Wehrmacht captured Švenčionys on June 27, 1941. Anti-Soviet insurgents were active in the area, bolstered by the desertion of many of the Red Army's Lithuanian 179th Riflemen's Division stationed at the nearby Pabradė military base. After the German takeover, the Lithuanians seized control of the administrative and police functions in a town which held a majority of Poles

---

162 Facsimile of the document is in Genovaitė Erslavaitė, Boleslovas Baranauskas, and Eusiejus Rozauskas, eds. *Masinės žudynės Lietuvoje*, vol. 2 (Vilnius: Mintis, 1973), 210.

and Jews. The anti-Jewish measures in Švenčionys followed a similar pattern as events in the other shtetls. The newly established police arrested scores of suspected Communists and pro-Soviet activists but soon turned most of their attention against the Jews. Records are scarce, but it is estimated that at least several hundred Jewish men perished in the genocidal wave which engulfed this region in September 1941.

Extensive massacres of Jewish men during the first month of the war occurred in and around Telšiai, the historic capital and cultural center of Samogitia (Žemaitija), home to about 1,600 Jews, a little more than a fifth of the town's populace. The four-hundred-year-old Jewish settlement was home to a world-famous yeshiva[163] and, despite emigration during the interwar years, had prospered economically. On the night of June 24–25, just before the Soviet retreat, the NKVD and Red Army soldiers tortured and killed seventy-three prisoners, including local intelligentsia and students, in a much-publicized atrocity in the woods near the hamlet of Rainiai. Later, local people drove Jews to the site and ordered them to exhume the bodies, as if in expiation of their collective "guilt." The persecution of Jews then intensified: on June 27–28, the "white armbands" drove the Jews of Telšiai out of the town to the Rainiai estate where the men and women were held in separate quarters. The newly established authorities confiscated Jewish property, much of which was reportedly simply stolen by the townspeople. Jews accused of Communist activities were taken to Telšiai prison. Benediktas Platakis, the commander of the makeshift camp, appointed a seven-man Jewish council, headed by the brothers Rabbis Abraham and Zalman Bloch, to tend to the Jews. According to several reports, in mid-July two SS officers arrived at the head of a unit of fifty to sixty auxiliary police and ordered the men to excavate large pits. For several hours, Jews were subjected to cruel and humiliating "gymnastics." A postwar interrogation relates that one of the men, Mejeris Šavelis, reacted to the torture by hitting one of the German officers who then promptly beat the impudent man to death. After the torments, the perpetrators shot between twenty and thirty men in the prepared ditches.

The mass killing of the Jewish men of Telšiai began during the third week of July (either on July 15 or July 20–21, depending on the source). The perpetrators were mainly drawn from the ranks of the Lithuanian auxiliary police, commanded by several German officers. The killers selected males older than

---

163 The yeshiva was closed by the Soviets in 1940, but in 1941 the school was reestablished in Ohio and is still in operation as the Rabbinical College of Telshe.

fourteen and convoyed them in groups to the killing fields near the Rainiai hamlet. It is estimated that the murder operation resulted in between 1,200 to 1,500 victims, including Jews from surrounding communities. Records indicate that on July 22, the Telšiai municipal government authorized the deputy police chief to transfer what remained of Jewish belongings from Rainiai to the town.[164] In nearby Viešvėnai the "white armbands" had established a camp for about five hundred to six hundred Jews who underwent much the same mistreatment as the inmates at Rainiai. During the third week of July a German-led contingent murdered more than two hundred men there.

"The Silenced Muse": The Murder of the Olkinas Family[165]

Matilda Olkinaitė's diary ends abruptly on February 28, 1941. We know that she continued her studies in the spring of 1941 and returned to Panemunėlis after the Nazi invasion. Because of the postwar testimony of Liza Abramson, published in 2005, much more is known about what happened to Matilda's brother in the first weeks of the war. Elijas Olkinas and his fiancée Liza were planning their wedding in Vilnius, but when the bombs fell, they decided to flee the city.[166] They rushed to the train station, but unable to fight through the crowds, decided to join thousands of others escaping eastward on foot. As Liza recalled:

> We were walking on the road along with thousands of people. People with babies and old men, who could barely walk, were on carts. Many were going on foot in the Eastern direction. The Soviet troops were retreating with us. It was accompanied with bombing, during which people hid away in the bushes by the road and in ditches. After the bombing not all of them came back to the road. It was dreadful and seemed interminable. We were let in some places to spend the night. We didn't have

---

164 Authorization of the Telšiai municipality of July 22, 1941, LCVA, f. 1075, ap. 2, b. 18, l. 133; cf. Bubnys, *Holokaustas Lietuvos provincijoje*, 458–463. On the inconsistencies of sources on Rainiai, see Aleksandras Vitkus and Chaimas Bargmanas, *Holokaustas Žemaitijoje: enciklopedinis žinynas* (Vilnius: Mokslo ir enciklopedijų leidybos centras, 2016), 425–432.

165 Laima Vincė, "Nutildyta mūza," in Olkinaitė, *Atrakintas dienoraštis*, 57ff., and Mindaugas Kvietkauskas, "Mėlynas," 40–45.

166 The couple's failed escape is based on Liza's memoir as related in Zhanna Litinskaya, interview with Liza Lukinskaya, Centropa Project, February 2005, https://www.centropa.org/biography/liza-lukinskaya.

money and Ilia's [Elijas's] pals paid for us. They were much older and had money on them. On our way retreating soldiers in passing cars told us that the Germans had entered Vilnius.

Days later, Elijas and Liza reached the village of Berezovki in Belarus, but like many others, they failed in their flight to safety. Overrun by the Germans, and after witnessing the selection and killing of Jewish men and Communists, they decided to turn back to Vilnius. The couple reached their "dear and favorite city" (Liza's words) after a harrowing journey but found it too dangerous to remain. They continued to Kaunas by skirting or bluffing their way through the roadblocks manned by Germans and anti-Soviet Lithuanian auxiliaries, until Elijas's luck ran out and he was arrested. Unharmed, Liza managed to make her way to her aunt Fanya's apartment in the city where she learned that "all [the] men were shot, and I should not hope to see Ilia again." Three days later, Elijas was released by the police and joined his fiancée. Aunt Fanya told Liza that someone in Šiauliai had seen her parents and brother leaving on a truck with the Soviet military with whom the family had been friendly during the Soviet occupation. (They survived the war.) In August, Liza, Elijas, Fanya, and another aunt, Ida, were incarcerated in the Kovno Ghetto where they shared a small apartment.

In the meantime, Matilda had returned to Panemunėlis. In early July the town's Jews were arrested and confined at the train station. A Lithuanian neighbor reported seeing Matilda there mopping the floor. When the guards briefly left the room, he urged Matilda to flee and hide among friends, but, as he remembered, "Matė didn't answer. She just began to scrub the prison's floor even more vigorously. I couldn't even get her to speak up, as to why she didn't want to get out of there."[167] After a few days, the Olkinases were transferred to the workers' quarters of the local estate. Noachas's friend Father Matelionis tried to save the family by subterfuge, convincing the guards to release them for a work detail in a nearby dairy, and then secreting the parents and their three daughters in an abandoned rectory. But the hiding place was soon discovered, and the "white armbands" threatened the priest. Noachas, fearing for his benefactor's safety, decided to return the family to the estate. It is likely that, at this point, Matilda turned over her poetry for safekeeping in the church.

---

167 As recounted by Juozas Vaičionis, *Iš prisiminimų* (Vilnius: Ciklonas, 2008), 87.

Most of the Jews of Panemunėlis were taken to the Rokiškis Ghetto sometime in July 1941 where, according to the testimonies of villagers who brought food to the inmates, conditions were dire. They perished in the massacre which took place outside the town in mid-August.[168] However, several Jewish families, including the Olkinases, never arrived in Rokiškis. They languished in the estate's workers' quarters which were described by one of Matilda's friends. "The conditions there were horrendous: there was manure everywhere, rotten potatoes and sugar beets. They would stretch out white sheets on the hay to lie down—that's how they lived."[169] Twelve-year old Ona, Grunia Olkinaitė's schoolmate, visited her imprisoned friend. One of the guards permitted the two girls to leave the compound and stroll in the nearby fields. Whenever they saw that the guard was a local acquaintance who would allow them in, Ona, her mother, and one other family brought food to their bereft Jewish neighbors.

Noachas Olkinas and Mauša Jofė (Moses Ioffe),[170] one of the town's two millers, were among the most prominent Jews in Panemunėlis, a fact which seems to have contributed to their murder at the hands of a criminal gang. According to witnesses, the killers were motivated by the mistaken conviction that the two families had hidden away abundant money and valuables which could be theirs for the taking. Available accounts of the massacre based primarily on the memories of the townspeople differ in some details but generally agree on how the events unfolded.

On a sunny and pleasant morning in mid-July people in Šeduikiškis village observed a group of "white armbands" arriving on bicycles on the road leading out of Panemunėlis. A few carried shovels. The men dismounted near a grove not far from the farmhouse of the Šarkauskas family and began digging, but the thick tree roots made excavation difficult. Undeterred, the workers went across the road to a more suitable site in the Kavoliškis forest, finished their work, and left. Soon after, the armed men pedaled back, accompanying an overloaded horse-drawn wagon, crowded with two families and their belongings, overseen by guards. The nine detainees were later identified as Noachas and Asna Olkinas, their three daughters, along with Mauša Jofė, his wife, the miller's sister and brother-in-law. According to people who saw the wagon on the road, the victims had been blindfolded. As the convoy approached a hillock, the horses were no

---

168 See below, Chapter 4.
169 As related by Ona-Genovaitė Šukytė-Grigėnienė, quoted in Vincė, "Nutildyta mūza," 71.
170 In one government document Ioffe's name was listed as "Elijas" (Eli).

longer able to pull the load, so the people were forced to get out of the wagon, then made to walk up towards a wooded spot nearby. There were two witnesses to what happened next. Farmer Šarkauskas, who told his family to hide, climbed atop a perch in the hayloft, from whence he was able to catch a glimpse of the unfolding horror. His eight-year-old daughter heard the shouts of the killers, the entreaties of the condemned, then the shooting amidst the cries of the dying. One account maintains that the victims had been stripped before they were shot. Years later, a witness remembered that the victims had been lured into their transport by their killers' false promises of safety, that they would be taken to the ghetto in Rokiškis. But Noachas Olkinas must have grasped his fate the moment the families were forced out of the wagon. Accounts from postwar interrogations point to the role of Henrikas Dūda, the leader of the Panemunėlis auxiliary police, a unit drawn from the "white armbands." Dūda had served in the police, both under the Smetona regime and as a member of the Soviet militia. During the German occupation he was also implicated in the murder of Jews in Belarus.[171]

While the final act of murder went largely unobserved, the same could not be said of the aftermath. The killers emerged from their mission into broad daylight visibly drunk and continued to badger farmers nearby for more alcohol. People recount that the pillowcases of the victims had been cut open, the feathers flying in the wind: the killers must have been looking for hidden treasures. The men sang and cavorted until dusk when they finally took to the road, urging the horses at full speed. One of the murderers was tied up and thrown onto the wagon by his mates; people later surmised that he had gone mad and, it was rumored, committed suicide. On the following day, Farmer Šarkauskas, his wife and a neighbor went to the woods and discovered a thin layer of newly shoveled soil barely covering what they realized were the bodies of their neighbors. The women covered the gravesite with branches and more earth, fearing that wild animals might disturb the grave. People reported finding remnants of clothing scattered about the site.[172]

---

171 He emigrated to the United States after the war and is almost certainly the same Henrikas Dūda who was on the list of suspected war criminals compiled by the U.S. Department of Justice.

172 The account here is reconstructed from the oral history interview with Ona-Genovaitė Šukytė-Grigėnienė Oral History / Accession Number: 2018.455.1 / RG Number: RG-50.030.0989 (October 4, 2018), https://collections.ushmm.org/search/catalog/irn628342 and the interview with Aldona Dranseikienė, Oral History / Accession Number: 1998.A.0221.110 /

Three months later, Mykolas Biržiška, the Rector of the University of Vilnius, signed Matilda Olkinaitė's formal dismissal from the Faculty of Humanities in accordance with new rules banning Jews from institutions of higher learning.

Ylakiai and Plungė: Harbingers of the Final Solution

The Nazis and their collaborators did not, as a matter of policy, systematically murder the women and children of Lithuania's provincial shtetls before August 1941, but there were at least two notable exceptions. One example is the extermination of the Jews of Ylakiai. The anti-Soviet insurgents had fought bloody skirmishes with local Communists and the retreating Soviet army before seizing control of this small town near the Latvian border. A witness recalls the detention of the Jewish men at the beginning of July: "One day the Jewish men were arrested and locked up in the school. Not arrested were Arkis and Aušeklis, because the first was old and sick, the other, a cripple. The famous doctor of Ylakiai, Joselevičius, was also not arrested. The Jews were detained very quickly, no one believed that they would be shot."[173] Other reports indicate that about three hundred Jews were corralled into the town's synagogue. The men were abused, their beards brutally shaved in public, as Germans photographed the spectacle. Available evidence indicates that the auxiliary police murdered at least four hundred Jews. Several sources recount Germans guarding the site and supervising the operation. The Jewish men were reportedly killed on July 6, the women and children, on the following day. Witness Vladas Vainutis recalled the death of the town's esteemed doctors, father and son, who had escaped the initial roundup:

> The Ylakiai doctor Joselevičius and his father were also brought to the killing site. Before his arrest, the young doctor had asked that they at

---

RG Number: RG-50.473.0110 (January 13, 2005), https://collections.ushmm.org/search/catalog/irn518532. Also, Kvietkauskas, "Mėlynas," 41–44; Vincė, "Nutildyta," 57–62, partly based on research and interviews compiled by the local historian and museum director, Violeta Aleknienė, as well as the testimonies compiled by the Moškėnai Soviet state farm ethnographic commission in Rokiškis district (Lietuvos TSR paminklų apsaugos ir kraštotyros draugijos Rokiškio skyriaus Moškėnų tarybinio ūkio kraštotyros organizacija), as compiled in Vladas Stašys, *Fašizmo aukų kapai Kavoliškio miške*, 1987 (unpublished collection).

173 As recounted in L. Drukteinienė, "Ylakių žydų bendruomenė," in *Mano senelių ir prosenelių kaimynai žydai*, ed. Linas Vildžiūnas (Vilnius: Atminties namai, 2002), 58.

least leave his small son alive, but the German answered, "Alle Kinder Kaput." While they were shooting the women and children, the old doctor was held at the gates of the cemetery, since they wanted to shoot him last. But they did not need to do this: [old] Joselevičius's heart just gave out. The younger Joselevičius was holding his three-year-old son. When they shot him, the little boy fell from his hands. They then also shot the child.[174]

According to one historian, the perpetrators of Ylakiai "were the first in Lithuania to get rid of their former neighbors." The Soviet-era monument at the site notes, "In this place the Nazis and their helpers murdered 446 Jews, twenty-five Samogitians [*žemaičiai*, that is, northwestern Lithuanians] and four Karaim" (although it should be noted that researchers have cast doubt on the exact numbers indicated). The killers plundered the property of the victims, reportedly an important incentive for participation in the massacre.[175]

The most stunning mass killing of the first month's terror was the murder of the Jews of Plungė, a center of Jewish learning and religious life since the sixteenth century. The auxiliary police exterminated the town's Jewish men, women, and children in mid-July 1941 in an operation whose scale was, until then, unmatched in the Lithuanian countryside. According to the tsarist census of 1897, the 2,500 Jews made up 55% of Plungė's population, although by 1941 emigration to the United States, South Africa, and Palestine had reduced the Jewish population to under two thousand. The community supported six synagogues, a yeshiva, and both Hebrew and Yiddish-language schools. An anti-Soviet partisan force was already gathering strength in Plungė and its environs when the Wehrmacht entered the town on June 24, 1941. Soon after, a small German military unit and the Lithuanian commandant of Plungė, Captain Povilas Alimas, who reportedly led a band of between 150 and two hundred men, took control and began arresting suspected Communists, former Soviet officials, and Red Army soldiers who had been cut off from their units. The Lithuanian auxiliaries took up police functions and carried out the roundup of the entire

---

174 A quoted in ibid., 59–60.
175 More in Valentinas Brandišauskas, "Mažeikių apskrities žydų likimas Antrojo pasaulinio karo metais," *Genocidas ir rezistencija*, 2, no. 20 (2006): 7–30; also, Brandišauskas, *1941 m. birželio sukilimas*, 114–116; cf., Holokausto atlasas Lietuvoje, accessed August 4, 2017, http://www.holocaustatlas.lt/LT/; "Execution of Jews in Ylakiai," yahadmap.com, accessed May 29, 2019, www.yahadmap.org/note #village/ylakiai-yelok-klaip-da-lithuania.975. A detailed account is also in Aleksandras and Bargmanas, *Holokaustas Žemaitijoje*, 123–129.

IMAGE 3.10.
The Destruction of a Community.
Top: A New Year's Hebrew-language greeting card with images of Jewish Plungė before the Shoah, 1935.
Middle: The former Plunge Beit Midrash in 2007.
Bottom: A view of the former synagogue and Beit Midrash buildings 2007. Jews were imprisoned in these buildings
before their murder in July 1941.
(Courtesy of Dr. Vilma Gradinskaitė.)

Jewish population during the first week of July, detaining the men in one synagogue, then herding women and children into another, holding the overflow in nearby houses. Witness accounts record the persecution of Jews, including beatings and public humiliations, as well as the imposition of meaningless and exhausting labor, all amidst widespread plunder. The persecutors stoked bonfires with religious books for their amusement. On July 15, 1941, Lithuanian police murdered an estimated fifty to eighty of Plungė's Jewish men near the village of Milašaičiai, six kilometers from the town.[176]

---

176 The commemorative stone there indicates eighty victims killed "by the Nazis and their local helpers"—see Holokausto Lietuvoje Atlasas, accessed July 20, 2019, http://www.holocaustatlas.lt/LT/.

MAP 7. Generalbezirk Litauen. Lithuania under German Occupation 1942. (Courtesy of Lithuanian Central State Archive.)

During July 1941 such selective executions and ad hoc ghettoization were features of antisemitic violence throughout the country, but Plungė stands out from the general pattern of events because of what followed. After the killings in Milašaičiai, the "white armbands" set fire to homes on Rietava Street, and then accused the Jews of arson. Following a meeting in which the leaders of the Plungė "partisans" informed the group that the Germans had ordered the killing of the town's Jews, the Lithuanian guards transported the victims to a killing site near the village of Kaušėnai, four kilometers northwest of the town where large pits had already been excavated in preparation. Jews were led to the pits in groups of ten to fifteen and ordered to strip to their underwear before execution. The shooters seized the victims' apparel as a reward for their work. Some of the condemned attempted to placate the killers at the pits by a last-minute attempt to convert to Christianity. In 1970 the priest Petras Lygnugaris told interrogators that the Lithuanian auxiliaries brought him to the killing site to baptize Jews who had asked for the ritual. This desperate gamble for a reported seventy to eighty people made no difference: after a brief delay, the killers led these new converts to the pits and shot them alongside the other Jews. (A few other such instances of instant "conversions" have also been reported.) Nearly 1,800 men, women, and children were buried in the pits of Kaušėnai. There are conflicting accounts about the dates of the Plungė atrocity and the role of individual commanders in the massacre, but most accounts identify the "white armbands" as the culprits.[177] Postwar Soviet investigations record the presence of a handful of Germans who oversaw the operation and provided alcohol to the shooters but did not engage in the killing themselves. Several sources indicate that local Germans were active participants.

It is essential to record and memorialize the numerous examples of widespread killing during the first six weeks of the war and occupation, and to document the sharp rise in antisemitic rhetoric and communal violence within Lithuanian society, phenomena which reached levels as yet unparalleled in Lithuanian history. One can only speculate about how many grasped that these blows presented a harbinger of the coming apocalypse. But the annihilation of the Jews of Plungė certainly revealed the possibilities of what has been characterized by Father Patrick Desbois as the "Holocaust by bullets"[178]—a crude formulation, perhaps, but one which encapsules the reality of the horrors which overwhelmed German-occupied Lithuania during the summer and fall of 1941. The gas chambers and the crematoriums, particularly at Auschwitz, have served as synonyms of the Shoah in popular culture and media, overshadowing the massive campaign of organized shooting operations which killed at least a third of all Holocaust victims in Europe and most of the Litvak population in the Baltics and Belarus.

---

177 Bubnys, *Holokaustas Lietuvos provincijoje*, 469–471 (dates provided: July 12–13, 1941); Vitkus and Bargmanas, *Holokaustas Žemaitijoje*, 405–411 (dates listed: July 15–18, 1941).

178 Patrick Desbois, *The Holocaust by Bullets: A Priest's Journey to Uncover the Truth behind the Murder of 1.5 Million Jews* (New York: Palgrave Macmillan, 2008).

4.

Concentration and Destruction: The Mass Murder Campaign in Lithuania, August–December 1941

Transition: From Selective Killings to Annihilation

On August 1, 1941, despite the pogroms, the operations in the border zone, the selective killings in the provinces, and the massacres at Plungė and Ylakiai, nearly 90% of Lithuania's Jews were still alive.[1] By December 1, 1941, when Karl Jäger forwarded his infamous report to Berlin, about four-fifths of the country's Litvaks were dead. At its core, the destruction of Lithuania's Jews involved a campaign of sustained mass shootings between mid-August and late October 1941, which effectively annihilated the country's historic Jewish shtetls. During the same period, the Nazis and their collaborators also massacred thousands of urban Jews during the establishment and consolidation of the major ghettos in Vilnius, Kaunas, and Šiauliai. The stages of identification, expropriation, and concentration of the Jewish population developed very rapidly in occupied Lithuania and were concurrent with the selective killings of June and July 1941. These processes were compressed, at times coinciding with one another, and clearly demonstrate a different evolution from the earlier developments in Germany after 1933. However, they were essential features in the history leading up to the annihilation of Lithuanian Jewry which gathered momentum in August 1941. In contrast to peacetime Germany of the 1930s, Lithuania was engulfed

---

1   This percentage is extrapolated on the basis of the official January 1941 estimate of the population of the Lithuanian SSR by nationality, the Jäger Report, the August 16, 1941, count listed by EK 3 in the USSR EG reports (*Ereignismeldungen*, 306–307), and the estimates of the June and July killings in the border zone.

in war, which at least in part explains the speed with which the identification and physical marking of Jews led to the destruction of entire communities.

The eradication of Lithuanian Jewry required considerable organization and planning. German officials agreed to rest their occupation policy on "four pillars" that would work in coordination to secure and exploit the occupied peoples in the East. The Wehrmacht was to "overpower" the foe in battle; Himmler's SS would take on the "political/police" campaign against the Reich's enemies; Hermann Göring would exploit the economy; and Alfred Rosenberg would oversee the reorganization of the political order in this part of the "New Europe."[2] Occasional conflicts among leading Nazi officials and struggles over jurisdiction between the different elements of the occupation authorities did not seriously hamper either the mass murder operations or the economic exploitation of the subjected peoples.

As noted above, the Wehrmacht's commandants in Lithuania instituted antisemitic measures against the Jews as part of their war against Germany's enemies by insisting on the identification and marking of Jews during the first weeks of the invasion. Pursuant to Hitler's decree of July 17, 1941, the transfer of control in the former Baltic states from the commandants to the ZV brought no relief to the suffering Jews: on the contrary, under von Renteln and his German officials, the new agency commenced a deadly new stage of persecution that rapidly escalated into a campaign of annihilation. The ability of the Nazi occupiers to employ collaborating structures facilitated the work. Two institutions were of particular importance: the Lithuanian police forces, especially the militarized TDA, and the local Lithuanian administration led by the district chiefs.[3]

In late July, units of the EG commenced an ominous operational expansion in the killing fields. Alex J. Kay has detailed the activity of Dr. Alfred Filbert's EK 9, a unit assigned to Army Group Center, which campaigned in southern Lithuania and beyond. After murdering some five thousand mostly adult male Jews in Vilnius by late July, Filbert's men moved to Belarus, where on July 30, 1941, the group massacred the entire Jewish community of Vileyka and then went on to kill women and children in other towns of the region. According to Kay, EK 9 was the first of the EG units to routinely add women and children to

---

2   See Dieckmann, *Besatzungspolitik*, 1:239ff.
3   For a more detailed listing of the military, police, and civilian institutions, see below.

their lists of victims.⁴ Jürgen Matthäus maintains that Himmler's encouragement, as well as initiatives by local commanders, was crucial in expanding the mass murder to entire communities, citing, as an example, the role of SS Cavalry units in the Pripet region of Ukraine which murdered at least eleven thousand Jewish men, women, and children by mid-August 1941, at an average rate of one thousand people per day.⁵ These egregious changes in the nature of the killings presaged the mass murder campaign that was being prepared for the Jews of northern Lithuania.

Preparing for Destruction: The Concentration of Rural Jewry, July–August 1941

Von Renteln's ZV brought Lithuania under a single authority headquartered in Kaunas that oversaw six commissioners (Gebietskommissar) who administered their assigned fiefdoms (*Gebietskommissariat*, GBK): two urban regions (G. *Stadt*, L. *miestas*) of Vilnius and Kaunas, as well as the four provincial regions (G. *Gebiet*, L. *apygarda*) of Vilnius-Land, Kaunas-Land,⁶ Šiauliai, and Panevėžys, which, in turn, contained their respective districts (G. *Kreis*, L. *apskritis*). Within the districts, the smaller Lithuanian units of administration (G. *Amtsbezirk*, L. *savivaldybė*) included mayors, rural townships (*valsčius*) elders, police chiefs, and other officials, all of whom reported to their district superiors, and, when necessary, to responsible German officials. The various agencies of repression and, ultimately, destruction worked within this administrative structure.

In July, the Lithuanian police and civil authorities, which had emerged in the wake of the anti-Soviet insurgency, had already begun establishing temporary Jewish ghettos, camps, and detention centers in the provinces, sometimes on their own, often with the direction or encouragement from the

---

4 Alex J. Kay, "Transition to Genocide: Einsatzkommando 9 and the Annihilation of Soviet Jewry," *Holocaust and Genocide Studies* 27, no. 3 (2013): 411–442.

5 See Jürgen Matthäus, "Controlled Escalation: Himmler's Men in the Summer of 1941 and the Holocaust in the Occupied Soviet Territories," *Holocaust and Genocide Studies* 21, no. 2 (2007): 218–242.

6 The "Land" appended to the title in German documents served to distinguish the provincial commissars from the commissars in charge of the two major cities (Kaunas-Stadt, Vilnius-Stadt).

Wehrmacht. The German civilian administrators replaced the initial patchwork of anti-Jewish measures implemented by local authorities (as in Joniškis) and German military commandants with a systemic policy of expropriation and concentration. On July 28, 1941, Hans Cramer, the Kaunas city commissioner, prohibited Jews from using sidewalks, public transport, and other facilities. A week later, he banned the return of Jewish refugees who had fled the city during the invasion. On August 4, 1941, Arnold Lentzen, the commissioner of Kaunas-Land, published a series of even more restrictive edicts and strict curfews. Within days, Lithuanian district chiefs issued directives to count the Jewish population in the provinces. In telephone messages of August 3 and 4, 1941, the Alytus district chief Stasys Maliauskas ordered a demographic breakdown of Jews by age. His subordinate in Butrimonys reported a count of ninety-four men and women fourteen to eighteen years old, 341 persons aged nineteen to fifty, and 164 Jews over fifty. The chief in Rudnia replied that "concerning the Jews there is one family, they are all wearing the Star of David and, when possible, are taken to work." From Birštonas came the news that there is only "one old woman, and then a man who is held in Alytus prison, so there are no more Jews of the ages indicated to report."[7] In total seventeen rural counties of the Alytus district sent in their numbers, including the historic shtetls of Merkinė and Varėna. On August 8, 1941, Maliauskas reported the material he had gathered to the newly created Department of Labor Management in Kaunas listing the total of provincial Jews for his district:

Age 14–18:	724
Age 19–50:	2,700
Age 50+:	1,224
Total:	4,648.[8]

During the first week of August Vaitiekus Bortkevičius, the Lithuanian chief of the Kaunas district in detailed bureaucratese ordered all heads of rural counties and police precincts to commence the concentration of his region's provincial Jewry:

---

7   Butrimonys rural county chief to Alytus district chief, August 4, 1941, LCVA, f. R-1436, ap. 1, b. 32 l. 129; Rudnia county chief message to Alytus district chief, ibid., undated l. 135, and message of September 6, 1941, ibid., l. 371; Birštonas message of August 5, 1941, ibid., l. 128; other locales are recorded in the archival file.

8   Maliauskas to Department of Labor Management, August 8, 1941, ibid., l. 156–157.

Kaunas, August 7, 1941

Republic of Lithuania
V. R. M. [Ministry of Internal Affairs]⁹
Chief of Kaunas District
General Section
No. 445

To all Heads of Rural Counties
And Police Precinct Chiefs

I order you, by working together, to set aside a part of the township [*miestelis*] for a Jewish ghetto, to fence it at their [the Jews'] expense and settle there all the rural county's Jews.

Persons of other races, who live with Jewish men or women as spouses, must sever such relationships. Those who do not, or who discontinue the relationship but continue physical or material relations, shall be treated as Jews and incarcerated in the ghetto along with their children.

The ghetto fences may be made of wire, boards, and posts.

The exterior security of the ghettos shall be organized from the partisans on a military basis. The purpose of the guard is to prevent the Jews from leaving the ghetto of their own accord and that passers-by should not be allowed to maintain contacts with those living in the ghetto.

After the Jews have been brought into the ghetto, they should be warned that any person making a willful attempt to leave the borders of the ghetto will be shot by the guards.

To maintain order within the ghetto, a police force of five to fifteen persons shall be organized among the Jews. The Jewish policemen are to be armed with wooden clubs.... Where there are still no Jewish committees, they [Jews] must be instructed to form such a committee within a strict timeline. The committee must consist of twelve persons. A copy of the list of committee members must be presented to both the chief of the police precinct and the head of the rural county. All the matters concerning the Jewish ghetto are to be handled by this committee.

The Jews will feed themselves at their own expense, but at reduced food rations and without a right to obtain the following food items: meat and meat products, milk and milk products, eggs, and fats. The ration available to the Jews is given to the committee, which will manage

---

9   The references to the "Republic of Lithuania" and the relevant "ministries" in some of the letterheads, particularly after the dissolution of the PG on August 5, 1941, do not reflect any existing government by that name.

the distribution. Until the Jews are driven into the ghettos, that is until August 15, then, where there are no Jewish food shops, they will be assigned a separate number of hours of the day, which are necessary for their consumption.

Lists must be created of all Jews of male gender of ages between twelve and sixty according to their work specialties, of which one copy must be held at the rural county office and another sent to me. The compiling of these lists shall be entrusted to Jews in the ghetto who are of the intelligentsia and the professions. The Jews can then be more productively utilized for labor.

These directives are to be carried out by the heads of the rural counties and the precinct chiefs by mutual agreement, and both [officials] will be held responsible [for carrying this out].

[signed] The District Chief[10]

By early August 1941, even before the establishment of the major urban ghettos, the German and Lithuanian police authorities in Kaunas had acquired, on the basis of collected reports, a demographic profile of the Jewish population in the provinces, most of whom had either been confined to temporary ghettos or were in the process of concentration in hastily established camps.

Hans Gewecke (1906–1991) headed GBK-Šiauliai, the largest administrative region of German-occupied Lithuania, which made up virtually all of the country's west and north with a population of more than 1.5 million until November 1941, when GBK-Panevėžys was carved out of the eastern half of his realm and placed under District Commissioner SS Major Walter Neum (1902–1976). Gewecke's administration took over during an ongoing discussion concerning the difficulties of maintaining the Jewish populace, particularly the problem of unemployable Jewish women and children. Nazi officials complained that in the Kretinga area, Jewish women who had been assigned to work among the farmers had simply absconded from their employers. In 1957, Pranas Lukys, the local Lithuanian Security Police chief, testified that Edwin Sakuth, the head of the Memel (Klaipėda) SD, often wondered aloud how it was that "the Jewish women and children, who were useless eaters [*unnötige Esser*], have still not disappeared." In the minds of the Germans tasked with administering the occupation, Lithuanian Jewry increasingly came to be seen as an economic dead weight, as well as a potential security threat and, in some cases,

---

10   As published in *Masinės žudynės Lietuvoje*, 1:290–291.

a flight risk.¹¹ Such deliberations portended ominous consequences for the vulnerable Jews.

Soon after Gewecke's arrival, the authorities in Šiauliai forbade Jews who had fled their townships during the fighting to return to their homes; landlords who allowed them back would be punished. Apart from the other discriminatory restrictions, the district's Jews were to begin wearing, as of July 25, 1941, a "yellow star of David ten centimeters in diameter," reaffirming a practice that had already been adopted in other locales. Furthermore, it was decreed that "persons of Jewish nationality who live in the small towns must move to an area designated by mayors and the heads of rural counties."¹² On August 6, 1941, Jonas Noreika replaced District Chief Ignas Urbaitis, who had carried out the first anti-Jewish measures ordered by Gewecke, but then unexpectedly resigned. Noreika issued Directive No. 429, "To All Rural County Chiefs and Mayors of Secondary Towns," concerning "properties left by Communist functionaries and citizens of Jewish nationality who had fled," ordering the officials to ensure the proper safeguarding of both the real estate and valuables in question. Paragraph 6 of the ordinance concerned the management of property abandoned by Jews who had already been corralled into ghettos: "Citizens of Jewish nationality who are being transferred to other places of permanent residence can take with them non-movable property as they see fit. On the other hand, real estate which is left without supervision is to be handled . . . [in the manner of those who had fled], while the movable property left behind is to be taken over by local governments." The same rule applied to the gardens and orchards of the dispossessed.¹³ By early August, ghettos and other restricted settlements had already been created in all but three of the thirty-seven concentration sites of the Šiauliai district listed in the registry created by the USHMM's *Encyclopedia of Camps and Ghettos*. (The exceptions were Kaltinėnai, Pajūris, and Tauragė.)

On August 13, Gewecke convened a conference during which Lithuanian regional officials and mayors received instructions on the final ghettoization plan for the region's Jews, followed by a written directive on the next day. Inasmuch as most towns in northern Lithuania had already established their own ghettos and camps, the obvious intention was to finalize and further consolidate the remaining Jewish population of GBK-Šiauliai. On August 22, 1941, Noreika

---

11 See Dieckmann, *Bezatsungspolitik*, 2:808.
12 Šiauliai district chief Announcement No. 6 [undated], author's archive.
13 Document in author's archive.

IMAGE 4.1.
Left: District commissioner of Šiauliai Hans Gewecke. Right: Prewar photo of Jonas Noreika, later district chief of Šiauliai during the German occupation.

issued a document which, decades later, was to resonate in a controversy assessing the collaboration of civilian officials in the persecution of Lithuanian Jewry:

> Chief of Šiauliai City and District
> August 22, 1941
> No. 962
>
> To All Rural County Chiefs and Mayors of Secondary Towns
> (Copy to Chiefs of Police Precincts)
> The Šiauliai District Commissar [Gebietskommissar] has ordered that all citizens of Jewish nationality, as well as half-Jews, must be removed from the district's rural counties and townships and settled in one neighborhood [L. *rajonas*]—the Ghetto. All Jewish property must be registered and secured through the efforts of the local governments.
>
> In relation to this, I order the following:
>
> 1. All Jews from rural counties and townships must be transferred to Žagarė town between the 25th and 29th of this month. Transport for the transfer will be provided by the appropriate local authorities.
> 2. Two copies of [lists of] Jewish properties must be presented to me by the 29th of August. The transferred Jews can take with them essential household goods and as much as 200 RM for each Jewish family.
> 3. In Žagarė the Jews must be settled in a separate neighborhood which must be enclosed by the 30th of August. The town council of Žagarė must provide for the enclosure of the Ghetto. The Jews must be taken under guard from the Ghetto area for work and then returned every day.

4. Citizens of non-Jewish nationality who are from the neighborhood assigned to the Jews are permitted to choose other places within the district. If anyone of the non-Jews is required to leave his real estate property, such a person is permitted to choose property of equivalent value left behind by the Jews whether in Žagarė itself or in other towns or townships.
5. The rural county chiefs and mayors are obligated to report the fulfilment of this order by the 29th of this month and relate [to me] what has been done on this matter, and how many Jews have been transferred. In addition, the mayor of Žagarė must report how many Jews in total have been settled in Žagarė.

[Signed]
J. Noreika
The Chief of Šiauliai City and District

[Signature illegible]
Secretary[14]

On August 25, Mayor Silvestras Rakštys reported to Noreika that 715 Jews had been settled in the Žagarė Ghetto in an area of 12,135 square meters. Within a week, as a result of Gewecke's and Noreika's directives, the ghetto population here grew to over 2,500.

The officials of Šiauliai district carried out a rough census of the population, including an estimate of the number of Jews. By the middle of August, the gathering of provincial Litvaks was well underway, and in some regions, nearly complete. It should be noted that any attempt at graphic representation of this process inevitably obscures the diversity of experience, so that some caveats are in order. The population of provincial ghettos was in constant flux as inmates were moved about, transferred to different locales, or killed in selective shooting operations. Thus, we are left with only approximations when attempting to establish the numbers of detainees. There are conflicting data concerning the establishment, duration, and inmates of the restricted settlements, particularly in remote rural areas. The problem is compounded by a lack of records and sources, sometimes limited to the recollections of a handful of survivors. Despite the scarcity of detail in many locales, the prevailing pattern of the operation intended to segregate Lithuanian Jewry is clear enough.

---

14 Document in author's archive, also published in *Masinės žudynės*, 2:226-227. On the controversy concerning Jonas Noreika, see Chapter 7.

4. Concentration and Destruction | 247

MAP 8. Ghettos in Lithuania and Western Belarus, 1941-1943
(Martin Dean, ed., *Encyclopedia of Camps and Ghettos, 1933–1945*,
vol. 2b: *Ghettos in German-Occupied Eastern Europe* [Bloomington:
Indiana University Press in association with the United States Holocaust
Memorial Museum, 2012], 1037).

Note: In reviewing the geographic concentration of the Jewish population it should be noted that in April 1942 part of what had been the General Commissariat of Belarus (GK Weissruthenien) was transferred to the Vilnius district and thus came under the jurisdiction of the General Commissariat of Lithuania (GK Litauen). The ghettos of this region were generally established later than in Lithuania and were not eradicated until later 1942 and early 1943. During this period Lithuanian civilian officials and police participated in their administration.[15]

---

15 Martin Dean, ed., *Encyclopedia of Camps and Ghettos, 1933–1945, vol. 2b: Ghettos in German-Occupied Eastern Europe* [Bloomington: Indiana University Press in association with USHMM, 2012], 1037.

TABLE 3. Concentration in the provinces July–October 1941
Šiauliai (GBK Schaulen)
Restricted Jewish settlements (ghettos, camps, temporary detention sites)
by district (GBK), duration, and estimated maximum number of inmates*

Panevėžys	July 17–August 23	7,000
Utena (including Šilinė forest camp)	July 14–August 29	3,500
Rokiškis	Early July–August 15/16	3,000
Ukmergė	August 5–September 26	3,000
Mažeikiai	Mid-July–early August	3,000
Telšiai-Rainiai-Geruliai	June 28–December 30	3,000
Biržai	July 26–August 4	2,500
Žagarė	August 2–October 2	2,500
Plungė	June 26–July 15	1,800
Pasvalys	Mid-July–August 26	1,500
Anykščiai	End of July–August 29	1,500
Raseiniai	Early July–September 6	1,500
Kupiškis	Early July–August	1,000
Kelmė	July–August 22	1,000
Kretinga	June 30–September	900
Salakas	August 9/10–August 26	800
Kuršėnai	July–August 29	800
Batakiai [Skaudvilė]	Mid-July–September 16	800
Šeduva	Mid-July–August 25/26	750
Radviliškis	July 8–August 29	750
Joniškis	Mid-July–September 1	700
Jurbarkas	Mid-July–September 12	700
Širvintos	July/August–September 18	600
Dukszty [Dūkštas]	Late August–September 21	600
Tauragė	September 6–September 16	600

* Inclusive of the territory transferred to GBK Panevėžys in November 1941. Sources: Martin Dean, ed., *Encyclopedia of Camps and Ghettos, 1933–1945*, vol. 2b (Bloomington: Indiana University Press in association with USHMM, 2012), 1031–1157; Arūnas Bubnys, "Mažieji Lietuvos žydų getai," *Lietuvos istorijos metraštis* (1999): 151–180; Bubnys, *Holokaustas Lietuvos provincijoje*; also, information gathered by Alfredas Rukšėnas for the IHC. For the long-term ghettos in the cities of Vilnius, Kaunas, and Šiauliai, see Chapter 5.

Obeliai	July–late August	500
Linkuva	Mid-July–late August	500
Seda	Early July–August 9	500
Rietavas (Ogiński estate)	June 27 – July 10	500
Viešvėnai	June 30–end of July	500
Vabalninkas	Mid-July–end of August	400
Dusetos	Early July–August 26	400
Krekenava	Early July–July 27	400
Žemaičių Naumiestis	Early July–September 25	400
Šiluva (Ribukai)	Late June–August 21	400
Darbėnai	July 1–September 22	400
Pakruojis	July 10–August 4	350
Užpaliai	Mid-July–late August	300
Vyžuonos	July–August 7	300
Ylakiai	June 26–July 6	300
Gargždai	June 30–September 14/16	300
Švėkšna	Mid-July– September 22	300
Kražiai	Mid-July–September 2	300
Pumpėnai	July 15–mid-August	250
Viekšniai	Mid-July–August 4	250
Joniškėlis	July–August 19	200
Pašvitinys	Early July–29 August	200
Akmenė	Early July–early August	200
Palanga (Valteriškė)	Early July–October 11/12	200
Kvėdarna	July–September	200
Alsėdžiai	July 5–mid-July	180
Užventis	Early July–July 30-31	150
Viduklė	Mid-July–August 22	150
Eržvilkas	Early July–mid-September	150
Vainutas	July 28–end of August	125
Subačius	Late July–end of August	100
Lygumai	Late July–early August	100
Pajūris	September	100
Kaltinėnai	September 4–September 16	50

Kaunas (GBK Kaunas-Land)

Marijampolė	Late July–September 1	5,000
Vilkaviškis	End of July–end of November	2,500
Kėdainiai	Mid-August–August 28	2,000
Lazdijai	September 1–November 3	1,600
Alytus	Early August–September 9	1,500
Šakiai	Early July–September 13	1,000
Kybartai	Mid-July–early August	1,000
Prienai	August 14–August 25	1,000
Seirijai	Early August–September 11	1,000
Merkinė	Early July–September 10	850
Butrimonys	End of August–September 9	750
Ariogala	Late July–August 30	700
Kudirkos Naumiestis	August 23–September 16	650
Virbalis	Early July–September 11	600
Vilkija	July–August 28	500
Krakės	Early August–September 2	450
Onuškis	September 1–September 30	300
Garliava	August 12–September 2	285
Vandžiogala	August 15–August 28	250
Babtai	August 11–end of August	200
Jonava	Late August–October 4	200
Zapyškis	Mid-August–September 4	180
Rumšiškės	Mid-August–August 29	140
Rudamina	July–September 15	80

Vilnius (GBK Wilna-Land)

Kaišiadorys	August 10–August 26	1,000
Pabradė	September 1–early October	1,000
Adutiškis/Hoduciszki*	August 15–September 26	1,000
Semeliškės	Early September–October 6	960
Maišiagala	End of July–September 28	700
Ignalina	September 5–late September	700

Švenčionys*	September 26–April 4, 1943	500
Trakai	September 1–September 30	500
Švenčionėliai/Nowe Święciany	Early August–September 26	400
Vievis	Early August–September 22	350
Žiežmariai	August 15–August 28	250
Darsūniškis	Early August–August 28	200
Daugeliškiai/Daugieliszki	July–late September	150

The Trajectory of Destruction: Northern Lithuania, August–October 1941

There is no written directive that unambiguously establishes the creation of the camps and ghettos as the intended precursor for the annihilation of Lithuania's provincial Jewry. Nonetheless, there is little doubt that by late July or early August the occupation regime had reached a decision on the ultimate fate of the restricted settlements. The ghettoization (concentration) and killing operations (extermination) which eventually encompassed the entire country first gained momentum in northern Lithuania. The sequence of events and geographic order of the escalating murder operations that ensued indicate a determined and well-thought-out program of destruction.

The massacre of the Jews in Mažeikiai foreshadowed the beginning of the end of Jewry in the Lithuanian countryside. On the morning of August 5, several officers from the German Security Police attached to the commando assigned to the area (Teilkommando 2), arrived to supervise the operation at the head of a force of the Mažeikiai auxiliary police. Workers had already excavated several large pits at the Jewish cemetery the day before. Jews were brought to the killing site in groups of ten, forced to undress, and executed at the edge of the pits. The German officers finished off some of the wounded with their side arms. The men were shot first, the women and children followed. The shootings continued on August 6: the final victims were a group of about sixty Russian and Lithuanian Soviet activists. The killers were reported drinking vodka during the action and, upon the completion of their task, were feted at a Mažeikiai restaurant. The Germans seized the valuables taken at the site, while the remainder of the victims' belongings were distributed later among the police rank and file. There has never been a reliable accounting of the number of people killed in the July and August massacres in Mažeikiai: estimates have ranged from two to four thousand deaths.[16]

The northern town of Biržai became the next venue in the transition to the Final Solution.[17] This picturesque historic seat of the Calvinist branch of the famous Radvila (Radziwiłł) family included about 1,500 Jews, a fifth of the town's population. On July 28, 1941, the mayor issued a curfew as well as an order for the town's Jews to move to a restricted neighborhood (*rajonas*) on the eastern edge of town, noting that Lithuanians living in the assigned area could "exchange real estate with the Jews by free [mutual] agreement."[18] In early August, the inmates of the local prison and Jewish workers dug two large pits in the Pakamponys woods some three kilometers outside of Biržai. On or about August 5 the Jews were driven into the synagogue, so that, as one witness reported, "not a soul was left in the ghetto." On August 8 German Security Police officers, most likely from EK 2, and the Gestapo representative from Šiauliai, Petras Požėla, arrived to take charge of an auxiliary unit from Linkuva, as well as police and men described as "white armbands" from Biržai itself, a force variously described as consisting of between fifty and eighty men. The killers convoyed the Jews through the streets to the murder site: the men in the lead in several groups, while the elderly, women, and children followed; invalids were the last to be taken. Townspeople watched the procession of the doomed. Some waived farewell to their neighbors. Guards forced the victims to shed their garments before they were shot. The extermination of the entire community was accomplished in eight hours. Postwar Soviet investigations determined that nine hundred children, 780 women, and 720 men perished that day, a number roughly corresponding to the prewar Jewish population of Biržai and its environs. Ninety ethnic Lithuanians were also reportedly among the victims. After the massacre, some local people plundered the clothing and bedding of the dead, something that one observer remarked "was a disgrace to behold."[19]

---

16 One testimony gives the dates of the massacre as August 6–8, 1941, and a death toll of 2,300. Cf. accounts in Bankier, *Expulsion and Extermination*, 128–132, Bubnys, *Holokaustas Lietuvos provincioje*, 259–260, and Dieckmann, *Besatzungspolitik*, 2:855.

17 A survey of the earlier history of the community is in Jurgita Šiaučiūnaitė-Verbickienė, trans. Lara Lempertienė, "Ocherki istorii evreiskoi obshchiny Birzhaia," in Kopchenova et al., *Birzhai*, 69–85; cf. Vladimir Petrukhin, "Rabbanitskiye i karaimskie obshchiny v srednevekovoi Litve: problem nachalnoi istorii," in ibid., 59–68.

18 *Naujosios Biržų žinios*, August 2, 1941, 2.

19 See the account of Regina Drevinskienė, in Kopchenova et al., *Birzhai*, 196–198.

An even larger operation was directed at the Jews in nearby Rokiškis. Here the shootings took place in full view of bystanders. Jürgen Matthäus has marked the Rokiškis operation as a "caesura in the history of the Holocaust."[20] Whether one agrees with this characterization or not, the terror of what happened is reflected in contemporary accounts, stunning even those who held little or no sympathy for the victims. A few days before the action, Soviet POWs were brought to the aptly named "Devil's Pit" (Velniaduobė) woods near the Bajorai village to dig several large trenches. On the evening of August 14, the heads of the local auxiliary police units were called to Lithuanian commandant Žukas's headquarters and told to gather the next day for a special task. On the following morning Žukas directed the police to escort the Jews from the ghetto to the killing sites. The people were told that they would be taken to work. About twenty-five men selected from the commandant's detail headed out to the pits in lorries where they were joined by a German mobile commando of about a dozen men armed with automatic weapons. The auxiliary police began moving the Jews to the pits, the able-bodied on foot, while the small children and elderly were driven to the death site by car or in horse-drawn wagons. The Jews were forced to remove their outer clothing and then shoved into the pits. The shooters stood at the edges and fired down at the people. On the first day, the Germans and Žukas's Lithuanians carried out the shootings as the auxiliary police from the surrounding communities guarded the site. On the following day, elements of the auxiliary police joined in the operation and, when finished, ordered the Soviet POWs to cover the corpses. Jäger's ledger listed the dead: "3,200 Jewish men, women and children, five Lithuanian Communists, one Pole and one partisan."[21] In one rather self-pitying passage in his report, Jäger described Rokiškis as *the* example of the roadblocks which needed to be overcome in achieving a "Judenfrei" Lithuania:

> *In Rokiškis 3,208 people had to be transported four-and-a-half kilometers, before they could be liquidated.* To be able to overcome this task in twenty-four hours, we had to assign more than 60 of the 80 available Lithuanian partisans for transportation and for cordoning off [the area]. The remainder of them, who, time and again, had to be relieved, carried out the work together with my men. Motor vehicles were only occasionally

---

20   Kay, "Transition to Genocide": 441n120.
21   Jäger Report, December 1, 1941, 2.

available. Attempts to escape, which took place every now and then, were prevented by my men at the risk of their lives.²² (Emphasis in original)

Despite the carnage at Rokiškis, the area around the town had not yet been "cleansed of Jews." Hundreds more men, women, and children were convoyed to Obeliai at the same Antanašė estate whence the able-bodied had once been taken to work in local farms. On August 25 about thirty men from Žukas's security force and several Germans arrived on the site. Once again, on the night before the action, Soviet POWs had excavated two large pits in preparation. The auxiliary police escorted the victims to the killing field located in the Degsnė woods where the more practiced killers from Rokiškis carried out the shootings, which lasted for most of the day. Jäger reported the Jewish victims of the Obeliai operation as 112 men, 627 women, and 421 Jewish children.²³ The victims' clothing and other belongings were brought back to the estate where the killers made off with the loot. A hundred ruble bonus was paid out to eighty-eight of the policemen for what was termed a "special assignment." The authorities then distributed the final wages to the "employees of the Jewish concentration camp of Rokiškis district."²⁴ There was no longer any need of accommodations for the area's Jews.

Hamann's Rollkommando next traveled to Ukmergė, located some ninety kilometers southwest of Rokiškis. The town was home to one of the oldest Litvak settlements with roots dating back to the sixteenth century, numbering nearly three thousand people before the invasion. The Jews had already suffered several large-scale massacres: the killing of 254 Jewish men and forty-two Jewish women on August 1, and then a further action a week later resulting in the murder of 620 Jewish men and sixty-two Jewish women. (A Communist political instructor and a "Russian Communist" were also included in this last tally). The ghetto established in late July later included Jews from the nearby communities of Širvintos, Musninkai, and Gelvonai. On August 19, EK 3 and local collaborators escalated the slaughter to include children: Jäger reported eighty-eight killed, along with 298 men and 255 women.²⁵

---

22 Ibid., 7–8.
23 Ibid., 3.
24 List of employees of the Rokiškis District Jewish concentration camp, LCVA, f. R-1515, ap. 1, b. 1, l. 1.
25 Bubnys, *Holokaustas Lietuvos provincijoje*, 509–519.

According to the Jäger report, the EK 3 led four shooting actions here between July 21 and August 11, which killed 1,314 people. The details show the progressive escalation of violence characteristic of the country at large.

TABLE 4. Panevėžys killings by victim category as reported by EK 3
July 21–August 11, 1941[26]

	Jewish men	Jewish women	Lithuanian Communists	Russian Communists
July 21–22	60	11	22	9
July 28	234	15	20	19
August 4	362	41	14	5
August 11	450	48	1	1
Total	1,106	115	57	34

In mid-August, the inhabitants of the Panevėžys Ghetto, their numbers swollen by the influx from the shtetls, were informed of their transfer to military barracks in Pajuostis (Pajuostė), about five kilometers outside the city. According to survivor Meir Gendel, a "Gestapo officer who had been assigned to guard the ghetto" assured Jewish leaders that the new facilities would provide ample food and more spacious accommodations. Despite the promises, the Jews were reluctant to leave the ghetto, concerned that the transfer was a ruse leading to something worse,[27] a fear likely amplified by the events in Biržai and Rokiškis (it seems impossible that the news of massacres in the district had not reached Panevėžys). Sometime in the third week of August, the police drove the ghetto inmates to Pajuostis, some on foot, others in a long caravan of commandeered horse-drawn wagons. Hundreds more Jews were brought to Pajuostis from surrounding communities. The story of one farmer, ordered to transport a Jewish family to their deaths here from the town of Pumpėnai, is recounted in a memoir published in 2011 and consistent with the experience of other "drivers":

---

26 Adapted from the December 1, 1941, Jäger Report.
27 Joseph Levinson, ed., *The Shoah (Holocaust) in Lithuania* (Vilnius: The Vilna Gaon Jewish State Museum, 2001), 109–110.

[The driver] Pulmickas was assigned to transport the Zeideris family. The Zeideris's took some things with them, the husband put on the new shoes made by J. Lapinskas. In Panevėžys they were told to take the Jews to a local station. There [the police] took away their belongings and pulled off their shoes. Zeideris came out of the station confused and overwrought, complaining about the lost shoes. From here, Pulmickas's wagon took them towards Pajuostė, where the site was surrounded by a fence with guards at the ready. The dogs were barking, the people crying. The guards ordered the Zeideris family to get out and took them beyond the gate. As Pulmickas turned back to [return home], he heard the shooting. Back home he was unable to eat for several days.[28]

On August 23, 1941, Hamann led his squad of men from EK 3 and a larger contingent of local police in what was the bloodiest murder operation of the summer of 1941 in the provinces. The Jews were taken in groups of two hundred and shot at pits prepared the day before in a forest next to the Pajuostis military complex. Soviet POWs filled the ditches after the massacre. Jäger reported the death toll of 7,523 Jews: 1,312 men, 4,602 women, and 1,609 children.

The massacre in Panevėžys was quickly followed by "actions" that annihilated three more Jewish communities. Jäger listed thousands of EK 3 victims with pedantic exactitude:

Šeduva (August 25–26): 230 men, 275 women, 159 children
Zarasai (August 26): 767 men, 1,113 women, 687 children
Pasvalys (August 26): 402 men, 738 women, 209 children.

Following this latest killing spree, Hamann's Rollkommando arrived in Kaišiadorys and Prienai on a special operation to urgently staunch the spread of infectious diseases, a problem they solved by annihilating the entire Jewish community in both towns. On August 29, Hamann's Germans and Lithuanian auxiliaries temporarily turned northwards to Utena where a month earlier they had reported their victims as 235 Jewish men, sixteen Jewish women, four Lithuanian Communists, and one criminal. A horrendous massacre now followed there and in nearby Molėtai: EK 3 reported that, along with TDA men

---

28   Cited from an account in Bubnys, *Holokaustas Lietuvos provincijoje*, 282.

from Kaunas and local auxiliary police, they murdered 3,782 Jews (582 Jewish men, 1,731 women, and 1,469 children).[29]

The majority of able-bodied Jewish men in the Telšiai region had perished in July 1941. The local police transferred the surviving older men, women, and children to a camp in the village of Geruliai about seven kilometers from Telšiai and placed them under guard. According to eyewitnesses, conditions there deteriorated throughout the weeks following the killings of the men. Despite a medical station and a German commandant's office located at the site, the greenhouses and farm buildings of the camp were overcrowded, filthy, and disease-ridden. The youngest children fell sick and died from diphtheria and typhus. Drunken German soldiers visited the camp at night and raped the women. On August 28, 1941, two lorries of armed men, mostly from the TDA and local police, arrived at Geruliai. The commander of the camp Platakis reportedly spent the night before the action drinking heavily with the arrivals, then met with the women leaders of the camp, demanding money and valuables, in return for which he promised to save their lives. The women collected thirty thousand rubles and dozens of wedding rings. On the next morning, the killing began. The killers escorted the camp inmates outside and separated the younger women from the older women and children. Some four hundred women were selected and sent to the newly established ghetto in Telšiai. The murderers then drove the remaining victims in groups to a nearby grove and began the massacre. The shootings dragged on for two days, resulting in the death of an estimated two thousand women and children. The killers went on a binge after the operation. Once the men had helped themselves to the money, jewelry, and other belongings of the dead, the clothing of the victims was taken to Telšiai and sold to the townspeople.[30]

On September 5, the Rollkommando and Lithuanian police revisited Ukmergė and rapidly completed the destruction of the community that they had left behind in August. On that day Jäger counted 4,709 Jewish victims (1,123 men, 1,849 women, and 1,737 children). On the following day the killers moved westward, eradicating the remnants of the Jewish communities in Raseiniai

---

29 Jäger Report, December 1, 1941.
30 Joshua Rubenstein and Ilya Altman, eds., *The Unknown Black Book: The Holocaust in the German-Occupied Soviet Territories* (Bloomington: Indiana University Press, 2010), 301–308; more details are in Bubnys, *Holokaustas Lietuvos provincijoje*, 457–462. The Telšiai killings of July–August 1941 do not appear in the Jäger Reports.

(sixteen men, 412 women, 415 children) and Jurbarkas (412 people). In mid-September, the largest concentration of northern Lithuania's Jewry existed fitfully in Šiauliai city, which became one of the three large long-term ghettos, and the town of Žagarė, the site of the final death throes of northern Lithuania's small-town Jewry. Jäger reported that on October 2 EK 3 and Lithuanian police killed, in Žagarė, 633 Jewish men, 1,167 women, and 496 children. The victims did not go quietly: "during the escorting of these Jews a mutiny broke out, which, however, was immediately suppressed and 150 Jews were shot forthwith. Seven partisans [sic] were wounded."[31] By November 1941, the once flourishing population of provincial Jewry which fell under the jurisdiction of GBK-Panevėžys counted 107 persons living in three rural counties (Subačius, Šeduva, Kupiškis).[32] The remainder of northern Lithuania's Litvak population hung on in the Šiauliai Ghetto or in hiding. There now followed a period of relative calm in the north. Jäger's commandos and their accomplices turned their attention elsewhere.

The Reivytis File: Organizing the Death of the Shtetls

The central and southwestern parts of the country included the Kaunas district (Kaunas-Land) and the Kaunas City district (Kaunas-Stadt). Kaunas was the seat of von Renteln's General Commissariat, the site of the headquarters of the Lithuanian Police Department, which administered the constabulary, as well as the headquarters of EK 3, which headed the strike force largely responsible for the operational leadership of the Holocaust in Lithuania during the summer and fall of 1941. Among the records relating to the genocide of Lithuanian Jewry is a file in the Lithuanian Central State Archive containing a cache of dozens of communications concerning nearly forty predominantly rural communities. The collection is of particular interest since, despite the limited geographic scope of these mostly Lithuanian-language documents, few archival sources so precisely capture the particulars of the genocidal process at the ground level, particularly the role of local police, the chain of command, and the day-to-day efforts of the bureaucracy in complying with orders.

---

31 Jäger Report, December 1, 1941.
32 Bubnys, *Holokaustas Lietuvos provincijoje*, 277.

4. Concentration and Destruction | 259

MAP 9. The Kaunas District (Gebietskommissariat). (Adapted from Martin Dean, ed., *Encyclopedia of Camps and Ghettos, 1933–1945*, vol. 2b: *Ghettos in German-Occupied Eastern Europe* [Bloomington: Indiana University Press in association with the United States Holocaust Memorial Museum, 2012], 1037.)

The chief executive officer and accountant of the destruction of Lithuania's provincial Jewry was Karl Jäger, the commander of EK 3 and author of the frequently cited surveys of genocide in Lithuania (namely, his reports to the RSHA of September 10 and December 1, 1941). But two other people stand out in the file. The first is the hands-on, daily manager of the killing operations, a rather low-ranking henchman from Kiel, twenty-eight-year-old SS First Lieutenant Joachim Hamann (1913–1945). An orphan of Baltic German parentage, Hamann received a chemist's training but, like many youths in depression-era Germany, had wandered rootless and unemployed until he found a home with the SA (the Sturmabteilung or "Brown Shirts) in 1931. He later joined the paratroopers as a volunteer, only to be thrown into the brig and cashiered for mistreating trainees. In 1938 Hamann joined the SS, then served with the Wehrmacht during the Polish and French campaigns, returning afterwards to Berlin to work in the Security Police and SD. To further his career with the SS, he attended evening classes in juridical studies at Berlin University. By April 1941 Hamann had been promoted to lieutenant and was assigned to EK 3. According to one of his bunk mates who testified after the war, the lieutenant's military and police training was supplemented by the appropriate worldview, personality, and enthusiasm for the task he was about to undertake: "Hamann gave me the impression of a fanatical persecutor of Jews who believed that he was fulfilling his duty for his people by these [anti-Jewish] measures."[33]

Forty-year-old Vytautas Reivytis (1901–1988), the director of the Lithuanian Police Department headquartered in Kaunas, had reason to think himself superior to Hamann in both rank and social status. The son of a respected patriot from Mažeikiai, Reivytis had entered police service in 1925, completing criminology studies in Kaunas and Berlin. He rose through the police bureaucracy, achieving a high rank in the railroad security service, while also working as an inspector and lecturer at the advanced school of police studies in Kaunas. During the 1930s Reivytis became an informer for the German military intelligence (Abwehr). An accomplished target shooter and ju-jitsu expert, who competed internationally with some success, as well as a well-known aviation enthusiast, Reivytis fit the Voldemarist image of a tough man of action. Rather than await his fate at the hands of the Soviets in June 1940, he fled to Germany. In July 1941 he received "Category II" German citizenship. There can be little doubt about the place in the Lithuanian chain of command which Reivytis held throughout the occupation, nor his subservience and loyalty to the Nazi cause during the

---

33 As quoted in Stang, *Kollaboration und Massenmord*, 157.

4. Concentration and Destruction | 261

IMAGE 4.2. Clockwise: SS Lieutenant Joachim Hamann, commander of the Rollkommando. SS Colonel Karl Jäger, commander of EK 3. First page of the Jäger Report detailing the mass murders of the summer and fall 1941.

war: he was decorated for his service in 1943 and as late as February 1944 applied for an upgrade of his German citizenship.[34]

The first page in the Reivytis file is Secret Order No. 3, a directive to subordinate district police chiefs for further distribution to precincts under their control. The stilted police vernacular outlines preparations for the destruction of provincial Jewry:

> Police Department
> Secret [Message] No. 3
> Kaunas, August 16, 1941
>
> To the Kaunas District Police Chief:
> Upon receiving this circular, in the places pointed out in the remarks, immediately detain all men of Jewish nationality from 15 years of age and those women who had become notorious in their Bolshevik activity, or

---

34 More on Reivytis's role during the German occupation is in Petras Stankeras, *Lietuvių policija 1941–1944 metais* (Vilnius: LGGRTC, 1998).

IMAGE 4.3. Vytautas Reivytis in 1934, German agent, Voldemarist and head of the Lithuanian Police Department during the German occupation.

who even now distinguish themselves by the same activity or insolence. The detained persons are to be gathered at the main highways, and when completed, this is to be immediately reported by special and most urgent means of communication to the Police Department. In the report, the number of such types of Jews who have been detained and collected is to be precisely indicated. It is necessary to ensure that the detainees are supplied with food and the appropriate security, for which the auxiliary police may be utilized. The [instructions in this] circular must be carried out within forty-eight hours from its receipt. The detained Jews must be guarded until they are taken and transported to the camp.

Note: to be carried out in the entire Kaunas District.

V. Reivytis

Director of the Police Department[35]

The police chief of Šakiai district, Balys Vilčinskas, noted and signed confirmation of the receipt on his copy of the circular: August 16, 1:35 PM.[36] Further instructions to the precincts, printed on half-page forms, ordered the rural police bosses to immediately carry out their instructions "without awaiting any specific order from their [local] police chief." Jews from smaller precincts were to be gathered at collection points located at crossroads convenient for transport. The precincts were told "to notify the Police Department, after gathering the Jews in the designated places." The reports on the resulting

---

35 LCVA, f. R-683, ap. 2, b. 2 [henceforth cited as the Reivytis File], l. 1 Responses to Reivytis's circular indicate that the instructions were received by some police chiefs before August 16, 1941. Some of the documents in the file have been published, most notably in the series of Soviet publications of the 1960s and 1970s.

36 Reivytis File, l. 48.

operation were to be delivered to Reivytis's office either by telephone or special courier.³⁷

The fate of less than a tenth of Lithuania's Jewish community is reflected in the file's correspondence, but the collection provides considerable detail about the method of the initial roundups, particularly the role of the lowest rung of officials who handled the concentration of the Jews. These obedient policemen may not have been the decision makers, but they were useful cogs in the machinery set into motion during the first bureaucratized stage of the Final Solution, which in concept, execution, and scale eclipsed both the pogroms of the first days and the mass killings of July. Most of the rural precinct chiefs were officials who had heeded the call of the PG and the anti-Soviet insurgency to return to the posts that they had held before June 15, 1940. Undoubtedly much of the

IMAGE 4.4. From the Reivytis File.
Clockwise: Order No. 3 issued by Director of the Police Department Vytautas Reivytis, August 16, 1941. Colonel Reivytis requests SS Lieutenant Hamann's permission to deal with the spread of typhus in Prienai, August 25, 1941. Police Chief Vincas Karalius reports on the destruction of the Jews of Šakiai, September 16, 1941. Kriūkai police report on the transfer to Plokščiai of "citizens of Jewish nationality," the five members of the Zaksas family, September 2, 1941. (Courtesy of Lithuanian Central State Archive.)

---

37 Ibid., l. 2–3.

populace, which had rejoiced at the departure of the Red Army, viewed these representatives of the First Republic as legitimate guardians of law and order. The experience of these veterans of Smetona's authoritarian regime inclined them to obey orders. They fell back to old habits and were not prone to taking initiative in solving problems.

Was Reivytis serious in limiting his instructions to adolescent and adult Jewish men and "insolent" women? Did his subordinates follow in the same spirit? The message from the head of the Paežerėliai precinct indicates a commitment to follow instructions to the letter, reporting to Reivytis about thirty-five detained persons (all women save one):

> All the citizens of Jewish nationality listed here were detained on August 17, 1941, in the town of Kriūkai and in the rural county of Šakiai district, and are being sent to the disposition of the Zapyškis precinct police chief. All the Jewish women have been notorious, and even now, when their husbands, brothers and children have been deported, they spread all manner of talk and even threats. They had all been notorious when the Communists ruled Lithuania.[38]

The bureaucratic language of officialdom was, for the most part, precise and laconic. In an Orwellian twist, many policemen remained loyal to the official discourse of the First Republic. Some simply referred to their victims as Jews, but the majority speak of the "Jewish nationality" of the detainees, or even more jarringly, as "citizens of Jewish nationality." Only two precinct heads in the Reivytis File utilized overt ethnic pejoratives, one reporting on August 19 that he had received the aforementioned "35 Jewish broads [L. *žydelkos*]" from Paežerėliai. Interestingly, the source of this scorn described his office as "the Head of the Zapyškis precinct of the Lithuanian National Soc.[ialist] Police," a bizarre formulation found nowhere else in the archives of Lithuania's native constabulary during the German occupation.[39] (Only two days previously, another officer, the acting head of the same precinct, had described his charges as citizens of Jewish nationality.) Still another precinct boss referred to "little Jews" (L. *žydeliai*), a condescending, but hardly vicious, slang expression widespread among Lithuanian Gentiles.

---

38   Ibid., l. 53–54.
39   Ibid., l. 64.

Whenever confronted with logistical problems relating to the order from Kaunas, the precinct chiefs sought clarification before proceeding with the roundup. One official requested further instructions since, as he put it, "among the Jews held at the Kazlų Rūda Jewish camp, 25 are ill or weak from old age. I ask for a directive on whether they should be kept in the camp or allowed to live at home."[40] On August 22, 1941, the precinct chief in Balbieriškis informed Reivytis:

> Sir, in answer to your secret message No. 3, I report that the Balbieriškis Police Precinct arrested and turned over to the Prienai Jewish ghetto a hundred Jewish men and six Jewish women. At the present time, in answer to your circular, there are only two Jewish men remaining in the town of Balbieriškis. They are the medical doctor Bielockis and the chemist of the leather factory, Jankelis Icikovčius, without whom the factory cannot operate, and a replacement for him, at this time, cannot be found.[41]

In at least one documented case, the victims fled the roundup, causing some frustration to the planners. According to an accounting completed in July, the Jieznas town council reported that Jews made up 236 of the town's 923 inhabitants. On August 16, the Jieznas precinct chief reported to Reivytis that he had sent sixty-three Jewish men and twenty-six women to Prienai. As the police began the arrests of Jews in response to the directive, many escaped. On August 29, Reivytis sent a caustic scolding to Stasys Krosniūnas, the Alytus district police chief, about the lax behavior of his subordinates: "the Police Department [in Kaunas] is unclear on whether, in the town of Jieznas, the Jews who are being hunted are still hiding, or are they hiding only when the police are looking for them?" Inquiring why the Jieznas precinct head "is still not executing the Police Department's Circular No. 3," and why the Department "is not receiving news of what has been done with the Jews in Birštonas," Reivytis told Krosniūnas: "I suggest that you, sir, supervise the work of your precinct chiefs more closely."[42] Krosniūnas responded defensively on August 30:

---

40   Ibid., l. 33.
41   Ibid., l. 77.
42   Ibid., l. 23, 84.

> In carrying out the Police Department's secret message No. 3, I report that when the arrests began..., the Jews of Jieznas precinct had scattered and gone into hiding. Later some of them returned to the town, but since the precinct chief was unable to communicate with the security police of Prienai region, and the borders of [security police] regions are not at all clear, and the circular had to be executed within two days, so the further arrests were made under the auspices of the Alytus region security police chief. All told 38 [Jews] were brought to Alytus by August 31 [sic]. Some of the Jews have not yet returned to the town but are living, according to what we have discovered, in the forests. The precinct chief has been ordered to round up the Jews from the forests by utilizing the auxiliary police.
>
> In the Birštonas precinct there never have been, and are not currently, any of the kinds of Jews indicated in circular No. 3. In all, one old Jewish woman lives in the town, who will be transferred to Alytus in the next few days. Upon receipt of circular No. 3, the Birštonas precinct chief should have reported its execution directly to the Department and later to me, but he reported it, as we found out, only to me. I received his message only after three days, but did not report anything to the Department since, according to the circular, this should have already been done by the precinct chief.[43]

After the admonitions from higher authority, the hunt for the Jews of Jieznas resumed with more determination. Survivors recount that the police discovered some Jews in hiding among local peasants and found more victims who had escaped to the woods. In the end, most did not elude the dragnet.[44] Some were reportedly sent to Alytus where they perished, while the remainder who had not been confined previously in Prienai were imprisoned: the men in the cellar of the county's administration building, the women and children in the synagogue. Jäger reported that by September 3, twenty-six men, seventy-two women, and forty-six children had been killed in Jieznas. According to postwar interrogations, two German officers from EK 3 (most likely from Hamann's mobile commando), as well as three Lithuanian officers and twenty TDA men, carried out the killings (these sources have provided a higher number of victims, some fifty men and nearly two hundred women and children). The

---

43 Ibid., l. 85.
44 Survivor accounts on Jieznas are in Bankier, *Expulsion*, 111–113.

auxiliary police guarded the murder site and several reportedly volunteered for the shootings.[45]

Some policemen apparently believed that their job was simply to watch the Jews until their prisoners would be taken off their hands to some unnamed "camp." The Zapyškis chief indicated that he was awaiting "additional orders."[46] In a number of cases, we find pedantically drawn up lists of the detainees by name, detailing age, sex, and even dates of birth: these would not seem to be the actions of officials expecting their victims' imminent demise. Self-delusion, the human inclination to evade responsibility, especially when one is not personally involved in the final and most gruesome outcome, is well known, and collaborating officials seemed particularly adept at applying this stratagem. Nothing, of course, lessens the responsibility of the rural police bosses who gathered the "citizens of Jewish nationality," and were thus complicit in their destruction. Moreover, in a small country, any ignorance concerning the ultimate fate of the detainees must have been fleeting. As the process unfolded, denial required purposeful evasion. In the Šakiai region, most of the Jewish men over fifteen years of age had been detained in the larger towns where hundreds of them had already been executed in July.[47] Elsewhere in the country, substantial numbers of the adult Jewish male population in question had already been murdered during the first six weeks of the occupation. Certainly, as August came to an end, even the thickest police head must have grasped that the Jews of the provinces were being corralled to their deaths. The arrival at the assembly points of the killing squads assembled in Kaunas, mostly the men from the EK 3 mobile unit and the TDA battalions, indicates that the decision to exterminate entire communities had already been taken by higher officials at the time Secret Order No. 3 had reached the police precincts listed in the Reivytis File.

One particular example from the countryside illustrates well the acceleration of the process of concentration and destruction. According to plan, the Jews nearest to Kaunas were to be gathered from the countryside and assembled in Jonava, Vilkija, Babtai, Rumšiškės, Zapyškis, and Garliava. In the latter case, the detainees created a logistical headache.

---

45 See Jäger Report, December 1, 1941. On Jieznas, see also Bubnys, *Holokaustas Lietuvos provincijoje*, 39–50.

46 Reivytis File, l. 44.

47 See Gertner testimony above, Chapter 3. In the sources, these men are sometimes listed as "deported."

IMAGE 4.5. Jewish men escorted to their deaths in Paneriai, ca. July 1941. Photographs taken by an unidentified German soldier.
(From the Archives of the YIVO Institute for Jewish Research, New York.)

On August 12, the head of the Garliava rural county reported that he had registered 285 Jews. Five days later the police reported that they had imprisoned seventy-three Jewish men and forty-six women from surrounding communities and imprisoned them in the town's synagogue. On August 20, the worried chief wrote Reivytis, requesting "an order on what to do with the detained Jews from Garliava town, its environs and the other rural counties." By the twenty-eighth of the month he was desperate:

> In supplementing my secret messages of August 17 and 20, registry No. 1, of this year, I ask you, Director, to give an order on what should be done with the Jews of Garliava town [and environs] who have been detained since August 17 and are being held in the Garliava town synagogue. Their feeding is difficult since the purchase of food products is being restricted and, furthermore, they do not have suitable accommodations.[48]

The police received their answer on the fate of the Jews held at Garliava soon enough. A few days later two lorries of TDA men arrived at the town's synagogue. After the Jews refused to excavate a pit outside the town, the police forced local workers to complete the job. They then convoyed the imprisoned men, women, and children to the pit where the TDA officers supervised the killings. Untypically, witnesses do not mention a German presence at the site.[49]

The other shtetls close to Kaunas presented relatively few logistical problems. Small communities could be eradicated by units dispatched to handle matters on the spot. According to the registration of Jews carried out by the Kaunas district authorities in July 1941, the small town of Kruonis contained a synagogue and twenty Jewish households with a total of 153 people. In his dispatch of August 17, the Kruonis police chief reported that he had taken no action on the Reivytis order since the problem lay elsewhere, shedding the responsibility for the Jewish men of his precinct:

> In response to the secret circular of August 15, I report that all the Jews of Kruonis rural county have been settled in the Darsūniškis church village [L. *bažnytkaimis*], which, as far as police responsibilities are concerned, has recently been placed under the jurisdiction of the Pakuonis police precinct. Furthermore, there are no more men of Jewish nationality of fifteen years and older, neither are there any women who were notorious by their Communist activity. In the entire Kruonis rural county there

---

48 Reivytis File, l. 57, 76, 83.
49 Arūnas Bubnys, "Holokaustas Lietuvos provincijoje 1941 m.: žydų žudynės Kauno apskrityje," *Genocidas ir rezistencija* 2, no. 12 (2002): 91–92. Some sources give a slightly higher figure than the numbers in the Jäger Report.

remain about fifty old women of Jewish nationality and about thirty children below the age of fifteen.[50]

Reports indicate that in mid-August most of the men of the town were shot during their transfer to Kaunas.[51] At the end of the month Hamann's Rollkommando arrived at Darsūniškis and murdered the remaining members of the community at the local Jewish cemetery: according to Jäger, ten men, sixty-nine women, and twenty children.[52]

Along the left bank of the Nemunas River lay the town of Zapyškis, once part of the estate of the Sapieha family and the site of a centuries-old historic church. It was home to some fifty Jewish families. On September 2, 1941, a unit of TDA men arrived in Zapyškis and, with the assistance from the local police, massacred 178 Jews, the majority of whom were women and children (including the aforementioned thirty-five "notoriously Communist women" from Kriūkai). The Germans at the scene photographed the killings.

In August 1941, ninety-three Jews were registered in Babtai, a town just north of Kaunas. On July 17, the local police executed eight Communists, including six Jews, as well as a Russian Soviet activist and his teenage son. A week earlier, in nearby Vandžiogala, Hamann's mobile commando and Lithuanian auxiliaries carried out one of the first mass killings of Jews outside Kaunas city, recorded by Jäger as the shooting of "32 Jewish men, two Jewish women, one Lithuanian woman, two Lithuanian Communists and one Russian Communist." The extermination of these communities followed in the wake of Reivytis's instructions. Between August 28 and September 2, men from the TDA First Battalion's Third Company killed, according to Jäger, eighty-three Jews from Babtai (twenty men, forty-one women, and twenty-two children) and 252 Jews from Vandžiogala (forty-two men, 113 women, ninety-seven children).[53]

The Nazi security forces held operational control over the operation, as evident in several German-language documents in the Reivytis File. On August

---

50   Reivytis File, l. 43.
51   Dov Levin cites accounts indicating that they were killed either at the city's outskirts or at the Fourth Fort. See "Translation of the 'Darsuniskis' chapter from *Pinkas Hakehillot Lita*," JewishGen, accessed October 29, 2019, https://www.jewishgen.org/yizkor/pinkas_lita/lit_00212.html.
52   Jäger Report, December 1, 1941, 4.
53   Ibid., 4.

16, 1941, a cautious precinct head from Raudondvaris responded to Reivytis's order by reporting "that there were no Jews of the category indicated in the circular" in his jurisdiction, with the exception of four Jews under the authority of the Security Police and four other Jews assigned to work for the "local German staff." Colonel Reivytis translated the message and forwarded the matter to SS Lieutenant Hamann for consideration.[54] Even more instructive of the German role was the situation in Prienai where Jews made up nearly a sixth of the town's estimated 4,200 inhabitants before the war. On August 14, the Prienai authorities established a ghetto, to which police convoyed Jews from nearby shtetls (including Jieznas, as noted above). But the situation took a dangerous turn and Reivytis was at a loss on how to handle the crisis. On August 26, 1941, he wrote to Hamann asking the lieutenant to resolve the issue:

> Supplementing my messages of August 18, 19, 20, 1941: since in Prienai the number of arrested Jews has reached 493 persons, I request from you an order to take away the detained Jews from their collection point as quickly as possible, because a contagious disease is raging among these Jews, as is the case in Kaišadorius [Kaišiadorys]. This presents a danger that the infectious disease will spread.[55]

Reivytis's Nazi overlords responded swiftly: on the next day, EK 3 dispatched forces to solve the problem of the afflicted Jews. The police rounded up and transported the victims of Prienai, both the healthy and sick, to two large pits which had been excavated the day before. Hamann's unit and a platoon from the First TDA Battalion led by Lieutenant Bronius Norkus carried out the shootings at a grove adjacent to military barracks outside the town. Four years later, a witness recalled:

> At about three or four o'clock we were allowed to take a look at the pits. At the time, lime was being poured on top of them [the victims]. Some of the bodies were still trembling and heaving because the lime was suffocating them. The people were piled up haphazardly like trees [cut down] in a forest. I recognized my former landlady and her daughter. Mrs. Katz and her seven-year-old daughter were lying next to each other. I was exhausted, and nearly fainting, I staggered home.[56]

---

54 Reivytis File, l. 27–28.
55 Ibid., l. 82.
56 Testimony of Marė Brasokienė, February 10, 1945, in Levinson, *Shoah*, 123.

A stark portrayal of the death of Lithuania's shtetls is the case of Vilkija, a town located eighteen kilometers west of Kaunas, where the roots of the Jewish community dated back to the end of the eighteenth century. On the eve of World War I, Jews made up over half of the town's population, but the tsarist expulsions of 1915 and the economic crises of the 1930s reduced the numbers considerably. Yet the community still maintained two synagogues, a Maccabi sports club, and several Zionist groups. After the Soviet takeover, the Communists nationalized Vilkija's small businesses, disbanded the Zionists, and banned Hebrew-language instruction in the schools. At the same time, Jews of a leftist or pro-Soviet orientation became more prominent in the town's public life evoking political tensions and resentments.[57] The Germans entered Vilkija on the second day of the war and immediately set up a commandant's post under a German officer, identified in postwar interrogations as one Missenbaum, who took command of the anti-Soviet insurgents.

On June 24, the commandant called together a meeting of prominent citizens and selected a "committee of activists" to take charge of the auxiliary police. On June 28, the "activists" shot twenty suspected Jewish Communists. In mid-July, the German commandant supervised the arrest of a further estimated 150–200 Jewish men and suspected Communists, also ordering the Jews to turn in all radios, photo cameras, and other electrical equipment. During the concentration of Jews in Kaunas district, the 222 adult Jews residing in the town paid a "contribution" of 21,400 rubles. By mid-August, the Jews of Vilkija and surrounding communities were incarcerated in a ghetto: some of the men in the Beth Midrash building, the women and children in the homestead of Shimon Fridland. A Lithuanian woman recalls that some of the Jewish girls' classmates brought food to the inmates.[58]

According to witnesses and the Vilkija precinct report, on August 18, 1941, 280 Jewish men and 120 Jewish women were taken under guard by lorries to Kaunas. The most likely scenario is that they were held there before their murder at the city's Fourth Fort. More is known about the fate of the Jews who remained behind. On August 28 local police convoyed the remaining Jews of Vilkija to a wooded site two kilometers outside the town. Men from the Third Company

---

57   See the Vilkija memoir of Bruno Ignatavičius above, Chapter 3.
58   Aleksandras Vitkus and Chaimas Bargmanas, *Vilkijos getas 1941 metais* (Vilnius: Mokslo ir enciklopedijų leidybos centras, 2019), 10–19.

of the First TDA Battalion from Kaunas were met at the site by several German officers and then proceeded to murder the victims.[59]

There is considerable material concerning the killings in Kaišiadorys, a large town and important rail junction some forty kilometers southeast of Kaunas, where the persecution of Jews began soon after the Nazi invasion. On orders of the Wehrmacht, the Trakai district chief[60] stipulated that weekly food rations for Jews be reduced to half of those assigned to Gentiles. In mid-August the police rounded up the Jews of the town, as well as those from other communities, into a makeshift ghetto of several houses and a local synagogue, reporting that they had arrested 536 Jewish males and 188 females (children were not separately listed). Afterwards hundreds more Jews were brought to the town from the nearby communities of Žasliai and Žiežmariai.[61] On August 26 the Rollkommando and the TDA men arrived in Kaišiadorys to carry out the murders: Jäger recorded the death of 1,911 Jews. The killings there were probably connected to the action in Prienai: infectious disease (most likely typhus) had been identified by the police among the incarcerated Jews. Considering the logistics of the operation, the massacre of nearly three thousand people in Prienai and Kaišiadorys seems to have been organized quickly as part of a single extended operation, allegedly to deflect the threat of an epidemic.

On August 20, EK 3 and the TDA killers turned towards the remaining Jews of Žiežmariai who had not been transferred to Kaišiadorys, as well as people from Rumšiškės: according to Jäger, they massacred twenty Jewish men, 567 women, and 197 children. On August 31 the Trakai district chief reported to his superiors in Vilnius that "in Kaišiadorys, Žasliai and Žiežmariai, there is no longer a single person of Jewish nationality," and requested instructions on how to handle the homes and household goods of the victims.[62]

---

59 Ibid., 22–24, 96–97.
60 During the German occucpation, Kaišiadorys, Žasliai, and Žiežmariai were under the administration of Trakai District within GK Wilna-Land, but the police were subordinate to Reivytis's department in Kaunas and the precinct was included in the distribution list for Secret Order No. 3.
61 Reivytis File, l. 35–37, l. 80.
62 As quoted in Bubnys, *Holokaustas Lietuvos provincijoje*, 501–502. Considerable detail is in the well-documented study by local historian Rolandas Gustaitis, *Kaišiadorių regiono žydai* (Kaišiadorys: Kaišiadorių muziejus, 2006), 50–55; 151–153; 215–217. A listing of the victims by name is in the English-language version of Rolandas Gustaitis, *Jews of the Kaišiadorys Region of Lithuania* (Bergenfield, NJ: Avotaynu, 2010), 206–113. For Jewish testimonies on Kaišiadorys and environs, see Bankier, *Expulsion*, 113–117.

In contrast to other towns, the Jews of Kėdainiai lived in their homes and were permitted to come and go without restriction until early August 1941 when District Chief Petras Dočkus ordered the Jews to be transferred to a temporary ghetto within the town. The Žeimiai precinct boss reported that Jews in his area had been duly sent to Kėdainiai on August 14, 1941, "in compliance with the order."[63] The district's police chief Antanas Kirkutis wrote to Reivytis that "all the citizens of Jewish nationality have been grouped together in three neighborhoods (L. *rajonai*): in Kėdainiai region, 913 persons, of whom 183 are women; in Ariogala region, 290 people, including 80 women; in Krakės region, 452 people, including 115 women."[64] During the second week of August the police ordered Jews to move to an area around the synagogue, then on August 16, following Order No. 3, separated the town's men, including teenagers, and some of the women, and brought them to the stables and farm buildings of the manor of former tsarist general, Count Eduard Totleben. On August 26, the remaining women in Kėdainiai town were taken there as well. According to postwar interrogations, rumors were rife that the Jews were to be sent to Lublin. At the same time local leaders convened a meeting during which, according to a witness, a German official (identified as a "commandant") read a statement affirming "the necessity to cleanse Europe of Jews, who are a danger to everyone."[65]

In preparation for this mission, Soviet POWs excavated a hundred-meter-long pit outside of the town. The organizers of the massacre selected twenty men who had served in the military to report for a "serious task" on August 28, a force that was supplemented by what witnesses reported as "German soldiers" (almost certainly Hamann's Rollkommando) and former "white armbands." Jäger listed that day's death toll in Kėdainiai as 2,076 victims. Witnesses recalled the local German chief of economic affairs Gevert Bellmer as particularly active in the Kėdainiai atrocity: he personally robbed the Jewish women of their valuables on the eve of the slaughter, and then commanded the shootings, finishing off the wounded as well. In a dramatic act of resistance, a former Lithuanian army officer, Codikas Šlapoberskis (Zadok Schlapobersky), attacked

---

63   Reivytis File, l. 20.
64   Ibid., l. 38.
65   Valentinas Brandišauskas, "Holokaustas Kėdainių apskrityje," *Genocidas ir rezistencija* 1, no. 17 (2005): 87–89.

the policeman Aleksas Čižas, dragged him into the pit and mortally wounded his executioner. Two Jews who tried to flee were hunted down and shot.[66]

The shtetl of Krakės was located about twenty kilometers northwest of Kėdainiai. During the first days of the war the local LAF chapter led anti-Soviet insurgents in carrying out the arrests of Soviet sympathizers and the internment of Red Army men cut off from their units. The men arrested two Jews, Doctor Boruchas Alperavičius and the tailor Fridmanas, as "Communist Party candidates" and sent them to Kėdainiai where they were executed. In early August Dočkus and Kirkutis declared that "the Jews are designated as dangerous, have no right to live freely with Lithuanians and must be isolated," which resulted in the establishment of a Jewish ghetto in this town of about 1,500 residents, whence the police also brought Jews from six surrounding communities. Sometime before mid-August Kirkutis arrived in Krakės and ordered the confiscation of Jewish-owned gold, silver, and other valuables. On August 17 precinct chief Teodoras Kerza reported to Kirkutis that "337 Jewish men and 115 Jewish women had been taken to the labor camp [per Reivytis's directive], all of whom have been housed in the monastery of Krakės town, held under guard, near the Krakės-Pernarava road."[67] Postwar interrogations confirm that adult men and women without small children were "taken to work" at the monastery. For the time being old people and women with children remained in the town's makeshift ghetto. As in the other towns, the Jewish community was forced to pay a contribution, which was collected by Kerza and transferred to the bank in Kėdainiai. The food situation among the detained Jews was dire, which some local people tried to ameliorate by surreptitiously bringing provisions to the ghetto inmates.

According to eyewitness testimony, about two weeks later, a truckload of about thirty to fifty Lithuanian TDA men arrived in Krakės, whose commander Lieutenant Barzda reportedly handed Kerza some sort of German-language notice with an official stamp authorizing the killing of the Jews. The officers ordered town officials to organize a workforce of locals to dig several large ditches about a kilometer from the monastery. On September 2, the auxiliary police

---

66 Additional details are in Bubnys, *Holokaustas Lietuvos provincijoje*, 131–141; Jager Report, December 1, 1941; Dieckmann, *Besatzungspolitik*, 2:881–883; cf. JewishGen, accessed October 22, 2019, https://www.jewishgen.org/Yizkor/lithuania3/lit3_001.html; Dean, *Encyclopedia of Camps and Ghettos, 1933–1945*, 1070–1071.

67 Reivytis File, l. 41.

convoyed the inmates to the pits, the men first, followed by the women. Finally, the perpetrators escorted the remaining Jews still in the town (who had been "unfit" for labor), including the children, to the killing site. Jäger reported that 1,125 people died that day, a figure that approximates the precinct's estimate of detained Jews. The police hunted down six Jews who had escaped to nearby villages and shot them on the spot. One Jew who had managed to survive the operation returned home and committed suicide. The authorities formed a commission to organize the sale of the victims' property. It is reported that Kerza's wife bought a closet, buffet table, and a bed.[68]

In Rumšiškės the police chief followed the instructions of Reivytis and the Kaunas district chief to the letter, separating out the physically able men before the killing operation. On August 19, he wrote Reivytis, with copies to the Kaunas district chief, that "in accordance with the instructions he had received" from the Police Department he could report that in the small town of Rumšiškės there were 140 persons of Jewish nationality: men, women, and children. They were placed in one neighborhood [rajonas] under the supervision of the police.

> On August 15 of this year, upon the arrival of units of the Germans and our army [the TDA men], and under the command of the expedition's chief Lieutenant [Jurgis] Skaržinskas, all persons of Jewish nationality between the ages of fifteen and seventy who had distinguished themselves by their pro-Communist activity and were dangerous to the current system and public order have been deported from Rumšiškės. About seventy persons have been taken away and there remain only seventy more who are left under guard, only children and old people. They have been gathered together and are settled in a separate area under [our] supervision.[69]

On August 23, the Jews were forced to pay a "contribution" of eight thousand rubles to the rural county treasury. On August 29, a TDA unit from Kaunas shot these remaining Jews on the outskirts of the town. Local officials reported

---

68 Brandišauskas, "Holokaustas Kėdainių apskrityje": 91–95; Bubnys, *Holokaustas Lietuvos provincijoje*, 138–152; also, Rūta Švedienė, ed., *Kėdainių kraštas svastikos ir raudonosios žvaigždžių šešėlyje* (Kėdainiai: Spaudvita, 2011), 29–32; Dean, *Encyclopedia of Camps and Ghettos, 1933–1945*, 1074–1075.

69 Reivytis File, l. 63.

to the Kaunas district chief that the property of the Jews was sold at auction, netting an additional 30,123 rubles.[70]

On August 15, 1941, the Josvainiai precinct reported to Kaunas that "the Jews within the borders of the Josvainiai town and local district were transferred to the Ariogala 'ghetto' in accordance with the Kėdainiai district chief's Order No. 7 ... of August 9."[71] Ariogala was one of the oldest settlements in Lithuania, located about fifty kilometers northwest of Kaunas. After the anti-Soviet rebels had seized the town, they proceed to execute eleven Lithuanian Communists and Soviet officials on July 4–5, and then shot another fourteen Communists and "Soviet activists" in mid-July, most of whom were Jews. The Ariogala police reported that as of August 17, 210 adult Jewish men and eighty women were being held at the town's synagogue "to be deported for manual labor,"[72] but this message did not include children, nor the Jews from Josvainiai. On September 1 two truckloads of TDA men under Barzda arrived in Ariogala. A large pit had already been excavated some two kilometers from the town. SS Lieutenant Dr. Alfons Scholz supervised the operation, carried out mainly by Barzda's men and several volunteers from the local police as well as former "white armbands." Jäger reported the Ariogala death toll as 207 men, 260 women and 195 children. One of the perpetrators interrogated in September 1944 provided an account:

> [Ariogala precinct chief] Čepas divided us into two groups. I found myself in the first group which was charged with guarding the women. We escorted them out of the ghetto and herded them to the southwestern part of the town. Along with the other partisans [police] we walked around them holding rifles at the ready. We took them to the execution site and sat them down by the ditch, then told them to lay down face first, one next to the other. We walked along and hit those women who did not want to lie down. After this, an officer in a Lithuanian lieutenant's uniform arrived and ordered them to hand over all the valuables. Afterwards he ordered the group of people to get up, undress and told them: "If anyone has any gold, give it up, otherwise you will wind up in the pit." Those Jews who had gold turned it over. Then that group was led to the pit where they were shot by people in Lithuanian uniforms. In this way, all the Jews were shot: the men, women, and children. ... On the next day I participated in the distribution of Jewish belongings. They gave

---

70 Bubnys, *Holokaustas Lietuvos provincijoje*, 120–121.
71 Reivytis File, l. 30.
72 Ibid., l. 30a.

me two coats, a women's fur coat, two pairs of women's small boots and a pair of women's shoes. Later I received from the warehouse of the Jewish ghetto two pillows, two blankets and some bedsheets.[73]

Two more documents are of note in revealing the progression of the genocide in the southwestern corner of Kaunas district. On August 17, officials in Šakiai wrote to Reivytis that they had implemented the gathering of the Jews from the shtetls of Paežerėliai, Jankai, and Lekėčiai. They summarized their previous actions: "In general, the Jewish men from the age of fifteen have already been deported for labor; there remain now only the sick, the women, and children. Most of the latter are in Šakiai and Kudirkos Naumiestis."[74] What this message does not reveal is that most of the "deported" men from Šakiai were shot by Lithuanian auxiliary police on July 5, 1941, in woods outside the town.[75]

The fate of the remnant of the Jewish community in these two towns is revealed in the second document, which must rank as one of the more cynical records of German-Lithuanian cooperation in the Final Solution:

Secret-personal

Republic of Lithuania [sic]
Šakiai, September 16, 1941
V. R. V. [Vidaus Reikalų Vadyba, Directorate of Internal Affairs]
Chief of Šakiai District

No. 3/sl. [secret]

To the Director of the Police Department:

In presenting this correspondence, I report to you, Director, that from this day, in the district entrusted to me, there are no more Jews. They were handled by the local partisans and the auxiliary police: in Šakiai, 890 persons on 9/13/41; in K[udirkos] Naumiestis, 650 persons on 9/16/41.

---

73 From the interrogation of J. Kripas, September 23, 1944, as cited in Brandišauskas, "Holokaustas Kedainių apskrityje": 90.
74 Reivytis File, l. 46.
75 Dean, *Encyclopedia of Camps and Ghettos, 1933–1945*, 1114, 1080. After this massacre, the perpetrators selected forty of the wealthier Jewish men and killed them as well. During the first week of July the Tilsit Gestapo and German border police also led a roundup and massacre of Jewish males older than fourteen with the help of local Lithuanian militia.

Before they were finally disposed of, and by order of the Gebietskommissar, his designated officials carried out searches of the persons and apartments of all the Šakiai and K[udirkos] Naumiestis Jews with the assistance of the local police and carted away the discovered money and other valuables. The remaining real estate and movable property is assigned to the security and care of the local government offices until further instructions from the [Gebiets] Kommissar.

A list of the Jews who have been disposed of by name, if it should be so ordered, I will present later.

The Gebietskommissar has been informed about this.
Attachments: 7 pages.

Vincas Karalius [signed]
Šakiai District Chief

Balys Vilčinskas [signed]
Police Chief[76]

TABLE 5. Concentration and destruction of rural Jewish communities in Kaunas GBK as recorded in the Reivytis File and the Jäger Reports
August 26–September 4, 1941

FROM: Precincts/Local Jurisdictions	TO: Murder Sites
Kaišiadorys town Žiežmariai Žasliai	**Kaišiadorys** August 26–27: 1,911 Jewish men, women and children
Balbieriškis Šilavotas Jieznas Stakliškės	**Prienai** August 27: 1,078 Jewish men, women, and children
Vilkija Čekiškės Veliuona Seredžius Lekėčiai	**Vilkija** August 28: 76 men, 192 women, 134 children

---

76   Reivytis File, l. 86.

Kėdainiai City Žeimiai Šėta other locales	**Kėdainiai** August 28: 710 men, 767 women, 599 children
Panemunė Pakuonis Garliava Rural County	**Garliava** August 28–September 2: 73 men, 113 women, 61 children
Krakės town Surviliškis Grinkiškis Baisiogala Gudžiūnai Dotnuva	**Krakės** September 2, 1941: 448 men, 476 women, 201 children
Zapyškis Jankai Paežerėliai/Kriūkai	**Zapyškis** September 4, 1941: 47 men, 118 women, 13 children

The banal bureaucratese of the Reivytis File reveals the role of rural police and civilian officials as they complied with the directives emanating from Kaunas to complete the concentration and expropriation of the Jews. During their brief captivity, the detained Jewish men and the "active Jewish Communist women" were held under a variety of conditions. Smaller groups were concentrated in synagogues (Ariogala, Garliava), public buildings, such as schools, and even monasteries (Krakės). Larger communities were herded into temporary camp sites and makeshift ghettos, or simply confined to designated areas. The deportation of the men and active female Communists to the holding areas, ostensibly for work, but ultimately to their deaths, was largely accomplished by mid-August. Left behind were the forlorn remnants of the region's Litvak world: scattered families, isolated in the provinces, deemed useless as labor. In the end, they were also caught up in the dragnet.

We can attach some names to the victims. The documents which encompassed the shtetls of Šiaudinė, Sudargas, and Kiduliai counted (as of August 26, 1941) 101 "citizens of Jewish nationality": sixty-one women and forty children, all meticulously listed by name, residence, date, and place of birth. The precinct in Gelgaudiškis reported three families deported on September 3: Hinda Kerbelienė (Mrs. Kerbel) was the mother of two boys, four and eight; Mina Šajavičienė's (Shayevich) daughters were eleven and seven; the largest family were the Kaplans, mother Feigė Kaplanienė had five daughters, the youngest of whom, Ženė, was ten months old. At the same time, the remaining seventeen Jewish citizens of the tiny hamlet of Plokščiai, all adult women except for the Budelskis sons, twelve and fifteen, were "handed over to the ferry at Gelgaudiškis and deported." The unfortunates of Plokščiai were joined by the Zaksas (Sachs) family of five from Kriūkai: the matriarch Haja, seventy-five, her 45-year-old daughter Reinė, and three grandsons, ages eleven through thirteen.[77] Their ultimate destination is unrecorded, but impossible not to imagine.

Accelerating Destruction: Jonava, Marijampolė, and Continued Operations in the Southwest

The concentration of Jonava's Jews began in early August. Kulvicas's police force transported most of the town's Jewish men and a few dozen women to the local military barracks, which was to serve as a ghetto, but, in fact, became a staging area for a shooting operation. On August 14, the guards escorted their charges to a wooded area about 1.5 kilometers from the town where workers had already excavated several large pits. The victims were told they would be put to work, but on their arrival they observed a unit of TDA men from Kaunas accompanied by German officers. Realizing what awaited them, a group of men tried to flee the scene but were shot down: only six managed to escape to the woods of whom only one, Nachumas Bliumbergas, survived the war to testify about the massacre. Jäger reported the death toll of this action as 497 men and 55 women. According to postwar Soviet investigations, the victims included a sizeable contingent of Party members and alleged pro-Soviet activists. Fearing for their lives, some Jewish families hid in the surrounding forests or sheltered with Christian friends in nearby villages. At least one report notes that the authorities then posted notices warning people not to hide Jews and offering a reward of food equivalent to the weight of any Jew turned over to the police.

Order No. 3 arrived at the Jonava precinct the day after this first killing action carried out by the unit from Kaunas. On August 17 the Jonava police chief informed Reivytis that "in response to your message of August 15, I am sending

---

77 Reivytis File, Reports of the Gelgaudiškis, Plokščiai, Paežerėliai precincts, and Šiaudinė, Kiduliai, and Sudargas list, l. 87–96. Some accounts indicate these people may have died in Šakiai, but that has not been established.

you the list of Jews who are *within the limits of the precinct entrusted to me*, and I report that they are being held in Jonava town and strongly guarded" (emphasis added). But the list of persons by name, age, and address included only eighty-three men, half of whom were over the age of fifty, and twenty women. Two days later the chief supplemented his report, attaching a list of eight men, all, except one, elderly.[78] These were likely the male survivors not chosen for the August 14 massacre. There is no mention of the remaining three-fourths of Jonava's Jews, primarily old men, women, and children. Available sources indicate that most remained in their homes; some people, left homeless after the June battle between German and Soviet forces, had found shelter at the main synagogue or at the Beth Midrash (house of study).

On August 22, District Commissar Lentzen ordered his Lithuanian subordinate Bortkevičius to complete the counting and concentration of the Jews of the countryside without delay, a directive which the latter immediately transmitted to the heads of the rural counties in the Kaunas district.[79] (One should note the coincidence with the order of the same day issued in Šiauliai by Jonas Noreika.) On August 23–24, the Jonava Jewish community was forced to pay a "contribution" of 120,000 rubles. Soon after this payment, most of the town's Jews were taken to the barracks that had held the victims of the previous massacre. There was widespread looting of the property left behind. According to postwar interrogations, sometime between August 31 and September 2, the new commander of Jonava's self-defense unit, Lieutenant Jonas Jurevičius, assigned sixteen of his men to serve as executioners, delegating the others to convoy duty. On the day of the killings, generous rations of hard liquor were distributed to the shooters. After the first groups of Jews were murdered, two officers from the Kaunas TDA and a German police official took over the operation. EK 3 reported that the Jonava action resulted in the murder of 112 men, 1,200 women, 244 children. A remnant of the community, less than two hundred Jews remained in Jonava and its environs until October 4 when they were taken to Kaunas where nearly all of them perished in either the Great Action of October 28–29 or in later killing operations.[80]

---

78   Reivytis File, l. 58, 66–72.
79   Lentzen to Bortkevičius, August 22, 1941, LCVA, f. R-1534, ap. 1, b. 186, l. 5; Bortkevičius to rural counties (undated), ibid., l. 8.
80   Account based on Dean, *Encyclopedia of Camps and Ghettos, 1933–1945*, 1059–1060; Dieckmann, *Deutsche Besatzungspolitik*, 2:873–876; Jäger Report, December 1, 1941; Bubnys, *Holokaustas Lietuvos provincijoje*, 108–111.

On September 1, 1941, Marijampolė, the major city of the Suvalkija (Užnemunė) region, witnessed one of the largest mass murders of 1941. On the eve of the war Jews constituted about a fifth of the population of more than fifteen thousand citizens. Only three of the nineteen precincts listed in Order No. 3 were located in the Marijampolė district (Germ. *Kreis*) of Kaunas-GBK so the documents in the Reivytis File do not shed much light on the final days of the Jewish community there, but postwar investigations, German documents, and eyewitness testimony lay out the process of destruction. As in the Jonava case, the concentration of the Jews of Marijampolė did not require the construction of an actual ghetto. At the end of August, on orders from Kaunas, police chief Vincas Buvelskis directed the expulsion of Jews from their homes to stables in the town's military barracks. Jews from Liudvinavas, Kazlų Rūda, and other nearby communities also arrived at the concentration point over the next few days. Rumors of an impending massacre were already circulating in the town, so officials attempted to allay the fears of the people by insisting that the concentration was a temporary solution awaiting the preparation of a permanent, "more livable" ghetto. Meanwhile, the precinct police chiefs were told to supply the necessary manpower for the upcoming operation. Buvelskis contributed twenty men from his municipal force, while one of the officers, Povilas Giržadas, was appointed to take command of the shooting itself.

On the morning of September 1, the Marijampolė district chief Vaclovas Goštautas, his deputy, Captain Vladas Klimavičius, and Buvelskis joined Hamann who arrived from Kaunas with a lorry of Germans armed with automatic weapons. According to EK 3 commander Jäger, the Marijampole massacre, like the other actions, were carried out by Hamann and "eight-to-ten trusted men from the Rollkommando in cooperation with Lithuanian partisans."[81] Historian Arūnas Bubnys has estimated that as many as two hundred Lithuanian police and some fifty Germans participated in the killings. At least one witness claims that some of the policemen asked to be excused from the task at hand but were threatened: "those who will not shoot, will themselves have to get in the pits along with the Jews."[82] (If true, this account would be one of the rare examples of such behavior by commanding officers.) The operation commenced at ten o'clock and continued until early evening. The police escorted Jews in groups to seven pits which had been

---

81 Jager Report, December 1, 1941, 1.
82 As reported in Bubnys, *Holokaustas Lietuvos provincijoje*, 246.

excavated at a hillside next to the Šešupė River. After the victims were forced into a prone position in the pits, Giržadas commanded the firing to begin with a signal from his whistle. The perpetrators shot the men first, then killed the women and children. The corpses were shoveled over with dirt by workers brought in from the town. Hamann's men walked around the edges of the pit finishing off the wounded. According to testimony from a statement on October 4, 1944, to the Soviet commission on Nazi crimes, the final stages of what was intended as a well-organized extermination mission came undone in a hellish scene:

> [T]owards the end of the massacre, especially during the murder of the women and children, this discipline fell apart. They began pushing people into the pits *en masse* and [after] covered them only slightly with dirt. They drove the condemned by force, using shovels and rubber clubs, pushing them into the bloody pits below. They hit the disobedient ones with shovels and rubber clubs, knocking out the brains and eyes of the infants. They clambered over the bodies. Most of the murderers were half-drunk, so that while shooting the condemned, their aim was poor. Many of the condemned wound up in the pit alive, either severely or only slightly wounded. A terrible screaming could be heard not only from the banks of the river, but from under the ground itself.[83]

EK 3 reported the death toll as "1,763 Jewish men, 1,812 Jewish women, 1,404 Jewish children, 109 mental patients, one German citizen married to a Jew, and one Russian."[84]

After the bloodshed, Hamann gave a congratulatory speech to the assembled killers and presented them with additional rations of alcohol. District Commissar Lentzen declared the belongings of the murdered Jews property of the Reich subject to further distribution with the permission of Nazi officials. In the rural counties, commissions were established to supervise the sale of Jewish furniture and other belongings to the local populace, a process begun in October 1941 and not completed until the following March. People who had lost their houses to the war, former prisoners of the Soviet regime, participants in the June insurgency, and the poor received a discount on the property of the dead. The total sales in Marijampolė amounted to nearly one hundred thousand RM, most of which was transferred to Lentzen's special account in Kaunas. In addition, it is recorded that Germans working in the ZV received from

---

83 As quoted in ibid., 246–247.
84 Jäger Report, December 1, 1941, 3.

Marijampolė's Jews, among other valuables, a total of "133 gold rings, fifteen silver rings, eighteen gold watches, eighteen silver watches, five gold bracelets, eight gold earrings, 24 gold teeth, 52 silver spoons, and twelve silver forks."[85]

The horror in Marijampolė was the apex of the genocide in Suvalkija, even as killing actions on a lesser scale there and in three other towns continued into September (see table below):

**TABLE 6. Jewish victims of EK 3
and police battalion operations in Southern Lithuania,**
September 9–12, 1941

		Men	Women	Children
September 9	Alytus	287	640	352
	Butrimonys	67	370	303
September 10	Merkinė	223	355	276
	Varėna I	541	141	149
September 11	Leipalingis	60	70	25
	Seirijai	229	384	340
September 12	Simnas	68	197	149

During this four-day killing spree the EK 3 found time to carry out the shooting of forty-three Russian villagers in Užusaliai as a "punitive strike (*Strafaktion*) against the inhabitants who had protected the Russian partisans and also were in possession of weapons."[86] In October Bortkevičius responded with a "mission accomplished" message to an earlier demand by Lentzen to provide a survey of Jews in his area: "In reply to your letter of August 22 of this year I inform you that in Kaunas District no Jews exist anymore. The last Jews from Jonava have been transferred to the Kaunas-Vilijampolė 'Ghetto.'"[87]

---

85 As certified by the Marijampolė District administration on December 30, 1941, Bubnys, *Holokaustas Lietuvos provincijoje*, 247–248.
86 Jager Report, December 1, 1941, 4. Most of the Užusaliai victims were from the Old Believer community which had settled here in the 1860s; they were widely viewed as supporters of Soviet power.
87 As quoted in Dieckmann, *Deutsche Besatzungspolitik*, 2:876.

A sizeable contingent of Kaunas-Land Jews still lived in Lazdijai, the southern corner of his district, where they constituted more than a third of the town's population of nearly three thousand. Following a visit by Lentzen on August 27, the persecution of Jews and the expropriation of property intensified: some of the Jews were detained, although they were allowed into the town during daytime hours. On September 1, the German commandant ordered the creation of a ghetto in the former Soviet military barracks in the hamlet of Katkiškės about two kilometers outside of Lazdijai. The ghetto began functioning in mid-September and soon was also home to Jews brought in from the surrounding communities of Rudamina, Veisiejai, and other settlements, which increased the population of detained Jews to about 1,500. The ghetto was surrounded by a high barbed wire fence and well-guarded by the auxiliary police. A Jewish council which included representatives from the surrounding shtetls handled day-to-day affairs within the encampment. Until late October able-bodied Jews were put to work sweeping the town square and landscaping the German cemetery. On several occasions, the adults were forced to perform humiliating "calisthenics," but the men of the Lazdijai Ghetto were not, as a rule, subjected to the selective shooting actions typical of the other provincial ghettos. Surviving records indicate that the local government kept detailed financial and administrative records: after the dissolution of the ghetto, the Lazdijai district chief requested a reimbursement of 1,132.75 RM from Lentzen's office for expenses incurred in feeding the ghetto inmates. Some of the townspeople smuggled food into the ghetto to supplement the rations which consisted mainly of bread.

At the end of October the Lazdijai police chief Povilas Braška assembled his men and informed them that the Germans were arriving in town and might need assistance for an unspecified action. The policemen were dismissed when no one arrived. A few days later, however, events were set in motion: the police corralled hundreds of local men and forced them to excavate two large pits not far from the ghetto. Given recent events in the area, the Jews grasped the consequences and almost two hundred fled the ghetto, but only several survived. Most were either shot during the escape or hunted down and killed later. On November 3, police chief Braška arrived to reinforce the ghetto guard detail and announced that troops would be deployed to kill the Jews. Soon a bus arrived with dozens of armed men from the First TDA Battalion in Kaunas, led by a car containing two German officers and a Lithuanian lieutenant.

Numerous depositions provide details of a massacre which echoed the horrors of the killings in Marijampolė two months before. As the killers assembled, the police brought in several cases of liquor and boxes of ammunition. The first victims were a small group of eight to ten patients and women with newborns from the hospital in Lazdijai. An old woman who was unable to climb out of the wagon was simply thrown into the pit along with her hospital cot. The police then convoyed the Jews from the barracks in the ghetto, forced them to strip to their underwear, and drove them barefoot over the snow-covered ground. The victims were pushed into the pits face down. On the command of Lieutenant Bronius Norkus, one of the practiced TDA veterans of such operations, the men from Kaunas fired into the people from above. The final group of victims escorted to the pits consisted of sick people and pregnant women. The killers walked along the edges of the ditches, finishing off the wounded. Several of the local auxiliary police convoying the victims also participated in the shootings. The police had brought in local workers with shovels to cover each layer of the bodies in preparation for the next group. One witness recounted that, as the bodies were covered up, a young boy of twelve sprang up from the dirt and begged in Lithuanian that he be left alive but was shot by a policeman. Witnesses who described the scene years later were still shaken. The entire killing operation lasted about five hours and afterwards the murderers celebrated with drink and song well into the night. According to Jäger, 485 men, 511 women, and 539 children died in the trenches.[88]

There are precise records concerning the disposition of the property of the Jews of Lazdijai district. By order of the military commandant in Marijampolė, all Jewish possessions were to be considered "the property of the German Reich." In practice, however, some of the carefully inventoried Jewish property was stolen, as evidenced by criminal investigations conducted by the Lazdijai police. Many other possessions, such as furniture and household appliances, were eventually sold off to the local populace, no doubt, in some cases to the victims' neighbors. It was an axiom that nothing should go to waste. New Lithuanian owners took over fifty formerly Jewish farms. The policeman Jurgis Nevulis "received" and signed for the farm of Z. Berkė, which included a sizeable plot of ninety hectares, a house, a barn, storage shed, two horses, and four cows.

---

88 The dozens of depositions on the Lazdijai massacre dating from 1944 to 1968 have been analyzed in Bubnys, *Holokaustas Lietuvos provincijoje*, 219–230; also cf. Valentinas Brandišauskas, "Lazdijų apskrities žydų likimas nacistinės okupacijos metais: nuo teisių apribojimo iki žūties, *Genocidas ir rezistencija* 23, no. 1 (2008): 58–75; Jäger Report, December 1, 1941, 5.

Nevulis's luck was short-lived: in 1944 the returning Soviet authorities expelled him from his newly acquired home.[89]

The Lazdijai massacre not only marked the end of provincial Jewry in Kaunas-Land but also substantially concluded the campaign to eradicate small-town Litvak society which had for centuries been part of Lithuania's social landscape.

Wilna-Land: The Destruction of Jewish Communities in Eastern Lithuania

In July 1941 the ZV established the Vilnius Region (Gebietskommissariat Wilna-Land) under Horst Wulff (1907–1945), which included the Jewish shtetls that had been part of interwar Poland and then were transferred first to Lithuanian and later to Soviet control in 1939–1940. As reported by Jäger, Hamann's mobile squad and a special commando unit (Teilkommando) of EK 3 headquartered in Vilnius killed more than sixteen thousand of the district's small-town Jews during a three-week murder campaign which commenced on September 20, 1941.

The predominantly Polish town of Nemenčinė was located some twenty kilometers northeast of Vilnius. During the first days of the war, the insurgents arrested Nemenčinė's prominent Soviet activists, including the Gordon brothers Kushel and Chaim, never to be seen again. Some of the rebels later joined the town's police force who, on the night of September 19, escorted Polish workers to woods three kilometers outside of the town to excavate a large ditch. The following day a force of about twenty men from the Special Platoon (the YB) arrived from Vilnius, commanded by the notorious SS Sergeant Martin Weiss (1903–1984) and Lieutenant Balys Norvaiša. The Nemenčinė police assembled the area's Jews in the town synagogue, estimated by survivors at about seven hundred, and, after robbing them of their valuables, escorted them out of the town. The people were told that they would be taken to the Vilna Ghetto, but when the column was ordered to turn towards the woods, the Jews grasped the ruse, as Sara Rudasehvski recalled a few years later:

> At least a hundred guards escorted us on the way. Among them I saw Antanas Paukštė. After we had gone some three kilometers from the town, [the guards] directed us to the right, to the woods. We then understood

---

89   Bubnys, *Holokaustas Lietuvos provincijoje*, 230.

that they are driving us not to the ghetto, but to our deaths. After walking about 300 meters from the road, we saw a freshly excavated ditch. Then the guards opened fire at our column. Some people fell, others ran to the side. I also began to run, and that is how I managed to save myself.[90]

According to reports, over a hundred Jews managed to escape. The remainder were surrounded by the police and YB men and driven towards the pits where they were shot in groups of ten, reminiscent of the tactic perfected in Paneriai. Jäger reported the death toll as 128 men, 176 women, and ninety-nine children.[91]

Two days later, the killers were sent to Naujoji Vilnia (P. Nowa Wilejka), located less than eight kilometers from the center of Vilnius. A count of the population in the late summer of 1941 indicates that 633 Jews lived in the rural county, and 515 Jews in the town itself. On September 2, 1941, local officials in the Vilnius district responded to an August 26 request from District Chief Bronius Draugelis to determine an appropriate site for a Jewish ghetto. Two locations were proposed, and the alternatives were carefully evaluated by the district engineer and his colleagues:

1. Ten kilometers in the direction of Nemenčinė. . . , we find the [former] Russian army camp. There are over a dozen buildings of which thirteen are heated and four are not. There are also five kitchens. It would be possible to fit all of the Vilnius district's Jews here, but it should be noted that the local inhabitants have terribly looted and trashed all the buildings: the window frames have been removed, the doors torn out, the heaters damaged. . . . So, if the Jews were to be settled here, it would be necessary to make major repairs.

2. About nine-and-a half kilometers in the direction of Šumskas . . . is the Vėliučionys estate, where the Poles had previously located a house of corrections, and the Russians had installed here some sort of military school. The estate was nationalized. There are several wooden structures and one large two-story stone building which could accommodate all of the Jews in the Vilnius district. There are also some farm buildings. Almost all the structures are in good condition, except for the ruined plumbing and electrical systems, so the Jews could

---

90 Testimony of Sara Rudaševskaja (Rudashevski), February 1, 1946, as published in *Masinės žudynės*, 1: 217–218.
91 Bubnys, *Holokaustas Lietuvos provincijoje*, 564–565; Jäger Report, December 1, 1941, 6.

be transferred here at any time. The Jews themselves could perform the still needed repairs. In our opinion, this place is convenient since it is close to the cities of Vilnius and Naujoji Vilnia, so that it would be easy to utilize Jewish labor for work in these cities. In addition, of all the places we have investigated, this one is most suitable for life in winter conditions.[92]

While the authors of the report intended the Jews to settle the ghetto for the long term, subsequent events made clear that this was not the intention of their superiors. On September 19, Draugelis, "on the order of the Gebietskommissar," issued detailed instructions to all the rural county chiefs with copies to the police precincts for the concentration of the district's Jews at the aforementioned Vėliučionys address. On the face of it, the document followed similar instructions from other officials in considerable detail: for example, for purposes of expropriation, there are the usual detailed inventories of Jewish real estate and properties left behind in their homes. There are several directives, however, that speak of an unusual sense of urgency and haste. Draugelis stressed that the order allowed for no exceptions: it was to include "even those Jews who are under the jurisdiction of the German military." In the words of the chief, local officials were to "strictly ensure that not a single Jew be left in place, and if such a Jew would be found, he must be immediately arrested and taken to the already indicated place of settlement of the Jews—the ghetto." There was also the warning: "For those inhabitants who hide Jews and their property.., they must be issued summons, and brought to me for punishment." To speed things up, Jews were allowed "to take only those possession, which they are able to carry, and, in a further clarification, "Jewish belongings abandoned on the way [to Vėliučionys] are not to be returned but brought back to the rural county office and placed in the warehouse [designated] for Jewish property." The timetable was exact: "The Jews must be driven into the ghetto by six in the morning on September 22."[93]

On the same day, the Vilnius police chief Antanas Iškauskas reaffirmed the deadline to the head of the Naujoji Vilnia precinct, restating "the order of the Vilnius Gebietskommissar, Mister Wulff" and informing him that his police would be assisting a unit of "forty soldiers of the self-defense battalion [a unit of

---

92   Message of Leonardas Palevičius et al. to Draugelis, September 2, 1941, in *Masinės žudynės*, 1: 208–209.
93   Vilnius District Chief Draugelis to the Naujoji Vilnia mayor and all rural counties, September 19, 1941, in *Masinės žudynės*, 1: 209–210.

the TDA] who will arrive at eight in the morning and are designated for Jewish transport and guarding of the ghetto." The Naujoji Vilnia police were informed that Jews from the Nemenčinė, Mickūnai, Šumskas, and Rudamina precincts would be sent to Vėliučionys as well. The final paragraph of Iškauskas's message is one of the more curious documents in the police files of the period:

> In transporting and guarding the Jews, the members of the convoy must not engage in violence, cruel behavior, verbal abuse, or seize Jewish property for themselves: persons who perpetrate such acts will be punished with the utmost severity. If an officer arrives with the self-defense unit at your precinct, it is the precinct chief who must command the convoy. In cooperation with the local government, the soldiers of the self-defense battalion must be provided lodging and food. The soldiers of the self-defense unit must remain until further notice. You are required to report on the completion of this task and all related events by noon of the 25th of this month.[94]

The police chief may have wanted to avoid the chaos associated with the undisciplined actions of the perpetrators which, by this time, had caused some unease. Or he may have felt some shred of empathy. Given the realities of Lithuania in the summer and fall of 1941, the former appears more likely.

The precise identity of the units that carried out the massacre at the Vėliučionys forest adjacent to the estate is unknown. Historians who have examined the available records conclude that the likeliest candidates involved a platoon-size unit of the First Police Battalion, which had been transferred to Naujoji Vilnia in late August, and the men of the Special Platoon (YB). Several witnesses testified that the latter group arrived by bus along with two SS-men and comprised most of the shooters. According to Jäger, the massacre occurred as scheduled on the supposed day of the establishment of the Jewish ghetto, September 22: 468 men, 495 women, and 196 children died.[95]

The largest action impacting the shtetls within the immediate vicinity of Vilnius occurred on September 24, 1941, when, according to Jäger, 512 men, 744 women, and 511 children were shot near Naujaneriai village, including the Jews of Maišiagala, Paberžė, Riešė, and other smaller communities. According to

---

94 Vilnius District Police Chief to Naujoji Vilnia precinct, September 19, 1941, in *Masinės žudynės*, 1: 211.

95 The details are analyzed in Bubnys, *Holokaustas Lietuvos provincijoje*, 561–564; Jäger Report, December 1, 1941, 6.

a 1969 interrogation, the YB men arrived on that day at the already excavated pits led by Weiss, Norvaiša, and Lieutenant Balys Lukošius. Weiss supervised the killings and executed the wounded, while Norvaiša gave the command to fire as the Jews were brought to the pits in groups. On the next day, the same unit moved to target the Jews held in Jašiūnai, a town located 20 kilometers south of Vilnius, where they killed 215 men, 229 women, and 131 children who had been gathered there from surrounding settlements.[96]

On September 27, the killing moved outwards from Vilnius in shooting operations that netted ever more victims. The town of Eišiškės (Eyshishok), sixty kilometers south of Vilnius, was a center of Jewish life in the region, celebrated in book and film, as well as in an acclaimed photographic exhibit of pre-Holocaust life at the USHMM. On the eve of the war this town of nearly three thousand had a Jewish majority, a sizeable Polish population, and a minority of ethnic Lithuanians. The Germans captured Eišiškės on the second day of the war and quickly established the military commandant's office and gendarmerie in the high school; a small unit of Lithuanian policemen arrived a few days later. During the first month of the occupation, the German detachment forced the Jews to repair roads. The usual identifying yellow badges were also introduced. On July 25, the Trakai district chief ordered all Jewish communities to elect representatives to better enact the directives of the authorities: in Eišiškiai the twelve-man council was headed by Abraham Kaplan. In mid-September, the German military left the town in the hands of the local municipal authority.

According to information gathered from witnesses, on September 21, a group of armed civilians entered Eišiškės and, together with the police, herded all Jews into three synagogues. At least several dozen Jews hid among neighbors or fled to the countryside. Townspeople noted the arrivals as Lithuanian speakers although their identity is not certain. Police from other areas of the district and the Eišiškės rural county police chief Astrauskas have been mentioned in some testimonies. Postwar interrogations also implicate the Vilnius YB. Germans were reportedly present and filmed the operation. Most accounts indicate that on the first day of the killings, Lithuanian "partisans"[97] convoyed about five hundred able-bodied men through the town as their Polish neighbors

---

96 Bubnys, *Holokaustas Lietuvos provincijoje*, 565–566.

97 It was common at the time for Jews and non-Lithuanian speakers to misidentify Lithuanian auxiliary police as "partisans," "Shaulists," or *šauliai* (members of the interwar Riflemen's Union—S. S.).

shouted to the victims, warning them of their impending doom. Over the next two days, old people, women, and children were put to death. Jews from the shtetls of Kalesninkai and Valkininkai were also among the victims. Finally, the killers went through the town hunting for Jews in hiding and looting what they could from the abandoned homes. Comparative analysis of different accounts suggests that the September 27, 1941, entry on Eišiškės in the Jäger Report, listing 989 men, 1,636 women, and 821 children among the dead, was in fact the cumulative total of a massacre which may have lasted as long as three days.[98]

Soon after, a similar action unfolded in historic Trakai, the renowned medieval residence of the Grand Dukes and the historic home of the country's Karaim community. In the fall of 1941, the population of Trakai was estimated at about 2,600. At the end of July, as in the other shtetls of eastern Lithuania, the persecution of the Jews intensified. The German military commandant ordered the reduction by half of the food rations to Jews. On August 16, Wulff issued instructions to the district chiefs of Vilnius, Švenčionys, and Trakai to commence the ghettoization of Jews and half-Jews and, a week later, directed local authorities to appoint officials for Jewish affairs.[99] In early September, the estimated four hundred Jews of Trakai, who had until then lived in their homes, were transferred to a ghetto where they were joined by about a hundred Jews from nearby Aukštadvaris, Lentvaris, and Onuškis. About a week after the transfer of the Jews, the Trakai district chief Mačinskas informed the town's police chief Kazys Čaplikas that his men would have to execute the Jews of the Trakai Ghetto. In a 1970 deposition Čaplikas claimed that he refused the order and, as a result, the action was delayed until Martin Weiss and a busload of YB-men arrived a week later. On September 30, 1941, as the local police guarded the site, the killers from Vilnius, according to Jäger, massacred 366 men, 483 women, and 597 children.[100]

---

98 The account is from witness statements in Bubnys, *Holokaustas Lietuvos provincijoje*, 502–505, especially the unpublished report by A. Peshko and A. Shalupayev compiled after the war.

99 Circular of District Chief Kostas Kalendra, August 18, 1941, LCVA, f. R-500, ap. 1, b. 1, t. 1, l. 138; Wulff to Kalendra, August 23, 1941, ibid, l. 233.

100 Jager Report, December 1, 1941, 6. The depositions of Čaplikas and a YB member are cited in Bubnys, *Holokaustas Lietuvos provincijoje*, 489–490. More details are in Neringa Latvytė-Gustaitienė, *Holokaustas Trakų apskrityje* (Vilnius: Valstybinis Vilniaus Gaono muziejus, 2002); cf. Dieckmann, *Besatzungspolitik*, 2: 902–903.

About sixty Jewish families lived in Semeliškės, located about forty kilometers southwest from Vilnius. On July 21, on orders from the Wehrmacht's commandant, the community of 261 Jews elected a twelve-man council headed by Rabbi Moishe Sheshkin.[101] In mid-September the Jews of the town, along with survivors from Vievis and Žasliai, were driven into a ghetto consisting of the synagogue, a school, and a few other buildings. As in Trakai, a squad of between twenty and thirty YB men arrived with a German commander to carry out the slaughter of the imprisoned Jews. After excavating a pit near a lake about two kilometers from Semeliškės, on October 6, the killers shot 213 men, 359 women, and 390 children.[102]

The genocidal wave in eastern Lithuania came to the town of Švenčionys, eighty kilometers northeast of Vilnius, on October 9, 1941. The persecution of the district's Jews had intensified in mid-August when Wulff ordered local municipal and rural county authorities to mark and segregate the Jews. At the end of September, the police escorted the Jews of Švenčionys and the entire rural county to the military training area near the town of Švenčionėliai (literally, "little Švenčionys"), some ten kilometers to the west. Several hundred Jews managed to escape eastward to Belarus where their chances for survival, at least for the moment, were considerably better. Lea Svirskaya described her ordeal on the day of the expulsion:

> On September 27 [1941], they began the action of driving [Jews] from their houses. They were searching for the Jews who had hidden among the Lithuanian homes. The people were allowed to take only that which they could carry. The children and the sick were taken in wagons, everyone else went on foot. We walked surrounded by the Lithuanian police, there were almost no Germans to be seen. It was dark when we arrived in Švenčionėliai. They led the Jews into a large building and pushed them inside. It was so crowded that there was only room to stand. Families held hands. The exhausted people fell over each other, and from every corner one could hear the Jews begging for water.[103]

---

101 Protocol of the Meeting of the Semeliškės Jewish community, July 21, 1941, LCVA, f-R-500, ap. 1, b. 1. 168.

102 Based on the 1970 depositions of J. Ragavičius and B. Kapačiūnas, as related in Bubnys, *Holokaustas Lietuvos provincijoje*, 490–491.

103 As related in Veronika Kumelan, ed., "Švenčionių krašto žydų tragedija 1941–1944," accessed May 24, 2020, https://www.gimnazija.svencioneliai.lm.lt/wordpress/wp-content/uploads/%C5%A0ven%C4%8Dioni%C5%B3_kra%C5%A1to_%C5%BEyd%C5%B3_tragedija.pdf.

An account published in 2002 relates what happened next. The barracks of the temporary camp in Švenčionėliai were surrounded by a fence and, after their arrival, the men were separated from their families. On the third day the Jews were allowed to go for water and to wash. Two Jews then arrived from Švenčionys and brought some food. The inmates elected a committee to distribute the food, but there was very little to eat, and the people began to starve. A high-ranking SS officer arrived at the scene later and announced that the Reich had imposed a "contribution" of a quarter of a million rubles to be paid in valuables and furs and threatened dire consequence for failure to comply. Within hours the required sum was delivered. Several families arranged their release from the barracks by bribing the German officer, among them, the family of survivor Svirskaya.[104]

In early October, the head of the district's police Januškevičius and two German security officials arrived at the Švenčionėliai encampment and informed the town's mayor and the local police chief that, in compliance with German orders, all Jews would have to be shot. Almost three hundred local men were ordered to dig a trench later estimated at two hundred meters in length, ten meters wide, and three meters deep. Most witness accounts relate that the killings commenced on October 8, 1941. The victims were led to the pit in groups of fifty, the men first, then the women and children. Workers were brought in to cover the bodies, as Leonas Meilus recalled:

> At the beginning of October, we were called in to see the local headman. There we were told to sign up for the task, for actually covering up the Jews. They collected us from work and told us to go to Švenčionėliai. It was pointless to resist. The trench was in square form, but I was unable to ascertain its depth since by the time we arrived, the pit was already filled with corpses. There were a lot of us there, covering up the bodies [with dirt]. The Jews were in their shirts, without outer garments. There were even those, who were wont to take Jewish clothes for themselves. The most difficult thing was to stand there helpless, when they brought an old woman and two children. The executioners killed the children with indifference. Along with those who were shot, they sometimes tossed into the pit a living person who would then try to get up, to escape the

---

104 Giedrė Geniušienė, "Nutrūkęs Švenčionių rajono žydų kelias," in *Švenčionių krašto žydų tragedija*, ed. Giedrė Ganiušienė (Švenčionys: Nalšios muziejus, 2002), 34–35.

clutches of death, but they would immediately finish off such a person either with a blow of the rifle stock, or with a bullet.[105]

Witness testimonies after the war report that some of the children were buried alive. The killers were men from the YB in Vilnius, led by the notoriously sadistic Lieutenant Šidlauskas, and assisted by over a hundred of the Švenčionys district police who guarded the murder site. According to Jäger's ledger, by October 9 the death toll included 1,169 men, 1,840 women, and 717 children.[106] The surviving Jews of the district were forced into a ghetto in the northwest corner of Švenčionys town which survived until the spring of 1943, an exception to the general rule of near total annihilation elsewhere in the provinces.[107] The men of the YB returned to their barracks in Vilnius, having left behind a dreadful milestone in the record of destruction. The murder of the Jews of Švenčionys and environs was the last major operation in the campaign of the mobile killing detachments in the countryside of eastern Lithuania. Except for a handful of harried survivors, the Vilnius region's shtetls had vanished in the killing fields.

Concentration and Mass Murder in the Cities: Kaunas, Vilnius, Šiauliai

In the history of the Holocaust in Lithuania, the fate of Jews trapped in the large cities is a different chronicle of agony, but no less cruel in its final chapter. In contrast to rural Jewry, who early on had been cynically portrayed as "useless eaters," the German need for labor meant at least temporary survival for many urban Jews. Aside from the violence of the pogroms, throughout July 1941 the German Security Police and Lithuanian police battalions had already carried out the well-organized execution of thousands of urbanites in Vilnius and Kaunas, primarily Jewish men and suspected Communists (the latter without regard to gender or nationality). In Kaunas, a reduction in anti-Jewish violence

---

105 "Švenčionių krašto žydų tragedija" [unpaginated].
106 Jäger Report, December 1, 1941, 6.
107 A readable account containing much interesting material on the Jews of Švenčionys and their destruction is the memoir of the granddaughter of Pranas Puronas, the Lithuanian Security Police chief of the region. Rita Gabis, *A Guest at the Shooters' Banquet: My Grandfather's SS Past, My Jewish Family, a Search for the Truth* (New York: Bloomsbury, 2016).

followed the massacres of July 4 and 6 at the Seventh Fort. Soon after, the city's Jewish leaders, including Leib Garfunkel, Doctor Efraim Rabinovich, Yankel Shmukler, Rabbi Samuel Sneg (Sniegas), and Yakov Goldberg, were called to a meeting with German officials to discuss the future of their community and its grim prospects in Lithuania. Sneg and Goldberg in particular had close ties to the prewar Lithuanian elite: before 1940, the former had been the Jewish chaplain in the Lithuanian army, and the latter had once headed the Association of Jewish Veterans of the independence wars. The men had shared a prison cell during the Soviet occupation. In Avraham Tory's account, the five men met with an unnamed German "general" who was the "Gestapo commander" who informed them that "the Lithuanians no longer wish to live together with the Jews" and were demanding the creation of a Jewish ghetto. The German commander told them that "There is an intense hatred towards the Jews among the Lithuanians, because all the Jews are Bolsheviks. After all, Lenin himself was a Jew." The group then met with Bobelis who told them that they must "haggle with the Germans" concerning the ghetto and gave Goldberg a letter certifying his rank as a former lieutenant in the Lithuanian army and his participation in the independence wars.[108] On the same day, Bobelis informed the PG cabinet that, according to Stahlecker, "the mass liquidation of Jews would no longer be carried out ... [but] in accordance with a German directive, a ghetto is being established for the Jews in Vilijampolė, to which all the Jews of the city of Kaunas must be moved within four weeks."[109]

On July 10, Bobelis and Kaunas mayor Kazys Palčiauskas issued Order No. 15 mandating the establishment of the ghetto, ordering "all Jews residing within the city of Kaunas to move to a designated neighborhood in Vilijampolė" by mid-August. Non-Jewish residents of the designated ghetto area were to be removed. As of July 12, Jews, "without regard to sex and age," were to wear a yellow Star of David patch. Jews were "allowed to walk the streets and appear in public places" between six in the morning and eight in the evening. They were forbidden "to hire the services of people of other nationalities." On July 25, the new Lithuanian commandant in Kaunas, Captain Stasys Kviecinskas, his

---

108 Tory, July 7, 1941, entry, in *Surviving the Holocaust*, 10–11; Arūnas Bubnys, *Kauno getas 1941–1944* (Vilnius: LGGRTC, 2014), 40–42; also, mentioned in Jacob Goldberg's 1948 memoir, in "Fun Letzte Churbn" (author's copy, an excerpt translated courtesy of CRH and Associates, 1983); cf. Dieckmann, *Besatzungspolitik*, 2:930–931.

109 Protocol of PG Cabinet meeting of July 7, 1941, in *LLV*, 50–51.

deputy Colonel Kalmantas, Mayor Palčiauskas, Reivytis, and other officials held an interdepartmental meeting finalizing the ghettoization process. The list of transferees compiled by the municipal authorities ran to forty-two archival pages. Officials meticulously recorded the addresses of the homes to be abandoned as well as the new, far more cramped accommodations.[110] In memorandums to both the municipality and the German Security Police, Jewish leaders protested the conditions of the transfer, noting that Vilijampolė was a notoriously poor neighborhood which could not easily accommodate twenty thousand Jews from the rest of the city, but their appeals went unanswered.[111]

Despite Stahlecker's earlier caveat, mass shootings resumed even as the concentration of the Jews of Kaunas gathered pace. The killing operations were now transferred to the Fourth Fort located in Aukštoji Panemunė on the left bank of the Nemunas River. On August 2, TDA men under the command of Barzda and Skaržinskas brought over two hundred people from Kaunas prisons to the fort where they were met by a dozen German police. EK 3 recorded the victims of the massacre: 179 Jewish men, thirty-three Jewish women, one American Jewish man, one American Jewish woman, and four Lithuanian Communists. A week later, the Third Company of the First Battalion convoyed more than five hundred Jewish men and women from prison to the same fort. The Germans reportedly brought liquor for the men and participated in the massacre. The women were shot first, the wounded dispatched by the TDA officers and Germans, this action then followed by the killing of the men. Soviet POWs were forced to shovel over the layers of the corpses. EK 3 registered 484 Jewish men and fifty women as the death toll for August 9, 1941.[112]

The establishment and closure of the Kovno Ghetto was effectively complete by mid-August. Crowded Vilijampolė was divided into two parts: the Large Ghetto, which abutted the Neris River, and the Small Ghetto, further inland. The two sections were connected by a walking bridge over Panerių Street.[113] The inmates had hardly been settled when an announcement from Captain Fritz Jordan, the officer in charge of "Jewish affairs" in Kaunas, invited

---

110 Documents in LCVA, f. R-1444, ap. 1, b. 6, l. 1–58.
111 Tory, *Surviving the Holocaust*, 14–17; Joachim Tauber, *Arbeit als Hoffnung: judische Ghettos in Litauen 1941–1944*, Quellen und Darstellungen zur Zeitgeschichte 108 (Berlin: De Gruyter Oldenbourg, 2015), 75.
112 Bubnys, *Kauno getas*, 28–29; Jager Report, December 1, 1941.
113 See MAP 11, Chapter 5.

the "intelligentsia" among the Jews to sign up for work in the city's archives, promising better working conditions and increased food rations. Nineteen-year-old Waldemar Ginsburg remembered this widely reported tragic episode:

> On August 18, three days after the closing of the ghetto, the SS and the partisans arrived to pick up 500 Jews for a specially demanding job: to sort out the records and files of the town hall. The Jewish council was told that the men must be well educated; the work would be indoors, and three meals would be provided. My classmate David and I decided to join the group, but I arrived late and was No 539 in the line. Only 534 men were taken, including David. They were not seen again. We assumed that they had been taken for forced labor. Sometime later, Lithuanian witnesses informed us of their fate. They were taken to the [Fourth] Fort and shot.[114]

For nearly a month, murder operations abated. On September 15, Captain Jordan issued five thousand certificates intended for skilled Jewish workers, which some inmates understood, correctly as "papers for life." On September 17, the patients and staff of the hospital located in the Small Ghetto, as well as Jews who did not possess the new work certificates, were assembled in preparation for a march to the Ninth Fort, but the process was interrupted when Captain Alfred Tornbaum, commander of one of the German police companies, called off the operation at Jordan's request. In any case, the reprieve was only temporary: on September 26, a large contingent of German and Lithuanian police stormed into the ghetto and rounded up hundreds of men, women, and children, listed in the EK 3 accounting as the sick and those "suspected of infectious diseases." The killers recorded 1,608 Jewish victims: 412 men, 615 women, and 581 children.[115] This was the year's final mass shooting at the Fourth Fort, but also a horrific beginning: the first such massacre of the city's children.

The terror intensified in October. In an action to be repeated in Vilnius, the Germans decided to reduce the population and size of the ghetto. One witness testified that during September Nazi officers supervised works around the Ninth Fort prison as the preferred site for executions: the area was cleared of brush and Soviet POWs excavated several large trenches.[116] In the early morning hours of October 4, 1941, about fifty German police and a hundred TDA men

---

114 Valdemar Ginsburg, *And Kovno Wept* (Nottinghamshire: Beth Shalom, 1998), 45.
115 Tory, *Surviving the Holocaust*, 37–39; Jäger Report, December 1, 1941, 4.
116 Interrogation of J. Barkauskas, November 30, 1944, as cited in Bubnys, *Kauno getas*, 32.

surrounded the Small Ghetto. The people were assembled in a square outside of the ghetto and subjected to a selection. Jews with the Jordan permits were allowed to leave for the Large Ghetto, while the remaining inmates were corralled for transport. At the same time, Germans turned their attention to the hospital and children's home located in the Small Ghetto: most of the children were loaded onto the trucks along with their nurses and taken to the Ninth Fort. Jewish workers were brought to the hospital grounds to dig a pit near the building. The killers threw old people, many patients, and some children into the ditch and shot them. Women who had just given birth, as well as patients and staff from the hospital's surgical ward, were allowed to proceed to the Large Ghetto. The Germans then set fire to the hospital, incinerating the patients who had remained and destroying most of the modern medical equipment which until then had been available to the Jewish community. According to a well-placed Lithuanian source, SS officer Went von der Ropp, a prominent member of Lithuania's ethnic German community before the war, witnessed the destruction of the hospital and later bragged about the murder of nurses and newborns at a dinner party.[117] The fate of the people transported to the Ninth Fort is noted in Jäger's ledger: "315 Jewish men, 712 Jewish women, 881 Jewish children (a punitive action [*Strafaktion*] because a German policeman had been shot at in the Ghetto)."[118]

On October 24, 1941, people in the Kovno Ghetto observed the visit of a Gestapo car which circled the area, as if on a reconnaissance mission. On the next day, SS Master Sergeant Helmut Rauca (1908–1983) and SS Captain Schmitz informed the Jewish council that, in view of the needs of the German war effort, the population of the ghetto would be divided into a larger area, which would contain able-bodied workers and their families, and a smaller ghetto which would house the rest. The former would receive larger food rations to sustain them in their work. The Nazis informed the council that all the families in the ghetto, without exception, were to assemble in Demokratų Square on the morning of October 28. Anyone found in hiding would be shot. Having already experienced the consequences of previous "selections," worried council

---

117 Related in Algirdas Mošinskis, "Liūdininko pasisakymas – II: žydų ligoninės sudeginimas," *Akiračiai* 10 (1984): 9. The narrator's wife, Halina Mošinskienė, was awarded the title of Righteous Among Nations at Yad Vashem in 1982.

118 Jäger Report, December 1, 1941, 5. Details are in Tory, *Surviving the Holocaust*, 40–43; Bubnys, *Kauno getas*, 32–33.

members sought assurances from Rauca who professed amazement that his motives were suspect.

But there was little that could be done to assuage the panic of the people who had already learned from Lithuanians outside the ghetto about the trenches prepared at the Ninth Fort. The leadership now faced the dilemma, well presented in the work of Lawrence Langer, of a "choiceless choice," that is, a decision that the victims of the Holocaust were compelled to make between two horrendous but unavoidable responses. The Jewish council in Kaunas consulted Rabbi Abraham Shapiro, whose examination of "learned books" led him to the conclusion that, as in previous cases, when an evil edict threatened the entire community, leaders were "bound to summon their courage, take the responsibility, and save as many lives as possible." Not everyone agreed: some supported the religious principle of "refusing compliance even on the pain of death."[119] On October 27, the council published an announcement in Yiddish and German, making it clear where the responsibility lay:

> The Council has been ordered by the authorities to publish the following official decree to the Ghetto inmates:
>
> All inmates of the Ghetto, without exception, including children and the sick, are to leave their homes on Tuesday, October 28, 1941, at 6 A. M., and to assemble in the square between the big blocks and the Demokratų Street, and to line up according to police instructions.
>
> The Ghetto inmates are required to report by families, each family, being headed by the worker who is the head of the family.
>
> It is forbidden to lock apartments, wardrobes, cupboards, desk, etc. . . .
>
> After 6 A. M. nobody may remain in his apartment.
>
> Anyone found in his apartment after 6 A. M. will be shot on sight.[120]

The scene that unfolded on the rainy autumn morning of October 28, 1941, has been described in a number of accounts. The ghetto inmates fully understood the gravity of the threat which faced them: as they gathered in the assigned square, the heads of families clutched any document which might prove their usefulness, or, in Tory's words, "some paper that might perhaps, who

---

119 Conversations as described in Tory's entry for October 28, 1941, in *Surviving the Holocaust*, 46–47.

120 As published in ibid., 47–48.

knows, bring them an 'indulgence' for the sin of being a Jew,"[121] including employment certificates, university diplomas, documents attesting service in the Lithuanian army. The thousands of Jews were surrounded by armed German police and TDA-men, waiting in the damp cold until 9:00 a.m., when Rauca arrived and positioned himself on a mound in the company of Jordan, Tornbaum, and Schmitz. The commander of the First TDA Battalion, Major Kazys Šimkus, stood nearby. The TDA men went through the empty homes, searching for anyone in hiding. After Rauca signaled for the Jewish leadership and ghetto police to step to the safe side, the selection began. As people began to grasp that the elderly, sick, and generally less fit were being shunted aside, they sought desperately to pass to the "good" side. Thirteen-year-old Irena Veisaitė had come to the square prepared to look older and fit for work:

> I dressed up in my mother's clothes, put on her brassiere and stuffed some socks into it so that my chest would look like a grown woman's. I remember how we stood in columns, generally according to our workplaces, as Gestapo officer Rauca walked the columns and indicated which Jews were to go to the left, which to the right. In other words, some were being sent to their death, while others were being given the chance to live a little longer. It was very cold. We stood there from early morning, waiting for Rauca to reach our column. Our "sorting" began as it was beginning to get dark, at around 4 p. m. I saw how Valdemaras [Ginsburg], Aunt Polia and Uncle Samuilas, her husband, were sent to the "good side," because they looked healthy and able-bodied.
>
> My grandparents were already over 70 years old. They looked quite frail, but I still had hope that I could save them. When Rauca approached us, I looked him straight in the eyes, perhaps with some kind of hypnotic power, so that he did not even notice my grandparents. I heard him say, "The girl has pretty eyes. Go to the right!" I remember how I dragged my grandparents, how we ran to the right and how my grandmother cried: "Don't rush so, my dear child. I can't run anymore!" But I continued to drag them with almost superhuman strength.... That time we were still destined to return to our ghetto quarters.[122]

---

121 Ibid., 49.
122 Aurimas Švedas and Irena Veisaitė, *Life Should Be Transparent: Conversations about Lithuania and Europe in the Twentieth Century and Today*, trans. Karla Gruodis (Budapest: Central European University Press, 2019), 62. Waldemar Ginsburg who wrote the memoir of the Kovno ghetto was Irena Veisaitė's cousin.

Seventeen-year-old Sara Ginaitė-Rubinsonienė, who was to later join the Jewish partisans, remembers that when Rauca arrived, a "deathly silence fell upon the crowd." Her own family seemed in dire danger: they had no work permits, and with her mother, aunt, and a small child, the four stood little chance of survival. Fortunately, they had befriended the affable young ghetto policeman David Glickman, who took them with him to the "good side." In effect, only the able-bodied, the relative few who had outsmarted Rauca's selection, and the handful who had fled before the roundup to hide among Lithuanian friends, escaped consignment to the lesser category of selectees who were not considered employable. The police marched those chosen for the "bad side" into the Small Ghetto where the Jews spent the night in confused despair, still hoping to survive amidst the chaos, some attempting to organize themselves in their new quarters. But the uncertainty lasted only through the night.

The following day would live in infamy. Hundreds of German police and men from the TDA's First Battalion's Third Company stormed into the Small Ghetto and commenced herding the crowd of an estimated 9,200 men, women, and children towards the Ninth Fort. Sara Ginaitė remembered the sight:

> The scene which I saw after I went out will never be erased from my memory. I still feel it, I can see it. Wherever you looked, wherever your gaze went, all one could see was but a dark mass of people. The crowds stretched all along Panerių Street, seemingly without beginning and end, and then near the ghetto gates on Varnių Street, it descended downhill. Surrounded by armed policemen, the people slowly moved towards the Ninth Fort. I stood there staring and could not believe my eyes. It seemed like a dream, not real, as if the police were convoying some black, unearthly massive black wave.[123]

The Great Action became the largest single massacre of civilians in Lithuania's history. Soldiers from the other TDA companies were already at the fort, prepared for action. As the massive column of the condemned approached the site, the killers began systematically escorting the people in groups of 150–200 to the trenches, each estimated at about two hundred meters in length. After each shooting, the layers of bodies were covered by the Soviet POWs brought to the site. Available evidence indicates that TDA officers who had

---

123 See Sara Ginaitė-Rubinsonienė, *Atminimo knyga: Kauno žydų bendruomenė 1941–1944 metų tais* (Vilnius: margi raštai, 1999), 78–81.

IMAGE 4.6. Posing for a group photo. Members of the Special Platoon (Ypatingasis Būrys) which carried out executions at Paneriai, 1941-1944. (Courtesy of Lithuanian Special Archive.)

gained extensive experience in mass killings actively supervised the operation. About twenty Germans also participated in the murders. The shootings continued until darkness fell. One of only two known survivors, fourteen-year-old Yudel Beiles (Judelis Beilesas) provided the sole eyewitness account of what happened when he and his parents arrived at the pits and observed an unexpected exchange between a doomed victim and her killer just before the shooting began:

> Surrounded by armed Lithuanian "partisans" [TDA men] and their dogs, we were told to undress. I felt a hand on my shoulder, and turned to see my father, holding his [Lithuanian Army] Volunteer Medal. He still thought I would survive, and asked me to protect this precious relic. I put it in the pocket of my undershirt, and said that perhaps we would all survive, that he'd have the pleasure of enjoying it for many years to come.
>
> A young woman with long brown hair stood close by. I had never seen a woman naked before. She recognized a university classmate—he was now a lieutenant, one of the murderers. She begged him to help her. The fellow stood with head bowed, muttering that he could do nothing,

that they were surrounded by Germans, that it was too late. She then reached out her hand and gave him her valuables, saying that she no longer needed them.

I stood with my mother and my father, at the side of a huge pit with water in the bottom. A German, armed to the teeth, raised his cap, and the "partisans" ran up and began jabbing at us with their bayonets, shoving us into the pit. People fell, cursing the killers. Then there were rifle shots, and the moaning of the wounded. The entire symphony was conducted by the one Nazi—raising and lowering his cap.

Among the cries and laments I thought I could hear my mother's quiet voice asking if I were still alive. I heard all the noise for some time, and then I fell into the pit; more and more people fell on top of me, blocking out the blue sky. . . . And then I passed out. I lay in the pit, unconscious, but alive. I don't know how much time passed before I finally came to, waking as if in a dream. At first I couldn't understand what had happened: I felt like my skin was on fire; I was pinned down by bodies and couldn't move. On top of me lay a five- or six-year-old girl, who had just recently been playing with her braids; now one of them was stuck in my mouth. Semi-alive people were moaning: "Oh Jesus, Mary!"— Lithuanians married to Jews were among the victims, and they called out to their own God. I began pushing away corpses, and nearly went mad with the burning sensation of the lime covering my body. I knew that I had somehow survived, and that I had to get out of there as quickly as possible. My head was spinning as I clambered over bodies.[124]

Beiles successfully returned to the ghetto, eventually found safety among rescuers, and survived the war.

Jäger recorded the death toll as "2,007 men, 2,920 women, and 4,273 children," noting that in this way, he had achieved the "cleansing of the Ghetto's superfluous Jews."[125] Following the action, a force of ghetto police was sent into the Small Ghetto to check if anyone had remained behind. On October 31, the Jewish police chief reported to the council that they had found nine bodies, which were then buried in the Jewish cemetery.[126] The policemen did, however, accomplish one surreptitious rescue: they found twenty survivors in the

---

124 Yudel Beiles, *Yudke*, trans. from the Lithuanian by Vida Orbonavičius-Watkins (Vilnius: baltos lankos, 2001), 39–40. On Beiles's survival, see below, Chapter 6.
125 Jäger Report, December 1, 1941, 5.
126 Bubnys, *Kauno getas*, 35–37.

abandoned buildings and smuggled them into the Large Ghetto dressed up in Jewish police uniforms.[127]

There were no further mass killings of Lithuanian Jews in Kaunas until March of 1944. But the men of the Ninth Fort had not yet finished their work. They found new victims beyond Lithuania's borders. On November 21, 1941, a train of German Jews from Berlin arrived in Kaunas. On November 25, Jäger reported the deaths of 2,934 Jews, including 175 children, described as "evacuees from Berlin, Munich, and Frankfurt am Main." On November 29, two thousand more such evacuees, this time from Vienna and Breslau (Wrocław), were killed at the Fort.[128] Just before he completed his December 1941 report, Jäger found time to record the Fort's final killing action for the year: "seventeen Jewish men and one Jewish woman who had violated the Ghetto laws; one Reich German who had converted to the Jewish faith and had attended a rabbinical school, then fifteen terrorists of the Kalinin group."[129]

When the Germans entered Vilnius in force on the morning of June 24, 1941, an estimated sixty thousand Jews were still in the city. Some three thousand had managed to flee eastward, but many people had crowded into town from the west, unable to proceed further, so it is difficult to arrive at an accurate count of Vilnius Jews during the first days of the war. Although the ghettoization of Lithuania's Jerusalem did not begin in earnest until September, plans to isolate the Jews were afoot by the first week of the occupation. On June 29, the Vilnius Citizens' Committee called for the establishment of a Jewish quarter and, on the next day, formed a working group to determine a site for the proposed ghetto. The city's German military conmmandant announced the first anti-Jewish restriction in Vilnius on July 3, 1941. On the next day, the Germans ordered the establishment of a ten-member Jewish council, which eventually grew to a body of twenty-four men headed by Shaul Trotzki. On July 11, the newly appointed commandant Max Zehnpfenning determined that at least twenty thousand Jews should be placed in the proposed ghetto. Despite these early plans for the concentration of the Vilnius Jews, implementation was delayed for two months.[130]

---

127 Dieckmann, *Besatzungspolitik*, 2:957.

128 Jäger Report, December 1, 1941, 5; A detailed analysis of the killing of the foreign Jews is in Dieckmann, *Besatzungspolitik*, 2:959–967.

129 Jäger Report, December 1, 1941, 5.

130 Dean, *Encyclopedia of Camps and Ghettos, 1933–1945*, 1148–1149; for details on German-Lithuanian preparations for the ghetto, see Dieckmann, *Besatzungspolitik*, 2:967–968.

In the meantime, vicious persecution of the Jews intensified. In July Alfred Filbert's EK 9 and the YB murdered an estimated five thousand of the city's Jews, almost all at Paneriai. After the takeover of the city by the ZV, Hans Christian Hingst (1895–1955), the head of the Vilnius city district (Wilna-Stadt Gebietskommissariat), imposed a five million ruble fine on the community. On August 9, a detachment of EK 3 took over responsibility for anti-Jewish actions from Filbert's men who had moved on to Belarus. Over the next three weeks the Germans and the YB men recorded their tally of victims as "425 Jewish men, nineteen Jewish women, eight Communist men, and nine Communist women."[131] According to Sakowicz, who observed the killings from his vantage point near the killing site, there were ten mass shootings at Paneriai during the month of August which resulted in some two thousand deaths, about a thousand of whom, by his count, perished before the arrival of EK 3.[132] Jäger's report and Sakowicz's observations seem to generally agree on the scale of the carnage for August 1941. At the end of August, von Renteln directed Hingst to hasten the establishment of a Jewish ghetto, the task eventually entrusted to the latter's deputy, the Austrian SS sergeant Franz Murer (1912–1994), who was to become the face of Nazi authority to the Jews of Vilnius. The ghetto was to include the old Jewish quarter in the city center.[133]

The establishment of the Vilna Ghetto came on the heels of a staged provocation. As if on cue, on the afternoon of Sunday, August 31, shots were fired in the heart of the city from a Jewish apartment, at the busy intersection of Didžioji and Stiklių Streets. German police and two Lithuanians rushed to the site of the incident and killed the two alleged attackers. On September 1, Hingst issued a proclamation prohibiting the Jews in the area adjacent to the incident to leave their homes in order "to protect the security of the population." The purpose of the edict was the expulsion and concentration of the people of the old Jewish quarter to facilitate murders at Paneriai which in scale were to eclipse the shootings of the previous weeks. Over the next two days, the Jews were quickly removed to Lukiškės prison, where they were robbed of their belongings and then transported to their deaths. EK 3 counted the Jewish victims shot by September 2: 864 Jewish men, 2,019 Jewish women, 817 children. In the colonel's

---

131 Jäger Report, December 1, 1941, 5.
132 See Sakowicz, *Ponary Diary*, 15–22.
133 Arad, *Ghetto in Flames*, 101–102.

words, this was "a special action [*Sonderaktion*] in retaliation, because Jews had fired on German soldiers."¹³⁴

Sakowicz recorded the horrific scene, adding information he had gathered from a second-hand source which he duly noted in his account:

> [T]here was a long procession of people—literally from the [railroad] crossing until the little church. . . . It took them fifteen minutes to pass through the crossing. There were, as it turns out, 4,000—so says Jankowski; others claim that it was 4,875. . . . When they entered the road (from the Grodno highway) to the forest, they understood what awaited them and shouted, "Save us!" Infants in diapers, in arms, etc.
>
> Eighty Shaulists did the shootings, while the fence around [the pit] was guarded by 100 Shaulists. They shot while they were drunk. Before the shooting they tortured men and women horribly (Jankowski). The men were shot separately. The way they shot, the group [of shooters] stood on the corpses. They walked on the bodies!
>
> On September 3 and 4 there was a brisk business in women's clothes! Next day a small child was found in the forest near the pit, playing in the sand. He was thrown into the pit and shot (Jankowski).¹³⁵

Incredibly, four women and two young girls managed to crawl out of the Paneriai pits after the shooting ended and found their way to a Lithuanian home where they found refuge and were then assisted in returning to the Jewish hospital in Vilnius. Word of this first mass killing of women and children in the city's history spread quickly. A further demoralizing calamity was the liquidation of the recently appointed Jewish council: clearly, they were no longer needed for what was to come.

At dawn on September 6, 1941, the Lithuanian municipal police, assisted by personnel from the TDA battalions stationed in the city, began the roundup of the Jews of Vilnius. The operation had been carefully planned and was

---

134 Jäger Report, December 1, 1941, 5.

135 Excerpt from Sakowicz, *Ponary Diary*, 28–29. Other sources also give a higher estimate of victims than that provided by Jäger. For example, the number of five thousand people expelled from their homes on September 1 is provided in Herman Kruk, *The Last Days of the Jerusalem of Lithuania: Chronicles from the Vilna Ghetto and the Camps, 1939–1944*, ed. Benjamin Harshav, trans. Barbara Harshav (New Haven: Yale University Press, 2002), 83. But Kruk also notes that it was hard to ascertain how many were shot. The men in Sakowicz's account were more likely the YB men or members of the TDA battalions than the so-called "Shaulists".

essentially complete by the next morning. The police convoyed the Jews into two quarters, the larger one, Ghetto 1 and the smaller one, Ghetto 2, which were separated by Vokiečių Street.[136] Between twenty-five thousand and twenty-nine thousand people were crowded into the first enclosure, while the latter ghetto housed nearly nine thousand people, but these numbers are, at best, rough estimates (the correspondence of German and Lithuanian officials on the numbers are inconsistent).[137] In a policy that recalled the process in Kaunas, the authorities began sorting the people, in effect, winnowing out those considered unemployable. In mid-September, the Nazis carried out two more mass murder operations. Sakowicz recorded the death of two thousand Jews on September 12, but without details; this was probably a reference to the 3,434 victims recorded by Jäger (993 men, 1,670 women, and 771 children). EK 3 listed an additional 1,271 victims killed on September 17, all Jews (337 men, 687 women, and 247 children), except for "four Lithuanian Communists."[138] While the number of victims and dates of the killings vary slightly in the sources, all confirm that the Nazis engaged in a sleight of hand. People without work permits were told of a transfer to Ghetto 2, but, in reality, they wound up in Lukiškės prison before being taken to Paneriai.[139]

In Vilnius, the Nazis initiated the process of consolidating the ghetto during the same week as the similar action in Kaunas. On Yom Kippur (Day of Atonement), October 1, 1941, SS NCO Horst Schweinberger came to the new Jewish council to demand the immediate gathering of one thousand Jews without work papers from Ghetto 1. In the meantime, German and Lithuanian police swept through Ghetto 2 rounding up nearly 1,700 people. The selection campaign descended into chaos: knowing what would happen, people lacking the requisite passes remained in hiding so that in the end many were seized for "evacuation" regardless of their status. In the confusion, dozens of people managed their release through connections or bribes.[140] It is estimated that this roundup of Jews

---

136 Kruk estimates that twenty-nine thousand Jews were driven into Ghetto 1 and eleven thousand incarcerated in Ghetto 2, equaling roughly two-thirds of the interwar Jewish population of Vilnius.
137 As discussed in detail in Dieckmann, *Besatzungspolitik*, 2:985–986.
138 Sakowicz, *Ponary Diary*, 29; Jäger Report, December 1, 1941, 6.
139 Arad, *Ghetto in Flames*, 133–135; cf. Kruk, *Last Days*, 112.
140 Noted poet Abraham Sutzkever's wife describes an instance of such bribery involving Schweinberger in Abraomas Suckeveris, *Iš Vilniaus geto* (Vilnius: Versus aureus, 2011), 40–42.

IMAGE 4.7. One of the burning pits at Paneriai where in 1943 and 1944 inmates working under Sonderkommando 1005A burned tens of thousands of the corpses of the victims. Photo depicts a research group of the Soviet Extraordinary Commission charged with investigating Nazi crimes working at the site in August 1944. (Courtesy of Vilna Gaon Museum of Jewish History.)

IMAGE 4.8. A restored burning pit of Sonderkommando 1005A as seen at the Paneriai Memorial Museum today. (Courtesy of Paneriai Memorial Museum.)

on the holiest day of the religious calendar led to the killings of between 3,700 and four thousand people on October 2 and 3, 1941.[141]

In a series of mass murders between October 4 and 21, the Nazis completed the destruction of Ghetto 2. On the heels of the Yom Kippur murders, during the night of October 3–4, Kruk's diary records two thousand Jews as "the number taken from Ghetto 2."[142] This corresponds closely to what Jäger reported as the death toll of victims killed on October 4: 432 men, 1,115 women, and 436 children. On October 15–16 German and Lithuanian police carried out another murderous selection in Ghetto 2 which, according to EK 3, resulting in the killing of 382 men, 507 women, and 257 children.[143] Fewer than four thousand people remained there. Many Jews attempted to escape the fate of their fellow inmates by crossing into Ghetto 1 or seeking refuge on the Aryan side.

On the evening of October 20, Petras Buragas, the Lithuanian liaison official for Jewish affairs under Franz Murer, visited the Jewish council to discuss the issue of a new series of identity papers which became known as the "yellow passes" (the notorious *gelbe Scheine*), a process ostensibly intended to simplify the system of work permits for employable Jews. The immediate effect of the new system was the liquidation of Ghetto 2. On the next day, hundreds of German and Lithuanian police swept through the area in an intensive manhunt and, by evening, had transported about 2,500 Jews to Paneriai, the number again correlating with the EK 3 murder count of 718 men, 1,036 women, and 586 children.[144] Sakowicz observed part of the massacre: "About 1,000 are transported, women and children among them. Because it was unusually cold, especially for the children, they permitted them to take off only their coats, letting them wait for death in clothes and shoes."[145]

The yellow passes became the means not only to select victims for the further elimination of "useless eaters" but also as a method to exert a particularly cruel means of control over those granted temporary reprieve: the realization that there would not be enough such passes for everyone provoked vicious competition to obtain the life-giving work permits, understandably arousing the worst instincts among desperate ghetto inmates. The fears of those who failed

---

141 See Dieckmann, *Besatzungspolitik*, 2:990–995; cf. Kruk, *Last Days*, 123.
142 Ibid., May 7, 1942 entry, 285.
143 As in Jäger Report, December 1, 1941, 6.
144 Ibid., 6.
145 Sakowicz, *Ponary Diary*, 34.

IMAGE 4.9. A reconstruction of the hiding places (malines) in the Vilna Ghetto where inmates sought to save themselves from the pits at Paneriai during police searches and selections. Displayed at the Jewish Information and Cultural Center, Vilnius. (Courtesy of Darius Sužiedėlis.)

to obtain the new passes were confirmed a few days later. On October 24, hundreds of police entered the ghetto in an operation that the people would experience time and again. During the hunt for those without the requisite papers, the security forces stormed through the houses searching for people, most of whom cowered in their basement and attic hideouts (*malines*), destroying and looting much of the Jews' property in the process. Some survived in hiding, but the arrested inmates were driven to Paneriai. In the final week of October, the YB men and German police murdered more than five thousand people. Jäger reported the tally as: 1,328 men, 2,739 women, and 1,247 children.[146] The murders of more than 2,500 women and children on October 25, were particularly wrenching, which Sakowicz described in his diary as the "terrible Saturday":

> At about 8:20 in the morning a long procession of the condemned appeared on the road near the little chapel. When they neared the crossing, I observed that it was made up exclusively of women—old and young, children in carriages, suckling babies. Some of them slept peacefully.... They walked quite slowly, their awful fatigue was reflected on their faces... [a] young Jewish woman, nineteen to twenty years old, in a gray overcoat and black fur collar, with a boy about three or four, in a blue

---

[146] Figures for October 25–30, 1941, according to the Jäger Report, December 1, 1941, 6.

coat, falls to the ground (full of mud), kisses the feet of the noncommissioned officer, and begs for her life, grasps his muddied shoes, and pleads. To free his leg he kicks her in the jaw with the tip of his shoe, freeing himself with the same leg from her grasp. On her torn cheek, blood rushes out, mixing with the mud.

The shooting carried on continuously until 5:00 p.m. Many wounded. At night they tried to escape. Shooting the whole night.[147]

Unlike in Kaunas, the mass murders of Vilnius Jews did not cease after the liquidation of the smaller ghetto. The Germans had kept up the fiction of Ghetto 2, now simply used as a staging area for further "cleansings" of Vilnius Jewry which continued on a lesser scale between early November and the end of the year. On November 3–5, 1941, YB men and police battalion units combed the ghetto searching for Jews without the proper work permits. EK 3 recorded the killing of 340 men, 749 women, and 252 children on November 6, 1941.[148] A number of smaller scale executions were carried out afterwards, culminating in a mass killing on December 22, 1941, of nearly four hundred Jews during what has been labelled the "Pink Pass" operation.[149] After the New Year, a period of relative calm within the now consolidated Vilna Ghetto ensued.

The last of the major city ghettos which survived into the latter period of the German occupation was established in Šiauliai. It is estimated that nearly 6,500 Jews, about a fifth of the city's population, lived in the city on the eve of the German invasion. Many Jews fled the advancing Wehrmacht but had been unable to reach safety in Soviet territory and were forced to turn back. By late July 1941, nearly one thousand Jews had already been massacred, most of them in Kužiai forest about twelve kilometers northwest of the city. As elsewhere, a number of onerous restrictions were levied against the Jewish populace within the first weeks of the occupation. In mid-July, the authorities ordered Jews to turn in their radios. On July 18, 1941, the mayor of Šiauliai Petras Linkevičius issued a comprehensive list of statutes "in consultation with the Military Commandant," which outlined a program of anti-Jewish discrimination and expropriation. Jews who had left the town during the fighting were prohibited from returning to their homes and were to wear a yellow badge. The people were

---

147 Sakowicz, *Ponary Diary*, 34–36.
148 Jäger Report, December 1, 1941, 6.
149 Named after the permits issued to family members of artisans and some others who had failed to obtain the previous yellow passes, see Arad, *Ghetto in Flames*, 162–163.

permitted to "walk the streets and appear in public" only from six in the morning until eight in the evening. Most ominously, Jews were required to move to "areas designated by the Šiauliai Municipality" between July 22 and August 22. 1941. The town of Žagarė, nearly fifty kilometers to the northwest, and the suburban neighborhood known as the Kaukazas (Caucasus), were the indicated sites. In order to assure an "orderly resettlement," the city's Housing Bureau was tasked with working out the details with "representatives of the Jewish community."[150]

Between July 19 and 22, the city carried out a compulsory registration of the Jews of Šiauliai. On July 20, 1941, the municipality's delegate for Jewish affairs Antanas Stankus provided the local LAF weekly "an explanation to [the people of] Šiauliai concerning the very sensitive issue of the Jews." According to the paper, the delegate was responding to "the inquiry of the editorial staff as well as to the entire Lithuanian community as to why the Jewish question in Šiauliai has taken longer than elsewhere in Lithuania." Stankus reassured the readers:

> The Jewish question is truly of preeminent importance, but until now the responsible institutions did not hasten to solve the problem since they were preoccupied with organizational matters. On the other hand, one cannot handle things in pell-mell fashion since, as we have heard, because things were done hastily elsewhere, misunderstandings have already arisen. It was necessary to choose a place of Jewish settlement, and to prepare and then implement a plan for the transfer. So that is how it was done.
>
> All the Jews of Šiauliai will be transferred to Žagarė within a month. The Jews who will be selected to remain temporarily in Šiauliai will be settled in the "Caucasus" [Kaukazas neighborhood]. The plan for transfer is already formulated and on July 19, a registration of all the persons of Jewish nationality will be carried out. The transfer will commence on July 22. Hence, the Jewish question on the scale of Šiauliai is being carried out in a systematic and radical fashion.[151]

On August 2, the mayor's Order No. 9 banned Jews from parks and recreational areas and prohibited their use of autos and public transportation. At the time,

---

150 See the original order as published in Irina Guzenberg and Jevgenija Sedova, eds. *Siauliu getas: kaliniu sarasai:1942* (Vilnius: Valstybinis Vilniaus Gaono žydų muziejus, 2002), 75.

151 "Žydų klausimas sprendžiamas planingai ir radikaliai," *Tėvynė*, July 20, 1941, 1.

data compiled by Lithuanian municipal officials and forwarded to Gewecke showed the city's population including 30,801 Lithuanians and 5,034 Jews.

After some negotiation with the German commandant, most of the Jews in the city itself were relegated to Kaukazas and to another area around Ežero-Trakų Streets, the two ghettos separated by Vilnius Street and housing an estimated four to five thousand of the city's Jews. The authorities had promised to set aside a third area in the Kalniukas ("Little Hill") neighborhood, but this turned out to be a cruel deception. The people destined for Kalniukas were taken to the hamlet of Bubiai where five hundred of them were murdered on August 14. Most of the Jews were moved into the ghettos by August 15, although the resettlement and isolation of the Jewish quarters were not officially completed until September 8, 1941. In November 1941 there were in Šiauliai a reported thirty-five thousand "Aryans" and 4,674 Jews.

In his December 1941 report on the mass murder of Lithuanian Jewry, Jäger concluded that he had accomplished his task, except for the ghettoized population: "Today I can confirm that the goal, to solve the Jewish problem for Lithuania, has been achieved by EK 3. *In Lithuania there are no more Jews, apart from Jewish workers and their families.* That is, in Šiauliai—4,500; in Kaunas, 15,000; in Vilnius, 15,000" (emphasis in original). Lithuania's urban Jewry had not suffered the near total annihilation characteristic of the country's shtetls, but the historic communities in the larger cities had been decimated.

Jäger's account of the remaining Lithuanian ghettos was incomplete. A Jewish ghetto in Švenčionys, which housed approximately six hundred survivors of the horrific massacres in their region, was not liquidated until the spring of 1943.[152] An even smaller ghetto in Telšiai, which housed the remnants of the killing operations in Samogitia, survived until late December 1941. On August 26, 1941, about five hundred women and girls from the Geruliai labor camp were incarcerated there in a few small houses. In mid-December Gewecke ordered the Telšiai police chief Bronius Juodikis to liquidate the ghetto by the New Year. On December 23–24, Lithuanian police massacred some four hundred women from the Telšiai ghetto. By some accounts, the killers were less than diligent in their task, and with the help of villagers in the area, nearly eighty-two people,

---

152 For more on the Švenčionys Ghetto see Chapter 5. Jäger's estimate of 34,500 Jewish survivors in the ghettos at the end of 1941 must be considered an undercount.

sixty women among them, survived the shootings; another source claims only thirty survivors.[153]

The Killing Fields of 1941: The Mortal Blow

In his December 1941 report Jäger had emphasized that the successful campaign to eradicate Lithuanian Jewry was primarily a "question of organization," which he summarized succinctly to his superiors in Berlin:

> The goal of making Lithuania free of Jews could only be attained through the deployment of a mobile commando [*Rollkommando*] with selected men under the leadership of SS First Lieutenant Hamann, who completely and entirely adopted my goals and understood the importance of ensuring the cooperation of the Lithuanian partisans and the competent civilian authorities.
>
> The implementation of such activities is primarily a question of organization. The decision to systematically make every district free of Jews necessitated an exhaustive preparation of each individual operation and reconnaissance of the prevailing circumstances in the applicable district. The Jews had to be assembled at one or several locations. Depending on the number, a place for the required pits had to be found and the pits dug. The marching route from the assembly place to the pits amounted on average to four to five kilometers. The Jews were transported to the place of execution in detachments of 500, at intervals of at least two kilometers.

The EK 3 commander noted that accomplishing such systematic slaughter was "difficult and nerve-wracking," presenting the Rokiškis massacre of August 15–16 as a particularly vexing example of what his men had to endure.[154]

The scale of the murders and the level of relative German and Lithuanian participation varied, but the overall pattern is recognizable. Forced labor, including local people, Soviet POWs, or, less often, Jews themselves, prepared the mass graves at designated sites on the outskirts of the shtetls, often near road junctions which facilitated the gathering of the victims. Lithuanian auxiliaries, drawn in part from former "white armbands" and, increasingly, from the TDA

---

153 Vitkus and Bargmanas, *Holokaustas Žemaitijoje*, 436–438.
154 Jäger Report, December 1, 1941, 7.

battalions, provided most of the manpower. With few exceptions, German police officials were present at the actions, usually as active participants but, in some cases, limiting themselves to various degrees of observation, control, and/or guidance. The perpetrators often subjected their victims to assault, rape, and robbery. Witness accounts invariably cite the liberal use of alcohol which helped dampen any feeling for the victims.

The escalation of the genocide from early August 1941 in terms of its geographic progression is clear enough. Until late August 1941, most of the killings of Jews in the Lithuanian provinces were centered in Gewecke's Šiauliai region, with some exceptions (for example, the shootings in Alytus and Jonava). Here the mass murder campaign dispatched over twenty-three thousand victims in four weeks. The murders then moved towards the southwest between August 26 and September 4, 1941: in a single week, Hamann's mobile commando and Lithuanian auxiliaries killed more than five thousand people. The killers then turned their attention to the Alytus region of the Vilnius district/commissariat, where the single-month's (September 9–October 9) recorded toll was over eighteen thousand Jews. The murders then escalated again in northern Lithuania (for example, Žagarė and Švenčionys) resulting in more than twelve thousand victims. The provinces with a substantial Polish presence in eastern Lithuania were among the last actions. Was this due to difficulties in policing a region with a history of Lithuanian-Polish tensions? The German were keen to prevent any conflict between Poles and Lithuanians in Vilnius, but there is no way to know for certain whether this was a consideration in the outlying areas.

The pace of the genocide accelerated decisively in August and continued at high intensity until the end of October. Nearly half of all victims perished during a four-week frenetic burst of murder between mid-August and mid-September. Most of the more than 200 killing sites were located in the provinces. The death toll of provincial Jews in the summer and fall of 1941 likely encompassed about one hundred thousand victims, an estimate found in a number of sources. It is unlikely to be much greater, considering that in January 1941, the number of Jews living outside the urban centers of Kaunas, Vilnius, Šiauliai, and Panevėžys was estimated at 105,000.[155]

---

155 A review of the older and newer estimates is in Dieckmann, *Besatzungspolitik*, 2:803–804.

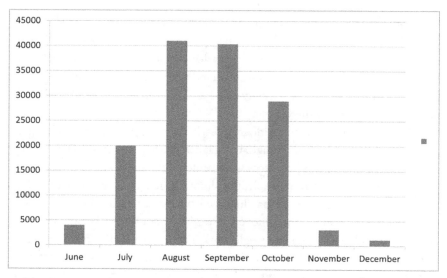

CHART 2. Timeline: Destruction of Jews in Lithuania, June–December 1941.

Most urban Jews died in sites located in Vilnius, in the pits of Paneriai, and in Kaunas, primarily at the forts (the Fourth, Seventh, and Ninth) that ringed the city. We know that nearly forty-five thousand Jews were murdered at these locales by the end of 1941. Among all the urban and rural dead, at least 110,000–120,000 were subjects of the First Republic (in police parlance, "citizens/persons of Jewish nationality"). The others were mostly Jews who until September 1939 had lived in the Vilnius region controlled by Poland, although as Litvaks they must be considered "Lithuanian Jews" by any reasonable historical definition.

"No More Jews": The Policy, Implementation, and Stages of Mass Murder

The killing operations of the summer and fall of 1941, particularly the massive campaign of destruction initiated in August 1941, were the result of policy decisions undertaken at the highest levels of the Reich's political leadership in Berlin and instructions emanating from the ZV which ruled the Baltics and Belarus. Jäger noted his subservience to Lohse in a caustic note appended to his infamous December 1, 1941, kill list in which he lamented to Stahlecker that he could not complete his work and was forced to spare the Jews now laboring in the ghettos:

> I also wanted to kill these work Jews, including their families, which however brought upon me acute challenges from the Civil Administration (the Reichskommisar) and the Wehrmacht and caused the prohibition (*Verbot*): the work Jews and their families are not to be shot![156] (Emphasis in original)

Between late June and the annihilation of the Jewish communities of Mažeikiai and Biržai in early August, German and Lithuanian police agencies carried out selective killing operations aimed primarily at Jewish men of military age and local Communists. Large-scale actions aimed at the annihilation of entire communities, including women and children, had not yet become the norm. (The massacres in Ylakiai and Plungė stand out as gruesome exceptions to the rule.) At the same time, the Germans and local civil authorities authorized the expropriation of Jewish property as well as their concentration into ghettos, temporary restricted quarters, and camps, which comprised the staging areas in preparation for the Final Solution.[157] The leading historian of German occupation policy in Lithuania has pointed out that, in hindsight, economic considerations were among the factors which strongly motivated "the economic, political and military decision makers" to take the final step towards the annihilation of provincial Jewry. Local Lithuanian authorities in the provinces had requested supplies of food for the remaining women and children in the towns. The German authorities countered that the Jews in the temporary ghettos were "useless eaters" and that they must be "liquidated." In the end, Hitler and Göring sent a clear message to Lohse's administration: "the Jews must disappear from the RKO."[158]

The German Security Police and SD, chiefly the staff of EK 3 in Kaunas, were the primary executors of the Reich's policy of genocide, their role particularly evident after the transition to wholesale murder in early August 1941. As an operational matter, considering the limited manpower of the Nazi police structures, the cooperation and assistance of other German and Lithuanian

---

156 Jäger Report, December 1, 1941, 7.
157 A review of this concentration process is in Dieckmann, *Besatzungspolitik*, 2:918–920; see also Bubnys, "Mažieji Lietuvos žydų getai": 151ff.
158 Dieckmann, 2:922–923. As an example of problems related to feeding the incarcerated Jews, see the message from the Garliava police chief to Reivytis, above.

institutions considerably eased the organizational problems encountered in the definition (marking), expropriation, concentration, and, finally, extermination of the Jews. The more important agencies which expedited the destruction process by providing logistics and personnel included:

1. The Wehrmacht, principally the Feldkommendaturen (military commandants' offices) and the security divisions, German police battalions, primarily the Eleventh and Sixty-Fifth,
2. Other police agencies, both civilian and military (for example the criminal police and Feldgendarmerie), and
3. The various sections of the German ZV (Zivilverwaltung).[159] The German policy makers and commanders also employed subordinate Lithuanian paramilitary forces, police, and administrative organizations including:
4. Elements of irregular forces which arose spontaneously or were quickly organized upon news of the Nazi invasion, such as the Klimaitis gang and other insurgents/partisans,
5. Units of the TDA, later termed the Self-Defense Battalions, often known in the literature as the Schutzmannschaften,
6. The Lithuanian Police department headquartered in Kaunas and the local constabulary reestablished after the Soviet retreat,
7. Agents and officers of the Lithuanian Security Police, and
8. Structures of the PG and LAF (until September 1941), including elements of the local Lithuanian administration, particularly the district chiefs and heads of municipalities.

In Lithuania the Germans found conditions uniquely suitable for engendering local collaboration which contrasted sharply with the situation in neighboring Poland. In the latter case, German occupiers, rather than the Polish police forces, provided most of the personnel involved in the mass murders of Jews which accelerated decisively in the summer of 1942. In Lithuania, the anti-Soviet insurrection and the quick return of pre-Soviet officials to their former stations allowed the PG to successfully recreate a rudimentary administrative structure initially modeled on the First Republic and manned by experienced officials down to the rural county level. With few defections, this system

---

159 On German forces see also, Kay, *Empire*, 90–91.

continued to function even after the dissolution of the PG on August 5, 1941, and its replacement with Kubiliūnas's more pliant advisory council. (The situation in the cities, where the German presence was stronger, was somewhat different, since in contrast to the provinces, the newly established municipal institutions had fewer analogues to those of interwar Lithuania.)

The desertion and mutiny of the Twenty-Ninth Territorial Riflemen's Corps, as well as the rapid assembly of the local police constabulary, created a pool of well-trained men, some of whom were directed to mass killing operations. The ability to exploit native police and collaborating local authorities greatly facilitated the Nazis' murderous plans. While the genocidal operations required a substantial administrative infrastructure, several of the subunits of the categories listed above played a disproportionate role in mass killings, such as the Klimaitis gang during the first days of the war, the Third Company of the First Battalion of the TDA, the infamous Special Platoon (Ypatingasis būrys) in Vilnius, and Hamann's Rollkommando. At the same time, a considerably larger number of Lithuanian auxiliaries took part in sporadic actions and served in secondary roles—guarding detainees, securing the perimeters at the pits, and hunting for Jews in hiding.

In his 1976 study on the documents of the Final Solution in Lithuania, the noted Holocaust survivor, partisan, and historian Yitzhak Arad outlines three stages of destruction, emphasizing the most intense period of mass carnage (June–November 1941). He considers the wave of anti-Jewish violence in the western borderlands of the USSR at the outset of the German invasion as a distinctive feature of the Shoah. At the time, Arad depicted the very first stage (June 23 to July 3) of the initial period of anti-Jewish actions as the time of "murders by the Lithuanians" but made no reference to the actions in Gargždai and the other border towns where Germans both led and participated directly in the killings. In his later comprehensive *Holocaust in the Soviet Union* (2009), Arad more accurately characterized the massacres of the Tilsit commando as part of the German-led "systematic and planned annihilation of the Jews" but differentiated these actions from localized pogroms, which he discusses in a separate chapter.

The summer and fall of 1941 marked a point of no return, the end of the centuries-old world of the Lithuanian shtetls. Arad's final two stages of destruction inflicted a different pattern of killing on the remaining urban Jews: first, selective actions carried out during the exploitation of Jewish labor (end of 1941–July 1943); secondly, and finally, murders committed during the dissolution of the ghettos (August 1943–July 1944).[160] Lithuania's urban ghettos comprised the last leg of the path to destruction, a somewhat slower and more deliberate genocidal process. Jews who had escaped the mobile killing units suffered in overcrowded quarters where they were subjected to compulsory labor, hunger, disease, and periodic killings aimed at reducing the number of unproductive inmates, the sick and frail, the old, and the very young. Outside the ghettos, a relative handful of at most several thousand people had escaped the dragnet, some hiding among sympathetic Gentiles, others languishing in makeshift camps in the forests. The Nazis' ultimate goal remained unchanged: extermination. But the tragedy of the ghettos should not overshadow an important development in the history of the Holocaust. Lithuania's ghettos gave birth to organized Jewish armed resistance, as well as to a remarkable campaign of preserving their cultural/spiritual world, a daunting struggle to remain human in a system designed to dehumanize Jews.

---

160 See Yitzhak Arad, "The 'Final Solution' in Lithuania in the Light of German Documentation," *Yad Vashem Studies* 11 (1976): 234–272; cf. Yitzhak Arad, *The Holocaust in the Soviet Union* (Lincoln: University of Nebraska Press, 2009), 89–95 (pogroms) and 141–162.

5.

Survival, Destruction, Struggle: Ghettos and Jewish Resistance

In creating the wartime Jewish ghetto, the Nazis introduced an institution that was radically different in function and purpose from the segregated communities of earlier centuries. After reviewing Isaiah Trunk's study of the Eastern European Jewish councils,[1] Raul Hilberg summarized the most important features of segregation under Nazi rule. As a polity, the ghetto was a "captive city-state, totally subordinate to German authority, while remaining a Jewish entity with traditions and expectations rooted in Jewish experience." Hilberg described the insoluble paradox facing Jewish leaders as "preservers of Jewish life in a framework of German destruction," who could not indefinitely serve their community and, at the same time, satisfy the occupiers' increasingly exasperating and cruel demands. As a socioeconomic entity, the ghettos inhabited a historic space "between prewar freedom and wartime annihilation." The constantly diminishing space and growing hunger created unprecedented social distress. An interim existence with no future (given the Nazis' ultimate intentions), ghetto life could be dismissed as a "mirage." Hilberg claimed that much of the educational and cultural life in particular "bordered on illusionary behavior," citing the example of the music school established in the Vilna Ghetto in the summer of 1942. Unlike a normal polity, he wrote, the internal Jewish administrative structures of the ghettos amounted to a "self-destructive machinery."[2] Hilberg's general description of the ghettos' institutional framework is a useful paradigm, although his harsh judgment on Jewish efforts to protect Jewish cultural identity is in contrast to memoirists and scholars who have argued that such activities constituted a form of "spiritual resistance." Not all Jewish leaders failed to understand the Germans' ultimate goals as implied in Hilberg's analysis.

---

1   Isaiah Trunk, *Judenrat: The Jewish Councils of Eastern Europe under Nazi Occupation* (New York: Macmillan, 1972).

2   See Raul Hilberg, "The Ghetto as a Form of Government," *Annals of the American Academy of Political and Social Science* 450 (July 1980): 98–112.

Following the onslaught of the summer and fall of 1941, the persecution of Jews entered a period during which the Germans pressed the ghetto inmates into service for the Reich's war industry. Although large-scale mass shootings abated, periodic killings continued to reduce the ghetto populations. Dissent and evasion of the rules were severely punished. Despair and isolation, vividly described by the survivors, inflicted severe strains on the mental and social lives of the prisoners. In the end, for most of the ghettoized Jews, hopes for survival proved illusory. In effect, as a temporary reprieve from annihilation, life for most of the Jewish inmates amounted to a bare subsistence in abysmally crowded quarters. And yet, the historical record left behind by the survivors reveals that many Jews trapped in the ghettos fought tenaciously to preserve meaningful communal life, to sustain a sense of dignity in the face of daily humiliation, and to organize passive and active resistance not only to fight back against their oppressors but also to provide a hopeful example to future generations.

While precise figures for the population incarcerated in Lithuania's ghettos are difficult to determine, the estimates do not vary much either in contemporary reports or in the most recent sources. On January 1, 1942, there were nearly twenty thousand Jews in Vilnius, between fifteen thousand and eighteen thousand in Kaunas, and another 4,500–5,000 in Šiauliai.[3] The smaller ghetto in Švenčionys housed about five hundred inmates. With the exception of several smaller labor camps these four ghettos were the only concentrations of Jews who survived the mass murder campaign of 1941. In April 1942, a part of western Belarus was transferred to the Lithuanian General Commissariat. Of this region's ghettos the largest, which at one time numbered some two thousand inmates, was located in Ashmyany (Oszmiana) (see Appendix 2). On June 21, 1943, Himmler decreed the reorganization of Ostland's ghettos as concentration camps under the direct control of the SS to take effect by August 1, although the implementation of this plan was delayed until October 1943.[4]

---

3   See Jager Report, December 1, 1941, 7; cf. Joachim Tauber's excellent overview of ghettoization in *Arbeit*, 67ff.

4   Tauber, *Arbeit*, 345.

The Vilna Ghetto: Lithuania's Jerusalem under German Control

The administration of the incarcerated Jews reflected a recognizable pattern regarding the role of the respective Jewish administrative bodies and the manner by which the Germans chose to control the Jewish communities trapped within. Hingst, the Vilnius city district commissioner, was responsible for implementing anti-Jewish policy, but it was his sadistic deputy Murer, renowned as the "butcher of Vilnius," who exercised minute control over Jewish life until he was replaced in July 1943. The Lithuanian Security Police (LSP) under Aleksandras Lileikis played a secondary role in assisting German tasks in the ghetto and are on record as hunters of Jews attempting to flee Vilnius.[5] The official Lithuanian liaison for Jewish affairs in Vilnius was Petras Buragas. The Nazis set the agenda and organized the economic exploitation of the labor force under their rule[6] but left much of the implementation in the hands of Buragas, the Lithuanian police, and the ghetto's Jewish administration albeit under the constant supervision and the cruel interference of Murer and his SS minions.

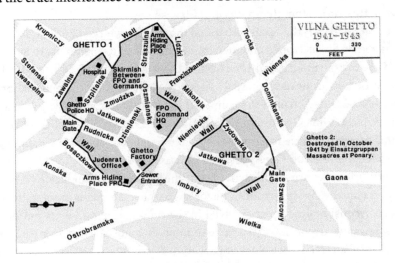

MAP 10. The Vilna Ghetto.
(Courtesy of United States Holocaust Memorial Museum.)

---

5 See, for example, the case of LSP officer Algimantas Dailidė, who in October and November 1941 participated in operations trapping Jewish escapees, as outlined in the "Report of Dr. Yitzhak Arad," attached to the filing in the U.S. District Case, Northern District of Ohio vs. Algimantas Dailidė (author's archive, obtained August 7, 1996).

6 See Tauber, *Arbeit*, 114–150.

Despite the similarities of the ghettoization process in Lithuania's three largest cities, the Vilna Ghetto differed from the ghettos established in Kaunas and Šiauliai in several important respects. Vilnius Jewry presented a different demographic profile from the other ghettos: most were Polish speakers who had been separated from the rest of Lithuanian Jewry in the First Republic, which, in the view of some Jewish historians, resulted in a lack of "a thoroughly Litvak experience." Furthermore, the Jewish councils in Kaunas and Šiauliai were remarkably stable in personnel throughout the occupation and had gained considerable trust among the people. The leaders here were long-respected figures with roots in their respective communities. In Vilnius, the Germans played a decisive role in choosing the council, finally selecting a leader from outside the community. Relying on testimonies and the works of ghetto historian-survivors, Dina Porat concludes that "as a result, the atmosphere, the inner relations, the feeling of public responsibility in Kovno and Shavli seems to have been ... different than in Vilna." Perhaps unfairly, in a play on German terminology, some Vilna Ghetto inmates nicknamed their leaders the *Judenverrat* (Jewish treason), rather than a *Judenrat* (Jewish council).[7]

In August 1941, the Nazis disbanded the first twelve-member Jewish council chaired by Shaul Trotzki and then executed most of its members. In September 1941 Anatole Fried became the head of the Jewish council in Ghetto 1, while Yitzhak Lejbowicz headed internal affairs in Ghetto 2. After the elimination of Ghetto No. 2, Fried chaired the council that administered the Jews in what remained of the Vilna Ghetto until the summer of 1942. In September 1941, the council formed a police force, which initially numbered about 150 men under the leadership of Jacob Gens (Jokūbas Gensas) (1903–1943), a captain in the former Lithuanian army. The activities of the Jewish ghetto police have given rise to a contentious spectrum of historical narratives ranging from its role as a corrupt collaborating force involved in the persecution and even murder of fellow Jews to surreptitious assistance to inmates, and even to active participation in anti-Nazi resistance. Survivor accounts from Vilnius generally record the behavior of the ghetto police in a more negative light than comparable memoirs from Kaunas. Herman Kruk, the noted chronicler of the Vilna Ghetto, observed that "The Jewish police created a full state machinery, with all the advantages

---

7   Dina Porat, "The Jewish Councils of the Main Ghettos of Lithuania: A Comparison," *Modern Judaism* 13, no. 2 (May 1993): 154, 157–158.

5. Survival, Destruction, Struggle | 327

IMAGE 5.1. Two views of the Rudnicki Street gate to the Vilna Ghetto.
Top: German, Lithuanian and Jewish police officers at the fence.
Bottom: Jewish and Lithuanian police guard the entrance to the Vilna Ghetto.
(United States Holocaust Memorial Museum Photo Archives #64118. Courtesy
of William Begell. Copyright of United States Holocaust Memorial Museum.)

and disadvantages of a normal state,"[8] but his view requires a caveat. The ghetto police found themselves in a uniquely dreadful circumstance as the only indigenous security force which the Nazis targeted for annihilation. For this reason, despite the reports of egregious conduct by some of the policemen, it would be simplistic and unfair to equate the situation of the ghetto police with that of other native collaborators.[9]

At its inception, the ghettos' Jewish bureaucracy included departments responsible for food, health, housing, and labor, to which it later added departments of finance, social welfare, education, and culture. The most vital institution of the council by far was the labor office (*Arbeitsamt*). The murderous selections carried out in the fall of 1941 in Vilnius, based on the various permits, known as *Scheins*, made clear that Jewish survival (at least for the time being) depended on the inmates' usefulness to the Reich's war economy. In April 1942, the labor office replaced the yellow work passes with new certificates which bore the stamp of the German social welfare office (*Sozialamt*).[10] Kruk assessed that at this point the area of the ghetto contained about 34,500 square meters of which only twenty-three thousand were available to live in. He estimated that in the period of September–November 1941 the twenty-nine thousand Jews crowded into the ghetto occupied a space that before ghettoization had accommodated no more than four thousand people.[11] In May 1942, the office reported 6,609 employees; in December, the number had grown to 8,874. In November 1942 Hingst provided additional guidelines on the employment of the Jewish workers: German and Lithuanian institutions presented orders to the council which, in turn, was responsible for providing the work force. By the summer of 1943 about fourteen thousand Vilnius Jews labored in the city's enterprises and in nearby labor camps.[12]

---

8   Kruk, *Last Days*, entry of May 14, 1942, 287.
9   A sympathetic and nuanced view has been articulated by the renowned artist and Vilna Ghetto survivor Samuel Bak, *Painted in Words: A Memoir* (Bloomington: Indiana University Press, 2001), 39–40.
10 Arad, *Ghetto*, 273–283.
11 Kruk, *Last Days*, entry of May 7, 1942, 282–286. The number of inmates provided here is somewhat larger than in other estimates.
12 Calculated utilizing labor office card files in Arūnas Bubnys, "Vilniaus žydų žudynės ir Vilniaus getas (1941–1944)," *Genocidas ir rezistencija*, 2, no. 14 (2003): 17.

Jacob Gens and the Deadly Price of Selective Survival

On July 11–12, 1942, Jacob Gens announced that, following Hingst's instructions, he was assuming leadership of the Jewish administration in the ghetto and appointed Fried as his second-in-command. Most of the heads of the various departments remained in place but were now reporting directly to Gens. The selection of David Salomon Dessler, aka Salk [Salek] Dessler, as Gens's deputy to oversee the police force had onerous consequences. The memoirs of ghetto inmates have described Dessler as a "scoundrel, traitor, and absolute nobody," infamous for his drunken gatherings paid for by goods stolen from the people. As historian Dina Porat explains:

> Salk Dessler, Gens's deputy, was in no uncertain terms a servant of the Germans, leading a life of debauchery with his cronies and uninterested in public matters. One wonders whether Gens, having realized Dessler was vile and utterly worthless, kept him as deputy so he could be the target for the ghetto's loathing or was forced by the Germans to keep him in place. Most of the policemen in Vilna, with the exception of those who belonged to the youth movements (chiefly Beitar) and of course with the exception of underground members, were drunk with the power they thought they had, and some of them acted with great cruelty ... [they] made people's lives miserable, such as the gate guard, which was a ghetto nightmare.[13]

The gate guards shook down workers who sought to smuggle food into the ghetto. Their behavior made them "the most hated group among the Jews of the ghetto." The inmate Grigory Shur reserved particular contempt for Meir Levas, who oversaw the Jewish police at the gate and was notorious for the beatings

IMAGE 5.2. SS Sergeant Martin Weiss who, despite his low rank, was the de facto commander of the Vilna Ghetto. (Courtesy of Vilna Gaon Museum of Jewish History.)

---

13 Dina Porat, *The Fall of a Sparrow: The Life and Times of Abba Kovner*, trans. and ed. Elizabeth Yuval (Stanford: Stanford University Press, 2010), 87.

he inflicted during searches of Jews returning to the ghetto from their work assignments, often under Murer's approving gaze.[14]

Even worse, Dessler's underlings undertook an increasingly active role in rounding up people for the periodic selections of Jews destined for destruction. In the early morning hours of July 17, 1942, with a prepared list in hand, his men collected some eighty-six elderly and sickly people, doing, as Kruk bitterly noted, what earlier had been the job of the Gestapo and Lithuanian police. A few days later, more were selected. The victims were purportedly taken to a rest home in Papiškės where they were to be examined by a German doctor. Two weeks later, amidst much consternation, news reached the ghetto that the unfortunates had been sent to Paneriai. Shur reported that afterwards Gens spoke to the heads of the work brigades claiming that he had resolutely rejected German demands to turn over the children, but would continue selections of the aged, infirm, and those who could not support themselves.[15] The stronger, healthier core of the Jewish nation would be preserved as long as possible.

IMAGE 5.3. Jewish officials of the Vilna Ghetto are seated in the audience at a sporting event. Jacob Gens seated sixth from left. (United States Holocaust Memorial Museum Photo Archives #64117. Courtesy of William Begell. Copyright of United States Holocaust Memorial Museum.)

---

14 Šuras, *Užrašai*, 82, 143; cf. Arad, *Ghetto in Flames*, 305.
15 Šuras, *Užrašai*, 72–75; cf. Kruk, *Last Days*, entries July 17–24, 1942, 330–335.

The most painful application of this principle was the participation of a detachment of Jewish police in an action against the Jews of Ashmyany in western Belarus where the inmates had been concentrated, along with Jews from the smaller ghettos of the region. In September 1942, the Jewish administration and police of these ghettos came under Gens's supervision. In mid-October 1942, about four thousand Jews were held in the already overcrowded quarters in Ashmyany. The Germans intended to alleviate this situation by liquidating at least 1,500 of the unemployable inmates and ordered the Vilnius Jewish police to participate in this heinous task. On October 23, 1942, Dessler's police handed over 406 mostly elderly Jews from Ashmyany to the death squads. On October 27, Gens chaired a meeting of Jewish leaders to explain "one of the most terrible tragedies of Jewish life—when Jews lead Jews to death," explaining that he had successfully cajoled and bribed Weiss not only to reduce the number of victims for the selection but also to avoid including women and children in the roundup. Gens made no attempt to diminish the emotional impact of his decision, but argued its necessity in view of two millennia of Jewish suffering:

> [I]t is my duty to dirty my hands, as the Jewish people are passing through their most terrible period now. At a moment when five million are no more, it is incumbent upon us to save the strong and young—not only in age but in spirit, and not to play with sentiments. I don't know if all will understand and justify this. . . . But this is the point of view of our police: to save what is possible, without regard for our good name and our personal experiences. Rosenberg recently said that it was the duty of the Germans to root out European Jewry. And so, to foil Rosenberg's statement, we shall fight today, and war sanctifies the means, even though they are sometimes very terrible. Much to our regret, we must fight with all our means, in order to grapple with the enemy. That is Jewry, a dauntless spirit, an everlasting faith in life. I accept responsibility for the *Aktion*.[16]

As noted by Arad, the actions of the Jewish police marked an "innovation" in the killing operations and identified Gens's approach as the "ideology of selective cooperation."[17] At first glance, the policy was a qualified success: for the price of 406 elderly and infirm Jews, the Ashmyany Ghetto purchased five months of relatively uneventful life. The stunningly cruel turn of events, however,

---

16 Taken from the protocol of the meeting published by Arad, *Ghetto in Flames*, 342–346.
17 See ibid., 349–351.

provoked painful soul-searching of all incarcerated Jews who faced the "choiceless choices" of existence on death row. Kruk wrote that many in the ghetto acquiesced in Gens's stand, accepting the "dictate of reality." For their part, the Jewish resistance groups had attempted to warn the Ashmyany victims.[18]

Grigory Shur bitterly condemned Gens's strategy. He observed Dessler's men after the action: "the appearance of the returning Jewish policemen with their Lithuanian uniform caps was disgusting." He went on to note that the entire expedition was a "terrible shame and disgrace."[19] The precocious fourteen-year-old Yitzhak Rudashevski observed with scorn the policemen's demeanor in his diary entry of October 18, 1942:

> In the evening—a sensation. The Jewish policemen have decorated themselves with new caps. Several walk by me: leather jackets, polished shoes and green, round caps with shiny brims and Stars of David. I hate them with all my heart, these ghetto policemen with their uniforms.... The whole ghetto feels hatred for them. They bring out feelings of revulsion, contempt, and fear, all together. The word in the ghetto is that they have received their uniforms because they are going to the Ashmyany ghetto, but no one knows for sure.

On the following day he wrote:

> Today, on orders of the Gestapo, thirty Jewish policemen are going to "work" in the small towns. Our humiliation and misfortune have reached the highest point. The Jews themselves have soiled their hands with the most dirty and bloody work: in this they will replace the Lithuanians. Our Jewish policemen are now heading to Ashmyany. They will herd the Jews of the surrounding towns to Ashmyany and there repeat the same bloody history as here in Vilnius. In all of this, our policemen will be the most active participants! I stand by the gates and people are pushing me aside, but I can see everything: thirty policemen, all in leather jackets and new caps, lined up and ordered about by that Gestapo dog, Martin Weiss. They are all climbing into the closed lorry. The entire ghetto is aflame because of this departure: how terrible is our misfortune, how great our shame and humiliation. Jews are helping the Germans to carry out organized, terrifying massacres![20]

---

18   Arad cites Kruk, Kalmanovitch, and Lazar (ibid., 347).
19   Šuras, *Užrašai*, 85–86.
20   Icchokas Rudaševskis, *Vilniaus geto dienoraštis*, trans. and introduction Mindaugas Kvietkauskas (Vilnius: Standartų spaustuvė, 2018), 117–118.

Whatever the clashing opinions about the leader's strategy of "selective cooperation" among the people, the hopes of assuring the survival of at least a healthy kernel of a future Jewish nation proved illusory in the face of the changing fortunes of war and the German determination to achieve the Final Solution, a reality that became ever more apparent as the mass killings, which had abated after the Ashmyany debacle, resumed in the spring of 1943. There is an eyewitness account of the first steps of this new wave of violence. At the end of 1942, the Jews of the Švenčionys Ghetto had enjoyed, in the words of Yitzhak Arad, a "sense of respite": a typhus epidemic had abated, while contacts with the anti-Nazi resistance and encouraging news from the front had lifted spirits. The tenuous sense of stability came to an end in early March 1943 when Gens, accompanied by Jewish policemen, visited the ghetto amidst rumors that the inmates would be transferred to Kaunas and Vilnius. The fifteen-year-old Arad joined the people who crowded into the town's remaining synagogue to hear the news:

IMAGE 5.4. Group portrait of members of the extended Rudashevsky [Rudashevskii] family in Vilnius, ca. 1936. The future diarist of the Vilna Ghetto Yitzhak Rudashevskii is seated in front. (United States Holocaust Memorial Museum Photo Archives #14728. Courtesy of Cilia Jurer Rudashevsky. Copyright of United States Holocaust Memorial Museum.)

There was absolute silence in the synagogue as the crowd waited tensely to hear the message Gens had brought. He opened with the words: "My Jewish brothers!" and went on to say that in view of the increased Soviet partisan activity in western Byelorussia [Belarus] and eastern Lithuania, the German government had decided to liquidate the remaining ghettos in the area . . . and transfer their 6,000 Jews to the ghettos in the large cities of Vilna and Kovno and to a number of labor camps in the vicinity of those cities. To reassure the Jews moving out of the small ghettos, the Germans had decided to make the Jewish police of the Vilna [G]hetto responsible for their transfer. Gens stated that he himself would accompany the Jews . . . , so they had nothing to fear. He called upon the people to facilitate the transfer and help him carry out his task. There were many places of work, he stated, in the Vilna [G]hetto, and manpower was needed. He described the intensive cultural life there—the theaters, choirs, orchestra, schools, and recreational facilities. Gens called on the people not to succumb to despair, but to bear the persecutions with dignity and patience and hope for a better future. We must go on clinging to life in the faith that this period will pass, and we will see better times.

Everyone listened intently to his words of encouragement, and all were influenced by his self-confidence. I must admit that what he had to say impressed me too, particularly his call to suffer with dignity, not give in, and hope for better days. The crowd dispersed very slowly as Gens and his men returned to the *Judenrat* offices. He had not said a word about the date of the transfer. The assumption in the ghetto was that it would take place in the course of a few weeks.[21]

Gens made similar assurances to the Jews of Ashmyany. Arad and a few of his comrades who had organized a resistance cell in Švenčionys decided not to wait for the transfer. On March 5, 1943, he left with a group of young fighters to join the resistance and save his life.

To promote the deception of an orderly evacuation both the Jewish administrations of the ghettos and German officials publicly assured the people of their supposed resettlement. By April 2, 1943, nearly three thousand ghetto inmates from Ashmyany, Mikhalishki, and Švenčionys had been transferred to Vilnius and the temporary labor camps in the area. The Vilna Jewish police assisted in boarding another contingent of ghetto inmates on a train at Soly that

---

21 Yitzhak Arad, *The Partisan: From the Valley of Death to Mount Zion* (New York: Holocaust Library, 1979), 93–94.

was ostensibly bound westward for Kaunas. On April 4, this transport stopped in Vilnius and took on another estimated three hundred Jews from Soly and Smorgony who had been staying in the Vilna Ghetto. Yitzhak Rudashevski observed the doomed people: "Standing at the gates I saw them packing their luggage. Cheerful and sprightly, they marched down to the train."[22] Gens boarded a car assigned to the Jewish police escort. The train left Vilnius, but then, unexpectedly, stopped at Paneriai where Gens and his police were forced to disembark and were driven back to the city. Unconfirmed reports suggest that railroad employees and Lithuanian police had warned the panicked passengers of their ultimate destination.

What followed was one of the bloodiest and chaotic murder operations of the Holocaust. At dawn on April 5, 1943, the German and Lithuanian police opened the locked railroad cars of the Soly transport and began herding the victims out into the open. In the ensuing pandemonium, hundreds attempted to flee into the woods, but only a few escaped the bullets. Many were shot on the spot, others were marched to the pits. In the meantime, the transport from Švenčionėliai had reached Vilnius. Gens was allowed to meet the train and succeeded in persuading the Germans to decouple several cars: one which carried the Švenčionys Jewish council, a few others that were destined for a local labor camp. It is reported that Gens assisted young men who had escaped from the train to reach the city's ghetto, but the remaining people were taken to Paneriai where the second action of the day proved even more chaotic than the first. Many tried again to flee the train, and at least some offered resistance.[23]

On the next day, the news of the massacres in Paneriai reached Kaunas where the Jewish council had been told to expect the arrival of at least two thousand Jews from the shtetls in eastern Lithuania and Belarus. The shock of the carnage was amplified by dramatic reports arriving from Vilnius, but it should be noted that the stories circulating in Kaunas are inconsistent with other accounts and should be viewed with some skepticism.[24] A German report to the RSHA in Berlin described about four thousand Jews receiving "special treatment" at

---

22 Rudaševskis, *Vilniaus geto dienoraštis*, 198.
23 See Arad, *Ghetto in Flames*, 355–367; Šuras, *Užrašai*, 106–111.
24 See Tory, *Surviving the Holocaust*, 269–292. Rumors that dozens of Germans and Lithuanian police had been killed in the operation at Paneriai by resisting Jews, or that some Lithuanians at the site had refused to take part in the massacre, and been executed in turn, would have constituted exceptional behavior unseen in other such mass murders carried out during the Nazi occupation.

Paneriai on April 5, 1943; other sources cite five thousand victims. Grigory Shur noted that what had transpired constituted "the worst day for the ghetto," not because the "murder of innocent people as such was news in itself, but the manner in which this *operation* was carried out really distressed the living" (emphasis in original).²⁵ On the next day, Weiss ordered a squad of Jewish policemen to accompany him to Paneriai to help bury the dead. Eyewitnesses reported local peasants robbing the bodies scattered about in the forest. The head of the German Security Police in Vilnius, SS Captain Rudolf Neugebauer, assured the leadership that their Jews were safe.²⁶

After these actions in Paneriai, the Germans began the liquidation of the rural Jewish labor camps in eastern Lithuania, relocating some of the inmates of the camps in Baltoji Vokė and Riešė to the Vilna Ghetto and sending most of the one thousand Jewish workers in Žiežmariai to Kaunas. In June and July 1943, the closing of the camps turned into more selective killings after SS NCO Bruno Kittel replaced Murer. Kittel fit the image of the cultured sociopathic Nazi, an accomplished actor, singer, and saxophone player in his twenties who performed on Vilnius radio. By this time, the German authorities considered the camps in the countryside insecure, too close to the surrounding forests where anti-Nazi partisans had grown in strength. In late June Kittel and his men came to Baltoji Vokė and executed sixty-seven inmates in reprisal for six escapees. A few workers fled after the killings, while the rest were transported to Vilnius. On July 8, 1943, Kittel arrived at the Kena camp where he warned the inmates to work hard and not to engage with the partisans; but even as he spoke, German and Lithuanian police surrounded the building and, after the commander had left the hall, massacred the assembled Jews. Kittel's group repeated the operation at the nearby Bezdonys camp, killing some 350 inmates. In late July, the German and Lithuanian police transported the Jewish workers of Naujoji Vilnia to Paneriai, in effect completing the closure of the rural Jewish labor camps in the region.²⁷

At this point, an estimated forty thousand to forty-four thousand Jews were still living as ghetto and camp inmates in Lithuania, of whom some thirty thousand were considered employable. The 1943 killings in Paneriai and in the camps greatly increased the anxiety among the people, and contemporaries spoke of a "dark cloud" looming over the sky. In contrast to the genocide of the

---

25 Šuras, *Užrašai*, 106.
26 Arad, *Ghetto in Flames*, 362–364.
27 Ibid., 367–372.

summer and fall of 1941, the Germans carried out the killing actions in the open and made few attempts to calm fears by hiding the truth from the victims, as they had done in the case of the ghettoized Jews in the summer and fall of 1941.[28]

The End of Jewish Vilna

The Vilna Ghetto did not long survive the fate of the region's labor camps. In early August 1943 the Germans, assisted by Lithuanian and Estonian police, violently herded several thousand Jews to the city's rail station for transport to Riga and points north. Since suspicion was rife that the transports were another ruse to send people to Paneriai, the Germans brought back letters from some of the deportees describing their new quarters in Vaivara, the transit camp in northeastern Estonia which processed incoming Jewish prisoners. A second transport of nearly 1,500 people was sent to Estonia on August 24, 1943. In the early hours of September 1, 1943, German and Estonian police surrounded the ghetto and initiated another roundup of Jewish labor which met with brief resistance from the United Partisan Organization (Fareynikte Partizaner Organizatsye, FPO), the Jewish underground. By the first week of September, the Germans had transported over seven thousand persons from Vilnius to camps in Estonia. About eleven thousand to twelve thousand Jews remained in the ghetto, and more than a thousand workers and their families were still housed in workstations around the city. On September 14, the German Security Police summoned Jacob Gens and Salk Dessler to their headquarters. Neugebauer and Weiss executed Gens, ostensibly for permitting the organization of Jewish resistance, an event which, according to Shur, stunned the people. Gens's Lithuanian wife and daughter escaped the city and survived the war. Dessler was allowed to return home and replaced Gens as the Jewish leader. On September 18, German and Latvian police invaded the ghetto again in search of workers; Dessler and his family fled to a hideout in the city, but they were soon captured and reportedly executed in Paneriai.[29] Kittel then appointed Boria Biniakonski as the nominal head of the ghetto, although at this point there was no longer any administrative order to the life of the community.

---

28 Tauber, *Arbeit*, 357.
29 Dieckmann, *Besatzungspolitik*, 2:1277.

On the morning of September 23, 1943, Kittel informed Biniakonski of the liquidation of the ghetto and then announced to the people that they were to be evacuated to Latvia and Estonia. German and Estonian police charged into the ghetto, while Ukrainian auxiliaries searched the hospitals and orphanages, separating the men from the women and children. People who tried to escape the roundup were shot on the spot. Most Jews obeyed the order to gather at the gates for transport, but many others hid in prepared hiding places (*malines*); most were eventually hunted down and either killed or escorted to the trains which left on the evening of September 24. About 8,500–9,000 Vilnius Jews were sent by rail to Estonia, while another approximately 1,400–1,700 inmates, mostly women, arrived in the Kaiserwald camp near Riga. German Security Police estimated that fourteen thousand Jews were eventually transported to Estonia. Nearly eight thousand "non-essential" people, the older women, mothers with children, and the disabled, were sent to their deaths. The number of Jews who survived the destruction of the Vilna Ghetto can be reasonably assessed at between two thousand to three thousand persons.[30]

The remnants of Vilna Jewry who had not been deported, or who had not succeeded in either escaping to the forests or sheltering in hiding, were concentrated in two remaining labor camps: the HKP (Heereskraftfahrpark) 562 motor repair facility and the Kailis clothing factory. About fifty inmates were assigned to work in the city's military hospital and another seventy were employed at the German Security Police headquarters.[31] A Wehrmacht engineering unit commanded by Major Karl Plagge administered the HKP and, according to German records, initially housed 1,243 Jews: 499 men, 554 women, and 190 children.[32] Among the latter was the ten-year-old artist prodigy Samuel Bak, whose drawings of ghetto life were to become world famous. In January 1944 Major Plagge managed to employ the women and older children in clothing repair services. The SS periodically entered the camp and carried out selective executions.

Kailis was an establishment consolidating several businesses which had been nationalized under the Soviets and, following the Nazi invasion, adapted for the

---

30   The numbers of victims are approximations. See Arad, *Ghetto in Flames*, 429–432; Dieckmann, *Besatzungspolitik*, 2:1280; Arūnas Bubnys, "The Holocaust in Lithuania: An Outline of the Major Stages and Their Results," in Nikžentaitis, Schreiner, and Staliūnas, *Vanished World*, 216–217; Anton Weiss-Wendt, *Murder without Hatred: Estonians and the Holocaust* (Syracuse: Syracuse University Press, 2009), 253–255.

31   Bubnys, "Vilniaus žydų žudynės": 28.

32   Tauber, *Arbeit*, 365.

production of winter clothing for the German army. From October 1941 until January 1942, it was under the direction of Oskar Glik, an Austrian Jew who had passed as an ethnic German with forged papers but was executed after the Gestapo discovered the deception. Nearly a thousand people, including worker's families, lived in the facility's buildings and maintained a kind of "mini ghetto," complete with a school, clinic, and its own police unit. During the liquidation of the Vilna Ghetto in August–September 1943 about six hundred people sought temporary refuge at the Kailis facility which was guarded by the Jewish police and thus easier to infiltrate. The Germans transferred a number of skilled workers to the HKP.[33] On March 27, 1944, the Germans entered the HKP and Kailis camps in force to carry out one of the infamous "children's actions" (*Kinderaktionen*) which marked the liquidation of Lithuania's ghettos and camps during the final phase of the war. The Nazis informed the mothers that the children would be taken for medical examination, and when some questioned the story, they were allowed to board the vehicles heading to Paneriai. A few children, including Bak, managed to evade the kidnappers. The perpetrators of the atrocity were Gestapo men and the SS; Lithuanian police, including the infamous Special Platoon; as well as Russian auxiliaries. Most accounts agree that Weiss and Richter led the operation which killed between two hundred and 250 children.[34] On July 1, 1944, Plagge announced to the remaining HKP workers that the Wehrmacht was retreating westward and that the inmates would be relocated by the SS within two days. Many Jewish workers grasped Plagge's revelation as a warning and escaped to their previously constructed hiding places. Two days later, the SS corralled some five hundred inmates who responded to the police roll call and took them to Paneriai, then continued to hunt down survivors in hiding, shooting those discovered on the spot. The murderous campaign was a startling example of Nazi fanaticism: the Germans and their collaborators continued to search for and kill Jews literally within earshot of approaching Soviet artillery as the Wehrmacht continued its losing battle for Vilnius.

The bodies of German soldiers still lay in the streets as the Red Army marched through the city on July 13, 1944. It was only then that hundreds of Jewish survivors emerged from the ruins or from the apartments of their rescuers. Among the latter was sixteen-year-old Irena Veisaitė, who was living with forged papers in the heart of the old town as the daughter of Stefanija Ladigienė,

---

33   Arad, *Ghetto in Flames*, 443.
34   Ibid., 441–442; cf. Tauber, *Arbeit*, 366; Bak, *Painted in Words*, 73–86.

the widow of the former commander of the Lithuanian army, General Kazys Ladiga (1893–1941). As the Soviets pushed toward Vilnius, and people were subjected to daily, frightening bombardments, the Ladiga family decided to shelter in the house of an acquaintance outside the city center. Despite Ladigienė's entreaties to accompany her, Veisaitė insisted on remaining as house sitter out of a sense of obligation to her rescuer, fearing for the property in the face of suspicious Polish neighbors (the Ladigas were the only Lithuanians in the apartment building). Left alone and trapped inside by the battles raging outside, Veisaitė saw the retreating Germans set fire to nearby houses, the heat from the flames peeling the apartment's wallpaper. As the shooting died down and Soviet soldiers appeared on the streets, she left the flat in the company of a family friend to rejoin her protector. She spoke years later about the horrors she encountered and the mixed emotions which they evoked:

> I can remember the terrible sights that we saw as we walked through the Old Town and then along the Neris River: collapsed buildings; streets scattered with the corpses of German and Russian soldiers, intestines and brain matter spilling from them; streams of blood, already dry, on the roads.... Fires were still raging in some places. The city looked so awful! But, strange as it may sound, life did not stop for a second. As we approached the Neris, at the spot where King Mindaugas bridge now stands, a boatman was already waiting to take people to the other side of the river. All you needed was a little bit of money. So, with the boatman's help, we found ourselves on the other side of the river, in Žirmūnai [to join the others—S. S.].
>
> It is difficult to convey the emotions that overwhelmed us in Mr. Stabinis's home. Everyone was exhausted from the long week of uncertainty. Mrs. Ladigienė could not forgive herself for leaving me to guard the apartment. When I saw them all alive and well, still sitting in the cellar, I began to shout quite hysterically. There are moments in life when one cannot control oneself... when one is simply carried by emotion. And Mrs. Ladigienė—as she told me later—was terribly frightened and even thought that my intense experiences had caused me to lose my emotional balance, or perhaps even my mind. In the end, we all simply embraced, crying and laughing from the joy of being reunited. For my part, I was happy that the apartment had been preserved, and a few days later we all moved back to Trakų Street.[35]

---

35 Švedas and Veisaitė, *Life Should Be Transparent*, 81–82.

The younger Samuel Bak recalled an eerily similar experience crossing a river to safety as he fled the city, holding on tightly to his mother's hand:

> I am unable to take my eyes from the intricate images of all those bombed sites. A few buildings that have lost their facades look like huge dollhouses. Single walls, sole remnants of rooms that used to stage dramas of life stand alone against the sky. My footsteps on something soft. It is the boot of a Russian soldier. Mother tries to pull me away, but the fascinating presence of the immobile man in uniform is paralyzing. I know that I must observe him attentively. He came for my rescue. He came from far, far away, and he paid with his life. Yet he never knew I existed. His open eyes look straight into the sky. Many more dead soldiers and civilians make up the macabre guard of honor....
>
> We must cross the river to get to Aunt Janina's house. The river flows steadily unhurried. Thousands of dead fish floating on the surface are sickeningly smelly. Close to where we stand the current gently caresses bodies of dead soldiers in Wehrmacht uniforms. An impulse of sweet revenge makes me stick out my tongue. An old man takes us into his dinghy and deposits us on the other shore. With a toothless mouth he thanks Mother for the few coins of Russian money that have survived in one of her jacket's pockets and have miraculously reappeared in the palm of her hand.[36]

The Life and Death of the Kovno Ghetto, 1941–1944

During the summer of 1941, Jewish leaders in Kaunas tried, without success, to intercede with both German and Lithuanian officials to ameliorate the dire conditions of the people in the congested Vilijampolė district, which had been designated for the ghetto. In the face of violence and systemic persecution, a committee headed by Grigory Wolf took charge of imposing some order on the Jewish community's transfer. At a dramatic meeting of the Kaunas Jewish community on August 5, 1941, Rabbi Shmukler of the Šančiai neighborhood told the people that "the German authorities insist that we appoint an Oberjude [head Jew]" to represent them and implored the gathering to choose the respected physician Elkhanan Elkes (1879–1944) as their leader.[37] Two weeks

---

36 Excerpts from Bak, *Painted in Words*, 43–45.
37 The meeting is described in Tory, *Surviving the Holocaust*, 26–29.

later, Hans Cramer, the city district commissioner, confirmed the makeup of the Council of Elders, the governing body of the ghetto, which Elkes led until the evacuation of Kaunas's surviving Jews in the summer of 1944. While most historical writing has examined the role of Dr. Elkes and the council, two Jewish officials with close ties to the Gestapo, Josef Caspi-Serebrowitz and Benjamin Lipzer (aka Beno Lipcer), also played an important role in the ghetto administration. According to a recent study, the latter determined much of what happened in the ghetto and controlled its police force, although some authors consider Lipzer's role as less significant.[38] In any case, Cramer held the ultimate power over the Jews. His deputy was another SA officer, the Lithuanian-born German Fritz Jordan. The Lithuanian liaison between Jordan and the council was Mikas Kaminskas.

On August 6, 1941, Jewish leaders approved the creation of a ghetto police force which began functioning on August 15 with sixty men headed by Michael (Moshe) Kopelman and his deputy, Michael Bramson (Mikas Bramsonas). Kopelman, a member of the council and a well-known Kaunas businessman, spoke fluent German; but he had no police experience, so he was forced to rely on Bramson who had served in the prewar army as one of its few Jewish officers and had been an active former member of the Lithuanian Jewish war veterans' association. On January 31, 1942, the records of the Jewish police indicated a force of 224 officers and support personnel.[39] In January 1942 a unit of the NSKK arrived from Hamburg and was assigned to guard the ghetto alongside the subordinate Lithuanian police who were rotated to their posts from the battalions stationed in Kaunas. After September 1942 guard duty was carried out by Lithuanian policemen under the command of Viennese officers. The guards were to play a critical role in choosing, as they saw fit, whether to allow food and other goods into the ghetto in return for bribes, or to punish smuggling activity.[40]

---

38 See Ilya Gerber, *Diary from the Kovno Ghetto August 1942–January 1943*, trans. Rebecca Wolpe, introduction Lea Prais (Jerusalem: Yad Vashem, 2021), 197–199, 31–36; for a different view, Dieckmann, *Besatzungspolitik*, 2:1058, 1536.

39 Samuel Schalkowsky, trans. and ed., introduction Samuel D. Kassow, *The Clandestine History of the Kovno Jewish Ghetto Police* (Bloomington: Indiana University Press in association with the United States Holocaust Memorial Museum, Washington, DC, 2014), 19, 78–79, 222; a brief biography of Bramson is in Vilius Kavaliauskas, ed., *Pažadėtoji žemė: Lietuvos žydai kuriant valstybę 1918–1940 m.* (Vilnius: Petro ofsetas, 2013), 214–215.

40 The Nazionalsozialistisches Kraftfahrkorps (NSKK) was a paramilitary organization that originally serviced the Nazi Party's motor transport but which during the war became increasingly involved in guard duty and other military tasks on the Eastern Front.

5. Survival, Destruction, Struggle | 343

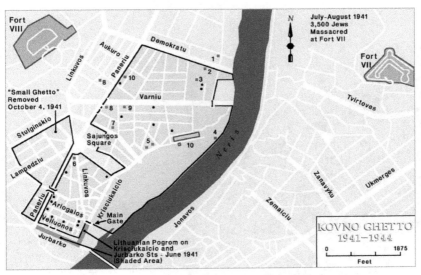

MAP 11. The Kovno Ghetto.
(Courtesy of United States Holocaust Memorial Museum.)

After the enclosure of the ghetto and the Great Action of October 28–29, 1941, the Jewish council was reorganized. By mid-1942 the ghetto administration consisted of nine departments: labor; food distribution; social welfare; registration; housing; health; economic; education; and police. The Jewish leaders recognized that as far as the Nazis were concerned, ghetto populations were useful only as contributors to the war economy and that maintaining minimal standards of health was critical in the struggle for survival. Infectious diseases were a threat to the very existence of the community. The medical staff under Dr. Moses Brauns treated cases of typhus in the patients' homes away from the prying eyes of the German and Lithuanian health inspectors. Soon the doctors faced another crisis. On May 28, 1942, Rauca summoned Elkes to announce that pregnancies would no longer be tolerated in the ghetto. Informed that termination after six months would endanger the lives of prospective mothers, Rauca relented; nonetheless, on September 7, 1942, ghetto women were strictly prohibited from giving birth. Given the overcrowding and difficult food situation, it is remarkable that the Jewish health service under the leadership of the famous surgeon Benjamin Zacharin managed to provide a wide array of services: in June 1942, the health department reportedly treated 9,187 ambulatory patients.[41]

---

41   See Bubnys, *Kauno getas*, 69–72; Tory, *Surviving the Holocaust*, 141–144.

IMAGE 5.5.
Top: View of Kriščiukaičio street in the Kovno Ghetto.
Middle: Street Scene in the Kovno Ghetto.
Bottom: Three Jewish ghetto officials stand at one of the gates to the Kovno Ghetto. (United States Holocaust Memorial Museum Photo Archives #81143, #05237 and #81158. Photos courtesy of George Kadish/ Zvi Kadushin. Copyright of United States Holocaust Memorial Museum.)

As in Vilnius, the council's labor office proved an essential cog in the daily functioning of the ghetto. During the first weeks of the occupation, a Jewish labor committee had tried to assign forced labor on a more rational basis as an antidote to the kidnappings of Jews for various demeaning jobs by so-called partisans as well as the Lithuanian and German police. Following the closing of the ghetto the Council of Elders formalized the labor office with an initial roster of thirty-one employees.[42] On September 15, 1941, Jordan provided five thousand work permits to be distributed to skilled craftsmen and physicians. A major part of the Jewish work force was assigned to the back-breaking work at the Aleksotas air base, which required an exhausting daily commute to the site and back. Ada Hirsz recalls the convoy of prisoners trekking some twelve kilometers to work which required hauling coal and heavy construction materials: "The work was very difficult and besides, the Germans repeatedly beat us for what they saw as an inadequate job, and also for the slightest offense."[43] Waldemar Ginsburg, the nineteen-year-old cousin of Irena Veisaitė, who also survived the Holocaust, was tasked with hewing wood and digging the airport's sewer lines, physically exacting work in harsh conditions in the raw weather of the fall of 1941. Nonetheless, his job allowed him to occasionally smuggle some logs into the ghetto to help stave off the cold of the approaching winter. Among Ginsburg's guards were Lithuanian police, German SS, and even teenage German Hitler Youth, whom he remembers as murderously brutal towards the starving Soviet POWs, but, at least in his experience, not particularly vicious to the Jewish laborers.[44]

A Jewish police report of April 22, 1942, listed 2,880 men and women working at the airfield.[45] At this point, Pavel Margolis headed the day-to-day mobilization of the Jewish workers and reported to Gustav Hörmann, the German chief of the ghetto's labor office (*Arbeitsamt*).[46] To offset the labor shortage created by the destruction of the shtetls, the massive death rates among Soviet POWs, and the setbacks on the Eastern Front, the Germans intensified their exploitation of the Jewish workers. On December 5, 1941, Cramer ordered the council to establish small manufacturing and service enterprises within the ghetto to

---

42 Bubnys, *Kauno getas*, 55.
43 Yad Vashem, M. 49.E ZIH (Żydowski Instytut Historyczny) Testimonies, Ada Hirsz, 15–16 February 1948 (Szczecin), 1.
44 Ginsburg, *And Kovno Wept*, 46–49.
45 Report to the Head of the Jewish Police, April 22, 1942, LCVA, f. R-973, ap. 2, b. 34, l. 448.
46 Tory, *Surviving*, 70; Tauber, *Arbeit*, 138.

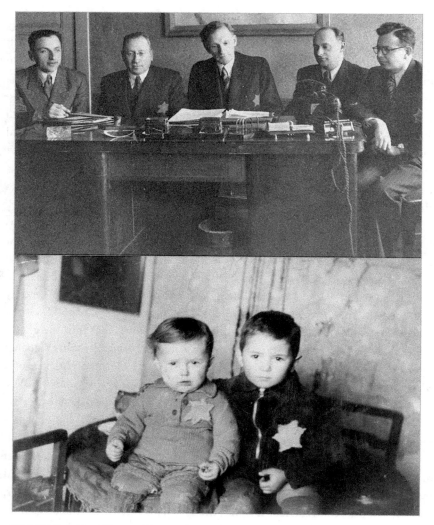

IMAGE 5.6. Top: Kovno Ghetto Council of Elders, left to right: Avraham Tory, Leib Garfunkel, Elkhanan Elkes, Yakov Goldberg and Zvi Levin.
(United States Holocaust Memorial Museum Photo Archives #77503. Courtesy of Yad Vashem Photo and Film Archives. Copyright of United States Holocaust Memorial Museum.)
Bottom: Portrait of two young boys wearing Jewish badges in the Kovno Ghetto, taken shortly before their round-up in the March 1944 "Children's Action." Pictured are Avram (5 years) and Emanuel Rosenthal (2 years). Emanuel was born in the Kovno ghetto.
(United States Holocaust Memorial Museum Photo Archives #06546. Courtesy of Shraga Weiner. Copyright of United States Holocaust Memorial Museum.)

process orders for the Reich, which within a year employed about 1,400 Jews. To reduce the long treks to more distant workstations, the Germans established labor camps outside Kaunas in Jonava, Palemonas, Kėdainiai, Kaišiadorys, and Babtai. In February 1943, the German Security Police reported that 9,600 Jews from Kaunas were employed at 140 sites, one-quarter of whom worked inside the ghetto. More than 60% of the laborers toiled in industries directly benefiting the Wehrmacht.[47]

Aside from the difficult conditions at the airfield, other jobs outside the fence provided opportunities for adding to the meager official rations. In November 1942, the young Ilya Gerber received a notice to work in "Boston," a former cloth-weaving factory transformed into an automobile repair shop. While saddened to leave his friends at the ghetto's vocational school Gerber was "pleased because this is one way that I can bring in some products and thereby help my family." The German supervisor, a "party member," turned out to be a "nice little guy" who assigned Ilya numerous jobs: a carpenter, a locksmith and mechanic. Lunchtime provided a chance for "business transactions":

> A few daring guys made a hole in the fence and from there go off in different directions. These guys bring back with them [quantities of] flour, beets, potatoes, macaroni, as well as other odds and ends. Obviously, they want to earn something for the risks they take. And truthfully, this isn't such a bad thing, for this is what one pays here for the following: fifteen rubles for potatoes; twenty rubles for beets; 700 rubles for butter; 140 rubles for macaroni; 60 rubles for rye flour, and 130 rubles for 2 kilograms of bread.[48]

The fact that prohibited commerce with the outside world was pervasive in the ghettos, as an existential practice in avoiding famine, in no way mitigated the deadly dangers inherent in the transactions. The process was never normalized. Unauthorize attempts to leave the ghetto in search of food carried deadly risks, as Gerber pointed out:

> Yesterday, they shot three Jews at the fence. They were either going there to trade or they were too close to the fence. One of them, a Jew of fifty years old, was killed on the spot. A bullet went through his forehead, the

---

47 Dieckmann, *Besatzungspolitik*, 2:1077–1082.
48 Gerber, *Diary*, 197–199, diary entries November 2 and November 5, 1942.

second hit him near his liver. The second victim was a woman. The bullet hit her hand, which had to be amputated. The third victim was a seventeen-year-old young man with the family name Kaplan. He was walking with his sister close to the fence. The bullet hit him in the leg. The woman and Kaplan are in the ghetto hospital.[49]

After the Great Action of October, the ghetto had entered an extended "quiet period," during which labor exploitation, rather than executions became the markers of "normalcy." (Mass killings at the Ninth Fort continued but were now focused on victims transported from Central and Western Europe.)[50] The Council of Elders estimated that within the ghetto itself the death rate between June 1942 and July 1943 averaged about twenty people per month.

The period of relative peace began to unravel during the spring of 1943. Escapes from the ghetto increased: some Jews found shelter with Gentiles, while others fled to the forests to join the resistance. Repression intensified as more Germans took up guarding the perimeter while the Jewish police enforced order inside the walls. The reorganization of the ghetto, as part of Himmler's decision to transform ghettos into concentration camps, was formally completed on September 15, 1943, with the appointment of SS Lieutenant Colonel Wilhelm Göcke as commandant who oversaw a Waffen-SS company to provide major security for the Kaunas concentration camp (KL Kauen). In the summer of 1944, just before the liquidation of the camp, Latvian SS legionnaires also joined the guard force.[51] During the reorganization, the Nazis dispersed more than 3,500 people to subcamps of the region where conditions of life were markedly worse. Until then the workers laboring at the Aleksotas airfield and elsewhere were generally escorted to the work site and back home or were kept there for a limited period of time. The former commuting system had made it possible to smuggle food and thus supplement the officially permitted near-starvation rations. By the spring of 1944, additional subcamps were operating in Pravieniškės, Šančiai, and Kazlų Rūda.[52] This dispersal of the inmates into subcamps led to the breakup

---

49 Ibid., 136, entry of October 2, 1942. Cf. Tory, *Surviving the Holocaust*, 138.
50 See above, Chapter 4.
51 Geoffrey P. Megargee, ed., *Encyclopedia of Camps and Ghettos, 1933–1945*, 4 vols. (Bloomington: Indiana University Press in association with USHMM, 2009), 1a:849.
52 The numbers are provided in Tauber, *Arbeit*, 348–349.

of families, exposing to mortal threat those unable to work and ending the once precarious but real stability of Jewish life in Vilijampolė.

On July 11, 1943, the commander of the German Security Police in Estonia, Dr. Martin Sandberger, toured Kaunas and reviewed the ghetto work force. The results of his ominous visit were to become evident only after the reorganization. The inmates of the Kaunas region were well aware of the brutal liquidation of the Vilna Ghetto. Their anxieties were realized when on October 24, 1943, Göcke forced the Council of Elders to provide the names of three thousand Kaunas inmates for transfer to a new camp. Suspecting that the council was not diligent in supplying the names, the Germans sent in a force of so-called "Vlasovites,"[53] who stormed the Kaunas camp on the morning of October 26 and dragged reluctant people from their quarters. As a result of this selection about two thousand able-bodied Jews were sent to work sites in Estonia. It is estimated that another estimated seven hundred people unfit for labor were sent to their deaths, probably in Auschwitz. After the reorganizations and deportations, nearly eight thousand inmates remained in the camps.[54]

The spring of 1944 brought a wave of violence to the Jews of Kaunas which in horror, if not scale, evoked the Great Action of October 1941. The terror began inauspiciously on the morning of March 27 when Göcke ordered the 140 Jewish policemen to assemble for inspection, ostensibly to participate in an air raid drill. The SS then surrounded the unit and transported the men to the Ninth Fort for interrogation by Bruno Kittel, who attempted to extract information about partisan activities and hideouts in the ghetto. Thirty-three Jewish policemen, including the entire leadership, were shot after a night of torture. At the same time, the Nazis carried out one of the most egregious acts of violence in the history of Kaunas Jewry. Groups of German police and Vlasovites, using dogs and axes, stormed through the streets of the Viljampolė camp invading homes and dragging away children and the elderly. Despite frantic resistance by the mothers about one thousand victims were seized on the first day and sent to Auschwitz. The next day, another eight hundred were taken to the Ninth Fort.[55]

---

53 Term used for members of General Andrei Vlasov's collaborationist Russian Liberation Army (Russkaya osvoboditel'naya armiya, ROA), assembled mainly from former Soviet POWs. In some sources, the ROA men are referred to as "Ukrainians."
54 Tauber, *Arbeit*, 350.
55 See Samuel Kassow's introduction "Inside the Kovno Ghetto," in Schalkowsky, *Clandestine History*, 1–3, on the estimates of victims of the Jewish police roundup and the children's

Waldemar Ginsburg remembers the heartrending disappearance of the children:

> On 27 March 1944 our brigade returned home from work early. There was a strange, frightening silence over the camp; no children to greet us, not a soul to be seen in the whole compound. Full of foreboding we waited for the counting to finish and rushed into the barracks. Our worst fears were confirmed. The children, the elderly, the sick and disabled were gone, snatched away in a most brutal manner by a detachment of Ukrainian militia, leaving behind the shocked and beaten-up camp workers who tried to resist. I started looking for Grandpa. It was in vain. I found only his belongings scattered around his bunk. Our camp was small—only 1200 people—and we all knew each other. As the workers started arriving, the panic, the frenzy increased. It was like a seething cauldron, people running around in all directions, searching, screaming, crying, and sobbing uncontrollably. For a long time this persisted. Some were seized with hysteria, some with impotent rage, others with paralysing numbness. As darkness fell, the first shock was over, but the night was punctuated by cries, sobs and screams. And Kovno wept.[56]

The situation of the Kaunas Jews deteriorated sharply after the March violence. The remnants of the police force were placed under the command of Chief Moshe Levin's deputy, Tankhum Aronshtam, regarded by most inmates as a decidedly unpleasant character. Security was tightened as the number of guards doubled. Prison clothing replaced civilian attire, while morning and evening roll calls were strictly observed, all in order to make escape more difficult. The Germans introduced a system of elders responsible for ascertaining that the people under their charge would not leave their assigned blocks. The Council of Elders was dismissed on April 5, 1944. Soon after the Nazis commenced disbanding the subcamps which had been part of the Kaunas system.

On July 5, 1944, a Latvian Waffen-SS unit surrounded Vilijampolė and on the following day Göcke announced that the Jews were to be transferred to Germany. The camp was officially closed on July 8, and over the next week 6,100 inmates were evacuated westward by barge and train. Many Jews sought to save themselves from deportation to their deaths by hiding in the available malines,

---

action. Sources differ on whether those seized on the first day were sent to Auschwitz or Majdanek. The roundup of the police is dated either March 26 or 27 depending on the source.

56 Ginsburg, *And Kovno Wept*, 89–90.

counting on the quick arrival of the Soviet forces to save them. But the chances for survival were slim. Under orders to raze the Kaunas camp, the SS destroyed the remaining homes with grenades and dynamite, then poured petrol over the ruins to incinerate anyone in hiding. Perhaps as many as two thousand Jews perished in this final spasm of violence.[57] One author described the aftermath of the last rampage of the SS in Vilijampolė/Slobodka: "After one week, the fire burned out, leaving a charred landscape of rubble and stone chimneys."[58] The Germans withdrew from Kaunas without offering serious resistance to the advancing Soviets, so the remainder of the city escaped destruction except for several government buildings demolished by the retreating Wehrmacht. On August 1, 1944, the Red Army entered Kaunas. A few hundred Jewish survivors emerged from the desolation. According to a listing compiled by Soviet authorities soon after they had secured Kaunas, 634 Jews were registered in the city.[59] The USHMM estimates that of the approximately forty thousand Jewish inhabitants who lived in Kaunas between the wars, only 5% survived.[60]

The Šiauliai (Shavl) Ghetto

After mid-September 1941, the Jews of Šiauliai largely evaded the deadly "selections" that had afflicted the ghetto inmates in Kaunas and Vilnius. On November 14, 1941, the municipality reported to Gewecke that 4,764 Jews (including an estimated 1,500 children) were living in the city's ghetto. In February 1943, the Šiauliai Ghetto officially counted 1,156 children under the age of fourteen, 3,383 adults under the age of sixty, and 236 older persons. Until August 1943 the ghetto was under the jurisdiction of District Commissioner Gewecke. Mendel Leibovitz (Mendelis Leibovičius) headed the Jewish council, assisted by inmates who had been prominent in prewar Šiauliai, including Aron Katz (Aronas Kacas), Aron Heller (Aronas Heleris), Berel M. Abromovich (Berelis Abramovičius), and the respected teacher Eliezer Yerushalmi, among others.

---

57   For a description of the operation, see Tauber, *Arbeit*, 367–369.
58   As described in USHMM, *Hidden History of the Kovno Ghetto* (Little, Brown and Company: Boston, 1997), 211.
59   Bubnys, *Kauno getas*, 116; cf. Megargee, *Encyclopedia of Camps and Ghettos*, 1a:850, which claims that nine hundred survived in the malines.
60   Dean, *Encyclopedia of Camps and Ghettos*, 1067.

IMAGE 5.7. Top: Gates of the Šiauliai Ghetto after its destruction (Aušra Museum Šiauliai);
Bottom: Marker indicating the site of the Šiauliai Ghetto.

In September 1941 Ephraim Gens (Efroimas Gensas), the brother of Jacob Gens, became head of the Jewish police in the Eżero-Trakų section of the ghetto. The area of the two-part Šiauliai Ghetto changed little over two years. In 1942–1943 several small satellite labor camps grew up nearby, including quarters for the workers at the Zokniai air base and the Linkaičiai armory. Most of the inmates toiled in work brigades assigned to the Frenkel leather factory, the airfield, and peat bogs outside the city. Some of the labor sites were seasonal, such as the peatbogs in Radviliškis, Pavenčiai, and Bačiūnai. The ghetto contained a food shop and a forty-bed hospital. Able-bodied adults received yellow work cards and their upkeep was financed by the German labor office. The food situation in the ghetto was dire and reached a situation of near starvation by January and February 1942.[61]

In May 1942, conditions stabilized to some extent: unemployed women and children received half of the so-called "Aryan" ration, while another two thousand employed Jews received the full bread and meat ration, but only half-rations of other products. Some 754 workers assigned to what was considered "heavy labor" were provided the same provisions as non-Jews.[62] Nonetheless, as in the other ghettos and camps, smuggling remained the only avenue for averting starvation, but attempts to bring food into the ghetto were among the most severely punished transgressions. This was made clear on August 20, 1942, when guards shook down a work detail of thirty Jews in the presence of Gewecke and other district officials, discovering contraband foods the prisoners had hidden under their clothing, including butter, beets, bread, apples, and carrots. Gewecke called in the Jewish council and demanded the arrest of fifty black marketeers to be turned over for execution. After a difficult all-night discussion, the council decided to resist the German demand and offered themselves in their place, effectively threatening to dismantle the Jewish administration. Gewecke relented and fined the Ghetto 20,000 RM. On May 31, 1943, Gewecke and a group of German officers supervised the search of Jews returning from work assignments to the ghetto and detained Becalel Mazoveckis, a former baker, and Lea Bayer, a music teacher, who were found concealing bread, cigarettes, and a half

---

61 See Christoph Dieckmann, "Erfahrungen von Juden im Ghetto Šiauliai 1941–1944," in *Lebenswelt Ghetto: Alltag und soziales Umfeld während der nationalsozialistischen Verfolgung*, ed. Imke Hansen et al. (Wiesbaden: Harrasowitz Verlag, 2013), 156; Dieckmann, *Deutsche Besztzungspolitik*, 2:1304; Leiba Lipšicas, "Šiaulių getas, 1941 liepos 18–1944 m. liepos 24," in *Šiaulių getas*, 14–15, 20.

62 Dieckmann, "Erfahrungen," 160.

kilogram of meat. Both were condemned to death. The Jewish council bribed the German officials and managed to save Bayer. On June 6, 1943, Mazoveckis's hanging was witnessed by the entire ghetto populace.[63]

In March 1942, the Germans prohibited births in the ghetto, threatening with death not only the mothers who violated the ban, but their families as well, threatening the adults of the ghetto with sterilization if the ban failed to do the job. Eventually, the Nazis decided that births would be permitted to go to term until August 15. The excruciating cruelty of the ban placed Jewish leaders in an impossible situation. During a meeting of the Jewish council on March 24, 1943, the officials learned that all members of a Jewish family in Kaunas had been shot as a result of violating a similar prohibition. Because there had been a number of pregnancies since the order's deadline, the council was faced with terrible choices: late-stage abortions, placing infants with Christians outside the ghetto, or even killing newborns.[64]

On September 17, 1943, in accordance with Himmler's policy, the Nazis converted the Šiauliai Ghetto into an affiliate of the Kaunas concentration camp. An SS unit numbering about thirty men eventually replaced the local Lithuanian police as the security detail. The Germans transferred about one thousand Jews from the Kaukazas section and housed them at the Zokniai airbase. The remaining inmates were crowded into the Ežero-Trakų section of the former ghetto. Nearly 2,500 other Jews were transferred to labor camps in Daugeliai, Bačiūnai, Pavenčiai, and Akmenė where they labored in factories and peat bogs, while some continued working in the Frenkel factory.[65] In November 1943, the dire consequences of the reorganization of the Šiauliai Ghetto confronted the Jews. The SS along with two companies of Vlasovites deported 796 Jews:

---

63 The story of the council's intended sacrifice has been disputed. See Lipšicas, "Šiaulių," 21–22; cf. the description by Dov Solonski, "A Smile from the Height of the Gallows," in *The Jewish Resistance: The History of the Jewish Partisans in Lithuania and White Russia during the Nazi Occupation 1940–1945*, ed. Lester Eckman and Chaim Lazar (New York: Shengold, 1977), 271–274.

64 See Eliezer Yerushalmi, "The Destruction of the Jews in the Šiauliai Ghetto and Surrounding Times," trans. Andrew Cassel, 20–21; Yerushalmi, Eliezer, "The Destruction of the Jews in the Šiauliai Ghetto and Surrounding Times" [trans. Andrew Cassel], JewishGen, accessed July 22, 2023, https://kehilalinks.jewishgen.org/shavli/YerushalmiUmkum.pdf; also, "From the Diary of Eliezer Yerushalmi: The Ban on Births in the Shavli Ghetto, 1942–1943," Shoah Resource Center, Yad Vashem, accessed July 1, 2021, https://www.yadvashem.org/odot_pdf/Microsoft%20Word%20-%205385.pdf.

65 Arūnas Bubnys, *The Šiauliai Ghetto* (Vilnius: LGGRTC, 2014), 34–52.

506 children under ten years old, sixty-eight children between the ages of ten and thirteen, 191 elderly people, as well as twenty-six sick and disabled inmates. Eliezer Yerushalmi described the ordeal:

> Friday, 5 November 1943. The darkest day in our unhappy ghetto life: they took our children from us. . . . Everywhere where it was possible to hide, they looked for children, and if they found them, they dragged them out, barefoot and without overcoats, to the square. There, grabbing the children by their hair and arms, they hurled them into trucks. They pursued little children who accidentally appeared in the streets or in the yards, shot at them, and caught them. The unfortunate parents ran after their captured children, lamenting and begging, but they were beaten and driven away.[66]

The ultimate fate of the children has not been documented in detail, although there is evidence that they were transported to East Prussia. In any case, it is certain that most were killed soon after their capture.[67] In early 1944 the prisoners who had been sent to work in the outlying labor camps were brought back to Šiauliai. As the Red Army approached in July 1944, the Nazis evacuated the city's remaining Jewish inmates.

The Final Stage: Deportations, Death, and Survival, 1944–1945

The thousands of Lithuanian Jews who were evacuated after the liquidation of the ghettos in 1943–1944 were dispersed on a journey of suffering and death which sent them to Latvia, Estonia, East Prussia, and even the German heartland. As difficult as it is to imagine, the inmates who had evaded the death camps now faced a situation which was even worse than the one they had left behind in Vilnius, Kaunas, or Šiauliai. Crowded into filthy barracks, they now underwent a confrontation with what has been described as "the experience of the inner world of the concentration camps," a brutal psychological and physical shock

---

66 Yerushalmi's text as cited in Levinson, *Shoah*, 137.
67 Dieckmann, "Ehrfahrungen," 175.

to an already traumatized society.⁶⁸ Gone were the familiar surroundings, social institutions, and family structures of the ghetto which, however fragile and precarious, had provided a modicum of stability and a sliver of hope to lives lived perilously close to the edge of destruction.

Many of the Vilna deportees arrived at the Kaiserwald (Latvian: Mežaparks) concentration camp near Riga which had been constructed in March 1943. The Nazis distributed the inmates to subcamps and work sites manufacturing critical components for the Wehrmacht, notably the battery factory next to the main camp which employed primarily women and girls. The fact that the foremen in charge of the work force were primarily convicted German criminals from the Reich, rather than the more familiar Jewish brigade leaders in Lithuania, placed the workers, especially women, under constant threat of violence. As the Red Army approached Riga, the Germans reduced the inmate population by shooting those unfit for labor. In August and September, the Germans began to evacuate most of the remaining nearly ten thousand Lithuanian, German, Hungarian, and Latvian Jews to the Stutthof concentration camp in East Prussia, most of them by sea via Danzig. A Soviet submarine reportedly sank one of the transport ships. The last detachment of 190 prisoners left the port of Riga on October 11, 1944.⁶⁹

In the fall of 1943 other contingents of Lithuanian Jewish evacuees began arriving in Vaivara, a transit center established in September 1943 which was also the headquarters of a complex of labor camps run by the infamous military-industrial complex known as the Todt Organization (Organisation Todt). While the SS administered the camps, much of the security was in the hands of Estonian and Russian police battalions. Lithuanian Jews deported from Vilnius and Kaunas comprised the majority of the evacuees and were eventually distributed to other sites in the region. The Jews and the Soviet POWs provided most of the labor in the petroleum works of the German company Baltic Oil (Baltöl) located in the eastern Estonian shale fields. The Estonian camps were considered critical to the war effort so able-bodied men were not, as a rule, subject to organized killings. However, the SS carried out selections of the old, sick, and

---

68 As pointed out in Tauber, *Arbeit*, 371. One survivor transferred to Kaiserwald in October 1943 from the Liepāja ghetto described his previous situation as "paradise in comparison" (cited in Dean, *Encyclopedia of Camps and Ghettos*, 1013).

69 Ibid., 370–372. See more on Kaiserwald in *Encyclopedia of Camps and Ghettos*, 1b:1229–1235, also Andrew Ezergailis, *The Holocaust in Latvia 1941–1944* (Riga: Historical Institute of Latvia and USHMM, 1996), 363–365.

children: some were killed outright, and over one thousand are on record as deported to Kaiserwald, a fate widely understood as death. In early 1944 retreating Germans began to evacuate the eastern Estonian labor camps. Many inmates died of exhaustion or were shot on the way as they endured forced marches westwards. Fewer than seven thousand inmates remained in the Vaivara camps in June 1944.

Klooga, located near the Baltic Sea coast thirty kilometers west of Tallinn, was considered one of the worst camps. Here the prisoners manufactured underwater mines for the German navy which demanded brutally exhausting work under harsh discipline. Klooga survivor Benjamin Weintraub recalled his journey from Vilnius and the harsh conditions which awaited him at his destination:

> After four days in stifling railroad cars, we arrived at the Vaivara camp. From here they took us to Klooga where we found out that we must forget our names, and that we all would receive a number. Everyone had to attach the assigned number on their back, sleeve, and knee. As prisoners, they shaved a line of hair from our forehead to the back of the head. The women's [heads] . . . were completely shaved. After the roll call, they took every last thing away from us and assigned us to our jobs. We had to haul fifty-kilogram cement bags from the factory to the train station, running one hundred fifty meters with the bag on our backs. The women, who were held in barracks separately, were ordered to dig up and haul rocks. We worked from six in the morning until six in the evening with a 45–minute break for lunch which amounted to a watery vegetable soup. If, after an exhausting day of work, we stood "incorrectly" in line, or were "otherwise" aberrant, the foreman would take notice and call us out during roll call. The SS men would drag the man onto a "bench" . . . and tie the "culprit's" arms and legs. One SS man would sit on his head, the other would whip him with a metal wire. What's more, the "culprit" would have to count the blows. If he lost track, the whipping count would begin anew.[70]

The contingent of Lithuanian Jews in Klooga grew smaller over time. Many workers weakened from disease and exhaustion, the mortality rate reportedly reaching 10% monthly. Periodic killings of the infirm, either by shooting or triage in the camp's hospital, also took its toll. Even as the Germans prepared to retreat in the face of the inevitable Soviet advance, the Nazis carried on their

---

70 As related in Suckeveris, *Iš Vilniaus geto*, 206.

brutal regime, in Kruk's words, "as if nothing has happened." By mid-summer it became clear that the camp's days were numbered. "It's symptomatic: evacuation to survive, surviving to die," was Kruk's entry of July 18, 1944.[71]

The Germans evacuated most of the prisoners of the Vaivara camp system to Germany. The removal of the inmates, however, was never completed and an undetermined number remained behind. The last entry in Kruk's diary is dated September 17. On September 19, 1944, with the sounds of Soviet artillery in the distance, the Klooga guards ordered about three hundred prisoners to bring logs into the camp from the nearby forest, shooting the workers once the job was done. SS troops then surrounded the Klooga camp and, in one of the most grotesque mass killings of the Holocaust, began dragging groups of inmates toward the logs which had been laid out in crisscrossed structures next to the camp buildings. The victims were shot and stacked in layers on the assembled pyres which were then set on fire. Pandemonium ensued: desperate inmates attempted to flee the scene as the troops fired on them with automatic weapons.[72] Estimates of the number of Jews slaughtered at Klooga have ranged between 1,500 and two thousand victims, the majority evacuees from the Vilna Ghetto.[73] Kruk managed to bury and thus preserve his priceless manuscript on the last days of Lithuania's Jerusalem before he was caught and perished in the flames. Less than a hundred of the prisoners, including Weintraub, evaded the killers, fitfully concealed in cellars and attics. They emerged from their hiding places on September 23, 1944, as the Soviet soldiers entered the camp, exactly one year after the destruction of the Vilna Ghetto. The prisoners who had not died during the forced marches or at Klooga were evacuated by sea, although several of the ships sank on the way to Danzig.[74] One can reasonably estimate that Litvaks made up at least five thousand of the more than 8,614 Jews known to have perished in the Estonian labor camps.[75]

During the late summer and fall of 1944, most of the Lithuanian Jews who survived the labor camps in Latvia and Estonia were deported to Stutthof, one of the harshest of the concentration camps whose six-year death toll is estimated to have exceeded sixty thousand victims. In Stutthof the SS exterminated those

---

71 See Kruk, *Last Days*, entries of July 7, July 14, and July 18, 1944, 694–695.
72 Suckeveris, *Iš Vilniaus geto*, 207; Weiss-Wendt, *Murder*, 314–315.
73 Ibid., 318.
74 See Megargee, *Encyclopedia of Camps and Ghettos*, 1b:1491–1496.
75 Based on the numbers provided in Weiss-Wendt, *Murder*, 351.

considered no longer useful by employing Zyklon B gas (during the summer of 1944), injections of poisons, as well as by individual shootings. On July 12–13, 1944, the camp recorded the arrival of 3,613 Jews from Kaunas. Another contingent of 1,172 Kaunas Jews disembarked at Stutthof three days later, and yet another 3,377 Jews from the city were transported here on July 17–19. Based on the available partial lists, it is probable that at least 85% of the convoys listed above were comprised of Lithuanian Jews. A recent study of the Kaunas evacuees suggests that the remainder were likely citizens of other European countries who had been incarcerated in Kaunas. The last sizable transport of approximately 1,300 Lithuanian Jewish prisoners arrived in Stutthof from Kaunas and Šiauliai on July 24. German documents indicate that Stutthof camp headquarters turned over 1,893 Jewish prisoners (801 women, 1,092 children) for transport to Auschwitz on July 26, 1944. On the next day, the list of those destined for the death camp was amended to include another 210 Jews from Šiauliai who were recorded as "passing through." A review of the archives of the Stutthof Camp Museum reveals that about 8,800 Lithuanian Jews were sent to Stutthof in July 1944, and that additional transports of prisoners arriving by train and by sea between August and December included another estimated 4,700 Lithuanian Jews. There was also a contingent of Vilnius Jews imprisoned in Stutthof, including some of the Polish Jews who had fled to neutral Lithuania in 1939–1940.[76]

The Jewish men in Stutthof were employed in the various workshops and industrial enterprises supporting the war effort. The fate of the Jewish women who had evaded the convoys to Auschwitz was markedly worse. Polina Zingerienė was taken off the train in Stutthof, while her brother and father continued on to Dachau. She remembered the cruel selection after the women disembarked: "I shall never forget that terrible sight when women without children were lined up on one side and mothers with children on the other. Some mothers would leave their children and run to the side of the women without children. Children were rushing about, screaming, crying, and looking for their mothers. Aunt

---

[76] This overview is based on figures compiled by Arūnas Bubnys and Stanislovas Buchaveckas, *Lietuvos žydai Štuthofo koncentracijos stovykloje 1943–1945m.* (Vilnius: LGGRTC, 2020), 15–20, 25–26, 50–51, 262–267. On July 30, 1944, Auschwitz sent a message confirming that it had received "only 1,892 prisoners." Cf. Megargee, *Encyclopedia of Camps and Ghettos*, 1a:859.

Liuba holding her little girl in her arms, said to me: 'My daughter and I are going to the gas chamber.'"[77]

The writer and critic, Balys Sruoga, one of Lithuania's best-known literati, and, like Krėvė, suspected of pro-Soviet sympathies, was one of the forty-six intelligentsia and officials who had been detained as hostages in Stutthof in March 1943 as punishment for Lithuanians' refusal to form an SS Legion.[78] Sruoga observed the condition of the Jewish women in his memoir, *Dievų miškas* (Forest of the Gods). Along with the other Lithuanian prisoners, he was housed in a barrack adjacent to the Jewish women's section of the camp. In a chapter, "A Flood of Jewish Women," he described the travails of mothers as they sought to hide their children from the prying eyes of Nazi officials. The conditions were abysmal from the start:

> [N]o lodgings had been prepared for them beforehand, so barracks had to be constructed quickly ... the women nestled in a structure without a roof or walls, often directly on the sand, covered only by the clear blue sky. Sometimes they were not even given a piece of bread for days at a time. The clothes they were wearing on arrival had to be confiscated, disinfected, and searched for possible valuables sown into the linings. Each gets a scanty, shabby dress with a six-pointed star on the breast and back. The overcrowding in the barracks was terrible; any attempt at hygiene was a story long in the past.[79]

The stronger women were put to work. Most received reduced rations which made them especially vulnerable to the typhus epidemic which swept through the camp in the fall of 1944. One of the methods of reducing the population among the weaker Jewish women was a stratagem of purposeful starvation. Sruoga vividly described the result:

> The women who were sent out to work left in good health; the [Germans—S. S.] didn't take the sick ones. They came back crippled, barely

---

77 Polina Zingerienė's account is in the bilingual compilation, LGGRTC, *Su adata širdyje: getų ir koncentracijos stovyklų kalinių atsiminimai. With a Needle in the Heart: Memoirs of Former Prisoners of Ghettos and Concentration Camps* (Vilnius: Garnelis, 2003), 372.

78 See below, Chapter 6.

79 Balys Sruoga, "Dievų miškas" in *Raštai*, ed. Donata Linčiuvienė, vol. 4 (Vilnius: Alma Littera, 1994), 499–500. The memoir has been translated into many languages, including English: Balys Sruoga, *Forest of the Gods: Memoirs*, trans. Aušrinė Byla (Vilnius: Vaga, 1996).

dragging their bluish, sore infested feet, stooped and skinny. . . . These women were crammed into the infamous Barrack Number 30. Some straw was strewn around, like in a barn for cows. That is where they lay. Centipedes ran about on their legs, but the women no longer had the strength to pick them off. Soon they began to herd other women into Barrack 30, the ones who were weak or ill. They went there, knowing that they were heading towards an inevitable and painful death. No one treated the women of Barrack 30, that was impossible in any case, nor did anyone give them anything to eat. . . . They died, atop one another. . . . So, the corpses lay there, alone or in heaps, waiting for the workers to transport the bodies to the crematorium or the tar pit. The winter of 1944–1945 was the leading producer of the dead, providing 200–300 corpses per day.[80]

Sonja Milner arrived in Stutthof from Kaunas in the summer of 1944 and remembered the appalling conditions in the camp as the months grew colder and the dehumanizing conditions turned the inmates against each other:

> They would wake us up in the morning and give us some coffee. And the lice would crawl all over us. Whenever we came across some pool of water, we would first take off our undershirts, wash them, and put them on again. Next, we would wash our dresses. We were half-naked and without shoes, and thus we worked until the frosts came. . . . The cold and frosts were so bitter that our hair would freeze to our cots. . . . We would get into a fight over a bit of soup. When, at daybreak, we would line up with our shovels and spades, we would fight over who would work at the most desirable positions, at the foot of the hill rather than on top of it. It was warmer below because the hill afforded some protection against the snow and the cold.[81]

Another surviving witness of what awaited the women in Stutthof was Liubovė Feldman-Glazer who arrived with her sister from Kaunas having lost her parents and niece in the March 1944 "Children's Action." Liubovė was separated from her sister whom she never saw again. For a while she worked in the fields outside the camp where she managed to dig up some beets and, when working in the camp kitchen, to pilfer some potato peels. Suddenly, one day she was assigned

---

80 Ibid., 501.
81 Sonja Milner, *Sonja: Survival in War and Peace*, ed. Goldie Wachsman (New York: Shengold, 1984), 34–35.

to a building which she instantly recognized as a "barracks for the condemned." She slipped out through a back window and escaped the fate of the dying women, but even in the other barracks, corpses would be taken out every morning. The inmates would try to keep the dead for a few days to get their assigned rations of bread and soup. "Toward the end of the war," Liubovė remembered, "we all looked like skeletons." She stayed in Stutthof to the bitter end. In May 1945, a German ship towed the POWs and female prisoners on a barge which the navy intended to sink out at sea. American planes bombed the German ship and the POWs managed to direct the barge back to shore where soldiers met them and gave them something to eat.[82]

Sruoga thought that the women who bypassed Barrack 30 on their way to the camp's gas chamber were the lucky ones. His fellow prisoner, Rev. Stasys Yla, was of a different cloth, and wrote from a different perspective albeit from the same vantage point. In his recollection, the gassing of the women was temporarily halted during the summer of 1944, but the killings resumed under a different subterfuge: the Jewish women were taken in groups to the camp infirmary ostensibly for medical checks prior to work assignments. Instead, they were taken to a room where a waiting SS office shot the victim from behind. The orderlies would haul off the bodies. News of what was really happening spread quickly. Yla could see what was happening:

> The Jewish women's camp next to us was growing significantly smaller, but the cries and screams of these poor women, as they were taken to their deaths, became ever more frequent. They seem to have grasped the horrendous reality. As they were loaded onto the wagons, they said their farewells to the daughters, friends, and acquaintances. Sometimes, it was hard to separate them. They wailed; their hands raised to the heavens.[83]

Not all of the Jewish women who perished in Stutthof have remained nameless. A few death notices have survived in the camp archives revealing the fates of some of the inmates. On October 23, 1944, four Jewish women of the camp's

---

82   *Needle in the Heart*, 77–80.
83   Stasys Yla, *Žmonės ir žvėrys dievų miške* (Putnam, CT: Immaculata, 1951), 363. English translation: Stasys Yla, *A Priest in Stutthof: Human Experiences in the World of Subhuman*, trans. Nola M. Zobarskas (New York: Manyland Books, 1971).

18th Block (Barrack) died: Dora Friedlander, Liuba Gluskin, Lobe Grimmer, and Herta Beer.[84]

The Jews who had survived the travails of Stutthof faced another horror when the Nazis decided to evacuate the camp in January 1945. The resulting death marches in the bitter cold were at times senseless since a part of the prison convoy was forced to return to the camp after failing to find a route westward to avoid the oncoming Soviet forces. SS guards gunned down the marchers if they faltered along the way. Other groups of prisoners wandered aimlessly, seeking shelter. In March and April 1945 about three thousand prisoners, mainly Jewish women, were evacuated by ships which came under attack from Allied bombers as a result of which some inmates drowned in the Baltic Sea. Given the circumstances, the stories of the women who outlived Stutthof are testaments to human endurance. Polina Zingerienė survived the wintry debilitating marches and lay near death in a barn outside Danzig after guards had abandoned her group of starving prisoners. On March 10, 1945, Red Army soldiers rescued the women. Polina refused the offer of a newly formed local Zionist group to go to Palestine and returned to Kaunas to raise a family. (Her older son was Markas Zingeris, 1947–2023, a prominent Lithuanian writer, whose younger brother is Emanuelis Zingeris, a member of the Lithuanian parliament, the Seimas.)

William Mishell, who had survived the Kovno Ghetto, was one of the nearly 2,000 prisoners, mostly men, who were sent on to the Dachau camp system in Bavaria. He survived the starvation rations, which he suffered alongside other Lithuanian Jews. On April 29, 1945, the Americans entered Dachau and William Mishell became a free man but in despair about the fate of his mother and sister who had been left behind in Stutthof. A few months later, he met an old acquaintance who had just come from Lithuania to the Jewish DP camp in Landsberg. "How long has it been since you left Lithuania?" Mishell asked. "The man answered: 'I left Vilna about two weeks ago. I assume that you know that your mother and sister are in Vilna.' I thought I would faint," Mishell recalled. His mother had survived the harsh labor regimen, while his sister Vera, who had been in ill health, had managed to get rare help from a sympathetic SS-man.[85] Yudel Beiles, the teenage survivor of the Ninth Fort, lived through Dachau as

---

84 Bubnys and Buchaveckas, *Lietuvos žydai Štuthofo*, 27–28. This book also contains the available lists of Lithuanian Jewish inmates incarcerated in Stutthof.

85 Mishell, *Kaddish for Kovno*, 369, 376–377.

IMAGE 5.8. Soviet investigators in the Klooga concentration camp examine corpses stacked for burning, September 1944. (United States Holocaust Memorial Museum Photo Archives #59484. Courtesy of Esther Ancoli-Barbasch. Copyright of United States Holocaust Memorial Museum.)

IMAGE 5.9. Soviet troops enter Vilnius, July 13, 1944. In the background the Town Hall, on the left an abandoned German artillery piece. (Photo ITAR-TASS, CC BY-SA 4.0 https://creativecommons.org/licenses/by-sa/4.0>, via Wikimedia Commons.)

IMAGE 5.10. Ruins of the Kovno Ghetto, August 1944. (United States Holocaust Memorial Museum Photo Archives #81133. Courtesy of George Kadish/ Zvi Kadushin. Copyright of United States Holocaust Memorial Museum.)

IMAGE 5.11. Three members of the Paper Brigade pose together on a balcony in the Vilna Ghetto. Left to right: Schmerke Kaczerginski, Rachel Pupko-Krinski, Avraham Sutzkever. (United States Holocaust Memorial Museum Photo Archives #64900. Courtesy of the Sutzkever Family. Copyright of United States Holocaust Memorial Museum.)

well and in his memoir described both the exhilarating freedom of his liberation and the harsh revenge that the former inmates inflicted on the local Germans.[86]

The few inspiring stories of endurance and survival, however, cannot obscure the devastating blow which the ghettos and camps inflicted on Lithuanian Jewry. A search through records of the Special Archive in Vilnius found evidence of 2,733 Jews returning home from Germany and other Nazi-occupied countries after the war,[87] but this survey sheds no light on the number of Lithuanian Jews, who like William Mishell, eventually left for the United States, Israel, and other lands.

The Struggle to Remain Human: Aspects of Social and Cultural Life in the Ghetto

In 1949 the economist Samuel Gringauz published a sociological analysis of the Jewish ghetto under Nazi rule. A survivor of the Kovno Ghetto and Dachau, Gringauz had become a leader among the Lithuanian Jews in Germany after liberation. Based in part on a lecture delivered the previous year at the YIVO in New York, the article used Kaunas as a case study in which Gringauz sought to go beyond, in his words, "factual accounts that narrate the external course of events in one ghetto or another," and, in their place, "provide an insight into the inner mechanisms of Jewish group life." He argued that, unlike the concentration camp, the ghetto "developed its own social life and formed a social community . . . a form of Jewish national and autonomous concentration." Gringauz acknowledged the specific outside pressures, namely the periodic killings, the constant hunger, cold and disease, as well as forced labor, which meant that physical survival "became the supreme value and hence the gage for all other values. . . [which] under such conditions took on a relative character." He also pointed out that although the ghetto was a transitional form of an artificially imposed social organization, "there were a series of moral, psychological, and social components, stemming from the pre-ghetto period, that were carried over into the ghetto." Former legal, social, and cultural institutions

---

86 Beiles, *Yudke*, 85–104.
87 Bubnys and Buchaveckas, *Lietuvos žydai Štuthofo*, 28–29.

survived in the ghetto even under "specifically abnormal and extraordinary living conditions."[88]

Jews could do little about the outside pressures that the Nazis exerted on ghetto society, except to attempt to placate their overlords, and temper, when possible, the worst consequences of the murderous selections and forced labor. On the other hand, the Jewish administration *within* the ghettos instituted a system of justice which sought to maintain moral norms and basic social cohesion. In February 1942, the Germans permitted the establishment of a judicial system in the Vilna Ghetto which until then had been in the hands of the ghetto police under Jacob Gens. The legal system employed judges, prosecutors, and defense lawyers whose activities were to be regulated by a fourteen-page constitution. Records indicate that 115 criminal trials took place in the Vilna Ghetto in the first half of 1942.[89]

Gringauz noted that in Kaunas, "amidst the general agony," there were still, for some time, functioning courts that dealt with criminal and civil cases, complete with defense lawyers representing the accused. This permanent court system was established by the Jewish council on December 8, 1941, replacing the so-called "rapid-response courts" established soon after the creation of the Kovno Ghetto.[90] Interestingly, Gringauz quoted what might be considered the Basic Law of the Kovno Ghetto: "The activity of the court is to be regulated by the material and procedural law of [interwar] Lithuania, as of June 15, 1940, insofar as the conditions of ghetto life, the principles of Jewish national discipline, and Jewish social ethics do not seem to demand any required deviation."[91] In Šiauliai, the court set up by the Jewish council also sought to preserve the norms which had prevailed before the war. The head of the court was David Getz who had once served as the district judge in the city.[92]

The first judge of the Kovno Ghetto court was Simon Bieliatzkin, a former professor of law at the University of Kaunas. According to Avraham Tory one of the firm rules of the Kaunas Jewish council was to "refrain from passing any

---

88 Samuel Gringauz, "The Ghetto as an Experiment of Jewish Social Organization (Three Years of Kovno Ghetto)," *Jewish Social Studies* 11, no. 1 (1949): 4–5.
89 Dina Porat, "The Justice System and Courts of Law in the Ghettos of Lithuania," *Holocaust and Genocide Studies* 12, no. 1 (1998): 60–61.
90 Schalkowsky, *Clandestine History*, 210.
91 Gringauz, "The Ghetto": 14.
92 Porat, "The Justice System": 53.

sentence which will bring a Jew into the power of the Gestapo."[93] The degree of support for any of the ghetto courts depended in large part on the public's attitude towards the Jewish councils and their police forces. The Kaunas council, with the respected Dr. Elkes at its head, had a high degree of confidence among the people which aroused little resistance to its decrees, relative to the other Lithuanian ghettos.[94] The Kaunas police force, despite the aforementioned roles of Lipzer and Caspi-Serebrowitz, also seems to have been viewed by contemporaries with considerably more understanding than its counterparts in Vilnius and Šiauliai.[95]

Not all Jews approved of the decisions of the courts and of the enforcement of the laws by the ghetto police. But there were dramatic incidents that showed that the ghetto inmates had not lost their desire for justice or a grasp of what constituted a moral order. On June 4, 1942, Gens ordered the public execution of six ghetto inmates for the murders of Yosef Gerstein and Herzl Lides. In Kruk's striking description of the event, he noted the approving reaction of the populace, "so great is the bitterness against the murderers and so great is the instinct to cleanse ourselves of the social and historical disgrace."[96] Crimes of such violence among Jews in the ghettos were rare. A more representative example of the problems relating to law and order are reflected in the records of the Kovno Ghetto police between April and December 1942. The documents reveal a total of seven hundred criminal cases, mostly instances of theft, fraud, and forgery, of which 424 were solved and another 222 transferred to the courts.[97] Any discussion of law and order within the ghetto must consider the unique context of life under German occupation. The courts and the police were forced to deal with problems that simply had not existed in the pre-ghetto experiences of the Jews. For example, given the fact that starvation was a constant threat to ghetto inmates, a fair and equitable distribution of the legally available food rations was essential. The authorities were thus forced to

---

93 As quoted in ibid.: 57.
94 Gringauz, "The Ghetto": 11.
95 One can compare Gringauz's evaluation of the Kaunas police with the caustic comments of Kruk in *Last Days*, entry of March 22, 1942, 244 and especially the entry of March 30, 1942, 255: "How wretched is the Jewish police . . . how rotten to the core is our ghetto kingdom." Also, cf. Šuras, *Užrašai*.
96 See details in Kruk, *Last Days*, 300–303.
97 Schalkowsky, *Clandestine History*, 343.

discipline the residents who falsified the number of household members to gain extra rations.⁹⁸

A viable public health system was essential, considering the constant threat of contagious diseases, especially the periodic outbreaks of typhus. In the Vilna Ghetto, although mortality from infectious diseases was estimated at five times the prewar rate, the health care system managed to avoid a catastrophe. One stroke of good fortune was the inclusion of the main Jewish community hospital within the ghetto, along with a skilled medical staff. The importance of this institution was well described by the pharmacist Balbierzyszki:

> All ghetto institutions were created in order to save Jews or to ease their fate. Every department was a battle station. But the hospital was exceptional; it was a defensive line, a true resistance movement, that fought not with arms and grenades, but with knowledge and with self-sacrifice, to snatch as many Jewish lives as possible from German hands.⁹⁹

The ruthless operations of the Jewish Sanitary Police were another reason for the relatively good public health situation in the Vilna Ghetto.¹⁰⁰ The cemetery section of the health department also benefitted the ghetto in an unusual way, as related by Solon Beinfeld: "The hearse that left the ghetto for the cemetery seldom came back empty. It was used routinely to smuggle food into the ghetto on its return journey. Thus, even the dead played their part in the battle for survival."¹⁰¹ In Kaunas, the public health infrastructure was not as robust, since the Jewish hospital had been burned during the massacre of October 4, 1941. Typhus had spread into the Kovno Ghetto in the autumn of 1942, but the efforts of the epidemiologist Dr. Moses Brauns not only kept the infections at bay with a minimum of lives lost, but also concealed the outbreak from the German authorities and the Lithuanian Board of Health. He knew that the Nazis would not hesitate to murder patients in order to "disinfect" Jews and

---

98 Ibid., 95.
99 As quoted in Solon Beinfeld, "Health Care in the Vilna Ghetto," *Holocaust and Genocide Studies* 12, no. 1 (1998): 69.
100 Ibid.: 71–74.
101 Ibid.; 91.

prevent the spread of disease to the more worthy population, especially German soldiers.[102]

The work of the courts, police, and health departments was essential in allowing a modicum of economic activity which enabled at least some ghetto inmates to experience a mirage of normalcy. In March 1942, Kruk described this deceptive semblance of normality in the trade carried out on the streets, and then added a discordant note about the relative economies of the ghetto and the outside world:

> In the beginning, people wandered about trading . . . a half-loaf of bread a quarter kilo of meat, a candle, a cigarette, some candy, etc. The seller could carry the whole "shop" in his hand. . . . Now people carry on free and open [commerce] in cigarettes, tobacco, matches, etc. You can see a basket of onions, a sack of potatoes, here stands someone with a big bundle of wood. . . . Little shops are open in the ghetto. Peasants who come in to take out our garbage bring merchandise into the ghetto and there is a trade . . . the likes of which has never been seen. By now they're dealing in live poultry, fish, etc. . . . Outside the ghetto, they say that the Jews in the ghetto live better than the residents of the city. There's some truth to that. In this respect, the ghetto is much livelier than are the inhabitants outside the ghetto."[103]

Nine months later Kruk observed that "Recently in the ghetto things really have been good . . . the residents of the Vilna Ghetto are really not living badly." He noted the availability of food, wood, and other essentials, concluding that life was "still bearable," and that "seldom does anyone die of hunger."[104] At first glance, these observations of relative normalcy seem to conflict with numerous accounts of inmates searching for food and struggling with constant hunger. Yet they are less surprising given the social stratification, an oft-described feature of ghetto life.

On the day before Kruk entered this last observation, the young Yitzhak Rudashevski saw something quite different as wet snow fell on the muddy street outside the Rūta store where a long line of people had gathered:

---

102 Tory, *Surviving the Holocaust*, 141–143.
103 Kruk, *Last Days*, entry of March 21, 1942, 242–243.
104 Ibid., entry of December 14, 1942, 426.

They are distributing horse meat and potatoes today. Two wagons stand outside, one with wet, frozen potatoes, the other with red, bloody horse meat. They are pouring the potatoes into the cellar. Jewish women in torn clothes are grabbing the ones that have fallen in the mud. The policemen are chasing them away, but suddenly they all again charge towards a few potatoes. There is also an uproar around the meat wagon. Here a few ragged boys with burning eyes are milling about. They're talking about something with the driver, a Christian boy with a quilted coat, big heavy shoes and a long whip. Soon I understand what is happening. The young driver turns around, tears off a piece of meat and puts it in a Jewish boy's pocket.[105]

Rudashevski also wrote about the difficulty of workers chasing after a mouthful of bread through deals with the Germans and by desperate exchanges with local peasants. He observed that "in general, people are impoverished, and a great many are simply suffering hunger."[106] Rudashevski's vivid account of the desperate women and boys would tempt one to conclude that there was little difference between ghetto life and the murderous struggle for survival in the concentration camps of 1943–1944, but this idea would have to ignore the role of cultural life in the ghetto. In his notable essay, Gringauz argued that the ghetto, in his words, a "social regime," was fundamentally different from the concentration camp which constituted an "individual regime." The former institution, he wrote, "developed its own social life and formed a social community," asserting that "one may speak of the *cultural miracle of the ghetto*" (emphasis in original).[107]

In terms of preserving a sense of Jewish identity, nothing proved more important than the struggle to maintain an education system. The schooling of children also implied continuity, a sense that there existed a future for the Jewish people, although this hope must have seemed illusory after the destruction of the ghettos in 1943–1944. The Vilna Ghetto registered between 2,700–3,000 school-age children during the first weeks, but by the winter of 1942, the number had fallen to about 1,500. After observing the opening of the girls' boarding school, Kruk reviewed the education situation in the ghetto in his diary entry of March 3, 1943: three grammar schools attended by

---

105 Rudaševskis, *Vilniaus geto dienoraštis*, entry of December 13, 1942, 159.
106 Ibid., entry of September 13, 1942, 95; entry of September 18, 1942, 99.
107 Gringauz, "The Ghetto": 5, 16.

1,245 children, secondary school classes enrolling 129 students, and a music school. There were daycare centers and orphanages. "The future historian, the future cultural scholar will often ponder this cultural wonder of the Vilna Ghetto," he wrote.[108] Before the liquidation, the educational system also included two kindergartens and a trade school. In Kaunas, two schools were opened in the fall of 1941, but on August 25, 1942, Cramer ordered them closed. The Germans did permit vocational training for the work force which created an opening for subterfuge. Fortunately for the students, the German official keeping tabs on the training did not carefully attend to details, and under the guise of providing technical skills, the teachers were able to provide "a Zionist education in the spirit of the Jewish heritage and our national aspirations."[109] Three hundred and fifty children were enrolled in the illegal schools in the spring of 1943.[110]

The struggle to preserve Jewish culture amidst a hostile environment meant an even fiercer attachment to the things which embodied Litvak identity. Some urban Jews rejected their adjustment to the Lithuanian majority's culture that had characterized the First Republic. Before entering the Kovno Ghetto, the sixteen-year-old Samuel (Shmuel) Schalkowsky, who like most Jewish youths in the city, could speak Lithuanian, suffered a "complete repression" of the language of his Gentile neighbors. He ascribed this to the trauma of hearing violent men in the streets as he hid in his house: "there are no visual memories," he remembered years later, "only the shouting in Lithuanian." Schalkowsky concluded, with some reason, that "knowing Lithuanian was, at least for me, not relevant to my survival efforts."[111] (Obviously the opposite was true for young Jews hiding in Lithuanian-speaking regions.)

Perhaps the most impressive cultural institution of the Vilna Ghetto was the Mefitse Haskalah library, commonly known as the "House of Culture." On November 27, 1941, Anatol Fried ordered the preservation of literary Judaica, paintings, and sculptures. When Kruk surveyed the holdings in September 1941, he found the library in disarray, the card catalog hauled away by the

---

108 Kruk, *Last Days*, 469.
109 The first visit to the vocational school by German officials is described in detail in Gerber, *Diary*, entry of October 5, 1942, 144–149.
110 Levinsonas, *Šoa*, 19–20; USHMM, *Hidden History*, 191–194; Tory, *Surviving the Holocaust*, entry of April 26, 1943, 307.
111 Quoted in Schalkowsky's preface to *Clandestine History*, xi.

Germans. Kruk immediately began restoring order to the collection and found a receptive audience. The insatiable demand for a connection with the Jewish word is described by historian David E. Fishman:

> Kruk and his staff would need to re-catalog everything from scratch. At first, he assumed that his task was to salvage the collection and serve as its custodian until the war was over. He didn't imagine that the throngs of frightened and confused people, looking for floor space to sleep and food to eat, would be psychologically capable of reading. But when the library began lending out select volumes on September 15, 1941, inmates "pounced on the books like thirsty lambs." "Even the horrible events they experienced could not stop them. They couldn't resign from the printed word." He called this "the miracle of the book in the ghetto."[112]

Even during the horrific month of September 1941, the library counted 1,485 readers. As the situation in the ghetto stabilized, the number of readers increased: according to the staff, between October 1 and before it was temporarily closed in December 1941 because of the typhus epidemic, 6,559 readers checked out over 25,552 books.[113] During the summer of 1942, about five thousand people visited the reading room every month.

On December 13, 1942, the library hosted a ceremony in the ghetto theater celebrating the loan of the one hundred thousandth book. The occasion was accompanied by "great pomp, and among the Yiddishist and cultural circles, made quite an impression." The festivities included a book exhibit and a lecture by Kruk who remarked that, despite all the ghetto's travails, "a cultural heart is beating here."[114] Young Rudashevski and his schoolmates, all avid readers, attended the celebration, writing on the occasion that "reading books in the Ghetto is the greatest pleasure for me. A book unites us with the world. The circulation of the 100,000th book is a great achievement for the Ghetto and the Ghetto has a right to be proud of it." The library had become a veritable

---

112 David E. Fishman, *The Book Smugglers: Partisans, Poets, and the Race to Save Jewish Treasures from the Nazis* (Lebanon, NH: ForeEdge, 2017), 37. Quotes are from Kruk's report of October 1942 in the YIVO archive.
113 Kruk, *Last Days*, entry of January 10, 1942, 169; cf. Kostanian-Danzig, *Spiritual Resistance in the Vilna Ghetto* (Vilnius: Vilna Gaon Jewish State Museum, 2002), 53–54.
114 Kruk, *Last Days*, entry of December 13, 1942, 424.

"anchor of ghetto life."[115] The only sour note in the celebratory atmosphere was the result of a survey conducted by the library staff which found that, much to the consternations of Zionists and Yiddishists, the majority of readers preferred Russian and Polish books to Yiddish and Hebrew ones.[116] The library also housed archival records and a department for scholarly research headed by Zelig Kalmanovitch. The ghetto archive contained directives from the German authorities orders of the Jewish council and police, as well as witness testimonies about the killing actions. At the beginning of 1942 Gens commissioned a team of writers to produce a history of the ghetto.

Artistic performances provided a significant source of social connection for the Jews of Vilnius. When in December 1941 Jacob Gens proposed introducing theatrical productions in order to lift the spirits of the inmates, his suggestion initially met a hostile reception among the Bund elite and Orthodox Jewish leaders. Invited to the first public performance in January 1942, Kruk reacted with disgust, considering it an insult to the survivors living in the shadow of Paneriai. Members of the Bund announced a boycott and leaflets were distributed: "You don't make theater in a graveyard."[117] Despite the initial resistance, Wolf Durmashkin organized and headed the symphony orchestra which began playing on March 18, 1942. The group grew from seventeen musicians to as many as forty and performed a total of thirty-five concerts. The ghetto also sustained two large choirs.[118]

In the Kovno Ghetto, despite resistance from the religious establishment on the principle that "in the cemetery you don't dance," musical instruments were smuggled into the ghetto through the sewage system. Elena Kutorgienė, who kept in close contact with Jews during the occupation, wrote: "The music of the symphony orchestra was for the inhabitants of the ghetto like mountain air

---

115 Rudashevski's quote is in Rachel Kostanian-Danzig, *Spiritual Resistance*, 56; cf. the overview in Fishman, *The Book Smugglers*, 42–51.

116 David G. Roskies, "Jewish Cultural Life in the Vilna Ghetto," in *Lithuania and the Jews: The Holocaust Chapter: Symposium Presentations* (Washington: Center for Advanced Holocaust Studies, USHMM, 2004), 40; cf. the December 13, 1942 statistical entry in Zelig Kalmanovich, *Hope Is Stronger Than Life: Vilna Ghetto Diary*, trans. Olga Lempert (Vilnius: The Vilna Gaon Museum of Jewish History, 2021), 160: 2 percent of the books in Hebrew, 17.6% in Yiddish, 70.4% in Polish.

117 Kruk, *Last Days*, entry of January 17, 1942, 173–174.

118 Kostanian-Danzig, *Spiritual Resistance*, 95–97.

for the consumptive."¹¹⁹ The violinist and conductor Michelis (Moišė) Hofmekleris, nationally acclaimed for his band's live and radio performances in prewar Lithuania, vigorously defended the role of music in the ghetto, asserting that "music is not just an expression of joy," and organized a symphony orchestra of thirty-five musicians and five singers who presented twice-weekly concerts. Hofmekleris also conducted the Jewish police orchestra. During the first concert in August 1942, at the first sounds of the prayerful "Kol Nidre," both the musicians and the audience broke into tears. In his diary entry for December 20, 1942, eighteen-year-old Ilya Gerber noted that the "mood in the ghetto is not very good and people are exchanging whispers and talking about the mass murders," but that the "musical ensembles were working full steam." The concert on that day, according to the diarist, was "well received by the audience," as Hofmekleris bowed "nicely to the applause."¹²⁰ The famous Slobodka yeshiva hosted the performances; seventy-seven concerts for the Jews and three for the local SS were performed in 1942–1943.¹²¹

On March 22, 1942, the auditorium of the former Vilna *Realgymnasium*¹²² staged the first children's recital in the ghetto: "The children were happy, as lively as in the good old days, and all those looking at them couldn't control themselves." Coming to terms with the milieu in which the children sang was initially difficult for Kruk who complained that, for him, the performance "made a grotesque impression."¹²³ Five days later Kruk commented on the concerts produced by the Second Police Precinct, which included some "well-performed numbers." "In short," he wrote, "the bleeding Vilna Ghetto . . . plays theater."¹²⁴ The outrage was understandable, but over time the mood shifted, and public cultural performances gained acceptance. During 1942 the Ghetto Theater presented 120 performances viewed by thirty-eight thousand spectators. In March 1943 the nine-year-old artist Samuel Bak opened an exhibit of sketches in the foyer of the ghetto theater. During the summer of 1944 survivors returning to the ruins of Vilnius managed to salvage much of the cultural heritage of the Vilna Ghetto

---

119 As quoted in Joachim Braun, "Music as Resistance, Music as Survival," in Gaunt, Levine, and Palosuo, *Collaboration and Resistance during the Holocaust*, 426.
120 Gerber, *Diary*, 226–227.
121 Levinsonas, *Šoa*, 21; Braun, "Music," 427; Ginaitė-Rubinsonienė, *Atminimo knyga*, 92–93.
122 A secondary school with a focus on modern science and languages.
123 Kruk, *Last Days*, entry of March 22, 1942, 243.
124 Ibid., entry of March 27, 1942, 250.

including more than two hundred posters of artistic events. The persistence of public cultural life is attested by one of the recovered posters, reading: "Vilna Ghetto Theater. Friday, July 9, 1943, at 21:30. For the third time: *The Ghetto in a Trick-Mirror*. Feuilleton, Satire read by Yosef Mushkat. Tickets at the theater desk." One week later, Yitzhak Wittenberg, the leader of the FPO, gave himself up to the Germans (see below), triggering a series of events that would lead to the destruction of the ghetto. The last recovered poster was dated August 3, 1943, notifying ghetto residents of "The Second Appearance of the Rhythmic-Plastic Arts Group under the directorship of Nina Gerstein."[125] (The posters were featured in an exhibition at the U.S. Capitol in September 1999.)

While the library, theater productions, and concerts in the Vilna Ghetto did much to keep up the spirits of the young (as frequently noted in Rudashevski's diary), a group of scholars and writers carried on a no less important discreet struggle to preserve the cultural heritage of the Jerusalem of the North, "the city of the book." These were the members of what has been dubbed the "paper brigade," of which two of the most prominent, Schmerke Kaczerginski and Avraham Sutzkever, were associated with the prewar literary Young Vilna (Jung-Vilne) movement. The nemesis of Vilna's Jewish intellectuals was Dr. Johannes Pohl, a former Catholic priest who had learned Hebrew during studies in Jerusalem in the early 1930s. An ardent antisemite, Pohl joined the Reichsleiter Rosenberg Taskforce (Einsatzstab Reichsleiter Rosenberg, ERR), the Nazi organization tasked with seizing cultural treasures in the occupied areas. The ex-priest presented himself to his superiors as a Hebraica expert who could loot the Jewish cultural treasures in Vilnius and eventually transport the relevant materials to the Institute for Research on the Jewish Question (Institut zur Erforschung der Judenfrage) in Frankfurt, a place dedicated to "the study of Jews without Jews" (Judenforschung ohne Juden). This attack on Jewish culture was combined with the ransacking and plunder of valuables and artifacts from the Great Synagogue. David E. Fishman succinctly summarized the operation as "a coordinated assault on the written Jewish word."[126] Avraham Sutzkever wrote that "Rosenberg's staff exterminated the Jewish word as assiduously as the Gestapo did Jewish lives." The rector of the University of Vilnius Mykolas Biržiška told the poet that after all the Jewish-authored books had been removed from the university, the Germans

---

125 See Jevgenija Biber and Rachel Kostanian, eds., *Vilna Ghetto Posters: Jewish Spiritual Resistance* (Vilnius: The Vilna Gaon Jewish State Museum, 1999).

126 Fishman, *Book Smugglers*, 30.

IMAGE 5.12. Samuel Bak who held his first artistic exhibition in the Vilna Ghetto at age nine. (Courtesy of Daniela Bak.)

IMAGE 5.13. Performance of the Kovno Ghetto orchestra, 1944. Michelis Hofmekleris is conducting. (United States Holocaust Memorial Museum Photo Archives #81073. Courtesy of Robert W. Hofmekler. Copyright of United States Holocaust Memorial Museum.)

searched for days afterward to find hidden writings and destroyed everything they could find. "Not a single Jewish children's book could be saved."[127]

The scholars, or "intellectual brigade," who sorted the Jewish treasures were assisted by the ordinary workers, or the "physical brigade," which provided technical support and transport. In the spring of 1942, the ERR office in Riga issued guidelines on separating Hebrew and Yiddish materials destined for Germany

---

127 Suckeveris, *Iš Vilniaus geto*, 121.

IMAGE 5.14. Portrait of partisan Sara Ginaitė, Vilnius, July 1944. The photograph was taken by a Jewish, Soviet major who was surprised to see a female, Jewish partisan standing guard. (United States Holocaust Memorial Museum Photo Archives #89040. Courtesy of Sara Ginaitė. Copyright of United States Holocaust Memorial Museum.)

IMAGE 5.15. A photograph depicting members of the Fareynikte Partizaner Organizatsye (FPO), a Jewish partisan organization in Vilnius during the war. (United States Holocaust Museum Photo Archives #37216. Courtesy of Irma Gurwicz. Copyright of United States Holocaust Memorial Museum.)

from those to be destroyed. In Vilnius, it was decided that only 30% of the books would be preserved, the rest turned into pulp as a business venture on the side. Kruk, the head of the group working under Pohl, decided that the often lax German supervision of the group would permit the smuggling of books into the ghetto for safekeeping, over the objections of Kalmanovich who thought that the materials would be safer in Germany where they could eventually be "rescued" by the Western Allies. Two of the most cherished volumes saved by the brigade were Theodore Herzl's diary and the record book of the Vilna Gaon's synagogue.[128] Not everyone appreciated the dedication of the intellectuals. As poets Sutzkever and Kaczerginski remembered: "Ghetto inmates looked at us as if we were lunatics. They were smuggling foodstuffs into the ghetto, in their clothes and boots. We were smuggling books, pieces of paper, occasionally a Torah scroll or mezuzahs."[129] In the end, valuable books and papers were, in fact, rescued and found their way to safety after the war.

Later authors, such as Raul Hilberg and Rich Cohen, as well as a few contemporaries, including Shmuel Kaplinski, the commander of the group "Towards Victory," dismissed the notion of cultural activity as part of the struggle against Nazism, arguing that such efforts served, at best, as a distraction, or, worse, as a narcotic that turned Jews away from the path of armed resistance.[130] But the intellectual elite of the ghetto understood well the concept of spiritual/cultural resistance. Max Viskind, the theater director, was firm about the role of fostering culture, asserting that "we must resist with this weapon to raise the spirit of the ghetto inmates."[131] The survivor Markas Petuchauskas who went on to become an authority on Lithuanian art and theater maintained that "physical resistance could not exist without this spiritual component, and the reverse is also true."[132] The emphasis on armed resistance underrates the daily efforts which sought to battle the constant humiliations of ghetto life. For example, there is the tactic designed by Sutzkever to avoid the obsequious practice of standing at attention when Germans entered the scholars' workstation: whenever one of them saw

---

128 See Fishman, *Book Smugglers*, 62–93.
129 Ibid., 133, photo: "Shmerke Kaczerginski and Abraham Sutzkever on the porch of their apartment in the Vilna ghetto."
130 Kostanian-Danzig, *Spiritual Resistance*, 20–21; cf. Rich Cohen, *The Avengers: A Jewish War Story* (New York: A. A. Knopf, 2000).
131 As quoted in Levinsonas, *Šoa*, 20.
132 Markas Petuchauskas, "Kultūros žemynas tilpęs teatre," *Kultūros barai* 1 (2003): 77–81.

a German approaching the building, someone would call out a signal and they would work in a standing position, so as not to have to rise. Fishman considers this "quiet resistance an affirmation of their human dignity and equality."[133]

Considering that the Nazis attacked not only the bodies of Jews, but Jewish identity itself, one can agree with Roskies that the very act of "a whole culture reconstituting itself in the face of total destruction" could be seen as part of the struggle against the Reich. Resistance to the Nazis was implicit in the very act of education as in the example of the Kaunas vocational school's secret curriculum of Jewish studies. In the opinion of Israeli musicologist Joachim Braun, the Jews of occupied Vilnius and Kaunas were unique: "In these two important East-European centers of Jewish culture, the ghettos turned into hotbeds of resistance—armed, spiritual, and musical."[134] Inasmuch as the cultural resistance discouraged apathy and anarchy and created a sense of solidarity, it encouraged the values without which people were unlikely to put their lives on the line to fight back. It is no coincidence that the origins of the FPO are intricately linked to the book smuggling operation and that two of its most illustrious fighters came from the ranks of the "intellectual brigade."[135]

From Ghettos to Forests: Jewish Armed Resistance

Aside from several reported instances of Jews attacking the shooters at the pits or attempting to flee the killing sites, the mobile units which carried out the massacres of the summer and fall of 1941 met no meaningful resistance. The contemptible accusation that the Jews went "like sheep to slaughter" ignores the efficiency of the militarized police operations and the environment of deep hatred that surrounded the vulnerable Jewish communities. Once the killing encompassed entire families as a matter of course in August 1941, the women in particular were faced with the heartrending duty to stay by their children and/or elderly parents. On the other hand, the spirit to fight back against the atrocities could not be suppressed for long. Sutzkever recorded perhaps the first

---

133 Fishman, *Book Smugglers*, 79. A case for the nonviolent spiritual resistance under the conditions of Nazi rule is in James Glass, *Jewish Resistance during the Holocaust: Moral Uses of Violence and Will* (Palgrave: New York, 2004), 5–6, 103–119.
134 Braun, "Music": 426.
135 Ibid., 94ff.

case of group resistance in Vilna on October 4, 1941, when the eighteen-year-old Moshe Frumkin, realizing that the Germans were escorting them towards Lukiškės prison, shouted to the people to escape: "Panic seized the column, women lay prone on the road, the elderly stood petrified, and the youngsters ran away. Schweinberger ordered his men to fire. Dozens of people fell dead, and the survivors were compelled to carry them. Nevertheless, dozens escaped, including Frumkin."[136]

In addition to the activities of the intellectual brigade in the Vilna Ghetto which disrupted German policies aimed at annihilating Jewish cultural identity, ordinary workers employed in the various labor brigades also sought to undermine the Nazis. Kovno Ghetto survivor Elja Ganz, who escaped death in Klooga by hiding in the barrack lofts, testified that "in many cases the Jews sabotaged the work by destroying the materials needed for bridge construction and other projects serving the war effort."[137] Many people working within the Jewish administrative structures also helped frustrate German directives. Kovno Ghetto policemen helped vulnerable inmates evade Rauca's selection during the Great Action in Kaunas in October 1941. Thanks to their efforts, some of them survived the Holocaust, including people who became prominent figures in Lithuanian life after the war. Gringauz stressed that these men distinguished themselves from the Jewish police forces of the other ghettos: "They shielded the partisan movement and participated in the resistance and rescue work in the ghetto. The entire police leadership died as heroes in Fort IX [Ninth Fort] of the Kovno citadel, martyrs to their social responsibilities."[138] There were contrary views. Ganz claimed that two of the Kaunas policemen, Uspitz and Arenstamm, delivered Jews to the Germans. Tory cites two shady characters who lived well and worked with both the Jewish administration and police, as well as the Gestapo: the aforementioned Caspi-Serebrowitz and Lipzer (Lipcer, also Liptzer).[139] However, despite some caveats, the generally positive view of the role played by the Kaunas Jewish police in the history of the ghetto must be taken seriously.

---

136 Sutzkever's account as published in Arad, *Ghetto in Flames*, 139.
137 Elja Ganz Testimony, Munich, September 2, 1946, Yad Vashem Archive, O.33, M.E. 3541063, File No. 1275, 2.
138 Gringauz, "The Ghetto": 14; cf. Katz, "Inside the Kovno Ghetto," 3.
139 Elja Ganz Testimony, 2; see Tory, *Surviving the Holocaust*, 44–45, 358–361, 220–221; Gringauz claimed that Lipzer was a criminal before the war (Gringauz, "The Ghetto": 8–9).

The Jewish armed resistance was chiefly a movement of the young. Obviously, the physical endurance required for combat and survival in the inhospitable conditions of the forest camps excluded the aged and infirm. But historian David Roskies also identifies a cultural factor which divided the generations in their effort to confront the relentless Nazi attack on the Jews. During one of the many well-documented discussions of the ghetto elite hosted by Jacob Gens, the older participants tended to measure the existential crisis of the Vilna Ghetto in terms of the centuries of past Jewish travails, which did not sit well with the youth:

> What wisdom, then, did the ghetto intelligentsia gain when taking the measure of history? Members of the older generation, led by veterans such as Feldstein and Kalmanovitch, were struck by the continuities, whereas the youthful members of the FPO (Abba Kovner, Shmerke Kaczerginski, Sutzkever, Kruk, Leon Bernstein) began to understand that what was happening now had never happened before.[140]

The youth were deeply steeped in Jewish history, but their inspiration from the past focused almost exclusively on examples of heroic battles against oppressors of the Jews.

Jews were unable to offer organized resistance to the initial attacks on their community in Kaunas during the first week of the war. Several acts of individual heroism against the Klimaitis pogrom in Vilijampolė/Slobodka have been recorded and there is evidence that some Jews fought hard to protect their families. Resistance groups began to form in the Kovno Ghetto in the fall of 1941.[141] Their membership came to some six hundred activists, including Zionist youth and a Communist-led group, the Anti-Fascist Military Organization (AMO), under the leadership of Chaim Yellin. At first, the activities of the anti-fascists dealt mainly with collecting information on the front and assisting inmates in evading deportation. They also carried out, whenever possible, acts of sabotage, especially at work sites employing Jewish labor brigades. The Zionists, under the guidance of their central governing body, the Matzok, were initially suspicious of the Communists but in time began to coordinate in joint operations. In 1943,

---

140 In his "Jewish Cultural Life," 36, Roskies describes the gatherings at Gens's apartments as "colloquia."

141 Dov Levin and Zvie A. Brown, *The Story of an Underground: The Resistance of the Jews of Kovno in the Second World War* (Jerusalem: Gefen, 2014), 56–57.

the factions came under the umbrella of the Jewish General Fighting Organization (Yidishe Algemayne Kamfs Organizatsiye). The majority belonged to the Zionist and Communist blocs; others were apolitical. Early attempts to establish permanent partisan bases in the forests around Kaunas failed.[142]

In 1943–1944, the Jewish resistance in Kaunas organized escapes into the eastern Lithuanian forests and western Belarus where conditions for guerilla activity were more favorable. An estimated 450 Jews fled from the Kaunas concentration camp and joined the partisans. Many were inexperienced youth: some perished during the escape attempts or were killed in the forests soon after joining the armed fighters. Matilda Olkinaitė's brother Elijas was among the resisters. After the massacre of his family near Panemunėlis, Elijas and his newlywed wife Liza had been living in the Kovno Ghetto. By the end of 1942 Elijas had joined one of the Kaunas underground groups and undertook increasingly dangerous tasks, including bringing weapons into the ghetto and maintaining contacts with friendly Lithuanians. In November 1943, Elijas said goodbye to Liza and left the ghetto with a small group in an attempt to reach an anti-Nazi partisan group known to be operating in the eastern forests. She never saw him again but was later told by his surviving comrades that Elijas had been killed in the spring of 1944: "He died by accident. A partisan squad, where he served, was [assigned] to a Belarusian village. At night, on the way back from the task, [he] said the password. The sentinel shot Ilia [Elijas] either because he didn't hear the password, or because it had been changed. He was severely wounded and passed away by the morning."[143]

Regardless of the difficulties in establishing itself in the Kaunas region, the Jewish underground continued to assemble weapons in several caches within the ghetto and trained for battle in at least seven locations. The group operated a radio receiver which provided a source of news about the situation on the front.[144] In the fall of 1943 the Kaunas resisters encountered another problem. With the help of an intermediary from the Lithuanian anti-Nazi underground, Yellin received a message from Gesa Glazer (Glezerytė, known by her guerilla

---

142 Ginaitė-Rubinsonienė, *Atminimo knyga*, 114.
143 Liza Lukinskaya interview (see citation above, Chapter 3). Sara Ginaite-Rubinsoniene's memoir relates that four fighters made it to the Death to Occupiers group in the Rudniki forest. She notes that "L. Olkinas was wounded not far from the partisan base in unexplained circumstances." This must be a reference to Elijas. Ginaitė-Rubinsonienė, *Atminimo knyga*, 126.
144 Levinson, *Shoah*, 261.

name, "Albina"), a veteran of the prewar Kaunas Communist underground and an emissary from the LCP Central Committee in Moscow who had parachuted into Belarus to help consolidate the Soviet-led partisan units. Glazer invited Yellin to Vilnius for consultations. He decided to make the dangerous journey and after two weeks of talks in the Vilna Ghetto, both of them returned to Kaunas to organize the armed underground. Despite skepticism from the local Jewish partisans, Glazer, who considered herself authorized by the LCP to give orders, insisted that the Kaunas group should cease efforts to reach the anti-Nazi fighters in their Rudniki (Rūdninkai) base and instead establish themselves in the vast forests of the Augustów region south of the city. Glazer's plan proved a deadly fiasco in view of the long distance to this destination in occupied Poland and insufficient arms for the partisans. In October and November 1943, eighty people slipped out of Vilijampolė: according to the Kovno Ghetto underground reports, forty-three were killed and eleven arrested by the Gestapo. Partisan Sara Ginaitė-Rubinsonienė claimed that only three of the seventy-one Kaunas fighters made it to the designated staging area; the others were either killed or captured and sent to the Ninth Fort.[145] Soon after, the Soviet partisan leadership permitted the Kaunas fighters to pursue their preferred route to the Rudniki forest.

One of the notable achievements of the Jewish underground in Kaunas was the escape of sixty-four prisoners of the Ninth Fort who had been tasked with the removal and cremation of the corpses from the site's mass graves, part of the Nazis' Operation 1005 intended to hide evidence of their crimes. On the night of Christmas 1943, all sixty-four prisoners, including the arrested underground members of the Kovno Ghetto, fled the fort after three weeks' meticulous preparation. The inmate Pinia Karkinovsky performed the most difficult work, utilizing primitive tools to drill holes in the steel doors of the prison. Historian Aya Ben-Naftali notes that this was the only example of a successful escape of an entire company of Jewish forced labor. Thirty-six of the escapees were soon recaptured and killed, but the others managed to reach safety (at least temporarily). Some of the escapees slipped into the ghetto where they composed a memorandum outlining the murders and cover-up operations at the fort. The

---

145 Šarūnas Liekis, "Jewish Partisans and Soviet Resistance in Lithuania," in Gaunt, Levine, and Palosuo, *Collaboration and Resistance during the Holocaust*, 469; cf. Sara Ginaitė-Rubinsonienė, *Atminimo knyga*, 117–120. Also, Eckman and Lazar, *The Jewish Resistance*, 65–66. A detailed account of the "failure of the Augustovo plan" is in Alex Faitelson, *Heroism and Bravery in Lithuania 1941–1945* (Jerusalem: Gefen, 1996), 192–202.

head of the Council of Elders and the Kovno Ghetto police hid the men until they could be smuggled out to the forests in the east.[146]

Of all the Litvak resistance movements, the one which emerged from the Vilna Ghetto has garnered the most worldwide attention and admiration. The Vilna fighters constituted the first Jewish resistance organization originating in the ghettos. During meetings in December 1941 surviving members of the Zionist youth movement Hashomer Hatzair decided that active resistance was the only response in the face of the mass murders of Vilna Jewry. The inspiration for battle was the uncompromising Ghetto Manifesto issued by the then twenty-three-year-old poet Abba Kovner, which was read at a gathering of Zionist groups, disguised as a New Year's Party, on the evening of December 31, 1941. The text, dated for the following day, is one of the most stirring resistance documents of the period:

> *Let us not go like lambs to the slaughter!*
> Jewish youth, do not believe the perpetrators. Of the 80,000 Jews of the "Jerusalem of Lithuania" only 20,000 have remained. We saw how they tore from us our parents, our brothers and sisters.
> Where are the men, hundreds of whom were kidnapped by the Lithuanian "Chapunes"?
> Where are the naked women, and the children, driven away on the horrible Provocation night?
> Where are the Day of Atonement Jews?
> Where are our brothers from the second ghetto?
> All those forced from the ghetto never returned.
> All the roads of the Gestapo lead to Ponar, and Ponar is death!
> Throw away illusions. Your children, husbands, and wives are all dead.
> Ponar is not a camp—everyone was shot there.
> Hitler has plotted to murder all the Jews of Europe. The Jews of Lithuania are doomed to be the first in line.
> *Let us not go like lambs to the slaughter!*

---

146 Aya Ben-Naftali, "Collaboration and Resistance: The Ninth Fort as a Test Case," in Gaunt, Levine, and Palosuo, *Collaboration and Resistance during the Holocaust*, 378–379. There is bitter disagreement on the portrayal of the escape and other aspects among some of the members of the Kaunas underground. The account of Aleks Faitelson in *The Truth*, and other venues, has been challenged by Sara Ginaitė-Rubinsonienė in her review of Faitelson's *Nepokorievshisya: Letopis' evreiskogo soprotivleniya* (Tel Aviv: n.p., 2001) in the *Yearbook of Lithuanian History* 2 (2001): 282–287, and in her "Memorandum to the Ninth Fort Museum in Kaunas" of July 2002 (copy provided to the author by Prof. Ginaitė-Rubinsonienė).

True, we are weak and helpless, but the only answer to the hater is resistance!

Brothers! Better fall as free fighters than live at our murderers' mercy! Resist! Resist to the last breath.

The 1st of January, 1942, Vilna, in the ghetto.[147]

Kovner was born in Sevastopol and, as the surname indicates, descended from a family of Litvaks who traced their origins to Kaunas. In 1926 the Kovners moved back to Lithuania where they settled in Vilnius, then Polish Wilno, where Abba attended the Hebrew gymnasium. Abba became a leader within the aforementioned Hashomer Hatzair. He considered himself a "citizen of Vilna" and was enthralled by its history, frequently referring to the founding legend of the city under Grand Duke Gediminas in the fourteenth century. When war broke out in September 1939 and transformed his beloved Vilnius, Kovner was already a published poet. Unlike some of his fellow Zionists, Kovner did not take the opportunity to leave for the USSR and was in Vilnius when the Germans arrived on June 24, 1941. In July 1941, as the wave of kidnappings of Jewish men intensified, Kovner and some of his friends found refuge at the Dominican Convent of the Little Sisters about six kilometers outside the city. In December 1941 Kovner left the nuns and entered the ghetto determined to join his people and organize a Jewish resistance movement. Anna Borkowska, the mother superior who had sheltered the Jews, later carried hand grenades under her habit to the Jewish fighters in the ghetto.[148]

The FPO, the organized armed resistance movement within the Vilnius Ghetto, was founded on January 21, 1942, bringing together the major political trends of prewar Jewish Vilnius: Socialist Zionists, right-wing Revisionist Zionists, Communists, and Bundists.[149] The group chose as its leader Yitzhak Wittenberg, a Communist, calculating that he would be useful in future dealings with the Soviets, a logical consideration given that ghetto inmates, including Jacob Gens, pinned their hopes for the survival of Lithuania's Jews on a Soviet victory. Josef Glazman, the well-liked deputy ghetto police commissioner, and

---

147 As translated by Dina Porat in her *The Fall of the Sparrow*, 71. See the extensive discussion of the dramatic background leading to Kovner's speech on pages 57–75.

148 See ibid., 3–56 for Kovner's early years and his refusal to leave Lithuania in the spring of 1941.

149 Arad, *Ghetto in Flames*, 234–238.

Abba Kovner joined Wittenberg in the leadership. The primary goals of the FPO were to organize mass resistance against any attempt to liquidate the ghetto, sabotage German industrial and military activities, and join the anti-fascist partisans' and Red Army's fight against the Nazis. An important underground group which became a rival of the FPO was the Second Struggle Group led by Yechiel Scheinbaum which comprised about two hundred members.[150] Gens, in his own fashion, coexisted with the underground, torn between conflicting emotions, his obligations to the ghetto as expressed in the policy of slowing down the destruction of its populace, and the desire to resist when "the end was near." The ghetto chief was aware of the hidden weapons and training which Kovner and the others utilized in preparation for a final showdown with the Germans.[151]

In June 1942, the FPO began to plot active military operations. Their first plan was to attack a German military train, but they lacked the necessary hardware. The "paper brigade," where Abba Kovner had found a position, assisted in the collection of explosives and munitions.[152] Vitka Kempner (who was to marry Kovner) and Rozka Korczak, two Polish-born young Jewish Zionists who had escaped to Vilnius in 1939 and had joined the FPO, assisted in putting together an explosive device (essentially a pipe bomb). On July 8, 1942, Vitka and three other FPO fighters slipped out of the ghetto and headed for a location along the train tracks leading out of the city. The group was armed with pistols and grenades; Vitka carried the bomb under her jacket. The plan worked: the explosion knocked the engine off the tracks, derailing the train. The Germans fired back, killing one of the attackers, a girl whom Kempner had brought with her who was likely the very first FPO fighter killed in action.[153] This operation is considered the first of its kind, carried out long before any substantial Soviet partisan movement had begun in Lithuania.

The FPO and other underground groups had succeeded in keeping their activities secret until the spring of 1943, when events took a particularly ominous turn. The mass killings in Paneriai resumed after the abolition of the

---

150 On the Struggle Group, see ibid., 264–270; cf. Lester Eckman and Chaim Lazar, *The Jewish Resistance*, 21–26.
151 Porat, *The Fall of a Sparrow*, 79–80, 103–104.
152 Fishman, *Book Smugglers*, 96.
153 Judy Batalion, *The Light of Days: The Untold Story of Women Resistance Fighters in Hitler's Ghettos* (New York: HarperCollins, 2020), 248–251. A slightly different version is in Porat, *Fall of the Sparrow*, 94–96.

Švienčionys and Belarusian Ghettos. The Warsaw Ghetto Uprising of April 19–May 16, 1943, resonated among the young FPO fighters. German repression intensified as Soviet partisans gained a foothold in eastern Lithuania and western Belarus while, at the same time, more Jews headed to the forests in the hopes of joining the Soviet partisans. The fifteen-year-old Yitzhak Arad and a group of friends in the Švenčionys Ghetto had organized a clandestine cell to steal and adapt arms from an arsenal of old weapons where they had been put to work by the Germans. When Gens arrived in Švencionys and informed the people that, because of increasing Soviet partisan activity in the region, they would be transferred to Vilnius and Kaunas, Arad's group decided to flee and join up with the Soviets who were already active in the Naroch forest in northwestern Belarus. On the night of March 5, 1943, the twenty-one young fighters slipped out of the town armed with two revolvers and a rifle. Arad described his elation and sense of purpose:

> Carefully, we went through the barbed wire to the open field west of the ghetto. I had a strange sensation as I went through the fence. Something fateful was taking place in my life. From this moment on my comrades and I were not humiliated Jews under Nazi rule, sentenced to annihilation, but free fighters who had joined the millions fighting the Nazi beasts on all fronts. I touched the revolver hanging at my belt and the grenade in my pocket. I felt great confidence. The ghetto was behind us, the forest and the unknown before us.[154]

The group eventually found the Soviet partisans' Chapayev unit commanded by Fyodor Markov, but Arad was later transferred to the Žalgiris group, a predominantly Russian and Lithuanian outfit.

In Vilnius events were coming to a head. On July 8, 1943, the Gestapo captured the Polish Communist Wacław Kozlowski who was a liaison with comrades in the Jewish underground. Under torture Kozlowski gave up Wittenberg's name, although it is uncertain whether the Germans uncovered the FPO at this point. The next day, Bruno Kittel issued Gens an ultimatum which created panic among the populace: Wittenberg's surrender or the destruction of the ghetto. It became clear in the hyper-charged atmosphere that the majority of the ghetto preferred the surrender of one man to the death of thousands, a situation which

---

[154] Yitzhak Arad, *The Partisan: From the Valley of Death to Mount Zion* (New York: Holocaust Library, 1979), 95.

threatened civil strife if the underground chose not to give up their leader. Faced with an impossibly cruel choice, Wittenberg appointed Kovner to the command and turned himself in. As the partisan leader headed to the ghetto gate to accept his fate, he walked through a crowd of weeping ghetto inhabitants and the salutes of some members of the underground. Overnight the Communist, who had been distrusted by some of his political rivals, became an icon of Jewish courage. Wittenberg died in Gestapo custody on July 17, 1943, most likely by suicide: his surrender and death became one of the most painful and controversial episodes in the history of the Vilna Ghetto resistance, not least of all for Kovner, who agonized about the tragedy for years afterward.[155]

It was the misfortune of the FPO that the group was unable to follow in the steps of the heroes of the Warsaw Uprising who had inspired them. On September 1, 1943, German and Estonian police began a mass roundup of Jews for deportations to Estonia. There was no question that this was the beginning of the end for the ghetto. Kovner decided to call for popular resistance, distributed another fiery manifesto, and gathered his FPO force for a last stand. The ghetto did not respond to Kovner's appeal. A brief shootout erupted when Scheinbaum opened fire prematurely and was killed by the Germans. On September 4, Kovner convened a meeting in which he admitted that there would be no battle in the ghetto, opening the way for the fighters to leave the city and head for the forests. Messengers from Markov and Glazman, who had left for the forests earlier, urged the underground to join their unit. By mid-September most of the Vilna underground departed the ghetto. Vitka Kempner was one of the most active of the FPO in organizing safe passage from the ghetto to the partisan bases.[156] The Paper Brigade's FPO members, Sutzkever, his wife Frydke, and Kaczerginski, made the difficult trek to the Naroch partisan base nearly two hundred kilometers northeast of Vilnius.[157] Other members of the Vilna Ghetto resistance left for the nearer Rudniki forest.

The Jews who made these fraught journeys in 1943 and 1944 found themselves in an indispensable, but at time contentious, relationship with the Soviet

---

155 Porat, *The Fall of the Sparrow*, 106–127; cf. the slightly different version in Arad, *Ghetto in Flames*, 387–395.

156 Porat, *The Fall of the Sparrow*, 138–144; Batalion, *Light of Day*, 250–251; Arad, *Ghetto in Flames*, 381–387.

157 Fishman, *Book Smugglers*, 111–120. For the early days in Naroch see also Eckman and Lazar, *The Jewish Resistance*, 40–44.

partisans who had been operating in Lithuania since 1942. Soon after the invasion, small groups of Party activists were sent from the LCP Central Committee in Moscow to reconnoiter the situation in Lithuania and begin the organization of a partisan movement in close cooperation with Belarusian comrades. The connection with Belarus was critical since the consolidation of the pro-Soviet Lithuanian partisan movement proceeded slowly: in mid-summer 1943 Party records show that the group numbered but 377 partisans, mostly escaped POWs and local Communist activists with limited armaments and few possibilities for effective combat.[158]

The Lithuanian Special Archive in Vilnius contains files compiled in 1944 and 1945 revealing the demographic breakdown of the anti-Nazi Soviet partisan units which operated under the jurisdiction of the LCP.[159] A total of 3,910 Soviet guerilla fighters were listed as having served in Lithuania during at least part of World War II including 35.5% ethnic Lithuanians, 37.8% Russians, and 17.3% Jews, with the remainder composed of other nationalities.[160] A quarter of these partisans were members of the Communist Party or the Komsomol. A list of the units of the Vilnius Brigade (the nomenclature for the Rudniki groups commonly used in Soviet sources) compiled in December 1944 showed that of 587 persons under the command of Marijonas Miceika, 8% were Lithuanians, 22% Russians, and 58% Jews. The Jewish fighters in particular were the youngest among the partisans: four were younger than eighteen, the majority in their late teens to early twenties. Most of the Jewish partisans lacked military training.

There were six predominantly Jewish groups of anti-fascist fighters embedded within three partisan brigades (Vilnius, Kaunas, Trakai). Archival sources give us a picture of their relative strength in numbers and combat capability:

(a) The Avengers under Kovner, who had moved from Naroch to Rudniki and whose core was the FPO, numbered 108 fighters, including 32 women in January 1944, virtually all Jews. Their armaments consisted of four

---

158 Šarūnas Liekis, "Soviet Resistance and Jewish Partisans in Lithuania," *Polin* 25 (2013): 334.

159 The most exhaustive study of the Soviet partisan movement in Lithuania based primarily on Party and partisan documents in the Lithuanian archives is Rimantas Zizas, *Sovietiniai partizanai Lietuvoje 1941–1944 m.* (Vilnius: LII, 2014).

160 Zizas, *Sovietiniai partizanai*, 249–251. The figures differ according to chronology and sources, but it seems safe to assume that the overall number never exceeded four thousand.

IMAGE 5.16. Left: Group portrait of partisans from the Vilna ghetto, ca. 1942-1944. (United States Holocaust Museum Photo Archives #33721. Source: Hebrew University of Jerusalem, Copyright Unknown.) Right: Yitzhak Arad (1926-2021), historian and chairman of Yad Vashem, who joined the partisans in 1943 from his hometown of Švenčionys.

IMAGE 5.17. Soldiers of the Red Army's Sixteenth Lithuanian Riflemen's Division in battle near Oryol, summer 1943. (Source—public domain.)

machine guns, 24 automatic weapons, and 34 Russian rifles. Between September 1943 and July 1, 1944, the unit derailed five trains, destroying 25 railroad cars and inflicting Axis casualties (reportedly including 200 Italian troops). The Avengers also eliminated two villages sheltering "white Polish" [Home Army] forces, disarmed five village militia groups, confiscating twenty rifles and other weapons, and cut 320 telegraph-telephone lines.

(b) The Towards Victory group labored under more difficult conditions. The group's official list counted 119 persons, of whom 106 are listed as Jews, comprising 75 armed fighters, but with only one automatic weapon, 15 rifles and the same number of pistols.

(c) The Death to Fascism unit, initially included 55 fighters armed with one machine gun, twelve rifles and ten pistols. In time, the unit expanded to 60 partisans with improved weaponry: two machine guns, 24 automatic weapons, 56 rifles, and 20 pistols. Ten fighters were reported killed. Jews made up two-thirds of the group, the rest were mostly Russophones.

(d) Death to Occupiers was founded in Rudniki in late 1943 by the Smirnov group of thirteen partisans affiliated with the Margiris faction. By early 1944 an influx of more than 300 Jews from the Kovno Ghetto transformed this unit into one of the largest partisan forces in the Rudniki forest. In mid-July 1944, the group listed 278 registered members.

(e) The Struggle Group which established itself in Rudniki in November 1943 under Aron Aronovich, consisted of 78 people, of whom 58 were listed as Jews, outfitted with twelve rifles and ten pistols. In January 1944, E. Liubetsky took over command.

(f) The Free Lithuania faction, led by escaped POW Russian officers, was established in early November 1943. According to an August 1944 official register, of the 96 partisans on the list, there were 55 Jews, 31 Russians, and one ethnic Lithuanian.

In the Rudniki forest Jews and Soviet POWs comprised the great majority of partisans throughout the war. By the summer of 1944, Jews made up a majority of partisans in the Vilnius Brigade, more than a third of the fighters in the Kaunas Brigade and about one-fourth of the Trakai Brigade.[161]

The relative strength of the pro-Soviet partisan movement and the national distribution of the fighters reflected the country's geography. Lithuanians

---

161 Ibid., 207–209; Liekis, "Jewish Partisans": 469–476.

predominated in the west. Here the partisan movement had little success, especially in the Suvalkija region. Small Jewish partisan groups sought but failed to secure a foothold in the vast Kazlų Rūda forest west of Kaunas.[162] The more numerous Soviet and Jewish guerillas in eastern Lithuania operated in a region with a majority of Polish and Belarusian speakers, interspersed with settlements of ethnic Lithuanians. Local outreach efforts never succeeded in attracting significant numbers of the local rural populace to the cause. The "Death to Occupiers" group of the Kaunas Brigade managed to attract only nine locals.[163] Very few Poles joined the Soviet-led movement: only eight were included in the Adam Mickiewicz group of ninety-five fighters (named after the most celebrated figure in Polish literature). Polish villagers were more likely to support the Home Army (Armia Krajowa), the most numerous and best armed anti-Nazi force in eastern Lithuania and western Belarus, which owed allegiance to Poland's government-in-exile in London and, understandably, viewed the Soviet ally of the Western powers with suspicion, if not outright hostility.

The Jews who fled to the forests to join the anti-Nazi resistance faced unique challenges both within and outside the encampments. From the Soviet leadership's point of view, the Jewish fighters, despite their contribution to the anti-Nazi movement, complicated the policy of "internationalizing" the partisan ranks which they considered essential for gaining support from the rural populace, the "sea" in which the guerillas swam (according to Mao's famous dictum). The central staff of the partisan movement in Moscow envisioned the creation of a mass movement uniting all nationalities under the leadership of the Communist Party, a goal that failed in eastern Lithuania and Belarus. As the front moved west, the LCP leadership sought to make the face of the partisan movement more representative by "distributing" Jews among different units, replacing their commanders, or moving the fighters to new locations.[164] Genrikas Zimanas (known as "Jurgis"), the LCP's de facto plenipotentiary charged with overseeing the Soviet underground in Lithuania, successfully pushed the Lithuanian Jews to abandon Naroch and transfer to Rudniki.[165]

The Jewish recruits within the broader Soviet partisan movement did not always receive the welcome they may have expected from their comrades in

---

162 Zizas, *Sovietiniai partizanai*, 226.
163 Ibid., 211.
164 Ibid., 213.
165 Ibid., 198.

arms. The commanders of the Soviet partisans were often reluctant to take in refugees from the ghettos and, when they did, demanded that they submit to units' discipline and, in some cases, rejected them if they did not bring weapons or valuables. Condescension towards the escapees from the ghetto was an oft-reported experience. In March 1944, Antanas Sniečkus, the head of the LCP, wrote to Zimanas about the criticism he had heard of Jews as ineffective soldiers, and also warned him to "be careful in employing people of Jewish nationality," because it was known to increase antisemitism in the ranks.[166] As a Jew, Zimanas was sensitive to the anti-Jewish bigotry among the partisans and the populace. In the summer of 1943, he penned a report admitting the problem, but singling out the Belarusian partisans who, he alleged, were "poisoned by antisemitic notions" and who often reportedly spoke of the Jews as if reading from a "Goebbels prayerbook."[167] There are credible reports of brutal, even lethal, attacks on Jewish partisans at the hands of their Soviet allies. One teenage escapee from the Minsk Ghetto confided to Belarusian Nobel laureate Svetlana Alexievich about his experience among the Soviet partisans, relating the murder of a sixteen-year-old "pretty Jewish girl" after she had become pregnant as a result of commanders who "took turns sleeping with her," this only one of the of killings of Jews in his unit.[168] According to historian Kenneth Slepyan, there is sufficient evidence to conclude that, taken as a whole, "antisemitism remained pervasive throughout the movement."[169] The rise of anti-Jewish sentiment during the war was noticeable not only among the non-Jewish populations of the Nazi-occupied territories of the East, but also in the Soviet rear, in part because the Kremlin no longer saw the struggle against antisemitism as a priority.[170]

While some Party functionaries believed that the Jewish fighters provoked negative reactions from the local populace, the failure to create a more represen-

---

166 Cited in ibid., 207.

167 Cited from Zimanas's July 16, 1943, report on the political and economic situation (ibid., 198–199).

168 See Svetlana Alexievich, "A Man's Story," in *Secondhand Time: The Last of the Soviets*, trans. Bela Shayevich (New York: Random House, 2016), 195–201.

169 Kenneth Slepyan, *Stalin's Guerillas: Soviet Partisans in World War II* (Lawrence: University of Kansas Press, 2006), 211; also see 147–149, 205–214. Cf. Kenneth Slepyan, "The Soviet Partisan Movement and the Holocaust," *Holocaust and Genocide Studies* 14, no. 1 (2000): 1–27.

170 As pointed out in Arkadi Zeltser, ed., *To Pour out My Bitter Soul: Letters of Jews from the USSR, 1941–1945* (Jerusalem: Yad Vashem, 2016), 19–20.

tative partisan force was in fact part of a larger problem. The anti-Nazi armed groups in eastern Lithuania confronted problems rooted not only in the difficult conditions of the German occupation but also in the region's long-standing national-political conflicts. Soviet POWs who had abandoned their farm jobs, as well as deserters from Ukrainian and Vlasovite collaborationist units, constituted a problematic element, some wandering the rural areas as bandits, others joining the partisans. Prone to violence against villagers with whom they had little in common, their behavior intensified anti-Russian sentiments, especially against the Old Believer settlements which were viewed as bases of Soviet power.[171] Security in the countryside deteriorated significantly after the summer of 1943, undermined not only by the growing activity of the partisans but also by the violence of rogue groups of escaped POWs, AWOL German soldiers, and local criminals. Neither the German nor the Lithuanian police forces ever entirely pacified rural Lithuania during the occupation. The village militias supported by the German and Lithuanian administration had significant popular support stemming from resentment at the general lawlessness and the requisitions exacted by the partisans. Further complicating the situation was the tendency of some Lithuanian-speaking villages to prefer the "Red partisans" as a lesser evil in comparison to the depredations of the Home Army units which often raided their homesteads, intensifying the decades of internecine rivalry which characterized the region's Polish and Lithuanian communities.[172] While there is evidence indicating that the Jewish and Soviet resistance movements encountered a friendly reception among some villagers,[173] this was hardly the norm in the Lithuanian countryside.

The well-documented conflicts between the Home Army and Jewish partisans added to the mix of clashing forces, a tragic example of which comes from the following deadly April 1944 encounter of two young fighters from different anti-Nazi camps. Yitzhak Arad described what happened as his party of Jewish partisans entered the house of a local woman "to wait out the daylight hours":

---

171 Zizas, *Sovietiniai partizanai*, 196–197. In the summer of 1941 German and Lithuanian authorities began the practice of assigning Soviet POWs to farmers as a solution to the labor shortage.

172 Well summarized in Liekis, "Soviet Resistance": 344–356. Cf. Saulius Sužiedėlis, "Vilniaus klausimas ir lietuvių-lenkų konfliktas ketvirto dešimtmečio krizės ir Antrojo pasaulinio karo kontekste," in *Lietuva ir Lenkija XX amžiaus geopolitinėje vaizduotėje*, ed. Andžej Pukšto, Giedrė Milerytė (Kaunas: VDU, 2012), 174–198.

173 See archival sources cited in Zizas, *Sovietiniai partizanai*, 215.

> The woman of the house was Polish. She and her two daughters seemed very upset at our appearance, which was not the usual reaction. Suddenly the door opened and a young man entered, a square Polish army cap on his head, captain's epaulettes, and a pistol in his officer's belt. His entrance was so sudden that we all remained rooted to our seats. He too was surprised but was the first to regain composure. He came to each of us, shook hands and turned to leave. I was nearest the door. I pointed my submachine gun at him and ordered him not to move. His unit of 300 [Home Army] fighters was temporarily camped a few kilometers away and he came to visit his mother and sisters every day. [We took the officer with us]. The following day in the forest we questioned the Pole about the Home Army and their collaborators in the area. At first, he refused to talk, but after rough treatment he broke down and told us a great deal about their activities. After intensive interrogation, the Pole was executed. He begged for mercy, but that did not help him.[174]

Contemporary pejoratives provide a sense of contempt between movements which ostensibly shared a common goal. In Jewish and Soviet parlance, the Home Army, the largest anti-German underground movement in Europe, were simply gangs of reactionary "White Poles." Not to be outdone, the Polish underground press came to refer to Communist partisan units as Bolshevik "gangs of saboteurs" (*bandy dywersantów*). The Vilnius region was reported to be "full of Soviet diversion gangs" in the summer of 1942. In another Polish underground press release of November 1943 Jewish partisans were described as "an organized element of the Communists in the forests."[175] Judeo-Bolshevik tropes persisted, but it should not be surprising that many Poles found it difficult to accept that the Soviet enemies, who had invaded their country in 1939 and then massacred much of the Polish officer corps, were now allies within "the anti-Hitlerite coalition."

The hostile and volatile environment in which they were forced to operate confronted the fighters with moral/ethical choices regarding the use of violence against the civilian population. The partisans' only reliable source of foodstuffs were the forced requisitions from the very people for whose freedom the struggle was being waged (at least according to the Party). The Lithuanian Soviet partisan Albinas Barauskas identified the question of "bread and guns" as the

---

174 Arad, *Partisan*, 161–162
175 See Adam Puławski, "Posrtrzeganie żydowskich oddziałów partyzanckich przez Armię Krasjową i Delegaturę Rządu RP na Kraj," *Pamięć i Sprawiedliwość* 2, no. 4 (2003): 271–300.

critical logistical problem facing the fighters.¹⁷⁶ The policy of what Slepyan has described as "organized looting" imposed hardships on the rural economies in the occupied territories, of which the Moscow leadership of the Soviet partisans were fully aware, and created a backlash among the people subject to requisitions.¹⁷⁷ Opposition to the confiscations was widespread: the peasants, it turned out, rarely gave up livestock and grain willingly to people they considered alien intruders.

A wave of German punitive expeditions (Operation *Sommer*) in August–September 1943 attacked suspected supporters of anti-Nazi partisans in eastern Lithuania, resulting in the burning of mainly Polish villages and the deportations of their inhabitants. On September 9, 1943, von Renteln informed Kubiliūnas that in the face of increasing partisan attacks on communications and transport, the Germans would employ collective punishment against civilians who failed to report on guerrilla activity in a timely fashion. When the German reprisals began to affect ethnic Lithuanian villages, the general councilors proposed the creation of "self-defense" units in place of the previous unarmed "night watch" patrols. In the fall of 1943 dozens of villages and small towns established militias to fight "banditry" and "Red partisans." In late October 1943, Zimanas reported to Sniečkus in Moscow that the people's anger at the behavior of rogue elements, which they linked to the partisan movement, was an even greater problem than the Germans and the Lithuanian police:

> [The people] do not know the partisans. Until now they have encountered only real bandits, who did not show their efforts against the Germans, but robbed, beat, raped, drank, and murdered.... They are afraid of us and often see the Germans as their defenders and protectors. The self-defense movement has achieved considerable success: around here, more and more villages are arming themselves.¹⁷⁸

The most violent clashes between the armed "self-defense" groups and anti-Nazi fighters occurred in the regions adjacent to the Rudniki forest, where the village militias resisted the partisans' efforts to requisition food. The case of the Lithuanian village of Daržininkai illustrates the complex interactions of the local

---

176 Albinas Barauskas, *Miškų frontuose* (Vilnius: Vaga, 1968), 171.
177 Slepyan, *Stalin's Guerillas*, 73ff.
178 Cited in Rimantas Zizas, "Vietinė savisauga (savigyna) Lietuvoje nacių Vokietijos okupacijos metais (1941–1944)," *Genocidas ir rezistencija* 1, no. 11 (2002): 84.

populace and the partisans. In mid-October 1943, the village militia opened fire on a group of Rudniki fighters who had come to demand supplies, killing their leader, Antanas Michalkevičius. Jewish partisans were not involved in the battle which followed, resulting in the burning of some twenty homes. There were no casualties, and the partisan force had to withdraw. The villagers rearmed and continued to operate. On February 15, 1944, the "Lithuanian partisan staff" sent a letter to the villagers, demanding that they disarm and "live together as Lithuanian brothers." Four days later the defiant villagers responded that they had been the victims of numerous robberies and refused to surrender. In May 1944, as the front approached and German power in the region visibly weakened, many of the village self-defense units began dispersing and giving up their weapons. The men of Daržininkai agreed to give up their arsenal on May 29, after which the partisans, including Jews from the Death to Fascism group, marched through the village in formation. Unfortunately, the peasants' troubles were not over: the next day, a Home Army unit attacked the village, beat the men and, according to one witness, "swept the place clean." But no one died in Daržininkai.[179]

It is difficult to precisely establish the extent of combat and civilian casualties in the Rudniki region during clashes between the popular militias and the partisans. In November 1943 Rudniki partisan leaders claimed that they had "disarmed" 124 members of the self-defense groups. On Christmas Eve 1943, five partisans from the Free Lithuania detachment, three Russians and two Lithuanian Jews, Mikhail Levin and Josef Milner, were killed in a firefight that defeated the Babrauninkai village militia. The more rigorous response of the Rudniki partisans beginning at the end of 1943 turned the tide against the village militias. Faced with the better-trained, armed, and motivated Soviet and Jewish fighters, many people became more cautious, particularly in view of the revenge that partisans threatened to exact if they continued the fight. In his letter to the Daržininkai villagers the partisan commander had warned the people that, if they did not submit, "you will perish together with your entire family. . . , only a cruel, sad picture of your village will remain, just as in Kaniūkai." At the end of the text was a postscript: "It should be clear to you. . . , no one takes in these

---

179 Rimantas Zizas, "Raudonųjų partizanų ir Pietryčių Lietuvos kaimų savisaugos ginkluoti konfliktai (Part One)," *Genocidas ir rezistencija* 1, no. 15(2004): 148–156.

dogs [the Kaniūkai villagers—S. S.], people are afraid that if they shelter them, the partisans will leave them without a roof."[180]

Kaniūkai (P. Koniuchy) was a settlement some forty-five kilometers south of Vilnius which, according to the population survey of 1942, had a mixed Polish-Lithuanian population of seventy-four households encompassing 374 people. The village was the object of the largest single operation of the Rudniki partisans against the self-defense forces in the region but is better known as the site of a massacre. Kaniūkai hosted a particularly active militia unit numbering as many as forty residents. In October 1943, the village fighters twice drove off a group of partisans who had tried to requisition food and warm clothing and, according to one postwar interrogation, killed two fighters from the Jewish Struggle Group. Other battles in the area between village self-defense and Lithuanian police forces interrupted food confiscations and killed several partisans. In reports to Moscow Zimanas described his Rudniki forces as desperately short of supplies. At daybreak on January 29, 1944, a detachment of an estimated 120 to 150 partisans attacked Kaniūkai and, after a forty-five-minute battle, destroyed the village. The Lithuanian police who rushed to the scene too late to engage the partisans found homes burning, most of the livestock slaughtered, and thirty-five villagers dead (mostly women and children).[181] Zimanas reported to Moscow two days later that a "joint unit of the Death to Occupiers, Margiris, and the General Staff special groups" had eliminated the most active [members] of the anti-partisan groups of the Eišiškės district, concluding: "The self-defense force has suffered numerous casualties. There are no losses on our part."[182] There were other such clashes. On April 12, 1944, units from the

---

180 Published in Rimantas Zizas, "Raudonųjų partizanų ir Pietryčių Lietuvos kaimų savisaugos ginkluoti konfliktai (Part Two)," *Genocidas ir rezistencija* 2, no. 16 (2004): 151–159.

181 The most thorough analysis of contemporary sources and postwar interrogations is Zizas, *Sovietiniai partizanai*, 464–494; also cf. his "Žudynių Kaniūkuose pedsakais," *Genocidas ir rezistencija* 1, no. 11 (2002): 149–165; cf. Chaim Lazar, *Destruction and Resistance: A History of the Partisan Movement in Vilna*, trans. Galia Eden Barshop (New York: Shengold, 1985), 173–175. For understandable reasons Soviet authors have either ignored the incident or tried to explain away the civilian deaths. For her part, partisan Rachel Margolis describes Kaniūkai as a "Nazi garrison" and provides an account of a huge battle which the partisans won "despite the enemy's superiority in numbers" (Rachel Margolis, *A Partisan from Vilna* [Boston: Academic Studies Press, 2010], 484, e-book). This description does not square with the voluminous evidence available in the archives of the Soviet partisan movement.

182 General Staff of the Lithuanian Partisan Movement (Zimanas) to Sniečkus, January 31, 1944, LYA, f. 1, ap. 1, b. 410, l. 173.

Rudniki partisans burned the village of Bakonoriškiai and surrounding settlements killing sixteen people, some of them civilians.[183]

Detractors of the partisans can find here an opportunity to besmirch the anti-fascist fighters, but it is important to understand the context of the violence. It would be specious to suggest that the unarmed people who died, the women and children in particular, were somehow less than innocent. To say this is not to suggest any equivalence between what happened in Kaniūkai, and the scale of the massive, singular crimes of the Nazis and their collaborators. As James Glass points out: "Partisan violence never produced indiscriminate consequences; it focused on specific ends." German violence, on the other hand, "destroyed anything in its way."[184] But it is also understandable that in 1944 the economically stressed people of the eastern Lithuanian countryside held a different view, caught as they were between the demands of the authorities and the confiscations of the anti-fascist partisans, which were often accompanied by violence, a problem throughout the western borderlands of the USSR.[185] The Soviet guerilla operations also had, at times, deadly side effects for the noncombatants. In June 1944, a German SS unit slaughtered the Lithuanian inhabitants of the village of Pirčiupiai as collective punishment for a Soviet guerrilla ambush of a group of German police, another reason for the people to resent the partisans. Even worse, after the anti-fascist guerrillas, the Home Army, and the Germans had left, there was still no respite from the lethal violence: tens of thousands died in the anti-Soviet guerilla campaign which followed the formal end of World War II. A precarious calm returned to the region only in the early 1950s.[186]

---

183 Rimantas Zizas, "Bakaloriškių sunaikinimas," in *Lietuva Antrajame pasauliniame kare*, ed. Arvydas Anušauskas, Česlovas Laurinavičius (Vilnius: LII, 2007), 489–506.

184 James Glass, *Jewish Resistance*, 83. The limited extent of partisan violence is also acknowledged by Zizas, who is otherwise critical of the Soviet resistance movement.

185 A well-sourced overview of the problem is in Alexander Statiev, "Soviet Partisan Violence against Soviet Civilians: Targeting Their Own," *Europe-Asia Studies* 66, no. 9 (2014): 1525–1552, although his extensive treatment of antisemitism and anti-Jewish violence in the ranks of the Soviet resistance (1537–1540) tends towards the apologetic.

186 On the postwar period, see below, Chapter 7.

Lithuanian Jews in the Red Army: The Sixteenth Division

The largest group of Jewish anti-fascist fighters from Lithuania did not go to the forests but confronted the Wehrmacht on the battlefields of the Eastern Front far away from their homeland. On December 18, 1941, the USSR State Defense Committee decided to form a Lithuanian Red Army division in the Moscow military district. The division was recruited from remnants of the former Twenty-Ninth Lithuanian Riflemen's Corps and refugees who had fled Lithuania during the German invasion. Jews who flocked to join the unit joked that it was designated as the "Sixteenth," since there were only sixteen actual Lithuanians in the division.[187] In fact, over a third of the division was Lithuanian, with Russians and Jews making up most of the remainder. The commanders were ethnic Lithuanian Communist generals: Feliksas Baltušis-Žemaitis (1942–1943), Vladas Karvelis (1943–1944), and Adolfas Urbšas (1944–1945). Jews comprised a third of the combat regiments and a majority of the engineering and political sections.[188] Jewish nurses made up a majority of the medical staff, more than 90% of whom were women.[189] More Jews served in the Sixteenth than in any other unit of the Red Army. Most reports indicate that interactions between the Jewish and Lithuanian soldiers, despite instances of antisemitism, were friendlier than relations between Jews and Gentiles in other Red Army units.[190]

The Soviet command threw the division into battle on February 21, 1943, at Alekseyevka, fifty kilometers southeast of Orel, where the unit suffered enormous losses. The division numbered nearly twelve thousand soldiers before it went into battle in Kursk in the summer of 1943. The news of the massacres of their families and friends back home greatly motivated the Jewish fighters who frequently volunteered for the most dangerous missions. On December 23, 1942, I. I. Draznin of the division's 156th Regiment wrote to Ilya Ehrenburg of his reaction to the Allied statement concerning the mass murder of Europe's

---

187 Justas Stončius, Hektoras Vitkus, and Zigmas Vitkus, *16–osios Lietuviškos šaulių divizijos kariai žydai: istorija ir atminimas* (Klaipėda: Klaipėdos universiteto Baltijos regiono istorijos ir archeologijos institutas, 2021), 17.

188 Ibid., 23.

189 Dov Levin, *Fighting Back: Lithuanian Jewry's Armed Resistance to the Nazis 1941–1945*, trans. Moshe Kohn and David Cohen (New York: Holmes & Meier, 1985), 61.

190 See the evidence in Stončius, Vitkus, and Vitkus, *16–osios Lietuviškos šaulių divizijos kariai žydai*, 58–74.

Jews ("this bestial policy of cold-blooded extermination") issued the week before:

> [W]e, Jewish fighters . . . [are] gathered to express our feelings regarding the declaration about the total liquidation of the Jewish population in Europe, in Hitler's Europe. At that time, our Lithuanian and Russian comrades expressed their protest separately against the atrocities of the fascist scum . . . we did not leave our dear ones just to save our own lives; we left in order to fight, in order to take revenge. Comrade Ehrenburg, convey to our high command that we are eager for battle and, like the day of salvation, we are awaiting the order to attack the Hitlerite monsters, to pay them back for everything—for the blood they have spilled, for the lives they destroyed, for the tears they caused old folks, for their shaming of our sisters.

At the end of his letter was a postscript to the famous writer: "Forgive me for my incorrect Russian language. I began studying it only in recent years."[191] The Litvaks who joined the Sixteenth Lithuanian Riflemen's Division of the Red Army may not have endured the logistical hardships of their partisan brethren in Rudniki, but they fought and died by the thousands in the war against Hitler.

Except for the Sixteenth Division, the Lithuanian Jewish resistance that went into the Lithuanian forests in 1942–1944 did not significantly affect major military operations, despite exaggerated claims in Soviet sources.[192] The total number of Lithuanian Jewish fighters probably did not exceed two thousand, less than 10% of all Jews in the partisan movement in occupied Soviet territory. But it would be wrong-headed to consider the contribution of the Jewish partisans purely in terms of military impact. The men and women who fought in the ranks were pioneers, and not just in their inspirational role as examples for future generations of Jews. Their combat experience and organizational skills proved invaluable in the coming struggle to establish a Jewish homeland. After the war, many former partisans and soldiers of the Sixteenth Division found their way to Palestine. They were joined by Abba Kovner whose writings inspired the troops during the 1948 Arab-Israeli War. On December 25, 1945,

---

191 Draznin to Ehrenburg, in Zeltser, *To Pour out My Bitter Soul*, 60–63.

192 For example, the claim that Soviet Lithuanian partisans killed fourteen thousand Germans and collaborators, and other inflated numbers in Povilas Štaras et al., ed. *Lietuvos liaudis Didžiajame tėvynės kare (1941–1945): dokumentų ir medžiagos rinkinys* (Vilnius: Mintis, 1982), 18.

after a long trek through Central Europe, Yitzhak Arad and fellow refugees ran the British blockade on the *Hana Senesh* and entered Mandatory Palestine. Arad joined the fight once again and rose to the rank of brigadier general in the Israeli Defense Force. The partisans from the ghettos could not prevent the annihilation of most of Lithuanian Jewry, but no one should question their contribution to the creation of the State of Israel.

PART THREE

RESPONSE, MEMORY, LEGACY

6.

Images of Blood: Perpetrators, Observers, Bystanders, Rescuers

Unlike the murders carried out in the industrial gas chambers of occupied Poland, the Holocaust in Lithuania attracted the attention of numerous observers in real time. News of the massacres spread quickly. Many bystanders had watched the police marching columns of Jews to the killing sites. There were eyewitnesses at the pits, especially in the provinces, so the first- and second-hand accounts related the unforgettable sights and sounds of the shootings to a wider public. Months after the killings, the gruesome reality of the mass graves continued presenting unavoidable reminders of the crimes, so the authorities undertook to protect the health of the public. On November 8, 1941, the Trakai district chief ordered the mayors of several towns to construct a 120 centimeter-high fence around the murder sites and to cover the grounds with lime, so that "people and animals" not disturb the mass graves.[1] The looting of the property of vanished communities, a widely reported spectacle, was a visually less egregious proof of mass murder, but one that troubled many observers. These unprecedented disasters evoked a range of reactions throughout society, ranging from revulsion at the brutality to satisfaction at the disappearance of troublesome neighbors. To some degree, the reactions to the mass murder of the Jews were linked to attitudes towards the Germans and to the shifting prospects of the war in the East, both of which underwent considerable change during the three years of the occupation.

---

1 Trakai district chief to the mayors of Žiežmariai, Semeliškės, and Eišiškės, November 8, 1941, LCVA, f. R-500, ap. 1, b. 4, t. 2, l. 794.

Political and Religious Authorities Welcome the Invaders

The rapid collapse of Soviet power at the war's onset enabled Lithuania's suppressed political and cultural elites of the First Republic to quickly reemerge as significant voices within the country, albeit with obvious limits to their ability to affect events. In addition to the reality of a new military occupation, the political elites faced divisions within the ranks: the mostly younger, radical elements in the LAF, and particularly the LNP, looked askance at the holdovers from the Smetona period, including former left-of-center politicians. Despite their differences, however, most leaders shared the spirit of the joyous crowds which celebrated the end of Communist rule and welcomed the German troops. At least initially, the leaders were able to address the public freely. In its first statement read on the radio and then published on June 24, 1941, the PG proclaimed the "restoration of a free Lithuania" in a solemn, if rather oddly worded statement: "The young Lithuanian State, facing the pure conscience of the entire world, enthusiastically promises to contribute to the construction of Europe on a new foundation."[2] The LAF, which announced the formation of the PG, was more explicit on the question of who would shape the future of the New Europe: "the Red Terror has been smashed by the courage and determination of the German army and nation," and thus had saved "European culture and civilization." The organization's activist leaders effusively welcomed Lithuania's new geopolitical realignment: "Long live friendly relations with Greater Germany and its Leader, Adolf Hitler."[3] The radical turn which began in Berlin in the fall of 1940 was now in full display for public consumption.

Caught in the euphoria of liberation from Stalinist terror, many of the supporters of the New Europe failed to appreciate the conundrum of offering themselves as junior allies to the Third Reich, although the real cost of their choices became apparent over time. Still others never acknowledged that the turn towards Germany had been a morally compromising proposition, let alone a political quagmire, an attitude evidenced in both contemporary messages and the postwar writings of the former LAF leader Kazys Škirpa,[4] as well as among the apologists for the LAF in the diaspora. Unlike Škirpa's cagey approach toward

---

2   "Atstatoma laisva Lietuva," *Į laisvę*, June 24, 1941, 1.
3   "Viskas Lietuvai," *Į laisvę*, June 24, 1941, 1.
4   Most notably in *Sukilimas*, the aforementioned memoir-cum-history, published in 1973 after Škirpa's retirement from the Library of Congress.

different constituencies, downplaying certain aspects of the LAF program, when necessary, the LAF-dominated regime went public in its embrace of the Third Reich. Even more vexing than the welcome to Germans as brothers-in-arms was the unabashed admiration that the LAF expressed for the ideology of its ally. The archives include a draft of a July 9 appeal from the Staff of the LAF directed to "Adolf Hitler, the Chancellor of Greater Germany." The message contained the usual grateful paeans to this "Great Creator of National Socialism" for liberation from the "hell of Jewish-international Communism." The writers also trumpeted the spurious claim of an LAF underground of 35,600 members, an insurgent force of some ninety thousand insurgents, as well as four thousand fallen LAF fighters. These sacrifices were intended to persuade Hitler that the Lithuanian nation was now "deserving of the restoration of our independent national state." The staff proposed that Hitler should appoint their leader, Škirpa, "the sincerest friend of the National Socialist German nation," to organize a Lithuanian volunteer corps which would be honored to fight alongside "the brave German army, inspired and strengthened by the noble ideals of National Socialism." The message was probably never sent, but the fawning idolization of the occupiers' world view is reflective of the authors' thinking which clearly placed them in an impossible quandary. The constant emphasis on an independent Lithuanian state, dramatically presented in the letter's final passage, as a "bequest [L. *testamentas*] to us from the [June] partisans," was in conflict with the authors' plea to the Führer: "We ask You, the Leader of the German Nation, to protect our country to be reconstructed in the spirit of National Socialism, and to respect our national aspirations."[5] No one at the time dared to point out that this kind of language was reminiscent of the speeches of the delegation of politicians and literati who had gone to Moscow to bring back "Stalin's sun" only a year before.

On July 11, 1941, Škirpa composed a list of political proposals that would form the basis (*Grundlage*) for a German-Lithuanian understanding/agreement (*Verständigung*) and which he planned to present to Hans Schütte, one of the colonel's German contacts in Berlin. The points were couched in diplomatic terms quite different from the overtly servile tone adopted by the LAF Staff and contained utterly unrealizable schemes for an expansion of Lithuanian territory

---

5   Lietuvos aktyvistų fronto štabas, "Didžiosios Vokietijos kancleriui Adolfui Hitleriui," July 9, 1941, Hoover Institution, Turauskas Collection, Box 5.

at the expense of Belarus, Poland, and even Latvia. The major points included a reference to National Socialism:

> The Basis for German-Lithuanian Understanding
>
> 1) Germany regards Lithuania as a free and independent state.
>
> 2) Lithuania recognizes the leading role of Germany in Europe and enters the German-led community of nations on the basis of equal rights with the others.
>
> 3) The following are the ties envisioned between Lithuania and Germany: a) an agreement on uniformity in foreign policy; b) a military alliance; c) close ties in transportation; d) an agreement on economic cooperation; e) cultural ties.
>
> 4) [To accomplish the above—S. S.]…, it is necessary to immediately transfer the government of the country to the newly formed Lithuanian government on whose friendly and loyal stance regarding Germany there can be no doubt. *This government is based on the Lithuanian Activist Movement which is very close to the valuable ideas of National Socialism* [my emphasis].

Aside from the ambitious territorial adjustments, Škirpa's proposals included the restoration of a Lithuanian army which would fight the "common foe in this war," a somewhat different offer from the volunteer corps proposed by the LAF Staff. To Škirpa's disappointment, no one in Berlin bothered to respond to his geopolitical fantasies.[6]

During its brief existence, the PG enjoyed significant confidence among the people. While the German military censors went to work within a few days of the invasion, they did not plant the antisemitic diatribes in the press nor the initial discriminatory laws against the nation's minorities.[7] Political leaders did nothing to discourage public expressions of anti-Jewish hatred; on the contrary, some continued to spout Judeo-Bolshevik themes. On July 2, 1941, the PG's minister of agriculture Balys Vitkus spoke on radio to the country's farmers about Lithuanian suffering "at the hands of Jewish-Bolshevik executioners" and

---

6 "Grundlagen der deutsch-litauischen Verständigung," July 11, 1941 (copy provided to the author by Liūtas Mockūnas and Alfred Erich Senn, also located at the Hoover Institution). In citing the document in his memoir, Škirpa, as one would expect, elided the sentence on National Socialism, as he did with other inconvenient passages when publishing extracts from the sources. See Škirpa, *Sukilimas*, 454–456.

7 See above, Chapter 3.

reminded his listeners of the German army's role in liberating European culture "from the threat posed by the Jews and their lackeys."[8]

The cultural and social influence of the Catholic Church was arguably unsurpassed by any other national body. The attitude of the clerical leadership largely mirrored the standpoint of the PG regarding the new political situation, albeit without the public endorsement of National Socialist values. The hierarchy were relieved at the collapse of the atheist Soviet regime in Lithuania and had reason to believe that the activities of the Church would suffer fewer restrictions under the Germans. While the occupiers generally refused to restore Church property seized by the Communists, and limited the activities of Catholic lay organizations, the clergy remembered the period as one in which "the Germans did not interfere in the affairs of the Church and did not obstruct pastoral work."[9]

The Church adopted a pragmatic approach to the new order which, to some extent, was not unlike the compromises it had accepted during the Soviet occupation. At that time, one of the country's leading prelate-politicians, Mykolas Krupavičius, had urged the faithful to adapt to Communist rule in areas which did not conflict with Church teachings, particularly regarding the rights of the working poor, a stance approved by the bishops. Krupavičius confided to an NKVD operative that in response to his parishioners' complaints about the regime's confiscations of their property, he had countered that Soviet Lithuania's limited sovereignty was far preferable to Nazi rule which would mean the end of the Lithuanian nation.[10] Nonetheless, the hierarchy's public pro-German statements and endorsement of the war against Bolshevism went considerably further than the accommodations made with the previous occupiers. On July 4, 1941, the highest-ranking churchman, Archbishop Skvireckas, Auxiliary Bishop Brizgys, and the general vicar of the Kaunas Archdiocese Monsignor Kazimieras Šaulys, broadcast on radio and disseminated in print a declaration which the country's metropolitan described in his diary as "corresponding to the wishes of the [unidentified] representative of Germany with whom [the text] had been arranged."[11] The Catholic leaders reminded the people that, in the face of

---

8   "Prof. Balio Vitkaus kalba, pasakyta liepos 2 d. ūkininkams per radiją," Į laisvę, July 3, 1941, 4.
9   According to Father Justinas Juodaitis as cited in Regina Laukaitytė, Lietuvos bažnyčios vokiečių okupacijos metais (1941–1944) (Vilnius: LII, 2010), 27.
10 Report of NKVD agent "Oscar" on conversations with Krupavičius in December 1940 and January 1941, LYA, f. K-1, ap. 10, b. 3, l. 78–83.
11 Skvireckas diary, in Brandišauksas, 1941 m. birželio sukilimas, entry of July 4, 1941, 275.

Bolshevik tyranny, "the eyes of the entire nation had been directed at Germany, and, in truth, the hopes of liberation were realized." The announcement praised the "sacrifices of the courageous German army and our patriotic youth... which opened a new life for our country." The prelates made clear who was responsible for saving the country and creating new opportunities for development, and also identified the beneficiaries:

> We must all get to work, gratefully trusting in the support of the German army which liberated us, and in the cultural support of the great German nation. The German army and nation are going forth to liberate Europe and the entire world from the threat of Bolshevism. So, dear kinsmen, let us all take up diligent and unified work to rebuild our land which had been plundered and destroyed by the Bolsheviks. The blessing of God, and the love of every Lithuanian for all Lithuanians... will lead to a beautiful future for our fatherland.[12]

A few days later, the EG reported that "Bishop Brizgys who occupies an essential position among the clergy, has been won over towards cooperation."[13] On July 11, 1941, Skvireckas and Brizgys added their signatures to a telegram thanking Hitler for Lithuania's liberation and promising to "struggle together against the Bolsheviks."[14] The Germans were keen to exploit the influence of the clergy to garner Catholic support for the war and to assuage the people's disappointment at Nazi reluctance to grant even a measure of political autonomy. The August 16, 1941 situation report of the EG noted approvingly the German authorities' "connections" with Bishop Brizgys "who had issued instructions for the priests that they were to abstain in the future from any political activity," and that "accordingly we can ascertain that the clergy will, at the moment, behave with total loyalty."[15]

The Nazis rarely punished priests for transgressions against the occupying authorities, and there was no systemic persecution of the clergy with one notable exception: the attack on Polish Catholics in the Archdiocese of Vilnius which led to the deaths of nearly a hundred priests and nuns.[16] This brutality

---

12 "Kauno Arkivyskupijos vyresnybės pareiškimas per radiją," Į laisvę, July 4, 1941, 1.
13 "Ereignismeldung 14 v. 6.7.1941," in Ereignismeldungen, 85.
14 Laukaitytė, Lietuvos bažnyčios, 42.
15 "Ereignismeldung 54 v. 16. 8.1941," in Ereignismeldungen, 302.
16 Laukaitytė, Lietuvos bažnyčios, 31, victims listed on pages 274–295.

was unsurprising, considering, as noted above, the Germans' sharply different treatment of the Polish and Lithuanian populations during the war.

Regardless of their internal political differences, the majority of what constituted the Lithuanian national leadership during the initial period of the occupation considered the decision to align their hopes for independence with Germany's victory in the East as a rational, inevitable geopolitical choice. They could not, however, avoid responding to the violence swirling around them. The ministers were clearly discomforted, if not distressed, by the killings of Jews and local Lithuanian Communists that erupted during the first days of the war. The men of the PG could clearly see that not only their German allies, but their own Lithuanian supporters, were carrying out the killings. During one of the cabinet meetings of the first week, the Minister of Communal Economy Vytautas Landsbergis-Žemkalnis, astounded by the beatings of Jews which he had observed in the streets, turned to Interior Minister Šlepetys demanding an explanation on why the latter had been unable to halt the violence. In a defensive retort, the colonel explained that under the wartime conditions it was difficult to restore the police force that had been disbanded by the Soviets. The justice minister recalled that Landsbergis's outburst "weighed heavily on all of us."[17] The cabinet recorded, albeit not publicly, their disassociation from Klimaitis and other rogue partisan elements and issued reprimands against lawlessness and vigilante justice.[18] During its final meeting on August 5, 1941, the PG claimed that it had lacked the power to prevent the massacres of the Jews in the provinces. One of the ministers claimed years later that historian Zenonas Ivinskis, an active member of the anti-Soviet resistance and the PG's liaison with the Germans, reacted with shock at the massacres and repeatedly urged the government to publicly condemn and disassociate itself from the violence against the Jews. But no such pronouncement was ever issued.[19] The responses to this challenge differed, although evasion in the face of the obvious criminality

---

17 Mečislovas Mackevičius, *Atsiminimai* (Vilnius: Lietuvos rašytojų sąjungos leidykla, 1997), 68–69. This is likely a reference to the aforementioned cabinet meeting of June 27, 1941.

18 See above, Chapter 3. There is also the claim that two Lithuanian generals had privately rebuked Klimaitis, as noted in Budreckis, *The Lithuanian National Revolt*, 63.

19 As reported by the PG's minister of industry Adolfas Damušis, in "Profesorius Zenonas Ivinskis," *Į laisvę* 54 (1972): 19. Damušis's account evades the issue of public disapproval by insisting that the PG did "everything in its power which was possible under the circumstances," a questionable assertion given the cabinet's antisemitic policy proposals.

of the lethal anti-Jewish violence was, with few exceptions, the dominant refrain evident in the written record of the observers themselves.

In early July, Jakov Goldberg, a former lieutenant in the Lithuanian army, a participant in the wars of independence, and a political prisoner of the Soviets during the first occupation, requested an audience with Jonas Matulionis, the PG finance minister, hoping for an intercession on behalf of the Jews. According to Goldberg, Matulionis explained his attitude, presenting it as a "moderate" alternative," given the passions of the moment:

> The Lithuanians are divided on the Jewish question. There are three main views: according to the most extreme view all the Jews in Lithuania must be exterminated; a more moderate view demands setting up a concentration camp where Jews will atone with blood and sweat for their crimes against the Lithuanian people. As for the third view? I am a practicing Roman Catholic; I—and other believers like me—believe that man cannot take the life of a human being like himself. Only God can do this. I have never been against anybody, but during the period of Soviet rule I and my friends realized that we did not have a common path with the Jews and never will. In our view, the Lithuanians and Jews must be separated from each other and the sooner the better. For that purpose, the Ghetto is essential. There you will be separated and no longer able to harm us. This is a Christian position.

In response to Goldberg's request to use his influence to stop the pogroms and shootings, Matulionis reportedly answered: "The wrath of the people is so great that there is no way to stop these acts. When you leave the city for good and confine yourselves to the Ghetto, things will quiet down.... I am speaking frankly with you."[20]

Goldberg and Rabbi Šmuelis Sniegas (Shmuel Abba-Snieg), who had once served as the Jewish chaplain of the Lithuanian army, then turned to General Stasys Raštikis (1896–1985), their former superior whom they knew from their days in the service, hoping for an intervention. The PG's defense minister, the popular former commander of the Lithuanian army (1935–1940) and husband of Smetona's niece, was arguably the best-known official in Ambrazevičius's cabinet. The Germans recognized the general's popularity among the Lithuanian public and had hoped to install Raštikis as the head of a council under their control in order to stymie any LAF attempts to establish an independent

---

20 Goldberg's account is in Tory, *Surviving the Holocaust*, entry of July 8, 1941, 13.

government. On the face of it, Raštikis seemed a perfect candidate: his relationship with Škirpa was known to be contentious. The General had studied at a German military academy in the early 1930s and had dealt with high-ranking German officers since his stint as prewar army commander (he briefly met Hitler in April 1939). On June 27, 1941, the RSHA flew him to Kaunas with Gräfe who was supposed to be the general's handler. But the plans to utilize Raštikis fell apart as the general showed no enthusiasm for his designated role as German puppet.[21]

In 1957 Raštikis published his version of what happened when Goldberg and Sniegas appealed to him for help. The story, as seen through the eyes of one of the First Republic's leading figures, is instructive:

> The Kaunas Jews who were to be driven into the ghetto chose a delegation which wanted to meet with the Lithuanian Provisional Government. Since they were unsuccessful in meeting with the other members of the government, the delegation contacted me by phone via my adjutant. I agreed to speak with them and received the delegation in my apartment. . . . Both delegates were old acquaintances of mine, Rabbi Sniegas . . . as well as the lawyer Goldbergas, a former Jewish soldier . . . who had been a political prisoner [under the Soviets—S. S.]. Both complained mostly about the horrendous living conditions in the ghetto. Almost prophetically, I directed their attention to the fact that their most urgent problem was not the difficulty of life in the ghetto, but the inhuman tendencies of National Socialism which could lead to the nearly complete liquidation of the Jews. The delegates completely agreed with my opinion. I explained to them that the Lithuanian Provisional Government was completely helpless and, just as with many other issues, could do nothing on the question of the Jews. It was not necessary to do much convincing; they themselves knew this perfectly well. Since I did not have any dealings with the Gestapo, I promised the delegates to raise the question in a sense favorable to them with the German military leadership. The delegates were satisfied and grateful for my determination to help on this matter.
>
> On the next day I went to visit General [Robert] von Pohl [commander of FK 821—S. S.] and proceeded to explain to him that the

---

21 On the German machinations, see Dieckmann, *Besatzungspolitik*, 1:432–436, Krausnick and Wilhelm, *Die Truppe*, 349–350; USSR Situation Report of July 4, 1941, *Ereignismeldungen*, 76. Raštikis kept a low profile in the PG and gradually withdrew from most public activities. The Soviets had deported his three young daughters and their grandparents to Siberia during the June 1941 roundups, and he may have feared that a more prominent political role might lead to retaliation against his family.

Lithuanian government and society were genuinely concerned about the German actions against the Jews. General von Pohl said that he could do nothing about this problem but suggested that I speak with General [Franz] von Roques [commander of Army Group North Rear Area]. I asked that von Pohl come with me to visit the general and he agreed so both of us drove to the former building of the Lithuanian general staff which were now the headquarters of General von Roques who received us in the offices of the former Lithuanian defense ministry. The participants in the discussion included me, Lieutenant General von Roques, Major General von Pohl, the chief of staff [Lieutenant] Colonel [Arno von] Kriegsheim,[22] the general's [von Roques's] adjutant. The adjutant took down our entire conversation by stenograph.

I began to tell them about the dissatisfaction and concern of the Lithuanian government and society about the German-initiated persecution and extermination of the Jews. The host [von Roques] interrupted my report: "You (Lithuanians) are not yet accustomed to this, but you will have to be..."

"No, Sir, General, we will not get used to this," I answered.

"But it is the Gestapo and not the German army which is doing this," they said.

"Yes, Sir, general," I replied, "but my government and I believe that during wartime, and especially here in Lithuania which is now closest behind the lines of military operations, the military administration should have the most, if not the highest, power."

Both generals grinned a bit. I continued speaking: "So, this is why I have come to you, Sir, to express all of our dissatisfaction and concern in this matter and to request that you cease the actions against the Jews which are continuing in Kaunas and in the provinces." I could tell that the general [von Roques] did not like my declaration, but he quickly recovered and began to justify himself by saying that [the killings] were within the jurisdiction of the Gestapo and the military was unable to have any great influence on this matter. General von Pohl agreed that this action by the Gestapo was unnerving the local Lithuanians. After a lengthier conversation, the host declared that he would inform the higher authorities about my statement and the mood of the Lithuanians. With this, the conversation ended. I was satisfied that I had achieved at least this much. But during our farewell, General von Roques unex-

---

22 Kriegsheim was among several German staff officers who shared Raštikis's concern about the killings and are on record expressing "discomfort over the murder of the Jews" (cited in Dieckmann, *Besatzungspolitik*, 1:236). Kriegsheim's "defeatist" attitudes led to his removal from his position as chief of staff in May 1942, followed by his dismissal from the Wehrmacht and the SS.

pectedly threw as if cold water on my head. When he took his leave and shook my hand, he said: "General, do not trouble yourself and don't worry, this whole action will soon be done with." So, it appeared to me that the highest-ranking military leader in Lithuania was speaking not about stopping the action [against the Jews—S. S.], but about its conclusion.

I accompanied General von Pohl in his car to Vienybė Square and from there walked to the Lithuanian government office. I was unable to report back any good news to the prime minister [Ambrazevičius]. . . . After a few days Rabbi Sniegas visited me again. All I could tell him was that I had tried to win some concession from the German military authority, but from what I could learn, there was little hope for optimism.[23]

There is no reason to doubt that the depicted meeting took place. Von Rocques's statement about the military's supposed inability to affect the massacres of the Jews is consistent with his complaint to von Leeb recorded in the latter's daily report.[24] But readers of Raštikis's four-volume memoir, an important historical source to be sure, will note the flaws inherent in the genre: there are occasional factual errors, a self-serving spin on political events, as well as the author's tendency to embellish his accomplishments. The account is self-serving, the conversations strike one as stilted and grandiose. And yet the description of the entire episode reveals a troubling ambiguity, characteristic of much of the political elite's response to the carnage, including the reluctance to acknowledge the fact of native participation in the killings of the Jews. It is characteristic that in the paragraph prefacing Raštikis's account of the meetings, one finds the archetypes of Jewish disloyalty and Lithuanian innocence, even as the minister recognized the evil around him:

> One of the most unpleasant questions of that time was the Gestapo-initiated actions against the Jews, particularly the mass shootings of the unfortunate Jews. This was a terrible business. Lithuanians had for centuries lived amicably with the Jews, and Lithuania had never seen such "pogroms" which earlier marked Poland, Austria-Hungary and even Russia itself. During the years of independence, the Jews themselves

---

23 Stasys Raštikis, *Kovose dėl Lietuvos*, vol. 2 (Los Angeles: Lietuvių dienos, 1957), 305–307. A visit by Raštikis on July 14, 1941, is noted in the daily journal of the intelligence unit (Abt. Ic) of Army Group North (NARA, Records of German Field Commands: Rear Areas, Occupied Territories and Others, Microcopy T501, Roll 2, Frame 752), indicating that contacts between Raštikis and German military officials were not unusual.

24 See above, Chapter 3.

called Lithuania the "small America" in which they prospered quite nicely. But during the first year of the Bolshevik occupation, it turned out that the Jews behaved very badly, and together with the Russian Bolsheviks inflicted many extremely painful wounds on the Lithuanians. And yet the Lithuanian nation did not intend to exact revenge on them, and to adopt the measures which the Germans had implemented, that is, to exterminate all the Jews. The action carried out by the Gestapo aroused the indignation of all decent Lithuanians, but no Lithuanian could halt this campaign. The Lithuanian Provisional Government was helpless and strictly disassociated itself from the German action.[25]

Thus, Raštikis portrayed his conversation with von Roques as a unified official stance against anti-Jewish violence, although this contradicted his own acknowledgement that other members of the government had declined pleas to assist the Jews. (It should be noted that the Jewish delegates visited the general in his apartment, rather than at the ministry.) There is no mention in this account of the rampant antisemitism described by his colleague Matulionis. In any case, none of the expressions of concern behind closed doors had any observable effect on Nazi policy, the extent of collaboration, or the spread of anti-Jewish hatred. The only recorded objection expressed directly to German authorities concerning the Jews was contained in a November 14, 1942, memorandum to von Renteln and Kubiliūnas's advisory council penned by former president Grinius, and two former ministers of agriculture, Krupavičius and Jonas Aleksa. Most of the text protested German colonization policies and the confiscation of non-German farms, stating only in passing, "The Lithuanian nation cannot assent to such methods [against farmers—S. S.], just as it cannot assent to the methods which have been applied against Lithuania's Jews."[26] The consequences for the signatories were not dire: Krupavičius and Aleksa were taken to Germany and held under house arrest; the aging Grinius was allowed to retire to a farm in the country. The memorandum has been lauded as a courageous act of defiance, but it was hardly a ringing protest against genocide.[27] Raštikis's trans-

---

25 Raštikis, *Kovose dėl Lietuvos*, 305. This passage contradicts the positive image of Raštikis found in Tory, *Surviving the Holocaust*, entry of September 28, 1943, 485–486.
26 Arūnas Bubnys, *Vokiečių okupuota Lietuva (1941–1944)* (Vilnius: LGGRTC, 1998), 355–356.
27 For example, Viktoras Petkus, "Pilietinės drąsos memorandumas. 1942–ieji. Lietuva," bernardinai, November 1, 2015, https://www.bernardinai.lt/2012-11-19-pilietines-drasos-memorandumas-1942-ieji-lietuva/.

parent balancing act involving unreconcilable elements became the standard for later apologia among much of Lithuania's political elite and among the LAF's postwar apologists: hand-wringing empathy for the victims, helplessness in the face of the carnage, accusations suggesting that Jews had brought on their misfortune by their pro-Bolshevik behavior, protestations of Lithuanian innocence, and emphasis on Germans as the sole perpetrators.

The response of the Catholic hierarchy to the persecution and mass murder of the Jews constitutes one of the thorniest problems in the history of the Church. The August 16, 1941, EG report provided the German view of the Church's stance regarding the Jews: "The position of the priesthood regarding the Jewish question is entirely clear. Bishop Brizgys has also forbidden all the priests from engaging with the Jews in any manner whatsoever." According to the EG, Brizgys had turned away Jewish delegations who had asked that he intercede with the German agencies. The document also noted that Jewish conversions to Catholicism had not yet been a factor, partly because the clergy were suspicious of such requests believing that Jews came to them "not because of religious reasons but because of the advantages connected with this."[28] Whether Brizgys publicly encouraged priests to shun Jews in need goes to the heart of the question of the Church's moral stance towards the victims of the Holocaust. The bishop has denied issuing such instructions arguing that he had no canonical authority to do so, and it is clear that on some occasions he received Jewish representatives, both during the initial days of the invasion and in the later period of the Nazi occupation.[29] There is evidence that, at the very least, he was aware of rescue attempts by nuns and priests in Kaunas. The case of Bishop Brizgys illustrates the political arrangement that confronted Lithuania's religious leaders under the Germans and the contradictions which ensnared them. Unlike the German and Lithuanian institutions implementing the policies of the occupation, the hierarchy had no say in the administration of the Jews, but the Church's social prestige was considerable. In several cases, bishops acknowledged the egregious violations of the teachings of the Church against murder and theft but, aside from notable exceptions among the rank-and-file clergy and several admonitions by individual bishops, the hierarchy's public

---

28 *Ereignismeldungen*, August 16, 1941, 306.
29 See Metropolitan Skvireckas's diary excerpts above, Chapter 3; also, Tory, *Surviving the Holocaust*, 312ff. Although the account in the August 16, 1941, USSR Situation Report may be exaggerated, one cannot fully rely on Brizgys's memoir.

stance in the face of anti-Jewish persecution was marked by caution. The behind-the-scenes approach negated most of the potential influence which the hierarchy might have exerted to turn the faithful away from participating in anti-Jewish violence.

The equivocal attitude of the metropolitan Juozas Skvireckas is recorded in his diary: concern at the violence against the Jews coinciding with stereotypes gleaned from Judeo-Bolshevik mythology. During the invasion and insurrection, the archbishop did not venture out from his mansion, since "everywhere there is fear that some maddened Jew could fire a shot in ambush."[30] Skvireckas took at face value reports of "a real battle of the Jews against the Germans and Lithuanians." His diary replicates antisemitic tropes, thoughts on Jews as particularly sadistic, and contains favorable references to Hitler and *Mein Kampf*. But the same Skvireckas, on learning of the Lietūkis killings, sent emissaries to intercede, albeit unsuccessfully, with the commandant of Kaunas.[31] On July 11, Skvireckas read the daily newspaper and noted what he described as the "terrible order against the Jews" announced by the Kaunas commandant and the city's mayor and copied the entire text to his diary.[32] On the same day a Jewish delegation visited the archbishop's assistant. The metropolitan described the meeting:

> The Jews attempted to seek intercession and even visited Bishop Brizgys who explained to them that the Jews probably are aware of the Catholic clergy's attitude about the Jews, but if the priests tried to publicly speak out in favor of the Jews, they could be lynched themselves. It is obvious that not all Jews are guilty, but the guilty ones have brought down Lithuanian society's hatred on all the Jews. The Jews should understand that at this moment, there is no benefit for them in forcing their way into the Lithuanians' midst, that it would be better for them to quietly remain alongside the Lithuanians, that it will be more tranquil for them, say, in Panevėžys or Šiauliai, where there have been no excesses against them, rather than in Kaunas, where at least 8,000 Jews have arrived from all different regions.[33]

---

30 Skvireckas diary entry for June 29, 1941, Brandišauskas, *1941 m. birželio sukilimas*, 272.
31 For more on this see the account above, Chapter 3.
32 Diary entry for July 11, 1941, in Brandišauskas, *1941 m. birželio sukilimas*, 284. The reference is to the announcement of the ghettoization of Kaunas Jews dated July 10, 1941, as published in "Kauno Komendanto ir Kauno Miesto Burmistro įsakymas," *Į laisvę*, July 11, 1941, 4.
33 Ibid., 284.

The minutes of the Lithuanian Bishops' Conference on August 6–7, 1941 recorded the hierarchy's decision, in view of the fact that "Jews, Russians and the followers of Bolshevism have been barred from public life, to demand that private Catholic schools be allowed to be established." The bishops also considered the "problem of Jewish Catholics" and decided to "write an appropriate letter to the government, interceding on behalf of Jews baptized before June 22, 1941, so that they would not be driven into the ghetto." The Bishops' Conference met again on October 7–8, 1941. One of the points on the agenda referred to the Jews: "H. E. [His Excellency] Bishop Brizgys informed us on today's conversation on the Jewish question with the First General Counsellor General Kubiliūnas from which it became apparent that the Germans had reserved for themselves the exclusive right to resolve the Jewish question."[34]

The pastoral letter of Bishop Justinas Staugaitis to the faithful of Telšiai diocese issued on July 12, 1941, remains, as of this writing, the episcopate's sole known official public warning against violence directed at the Other during the initial period of the occupation (which in the context of the then prevailing situation could only have meant Jews, Russians and accused Communists):

> When the Red Army overran our country and introduced the Bolshevik order, we did not need to look for activists in Russia: Bolshevism, unfortunately, was carried out by Lithuanians themselves. . . . Let us not also forget, that every human being, whether one of our own or an outsider, whether friend or foe, is the same child of God, that is, our brother. If he is suffering, it is our duty to help him as much as we can . . . [The criminals should be prosecuted—S. S.] by organs of public authority. . . . God keep you from revenge and licentious violence.[35]

Witnesses reported that in September 1941 during a pastoral visitation to Linkuva, the bishop of Panevėžys Kazimieras Paltarokas preached a sermon condemning "radical activists who had soiled their hands with Jewish blood."[36] Two sources claim that the bishops had forwarded a memorandum protesting the slaughter of the Jews, but this remains unconfirmed and is contradicted by a 1976 letter from Brizgys to Domas Jasaitis, a doctor who had sheltered Jews in Šiauliai. Brizgys maintained that the hierarchy had not issued any "decrees"

---

34   Both documents published in Laukaitytė, *Lietuvos bažnyčios*, 240–245.
35   Staugaitis letter of July 12, 1941, LVIA, f. 1671, ap. 5, b. 63, l. 16.
36   Laukaitytė, *Lietuvos bažnyčios*, 108.

on the matter of the Jews but had taken steps to encourage and even organize rescue efforts.[37]

As the massacres in the countryside intensified during August, some members of the elite became concerned about the effects of the genocide on the reputation of the Lithuanian people. On September 19, 1941, Archbishop Skvireckas recorded his recollection of a meeting with the former acting head of the PG who came to see the metropolitan on an urgent matter:

> I was unable to guess what these important matters were, but Bishop [Antanas] Karosas quickly noted that Dr. A[mbrazevičius] wanted to talk about the Jews. As it turned out, the former prime minister of the Provisional Independent Government had come to propose some sort of action on the problem of the murders of the Jews. Well, as it is becoming increasingly obvious, the Germans want to place the entire blame on the killing of the Jews on Lithuanians themselves, the Lithuanian partisans. The partisans are so enraged and set against the Jews that they strive to participate in the shooting of the Jews and even sign up to do so voluntarily. The Germans are filming the shootings, and in these films the Lithuanian partisans with yellow markings are prominent. Dr. A. has seen one such execution himself in which Lithuanians indeed participated, maybe having received some more beer mixed with whiskey. The shootings are done without any court proceedings, and it is not clear under whose orders. With the end of the war and with some sort of [sic] English victory, the Lithuanians could receive a very large accounting for these massacres, since there will not be any evidence that they did not do this and are not the ones at fault; thus, [Dr. A proposed—S. S.] to proclaim a protest against these killings which would be signed by the most famous people in Lithuania, such as the former President of Lithuania Dr. [Kazys] Grinius and myself as the Archbishop of Kaunas....
>
> On the question of whether there will be evidence that Lithuanians did not approve of the massacres, I said that the priests on more than one occasion have already spoken out against them and have fallen into disfavor with the Germans, that I had already spoken out against the massacres which are contrary to Christian morality through representatives of the Red Cross and made efforts that this attitude of mine would be known to the partisans' staff, that I had written a very serious letter

---

37 As claimed by Brizgys in his *Katalikų bažnyčia*, 123 and by Vincentas Borisevičius during his interrogation by Soviet security in 1946. Cf. Brizgys to Domas Jasaitis, November 25, 1976, as published in Dalia Kuodytė and Rimantas Stankevičius, eds., *Išgelbėję pasaulį ... Žydų gelbėjimas Lietuvoje (1941–1944)* (Vilnius: LGGRTC, 2001), 112.

concerning Jewish Catholics and persons of mixed Jewish marriages, that the bishops will find a way to inform world opinion, in their own way, as to what they think of the killings and who are the true culprits. I added that even among the partisans there are people openly resisting those who force them to be murderers. I mentioned to him that hardly anyone will believe what the Germans are proclaiming for purposes of propaganda, since they lie too insolently, and I pointed out that [my] conversation with Reichskommissar [Hinrich] Lohse which was published in the newspaper was all an invention from A to Z.[38]

Skvireckas evaded the call for such a historic public protest with an additional argument by remarking that while it was proper for political leaders like Grinius to make such statements, a religious leader must stay clear of political matters and avoid actions that "needlessly bring German hatred against the entire Curia."[39] But as historian Valentinas Brandišauskas has noted, Skvireckas, "did not avoid other statements on public issues, especially if they concerned the struggle against the evils of Communism."[40] In March 1942 Skvireckas penned a letter of protest to Reichskommissar Hinrich Lohse opposing the closure of the humanities and theological faculties of the University of Kaunas but in an obsequious style that gratefully acknowledged the Germans' "liberation of small nations from the Judeo-Bolshevik yoke."[41]

The hierarchy was careful to take notice of the occupation's anti-Jewish regulations and circulated the appropriate information to the clergy, for example, on the issue of accepting Jewish converts into the Church. Contrary to initial German reports, a number of "quick Jewish baptisms" were recorded in the summer and fall of 1941, doubtless inspired in part by the desire of the converts to escape the death squads and assisted by the lax attitude to canonical rules on the part of accommodating priests. There is no reliable data concerning the number of such opportunistic conversions, but several have been documented.

---

38 Copy of notes from the Archive of the Kaunas Curia [Kauno Arkivyskupijos kurijos archyvas], provided to the author by Dr. Arūnas Streikus. A more detailed and critical analysis of Skvireckas's attitude towards the Jews is in Valentinas Brandišauskas, "Holokaustas Lietuvoje: istoriografinė situacija ir pagrindinės problemos," *Lietuvos Katalikų mokslo akdemija. Metraštis* 14 (1999): 140–150.

39 From the above cited excerpt in Skvireckas's notes.

40 Brandišauskas, "Holokaustas": 143–144.

41 Letter of the Archbishop of Kaunas and Metropolitan Juozapas Skvireckas to Lohse, March 21, 1942, published in Laukaitytė, *Lietuvos bažnyčios*, 262.

Some were doubtless unreported by priests who did not want to create a paper trail, a phenomenon soon noted by the authorities. In November 1941 the Lithuanian Security Police chief of Panevėžys demanded that Bishop Paltarokas immediately provide a list of all "Israelite" converts, but, in this case, the diocese refused, citing a lack of records.[42] Nevertheless, responding to pressure from the authorities, in March 1942 Msgr. Kazimieras Šaulys reminded the deacons of the Kaunas Archdiocese not to baptize adults without episcopal permission, making clear the purpose of this caution: "Furthermore, on this occasion it is necessary to remind you of the instructions of the civilian authorities forbidding inhabitants, thus also the clergy, from associating with Jews." Two weeks later the monsignor reasserted this warning, adding: "For reasons known to everyone, persons of Jewish nationality are subject to the rules which apply to prisoners of war. Civilians are prohibited to associate with them in any way. The clergy of the diocese are warned to strictly observe this prohibition."[43] In any case, many clergy, including Bishop Brizgys, ignored both the letter and spirit of the various regulations concerning contacts with the Jews and, despite the strictures, some priests continued baptisms of Jews.

In Lithuania, authenticating one's religious affiliation could be of critical importance to Jews who sought to evade the authorities, especially to young people born during the interwar years. The First Republic's government did not, as a rule, require civil registry, but rather paid the clergy of the respective confessions to provide documentation confirming marriages and births; thus, the signatures of priests and rabbis were crucial to affirming one's identity. (Compulsory civil registry was introduced in August 1940 after the Soviet annexation of Lithuania.) False birth and/or baptismal certificates for young Jews in hiding were potential lifesavers.

In general, the hierarchy sought to persuade the police to allow the Church itself to discipline priests who ran afoul of the regulations of the ZV and police. For example, the pastor of Alsėdžiai, Vladislovas Taškūnas, protested the killings of Soviet activists and Jews in sermons and had attempted to intercede on behalf of the victims. He refused to hear the confession of one of the local killers. Taškūnas was arrested in June 1943 after being denounced for sheltering

---

42 Laukaitytė, "Katalikų bažnyčia bažnyčia Lietuvoje 1941–1944: požiūris į žydų genocidą ir krikštą," *Lituanistica* 70 (2007): 7.

43 LCVA, Kazimieras Šaulys to the Deaconate, March 20, 1942, and April 8, 1942, f. 1671, ap. 5, b. 134.

IMAGE 6.1. German and Lithuanian police officials at a conference in Kaunas, 1942. Vytautas Reivytis is seated in the first row, fifth from left.

IMAGE 6.2. A member of the Lithuanian auxiliary police, who has just returned from taking part in the mass execution of the local Jewish population in the Rašė Forest, auctions off their personal property in the central market of Utena. (United States Holocaust Memorial Museum Photo Archives #25736. Courtesy of Saulius Beržinis. Copyright of United States Holocaust Memorial Museum.)

a Jewish girl in the parish rectory. After considerable efforts from the hierarchy on his behalf, the priest was released, but as canonical punishment for violating the restrictions on "political activity," was assigned three months of confinement in a monastery and then transferred to lesser duties.[44]

The moral confusion that afflicted the attitudes of churchmen towards the destruction of the Jews can also be gleaned from their contorted debates on the disposition of Jewish property, evident in the records of several deaneries (L. *dekanatas*)[45] in which the issues were raised amidst disagreements and "difficult discussions." Father Jurgis Jasukaitis stated the obvious to a conference of priests in Šiauliai in July 1942: "It is no secret that in this war a great tragedy has befallen the Jewish nation, which has been murdered, while the property left behind is being distributed among Germans and Lithuanians." He noted the abundance of goods in black markets, many of which were acquired through the "persistent and even envy-driven robbery of Jewish property, and by the misappropriation of the possessions of the deportees [to the USSR—S.S.]."

Since most of the Jewish property owners were already dead, the question turned to restitution. Jasukaitis's convoluted solution would be of interest to ethicists. Partisans who had fought honorably against the Soviets were entitled to reasonable compensation from properties seized, although those who had "grabbed too much, should have the duty, according to their means, to assign something to support the poor, or other charitable purposes, even in the absence [sic] of the owner." Jasukaitis's attitude was harsher towards those who joined the partisans "to rob Jewish property, rather than for love of country, or shocked by the Red terror." These were the culprits, according to the priest, "who had robbed the most Jewish belongings" and thus should be warned to "assign to charity a substantial part of what they had taken." In sum, robbers could be given partial absolution by turning over ill-gotten gains to the poor. In the discussion following this presentation the monk Bernard opined that "it is difficult to decide who should receive the property left behind by the Jews," but then added: "If the Germans are misappropriating this property, it is better for us, because it is they who are taking the responsibility for their actions."[46]

---

44 Laukaitytė, *Lietuvos bažnyčios*, 31, 181, 273. Cf. the reference to the pastor of Alsėdžiai below.
45 A Church administrative unit below that of a diocese, usually consisting of several parishes.
46 From the records of the conference of the Šiauliai deanery of July 12, 1942, as cited in Brandišauskas, "Holokaustas": 148–149.

Father Alfonsas Keturakis explained his own pastoral tactic in dealing with the problem at a meeting of the Krakiai deanery:

> What is to be done with the property of the thousands of Jews looted by the people? One should make restitution. But the question arises: to whom? To the church, the state or in terms of [the principle of] *piis causis*? I would do the following: I would ask the penitent, did he take the object out of extreme necessity, just to live, are he and his family in tatters or do they walk barefoot? So, such a person does not need to do restitution, but he should understand that he has done a bad thing, and his penance should be to pray, for the fatherland, for peace, for the Holy Father, and even for the Jews. Actually, I would ask these same Jews: what is to be done with the property left behind? I think that they would all say, let those who have nothing, or who live in complete poverty, let them use our property.[47]

In January 1943 Lithuania's bishops sent a message to the faithful: "With ever greater impudence the property which had been rightfully acquired by persons of non-Lithuanian nationality is being stolen. This shows terrible contempt for Christian morality." The hierarchy admonished the people that "such behavior denigrates and insults our nation," concluding that "We must be just to all and remember the rule: do not do to others what you do not wish done to you."[48] But the stern warning did not specifically mention the murdered Jews, although some Catholics may have made the connection. In the context of this later period of the occupation, the bishops may also have been referring to the abandoned homesteads of deported Polish farmers who fell victim to the German colonization drive in Lithuania.[49]

---

47   As quoted in ibid.: 149–150.
48   Bishops' letter, January 1943, LCVA, f. 1671, ap. 5, b. 65.
49   On the expropriation of Jewish property see the account and documents in Valentinas Brandisauskas, "Lietuvos žydų turto likimas Antrojo pasaulinio karo metais," *Genocidas ir rezistencija* 1, no. 15 (2004): 86–107.

A Priest among Perpetrators:
Father Zenonas and the Twelfth Battalion

A few Lithuanian clergy, with Bishop Teofilius Matulionis (1878–1962) at their head, proposed to take up missionary work among Christians in the East who, in their view, had been decimated by decades of atheistic Soviet rule. The German authorities the German authorities opposed Catholic missions in the occupied territories.[50] However, the men of the so-called Lithuanian Self-Defense Battalions (L. savisaugos batalionai, Germ. Schutzmannschaften, LSD) sent to the German-occupied areas of Belarus and western Russia were another matter and here the Church eventually found some grounds for pastoral work. The LSD which eventually numbered some twenty battalions with an estimated eight thousand men was based on the model of the TDA units established during the first weeks of the invasion.[51] In popular slang, they were often derided as "self-strangling" (savismaugos) battalions, a play on the term "savisaugos" (self-defense), that is, oppressing their own people. The Second LSD Battalion was renamed the Twelfth in the fall of 1941.

In December 1941 Metropolitan Skvireckas was shown a letter from an officer of the Twelfth LSD Battalion, which had been stationed in Minsk since early October 1941, urgently outlining the problems of the Catholic "Lithuanian soldiers and civilians." The men had no one to administer to their "spiritual needs," especially in view of the approaching Christmas season. Skvireckas authorized Rev. Zenonas Ignatavičius (1909–1975) to take up the challenge. Ignatavičius's status in Minsk was initially uncertain: he had no formal agreement with German or Lithuanian police authorities. It was only in September 1942 that the commander of the Kaunas LSD district approved Ignatavičius and five other priests as chaplains to the Lithuanian battalions in the field.[52]

Ignatavičius's diary of his time in Belarus is the only eye-witness account of its kind by any of the assigned priests, a valuable source given the nature of the operations conducted by the men assigned to his spiritual guidance.

---

50   See the interesting study of Regina Laukaitytė, "Lietuvos bažnyčių misijos okupuotose SSSR srityse 1941–1944 m.," *Lituanistica* 63 (2005): 1–14.

51   See above, Chapter 3.

52   Details on the appointments of the chaplains are in the statement of the LGGRTC, "Dėl kunigo Zenono Ignatavičiaus veiklos nacių-sovietų karo metais," dated May 14, 2019 (copy of the document provided to the author by the LGGRTC).

6. Images of Blood | 427

IMAGE 6.3. German officers review a Lithuanian militarized police battalion in Vilnius. (Source—public domain.)

The Twelfth LSD Battalion commanded by Major Antanas Impulevičius had already carried out massacres in Lithuania during the summer of 1941. The unit gained a reputation as prolific executioners, their outrages well known to the local authorities and Belarusians, the knowledge eventually spreading from a select few to a wider circle of people back home in Lithuania. While stationed in Minsk, Impulevičius's force of nearly 450 men reported to Major Franz Lechthaler who commanded the Eleventh German Reserve Police Battalion which consisted of 326 militarized police.[53] The German and Lithuanian police battalions, along with Belarusian auxiliaries, reportedly killed more than fifty thousand Jews, Soviet POWs, and alleged Communists and participated in the hanging of dozens of persons during the peak of the massacres between mid-October 1941 and the end of the year. The Twelfth was almost certainly the unit which, together with Lechthaler's men, massacred an estimated three to four thousand Jews on October 27–28, 1941, in Slutsk, provoking the infamous report of Heinrich Carl, the district commissar, who was appalled by the brutality of the

---

53 Christian Gerlach, *Kalkulierte Morde: Die deutsche Wirtschafts- und Vernichtungspolitik in Weissrussland 1941–1944* (Hamburg: Hanburger Edition, 1999), 612.

IMAGE 6.4. Prewar photo of Major Antanas Impulevičius, who later commanded the 2nd (12th) LSD Battalion during the German occupation of Lithuania and Belarus.

operation.[54] A statistical overview of nearly twenty Belarusian locales in which men of the Twelfth are known to have been active indicates that the Lithuanian unit was responsible for more than a third of the deaths during the period in question. The killings abated after November 1941, but the battalion continued both anti-partisan operations and the guarding of POW camps, activities which continued to result in civilian casualties, including the murder of Jews, albeit on a smaller scale.[55]

On December 21, 1941, Ignatavičius left for Minsk. His arrival coincided with a period of relative calm and the priest found a place as pastor of SS. Simon and Helen, a Belarusian Catholic parish. He celebrated three Masses on Christmas morning; the third one, to the gathered "Lithuanian civilians and soldiers," held for him special significance: "I thought that this was the first time the Lithuanian religious hymns resounded at SS. Simon and Helen's Church in Minsk. . . . This was deeply emotional for me." Ignatavičius's joy was short-lived. The next day the parish organist informed him of a gruesome discovery: "in

---

54 The circumstances of the operation and Carl's report are in Christopher Browning, *Ordinary Men*, 19–25. An account of the Slutsk massacre based on postwar interrogations of the Lithuanian battalion members is in Alfredas Rukšėnas, "Kauno Tautinio darbo apsaugos, 2-ojo pagalbinės policijos tarnybų bataliono karių kolektyvinė biografija" (PhD diss., Klaipėda University and Lithuanian Institute of History, 2013), 187–191.

55 An operational history of the Twelfth Battalion is in Andriejus Stoliarovas, "Lietuvių pagalbinės policijos (apsaugos) 12–asis batalionas," *Karo archyvas* 23, no. 1 (2008): 263–315; cf. Alfredas Rukšėnas, "Kauno 2-asis pagalbinės policijos batalionas ir gyventojų žudynės Baltarusijoje," in *Holokaustas Lietuvoje 1941–1944 m.*, ed. Arūnas Bubnys (Vilnius: LGGRTC, 2011), 424–469.

woods outside Minsk they found the body of my fellow priest Father Hlakauskas [Glochewski] riddled by Gestapo bullets."[56] After some effort, Ignatavičius acquired a military uniform which one of the soldiers managed to make into an apparently legitimate chaplain's garb. As he spent more time among the men, the priest became disheartened by the moral quagmire in which the battalion operated, recording in numerous entries the alcoholism and misbehavior of the troops. During a visit to headquarters after the New Year, he found the commanding officer drunk in bed. A lieutenant sitting nearby complained while gesturing to the collapsed soldier: "What's the purpose of being in the battalion? If I could, I would leave. The worst thing is that there's no order among us."[57] Weeks later, the priest overheard conversations among the enlisted men about their "great dissatisfaction with their drunken superiors," including Major Impulevičius, some joking that they would pay five marks for tickets to a show in which officers could be observed "in a sober state."[58]

But the reality was far crueler than simply indiscipline or lax morality. Ignatavičius recorded an impression as he walked near the church on an early January morning, making it clear that he already knew the worst: "I encountered Jews being convoyed from the ghetto. Upon seeing my military uniform, they raised their caps. It seems they are afraid since, in some places in Belarus, Lithuanian solders are shooting Jews in the towns."[59] A week later Ignatavičius returned to his native town of Vilkija to visit family. Before he left, he called on the local pastor, one Father Bikinas, and in a frank conversation expressed his forebodings about what lay in store: "The future of Lithuania is very dark. . . . If we just take this [past] summer, many bloody and terrible crimes have been committed by the children of Lithuania. May God stay His punishment against them!"[60] Three days later, Ignatavičius was back at Minsk train station, where he found "a huge crowd of Nazis." The priest struck up a conversation with a fellow passenger,

---

56 Zenonas Ignonis, *Praeitis kalba; dienoraštiniai užrašai. Gudija 1941–1944*, ed. Klemensas Jūra (Brooklyn, NY: Pranciškonų spaustuvė, 1979), 13–14.

57 Martynas Mažvydas National Library of Lithuania, Rare Books and Manuscript Section [Lietjvos Martyno Mažvydo Nacionalinės bibliotekos Retų knygų ir rankraščių skyrius], F223 "Kunigo Zenono Ignatavičiaus 1942 metu žiemos dienoraštis 1942.I.3–1942.III.9," diary, January 3, 1942, 5–6. Transcribed from the original notebook by Egidijus Saulius Juodis.

58 Ibid., February 28, 1942, 21.

59 Ibid., January 3, 1942, 6.

60 Ibid., January 12, 1942, 16.

a Lithuanian officer whom he thought an "honorable man," and invited the soldier to spend the night at the local rectory. His guest told Ignatavičius that he was troubled by a conversation with one of his men who had been on the train and had talked about his goal: "to kill some Jews whom he had seen and come to know, and then steal their valuables."[61]

On Sunday, March 1, 1942, Father Zenonas delivered a Sunday sermon to the soldiers "on these troubled times." He emphasized St. George as a model soldier, "a knight without fear," explaining that "in raising this thought, I had in mind that the Lithuanian soldiers would no longer be forced to participate in this work of incredible cruelty—the shooting of the Jews. Maybe God will grant that they will understand my thoughts and will not carry out someone's terrible orders."[62] Whether the men understood the message is uncertain. On the following day, the distressed chaplain recorded a conversation in headquarters about "the attitudes of several (perhaps seven) soldiers": "They no longer wished to serve in the battalion and hadn't signed any promises to the Germans," he wrote, "but if it's about shooting Jews, that's OK, they will be the first to go ... among those assigned to guard the Minsk ghetto, no one is found who is sick or unable. You see, they can get some stuff there." In the same day's entry, he recorded what had happened outside his rectory:

> After about six in the evening continuous shooting resounded in the city. As it turned out, Jews were driven in groups out from the ghetto in various directions. Some of them were running away. The Germans, the Belarusian police and three men wearing Lithuanian uniforms (robbers!) were shooting at the escapees. I could barely stand to listen to our young sacristan's tale: a young Jewish boy, maybe about sixteen, had rushed in, white as a sheet, coatless, asking for a cloak. He did not get one and ran out; clearly, he had escaped from the ghetto. Many Jews lay dead in the street.[63]

During his service in Minsk, Ignatavičius visited his family in Vilkija whenever able, usually traveling on the popular Nemunas River steamboat route. On a trip to visit his mother on July 1, 1943, he felt despondent, sensing a lack of

---

61 Ibid., January 15, 1942, 17.
62 Ibid., March 1, 1942, 21.
63 Ibid., March 2, 1942, 23. See Gerlach, *Kalkulierte Morde*, 691. This event refers to the massacre of March 2–3, 1942, which, according to German sources, resulted in the killing of 3,412 inmates of the Minsk Ghetto with the purpose of solving "food shortages."

"spiritual contentment" among the people, and then added a possible reason: "The days of the bloody massacres are really not so distant, and thus a cloud of guilt oppresses our nation. The nation did not carry in itself the necessary Christian morality."[64] In another passage from the chaplain's writings we find a much harsher, specific condemnation:

> During the summers they [the Jews] used to always be the most frequent travelers to the resorts along the Nemunas. Today they are not among the passengers, and I thought in horror that, perhaps for centuries, there will be talk of this bloody past. With the greatest pain in my heart, I have heard many stories of what cruelties were carried out not only by the Germans, but by Lithuanians themselves. A terrible indelible stain on the unblemished history of my nation. No reasons, no arguments will ever either justify or cover up this terrible crime.... We will always know that the majority of these cruel and terrible executioners, murderers of the innocents of the Jewish nation, arose from the ranks of the serene [sic] Lithuanian nation.[65]

In Vilkija, Ignatavičius strolled through the town and encountered an old acquaintance which only further aggravated his mood:

> I visited my former acquaintance, the postal official Rimkus. He lives in the very beautiful home seized from the Jews. All this comfort stirred in me a mood as if in a funeral. Even though everything looks splendid, I wouldn't live a single day in such a home, acquired through the blood of innocent people. God save us from such a terrible sin. When you walk along the town's streets and you see your nation's people living in the homes left by the Jews, you feel that they have entered such apartments through the blood and the corpses of innocents.[66]

Clearly, some of the rank-and-file Lithuanian clergy, who observed atrocities more closely than the hierarchy, were distraught at what they saw and heard, nor were they blind to the crimes of their parishioners.

---

64 Extract from a copy of another section of Ignatavičius's diary/notes dated July 1, 1943, provided courtesy of the LGGRTC and the Lithuanian Institute of History.

65 As published in Ignonis, *Praeitis kalba*, 162–163.

66 Ibid., 163. Ignatavičius's nephew and Vilkija native Egidijus Saulius Juodis and the town's memoirist, the pharmacist Jonas Grinevičius, believe the opulent home in question probably belonged to the local physician, Dr. Gershon Shpunder. The exact timing of this visit is unclear.

The violent images and stories, as well as the indignities which the Germans inflicted on the Lithuanians of the battalion he served, impacted Ignatavičius's once positive views of the Germans. "How we all waited for them," he wrote, and recalled how the invaders "had brought all of us under their influence with open goodness and honorable behavior." But three months after his arrival in Minsk Ignatavičius lamented: "Their arrogance brings fear rather than friendship . . . until now I had thought of them as human beings." He came to view Nazi fanatics, such as the General Commissar of Belarus Wilhelm Kube, as ignorant degenerates ("how can a pig understand the worth of pearls?").[67] Ignatavičius's disenchantment with the aftermath of the German liberation from the Soviet yoke and growing suspicion of the Reich's policy towards the occupied peoples of the East had, by this time, become commonplace.

And yet moral indignation at genocidal consequences coexisted with prejudicial stereotypes, including the ubiquitous charge of Judeo-Bolshevism. In the same entries acknowledging atrocities against Jews, the diarist Ignatavičius reported on a conversation with a nurse who had told him of a Jewish doctor, still working in a Minsk hospital, who hoped that "when the Bolsheviks arrive, the entire Lithuanian nation will be slaughtered, along with the Latvians and Estonians." The priest's response is revealing: "The poor Jews! They still can't help thinking about their Bolshevik-Jewish trade."[68] Ignatavičius noted that "the Jews had been horrible during the Soviet times in Minsk," but that the public massacres would create revenge, "blood from the other side."[69] He contrasted the fanatical but brave Communists, who fought to the death with their captors, to the Jews who allegedly "went like goats when driven to their deaths." Like many of his contemporaries, Ignatavičius considered Bolshevism as the primary danger to his nation and faith, noting that, regarding the execution of Communists, he was "willing to justify the death penalty, for there are criminals, especially among the NKVD-Communists, whose crimes are so great that they can be redeemed only by blood."[70]

A sympathetic chronicler of the chaplain's life questioned whether he faced a "moral collision," whether it was proper "for a priest to associate with such

---

67 National Library, "Kunigo Zenono Ignatavičiaus 1942 metu žiemos dienoraštis," March 4, 1942, 26.
68 Ibid., January 3, 1942, 6.
69 Ibid., February 26, 1942, 19.
70 Ibid., March 4, 1941, 25.

soldiers," suggesting that the job of the priest is to confront the sinners, not the just.[71] But this scriptural solution fails before the reality that the very presence of the priests, particularly the dispensing of sacraments to the killers, lent an air of normalcy to the operations of the battalions. The attitudes are thus as jarring as they are contradictory: flashes of horror at the murders, shame at the behavior of his countrymen, but inevitably intermingled with the ever-present antisemitic images and grievances stemming from the Soviet experience. The personal struggles of Zenonas Ignatavičius place under a microscope the conundrum which, in retrospect, constitutes one of the most troubling legacies of the response of the institutional Church to the Holocaust in Lithuania and elsewhere in German-occupied Europe.

The intriguing case of Metropolitan Andrey Sheptytsky of Lviv is worth considering in this regard: here was a public shamer of the killers of Jews, a savior of Jewish children, and the older brother of the monk Klymentiy Sheptytsky, one of Yad Vashem's acknowledged Righteous Gentiles. This highest-ranking Greek Catholic clergyman also blessed the Ukrainian Waffen-SS "Galizien" Division as it went into battle in 1943, purportedly to save their homeland from Bolshevism. Many people (as well as Americans steeped in the "good war" narrative) understandably view such responses to evil as incomprehensible. But as Timothy Snyder has noted, Sheptytsky's stance was not, and is still not, counterintuitive to much of the populace trapped in the realities of the "lands between," the murderous battleground between Nazi Germany and Stalinist Russia during World War II.[72] But unlike Sheptytsky, Lithuania's Metropolitan Skvireckas chose not to confront the Germans or even to publicly acknowledge the genocide. His assistant and the de facto administrator of the Archdiocese of Kaunas, Bishop Brizgys, pro-German in political orientation, also evaded public condemnation of the massacres, although he knew of rescue efforts by

---

71 Egidijus Juodis, "Zenonas Ignatavičius, ar galima išlikti žmogumi, kai aplink vien neteisybė (2020)," Dievas tėvynė, accessed May 25, 2021, http://www.prodeoetpatria.lt/index.php/baznycia/21–knygos-tikejimas-baznycia/326–egidijus-juodis-zenonas-ignatavicius. Reference is to Luke 5:32: "I have not come to call the righteous but sinners to repentance."

72 See Timothy Snyder, "He Welcomed the Nazis and Saved Jews," *New York Review of Books*, December 21, 2009, http://www.nybooks.com/blogs/nyrblog/2009/dec/21/he-welcomed-the-nazis-and-saved-jews/. See Chapter 7 for a more extensive discussion of the clashing national narratives on the war.

rank-and-file religious, while maintaining contacts with Jewish leaders from the ghetto.[73]

In general, the hierarchy's position can be described as one of active public support for the "war on Bolshevism" and a pragmatic rational defense of the institutional interests of the Church, while seeking to affirm its spiritual mission. This canonical response, reminiscent of the caution of Pius XII, contrasted sharply with the actions of those priests and nuns who assisted Jews and some who spoke out against the killings.[74] Lithuanian historians who have studied the response of the Church have noted the cost of this ambiguity to the reputation of the Church. Valentinas Brandišauskas saw the tendency to "condemn not the murders themselves, but excessive misappropriation of others' properties," as an example of the "undermining of the enormous moral authority of the Church, and its failure to adequately apply it [to the situation—S. S.]." Although Church leaders avoided pouring "fuel on the fire" by publicly employing Judeo-Bolshevik stereotypes, they also evaded any statements on the "Jewish question" which would place them in conflict with German authorities.[75] A historian of Lithuanian Catholicism during the period of foreign occupations summarizes the failure of the Church hierarchy to find its voice concerning the persecution and murder of the Jews: "In none of their public texts, neither in their circulars to the deaneries, nor in their pastoral letters to priests and the faithful, nor in their writings which they sent to Pope Pius XII via trustworthy couriers, nowhere did Lithuanian bishops mention the tragedy of the Jews."[76] In a revealing contrast to their caution regarding the Jews, during their annual conference in October 1943 the bishops reacted quickly to another moral issue, Dr. Jonas Šliūpas's proposal, published in a Lithuanian medical journal, advocating the euthanasia of "defective people," such as deformed infants, psychiatric patients, and the incurably sick. In the final agenda item in the conference minutes, the

---

73 See Tory's account in *Surviving the Holocaust*, 312–317. More details about rescue efforts approved by the Kaunas Archdiocese are in Brizgys, *Katalikų bažnyčia*, 182–183, although the bishop's memoir-cum-study must be viewed with caution.

74 See Arūnas Streikus, "Bažnyčios institucija nacių okupacijos laikotarpiu Lietuvoje," accessed May 4, 2021, https://www.komisija.lt/wp-content/uploads/2016/06/A.Streikus_Baznycia-naciu-okupac.-laikotarpiu.pdf.

75 See Brandišauskas, "Holokaustas": 150–151, also Laukaitytė, *Lietuvos bažnyčios*, 105–109; cf. the April 14, 2000, statement of Lithuania's bishops, below, Chapter 7.

76 Laukaitytė, "Katalikų bažnyčia": 4. Staugaitis's July 1941 pastoral letter against violence is an exception to this general rule.

hierarchy "sharply condemned" the plan and approved sending a congratulatory note to a group of doctors in Kaunas who, in the same journal's next issue, rejected Šliūpas's "radical plan" as immoral and "contrary to the ethics of the medical profession."[77]

In the end, with few exceptions, the Lithuanian clergy were little different than most of the Church hierarchy throughout Europe which considered Nazism as the lesser of the two evils, and in doing so proved incapable, in the words of historian Lauren Faulkner Rossi, of facing the truth that "to accommodate or compromise with a racist, genocidal regime was antithetical to everything their faith stood for."[78] Despite their expressed misgivings about the violence, most political and religious leaders chose not to issue public condemnations that might have persuaded at least some of the young men who had volunteered or been co-opted into participating in the killings to rethink their behavior. During the final sitting of the PG, the acting prime minister Ambrazevičius, in a comment that was so short as to be an aside, regretted that the PG "could not affect" the massacres of the Jews in the provinces, hardly a denunciation of the slaughter of thousands of the country's citizens. In short, the institutions that claimed responsibility for the restoration of a liberated nation failed to send a clear message to the people. Given the realities of the Nazi occupation, preventing the Holocaust would have required unimaginably herculean efforts on the part of the Lithuanian people, but publicly expressed opposition to the massacres, a task within the powers of the elites, would have preserved national honor and probably encouraged more effective rescue efforts.

The People High and Low:
Hatred, Satisfaction, Indifference, Shame, and Horror

An evaluation of responses to the Holocaust during the occupation on the part of Lithuanian society at large presents obvious hurdles for the historian. How prevalent were the attitudes ranging from condemnation, sympathy, and

---

77 More details on this plan from the formerly liberal and humane Šliūpas are in Perrin, "Lithuanians in the Shadow," 246–248. The conference protocol is published in Laukaitytė, *Lietuvos bažnyčios*, 253–257. Cf. Brizgys, *Kataliku bažnyčia*, 161–162.

78 As cited in the conclusion of Lauren Faulkner Rossi, *Wehrmacht Priests: Nazism and the Nazi War of Annihilation* (Cambridge, MA: Harvard University Press, 2015), 255.

indifference to actual acceptance and approval of the genocide? There were no professionally conducted opinion polls in 1941. The study of attitudes differs from the investigation of observable actions. Research on what can be considered a nation-wide response, or a range of collective memories of the Holocaust, is inherently different from the kind of documentary evidence generally employed in describing the perpetrators. Killers acted more or less in the open, their actions documented in police reports. Rescuers were forced to work in the shadows. Whether one considers the immediate reaction to the murders, people's reflections on its aftermath, or the development of postwar memory, the spectrum of responses is wide. Attitudes can be inconsistent and even counterintuitive: some views persisted, while others changed over time.

The accounts of the security services and the reports produced by agents on the ground may constitute important evidentiary tools in gauging the "mood of the times," but much of their value depends on the professionalism and/or bias of those spying on the people. The permitted press, even if censored, gives us some insights but is a problematic source. The authorities' pressure on the local media to portray German policies in a favorable light were constant, directed by the Deutsches Nachrichtenbüro (DNB), which replaced the Lithuanian ELTA news service on August 14, 1941. The negative reports on the Western allies published under pressure from Nazi censors were not widely shared among the general public, as admitted in the extant German Security Police reports. There is no doubt, however, that the persistent anti-Jewish vitriol in the press genuinely expressed the sentiments of many writers and editors, such as Simas Miglinas, the antisemitic editor of the Šiauliai weekly *Tėvynė* (Fatherland).[79] The nearly forty permitted periodicals reached a large segment of Lithuanian society. At one point, the daily *Į laisvę*, and its replacement *Ateitis* (1943–1944), ran as many as ninety thousand copies.[80] The antisemitic screeds, including grisly depictions of "Jewish crimes," created an atmosphere conducive to dehumanizing the victims of the Holocaust.

Analysts who have studied the press notice a marked shift in the thematic emphasis of antisemitic rhetoric after the first two months of the occupation. The change reflected the success of the more extreme LNP which decisively

---

79 Algis Kasparavičius, "From the Lithuanian Press about the Jews during the Nazi Occupation 1941–1942," in Levinson, *Shoah*, 227–228.

80 See Mantas Bražiūnas, "Legalios spaudos ir valdžios santykis Lietuvoje vokiečių okupacijos metais (1941–1944)," *Žurnalistikos tyrimai* 7 (2014): 195–218.

defeated the LAF in the internecine power struggle and gained control of much of the Lithuanian administrative structures of the occupation as well as influence in the editorial offices of Lithuanian newspapers. The extremists sought favor with the occupiers by adopting much of the Nazi world view as their own. Localized Judeo-Bolshevik narratives on Jewish betrayal and cruelty continued, but themes that previously had not dominated antisemitic Lithuanian discourse became more frequent, such as the emphasis on global Jewish conspiracies, working in concert with Anglo-Saxon "plutocracy" and freemasonry.[81] "England's War is a Jewish War," declared *Į laisvę* on October 21, 1941; and then a few days later, it stated in a front page column, "Let Us Think Racially," arguing that "the current war is a race war," with the Jews fighting a "hopeless war against the Germanic race."[82] In any case, the public space of the Nazi occupation, including the period of the PG, allowed for only anti-Jewish narratives. Except for some of the clergy speaking from the pulpit, public denunciations of the massacres could easily be stopped by the censors. Only the collaborators willing to repeat German talking points could speak openly without fear of sanction.

Other sources are also problematic as reliable indicators of the popular mood. Most ghetto inmates and especially the hunted Jews in hiding believed, understandably, that most of the world was against them. Those who pitied the victims may have assigned their own feelings to fellow bystanders. People who helped the victims despite a hostile environment may have believed that they were but a lonely few, although rescuers who passed on their charges to others might have concluded that the network of righteous was larger than in reality. Diaries, memoirs, and other so-called anecdotal evidence are by their nature "snapshots," the opinions shaped by the authors' predilections. Educated observers often wrote down what they saw, but the voices of ordinary people are often accessible only in recorded oral testimonies years after the fact. The historian is left to mine the available, albeit admittedly challenging sources for insights into what people thought at the time.

---

81 Mantas Bražiūnas, "The Darkest Page in the History of Lithuanian Journalism: Anti-Semitism in Legal Press during the Second Half of 1941," *Journalism Research: English Edition* 10 (2016): 127–139. Also, Brandišauskas, *Siekiai*, 133–134 and Linas Venclauskas, "Stereotipų mįslės: antisemitizmas Lietuvos ir Prancūzijos spaudoje 1940–1942 metais," *Darbai ir dienos* 34 (2003): 321–348.

82 "Anglijos karas – žydų karas," *Į laisvę*, October 21, 1941, 2; ibid., "Galvokime rasiškai," October 24, 1941, 1.

The irregulars (for example, the Klimaitis gang), the fighting units of the June insurrectionists, and the various police and administrative agencies created after the invasion represented a cross-section of Lithuanian society. The killers undoubtedly shared anti-Jewish prejudices as well as Judeo-Bolshevik ideas, which had become widespread before the Nazi invasion. In an interview in the 1997 documentary *The Nazis: A Warning from History*, Petras Zelionka, a member of one of the most active killing units (Third Company, TDA Battalion), told his questioner that he considered Jews especially "selfish." His matter-of-fact description of the murder of children was one of the most cold-blooded admissions by shooters: "This is a tragedy, a great tragedy. How should I put it to you? How can I explain? It's a kind of curiosity. You just pull the trigger, he falls, and that's it. Some people are doomed, and that's that."[83] One of the TDA men admitted that he "had been raised to fear and hate Jews." In another case, to encourage the shooters, one of the officers told his men that Jews had exploited them and betrayed them after the Soviet invasion.[84]

For some of the killers, violence satisfied an intensely personal need for revenge. Captain Bronius Kirkila, who had been tortured during interrogations and whose wife and daughters had been deported by the Soviets on the eve of the war, was an active leader of the actions at the Seventh Fort. On July 12, 1941, Kirkila committed suicide.[85] A similar tale of revenge is related in the confession of a former Lithuanian army NCO arrested by the Soviets and whose family had also been deported and who expressed his fury by beating to death the Jewish men at the Lietūkis facility. "You people are always talking about the garage," he complained at a dinner gathering where the subject came up. "After I left the [Soviet] prison, I was overcome by revenge . . . I lost control. So, go ahead and judge me."[86] Such recorded personal experiences were relatively few but

---

83 As cited from the video by the series author and producer Laurence Rees, "How Curiosity Killed," Historynet, October 8, 2012, https://www.historynet.com/how-curiosity-killed.htm.

84 Rukšėnas, "Kauno tautinio darbo," 240–241.

85 An interesting albeit somewhat speculative account of Kirkila is in Simonas Jazavita, "Dviejų Lietuvos kariuomenės kapitonų likimas dviejų diktatorių pakto fone," Bernardinai, August 26, 2019, https://www.bernardinai.lt/2019–08–26–dvieju-lietuvos-kariuomenes-kapitonu-likimas-dvieju-diktatoriu-pakto-fone/; cf. Alfonsas Eidintas, *Žydai, lietuviai ir Holokaustas* (Vilnius: Vaga, 2002), 172, 237, 263.

86 The conversation is recalled in Henrikas Žemelis, "Juodasis Lietuvos istorijos puslapis," *Akiračiai* 5 (1998): 8.

similar narratives circulated among those who sought a justifying rationale for the murders.

Aside from impulses towards revenge and antisemitic delusions, the participants in the persecution of the Jews often admitted to robbery as an important motivator, in some cases portraying it as a form of distributive economic justice. Some sought to improve their station in life. Juozas Gruodis joined the auxiliary police for a better job, so that "he would not have to do physical labor." For his part, Antanas Šėgžda was more explicit. The benefits accrued during the killings were mundane but important to his new lifestyle which he described in his post-war interrogation:

> We would take away [from the Jews—S. S.] their money and valuables, and then pile the clothes in a heap, after which we would transport them to a warehouse from where we would distribute them to people who had suffered from the war. From these [goods] my mother gave me a new blue wool coat, for which under current prices, one would have to pay some 1,500 rubles. Also, from the Jews... I gained money in considerable sums, that is, that was done when they brought a group of Jews to the already excavated pits to be shot, so they were told to give me the money, as death awaited them in any case, and so they would give me money from which I bought a hat for fifty rubles. In Kaunas I bought a violin for 700 rubles, and I also used the money to eat.[87]

Some shooters claimed that they feared punishment if they refused orders, citing threats from their officers. These excuses, however, fly in the face of considerable evidence indicating that when faced with evasion or outright refusal to participate in the killings, commanders tended to allow reluctant soldiers to step aside, although there were a few exceptions.[88] In Jonava, a member of the Lithuanian unit involved in the first shootings was locked up in the German commandant's jail for demonstrating "weakness" during the operation. The Jonava police precinct chief Juozas Stankevičius informed his Kaunas superiors

---

[87] An example from interrogations conducted in 1960 and collected in Aušra Pažėraitė, "Žydų žudynių dalyvių motyvacija," Report presented to the IHC [undated], 20.

[88] This is borne out not only in Western studies, such as in Christopher Browning's *Ordinary Men*, but in specific situations during actions of the Twelfth LSD Battalion as recounted in Rukšėnas, "Kauno Tautinio darbo," 237–238. Cf. Blynas, *Karo metų*, entry of November 6, 1941, 224, in which he describes the refusal of the battalion's men to shoot four captured Russians, after which the Germans simply released the condemned prisoners, ending the incident.

that the people were unhappy with the killings in their town. In November 1941 Germans arrested this complainer who served half of a two-year prison sentence in Kaunas.[89] The massacres evoked revulsion among some of the policemen. The records of the TDA battalions in Kaunas record an upsurge of requests for family and hardship leave after the mass shootings at the city's forts during the first week of July, a trend which continued in later months. As one officer reported: "I have noted that some men who wish to leave the Battalion without serious justification, purposefully break discipline in order to be expelled..., [and are] helped in this by their superiors."[90] The use of alcohol as both a stimulator towards brutality and as a moral anesthetic to suppress normal instincts of aversion during the bloody operations has been noted in studies dealing with mass shooting operations and is so frequent in Lithuanian accounts as to indicate routine behavior.

Among the recorded commentators on the genocide were several intellectuals who, while avoiding public statements on cleansing the country of the Jews, made no bones about their feelings in support of what the German and Lithuanian killing units were accomplishing in the field. Rapolas Mackonis, the editor of the daily *Naujoji Lietuva*, blamed the Jews themselves for their fate. With full awareness of the escalating massacres in the provinces, on August 25, 1941, he wrote in his diary that:

> [E]very day we receive fresh news of the severe settling of accounts with the Jews. If that were done only in one or another small town, we could call it an incident or just hooliganism. But when settling with the Jews encompasses the entire country, then cleansing ourselves from them is a historic necessity. For centuries the Jews, like lice... had covered the body of Lithuania, sucking out her life juices.... But the moment has come for disinfection and that is what is being done without any thought of the consequences.[91]

---

89   As reported on the basis of postwar interrogations and testimonies in Bubnys, *Holokaustas Lietuvos provincijoje*, 110–111. In his 1954 interrogation protocol Stankevičius testified that his intervention persuaded the Germans to approve the deportation of the surviving Jonava Jews to the Kovno Ghetto, thus granting the victims a temporary reprieve.

90   Lieutenant Aleksandras Stančikas Report, September 23, 1941, LCVA, f. R-1444, ap. 1, b. 5, l. 308.

91   Mackonis diary, entry for August 25, 1941, l. 60.

On September 6, the journalist, one of a handful of Lithuanian intelligentsia, who had lived most of their adult lives in the city, observed the ghettoization of the Jews of Vilnius:

> Today from early morning the Jews are being transferred from all parts of the city to streets in the center which have been designated for their ghetto. The more sensitive among us are disturbed that our police are carrying out the transfer of the Jews. What strange thinking! Whoever owns the police, those are the ones that carry out all the orders. Of course, Lithuanians do not make for a pleasant picture. But the concentration of the Jews into the ghetto had to be done sooner or later, because the time has come to take care of this element which, like a parasite, has fed off the Lithuanian body for many centuries.[92]

Mackonis continued his antisemitic commentary even after the destruction of most of the Litvak community. In June 1942, commenting on the approaching anniversary of the Nazi-Soviet war, he mused about "the size of Poland which the Jews will be willing to grant [Gen. Władysław] Sikorski," the head of the Polish government-in-exile. Mackonis affirmed a well-known American trope by adding that the *New York Times*, which was "established and edited by the Jews," openly advocated for the Soviet possession of the territories the Kremlin had gained before the war. "So, it seems," he wrote, "that Lithuania is also to be sold. On the other hand, no surprise here since, for the Jews, the business of selling one or another nation into slavery poses no difficulty."[93]

The Rokiškis massacre of mid-August 1941 shocked even the secretary general of the LNP. On the eve of the operation Zenonas Blynas recorded in his diary a conversation with the district chief:

> I advised him to make sure not to needlessly destroy Lithuanians. Care should be taken regarding repressive actions against the Communist Youth [Komsomol]. I reminded him of the Jews, Russians, and Poles, and advised him to remember that there are only two million of us, there will be enough others to go after us . . . , let's not slaughter each other.
>
> He says that tomorrow 9,000 Jews must be shot in Rokiškis. They [will] dig a three-meter ditch, bring in a hundred Jews, put them in the

---

92 Ibid., entry for September 6, 1941, l. 64.
93 Ibid., entry for June 12, 1942, l. 117–118.

ditch, threaten that whoever gets up will be shot, then a few people with submachine guns fire crisscross at the backs, they will then pour on a layer of 20–30 cm sand... then they lay down another line [of people].... Once [earlier] they had brought in 600 Jews and ordered them out of town. After a few kilometers they were ordered to put down their sacks and take off their outerwear. The Jews understood their fate, there were tragic scenes. This even affected the people who carried out the action. Supposedly there are 2,000 people (old people, women, children) who are left for the "second group"—for humanitarian reasons, so that there would be no need to bother with the children.... But now they are handling the healthier ones, the young men.[94]

A week after the killings, Zenonas Blynas received a report from a colleague. His earlier matter-of-fact tone outlining the technical details of the planned massacre, replete with irony concerning "humanitarian" aspects, changed sharply. He wrote down his thought after a leisurely stroll:

I visited the cemetery, then went to the bridge near Aleksotas, after which I went to the "ghetto" where there is also a bridge: the only place where Jews can stand above the Aryans....

Yesterday [Klemensas] Brunius told me the story of the massacre in Rokiškis, which was carried out in the open. After being half-undressed, the Jews had to jump into a pit three meters deep. They were then shot at by men walking along the trench, the [victims'] brains and blood were spattering, the men, the shooters, were covered in blood. The women yelled and screamed. People from the area had gathered to watch. At first, they laughed, smiled in a happy manner, but then they became horrified, the Aryan women began screaming. A massacre. Disgraceful.

The local chief is a Judas. I had said before, that if the Germans are doing this by our hands, then everything must be done calmly, not in public, without scandal. But that traitor did everything to the contrary. I will remember him... that villain.[95]

On November 6, 1941, Blynas reported sarcastically on one of the notorious officers who had distinguished himself as one of the TDA Third Company's prolific killers who was now serving with the Twelfth Battalion in Belarus:

---

94 Blynas, *Karo metu*, entry for August 14, 1941, 128. Reference here likely concerns two massacres: the smaller action of July and the massacre of August 15–16 which involved over three thousand victims. The nine thousand figure may refer to the entire district.

95 Blynas, *Karo metu*, entry for August 24, 1941, 147.

> [Lieutenant] Barzda has returned from the Minsk-Borisov-Slutsk region. The Lithuanian battalion has shot more than 46,000 Jews (from Belarus and some brought from Poland), Russian Communists and Russian POWs. They hanged more than ten people. Hundreds of Germans took pictures of the battalion's Lithuanians who took part in the hanging. It is said that the Vilnius battalion is heading to Lublin ... for honorable duties. ... So there, these German gentlemen are so full of honor. The Ukrainians, Latvians and Estonians don't have to shoot. We alone must do the shooting.[96]

A month later, Blynas evaded a request from a woman acquaintance who was seeking help in the case of a Jewish doctor. His reply was telling:

> She asked me to come by. I refused. It's a stupid affair. Perhaps, a provocation? For me, only a certain principle actually matters—not the rescue of one, or a few, Jews. I cannot stand the fact that Lithuania is being transformed into a morgue, a cemetery, that they force [us] to regularly shoot Jews who had left Germany with visas, that we shoot others, that we are becoming salaried butchers, that [they] film us, but the Germans don't film themselves. I hate this vile business.[97]

In January 1942 Blynas was enraged at the killings of members of the Sokol, the Czech resistance, who had been brought to Lithuania, hurling "eternal damnation" on the officers who participated.[98]

The LNP's general secretary's disgust and embarrassment should not be confused with sympathy for the defenseless Lithuanian Jews (he was obviously more troubled by what had happened to the Czechs, and to German Jews with visas). This was self-pitying shame without moral substance: if the Germans want to kill the Jews, they should do it themselves. Blynas did show some alarm at the potential danger to his own kind. As the massacres expanded in September, he had a conversation with LNP colleagues and gloomily concluded: "My thesis is that now it's the Jews, then the Poles, afterwards the Lithuanians. (This was explained by a German soldier). The remaining Lithuanians will shine

---

96   Ibid., entry of November 6, 1941, 224. The reference to Lublin probably concerns the unit sent to the Majdanek camp in Poland.
97   Ibid., entry of December 13, 1941, 258. The reference here is to the killing of German and Austrian Jews at the Ninth Fort.
98   Ibid., entry of January 12, 1942, 282.

German shoes."⁹⁹ For their part, the most extreme among the Voldemarists, the Iron Wolves, had no qualms about murder: according to Blynas, in a meeting among top LNP officials, the Abwehr agent Jonas Pyragius, in response to complaints about the humiliating tasks assigned to Lithuanians, "defended the shooting of the Jews."¹⁰⁰

When the noted writer Kazys Boruta (1905–1965) expressed to Blynas his "indignation at the shootings of the Jews," the LNP leader responded: "I think it's better that they shoot Jews rather than Lithuanians!"¹⁰¹ Blynas was also keen to make sure that everyone understood the real source of Lithuanian antisemitism. In one passage, after a "thorough discussion on the massacre of the Jews" at a meeting of LNP officials, he noted: "In today's issue of *Į laisvę* there is an interesting stanza in [poet Bernardas] Brazdžionis's poem, "I Call upon the Nation," adding that the cited selection "is probably about Jewry":

> I call in the name of your land of sorrows,
> In the voice of the castle hills, meadows, and forests
> Do not take revenge, so that the stain of hot blood,
> Not fall as a curse on your children's children.¹⁰²

Blynas was annoyed at the implied critique from a Catholic poet and threatened a rejoinder: "When our own [LNP] newspaper is published, we will put out in public all the prewar declarations of clerical 'antisemitism.' Let not the guilt they direct at us be ours alone. Those Christian Democrats."¹⁰³

For some, however, even a smidgeon of shame or concern was too much. A travelogue dated July 15, 1941, by a student, one V. Jurgutis, titled "The Whirlwind of War in Samogitia," contains a blend of satisfaction and contempt at the disappearance of the Jewish men. The traveler reported that locals in Samogitia were still complaining that Jews had threatened them and had allegedly burned

---

99   Ibid., entry of September 9, 1941, 171.
100 Ibid., entry of December 7, 1941, 252.
101 Ibid., entry for July 23, 1941, 77. One of Lithuania's foremost literati, Boruta is thought to have authored the phrase "bringing Stalin's sun to Lithuania," proclaimed in July 1940. During the German occupation he is known to have assisted Jews. The NKVD imprisoned Boruta in 1946–1949 for alleged contacts with the anti-Soviet resistance.
102 Bernardas Brazdžionis, "Šaukiu aš tautą," *Į laisvę*, August 30, 1941, 4.
103 Blynas, *Karo metų*, entry for August 30, 1941, 157. The LNP considered Christian Democrats, a dominant force in the LAF, as an insufficiently radical Catholic-dominated political organization.

towns and villages. And yet, in the new order, Jurgutis observed that local farmers had discovered, to their liking, that the Jews were "unnecessary." The open-air markets were doing fine without the traditional input of Jewish commerce. In a jocular, cynical tone the young man wrote: "Truly here in Samogitia even the Jewish seed is gone: all the men, have been 'put in their place,' as they say in the Samogitian dialect, for their various misdeeds: only the women and children are left. They are corralled in temporary camps and are guarded by TDA officials and perform all kinds of work."[104] A farmer from Vilkija who spoke with Blynas held a more pragmatic view of the destruction of the Jews. He told the LNP leader that "East Prussia is less thickly settled than Lithuania. After the massacre of the Jews, about 10% of the population, Lithuania will be less inhabited. Germans will be sent to the Jewish homes and the state farms. The Germans will dominate and thus will Germanize Lithuania." Blynas recorded that his interviewee had "shot four Jews himself the other day. [According to him—S. S.] there will be no more Jews in Vilkija."[105]

The normal human response of distress to the killings is recorded in a number of sources. A young witness from Vilkija reported the same unease after watching two young men with guns escort the young Jewish Komsomol activist Rufkė to a nearby rivulet, the victim carrying a shovel on his shoulders. Then there was shooting. The observer remembers that "the more serious people" in the town complained about the murder as legally unwarranted, others were unhappy with the unseemly burial.[106] Aside from writing on the opinions circulating among the nationalist and literary elites, Blynas recorded an interesting conversation reflecting the reaction of some people in the provinces:

> Today a man came from Joniškis saying that the villagers are finding it difficult to get accustomed to the massacre of the Jews. In the villages, where the Jewish terror [sic] was not as rampant as in the towns, the killings are creating a depressing and heavy atmosphere. People say it would be better to take the Jews for work and shoot only the Communists. It's unfortunate that there is too much shooting and that it is done by

---

104 LMAVB RS, "Karo viesulas žemaičiuose," f. 22–1754, l. 14–17.
105 Blynas, *Karo metų*, entry for August 16, 1941, 132.
106 Jonas Grinevičius, "Vilkijoj, Vydūno alėjoj matyta, girdėta ...," 47 (unpublished manuscript, ed. Egidijus Juodis). According to the memoir, Rufkė's body was exhumed and reburied in the Jewish cemetery.

Lithuanians, especially if it is true that the Germans are filming the actions.[107]

Matilda Olkinaitė's school friend remembered her initial disbelief as rumors circulated among the adults of the town that the Jews would be shot: "how can they just shoot living and breathing people, for what? Such nonsense." After the killings began the witness recounted that "no one raised a ruckus about the killings, everyone was concerned with their own situation."[108] Another witness from the area recalled the contempt with which the villagers tended to view the so-called "white armbands," telling of village women singing derisive ditties about the killers, while others would sarcastically question the men on whether they had found enough "golden Jewish teeth."[109] Ever since the mass murder campaign of 1941, the pejorative term for the executioners, "Jew-shooters" (L. *žydšaudžiai*), had gained currency as an expression of opprobrium.

Some writers of the time, including people who had initially welcomed the insurrection and the Germans' supposed liberation of the homeland, recognized that a terrible crime had taken place. In July, Marija Gimbutas, the anti-Soviet student rebel, enjoyed her honeymoon: "We, the exhausted partisans, have arrived in Palanga from noisy and dusty Kaunas. Here, like nature's children, we are ruling the seaside." Her sunniness was short-lived. On September 3 she wrote in her diary that she was tired of "the damned and stupid twentieth century." Two weeks later she had given up: "That 'cultured' world of today is horrible and terrifying. Such mass murders . . . Bolshevism has swallowed up so many small nations, along with the scholars and artists. The same is happening now with the Jews."[110]

The Finance Minister Matulionis, who in July 1941 had suggested to Goldberg that the Kovno Ghetto was a just solution for the safety of both Jews and Lithuanians, continued as chief financial advisor in Kubiliūnas's collaborationist council after the dissolution of the PG. Summarizing the situation at the end of

---

107 Blynas, *Karo metų*, entry for August 13, 1941, 128.
108 Interview with Ona-Genovaitė Šukytė-Grigėnienė, USHMM, Accession Number: 2018.455.1 / RG Number: RG-50.030.0989, October 4, 2018, https://collections.ushmm.org/search/catalog/irn628342.
109 Interview with Aldona Dranseikienė, USHMM, Oral History / Accession Number: 1998.A.0221.110 / RG Number: RG-50.473.0110, January 13, 2005, https://collections.ushmm.org/search/catalog/irn518532.
110 Gimbutienė, *Dienoraštis*, 101.

1941, he described the problem of former Jewish bank accounts, securities, and confiscated valuables, which to his resentment, were to be turned over to the German Security Police. He then added: "Such is the case with their [Jewish] property. Concerning what happened to the people themselves, that is, in any case an indescribably cruel and horrible stain on the twentieth century." Matulionis noted that Jews were being brought to Lithuania ostensibly for "work," but in fact to their deaths. "People are speaking about this a good deal," he wrote, "they are fearful and engaging in conjecture." He lamented that Lithuania, once famous in Europe as a "second Palestine," and Vilnius as a second Jerusalem, had become "a cemetery for Europe's Jews." But he made no mention of the culprits, instead concluding his thoughts with a cliché about the unpredictable and inscrutable laws of nature.[111]

The change in mood did not escape German observers. In February 1942, Josef Wutz of the ERR in Kaunas, reported on growing anti-German sentiment in the populace, one aspect of which concerned the Jews:

> Furthermore, the current attitude towards the Jews is typical [of the change—S. S.]. It is true that earlier [during the interwar period—S. S.] Lithuanians had kept their distance from Jews, closing official positions, allowing Jewish officers only as a great exception, and had, partly on their own initiative, risen up against the Jews in June 1941. These feelings have also shifted given the fact that National Socialism brought about a radical settlement of the Jewish question. Increasingly it happens that today Lithuanians help the Jews, supporting them in their flight from the ghetto, taking them in, legalizing them through false passports, etc. The German authorities have waged an increasingly intense battle against these phenomena. The reason for this change among Lithuanians? The overwhelming part of the population harshly judges the mass shootings of Jews which are being carried out. The Lithuanian points out that only the truly guilty should be shot, but not, under any circumstances, the women, and children. Furthermore, many female employees of the ZV appear on the streets in furs that once belonged to Jewish women. Lithuanians see this as a betrayal of principles and a lack of race-consciousness. They are especially exasperated over the fact that many German Jews from the Old Reich (*Altreich*) [Germany] were also shot, and in which the recruited unsavory Lithuanian elements assisted. All of

---

111 Matulionis, *Neramios dienos*, 26–27.

this has led Lithuanians to begin to see the Jews as martyrs and to help them in the manner and means noted above.[112]

Wutz's observations on Lithuanian attitudes to the Jews was a part of a larger "attitude/mood report" (*Stimmungsbericht*) on Lithuanian views of German occupation policy, which he concluded had changed markedly since the early days of the invasion. The chronicler Kruk also noted in his diary the growing Lithuanian resentment of German control. He noted in December 1942 that twenty-three garden workers who were detained "told of extremely friendly relations with the staff in Lukiszki (Lukiškės) prison." Kruk added: "The same with the relations to Jews in all other Lithuanian offices. The Lithuanians are really turning themselves inside out to demonstrate their friendship to the Jews."[113]

Descriptions provided by observers as disparate as Wutz and Kruk are recorded snapshots and may not be reflective of typical attitudes widespread in society, but their accounts should not be dismissed out of hand. Whether the anti-German mood noted by many observers constituted a meaningful departure from the rise in public antisemitism which had characterized the late 1930s and especially the first Soviet occupation is another question. Here the evidence is not encouraging.

Disenchantment with Germany and Views of a Jewish Future

According to Hitler, the Baltic peoples were, at best, destined for a future of toil within the anticipated thousand-year Reich. Nazi ideologues made it clear that the majority populations in the former Baltic states were racially subordinate to Germans, albeit ranking Estonians closest to the Aryan ideal, somewhat higher than Latvians. For their part, Lithuanians occupied the lowest rung on the Baltic racial ladder.[114] Nonetheless, during the occupation the Germans granted

---

112 Quoted from "Politische Stimmungsbericht Nr. 1 aus dem Generalkommissariat Litauens," February 26, 1942, Centre de Documentation Juive Contemporaine (Paris), Rosenberg Collection, CXLIV-430, 10–11. My thanks to the Communauté Lithuanienne en France for mailing a copy of the document after my visit to the center.

113 Kruk, *Last Days*, entry of December 29, 1942, 435.

114 On the interesting use of Nazi archeology and historical scholarship to create a legitimizing rationale for the Germanization of the Baltics, see Malte Gasche, "Die Instrumentalisierung des Prähistorie im Reichskommissariat Ostland 1941 bis 1944," in *Reichskommissariat Os-*

Lithuanians a privileged position over the other indigenous nationalities (except, of course, over Lithuania's German minority). In contrast to the interwar period, this relative advantage was explicit, openly proclaimed, and enforced by regulation. As the police chief Antanas Audronis explained in a speech to the precinct chiefs of Alytus district on July 16, 1941: "Germans and Lithuanians make up the first class of citizens, Poles and Russians are second-class, while the Jews are last among all the nations." He noted that "the German military leadership in Lithuania has determined weekly per capita food rations." Jews were assigned half the amount due the others.[115]

Audronis's audacious claim of German and Lithuanian parity, however, did not reflect reality. The German award of privilege was both temporary and conditional. Nazi authorities did not hesitate to employ force when Lithuanians became incalcitrant. It was also decidedly insincere, given the Nazi designs for the ultimate Germanization of the Baltic littoral openly expressed in a 1942 article in *Das Schwarze Korps*, the official newspaper of the SS, which proclaimed the peoples of the East inferior beings destined to submit to biologically superior German folk who would colonize the region. The editors of *Naujoji Lietuva* translated and reprinted the article in full. The Germans considered this republication in the Vilnius daily a provocation and responded to the dismay among the intelligentsia with unconvincing explanations.[116]

Nazi racial arrogance and the dismissive attitude of the occupiers regarding Lithuanian political aspirations dashed hopes for even nominal independence. In his report Wutz wrote that "without a doubt the mood of the [Lithuanian] population vis-a-vis the Germans has noticeably worsened in the last quarter," and that "the national demands for the regaining of independence or, at the very least, a recognition of cultural autonomy, are equally strong among all strata [of the population—S. S.]." His judgment was not an outlier. German reports on the mood of the populace after the initial phase of the occupation often remarked on the growing conviction among Lithuanians that Germany had lost the war as well as their tendency to view favorably the prospects

---

tland: *Tatort und Erinnerungsobjekt*, ed. Sebastian Lehman et al. (Paderborn: Ferdinand Schöningh, 2012), 171–187.

115 Audronis to Precinct Chiefs, July 16, 1941, as published in Brandišauskas, *1941 m. birželio sukilimas*, 196–201.

116 The article "Germanisieren?," *Das Schwarze Korps* 34 (August 20, 1942) was translated and reprinted in Lithuanian in "Germanizuoti?," *Naujoji Lietuva*, September 10, 1942, 2.

of an Anglo-American victory. In the spring of 1943 popular resistance caused the collapse of the German administration's highly touted campaign to create a Lithuanian SS legion, which in turn led to a crisis in German-Lithuanian relations.[117]

Worries about a future under the Nazis were shared even by those who had initially welcomed the actions against the Jews. Only a month after he approvingly noted the ghettoization of Vilnius, Mackonis wrote in his diary: "We cannot imagine Lithuania's fate should the Germans lose. But then what fate awaits her if the Germans win? This is the fundamental question which, as far as I can see, troubles all of society."[118] Three months later he observed "the changing attitude towards the Germans," reporting that, according to visitors from Kaunas, there was "increasing sympathy for the Anglo-Saxons there," largely because the Germans had refused to commit to any clear policy toward Lithuania, while at the same time demanding a great commitment from the people.[119] On February 1, 1942, he opined that "the majority of the Lithuanian intelligentsia do not like the Germans and probably do not wish for them to be victorious."[120] Months later, someone who wrote from an entirely different perspective noted the phenomenon among ordinary people. Zelig Kalmanovitch's diary records his discovery of a note while "sorting Jewish books . . . I saw the letter of a girl hiding with a Lithuanian farmer. Hundreds have survived taken in by clerics and villagers. The farmers already wish to be rid of the current masters, like they wanted to get free of the previous ones [that is, the Soviets—S. S.] two years ago."[121]

At the same time Škirpa wrote to Turauskas from his internment in Bavaria, still arguing to maintain a pro-German course and expressing his disappointment in the shifting mood back home:

> Lithuania finds itself, in one way or another, completely under the control of Germany and this fact cannot change, unless the Germans lose the war . . . , which today cannot be confirmed and is only speculation. I consider any turn of our policy against Germany, which unfortunately

---

117 See Saulius Sužiedėlis, "The Military Mobilization Campaigns of 1943 and 1944 in German-Occupied Lithuania: Contrasts in Resistance and Collaboration," *Journal of Baltic Studies* 21, no. 1 (1990): 33–52.
118 Mackonis diary, entry of October 11, 1941, l. 74.
119 Ibid., entry of January 8, 1942.
120 Ibid., entry of February 1, 1942..
121 Kalmanovich, *Hope*, February 1, 1942, entry of August 13, 1942, 127.

some voices are already suggesting, too premature, fundamentally mistaken, and dangerous to our nation's very existence. Such a change would have no practical benefit for Lithuania's reconstruction. In return for such courage, English and American propaganda would applaud us nicely but that would be all, since obviously our fate is not in the hands of the [Western] Allies. On the contrary, this would destroy the sympathies which we have won among the Germans for the courage and solidarity we have shown in the war against Bolshevism. Furthermore, it would destroy the bridges for political bonds with Germany in the future and would provide the local [German] imperialists with an excuse to suppress our nation even more, or even to undertake extreme measures, such as physical annihilation, or to use force to push us further east, not awaiting the end of the war.[122]

Skirpa's long-held fantasy that Lithuania could survive with the help of "good Germans" who would fend off the "bad ones" revealed his increasing isolation from the mood back home.

Despite the deterioration in Lithuanian-German relations, the thinking of some elite circles regarding relations with other nationalities continued to take a radical turn. The Russians were widely viewed as second only to the Jews as active supporters of Bolshevism and potential targets for expulsion. The underground press and police reports described occasional attacks on Russian homesteads. Particular animus was directed at Old Believer settlements which were seen as communities supportive of Soviet partisans. In eastern Lithuania, the Lithuanian administration's anti-Polish measures can be seen as a more extreme form of the "Lithuanianization" policies of 1939–1940.[123] In August–September 1941 a Catholic philosopher published in *Į laisvę* two articles acquainting readers with the "ideological foundations of National Socialism." Hitler, he wrote, had "enabled the German Nation to emerge onto the road of the current series of victories which are joined by all European nations seeking a new future." The second installment on Nazi thought explained the insidious influence of the "eternal Jew" as a "destroyer of all authentic culture."[124] In 1942–1943

---

122 Škirpa to Turauskas, January 20, 1942, Turauskas Collection, Box 3.
123 Rimantas Zizas, "Tarpnacionalinė situacija Vokietijos okupuotoje Lietuvoje 1941–1944 metais," in *Epochas jungiantis nacionalizmas: tautos (de)konstravimas tarpukario, sovietmečio ir posovietmečio Lietuvoje*, ed. Česlovas Laurinavičius (Vilnius: LII, 2013), 72–73, 77–106.
124 Juozas Girnius, "Idėjiniai nacionalsocializmo pagrindai," *Į laisvę*, August 30, 1941, 3; ibid., September 4, 1941, 3.

a series of documents and studies titled *The Lithuanian Archive: The Year of Bolshevism* were published by a "Bureau of Studies," which purported to reveal the crimes of the first Soviet occupation. The fourth volume came out in a print run of twenty-five thousand copies. While most of the archival material on Communist misdeeds was authentic, the articles based on the research, as well as the memoirs on the first Soviet occupation, echoed themes of Jewish betrayal and persecution of Lithuanians, reinforcing Judeo-Bolshevik narratives.[125] But as disenchantment with German policies became more evident, the officially permitted press increasingly lost its role as the sounding board for what most Lithuanians were thinking.

The center-left underground newspaper *Nepriklausoma Lietuva* (Independent Lithuania), the first Lithuanian anti-Nazi periodical published by a small group of Populists and Social Democrats, appeared in November 1941, advocating support for the Western Allies. Several other Lithuanian anti-Nazi underground organizations emerged during 1942 and began distributing numerous publications which eventually reached a readership of, at a minimum, tens of thousands. The two largest groups replicated the competing Catholic/Christian Democratic vs. Voldemarist political trends of long standing. The former was represented by the Lithuanian Front (LF) which emerged from the clerical wing of the LAF and produced an underground version of *Į laisvę* after the Nazis closed the legal daily in December 1942. Initially, the LF found it difficult to give up on an anti-Bolshevik alliance with the occupiers. The new *Į laisvę* noted regretfully: "We do not consider our purpose to stab in the back the Germans who have found themselves in a difficult situation. We are not enemies of the German nation, but we maintain that the Zivilverwaltung is the major obstacle to good Lithuanian-German understanding."[126] The rest of the underground press took on a sharper anti-German stance, evoking at times the historic animosity between the Lithuanians and their historic Germanic enemy, as personified by the ravages of the Teutonic Knights and Bermondtists. Finally, the underground press tarred the occupiers with the ultimate insult: the Nazis, it was said, were no different from, and at times even worse, than the Bolsheviks.[127] On the second anniversary of the war, *Nepriklausoma Lietuva* wrote that: "To separately

---

125 Juozas Balčiūnas, ed., *Lietuvių archyvas: bolševizmo metai*, 4 vols. (Kaunas: Studijų biuras, 1942–1943).
126 "Kelias į nepriklausomybę," *Į laisvę*, August 14, 1943 (extra ed.), 1.
127 Sužiedėlis, "Military Mobilization Campaigns": 38–40.

consider the Bolshevik and German occupations makes no sense since they are similar in their goals towards Lithuania."[128] In one of their final issues, the paper equated both Soviet and Nazi regimes as equally murderous systems.[129]

Oddly enough, the most strident anti-German propaganda came from the radical right of the political spectrum. A part of the LNP, which had formerly been the most pro-Nazi group, joined the ardently nationalist Lithuanian Union of Freedom Fighters (Lietuvos laisvės kovotojų sąjunga, LLKS) which coalesced into the militarized Lithuanian Freedom Army (Lietuvos laisvės armija, LLA). The sharper anti-Nazi tone was also shared by the liberal Populists who supported a return to multiparty democratic rule in sharp contrast to the LAF program of 1940–1941. In February 1944, the different factions, except for the LLA, united under the umbrella of the Supreme Committee for the Liberation of Lithuania (Vyriausias Lietuvos išlaisvinimo komitetas, VLIK).[130]

Closer analysis of the Lithuanian anti-Nazi movement is beyond the scope of this study, but several of its aspects are relevant to understanding the evolution of elite and popular attitudes during the German occupation. The consensus among the different underground groups was that while Nazi plans for German colonization in the East posed a long-term threat, a second Soviet occupation remained the immediate danger, which obviated any actions that would benefit Soviet military advances. In this view, armed struggle against Nazi power was counterproductive. The strategy was to sabotage anti-Lithuanian Nazi policies and consolidate the human resources of the nation, while awaiting favorable geopolitical developments. Cooperation with the two other major anti-Nazi movements was briefly considered but proved impossible since their goals were perceived as antithetical to Lithuanian national interests: the Polish Home Army laid claim to Vilnius, while the Soviet partisans opposed the country's independence. The confrontation with Poles was excruciatingly difficult in two respects. The operations of the Home Army and the resulting interethnic violence which peaked in 1943–1944 endangered Lithuanian control of the Vilnius region. In addition, the potential influence of a resurrected and vengeful Poland allied with Britain and the United States threatened Lithuania's future status as an independent state. These fears were not unfounded given the

---

128 "Dvejos skaudžios metinės," *Nepriklausoma Lietuva*, June 15, 1943, 1.

129 "Barbariški žiaurumai," *Nepriklausoma Lietuva*, April 16, 1944, 4.

130 A brief history of the Lithuanian anti-Nazi resistance is in Arūnas Bubnys, *Lietuvių antinacinė rezistencija 1941–1944* (Vilnius: Komprojektas, 1991).

proposals in the underground Polish press to federate Lithuania with Poland after the war. Future relations with the country's Russians and Germans presented few headaches: the former were traitors relevant only in the context of a second Soviet occupation; the latter were Teutonic colonizers who would be expelled once Germany was defeated by the Western Allies.[131]

What of Lithuania's historically largest minority? Given that the genocide of the Jews was indisputably the most violent event in the country's modern history, one would expect some thoughtful examination of the consequences of this unprecedented trauma, even if, as a result, Litvaks no longer represented a future socioeconomic or political force. Despite occasional expressions of distress and shock, the Holocaust did not signify any fundamental shift in the thinking of most of the Lithuanian leadership which regarded the Jews as the Other. Inasmuch as the illegal press provided the only sounding board that provides a record of uncensored opinion among the politically conscious citizenry, it must serve as the available barometer for gauging prevalent views on the situation of the Jews. Most of the anti-Nazi propaganda that appeared in the underground press dealt with German restrictions on Lithuanian cultural life, forced labor to the Reich, expropriations and pillaging of the agricultural economy, and the 1943 Nazi mobilization campaign which aimed to create a Lithuanian Waffen-SS formation. The empathy towards ethnic Lithuanian victims was manifest. A brief report on the arrest of the pastor of Žiežmariai, Msgr. Bernardas Sužiedėlis, following the forceful invasion of his church by German gendarmes in September 1943, spoke vividly of the violent seizure of "young and beautiful girls kneeling at Mass," dragged off to forced labor.[132] Commenting on the same incident, which one should note was not usual German practice in relation to churches, the underground youth paper *Atžalynas* (Seedlings) declared: "Nazi atrocities have crossed all boundaries."[133] *Į laisvę* noted that "the German atrocities have reached a hitherto unheard-of fury, exceeding by far the cruelties of the [previous] Bolshevik deportations."[134] There was no need,

---

131 On the Polish conundrum, see Saulius Sužiedėlis, "Vilniaus klausimas": 187–198; also, Krzysztof Buchowski, *Litvomanai ir polonizuotojai: mitai, abipusės nuostatos ir stereotipai lenkų ir lietuvių santykiuose pirmoje ir antroje XX amžiaus pusėje*, trans. Irena Aleksaite (Vilnius: baltos lankos, 2012), 431–494; cf. Zizas, "Tarpnacionalinė situacija," 77–106.

132 "XI. 9 areštuotas klebonas prelatas Sužiedėlis," *Į laisvę*, November 23, 1943, 3.

133 "Kronika," *Atžalynas*, October 30, 1943, 3; cf. the commentary on the Žiežmariai and other incidents in Laukaitytė, *Lietuvos bažnyčios*, 29–31.

134 "Siaubingi vokiečių banditizmai," *Į laisvę*, August 28, 1943, 3.

however, to exaggerate the cruelty that the Nazis inflicted on the Lithuanian villagers of Pirčiupiai on June 3, 1944, when, in a reprisal for a Soviet partisan attack on a German convoy, the SS massacred some 120 people, most of whom were locked in buildings and burned alive. In a report titled "Germans Have Exceeded the Bolsheviks in Cruelty," the press called for "vengeance from the heavens." *Į laisvę* described how "the SS bandits . . . , the brown barbarians, threw infants into the fire."[135]

The travails of Jews, on the other hand, were usually reported in a factual tone with minimal editorial comment. In September 1943, *Į laisvę* printed a single paragraph on the ongoing, as yet incomplete, destruction of Jews titled: "Jews No Longer Seen in Vilnius."[136] In November 1943, in a section titled, "Jews Are Being Deported and Shot," the paper related that on October 25–27 the Germans had deported four thousand Jews from the Kovno Ghetto, noting that the women and children were being sent to Poland, where "it can be surmised that the crematorium awaits." In Warsaw, it went on to report, the "Germans are rapidly completing the construction of several crematoria, which will 'process' 1,500 corpses per day." The most horrific event of the paragraph resulted in the most laconic sentences: "In early November eight truckloads of Jews unfit for work were driven out to various places and shot."[137] In March 1944, *Į laisvę* described the atrocities in the Kovno Ghetto with more understanding. "The children were seized by their hands, feet, and hair, and thrown into lorries like some deadwood. They were then exterminated near the Ninth Fort."[138] *Nepriklausoma Lietuva* went further than most in a 1943 article titled "The Murder of Nations":

> It is nauseating to listen to the Germans pretending to defend people . . . they themselves have covered all of enslaved Europe with huge cemeteries, death camps and gas chambers. These [German] knights have murdered all the Jews of Poland and exterminated a part of the Polish nation . . . they shoot little children and feeble old people. In Poland, the slaughter is complete. And now the Jews of the Balkans are being murdered.[139]

---

135 "Vokiečiai savo žiaurumu pralenkė bolševikus," *Į laisvę*, June 20, 1944, 2.
136 "Vilniuje nebematyti žydų," *Į laisvę*, September 17, 1943, 3.
137 "Vežami ir šaudomi žydai," *Į laisvę*, November 23, 1943, 4.
138 "III. 27 ir 28 gestapo žinoje. . . ," *Į laisvę* April 3, 1944, 2.
139 "Tautų žudynės," *Nepriklausoma Lietuva*, July 15, 1943, 3.

Demeaning references to Jews persisted even in the rhetoric aimed at the Germans. The press ridiculed the notoriously corrupt Nazi district commissioner Hans Cramer as a German who combined the qualities of "a general, a Jew and a Gypsy." In a special edition laying out the necessary response to German repressions stemming from the failed SS mobilization in the spring of 1943, Lithuanian bravado against the Germans was compared to the behavior of Jews: Lithuanians would respond to Nazi behavior with courage since, it was said, "in our history and in the present, we have a notion of honor and freedom, so we must say to them [Germans]: We are not Jews and will not dig our own graves."[140] In a bitter article against the despised German settlers (*Umsiedler*), *Į laisvę* wrote that they should be held responsible for the crimes of the occupation: "It depends on the *Umsiedler* themselves if they will become a tolerated element or whether they will be hated even more than the Jews during the time of the Bolsheviks."[141] The radical right retained its old habits even as they turned against the Germans. "What did the Germans bring us?" asked their mouthpiece *Laisvės kovotojas* (Freedom fighter). "The 'European freedom' that they have granted us is little different from Jewish-Bolshevik tyranny."[142]

Even in commentary that avoided anti-Jewish stereotypes, the limited coverage of the destruction of the Litvaks focused not on the catastrophe at hand but on calculations concerning the future, including the impact which the charges of Lithuanian collaboration would have on the country's political prospects. On December 30, 1942, *Nepriklausoma Lietuva* commented on the future of minorities in Lithuania. "The Lithuanian Nation," it wrote, "has long lived together with the Poles and Jews. She knows them well and has the means to protect herself. These means are completely different from those employed by the Germans. In defending the national interests, [Lithuanians] do not accept methods whose purpose is to destroy other nations."[143] In May 1943, the Polish covert radio station Świt accused the Lithuanian underground press of silence on the massacre of Warsaw's Jews, claiming that such behavior was founded on Lithuanian approval of the extermination of Jews. *Į laisvę* was repelled by such "disgusting slander":

---

140 "Mobilizacija ir kas toliau?" *Į laisvę*, March 17, 1943, 1.
141 "Kovojanti tauta turi ruoštis," *Į laisvę*, June 26, 1943, 4.
142 "Į lietuvių tautą," *Laisvės kovotojas*, March 1, 1943, 1.
143 Quoted in Linas Venclauskas, "Lietuvos įvaizdžiai antinacinėje lietuvių spaudoje," *Genocidas ir rezistencija* 1, no. 15 (2004): 79.

> More than 80 thousand Lithuanian Jews were murdered. Germans alone were in command of the shootings and of the rabble dressed in Lithuanian uniforms, all sorts of John Doe types (*jankai ir jaskiai*), whom the Germans got drunk and allowed them to rob the victims. The Lithuanian nation has disassociated itself from these mass killings. The Lithuanian Provisional Government has not issued a single statute against the Jews [sic] although the entire nation felt the fresh injury [of the Soviet occupation—S. S.] and awaited justice to be handed down to that part of the Jews who helped the Bolsheviks torture Lithuania.[144]

In October 1943, *Nepriklausoma Lietuva* rejected Polish accusations against Lithuanian participation in the murders of Jews: "If they [the Poles—S. S.] attempt to put the blame on Lithuanians for the murder of the Jews—well, such a reproach would be about as valid as any attempt on our part to place blame on the Poles for the crematoria in Auschwitz, where masses of Jews are being burned. Just because Auschwitz is in Poland this does not necessarily mean that Poles must bear the responsibility for it, even if some Polish officials might be involved." The real evidence of Lithuanian tolerance towards Jews, the paper asserted, "can be found in the life of the prewar period: Jews had no experience of antisemitism in Lithuania" and in an acerbic aside, concluded that, as far as Poles were concerned, "it would be better not to talk about the [interwar] situation in Poland."[145] In their defensive stance, the underground press anticipated the arguments that would roil Lithuanian society long after the war. In any case, for those Lithuanians who chose to view their situation in pragmatic terms, the Jews were no longer a serious problem: other challenges awaited the nation.

The predicaments of people caught between the hammer and anvil were real enough, but pragmatic calculations in the face of massive death must be seen, at best, as profoundly amoral. The impact of two occupations is reflected in vividly existential terms in the person of the writer and journalist Rapolas Mackonis who, as noted, had recorded his joy at the German liberation of Vilnius. Some would prefer to forget his response to the first days of the Soviet occupation of a year earlier as he welcomed the People's Government, denigrating Smetona

---

144 "Ar ir lietuviai terorizuos?‚" *Į laisvę*, May 25, 1943, 3–4. The terms, translated here idiomatically as "John Doe types," imply that the killers may not have been ethnic Lithuanians.
145 Cited from the October 15, 1943, issue of *Nepriklausoma Lietuva* in Venclauskas, "Lietuvos įvaizdžiai": 80.

("The President is Dead! Long Live Lithuania!") and praising the "revolution."[146] Under the Germans, Mackonis edited the antisemitic Vilnius daily *Naujoji Lietuva* until his arrest and subsequent incarceration at the Stutthof concentration camp in March 1943 as part of the Nazi crackdown following the failed SS mobilization drive. In the spring of 1945 Mackonis found himself huddled in a barn with other hungry inmates who had survived the camp's evacuation and subsequent death march. He described yet another liberation:

> Nearby we hear explosions. The walls are shaking, the doors are blown off. The shooting is getting closer and more persistent. We hear the obvious thunder of tanks. "The Swabians are holding on," [some are saying]. "No, it's not the Swabians, they're Soviet tanks. Soviet ones? Can it be? No, they're really Soviet." The roaring of the tanks comes closer, the shooting stops. Some of our fellow inmates, out on the street, are enthusiastically shouting, "hooray." Our barn is filled with enthusiasm and joy. We fall into hugs and kisses. Some are crying with joy. Thus, with the first rays of the sun on this day, April 12th, we are human again. An hour ago, we had been slaves, awaiting a terrible death, and now in small groups we come out of the barn as if resurrected. Huge tanks are rolling along the narrow streets of the small town. One of them comes to a stop. A young soldier leaps out of the tank. He distributes cigarettes, and we sincerely shake his hand.[147]

Following his liberation from the SS Mackonis chose to remain in Poland. In 1952 he was arrested by Soviet security and sent to the Gulag. He died in Vilnius in 1982.

Occupiers, Collaborators, Relationships: Questions of Power and Responsibility

Few issues arouse as much passion as collaboration under foreign rule. The case of the killer at the pits is an easy one, condemnation the only proper

---

146 On Mackonis's behavior in 1940 see Mantas Bražiūnas, "Žurnalistikos laukas okupuotoje Lietuvoje" (PhD diss., University of Vilnius, 2017), 90–93.

147 Rapolas Mackonis, *Amžiaus liudininko užrašai*, ed. Birutė Mackonytė (Vilnius: Lietuvos rašytojų sąjungos leidykla, 2001), 426–427. Among some Lithuanians, "Swabian" can serve as a condescending term denoting a simpleton.

response. Other cases are more confounding. An American scholar described her grandfather, one Milivoje Jovanović, a Serbian police official in Belgrade, who established and briefly oversaw an office of Jewish affairs during the German occupation. Jovanović implemented repressive measures but eventually fell out of favor with the Germans. His story, she wrote, "reflects the complex nature of collaboration and rescue, responsibility and memory," listing the various motives for helping the occupiers: ideological affinity, careerism, fear, simple inertia.[148] Collaboration is, of course, above all a relationship, but one which is rarely static, subject to change over time.

To understand the interactions between Germans and Lithuanians during the years of occupation requires addressing two issues: ideological intent and power. In terms of shared purpose, many non-Communist Lithuanians supported the Reich's goal of crushing Bolshevism, and considering the popularity of Judeo-Bolshevik notions, proved susceptible to imagining a new social order without Jews. Lithuanians, however, did not draft plans for a Final Solution, despite the vile rhetoric of the press following the invasion. The PG approved the segregation and legal discrimination of "citizens of Jewish nationality," but the leaders neither intended nor supported mass extermination. (The genocidal language of Voldemarist radicals in Berlin was an early outlier.) The LAF had indeed proposed a goal of what we now label "ethnic cleansing," the forced removal of a nationality from a specified territory, either through terror or forced deportation. Ethnic cleansing (displacement) and physical annihilation are activities that are significantly different, although it is also true, according to Norman Naimark, that the former can, under the right circumstances, "bleed into genocide as mass murder is committed in order to rid a land of its people."[149] History will, however, record that most Lithuanian leaders remained, with few exceptions, silent regarding anti-Jewish violence and did nothing to restrain antisemitic propaganda. As the war continued, identification with German policies waned: in the end, the majority of Lithuanians concluded that the only shared purpose with the occupier that was of any use for the national cause was halting a Soviet invasion. But anti-Jewish attitudes persisted, even as the

---

148 Jelena Subotić, *Yellow Star, Red Star: Holocaust Remembrance after Communism* (Ithaca: Cornell University Press), xiv.
149 Norman M. Naimark, *Fires of Hatred: Ethnic Cleansing in Twentieth-Century Europe* (Cambridge, MA: Harvard University Press, 2001), 3–4. Of course, to people suffering the physical and emotional impact of cruel and lethal policies, such academic distinctions can be meaningless.

anti-Nazi underground press disingenuously sought to put the blame for the genocide solely on the Germans and their gaggle of lackeys.

The German police and administrative personnel and their Lithuanian counterparts were connected and performed similar functions. There were far fewer German officials than Lithuanian personnel in the country, a situation that prevailed in most of the German administrative structures of the occupied East. But the respective German and Lithuanian institutions were not equivalent in power regardless of how few were the foreign supervisors, or how willingly the more numerous subservient native officials enacted decrees. Even when collaboration was granted freely, as was usually the case, there was never much question of who acted as superior, and who followed as subordinate. The notions of assistance or cooperation, without proper qualification, do not fully convey the situation of disempowerment in an occupied land. When Colonel Reivytis encountered what, in the scheme of things, was a relatively minor matter, he sought direction from an SS lieutenant many years his junior. In one account from the Kovno Ghetto, an SS man, in response to Jewish complaints, detained a Lithuanian policeman who had murdered a ghetto inmate and then sent the culprit to the Ninth Fort.[150] There are accounts of German officers arresting and, on at least several occasions, executing undisciplined Lithuanian police battalion members.[151] Passive resistance, such as the refusal to mobilize an SS legion in the spring of 1943, or the subsequent negotiations with Germans at the so-called Lithuanian Conference in April 1943, did not significantly change the status of relative power. In the latter case, the Lithuanians were faced with the threat of a General Government-style occupation if they did not submit to the demands of Reich officials. In the end, despite their relatively lean police presence in Lithuania, the Germans had no trouble suppressing the Local Force (Vietinė Rinktinė) in 1944, executing some eighty-six recalcitrant Lithuanian volunteers.[152]

As Jan T. Gross has noted, the essence of collaboration, commonly understood in the pejorative sense of harming one's fellow citizens, lies in the granting of authority to the occupier in a situation of an "uneven distribution of

---

150 Gerber, *Diary*, entry of November 15, 1942, 202–203.
151 The Rev. Zenonas Ignatavičius recorded ministering to them before their executions.
152 The reference to the veiled threat to place Lithuanians into a situation "like that of the Polish nation" is recounted in Matulionis, *Neramios dienos*, 238. See also, Sužiedėlis, "Military Mobilization": 36–44. There is now a monument to the Local Force soldiers at Paneriai.

power," rather than merely providing administrative "expertise and information."[153] There is no doubt that Lithuanian collaborators played an important supportive role in the Holocaust. Whether their assistance was indispensable in accomplishing the Nazis' ultimate goals is another, probably unanswerable, question.[154] It is easier to deal with the problem of moral agency. Lithuanians working in collaborationist structures had real choices: whether to protest the murders, refuse to participate, resign, evade unnecessary cruelties, or even attempt rescue. Moral decisions could have been made even if they would not have substantially affected the ultimate outcome, particularly after "the thin line between mass persecution and genocide was irrevocably crossed."[155] Nonetheless, recognizing the culpability of indigenous perpetrators in the Holocaust should not lead to confusions about the power relationship between the occupiers and the occupied. It is clear that ultimately, the fate of Europe's Jews depended on decisions made in Berlin. The historical record also reveals that the operational agency of the Final Solution in Lithuania was largely in the hands of the high-ranking German officials who oversaw the country's occupation.

There was one notable exception to this disparity in power. The survival of Jews hiding in city apartments, former shtetls, villages, and forest hideouts depended not on the occupiers, but almost entirely on the behavior of the surrounding Gentile population.

---

153 Jan Tomasz Gross, *Polish Society under German Occupation: The Generalgouvernement 1939–1944* (Princeton: Princeton University Press, 1979), 117, 119.

154 The experience of German Police Battalion 101 in Poland suggests that the Nazis were quite capable of shooting and transporting to death camps tens of thousands of human beings without employing significant local forces and in situations where the cooperation of local officials was helpful, but not essential to the killing process. See Christopher Browning, *Ordinary Men: Reserve Police Battalion 101 and the Final Solution in Poland* (New York: HarperCollins, 1991).

155 As noted in the insightful presentation by Joachim Tauber, "The Significance of June 22nd, 1941: Thoughts on the History of the Second World War and the National Socialist Annihilation Policy" (paper presented at the conference "A Divisive Past: The Soviet-German War and Narratives of Mass Violence in East Central Europe," sponsored by the Lithuanian Institute of History, the Ministry of Foreign Affairs, and the History Faculty of the University of Vilnius, June 4–5, 2021).

Empathetic Helpers and Righteous Gentiles: Assistance and Rescue in Lithuania

Jacob Goldberg underwent a disorienting experience at the outbreak of the war. He had broken out from a Soviet jail along with other political prisoners but was then almost immediately arrested by the anti-Soviet insurgents and jailed again with his family. Two days later, he was recognized by the new prison director, a fellow former officer in the Lithuanian Army, and released, saving him from the Seventh Fort.

Evaluating the measure of assistance that Lithuanians provided to the Jews is a daunting task. As of January 2022, the registry of Righteous Gentiles held at Yad Vashem contained 924 names under the heading of "Lithuania," constituting the second (after the Netherlands) highest ratio of rescuers to the general population on this honored list.[156] Most are ethnic Lithuanians, along with people whose surnames are of Polish or Belarusian origin. Among the recipients of the Lithuanian government's Cross of Saviors (Žūvančiųjų gelbėjimo kryžius) are 1,663 persons recognized for their efforts to save Jews (as of September 2023), although some of the rescuers are also included in the Yad Vashem archive (for example, Stefanija Ladigienė who rescued Irena Veisaitė). The cross is usually presented by the president at an annual ceremony in Vilnius on September 23, the Day for the Commemoration of the Genocide of Lithuanian Jews.[157] There are also unacknowledged rescuers who appear in diaries, memoirs, interviews, and testimonies, although here the historian must exercise care: some storytellers are less than reliable, while others may be motivated by a desire to repair the national reputation. In any case, the approximate number of Gentile families in Lithuania who sheltered and/or rescued Jews during the Holocaust has been estimated at about 2,300.[158]

Many people went beyond mere disapproval of the killings and extended a helping hand to their distressed Jewish neighbors, or other persecuted strangers, including Soviet POWs. Zelig Kalmanovich stayed in an underground

---

156 Calculated on recipients of the award per one hundred thousand inhabitants according to the 1939 estimate of the population in the listed countries.

157 "Žūvančiųjų gelbėjimo kryžiumi apdovanotų žydų gelbėtojų sąrašas," Vilniaus Gaono žydų istorijos muziejus, accessed November 29, 2023, https://www.jmuseum.lt/lt/zuvanciu-ju-gelbejimo-kryzius/i/2335/zuvanciuju-gelbejimo-kryziumi-apdovanotu-zydu-gelbeto-ju-sarasas/.

158 According to approximations of researchers at the Vilna Gaon Jewish Museum.

shelter in Vilnius during the first week of the invasion, recalling that "Our Polish neighbors were especially helpful in obtaining vegetables and more."[159] Yudel Beiles who had survived the October 29, 1941, mass shooting at the Ninth Fort fled to a small house nearby where an elderly couple provided the blood-soaked youth with fresh clothes and food before sending him on his way. While such actions did not constitute rescue, they were not without some risk to the helpers. Some women who undertook to feed imprisoned Jewish children grew close to them and sought to have them adopted, usually unsuccessfully.[160] There is, of course, no way to quantify the extent of such assistance, but considerable anecdotal evidence, especially from survivors who had no particular reason to feel kindly towards Lithuanians, indicates that it was not uncommon.

The authorities noticed that some non-Jews were not abiding by the strict curfews and other restrictions which had been imposed on the Jews, as well as the prohibitions against contacts with the POWs. On October 25, 1941, the daily *Į laisvę* wrote on its first page about the lack of proper understanding among people who had not yet internalized the new order and who had failed to appreciate the dangers posed by the nation's enemies:

> What is going on? In some shops one can see the yellow-starred Jews pushing their way forward towards the salesclerks, who then go out of their way to quickly satisfy every wish of these "honored clients." You can see columns of POWs on the streets, marching along, those who just recently fought us in the most despicable and perfidious manner. And guess what? One can't believe one's eyes: there are people—and not just a few—who run up to the columns of prisoners, peppering them with food and cigarettes. When they are caught, they argue, well you see, these are people after all. Any decent person who has any self-respect cannot and should not tolerate such behavior towards the POWs and the Jews of the ghetto. Whoever helps the Jews and POWs is expressing solidarity with them and will be treated accordingly. By behaving in this fashion, they place themselves beyond the bounds of our community, because today we follow the slogan: *it's either us or them!*[161] (Emphasis in the original)

---

159 As remembered in his entry of June 22, 1942, published in Kalmanovich, *Hope*, 47.
160 As in the case of Ona Balsienė in Vilkija, reported by Grinevičius, "Vilkijoj," 51.
161 "Kas yra?" *Į laisvę*, October 25, 1941, 1.

In Rokiškis, the local commandant threatened public censure for those who allowed Jews to avoid onerous work requirements. The German official Wutz noted that Lithuanian assistance to Jews had become more common by early 1942.[162]

On September 10, 1941, Major Arno Brendel, the Wehrmacht's commandant in Šiauliai, wrote to Gewecke describing the reaction of people who had gathered to watch a column of fifty Russian POWs. Women of all walks of life, Brendel observed, gathered on the sidewalks and "threw all manner of food, apples, bread and sausages" at the men. The column came to a halt as a wild scene unfolded. The escort was unable to control the Russians as they scrambled to pick up the food. The Lithuanian men took no action to control their womenfolk and simply "observed this shameless and unworthy behavior." Such was the ungrateful behavior of the folks who had been liberated from the "Bolshevik yoke," Brendel concluded.[163] In the summer of 1943, the family of Juozas Lukša-Daumantas, a leader of the postwar anti-Soviet resistance, took in Vasily, a starving nineteen-year-old Russian POW escapee wandering the countryside, and helped him evade capture until the return of the Soviets a year later.[164] It is possible that people may have shown more sympathy for the bedraggled young POWs than for the Jews; nonetheless, the ordinary impulse towards empathy boded well for those Jews who had the fortune to meet up with the right people.

Elijas Olkinas's wife Liza recalls how the wife of "some Fascist boss" had allowed her to use the telephone: "I called my Lithuanian friend [who] brought me food a couple of times." A German guard allowed her to surreptitiously collect apples. Afterwards, she encountered a "Lithuanian solder" whom she had once met as a child: "he recognized me, gave me a large chunk of bread and sausage, and saw me off to the gate of the ghetto."[165] Elja Ganz remembered a time when the "provisions/food situation improved since the Lithuanians often helped with the smuggling of food." At other times, she writes, Lithuanians sold food.[166] As noted, neighbor women provided food to the Olkinas family in Panemunėlis. Sometimes helping Jews took the form of spiritual rather than

---

162 See above.
163 Brendel to Gewecke, September 10, 1941, LYA. f. 3377, ap. 58, b. 1040, l. 10–10a.
164 Juozas Daumantas, *Partizanai*, 3rd ed. (Vilnius: Į laisvę fondas, 1990), 15.
165 Litinskaya, Zhanna, interview with Liza Lukinskaya, Centropa Project, February 2005, https://www.centropa.org/biography/liza-lukinskaya.
166 Elja Ganz testimony, 1–2.

material assistance. The Jewish peasant Yoyel Levin hid out among his neighbors rather than go to the ghetto. During a routine search, Yoyel was murdered and buried by the side of the road. The peasants apparently understood what their dead neighbor would have wished and went to the village elder to ask permission to dig up the body and bring it to the Jewish cemetery in Vilnius. Kruk recounts that "The corpse was accompanied to the cemetery by a few Christian peasants, who brought sheets to bury him in linen according to Jewish law."[167] By themselves, these empathetic helpers could not affect the ultimate fate of the persecuted Jews, but their efforts should not be ignored in the historical record.

In Lithuania rescue efforts to assist Jews in escaping Nazi persecution can be traced to the crisis which resulted from the influx of thousands of refugees who fled the German-Soviet invasion of Poland in September 1939. In January 1940, the Lithuanian government's commission on refugees reported the registration of 34,939 arrivals, of whom 13,469 were listed as Jews. At least ten thousand Jewish refugees were registered in Vilnius, of whom about 75% were single men reflecting the predominance of Polish yeshiva students. The first contingent arrived from Kleck on October 14, 1939. More came to escape the clutches of "godless Communism" when in November 1939 Moscow announced that Soviet citizenship would be granted to the inhabitants of the annexed Polish territories. At the time, only about five hundred of the registered refugees were children.[168] Many of the refugees were Zionists who hoped to find a way to Palestine, among them, the future prime minister of Israel, Menachem Begin. Neutral Lithuania across the border seemed at the time a reasonably secure refuge.

Hundreds of Jewish refugees were able to leave Lithuania before the Soviet invasion of June 1940 with the cooperation of the government and the help of the Hebrew Immigrant Aid Society (HIAS) and other Jewish groups in a complicated arrangement which allowed their departure to Sweden via Kaunas and Riga.[169] A more important initiative to find a way out for the refugees originated with Lithuanian authorities in late 1939 through the head of its mission in Moscow, Ladas Natkevičius, who had been imploring the Kremlin to grant Jewish migrants transit through Odesa to Haifa, offering to provide Polish citizens with

---

167 Kruk, *Last Days*, 289, entry of May 14, 1942.
168 Strelconvas, *Geri, blogi, vargdieniai*, 110.
169 Levin, *The Lesser*, 205–206.

new Lithuanian passports or other necessary permits for the journey. Records show that by the end of April 1940, the Soviets were ready to consider the plan. On July 29, 1940, while Lithuania was under Soviet control but not yet incorporated into the USSR, Stalin signed a document "permitting the Jewish refugees from the former Poland now staying in Lithuania to transit via the USSR." The refugees were now free to use their Lithuanian safe conduct passes to get out. People in Kaunas often say that this was the beginning of their city's transformation into the "Casablanca of the North," evoking the classic 1942 film.[170] The Kremlin's liberal attitude towards the refugees seems out of character. Dov Levin has suggested that Stalin's motives were pragmatic: an easy way to rid themselves of a non-productive and potentially hostile element which was not keen to accept Soviet citizenship. An added bonus was the opportunity for Lavrenti Beria, head of the NKVD, to infiltrate Soviet agents into the groups leaving for the West, as in the case of the brothers from Vilkaviškis, Jack Soble and Robert Soblen, who were arrested for espionage in New York in 1957 and 1960 respectively.[171]

Such was the background for the rescue efforts that have come under the heading of the "Visas for Life," the diplomatic effort to provide an exit for Jews escaping the Soviet Union, but which in the end enabled them to avoid death in German-occupied Europe. The first consular official to sponsor the program in Lithuania was Jan Zwartendijk, the Philips Company's manager in Lithuania, who was appointed acting consul in Kaunas in June 1940 to represent the Dutch government-in-exile. Despite the fact that he had no permission from Dutch colonial officials to act, during the summer of 1940 Zwartendijk issued some two thousand travel permits for Jews to travel to Curaçao where visas were not needed as long as it was understood that the refugees' true destination lay elsewhere.

The better-known diplomat rescuer who granted life-saving visas was Chiune Sugihara, a specialist in Soviet affairs, who took over the Japanese Consulate in Kaunas in October 1939. Sugihara's job was to collect information on German-Soviet relations and maintain contact with Polish intelligence

---

170 Ilya Altman, "The Issuance of Visas to War Refugees by Chiune Sugihara as Reflected in the Documents of Russian Archives," *Darbai ir dienos* 67 (2017): 233–234; Also, Kasparavičius, "Lietuviai ir žydai," 149–150. See examples of the various transit documents in *Šiaurės Kasablanka. Kaunas 1939–1940: Parodos katalogas* (Kaunas: Sugiharos fondas, 2018).

171 Levin, *The Lesser*, 215–217.

operatives.¹⁷² After his arrival, Sugihara began issuing visas that would permit holders to leave Lithuania. The Japanese diplomat left Kaunas for Prague on September 1, 1940, but continued to provide information on the refugees to his superiors in Tokyo. Perhaps, the most unusual case of rescue in this context is that of the Kaunas-born Jewish couple, Abraham and Gusta Lipetz, and their three sons, who found their way to Manila after a fantastic journey via Belgium, France, Algeria, Morocco, Portugal, America, and the Panama Canal.¹⁷³

The estimates of the numbers of Jewish refugees whose lives were saved by the efforts of the Kaunas diplomats vary widely, raising questions about the assumptions and methods on which the statistics have been collected. A message of February 28, 1941 from Sugihara to Tokyo included a thirty-one-page list of Polish and Lithuanian refugees of whom 1,500 were Jews. Sugihara himself suggested that 4,700 managed to successfully reach their destinations, mostly in the Far East. Hillel Levine's estimate that the diplomatic operation resulted in as many as ten thousand rescues must be considered improbable. The oft-cited number of six thousand is likely a "rhetorical figure," generally accepted in popular discourse but not necessarily precise. It has been based on the notion that the visas and tickets on record were issued to family units, not individuals, and thus assumed a significant contingent of children. The Russian historian Ilya Altman notes that at most 2,500 refugees purchased tickets from Kaunas or Vilnius to Vladivostok in 1940–1941. According to his review of the relevant documents in Russian and Lithuanian archives, the number of children traveling to the Far East on these trains was insignificant. The question of the number of people saved by Sugihara must be considered as yet unresolved.¹⁷⁴ The "Visas for Life" rescue story has produced a number of popular and academic works. But as Lithuanian historians have noted, much of the history of the Sugihara episode in particular was written before the post-1990 opening of

---

172 Gerhard Krebs, "Germany and Sugihara Chiune: Japanese-Polish Intelligence Cooperation and Counter-Intelligence," *Darbai ir dienos* 67 (2017): 215–230.

173 Ber Kotlerman, "Phillipine Visas-for Jews from the Perspective of the Unanswered Letters of 1939 to President Quezon," *Darbai ir dienos* 67 (2017): 285.

174 Chiharu Inaba, "Documents Related to Visas for Life and Historiography of Chiune Sugihara," *Darbai ir dienos* 67 (2017): 265–267; Hillel Levine, *In Search of Sugihara: The Elusive Japanese Diplomat Who Risked His Life to Rescue 10,000 Jews from the Holocaust* (New York: The Free Press, 1996), 285–286n7. Questions on some other details of the Sugihara narrative are raised in Bernaras Ivanovas, "Chiune (Sempo) Sugiharos veiklos Kaune 1930–1940 m. probleminiai aspektai," *Genocidas ir rezistencija* 1, no. 9 (2001): 7–14. Ilya Altman, "The Issuance of Visas": 231–237. Cf. Levin, *The Lesser*, 208.

the Soviet-controlled archives, so that that the particular Lithuanian political and diplomatic context in which the rescue took place was either minimized or ignored.[175]

Sugihara and Zwartendijk fully deserved the title of Righteous Gentile, but like the other diplomats (such as the Portuguese consul Aristides de Sousa Mendes), they risked bureaucratic sanctions rather than life-threatening consequences. Even if the Nazi occupation regime in Lithuania was far less brutal than in neighboring Poland, the Lithuanians who chose to shelter Jews placed themselves in danger. Authorities sometimes levied fines on people who violated rules and sold food to Jews. In two known cases, German and Lithuanian police severely beat women who had tried to intercede on behalf of persecuted Jews. Some rescuers gave up their lives for the cause. In the summer of 1941, the Kaunas doctor Vytautas Žakavičius was executed for protecting his Jewish friend. On January 31, 1942, the actor Vytautas Juodka was killed by the Gestapo together with the two Jewish women he had hidden in his home. A sentry at the Kovno Ghetto shot V. Kukta as he tried to pass food to an inmate. At least a dozen Lithuanian Gentiles are known to have been put to death for saving Jews.[176]

Elena Kutorgienė, a well-known Righteous Gentile, took more risks than most, sheltering Jews in her Kaunas apartment and sending them on to safety. Kutorgienė hoped that news of the mass killings of the summer and fall of 1941 would stir the outside world to action. On October 7, 1941, she wrote in her diary: "Maybe the world community does not know what is transpiring here. We must inform, organize protests, search for ways to fight back wherever possible." Elena's son Viktoras composed an extensive account of the murders in English which concluded with a passionate plea to help the Jews. The plan was to smuggle the document to the West with the help of soloist Vincė Jonuškaitė-Zaunienė who was heading out of the country on a concert tour of Sweden and Germany. She is reported to have delivered Kutorga's message to the American Embassy in Berlin just before the United States entered the war. There is no evidence of

---

175 See Simonas Strelcovas, "Pabėgeliai, vizos, gelbėtojai?," *Darbai ir dienos* 47 (2007): 62–73; also the more recent study, Strelcovas, *Geri, blogi, vargdieniai*, 11–19, 112–118.

176 Kazys Rukšėnas, "Del Lietuvos žydų gelbėjmo hitlerinės oklupacijos metais (1941–1945)," in *Lietuvos istorijos metraštis* (1978): 46–47. Cf. Rimantas Zizas, "Persecution of Non-Jewish Citizens of Lithuania, Murder of Civilian Population," in Zizas et al., *Karo belaisvių*, 372–377.

IMAGE 6.5. Visas for Life. Clockwise: Chiune Sugihara, the Japanese consul in Kaunas, who distributed life-saving visas to Jewish and Polish refugees. Jan Swartendijk, the Netherlands honorary consul who provided transit papers to Curaçao. Refugees seeking assistance at the Japanese Consulate, July 1940 (Courtesy of Nobuki Sugihara). The former Japanese Consulate in Kaunas, currently the Sugihara House Museum (author's photo).

what happened afterwards. A German version of the document was found in the Russian State Archive and published in 1993.[177]

---

177 The quotes in the diary and the story of the document are taken from Ilya Altman, "Dokumenty rossiiskikh arkhivov o Kholokoste v Litve" (report presented to the International Holocaust Conference, Vilnius, September 2002). Author's copy of the distributed text. Viktoras Kutorga's report is available in English in Rubenstein and Altman, *Unknown Black Book*, 278–287.

IMAGE 6.6. Ona Šimaitė, the librarian who helped the Paper Brigade in the Vilna Ghetto and rescued Jews. After her arrest by the Gestapo, the Rector of Vilnius University Mykolas Biržiška organized a bribe which saved her from execution. Ona was subsequently sent to Dachau. (Courtesy of the Vilna Gaon Museum of Jewish History.)

IMAGE 6.7. Stefanija Ladigienė (left) and Juozas and Ona Strimaitis who rescued Irena Veisaitė from the Kovno Ghetto. (Courtesy of Vilna Gaon Museum of Jewish History.)

Another well-known rescuer was Ona Šimaitė, by all accounts a selfless soul who worked as a librarian at the University of Vilnius. Here she met Jacob Gens's Lithuanian wife who provided her with a permit to enter the ghetto. Šimaitė assisted Sutzkever and the Paper Brigade in securing Jewish cultural treasures, which she would smuggle out and hide in her home and other locations. She is credited with saving the notes of the Vilna Ghetto chronicler Grigory Shur by hiding them under the floorboards of the university library. She also used her cover to bring food and news of the outside world to the Jews and, on many occasions, provided forged papers to help ghetto inmates escape. Šimaitė's turn towards the rescue of people occurred by chance when the rector of the university, Mykolas Biržiška, asked Ona to deliver some money to one of his former students in the ghetto. Here the librarian met the sixteen-year-old inmate Sala Vaksman whom she managed to smuggle out to the Aryan side in September 1943 as the liquidation of the ghetto threatened. In April 1944, a neighbor denounced the rescuer to the Gestapo. The police seized the materials Šimaitė had hidden for the paper brigade and severely tortured her but were unable to extract any useful information. Ona Šimaitė survived Dachau and lived in France after her liberation.[178]

---

178 Fishman, *Book Smugglers*, 201–203; Šuras, *Užrašai*, 16. Dalia Kuodytė and Rimantas Stankevičius, eds., *Išgelbėję pasaulį . . . žydu gelbėjimas Lietuvoje* (Vilnius: LGGRTC, 2001),

IMAGE 6.8. The Rev. Bronius Paukštys (left) who saved many Jewish children from the Kovno Ghetto and Bishop Vincentas Borisevičius who sheltered Jews in Telšiai.

Although the country's elites had stayed largely silent during the Holocaust, a number of prominent citizens undertook to rescue Jews. The former president Kazys Grinius and his wife Kristina were recognized by Yad Vashem in 2015. At least two rescuers were family members of Lithuanian officials working under the Germans. Ona Landsbergienė, the wife of the PG's minister of communal economy, Vytautas Landsbergis-Žemkalnis (and the mother of the first head of state of the Second Republic in 1990–1993, Vytautas Landsbergis), rescued the pediatrician Fruma Gurvičienė and her daughters Bela and Eta. Jadvyga Jablonskienė, the sister of Stasys Žymantas Žakevičius, a prominent LAF member and head of the Vilnius Citizens' Committee in June and July 1941, smuggled Sulamita, the baby daughter of the Kaunas tailor David Vilenchuk (Dovydas Vilenčukas) out of the Kovno Ghetto. After the Soviets arrested Jadvyga in 1945, her mother protected Sulamita, now renamed Dalia, until her father, having survived Dachau, returned to reclaim his daughter in 1946. Jadvyga died in a Soviet prison in December 1948. Both she and Ona Landsbergienė are now in the Righteous Gentile pantheon.[179] Other prominent people also took part in rescue. The Šiauliai doctor Domas Jasaitis and his wife Sofija, mentioned in several accounts as friendly to Jews, took in the young girl Chana. Since the doctor worked in a busy clinic, the couple feared discovery and, after an unsuccessful attempt to "plant" the child in a village outside the city, found permanent shelter with the Dambrauskas family near Mažeikiai. Chana's mother and older sister survived Stutthof and returned to Lithuania; the remnants of the family eventually emigrated to Israel. A friend of Sofija, Janina Luinienė, who worked in the clinic along with the local nursing sisters of

---

84–89; Julija Šukys, "Ona Šimaitė and the Vilnius Ghetto: An Unwritten Memoir," *Lituanus* 54, no. 2 (2008): 5–25; cf. Julija Šukys, *Epistophelia: Writing the Life of Ona Šimaitė* (Lincoln: University of Nebraska Press, 2012).

179 Kuodytė and Stankevičius, *Išgelbėję*, 156–158.

the Order of the Sacred Heart, also helped rescue Jewish children.[180] Among the most prominent cultural figures who assisted Jews were the writer Balys Sruoga and his historian wife Vanda, as well as the feminist writer Sofija Kymantaite-Čiurlionienė, the widow of Lithuania's revered painter and composer Mykolas Čiurlionis.[181]

There were some counterintuitive cases. The Lithuanian chief of the Vilnius district Kostas Kalendra, who promulgated antisemitic decrees, assisted the family of the art and theater critic Markas Petuchauskas and another Jewish family who were acquaintances from the chief's days in Šiauliai (Kalendra had been district chief there in 1934–1937; at the time, Petuchauskas's father Samuel was the city's vice-mayor).[182] Bobelis, the Kaunas commandant, released some Jews from the Ninth Fort. In these latter two cases, the onetime help seems to have been extended based on previous relationships or to former fellow soldiers.

The role of the clergy was an important factor in rescue efforts. There were several instances in which priests directly confronted the executioners, recorded in the towns of Varėna, Plungė, and Alsėdžiai. In the latter case, survivors recall that the "Roman Catholic priest and prelate" stood among the Jews and prevented the police from carrying out the killing.[183] None of these rare interventions saved the victims in the end, but rectories, monasteries, and convents offered relatively more long-term safety. Priests interested in helping Jews also knew those parishioners who could be trusted. Since there was no civil registry in Lithuania before 1940, clerics could act as "forgers" of critically needed baptismal and birth documents. Some religious people were motivated by a desire to "save souls," but the result was rescued lives, nonetheless. Bronius Paukštys (1897–1966) was an erudite and well-traveled Catholic priest who worked to rescue over a hundred Jewish children and dozens of adults. As dean of the Holy Trinity parish in Kaunas, Paukštys, assisted by his brother Juozas, was in a position to produce birth certificates and baptismal records for the Jews from the Kovno Ghetto. The brothers hid Jews on the church grounds, and when

---

180 "Rescued Lithuanian Jewish Child Tells about Shoah: Jasaitienė Sofija—Domas Jasaitis," Vilna Gaon Museum of Jewish History, accessed November 29, 2023, http://rescuedchild.lt/content.php?id=5252; cf. Kuodytė and Stankevičius, *Išgelbėję*, 220–221.
181 Ibid., 116–123.
182 Ibid., 125–126, also mentioned in Markas Petuchauskas, *Price of Concord* (Vilnius: Versus Aureus, 2015), 42.
183 Testimonies of survivors as recorded by Lazar Yerusalimsky in Rubenstein and Altman, *Unknown Black Book*, 308.

discovery was imminent, found safe houses with farmers in Suvalkija.[184] In contrast, Bronius Gotautas, the nearly illiterate, devout son of peasants known as "the brother," worked as a servant for the Capuchin monks in Petrašiūnai. He was often seen in his ragged clothes doling out food and medicine to the Jews. Gotautas collected unused documents from local offices and rectories and took them to forgers for distribution. In the hospital where he worked as an orderly, he helped shelter Jews. He was arrested in Kaunas on July 22, 1944, and was deported to one of the subcamps near Natzweiler. Gotautas died in a Salesian nursing home in Germany in 1950 (and became a Righteous Gentile in 1974).[185] Rev. Juozas Želvys of Saint Anthony's in Kaunas helped escapees from the ghetto, sometimes using as a contact his parishioner, the teacher P. Švegžda, who operated a small shop next to the church. Two high-ranking prelates have been documented as having sheltered Jews: the bishop of Telšiai, Vincentas Borisevičius (1887–1946), and the bishop of Kaišiadorys, Teofilius Matulionis, who is credited with assisting the rescue of the Israeli concert pianist Esther Yellin (b. 1940), the niece of anti-fascist fighter Chaim Yellin, by placing her, along with a few other children, with Benedictine nuns under his charge. Unfortunately, Esther was the only one in the group to survive.[186]

The experience of the Bak family, which also found shelter in convents, exemplified the difficulties facing the rescuers and their charges. In the fall of 1941, Samuel Bak and his parents, along with two other men, escaped ghettoization by hiding in Maria Mikulska's Benedictine Convent in the heart of Vilnius. After several months of quiet, the Germans expelled the nuns to a labor camp, while the concealed survivors barely managed to escape the building in the freezing cold. Their only choice, as Bak explained in noting the irony, was "to seek refuge in the ghetto as a place of last resort." By chance the family was able to slip in with a group of Jews returning from work and found a place in the ghetto. After escaping from the roundup of the children at the HKP camp Bak and his mother managed to make their way to the Benedictine Convent once again. The building had been turned into the headquarters of the ERR where confiscated Jewish

---

184 Paukštys's exploits are described in Ilya Ehrenburg's and Vassily Grossman's *Black Book of Soviet Jewry*, 377–378; cf. Viktorija Sakaitė, "Žydų gelbėjimas," *Genocidas ir rezistencija* 2, no. 4 (1998): 93–94.

185 Kuodytė and Stankevičius, *Išgelbėję*, 227–241

186 Yellin's testimony is Solomonas Abramovičius and Jakovas Zilbergas, eds., *Išgelbėti bulvių maišuose: 50 Kauno geto vaikų istorijų* (Vilnius: Siaures Jeruzale, 2014), 269–277.

materials were stored, and it was the Baks' fortune that some of the former nuns, including Sister Maria, had been released and were employed as hired help at the facility. The nuns persuaded a group of Jews hiding among the piles of books and archival manuscripts to take in the mother and child despite the danger. It was here under the watchful eye of Mikulska, the historian Rev. Juozas Stakauskas, and the engineer Vladas Žemaitis that the Baks endured until they were able to emerge from hiding as the Red Army entered the city in July 1944.[187]

After the war, some Lithuanian sources exaggerated the role of some members of the clergy who, on closer inspection, had not been rescuers.[188] Nonetheless, the collected material on Lithuania's clergy indicates that scores of priests and many nuns participated in some manner in the rescue of Jews. Although hundreds of ordinary people received Yad Vashem and Lithuanian government awards for their dedication, many rescuers remain nameless. Kruk described the practice of ghettoized Jews seeking to save their children by "settling" them with Christian parents on the outside: "Often Christian neighbors did this themselves, on their own initiative. People took Jewish children, often converted them, kept them in their homes, and brought them up." Kruk described the case of an "intelligent woman" from his neighborhood whose only child lived with a Christian in the village. "The mother will risk her own life," he remarked, "but not play with the fate of her child." Such cases were not uncommon, although it is difficult to accept Kruk's claim that "thousands and thousands" of children were sent out in this manner.[189]

In the Šiauliai Ghetto two-year-old Rosalyn (Reyzele) Kirkel was hidden in the attic during the children's action of November 5, 1943, and told to be quiet as her parents went out to work. Her brother was seized by the police and perished, but Rosalyn and her sister managed to evade the roundup. The desperate mother persuaded a widowed friend in the ghetto who had Christian in-laws to arrange a home for her smallest child. The woman turned to her father-in-law's relatives and found a childless couple ("simple Catholic people, not at all wealthy") who agreed to take little Reyzele. She came to see Vincentas and

---

187 Sofija Binkienė, *Ir be ginklo kariai* (Vilnius: Mintis, 1967), 50–53, 55, 58. It was not uncommon for Jews hiding under extreme conditions to seek the ghetto as a place of relative safety. Unfortunately, unscrupulous writers have noted this fact to argue that the authorities *intended* ghettos as havens protecting Jews from Gentile violence.

188 See the analysis in Laukaitytė, *Lietuvos bažnyčios*, 114–117.

189 Kruk, *Last Days*, entry of May 3, 1942, 279.

Image 6.9. Two young girls in the Kovno Ghetto wearing Stars of David that were fashioned out of wood by their uncle, July 1943. Henia Wisgardisky (right) and her cousin, Bluma Berk were smuggled out of the ghetto, hidden by Lithuanian families and survived the war. (United States Holocaust Memorial Museum Photo Archives #10945. Courtesy of Henia Wisgardisky Lewin. Copyright of United States Holocaust Memorial Museum.)

Elena as her parents until her father returned to Lithuania in February 1946 to reclaim his daughter. The now five-year-old girl had no memory of this stranger and had to be dragged away from her rescuers.[190] One of Lithuania's child survivors of the Holocaust was the renowned writer Icchokas Meras whose short stories and novel *Stalemate* were one of the few examples of Soviet-era Lithuanian-language literature dealing solely with the Jewish experience of the Holocaust. Meras and his sister were picked up by women during a summer 1941 shooting operation near Kelmė after the guards left some of the condemned children unattended. Mrs. Dainauskas, the matriarch of the family who took him in became, in the writer's words, his second mother; his first, lost to him in the killing fields.[191]

One of the many fascinating stories involving children ended in what can be termed a "reverse rescue." Despair seized mothers in the Kovno Ghetto and concentration camp as the inmates learned of the Šiauliai children's action of November 1943 and feared the worst. Judita Kamber, the mother of a toddler named Ilana, bribed a guard with her wedding ring and took her to a Polish woman who refused to take the girl because her shelter was already overcrowded with hidden children. A desperate Mrs. Kamber persuaded Doctor Elkes to sedate Ilana and carried her out of the ghetto in a potato sack, leaving the child at the doorstep of the reluctant woman come what may. Moved by the mother's

---

190 "My Mother Smuggled Me out of the Shavl Ghetto," Yiddish Book Center, accessed May 10, 2021, https://www.yiddishbookcenter.org/collections/oral-histories/excerpts/woh-ex-0002669/my-mother-smuggled-me-out-shavl-siauliai-ghetto-hidden-jewish-child-during-holocaust.

191 See the writer's account in "Icchokas Meras and the Holocaust: Terror and Salvation in Contemporary Lithuanian Literature," *Lituanus* 27, no. 3 (1981): 5–6.

plight, the unnamed Polish rescuer found Ilana a home with a childless Lithuanian couple, Bronė and Kazys Liutkus. After the Soviets entered Kaunas, Ilana's engineer father Markus, who had been conscripted by the Red Army on the first day of the war, returned and claimed his daughter. Judita Kamber survived Stutthof and was reunited with her husband and father. The story took an odd turn when in 1946 Bronė Liutkienė appeared at the Kambers' doorstep with a small two-year-old boy and asked for refuge: she had received a warning that the couple were on a list to be deported. Markus Kamber sheltered the woman and boy, protecting them from Soviet officers who were searching for people on the deportation registers.[192]

In addition to individual acts of rescue, small groups and informal networks that depended on the cooperation (and silence) of those in the know also assisted Jews. The best organized and effective rescue of children was the result of the cooperation of Jewish parents in the Kovno Ghetto and willing Lithuanians. Rev. Stanislovas Jokūbauskis helped Yudel Beiles organize the operation. It is estimated that between 250 and four hundred children were smuggled out to the Gentile side although the precise number who remained successfully hidden and then survived is unknown.[193] The Jewish police helped ten-year-old Ella Griliks to slip out of the ghetto with her mother:

> A Christian youth who was waiting for us took us to his home.... I stayed there for two days.... My mother came to me and took me to the Christian orphanage. I was there for two or three days, until they gave me to a farmer. They disguised me as a Russian girl because I spoke Russian well. The farmer took me to a village near Aukštadvaris and put me into a children's home. I worked there with the other children, peeling potatoes and in the field. The children did not know I was a Jew, but the adults did know. There were other Jewish girls at this home, younger than me. I realized this by their faces. They did not know I was Jewish. We never talked about it.[194]

During the Soviet period, the history of sheltering Jews was not a priority for historians. Many rescuers were clearly people with "bourgeois nationalist"

---

192 The story is in Abramovičius and Zilbergas, *Išgelbėti bulvių maišuose*, 137–144. English version: Solomon Abramovich and Yakov Zilberg, eds., *Smuggled in Potato Sacks: Stories of the Hidden Children of the Kaunas Ghetto* (Edgware: Valentine Mitchell, 2011).

193 Abramovičius and Jakovas Zilbergas, *Išgelbėti bulvių maišuose*, 13; Beiles, *Yudke*, 68–75; cf. Levin and Brown, *The Story of an Underground*, 48–49.

194 Testimony cited in ibid, 49.

backgrounds, so they were mentioned sparingly in the very first Soviet book devoted entirely to rescue in Lithuania written by Sofija Binkienė, herself recognized by Yad Vashem in 1967.[195] In one of the rare Soviet Lithuanian academic surveys of the subject, the Germanist Kazys Rukšėnas, while presenting substantive material, singled out the role of Communist activists and "working class" elements.[196] The wrong kind of rescuers suffered more than just condescension at the hands of Soviet-era authors: after the war, some were arrested and found themselves on the way to prison or the Gulag. This was the fate of Rev. Paukštys, Stefanija Ladigienė, Jadvyga Jablonskienė, and the nurse Nelė Vukonytė, among others. In 1946 the Soviets executed Bishop Borisevičius.

With the restoration of independence in 1990, much new material has been published on Lithuanian attempts to save Jews. The Vilna Gaon Jewish State Museum in Vilnius has produced a mass of previously unavailable Jewish and Gentile testimonies. The new attention has not been without problems since there is at times a tendency among Lithuanians to utilize rescue stories as tools in the argument over the extent and nature of participation in the atrocities. Moreover, the motivations of rescuers were complex and inhabited a gray zone, a spectrum from altruism to less admirable incentives. Antisemitic rescuers (first noted by Nechama Tec), seemingly an oxymoron, are not such a strange phenomenon if one considers some historic analogues. (Many, if not most, American abolitionists, even the most passionate, can easily be classified as racists by today's more exacting standards.) Nevertheless, in one important way, the rescuers comprised a uniquely courageous cohort in German-occupied Lithuania. Unlike the underground press, the rescuers were unconcerned with geopolitical calculations. For them, it was enough that Jews were human beings. The political elites, even when they expressed regret at the destruction of the Litvaks, never used their public voice to call on the people to assist their fellow citizens. What is strange is that as of this writing those who saved Jews have only now begun to be acknowledged in marble. A street was named after Ona Šimaitė, and on September 21, 2018, a stone marker was unveiled in Vilnius announcing that "in this place a monument will be built commemorating rescuers of the Jews."[197]

---

195 Sofia Binkienė, *Ir be ginklo kariai*.

196 Rukšėnas, "Dėl žydų," 36–49.

197 "Rescuers of Lithuanian Jews Awarded and Honored," Vilna Gaon Museum of Jewish History, September 28, 2018, https://www.jmuseum.lt/en/news/item/787/.

7.

The Past as Legacy and Conflict: Wartime and Holocaust Narratives in Lithuania

Lithuania's population statistics of the postwar period reflect the devastation of the country's Jewry. At the end of 1945 there were an estimated ten thousand Jews in Lithuania of whom almost a fifth had survived as either partisans or in hiding among rescuers; the remainder were mainly returnees from the Soviet Union. The census of 1959 counted 24,672 Jews in the Lithuanian SSR, the majority in Vilnius.[1] Of this number, less than half had Litvak roots. About fifteen thousand to seventeen thousand Jews left Lithuania between 1959 and 1990; by 2009 the Jewish population in Lithuania was estimated at less than five thousand. According to the 2021 census, Jews constituted about 0.1% of the country's population, or about three thousand persons. The community remains active in politics as well as social and cultural life, but the slow drain of emigration has continued.

The Shoah represents the bloodiest page in the history of modern Lithuania. The genocide of the Jews should thus logically occupy the central place in the memory of the nation's twentieth-century experience of wars and foreign occupations. This has not yet happened, although perceptions of the Holocaust have changed significantly and well-researched Lithuanian academic works on the Nazi period have proliferated since the 1990s.[2] The history of the vanished Litvak world has evoked interest but has also presented Lithuanian society with controversies, some of which have resonated internationally. The history of the destruction of Lithuanian Jewry is situated within a difficult conversation on

---

1   Atamukas, *Lietuvos žydų kelias*, 297–298, 314–315.
2   These issues are examined in Hektoras Vitkus, "Holokausto atminties raida Lietuvoje" (PhD diss., Klaipėda University, 2008).

the history of Jewish-Lithuanian relations and is closely linked to the broader transformation in society's divergent collective memories of the war which has characterized the post-Soviet era.

Displaced Persons and Memories of Blood: Recriminations among the Ruins

The partisans who fled the ghettos had firsthand knowledge both of the destruction of Lithuanian Jewry and the extent of native collaboration in the process. Soviet media had broadcast accounts of fascist atrocities and news of the mass killings had leaked to the Western allies, but for the thousands of Jews who returned to the country following the Red Army's offensive in the summer and fall of 1944, the direct visual experience of the destruction was, without a doubt, the singular trauma of their lives. The returnees could see that the world of the Litvaks that they had left behind was no more. Many Jews, especially the partisans and soldiers of the Sixteenth Division, were eager to exact retribution against the murderers of their communities: for the many who lost family members, the desire for revenge was acutely personal and on occasion achieved.[3] The survivors who had endured Stutthof and Dachau and had chosen to return from Germany often found their homes in the possession of Gentile neighbors unwilling to surrender their new-found properties. Some rescuers who had saved Jewish children were not inclined to give up their charges easily.

At the same time, nearly one hundred thousand Lithuanians fled west to escape the advancing Soviet forces, the majority of whom came under western Allied control in Germany when the war ended. An estimated sixty thousand Lithuanians eventually populated the Displaced Person (DP) camps in occupied Germany. These refugees had good cause to fear the Soviets for reasons that most people would consider understandable: one year of experience under Stalinism was motive enough to flee. Most did not head West "to help the Germans," as some have alleged,[4] but bolted in that direction to seek protection of the advancing British and American forces. But there was no denying that some DPs had maintained what any Allied officer would have considered egregious

---

3   Stončius et al., *16–osios Lietuviškos divizijos*, 92–96.
4   For example, Allan A. Ryan, *Quiet Neighbors: Prosecuting Nazi War Criminals in America* (San Diego: Harcourt Brace Jovanovich, 1984).

collaboration with Nazi authorities during the German occupation, among whom were persecutors of Jews and even murderers who were now masquerading as victims who presented themselves to their fellow refugees as Lithuanian patriots.

The political leaders in the Lithuanian DP camps were concerned that accusations levied against them for collaboration with the Germans would complicate relations with the Western occupation authorities. The more astute refugees realized that in post-Nazi Europe, antisemitism had become a greatly devalued currency, although some continued to push Judeo-Bolshevik narratives, albeit mainly among themselves. Pro-German attitudes, such as had been displayed by Škirpa, were now a political impediment; also, strident anti-Communism did not necessarily play well as long as the Grand Alliance held together in the war's immediate aftermath. In 1946, the former secretary and head of the press section of the German-era Lithuanian Police Department published a short history titled the *Lithuanian Struggle against the Nazis*, which detailed opposition to German colonization and the Nazi deportation of workers to the Reich. Bronius Kviklys described the Lithuanian constabulary of 1941–1944 as secret anti-Nazi resisters who "guarded the interests of the country and battled against the German occupiers just as did the entire Lithuanian nation."[5] The author addressed the Holocaust in a section titled "The Evil Deeds of the Nazis: The Extermination of the Jews," which concluded that the "agony of this nation under the Nazi occupation" was an unprecedented crime in the "centuries of human suffering and struggles." The culprits were identified as Germans and rogue elements, possibly non-Lithuanians, "dressed up in Lithuanian uniforms." Contrary to fact, the author claimed that the PG had not passed any antisemitic statutes.[6]

While Lithuanian DP leaders gradually learned how to approach the Allied occupation authorities, they failed to grasp the pain and anger that animated their country's Jewish survivors. Initially, a few hopeful Lithuanian representatives thought that good memories of a shared life in the First Republic would mollify hurt feelings; others began to collect stories of rescue. Mykolas

---

5   Bronius Kviklys, *Lietuvių kova su naciais 1941–1944* (Memmingen: "Minties leidinys," 1946), 32.

6   Ibid., 16–20. This implausible narrative circulated outside Lithuania as well. In reports written in 1942, the anti-Nazi German Catholic social worker and rescuer Margarete Sommer repeated the canard about German SS men and SD officers dressed up in Lithuanian uniforms "to prove that Lithuanians, not Germans, shot the Jews." Cited in Rossi, *Wehrmacht Priests*, 58.

Krupavičius, the chairman of VLIK, which viewed itself as a kind of government-in-exile, hoped that Jews could support Lithuanian national goals, apparently under the notion that peace making in post-World War II Europe would follow the trajectory of the diplomacy which had produced the Versailles settlement of 1919. He was also concerned about the possibility that some Lithuanian DPs might face arrest and/or prosecution for their roles during the German occupation. The fears were well founded: aside from the Soviet delegations which visited Baltic DP camps to persuade the refugees to return home (without much success),[7] a secret group of Soviet SMERSH counterintelligence operatives had been active in Germany since early 1945 targeting alleged Baltic traitors to the Soviet Union. In December 1945 they kidnapped the former general counselor Petras Kubiliūnas who had found refuge in the British Zone and spirited him off to Moscow where he was executed in August 1946. While not all Lithuanian DPs may have viewed Kubiliūnas with sympathy, the refugees were concerned, with good reason, that the Kremlin's agents would act against anti-Soviet leaders without regard to their behavior during the German occupation.[8]

On November 29, 1945, Krupavičius and former Lithuanian diplomat Antanas Kalvaitis visited the offices of the Central Committee of Liberated Jews in Munich headed at the time by Zalman Grinberg, former director of the Kovno Ghetto hospital. The two visitors spoke with the engineer Leibovičius (Leibovich), the head of the committee's educational section, a graduate of the University of Kaunas and a survivor of the Šiauliai Ghetto. The meeting did not go well, although the memorandum of the talks noted that the hour-long conversation occurred in a "relatively favorable atmosphere." When the monsignor asked whether Jews and Lithuanians would work together in the struggle for restoring Lithuanian statehood, Leibovičius replied that "the wounds inflicted on the Jewish nation in Lithuania have not yet healed," so that any discussion of a common front for independence was premature. Kalvaitis complained that Jewish DPs had been petitioning authorities to open war crimes cases against his countrymen to which Leibovičius replied that "it is no secret that among Lithuanians there are hiding many persons who actively participated in liquidating Jews," singling out the former mayor of Šiauliai, Petras Linkevičius. Leibovičius reiterated what was to become a widespread storyline

---

7   Unlike other refugees from the USSR, Baltic DPs were not considered Soviet citizens and were, as a rule, not subject to forced repatriation.

8   As in the Soviet arrests of rescuers, above, Chapter 6.

among surviving Litvaks: "In some small Lithuanian towns, for example, Pakruojis, Joniškis, and Joniškėlis, Lithuanians liquidated the Jews themselves even before the Germans arrived."⁹ Krupavičius was not the best envoy to deal with the Jews considering the views he expressed in a 1946 political report to the VLIK, in which the monsignor claimed that it was understandable why many of his people saw Jews as "especially cruel during the last days of the Bolshevik rule," that Jews had attacked the anti-Soviet insurgents and German soldiers, and that they had played a major role in "torturing and murdering" Lithuanians.¹⁰

IMAGE 7.1. Avraham Sutzkever stands in front of the ruins of the ghetto school in Vilna, ca. July 1944. (United States Holocaust Memorial Museum Photo Archives #64905. Courtesy of the Sutzkever Family. Copyright of United States Holocaust Memorial Museum.)

---

9 Citations taken from Krupavičius's report of the meeting, "Pro Memoria," in Vytauto Didžiojo Universiteto išeivijos studijų centras [Vytautas Magnus University Center for Diaspora Studies], Manuscript f. 1, ap. 1–7, b. 19669–2499, l. 1–2. In a text written later and edited after his death by Bishop Brizgys, Krupavičius's recollection of the meeting changed, referring to the Jewish official as "Davidovičius from Šiauliai." Prel. M. Krupavičius, "Lietuvių ir žydų santykiai Hitlerio okupacijos laiku," *Laiškai lietuviams* 37, no. 5 (1986): 171. The contemporary "Pro Memoria" is probably more reliable. Cf. Alfonsas Eidintas, *Lietuvos žydų žudynių byla* (Vilnius: Vaga, 2001), 337.

10 As cited in Eidintas, *Žydai, lietuviai ir Holokaustas*, 185.

7. The Past as Legacy and Conflict | 483

IMAGE 7.2. Survivors from Vilnius gather for a memorial service in Munich, 1948. (United States Holocaust Memorial Museum Photo Archives #61701. Courtesy of David Rogow. Copyright of United States Holocaust Memorial Museum.)

The majority of Litvak survivors who had been liberated from the German camps came together in the Association of Lithuanian Jews but chose not to repatriate to a land of blood-soaked memories. They had little patience with the sanitized history and Judeo-Bolshevik memes that circulated among some of the Lithuanian refugees. In April 1947 the association, constituting, in their words, the "tiny remnant of the more than 160,000 Lithuanian Jews," met in Munich and issued a resolution concerning "the crime of a large part of the Lithuanian nation in murdering the Jews of Lithuania." They made clear their feelings towards their erstwhile fellow citizens: "All elements of the Lithuanian nation (intelligentsia, officials, farmers, craftsmen, workers, etc.) actively participated together with the Nazi bandits in murdering Lithuanian Jews, especially in the provinces." The resolution also claimed that many of the murderers were living as refugees in Germany and Austria, enjoying the hospitality of the UNRRA.[11]

---

11   The Resolution of the Meeting of the Association of Lithuanian Jews, April 15, 1947, in Munich, translated and published in Eidintas, *Byla*, 340–341; the German translation is in Dieckmann, *Besatzungspolitik*, 1:14.

IMAGE 7.3. Top: View of the Landsberg DP camp, ca. 1945–1948. (United States Holocaust Memorial Museum Photo Archives #82282. Courtesy of Herbert Friedman. Copyright of United States Holocaust Memorial Museum.) Bottom: Jewish DPs gather in front of and inside an open truck in the Landsberg DP camp. (United States Holocaust Memorial Museum Photo Archives #60794. Courtesy of Rivka and Shlomo Baran. Copyright of United States Holocaust Memorial Museum.)

IMAGE 7.4. A gathering of Lithuanian DPs in Hanau, Germany, ca. 1948. Seated sixth from left: Rev. Mykolas Krupavičius (in mufti) who sought a dialogue with Jewish DPs. Seated third from right is the Rev. Stasys Yla, Stutthof survivor and author of the memoir *Forest of the Gods* (Author's archive).

Perhaps it was fitting that the Lithuanian-Jewish arguments about the war and Holocaust were articulated in the DP camps of the country which was the source of the genocidal racial ideology leading to the Shoah. These documents of the 1940s pointed the way to the acrimonious narratives of collective guilt, inspiring struggles over history and memory which would continue for decades.

Commemorations in Stone: Contested Memories

The Jews of the USSR experienced antisemitism at the hands of Soviet authorities during World War II (for example, the often dismissive treatment of Jewish partisans) and the Stalinist aftermath (for example, the "Doctors' Plot"). Soviet officialdom resisted certain wartime narratives, including the Jewish specificity of the Holocaust, which challenged the myths of class solidarity and the USSR's multinational harmony. Historian Justas Stončius's comprehensive recent study of Soviet-era antisemitism in Lithuania noted that the Kremlin's policy towards Jews constituted a "balancing act between two contradictory positions": on the one hand, formal commitment to equal rights of the USSR's nations, including Jews, and, on the other, strident anti-Zionist incitement. Thus, in 1948 Stalin ordered the murder of Solomon Mikhoels, the chairman of the Jewish Anti-Fascist

Committee, and then famously provided his victim with a solemn state funeral.[12] In a scathing indictment, Stončius noted the impact of antisemitic policies in Lithuania following the Soviet return in 1944:

> The Soviet occupation regime in Lithuania did not create conditions to present Jewish-Lithuanian relations in a context of either academic study, or of moral values. Holocaust memory was harshly refashioned, there was no public condemnation of antisemitic incidents. Instead, the regime utilized propaganda campaigns (for example, against cosmopolitanism, Zionism, etc.) to form negative images and mistrust of Jews. It is evident that this language of hatred left its footprint and influenced those elements of society which were receptive to narrow (irrational) beliefs.[13]

Narratives of the war and the commemoration of the destruction of the Jews became, in themselves, ideological battlefields, for many, an "unwelcome memory." This troubled past, as well as the later anti-Jewish policies of the Kremlin that gave rise to the refusenik movement, have resulted in a widespread fallacy that "Jewish social life was fundamentally impossible in the USSR." This mistaken belief was extended to include the misconception that memorialization of the Holocaust simply was not possible in the USSR and that it became a phenomenon only after perestroika and the collapse of Communism. As Arkadi Zeltser has confirmed in a recent study, "not only did a space for memorialization of the Holocaust victims exist in the Soviet Union, but Soviet Jews also took an active part in building it." There are records for at least 733 sites in the territory of the former USSR where Jews themselves built monuments to the victims.[14] The surviving Lithuanian Jews sought recognition of their experience under the Nazis as a priority. Commemoration began in 1944 when the Lithuanian Jewish Museum, the only such institution in the USSR, was founded by the former partisans Sutzkever, Kovner, and Kaczerginski who collected cultural materials and documents in their apartment at 15 Gedimino Avenue:

---

12   See Justas Stončius, *Neapykantos ribos: antisemitizmas Lietuvoje 1944–1990 metais* (Klaipėda: Klaipėdos universiteto leidykla, 2022), 8–9, 29. Stončius argues that the very term "Soviet antisemitism" does not fit neatly into the 2016 working definition of antisemitism of the International Holocaust Remembrance Alliance (IHRA).

13   Ibid., 9–10.

14   Arkadi Zeltser, *Unwelcome Memory: Holocaust Monuments in the Soviet Union* (Jerusalem: Yad Vashem, 2018), 19–26.

by September 1944 they had enlisted twenty-nine volunteers.[15] The Museum organized the first postwar exhibition of its kind, titled "The Brutal Destruction of the Jews during the German Occupation." However, in June 1949 the Soviet Lithuanian government effectively liquidated the Museum during the reorganization of cultural institutions.[16]

Jewish survivors sought to memorialize their grievous losses in stone but had to contend with the fact that Soviet authorities also undertook a commemorative policy regarding the mass murders. On August 23, 1944, as the inspection of the killing site by the Extraordinary Commission approached its end, Soviet Lithuanian leaders convened a mass demonstration at Paneriai, the first revelation of the site to the public. Mečislovas Gedvilas, the then head of the government of the Lithuanian SSR, spoke to the gathering. Based on a draft of the speech found in the archives, Gedvilas laid out what was to become the regime's basic approach to commemoration, one in which the Jewish dead were both "Sovietized and Lithuanianized," that is, appropriated for a "de-Judaized" narrative. The premier identified the victims as "people of all social strata and nationalities: men, women, old people and children, workers, peasants, professors and priests, Jews, Lithuanians, Poles, and Russians—all driven into a common grave by the Hitlerite beasts." According to Gedvilas, all strata of the Lithuanian nation had wholeheartedly resisted the German occupiers who had, as a result, "failed to sully the name of the Lithuanian nation and force it to its knees."[17] In a report written the same day and published on August 25, the writer Antanas Venclova posed the question "Whom did the Germans kill?" and answered: "The Jews? Yes. They wiped out Jewish professors, doctors, writers, artists, workers—people of all professions. But not only Jews were killed in the fields of Paneriai." Venclova then enumerated as victims the sons of Lithuanian peasants "who had refused to join the German Army," Polish priests and nuns, Latvians and Estonians who had resisted the Nazis.[18] Even the Communist Kaczerginski

---

15 Fishman, *Book Smugglers*, 146.
16 Saulius Sužiedėlis and Šarūnas Liekis, "Conflicting Memories: The Reception of the Holocaust in Lithuania," in *Bringing the Dark Past to Light: The Reception of the Holocaust in Postcommunist Europe*, ed. John-Paul Himka and Joanna Beata Michlic (Lincoln: University of Nebraska Press, 2013), 323.
17 Cited from the draft of the speech in Zigmas Vitkus, *Atminties miškas: Paneriai istorijoje, kultūroje ir politikoje* (Vilnius: Lapas, 2022), 83–85.
18 Antanas Venclova, "Žudynių laukai Paneriuose," *Tiesa*, August 25, 1944, 3.

joined in the more inclusive "Lithuanization" of the Paneriai victims in the Lithuanian Soviet press.[19]

On at least one point, Venclova engaged in a sleight of hand: the eight-six Lithuanian "peasant sons" executed at Paneriai by the SS were among the nearly twenty thousand men who only six months earlier had volunteered to defend Lithuanian territory against the Soviets as part of the so-called Lithuanian Local Force (Lietuvos Vietinė Rinktinė), and then had mutinied against the Germans for reasons that had no connection to the anti-fascist resistance.[20] This deception was understandable: Lithuanian Communists had their own particular incentives to avoid a detailed story on the destruction of the Jews aside from mimicking Moscow's official line. The welcome that many Lithuanians had given the Germans at the war's outset, the strong anti-Soviet mood among the masses and the collaboration of thousands of ostensibly Soviet citizens in the Holocaust, as well as the bloody interethnic strife which pitted Lithuanians, Poles, and Russians against one another, contradicted the storyline trumpeting the solidarity of the Soviet nations in battling fascism. It would take several years to construct coherent ideological propaganda to obfuscate an inconvenient past widely seen and shared by the populace.

And yet, just as in most of the formerly German-occupied Soviet Union, the Jewish community engaged in a "self-organized" effort to commemorate the destruction in ways that could mark the Shoah as a crime directed at the Jews.[21] In Lithuania, the Party initially tolerated Jewish religious and commemorative activity, perhaps, in part because the regime struggled to assert Soviet power in the face of a widespread guerrilla insurgency. On March 12, 1948, the Soviet Lithuanian government approved the plan for a Jewish memorial at Paneriai. The community began a fund drive and within a few months erected an obelisk-like structure with biblical inscriptions in Hebrew, as well as texts in Yiddish and Russian, which made clear that this was a monument built by Jews, for Jews.

---

19 See Vitkus, *Atminties miškas*, 88–90.

20 The battalions of the Local Force were created in February–March 1944. The Germans disbanded the force in May 1944 and arrested the Lithuanian officers who had ordered their soldiers to stand down. Most of the enlisted men successfully deserted, but several thousand were dragooned into Wehrmacht anti-aircraft units or sent to labor in Germany. See Arūnas Bubnys, *Vokiečių okupuota Lietuva*, 407–423. Useful documents are in Antanas Martinionis, *Vietinė rinktinė* (Vilnius: Kardas, 1998), although the study itself is marred by its hagiographical and celebratory tone.

21 Zeltser, *Unwelcome Memory*, 228–246.

A similar monument was built in Zarasai in August 1948 with inscriptions in Yiddish and Russian designating Jews as the victims, and another monument in Panevėžys at about the same time.[22]

As early as October 1944 Moscow's overseers in Lithuania had sent an extensive and sharp critique of the "leadership of the Central Committee of the LCP (b)" to Georgi Malenkov, then secretary of the Central Committee of the AUCP (b), complaining that the Lithuanian Communists not only failed to organize the struggle against anti-Soviet "bourgeois nationalists" but had actually obstructed the campaign. The authors accused their comrades of excessive attention to the needs of the Jews and alleged excessive Jewish influence in the Party ranks:

> In solving the Jewish question, the Central Committee of the LCP(b) essentially follows the lead of the Jewish community ... [which in Vilnius] numbers about 2,000 people and is basically under the influence of the rabbis. The community demands that the Lithuanian Party and government organizations create special Jewish schools, children's homes, and kindergartens exclusively for Jewish children. The LCP(b) and, personally, Comrade Sniečkus gave their assent, rather than explaining that this is unnecessary and harmful for the Jewish children themselves.... The Jewish community demanded that funds be taken from the budget of the Narkompros [Peoples Commissariat of Education—S. S.] and the museum of the Jewish community for building Jewish cultural monuments. The LCP(b) agreed to this as well.
>
> The Jewish Communists working in Lithuania ... not only do not fight Bund-like tendencies or explain the fallacy and harm in creating special Jewish organizations, but themselves have been active organizers in the effort. The Jewish Communists who work in leading positions in Lithuania carry out the selection and appointment of cadres on a narrow nationalistic basis. Comrade Yoffe [Moisiejus Jofė], the chief of Glavlit [censorship office] of the Lithuanian SSR, assembled 80% of his staff with Jews. The head of the Vilnius City Committee's organizational section Comrade Vinitskus [Jankelis Vinickis] signs off and sends to the Narkomat [government] all those Jews who request material help. Among them are Jews who had been imprisoned in the Soviet Union for their attempts to escape to Poland after the Red Army arrived in Lithuania in 1940.[23]

---

22   See the photo in ibid., 201, also 331–332; Vitkus, *Atminties miškas*, 102.

23   From the message of the officials responsible for cadres' policy of the AUCP(b) Central Committee Kaloshin and Nikolai Mayorov to Malenkov, October 15, 1944, as published in

It is striking that Stalinist officials would employ themes of Jewish dominance within the Party that echoed the antisemitic propaganda emanating from the LAF.

The attempts to impose stronger anti-Jewish measures had a limited effect during the first postwar years, likely due in part because of the strong local position of Antanas Sniečkus, whose two successive wives were Jewish, and who was one of the longest serving Party bosses in history. In effect, the government institutions and society "did not always pay mind to the ideological doctrines and the policies of historical memory."[24] But the relative tolerance towards Jewish commemoration was short-lived. In January 1949 the head of the Soviet Lithuanian MGB Dmitry Yefimov complained to Sniečkus about the monument in Paneriai criticizing both its inscriptions and structure which, in his words, were "purely religious and did not reflect anything that was Soviet," insisting again that "the Germans shot not only Jews, but Russian, Lithuanian, Belarusian and other Soviet patriots."[25] The Yefimov letter coincided with the growing anti-Zionist campaign in Soviet media which followed the creation of Israel.[26]

The consequences for the Jewish Paneriai monument were not long in coming: by 1949 the Soviets decided that the message it conveyed was unacceptable. In 1952 this memorial to one of the best-known killing fields of the Holocaust was replaced. The Hebrew and Yiddish inscriptions were changed to Russian and Lithuanian texts commemorating the massacres of "peaceful Soviet citizens,"[27] a formulation that would increasingly be applied to numerous other local memorials. In Panevėžys, the Hebrew inscription on the memorial marked the site of martyred Jews "murdered in these four mass graves by the Lithuanian-German fascists in August 1941."[28] This, as historian Zigmas Vitkus

---

Mindaugas Pocius, ed. *Lietuvos sovietizavimas 1944–1947 m.: VKP(b) CK dokumentai* (Vilnius: LII, 2015), 125–126.

24 Hektoras Vitkus, "Memorialinių vietų veiksnys holokausto atminimo kultūroje: sampratos gairės ir tyrimo metodai," *Genocidas ir rezistencija* 1, no. 9 (2006): 87. Cf. Stončius, *Neapykantos ribos*, 114–115.

25 From the message of major general Dmitry Yefimov to Sniečkus, January 26, 1949, as cited in Vitkus, *Atminties miškas*, 101–102.

26 Hektoras Vitkus, "The Use of Holocaust Memory in Soviet Lithuania: An Ideological Aspect," in *Holokaustas nacių okupuotose Rytų ir Vakarų valstybėse: tyrimai ir atmintis. The Holocaust in the Eastern and Western European States: Occupied by the Nazis: Studies and Memory*, ed. Vygantas Vareikis (Kaunas: Spindulys, 2017), 303–304.

27 A detailed study of the replacement is in Vitkus, *Atminties miškas*, 104–108.

28 Zeltser, *Unwelcome Memory*, 201.

notes, contradicted the safe Soviet narrative on local collaboration: the killers had to be generic "bourgeois nationalists," certainly not ordinary Lithuanian citizens of the USSR. Despite the obstacles, the Jewish community continued its efforts to memorialize the Holocaust as a Jewish loss, building markers in Kupiškis (1952), Ukmergė (1953), and as late as 1957 in Šakiai, and 1958 in Šiaudvievčiai.[29] Soviet commemoration policy, while de-emphasizing the genocide of Jews as *the* central historic feature of the German occupation, was at times ambivalent, allowing for limited recognition of Jewish suffering. In the post-Stalin era, aspects of Holocaust history and commemoration were allowed into Lithuanian public life. The Paneriai and Ninth Fort museums provided the main venues for a censored Soviet commemoration of the Holocaust. The ambivalence of official Soviet commemoration policy regarding the Holocaust contrasted sharply with the official memorialization of the Lithuanian villagers slain at Pirčiupis. After the war, the village became the site of an important memorial which included a giant sculpture of a grieving woman, the celebrated *Mother of Pirčiupis*.[30]

The Holocaust and the War:
Soviet Lithuanian Literature and the Arts

After the war, the Soviets suppressed much of what remained of Litvak religious and cultural life although Lithuanian Communists provided a brief hiatus of relative tolerance in the immediate aftermath of the second Soviet occupation. For example, in September 1944 the Kaunas Party leaders allowed Rabbi Efraim Oshry to restore two synagogues to service, but the permissive atmosphere here was short-lived. A year later, the city's Party boss ordered the Jewish religious leaders to abandon the choral synagogue (Ožeškienė Street) so that (incredibly) the premises could be utilized as a German POW station. On September 10, 1945, Jewish representatives protested to Justas Paleckis, the head of the Lithuanian Soviet government, proclaiming that the "community sees the demand to quarter the murderers of 200 thousand Jews at the site of

---

29   Subotić, *Yellow Star*, 170–172.
30   A detailed history of this memorial is in Ekaterina Makhotina, *Errinerungen an den Krieg – Krieg der Erinnerungen: Litauen und der Zweite Weltkrieg* (Gottingen: Vandoenhoeck & Ruprecht, 2017), 153–172.

the Jewish temple as an insult to the Jewish faith and our self-respect." Paleckis quickly reversed the decision, but the Kaunas Party continued the pressure, eventually transferring the synagogue's courtyard to a kindergarten. In May 1952 the government closed all Jewish cemeteries in Kaunas to visitors.[31]

Repression grew as the control over Lithuania's Jewish community tightened. The Great Synagogue in Vilnius was torn down rather than restored, and religious life was curtailed. The last Yiddish primary schools were closed. Jewish tombstones were utilized as construction materials, while one of the city's prominent landmarks, the Palace of Sports and Culture, was built at the site of the historic Jewish Šnipiškės cemetery in Vilnius. The Stalinist antisemitic and anti-Zionist campaigns which began in the late 1940s and then culminated in the attack on the Jewish Anti-Fascist Committee in the early 1950s, created an atmosphere that further obviated a thorough investigation of the Holocaust in the USSR although there were some earlier exceptions to this neglect. In 1943 Elis Sarin published *The Hitlerite Massacre in Lithuania*, and in 1946 Avrom Sutzkever followed with *The Vilna Ghettto*, both books printed in Moscow and read in Yiddish by many Lithuanian Jews.[32] The diary/memoir of inmate and Stutthof survivor Marija (Maša) Rolnikaitė, sometimes referred to as Lithuania's Anne Frank, first published in 1965 and later in numerous translations to a wider audience, was also somewhat of an outlier. According to Anja Tippner, Rolnikaitė was "one of the few, if not only, authors whose oeuvre consisted almost entirely of texts that deal with the Holocaust and that were published in the post-Stalinist Soviet Union."[33] As a general rule, however, until the late 1980s, the wartime suffering of the Litvaks, whether in Lithuanian academe, popular histories, literature, or the arts, was told within the historic framework of the struggle against fascism during the Great Patriotic War, the official term for World War II. The Jewish authors and anti-fascist partisans Mejeris Eglinis-Elinas and Dimitrijus

---

31 As related in Regina Laukaitytė, "Žydų religinis gyvenimas Lietuvoje 1944–1956," *Lituanistica* 58 (2012): 297. To this day the synagogue in question serves as the city's Jewish community center.

32 Zeltser, *Unwelcome Memory*, 120.

33 Anja Tippner, "Conflicting Memories, Conflicting Stories: Masha Rol'nikaite's Novel and the Soviet Culture of Holocaust Remembrance," *East European Jewish Affairs*, 48, no. 3 (2018): 372–390. Cf. the analysis of Rolnikaitė's place in the Russian "usable past" of the Holocaust in Anja Tippner, "The Writings of a Soviet Anne Frank? Masha Rolnikaitė's Holocaust Memoir *I Have to Tell* and Its Place in Soviet Literature," in *Representations of the Holocaust in Soviet Literature and Film*, ed. Dan Michman and Arkadi Zeltser (Jerusalem: Yad Vashem), 59–80.

IMAGE 7.5. Three stages of commemoration at Paneriai. Top: Monument constructed by the Jewish community in 1948 and subsequently demolished. (Courtesy of Vilna Gaon Museum of Jewish History.) Middle: The Soviet obelisk built in 1952 (left) with a de-Judaized inscription dedicated to the "Victims of Fascist Terror, 1941-1944." (Courtesy of Darius Sužiedėlis.) Bottom: The memorial built in 1991 after the restoration of Lithuania's independence inscribed in Hebrew and Yiddish and now the site for the annual Day of Commemoration of the Genocide of Lithuanian Jews on September 23, the anniversary of the destruction of the Vilna Ghetto. (Courtesy of Darius Sužiedėlis.)

Gelpernas commemorated the fighters of the Kovno Ghetto in a short history intended for Lithuanian readers.[34] As with other literature in this vein, the German occupation, as well as the persecution and murder of the Jews emphasized the role of Party activists and Communist ideology in the anti-fascist struggle.

---

34 Mejeris Eglinis-Elinas and Dimitrijus Gelpernas, *Kauno getas ir jo kovotojai* (Vilnius: Mintis, 1969). Rolnikaitė's memoir, Marija Rolnikaitė, *Turiu papasakoti* (Vilnius: VPMLL, 1963) has been translated into many languages and was republished as Maša Rolnikaitė, *Turiu papasakoti. Dokumentinė apysaka* (Vilnius: Inter Se, 2021). See the publications listed in Vytautas Toleikis, "Repress, reassess, remember: Jewish Heritage in Lithuania," *Eurozine*, November 27, 2008, http://www.eurozine.com/articles/2008-11-27-toleikis-en.html.

In this context, the fate of Soviet Holocaust narratives in Lithuanian literature and the arts is instructive. Olga Gershenson opened her study of Soviet cinematic depictions of the Holocaust by subtitling her first chapter "Jews without the Holocaust and the Holocaust without Jews."[35] But, as Gershenson points out, the idea that the Holocaust was not represented in Soviet film is simplistic. The story of Jews during the Holocaust was not subject to an outright taboo, but two factors subverted a historically authentic presentation of the Shoah. The first—universalization—submerged the Jewish experience within a general narrative of the war. "The trope of Jewish suffering," explains Gershenson, "is recruited to tell someone else's stories"—essentially, that of the Soviet peoples at large. Jewish anti-fascist fighters are lost among the Russians, Ukrainians, and war heroes of other nationalities. The second problem—externalization—exploits concentration camp imagery that avoided highlighting the "Holocaust by bullets," the manner in which most Soviet Jews lost their lives, in effect, "[locating] the Holocaust outside Soviet borders." The latter practice had the added benefit of "conveniently avoiding the difficult questions of local collaboration and historical responsibility."[36]

During the Thaw of the Khrushchev years, Soviet Lithuanian filmmakers and authors learned the limits of presenting Jewish themes during the most violent period in the nation's history. In 1961 Lithuania's premier film director Vytautas Žalakevičius and the noted Lithuanian Jewish writer Grigory Kanovich (Grigorijus Kanovičius, 1929–2022) wrote a screenplay *Gott mit uns*, which addressed rescue efforts, local collaboration, and the murder of Jews in the Lithuanian countryside. The text's portrayal of a Catholic priest as a rescuer, and insufficient attention to "universal humanism" at the expense of "the Party truth," worried censors in Vilnius, but the decision to reject the project was made in Moscow where officials made clear that certain Holocaust themes on film would not be allowed. The screenplay was ultimately published in *Pergalė*, the monthly journal of the Writers' Union of the Lithuanian SSR, which prevented it from gaining wider distribution in the rest of the Soviet Union.[37] Despite the LCP's somewhat longer leash, the pressure from Moscow on Lithuanian

---

35 Olga Gershenson, *The Phantom Holocaust: Soviet Cinema and Jewish Catastrophe* (New Brunswick: Rutgers University Press, 2013), 1–2.
36 For Gershenson's conclusive analysis, see ibid., 223–228.
37 See the detailed story of the screenplay and how Gershenson discovered the "lost" original in a Moscow archive in ibid., 71–82.

cultural matters encouraged a strategy of self-censorship. (Some writers simply practiced "writing to the desk drawer," a tactic which, in the parlance of the time, preserved artistic integrity by hiding manuscripts in the hopes of publication in a less oppressive future.)

Two films that followed *Gott mit uns* also suffered the cutting room floor. In 1963 film director Raimundas Vabalas released *Žingsniai naktį* (Footsteps in the night), which dealt with the inmates' escape from the Ninth Fort. The movie erased most Jewish references and "internationalized" the event as a major wartime episode, the cuts largely due to vehement objections from the hardline Soviet film critic Mikhail Bleiman. Despite script writers' efforts to adjust to the Party line, cuts and changes to Almantas Grikevičius's 1969 film *Ave vita* resulted in a considerable distortion of the historical record. The screenplay, once again by Žalakevičius and Kanovich, originally intended to present the story of a Jewish survivor who returns annually to Vilnius to revisit the death march from the ghetto to Paneriai. The authors "de-Judaized" the story by eliminating the yellow star and making the survivor a Lithuanian. The writers did, according to Kanovich, choose an actor who "looked Jewish," and provided him an unusual, foreign-sounding name (Cezaris). Gershenson describes her own viewing of yet "another film about the Holocaust without Jews" in which the German occupiers are identified as the sole culprits:

> Precautionary self-censorship was not enough. The film was still, in the words of Kanovich, "anatomized," and had entire plot elements taken out. In the final cut, [the film's hero—S. S.] Cezaris is haunted by wartime memories upon his return to Lithuania. As he and his survivor friends walk a contemporary cobblestone street, he keeps hearing German orders, until his flashback takes over, and the screen is filled with people marched by the Germans through the same streets. There are no Jewish references. It is entirely unclear why the Nazis arrested these Lithuanians, and, in a later scene, why the Lithuanians are killed in a mass machine-gun operation. The plot makes sense only if the characters are Jewish.[38]

The child survivor Icchokas Meras (1934–2018) made his literary debut in 1960 with a collection of autobiographical short stories which recounted the travails of a Jewish child and the boy's rescue in his hometown of Kelmė in the summer of 1941. In 1963 Meras published his novel *Lygiosios trunka*

---

38   Gershenson, *The Phantom Holocaust*, 87.

akimirką (which appeared as *Stalemate* in a 1980 English translation), one of the first Soviet novels on the Holocaust, and the first such work in the Lithuanian language.[39] Two years later, he followed with a second short novel-ballad *Ant ko laikosi pasaulis* (That which holds up the world), depicting a Lithuanian peasant women named Veronika who nurses a rescued Jewish baby.[40] Meras's treatment of the Shoah, *Stalemate* in particular, was uniquely free of ideological cant and devoid of socialist realism, which led to sharp criticism when the novel was presented in Moscow; an ideologically revised Russian edition was published in 1965. The situation improved in 1966 when *Ant ko laikosi pasaulis* was published in the Russian literary journal *Yunost'* which boasted a circulation of millions. In 1966, even as the cultural Thaw began to slacken, both novels were published in a Russian-language print run of one hundred thousand, the *Stalemate* content restored to its original, uncut version. However, attempts to present *Stalemate* on film met a different fate. A group from the Lithuanian Film Studio visited Moscow and enlisted the help of dissident director Mikhail Kalik to help them produce a screenplay of the novel in consultation with Meras. The project died amidst wrangling between the studio and the censors. *Stalemate* never made it to cinemas, but an award-winning version of the novel appeared on stage in a prestigious Moscow theater in 2010.[41] As for Meras, despite writing only in Lithuanian, he achieved success in translation, both within the Soviet Union and internationally, but his ensuing conflict with Soviet censors led him to join the flow of Jewish emigrants to Israel in 1972.

Changes: Commemoration and the Arts after Perestroika

In 1985 Mikhail Gorbachev (1931–2022) came to power in the USSR and initiated a policy of openness (glasnost) which removed the remaining shackles on commemoration of the Holocaust as a specific Jewish tragedy. On May 5, 1989, the founding meeting of the Cultural Association of Lithuanian Jews was held

---

39 Icchokas Meras, *Geltonas lopas* (Vilnius: Vaga,1960) [republished in 2005]; also, Icchokas Meras, *Lygiosios trunka akimirką* (Vilnius: Vaga, 1963). English version: Icchokas Meras, *Stalemate*, trans. Jonas Zdanys (Seacacus, NJ: Lyle Stuart, 1980). Meras's works have been published in eighteen languages.
40 Icchokas Meras, *Ant ko laikosi pasaulis* (Vilnius: Vaga, 1965).
41 The account is in Gershenson, *The Phantom Holocaust*, 102–114.

in Vilnius and the group began publishing the newspaper *Lithuania's Jerusalem* in Yiddish, Lithuanian, and Russian. Grigory Kanovich gave the opening address and reminded his audience of the oppressive Stalinist past:

> Who could have imagined that, almost immediately after the fireworks display that marked the victory over Nazi Germany, a new lengthy era of legally sanctioned antisemitism would begin? Remember the Jewish Anti-Fascist Committee, whose members were purged and later arrested and shot! . . . Remember the Jewish Museum in Vilnius, which was shut down; remember the closing of the boarding school, where the surviving children received instruction in their own native tongue. These were the last Yiddish-language lessons in the Soviet Union. The apparatus of terror crushed not only Solomon Mikhoels, but our entire people, our language, our national traditions, our cultural values.

According to Ekaterina Makhotina, Kanovich's statement clearly expressed the hope that a "rebirth of Jewish national consciousness and the creation of an authentic Jewish culture" would follow the years of postwar repression. His anti-Soviet diatribe would have been welcomed by much of Lithuanian society which shared painful memories of Stalinist rule.[42]

The restoration of Lithuanian independence and the renewed activism of the Jewish community created the conditions for the reestablishment of the Jewish Museum in 1991, formally rededicated as the Vilna Gaon State Jewish Museum in 1997. An exhibit featuring the Holocaust, the first in the former Soviet Union, was opened in the same year. Other early programs at the museum included a memorial to the Righteous Gentiles of Lithuania in 1990, a display on the Jews of Vabalninkas in 1992, as well as one on "Jews in the Struggle against Nazism." In 1988, a new monument to the July 1941 massacre in Ylakiai replaced an older memorial to the "Soviet people" with one which acknowledged the killing of hundreds of Jews.[43] In May of that year, a Soviet official addressed a spontaneous gathering in Paneriai and proclaimed that Jews constituted the overwhelming majority of the victims.[44] Over the next decade, Jewish organizations created a comprehensive registry of Holocaust sites, while new plaques and signs

---

42 The speech is cited with commentary in Ekaterina Makhotina, "Between 'Suffered' Memory and 'Learned' Memory: The Holocaust and Jewish History in Lithuanian Museums and Memorials After 1990," *Yad Vashem Studies* 41, no. 1 (2016): 221 222.
43 Subotić, *Yellow Star*, 172.
44 Vitkus, *Atminties miškas*, 236.

stressing the Jewish specificity of the Holocaust were installed in many locations with the assistance of local governments.[45] A new monument next to the Paneriai Memorial Museum was donated by Holocaust survivor Yeshayahu Epstein. An easily accessible online atlas of Holocaust sites in Lithuanian and English provides information on the number of victims, references to the Nazis and their collaborators, and a travel guide to mass graves and local monuments.[46]

The most important center of Holocaust commemoration is the permanent Holocaust Exhibit in the "Green House" section of the Jewish Museum. The main building of the Gaon Museum also houses the "Alley of the Righteous."[47] In September 1999 the "Vilna Ghetto Posters" exhibit traveled to the US Congress where it was celebrated in a program featuring speeches by California Rep. Thomas Lantos and Stuart Eizenstat. Another main function of the museum is the preservation of the Jewish cultural and religious heritage destroyed in the Shoah, including a memorial to the Great Synagogue and the restoration of the Kalvarija synagogue with help from American-donated funds. In 2002 the Jewish Museum commemorated the Jewish soldiers who fought and died in the wars for Lithuanian independence in 1918–1920. The museum has also published numerous studies, mainly in English, Russian, and Lithuanian.[48] There are plans to redesign the area around the Paneriai killing site and, for its part, the government has renovated the Museum of the Ninth Fort, adding new exhibits. The Soviet ideological verbiage which formerly greeted visitors has been removed or reedited. In 2018 construction began on the Lost Shtetl Museum in Šeduva, dedicated to the life and death of the town's Jewish community, the most ambitious and comprehensive commemorative project on provincial Lithuanian Jewry to date. The endeavor is headed by Sergejus Kanovičius (Sergey Kanovich), the son of the renowned Litvak writer Grigory Kanovich.

---

45 See the listing in Josifas Levinsonas, ed. *Skausmo knyga. The Book of Sorrow* (Vilnius: Vaga,1997).

46 Holokausto Lietuvoje Atlasas, accessed July 20, 2019, http://www.holocaustatlas.lt/LT/.

47 The Righteous are listed and described in an ongoing series published by the museum: Viktorija Sakaitė, comp., Dalija Epšteinaitė, ed., *Gyvybę ir duoną nešančios rankos. Hands Bringing Life and Bread*, 4 vols. (Vilnius: Vilna Gaon Jewish Museum, 1997–2009). The most comprehensive listing of rescuers in the "Alley of the Righteous" is on the Museum website: https://www.jmuseum.lt/en.

48 For a brief history and more information on the Jewish Museum see the institution's website: http://www.jmuseum.lt.

The Jewish community has long sought official state recognition of the Holocaust, the goal realized in 1990 with the naming of September 23, the anniversary of the destruction of the Vilna Ghetto, as the National Day of Commemoration of the Genocide of the Jews. Since 1994 the date is solemnly remembered at the Paneriai Memorial with an annual service which has been attended by the head of state and other high officials. An awards ceremony at the Presidential Palace recognizes those who rescued Jews during the war. The government and public organizations regularly organize commemorative events on this date throughout the country, including visits to the killing sites of 1941 and activities in schools aimed at fostering interethnic tolerance.

Commemorative activities and monument reconstruction constituted the least difficult part of the Lithuanian public's encounter with the Holocaust. The bitter divide which separated the memories of Lithuanian and Jewish DPs in postwar Germany were indicative of a much broader clash of contrary visions embedded in the memories of the country's various national communities, as well as in the views of political and ideological groups, which to this day bedevil attempts to produce a shared commemorative history. For Jews, the Holocaust, especially the painful experience of the participation of fellow citizens in the killings, remains the inescapable reality of the period. In the Baltics, many Russophone residents cling to heroic memories of the Great Patriotic War as an essential part of their identity. Polish memories of the war are less categorical, complicated by the bloody ethnic conflicts of the 1940s in eastern Lithuania and west Ukraine and, of course, by the 1940 Soviet massacres of the nation's officers in Katyn and elsewhere. But in contrast to the majority of ethnic Lithuanians, these well-entrenched narratives recognize Nazi atrocities and heroic anti-fascist struggles as integral parts of the wartime experience. The Soviet victory, the Warsaw uprisings of the Jewish ghetto fighters (1943), and the Home Army (1944) won worldwide admiration. Edward Zwick's 2008 well-received movie *Defiance*, filmed partly in Lithuania, underscored the Jewish struggle against Nazism. Importantly, the enormous suffering of Jews, Russians, and Poles during the German occupation contained elements of redemption. The state of Israel created a sovereign home for a people who had been destined for extinction. The restoration of a nominally independent Polish state with its ancient "restored" western borderlands partly compensated for the devastation and territorial losses inflicted by foreign invaders. The Soviet Union emerged as a great power which could credibly claim a central role in the defeat of Nazism. At the same time, the paean to the "Greatest Generation" and to rescuers mirrored in the films of Steven Spielberg (*Schindler's List, Saving Private Ryan*) provided Americans an uplifting coda to the war's travails.

None of these storylines have gained much traction among the many Baltic citizens whose experience of World War II and its aftermath were radically different, and for whom the period of 1939–1945 does not instinctively bring to mind German barbarism, armed anti-fascist resistance, or, for that matter, any redemptive postwar outcome. Lithuania's national communities have thus been emotionally committed to what are different and nearly irreconcilable Lithuanian, Russian, Polish, and Jewish versions of the war's meaning and impact, not to mention the generational and ideological divides at play in Baltic societies. With the exception of the hard right, Western-oriented urban youth and intelligentsia have tended towards a more open-minded and nuanced view of the wartime past. The aging veterans who served in the Red Army and part of the impoverished rural populace mired in nostalgia for the Soviet period still find comfort in stories of the Great Patriotic War, but in the Baltics these groups have been marginalized, exert little social influence, and fewer and fewer of their number are still alive. Regardless of the conflicting memories, however, it should be obvious that no meaningful discussion of remembrance is possible without appreciating the authentic, lived individual and group experiences, even if they tend towards discomforting and one-sided narratives.

Writing History: Soviet Lithuania and the Émigré Diaspora

The politicized context of wartime remembrance and the resulting contradictory perspectives in Lithuania have impacted every aspect of the historiography of the Second World War both in academia and in the society at large. The issues that have challenged the ongoing national conversation about the Holocaust include: postwar storylines concerning the Shoah, especially the arguments over native culpability in mass murder; new revelations about the wartime past in both the academy and the public sphere; the domestic and international political and cultural dynamics, which affect the memory of foreign occupations; and the ongoing debate on the relative historical impacts of Communism and Nazism in a region which endured both.

Three views of the Holocaust dominated popular and academic historical writing on wartime Lithuania until the late 1980s. Allowing for some simplification, they can be defined as the Soviet, émigré, and Western perspectives.

Despite their limitations, the three conflicting approaches reflected what their respective constituencies in the public domain generally regarded as acceptable narratives and, to some extent, circulated in scholarly works. The first two accounts exacerbated ideological conflict within Lithuanian society. Soviet historical works emphasized the service of Lithuanian "bourgeois nationalism" to the Nazi cause, seeking to discredit both the anti-Communist diaspora in the West and the postwar armed struggle against the Soviet occupation. A notably different book was the collection of rescue accounts by Righteous Gentile Sofija Binkienė which did mention instances of "bourgeois" assistance to Jews in hiding.[49] Such publications, however, were exceptions that did not change the main thrust of the Soviet narrative on the Nazi occupation. The anti-émigré propaganda peaked during the 1960s and 1970s with the campaign to "unmask" Lithuanian refugees and other DPs as Nazi war criminals hiding in the West, which coincided with high-profile Soviet trials of former police battalion members involved in mass shootings of the Jews.[50] In 1960 the journalist Stasys Bistrickas, a veteran of the Sixteenth Division, penned a booklet on the crimes of the Nazis and collaborators at Paneriai, warning of the "spider of fascism raising its head in West Germany," and of the killers "hiding across the Atlantic."[51] This was one of the earliest publications in the Facts Accuse (Faktai kaltina) series and other related mini-studies, including English-language booklets adapted to the needs of the Cold War. One such 1964 product of this latter genre, published in three thousand copies and sold for one kopeck, came with the sensational title "He Kissed the Swastika," purportedly exposing Bishop Brizgys as "a Hitlerite henchman and war criminal."[52] In 1972 American and Canadian readers were presented with a warning: *They Live in Your Midst*, a list of the names and addresses of fourteen alleged Lithuanian war criminals living in North America. One of the accused was Henrikas Dūda, implicated in the murder of the Olkinas family of Panėmunelis.[53] Vytautas Žeimantas, one of the most prolific authors

---

49 Binkienė, *Ir be ginklo kariai*.
50 See Eusiejus Rozauskas, ed., *Nacionalistų talka hitlerininkams* (Vilnius: Mintis, 1970). An example in English stressing the services of the purported "Nazi fifth column" during the German occupation is Eusiejus Rozauskas et al., eds., *Documents Accuse* (Vilnius: Gintaras, 1970).
51 Stasys Bistrickas, *Ir sušaudytieji prabyla* (Vilnius: VPMLL, 1960), 5.
52 *He Kissed the Swastika* (Vilnius: Mintis, 1964), 16.
53 Leonas Jonaitis, *They Live in Your Midst* (Vilnius: Gintaras, 1972), 40–42. Dūda was ostensibly living in Detroit under the name Henry Pivoriūnas, although people who knew the

exposing Nazi collaborators hiding among the Lithuanian diaspora, published numerous articles and several books until 1988 when his last opus, ironically titled *The Process Continues*, added the sensational (and false) charge that Bishop Brizgys had "urged the annihilation of the Jews."[54] But the campaign against émigré nationalists ceased soon after. As perestroika and glasnost gathered steam, the Party lost control of the Lithuanian media. Attention increasingly turned towards revelations of Stalinist crimes and demands for national sovereignty. Tellingly, Žeimantas quickly abandoned Nazi themes. The once feted Soviet journalist became an award-winning editor of the patriotic conservative daily *Lietuvos aidas* (Lithuanian Echo), his previous work forgotten (or, perhaps, forgiven) by his colleagues in the Lithuanian Journalist Association.[55] This was not the only case of conversion from Party propagandist to patriot as the LCP's power waned and the USSR unraveled.

In the Soviet Union, the Great Patriotic War had been presented as a continuation of the heroic struggle of the Soviet nations against the historic Teutonic aggressor under the leadership of the Russian tsars.[56] Historian Juozas Žiugžda undertook to closely follow this narrative and was instrumental in overseeing that his Soviet Lithuanian colleagues closely followed the Party line.[57] There was little room in this historiography for a serious examination of the reasons for the welcome which the Nazis received from the peoples of the lands annexed by Stalin in 1939–1940. One review of Soviet publications on Nazi war crimes in Lithuania, including works on the mass murder of civilians, lists forty-four

---

man do not remember him using an alias. The Olkinas killings are not mentioned in the publication.

54   Vytautas Žeimantas, *Procesas nesibaigia* (Vilnius: Mintis. 1988), 243; cf. his "Kryžiumi laimino svastiką," *Tiesa* December 8, 1985, 2; also, Vytautas Žeimantas, *Teisingumas reikalauja* (Vilnius: Mintis, 1984).

55   On Žeimantas's transformation, see Ipolitas Skridla, "Sukaktys, jubiliejai," accessed May 15, 2021, http://www.lzs.lt/lt/naujienos/sukaktys_jubiliejai/archive/p85/kolega_vytautas_ zeimantas_desimtmeciai_atiduoti_zurnalistikai.html.

56   See, for example, the odd monograph of the otherwise respected medievalist Vladimir T. Pashuto, *Geroicheskaya borba russkogo naroda za nezavisimost' XIII v.* (Moscow: Gos. Izd-vo polit. lit-ry, 1956). Cf. Makhotina, *Errinerungen*, 113–115, on the 1960 celebration of the 550th anniversary of the defeat of the Teuronic Knights at the Battle of Grunwald presented as a testimonial to historic Russian-Lithuanian friendship and a battle of "fraternal peoples" against Western aggression.

57   On Žiugžda's domineering role between 1948 and 1970, see Makhotina, *Errinerungen*, 85–86.

books and seventy-eight articles which appeared between 1940 and 1975. The Lithuanian Party boss Antanas Sniečkus authored the first book, titled *Lithuania Battles the German Occupiers*, published in Moscow in 1944. Most of these works, including those which specifically mentioned Jews as victims, would not have passed muster as academic studies as that concept is understood even within the restricted world of Soviet universities and research institutions.[58]

It was the misfortune of Soviet Lithuanian historiography that even well-documented historical studies could not escape the Party's ideological shackles, as in the case of the two-volume collection of documents of German and Lithuanian sources titled *Mass Murders in Lithuania*.[59] The hundreds of pages of detailed reports on the role of the Nazi and collaborationist structures in the destruction of Jews were unprecedented at the time and many historians still cite the published documents. At the same time, the rector of Vilnius University, Juozas Bulavas, who had been expelled from the Party in 1958, wrote a useful survey of German rule in Lithuania.[60] But such works were exceptions. The Party's caution regarding the history of the Soviet and Nazi occupations can be seen in the fact that the most comprehensive Soviet-era examination of the crimes of the Nazi occupation, the doctoral dissertation of the Germanist Kazys Rukšėnas approved by the Lithuanian Institute of History in 1970, was never published.[61]

Soviet hardliners were prescient censors: their fears that any transparent and public discussion of wartime history would be politically catastrophic were fully vindicated when nearly a million pro-independence demonstrators joined in the Baltic Way of August 23, 1989, to protest the Molotov-Ribbentrop Pact in the largest political demonstration in the history of the USSR. To many observers, this massive show of defiance signaled the collapse of the Party's authority in the Baltics and, along with it, any remaining credibility of the Communist establishment's historical narratives. The result was that for much of the population at large, and anti-Soviet dissidents in particular, it was difficult to

---

58 See Michael Kors, "Die offizielle Darstellung des Holocaust in der Sowjetzeit (1945–1990)," in *Holocaust in Litauen: Krieg, Judenmorde und Kollaboration im Jahre 1941*, ed. Vincas Bartusevicius, Joachim Tauber, and Wolfram Wette (Koln: Bohlau, 2003), 247–261.

59 A number of documents from this collection are cited in this study.

60 Juozas Bulavas, *Vokiškųjų fašistų okupacinis Lietuvos valdymas 1941–1944 m.* (Vilnius: LTSR Mokslų Akademija, 1969).

61 LMAVB RS, f. 26–1475: Kazys Rukšėnas, "Hitlerininku politika Lietuvoje 1941–1944" (PhD diss., Lithuanian SSR Academy of Sciences, Vilnius, 1970).

separate what passed as useful historiography from the cruder propaganda. It did not help matters that one of the editors of the second volume of *Mass Murders*, Boleslovas Baranauskas, was a veteran officer of the NKVD with a violent reputation.

Initially, the main concern of the civic society which emerged from the Baltic independence movements was the correction of the historical record regarding the Kremlin's seizure of the Baltic states in 1940, and other Stalinist crimes. While this was a welcome development, an unfortunate side effect of the wide-spread allergy to the Soviet story was a knee-jerk rejection to even those aspects of the narrative which contained important historic insights, for example, the colossal scale and unique nature of Nazi atrocities. The bitter opposition to the Soviet version of the past inadvertently created significant obstacles to dealing with the history of the Holocaust. The Soviet system had protected Lithuanian society from cultural processes in the West including the transformative postwar examination of the Holocaust in both scholarship and popular media. After the collapse of the USSR, Lithuanian citizens were disoriented to discover an outside world bearing little resemblance to either their images (and for older people, the memories) of life in the West, or to the Communist image of corrupt capitalism. The struggle to overcome this confusion came to the fore in the 1990s.

The most problematic version of the Holocaust and communal violence during the occupations emerged among the exiles who fled West in the summer of 1944 and then emigrated from the DP camps, mostly to the already established Lithuanian communities in the United States and Canada. This diaspora reacted fiercely to Soviet and Western accusations of Nazi collaboration and proved largely immune to serious inquiry into the Holocaust for at least three decades. The majority of Lithuanian refugees, including many of their descendants, found it hard to accept the Western narrative of the war, including the acknowledgement of the Soviet Union's immense contribution to the defeat of fascism, and many failed to fully acknowledge Nazism's genocidal nature. Most of the émigré narratives rested on an intensely anti-Soviet perspective and a denial of native participation in the murder of the Jews accompanied, at times, by open or disguised antisemitism. The Lithuanian exiles' response to the Holocaust differed, however, from the denial of the so-called "revisionists" in the West: it did not question the fact of the Holocaust as such, but rather, its manner, usually insisting that the native killers constituted but a handful of a criminal rabble. Accustomed to a self-perception as victims, the older generation in particular reacted vehemently to any suggestion of Lithuanian guilt. A not untypical summary of the bloodiest period in the nation's modern history is found in a brief historical overview published in the United States during the early 1970s:

> In June 1941 Hitler turned on Stalin and German armies attacked Russia. The Nazi armies marched through Lithuania and established a military occupation which lasted until 1944. During all this time the Lithuanians were again forced to feed the invaders. Thousands of Lithuanian young men were deported to Germany for forced labor. Many Lithuanian Jews were executed by the Nazi regime.[62]

There were a few exceptions to the general attitude of apologia and defensiveness concerning the Holocaust. In November 1977, the Lithuanian Israeli writer and Holocaust survivor Icchokas Meras arrived in Chicago to accept an award from the Lithuanian Writers' Association granted for a novel published in the United States by a Catholic printing press. An overflow crowd at the Lithuanian Youth Center attended Meras's speech in which the author spoke of his rescue and addressed "my relations with Lithuania and Lithuanians."[63] But such positive Jewish-Lithuanian interactions were infrequent. In October 1978, the émigré organization Santara-Šviesa, a coalition of liberal-minded intelligentsia, many of whom were products of American graduate schools, published a discussion held during its annual conference on "The Jewish Question in Our Society and Media." The session criticized "popular assertions," including antisemitic tropes circulating in the Lithuanian diaspora, citing the following: a) any discussion of Lithuanian crimes against Jews must consider Jewish crimes against Lithuanians, since Jews were the dominant force in Soviet security forces; b) Jews as a group had betrayed Lithuania in 1940–1941, had been active in deporting Lithuanians, but themselves had not been subject to Soviet repressions; c) the killings had been carried out by Germans with the help of some rabble who were dressed up in Lithuanian uniforms; d) all DP emigrants accused of crimes during the Holocaust were innocent victims of Soviet propaganda;

---

62   Joseph B. Končius, *History of Lithuania* (Chicago: Lithuanian-American Community, n.d.), 131.

63   The novel is Icchokas Meras, *Striptizas, arba Paryžius-Roma-Paryžius* (Southfield, MI: Ateitis, 1976), republished in Vilnius in 2008. The speech is in "Icchokas Meras and the Holocaust," 5–6.

e) depictions in the popular press of atrocities by the Lithuanian SS in Poland and Belarus were slanderous, since there were no such SS units; and f) Jews, influential in the Western media, failed to give proper credit to Lithuanian efforts to save Jews and minimized the crimes of the Communists. The discussants at this meeting, which included the prominent poet and Yale professor Tomas Venclova, as well as the dissident Aleksandras Štromas, whose father had been killed in the Lietūkis massacre, pointed out that only one in the list of opinions (concerning the SS) had any basis in fact.[64] Suggestions by Lithuanian American liberals that, despite the manipulation of the Holocaust by the Soviet regime and others with political agendas, society needed to own up to an unpleasant past were met with charges of pro-Soviet bias, if not downright treason to the cause of the nation's freedom. Resistance to any hint of Lithuanian culpability for the Holocaust was further inflamed by the defensive reaction of many émigrés to the denaturalization and deportation cases against a number of former DPs by the U.S. Justice Department's Office of Special Investigations which charged them with concealing their Nazi collaborationist past. The investigations were spurred by the pro-Soviet journalist Charles R. Allen, Jr., implicating the PG in the persecution of Jews. The resulting publicity led to the passage of Congresswoman Elizabeth Holzman's 1978 amendment to the Immigration and Nationality Act which authorized the Department of Justice to prosecute, denaturalize, and deport persons who had misrepresented their service to Nazi Germany and had immigrated to the United States.[65]

The main thrust of the émigré memoirs, articles, and historical surveys of the Nazi occupation sought to defend the reputation of Lithuanians who had served in official capacities under the German occupation. One of the most contorted interpretations among diaspora writers was the notion that the June 1941 insurrection was aimed at the Germans as much as the Soviets, an explanation that flies in the face of the PG's rhetoric at the time. A major publisher of such and similar material was the quarterly journal *Į laisvę* published by the Friends of the Lithuanian Front (Lietuvių Fronto bičiuliai) and initially edited by the former PG acting premier Juozas Ambrazevičius-Brazaitis with

---

64 "'Žydų klausimas' mūsų spaudoj ir visuomenėj," *Akiračiai*, no. 9 (103) (October 1978): 8–9. The outrage at the SS charge was a response to the 1978 blockbuster NBC miniseries *Holocaust* in which a Jewish resister urges the killing of a "Lithuanian SS officer" during the Warsaw Ghetto Uprising.

65 See Charles R. Allen, Jr., *Nazi War Criminals among Us* (New York: Jewish Currents, 1963).

contributions from, among others, former members of the LAF. The journal abandoned the blatant antisemitism of the 1941–1942 newspaper and included studies from younger intellectuals who had no connection to the organization founded in Berlin, but the editors never permitted a straightforward account of the genocide of Lithuania's Jews. Former LAF leaders did admit that the LAF program had, in fact, contained "totalitarian tendencies with a leader, and with allusions to racism which were fashionable at the time."[66] For his part, Škirpa, in his memoir, simply elided antisemitic passages from LAF documents which he included in his volume on the uprising of 1941, while Bishop Brizgys's study of the Catholic Church in 1941–1944 defended the hierarchy's response to the Holocaust.[67] The émigré approach marked by apologia and, not infrequently, anti-Jewish prejudice found a response among some anti-Soviet dissidents, but it also evoked a sharp rebuke from others in the samizdat community, including Tomas Venclova and Antanas Terleckas.[68]

The utter incompatibility of the Soviet and diaspora narratives is reflected in the dishonest and one-sided treatments of history that occurred in the same wartime space. An encyclopedia of Lithuanian geography published in Boston contained an entry on Pravieniškės which detailed the massacre of more than two hundred prisoners and guards at one of Lithuania's better-known penal colonies carried out by a Soviet armored unit on June 26, 1941. "The massacre at Pravieniškės greatly agitated all of Lithuania," the entry concluded. "However, there was no international intervention, the criminals were neither identified nor punished."[69] One would never know that Pravieniškės served as a labor camp and killing site during the German occupation. A Soviet Lithuanian encyclopedia simply states that "the Hitlerites and local bourgeois nationalists established a concentration camp in Pravieniškės in 1941," and then enumerated the fascist

---

66 As quoted in Brazaitis-Ambrazevičius and Pilypas Narutis, "Lietuvių aktyvistų frontas," in *Lietuvių enciklopedija*, vol. 16 (Boston: LE leidykla, 1958): 27.

67 As in Škirpa, *Sukilimas* and Brizgys, *Katalikų bažnyčia*. For a brief overview of diaspora historical writing on the Holocaust see Eidintas, *Lietuvos žydų žudynių byla*, 203–215; Liudas Truska, "Litauische Historiographie über den Holocaust in Litauen," in Bartusevičius, Tauber, and Wette, *Holocaust in Litauen*, 264–268; Dieckmann, *Deutsche Besatzungspolitik*, 1:17–18; Brandišauskas, *Siekiai*, 8–21.

68 The debate between Tomas Venclova and the dissident Žuvintas (pseudonym) along with the comments of Antanas Terleckas were republished in Eidintas, *Lietuvos žydų žudynių byla*, 403–429.

69 Bronius Kviklys, comp., *Mūsų Lietuva*, vol. 2 (Boston, LEL: 1965), 376. This entry exaggerated the number of victims, listing four hundred dead.

crimes.⁷⁰ This is not the only case of memories (and monuments) sharing space. On June 26–27, 1941, retreating NKVD troops massacred hundreds of prisoners at Chervyen (Cherven) southeast of Minsk, including scores of Lithuanians evacuated from Kaunas prisons. After clearing the Chervyen ghetto, German and Belarusian police murdered an estimated 1,400 of the inmates in February 1942.⁷¹

Scholarship on a New Path: The Benefits and Predicaments of Looking West

In Lithuania, a different approach to the history of the Holocaust became possible with the collapse of Soviet rule. The opening of the archives and the academic freedom that came with independence provided the necessary preconditions for serious Holocaust studies. A growing number of Lithuanian scholars began to investigate the social and cultural history of the country's Jews. Mainstream academics of the post-1990 generation working in the major universities, research institutions, and museums, such as the Lithuanian Institute of History and the Ninth Fort Museum, went far beyond the official censorship of the Soviet period and the self-imposed limits of the émigré narratives and began to examine issues which much of the previous generation had preferred to set aside. To fully appreciate the novelty of this change, one should note that the concise 1923 scholarly history of Lithuanian Jewry from the fourteenth to the nineteenth centuries penned by Augustinas Janulaitis (1878–1950) had been the sole such monograph of an ethnic Lithuanian historian devoted to the subject. The erudite professor's hope at the time that the story of the Litvaks would become an integral part of "Lithuanian social history" had found no takers among the scholars of the First Republic.⁷²

In 1991 the first conference which included Jewish and Lithuanian historians was held in New York and was attended by two academics who were to play an important role in expanding knowledge of the Holocaust in Lithuania:

---

70 Lietuvos TSR MA, *Mažoji lietuviškoji tarybinė enciklopedija*, vol. 2 (Vilnius: LTE, 1968). Two hundred Jews were murdered there on September 4, 1941.

71 Arvydas Anušauskas, *Lietuvių tautos sovietinis naikinimas 1940–1958* (Vilnius: Mintis, 1996), 117–132; Dean, *Encyclopedia of Camps and Ghettos*, 1663–1664.

72 Janulaitis, *Žydai Lietuvoje*, 3.

Egidijus Aleksandravičius of Vytautas Magnus University in Kaunas, and Alfonsas Eidintas, deputy director of the Lithuanian Institute of History and later ambassador to Israel. In October 1993 a conference organized by the Lithuanian State Jewish Museum on the fiftieth anniversary of the destruction of the Vilna Ghetto provided an opportunity for Lithuanian and international scholars to publicly face the myriad issues of Jewish life and death in Lithuania. A bilingual publication of the conference included sharp exchanges and conflicting points of view.[73] In January 1995, a young researcher at the Lithuanian Institute of History defended a dissertation on the anti-Soviet Lithuanian underground of 1940–1941 which included an evaluation of events surrounding the first weeks of the Nazi occupation.[74] Valentinas Brandišauskas punctured myths surrounding the uprising of June 1941 and noted the antisemitic policies of the PG. Virtually unnoticed outside Lithuania, this work, while modest in scope compared to studies that have appeared since, was a significant step. In 1996 Liudas Truska published a political biography of Antanas Smetona, which included one of the first analyses of the interwar period's most important politician's policies and attitudes towards the Jews.[75] In September 1997, an academic conference on the history of the Jews and the Holocaust at the seaside resort in Nida was the first such gathering convened at Lithuanian initiative and included internationally recognized scholars Jonathan Steinberg, Ezra Mendelsohn, and Dina Porat. On April 23, 1999, a remarkably open discussion on the Holocaust took place in the Seimas attended by politicians, historians, archival researchers, and jurists.[76]

In effect, serious Lithuanian-language scholarship on the Holocaust and public discussion of the Shoah ceased to be a novelty and had a beneficial effect on the study of Lithuanian-Jewish relations generally as younger scholars in particular took an interest in the past of a vanished community. A number of young academics studied Hebrew and Yiddish to better access the relevant sources. In the April 2022 issue of *Jewish Currents* historian Michael Casper, a critic of the Lithuanian government's approach to the Holocaust, acknowledged that "increasing numbers of Lithuanians are opening up to the truth

---

73 Emanuelis Zingeris, ed., *Atminties dienos: The Days of Memory* (Vilnius: baltos lankos, 1995).
74 Published in Valentinas Brandišauskas, *Siekiai*. For purposes of disclosure: I was the chair of Dr. Brandišaukas's doctoral committee.
75 Truska, *Antanas Smetona*, 296–305.
76 *Lietuvių-žydų santykiai. Istoriniai, teisiniai ir politiniai aspektai. Stenograma.* (Vilnius: LRS, 1999). See http://www.genocid.lt/GRTD/Konferencijos/lietuvi.htm.

about their country's wartime history" and described the "renewed local interest in, and respect for, the 700 years of Jewish history in Lithuania" as a veritable "renaissance in Jewish studies."[77] New works appeared on the anti-Judaic policies of the Catholic Church, the emergence of modern Lithuanian antisemitism, and the development of Jewish-Lithuanian relations between the wars. The years of the First Republic (1918–1940) came to be seen as a significant transformation affecting the country's inter-ethnic relations. The social and political shock of the international crises of the later 1930s, as well as the first Soviet occupation of 1940–1941 received particular attention.[78] Inasmuch as the persistence of Judeo-Bolshevik narratives distracted from appreciating the gravity of the Holocaust, rigorous study which would demythologize the role of Jews in the demise and Sovietization of independent Lithuania proved essential in disputing politicized extremist narratives, for example, the so-called "theory of two genocides," which repeated the shopworn tale of Jewish betrayal in 1940–1941 as a "genocide against Lithuanians," which, in turn, ostensibly provoked the anti-Jewish violence during the German occupation. This still extant antisemitic narrative is an increasingly marginalized polemic more common to the far right, rather than an academic hypothesis, rejected or ignored by most mainstream academic institutions and scholars.[79]

Many younger Lithuanian historians undertook graduate studies and fellowships at major European and American universities. The impact of Western research on German occupation policy, once available only in the restricted "special sections" of Soviet research libraries, shaped much of their evolution to a better understanding of Nazism. Historians in the United States, Europe, and Israel had employed a mass of primary sources on the Holocaust, not only the German documents so thoroughly mined by Raul Hilberg, but also the thousands of eyewitness reports and survivors' testimonies collected after the war. Israeli historians in particular, including Yitzhak Arad, Dina Porat, Dov Levin, and others, have written histories and case studies of the situation in Lithuania based on these essential sources. The ability to engage with the West was

---

77　Michael Casper, "World War II Revisionism at the Jewish Museum," *Jewish Currents*, April 21, 2022, https://jewishcurrents.org/world-war-ii-revisionism-at-the-jewish-museum.
78　An overview of Lithuanian historiography before 2010 is in Darius Staliūnas, "Žydų istorija lietuviškosios istoriografijos kontekste," in Šiaučiūnaitė-Verbickienė, *Abipusis pažinimas*, 120–133.
79　See below.

a crucial opportunity for Lithuanian researchers. It became clear that no meaningful history of the Holocaust in Lithuania was possible without a grounding in the historiography which Western scholars have amassed over the decades, including studies of indigenous collaboration in Axis-occupied Europe.

Familiarity with Western scholarship was an essential learning experience and undoubtedly enhanced the historical knowledge of Lithuanian academics, but the encounter with the outside world also presented challenges. Lithuanian historians found that in some texts on Jewish history, Lithuanians were either largely absent or appeared as one-dimensional figures: antisemitic peasant traders, Holocaust perpetrators, occasionally as heroic saviors. For example, an otherwise competent historical survey by a noted Israeli historian, intended to enlighten the general public, titled the *Short History of Jews in Lithuania*, translated and published in Vilnius in 2000, contained not a single citation from a Lithuanian archival document or a Lithuanian-language monograph and made no mention of Antanas Smetona who ruled Lithuania for most of the First Republic.[80] Perhaps, a more nuanced history of the peoples' relations reflecting evolving forms of cultural and social interaction is a past which is easy to miss in the shadow of the Shoah.

At times, East-West scholarly engagement came across as a one-way street within an atmosphere of tutelage rather than an exchange of knowledge: in some cases, Western scholars and journalists who lacked sufficient expertise in the history of the region expounded to Baltic colleagues on the details of the Holocaust in their countries.[81] While there was general agreement on the basics of the wartime past, the Lithuanian understanding of certain historical events diverged from Western accounts. Lithuanian researchers based their work on a mass of previously restricted in-country documentation which few Western historians had had the means to investigate, especially during the first decade of independence. As a result, some of the Western academic writing on World War II and the Holocaust lacked a grasp of important aspects of Lithuania's modern

---

80 Dov Levin, *Trumpa žydų istorija Lietuvoje*, trans. Jonas Morkus (Vilnius: Studija 101, 2000). On some of the superficial Western and Israeli writing on Lithuanian antisemitism see Stončius, *Neapykantos ribos*, 24–26.

81 This kind of condescending practice has recently been dubbed "Westsplaining," a term conceived by East European academics and popularized after the Russian invasion of Ukraine in 2022 to describe the tendency of some Western commentators to impose their analytical schemes onto issues involving Central and Eastern Europe without sufficient grounding in the political and/or historical realities of the region.

history, flaws which not only impacted both academic and popular accounts of the past but led to deleterious politicized polemics as well.

The dearth of relevant primary sources was evident even in specialized Western studies on the Holocaust. In 1996 historian Knut Stang published an investigation of the Hamann mobile commando under the respected Peter Lang imprint. As important sources, Stang cited Soviet-era publications which had edited out inconvenient passages from archival documents. Aside from other problems, the book featured a startling incompetence in the details of geographic and institutional terminology which could easily have been avoided by employing a Lithuanian research assistant and a closer look at the relevant archival sources.[82] An American history of the massacre of the Lithuanian Jews which appeared in 2008, while superior to Stang's monograph, employed few of the available post-1990 peer-reviewed scholarly studies in Lithuania or the works of Western scholars who had examined formerly closed archives.[83] Experts on antisemitism, the war, and the postwar period sometimes also misstated easily verifiable facts. In his study on U.S. policy towards survivors of the Holocaust, historian Leonard Dinnerstein cited an American specialist of postwar Germany in concluding that "most" Baltic DPs had been members of the Nazi Party. (Except for Baltic Germans, ethnic Balts were, as a rule, ineligible for membership in the NSDAP.)[84] Narrow expertise in archival work was no guarantee in avoiding popular but mistaken stereotypes. During the largest Holocaust conference ever held in the Baltic states, a Yad Vashem researcher insisted that the Germans acted primarily as "observers" and recorders during the massacres of the summer and fall of 1941, taking at face value testimonies which, according to her, proved that "only Lithuanians carried out the slaughter, and if there were Germans present, they were there as spectators . . . [they] stood aside and took photographs." This prospect of a "German-less" Holocaust

---

82 See Stang, *Kollaboration und Massenmord*; cf. my review in the *Journal of Baltic Studies* 29, no. 1 (1998): 84–88; also, the criticism in Arvydas Anušauskas, "Kolaboravimas ir masinės žudynės," *Lietuvos rytas*, January 15, 1998, 11–12.

83 Karen Sutton, *The Massacre of the Jews of Lithuania* (Jerusalem: Gefen, 2008), an updated version of Karen Friedman, "German/Lithuanian Collaboration in the Final Solution 1941–1944" (PhD diss., University of Illinois-Chicago, 1994).

84 Leonard Dinnerstein, *America and the Survivors of the Holocaust* (New York: Columbia University Press, 1982), 22. The source of this assertion is a statement by an American officer uncritically related in Edward N. Peterson, *The American Occupation of Germany: Retreat to Victory* (Detroit: Wayne State University Press, 1977), 295.

drew criticism from the international scholars in attendance.⁸⁵ Even professional historians well versed in the history of the region cannot be expected to be thoroughly immersed in all minutiae of their specialty, but what can appear to a casual reader as inconsequential errors can lead to the continued acceptance of stories abandoned by Lithuanian researchers with better access to primary sources. Timothy Snyder's path-breaking *Bloodlands* mistakenly asserts that Kazys Škirpa had "returned [to Lithuania] with the Germans" and had authored "broadcasts to spur mobs to murder."⁸⁶ Because such questionable assertions appeared in academic studies, they gained traction among the less informed.

One of the problems in writing the history of wartime Lithuania is the persistence of previously accepted, but unfounded, statistics which have been corrected thanks to new investigations. In recent years, archival research has corrected the inflated number of thirty thousand to forty thousand victims of the Soviet deportations in 1941, among whom Jews were said to constitute nearly a quarter of the victims, revealing, rather, roughly eighteen thousand deportees taken during June 14–17, 1941, of whom about 10% were Jews. Other misstatements have resulted in exaggerations concerning the magnitude of the June Insurrection. The myth of the one hundred thousand anti-Soviet rebel participants in the uprising that coincided with the outbreak of the war has been utilized as evidence of either great patriotism (apologetic Lithuanian authors) or extensive collaboration (several Jewish writers). The actual number of insurgents was at least five times less. The pogroms during the first week of the invasion were less extensive than sometimes asserted. The widespread belief that Lithuanians murdered thousands of Jews before the arrival of the Germans in June 1941 must now be reevaluated in the light of new evidence.⁸⁷ Recent studies no longer accept the previously oft-repeated numbers of victims buried at Paneriai, with some sources assuming a figure closer to half of the rhetorical

---

85 Elisheva Shaul, "Jewish Testimonies in Yad Vashem Archives as a Source for the Study of the Holocaust in Lithuania" (report presented to the International Holocaust Conference in Vilnius, September 2002). Author's copy of the distributed text. I observed the reaction of German and American attendees to Shaul's paper firsthand.

86 Timothy Snyder, *Bloodlands: Europe between Stalin and Hitler* (New York: Basic Books, 2010), 192. The Germans interned Škirpa for the duration of the war. There is no evidence that he broadcast over the radio.

87 See the interview with Christoph Dieckmann: Yad Vashem, "The Holocaust in Lithuania," YouTube Video, 16:45, March 4, 2013, https://www.youtube.com/watch?v=HH2ocwBu-FEA.

estimate of one hundred thousand that Sniečkus and the Soviet Extraordinary Commission first announced in 1944. The claim that some twenty thousand ethnic Poles were buried here has been shown to be off the mark by a factor of ten.[88] That such corrections are not always easily accepted was starkly revealed in the hostile reaction in some quarters to the revelations by Yehuda Bauer and others that about 1.1 million people perished at Auschwitz rather than the previously announced figure of four million.

Even seemingly minor inaccuracies in scholarly works can lead to narratives which, as if in the parlor game of telephone, can result in distorted repetitions until the end result becomes unrecognizable as history. In his indispensable pioneering study of the Holocaust Raul Hilberg described the infamous pogrom leader Klimatis [sic] "as the chief of the Lithuanian insurgents," although German documents make clear that this culprit led only one "undisciplined" group, which, according to recent studies, constituted at most less than a tenth of all the fighters in Kaunas. The consequence of what most readers probably would have considered, in the broader scheme of things, a minor misreading of a German document evolved over time. In 1983 Canadian journalist Sol Littman misunderstood this factoid about the Kaunas insurrection and promoted the murderer of Vilijampolė to "temporary leadership of the provisional government." Two *Los Angeles Times* journalists, anxious to discredit the Sąjūdis independence movement as a supposed extremist threat to the Soviet reform movement and the peace of Europe, took this spectacular promotion further and raised Klimaitis to the rank of "national hero." (In fact, even LNP leaders considered Klimaitis a crackpot.) [89] Interestingly, none of this publicity carried any consequences for Algirdas Klimaitis who seems not to have attracted the attention of Nazi hunters, and despite a postwar German investigation,[90] lived quietly under his own

---

88 See Stasiulis and Šepetys, *Nusikaltimų pėdsakai*, 11–12 which suggests the possibility of as many as eighty-three thousand victims, while a lower number is in the November 2013 report of the LGGRTC to Vice-Minister R. Jarockis, "Del Paneriuose 1941–1944 nužudytų žmonių skaičiaus," which estimated as few as fifty thousand dead. Cf. Monika Tomkiewicz, *Zbrodnia w Ponarach 1941–1944* (Warsaw: Instytut Pamięci Narodowej, 2008), 208–251.

89 Hilberg, *Destruction*, 203; Sol Littman, *War Criminal on Trial: The Rauca Case* (Toronto: Lester & Orpen Dennys, 1983), 42; Benjamin Frankel and Brian D. Kux, "Recalling the Dark Past of Lithuanian Nationalism," *Los Angeles Times*, April 29, 1990, M2. See Blynas, *Karo metų denoraštis*, diary entries for 1941, 104, 139–140, 156, 166–167, 172, 199, in which the LNP official found Klimaitis "an odd character," "an idiot," a self-important political intrigue artist, and probably a German agent.

90 Dieckmann, *Besatzungspolitik*, 2:1560.

name in the German Federal Republic until his death in Hamburg in 1988. The Klimaitis episode showed that the issue of native collaboration in the Holocaust could acquire international significance, both in the way World War II was remembered and as a political weapon.

In some cases, academics and writers with insufficient knowledge of East European history asserted generalizations which were either mistaken or shed little light on the nature and extent of collaboration. Amos Perlmutter, a well-regarded scholar of Middle Eastern studies, asserted that "most Lithuanian people were perpetrators and collaborators of the Nazis" and asserted that they "played an important role in transferring Jews to Auschwitz."[91] A popular history of the Holocaust published in the United States indicted nations in the broadest terms: "The Baltic and Ukrainian populations collaborated voluntarily with the Germans in murdering the Jews."[92] An image in a 1998 article by a respected Australian scholar of the Holocaust depicted a young killer in the notorious Lietūkis massacre of June 27, 1941 as a "nationalist," although nothing in this well-known Holocaust photograph indicates why the perpetrator would deserve a political characterization. Curiously, the same snapshot had provoked a bizarre exchange involving identity politics. A Jewish survivor compared photographs and, on the basis of facial recognition, asserted that the youth in question was none other than Juozas Lukša (1921–1951), the celebrated hero of the postwar anti-Soviet resistance. Some Lithuanians, comparing extant wartime photos, have insisted that the person depicted is SS officer Joachim Hamann dressed up as a local hoodlum. As of this writing, no mainstream historian has taken these claims seriously.[93]

The controversy over the Lietūkis photos may seem trivial, but the point it illustrates is not. The impressive multivolume *Encyclopedia of Camps and Ghettos* published in 2012 contains numerous entries in which persecutors and killers

---

91   Amos Perlmutter, "Act of Repentance for Lithuania?," *Washington Times*, December 28, 1996, A11.

92   Lucy Dawidowicz, *The War against the Jews 1933–1945* (New York: Bantam, 1975), 541.

93   The photo is published in Konrad Kwiet, "Rehearsing for Murder: The Beginning of the Final Solution in Lithuania in June 1941," *Holocaust and Genocide Studies* 12, no. 1 (Spring 1998): 15. The perpetrator stares into the camera above the caption: "Lithuanian nationalist poses with the iron bar he used to kill Jews at the Lietukis [sic] garage, June 27, 1941." On the Lukša identification see Faitelson, *The Truth*, 34. On Hamann, cf. Algimantas Liekis, *Lietuvos laikinoji vyriausybė (1941 06 22– 0805)* (Vilnius: Lietuvių tauta, 2000), 254. I have personally heard stories about Hamann and other Germans "dressed up as Lithuanians."

of the Jews are described as "Lithuanian nationalists."[94] In fact, the nationalists were never a monolith: they argued over future visions of their state and nation and behaved accordingly. During World War II, some Lithuanian nationalists turned into murderers, others served in various posts under both the Soviet and German occupations, still others observed the atrocities of the occupiers, and there were those who fought the foreigners and even rescued Jews (including relatives of people who worked in collaborating institutions).[95] Notably, the same pigeonholing is at times applied to victims, as in the tendency to describe the region's prisoners and other civilians massacred by the retreating Soviet forces in June 1941 as "nationalists" (implying that the dead were, perhaps, not quite so innocent).

The issue is not whether there were nationalists among the perpetrators and victims, of which there certainly were many, but whether casually classifying people utilizing potentially prejudicial terminology is a useful approach. The nationalist label is, at best, inadequate when divorced from its historic context and attached to vastly dissimilar people. Presenting perpetrators of the Holocaust as an undifferentiated generic mass not only risks trafficking in collective guilt but also fails as a historic narrative. It does nothing to explain the animosities and social conflicts which motivated anti-Jewish violence in the occupied territories and shirks the more difficult task of thoroughly examining the specific classes of perpetrators, whether anti-Soviet rebels ("white armbands"), civil officials, police battalions, or local rabble. Aside from the broad brush, some of the oft-repeated terms used to describe collaborators in the German occupied territories in scholarly works have their limits as useful descriptors of the persecutors and murderers of the Jews. The persistence of the term "partisan" long after the end of the anti-Soviet uprising obscures the structures and functions of the local administration, the constabulary, and the militarized police formations which carried out most of the atrocities during the late summer and fall of 1941.[96]

---

94 "Lithuanian nationalists" appear dozens of times in entries on Lithuania, most written by historian Alexander Kruglov. See the entry on Alytus in Dean, *Encyclopedia of Camps and Ghettos, 1933–1945*, 2b:1039: "On June 25, 1941, several hundred Jews were taken to Suwałki by Lithuanian nationalists for forced labor and killed." This account is factually problematic. Suwałki had been in German-occupied Poland since October 1939. There are no records of Lithuanian insurgents/militia operating in this area during the first days of the Nazi invasion.

95 See above, Chapter 6.

96 See above, Chapter 3.

Aside from insufficient attention to salient details of Baltic history, two unavoidable practical difficulties affected Western writing on the Holocaust in Lithuania: the limited access to Soviet-controlled archives before 1990 and the unfamiliarity of most foreign researchers of that time with the indigenous languages of the Baltics, aside from a few specialists such as Alfred E. Senn (1932–2016) of the University of Wisconsin. The latter deficiency denied linguistically challenged Western scholars access to the archival collections of local institutions of the interwar years and the occupations of 1940–1945, as well as to the hundreds of academic monographs and articles on these periods published in Lithuania since the mid-1990s. Another problem stems from the fact that a different rule tends to apply to works on smaller countries where an adequate command of sources in the official languages is not seen as particularly important (few academic presses would publish a study of the Vichy regime by researchers without at least a reading knowledge of French).

None of the issues noted should be seen as undermining the conclusions of Western studies regarding the extent and nature of the Holocaust in Europe, particularly those contained in the histories of giants in the field such as Raul Hilberg and Yehuda Bauer. The mistakes that have populated some of the Western narratives and even peer-reviewed scholarly works needed correction, first, as an antidote to stereotypes about the "good" West as opposed to the "bad" East; second, because even minor errors promoted mistrust of academic scholarship which plays into the hands of Holocaust trivializers and right-wing commentators who resist any history which includes a realistic account of Lithuanian collaboration in the Holocaust.

Fortunately, Western historical writing on modern Baltic history has undergone positive changes since the turn of the century as more visiting scholars developed closer ties to Lithuanian academic institutions and acquired the requisite linguistic ability to dig into the voluminous archival records available in the country as well as the opportunity to access indigenous scholarship on Jewish history and the Holocaust. Mordechai Zalkin, Anna Verschik, Theodore Weeks, and Klaus Richter, among other professional historians, have published well-sourced studies emphasizing the complex and changing cultural and literary interactions of Jews and Lithuanians in a modernizing society, placing both communities squarely within the country's social fabric. Joachim Tauber and Christoph Dieckmann have utilized their thorough knowledge of both German- and Lithuanian-language primary and secondary sources to clarify in great detail the history of both Nazi policies and of native collaboration in the destruction of Lithuania's Jews. Lithuanian scholars, academic institutions, museums, and research centers have continued fruitful cooperation with foreign colleagues in furthering research on uniquely Lithuanian aspects of the history of the war years and of the Holocaust. This process means that the older divide between "Western" and Lithuanian academic perspectives is fading, and may, in the end, disappear altogether.

It should be noted that Lithuanian scholars have recently turned their attention to two other aspects of wartime history which lie outside the main focus of this study and which had not until very recently attracted much attention in Lithuania. The violence against accused non-Jewish Communists and other civilians, particularly during the first part of the occupation, was long an object of some academic interest, but the mass murder of Soviet POWs, one of the greatest atrocities of the period, did not much resonate with the country's post-Soviet public. In 2005 the IHC commissioned a study by historian Christoph Dieckmann which outlined the situation of the POW camps in Lithuania. In the Kaunas region, it is estimated that between September 1941 and July 1942 nearly twenty-two thousand prisoners died, some by shooting, most as a result of disease and starvation. At least twenty thousand men died in the Alytus POW camp by the end of the war. Dieckmann has calculated that at least 168,000–172,000 POWs perished in German captivity in camps located within the territory of the current Republic of Lithuania.[97] Another long-neglected atrocity that historians and anthropologists have long ignored is the fate of Lithuania's Roma community. In 1936 nearly 1,500 Roma lived within the borders of the First Republic and, according to a concise IHC study, at least a third of the community was murdered during the occupation, a large number at the Pravieniškės labor camp, while most of the remaining people were deported to Germany and France.[98] Agnieška Avin, Ausra Simoniukštytė, and Jolanta Zaborskaitė as well as other researchers have expanded knowledge of the Roma by producing a bilingual oral history of the community's experience during the war.[99] Two recent publications have described the murder of the

---

97 Christoph Dieckmann, "The Murder of Soviet Prisoners of War in Lithuania," in Dieckmann et al., *Karo belaisvių*, 221–264.

98 See Vytautas Toleikis, "Lithuanian Roma During the Years of the Nazi Occupation," in Dieckmann et al., *Karo belaisvių, Karo belaisvių*, 267–287.

99 See the interactive study available online: Agnieška Avin, Kirill Kozhanov, and Gopalas Michailovskis, comps. *Litovskone romengiro rakiribnytko / Lietuvos romų sakytinės istorijos*

Roma of Panevėžys and presented the suffering of this minority as the country's "forgotten Holocaust."[100] Since 2009 the Lithuanian Roma and supportive groups have commemorated the International Day of Remembrance for Roma Victims of the Holocaust on August 2, and there is now pressure on the government to seek official recognition for the event.[101]

Perpetrators Exposed, Victims in Opposition: History, Politics, and Nationalism in the 1990s

The dismantling of official censorship during the late 1980s and the subsequent political crises which destroyed the USSR created a radically new situation regarding popular attitudes on the history of the war and foreign occupations. Naturally, most Lithuanians at home and in the diaspora welcomed this change that revealed long-suppressed evidence of Stalinist atrocities, but access to the archives also disclosed documentation on the years of Nazi rule in which Lithuanians appeared as perpetrators rather than victims. The domestic turmoil that accompanied Gorbachev's reforms of the 1980s impacted the process by which Holocaust history became a "wedge issue" in Lithuanian society. The initially positive international press coverage of Lithuania's democratic independence movement, Sąjūdis, reinforced a national self-image of heroes and martyrs. But the good feelings did not last. The faith in Gorbachev's policies in the Western press, particularly within certain media and academic circles, led to fears that impatient Lithuanian nationalists were destabilizing the Soviet Union and thus endangering perestroika and even world peace. Some commentators claimed that Vilnius, not Moscow, was the problem. In this view, Gorbachev, in preserving the Union against "secessionists," was following the example of

---

archyvas (Vilnius: Romų visuomenės centras, 2022), https://tmde.lrv.lt/uploads/tmde/documents/files/Romu-istorijos_elektronine-compressed.pdf.

100 Vida Beinortienė and Daiva Tumasonytė, eds, *Panevėžio romų kančių keliai 1941–1945. Exploring the Untold Suffering of the Roma People of Panevėžys: 1941–1945* (Panevėžys: Komunikacijos centras, 2016).

101 "Romų holokaustas Lietuvoje," Romų Platforma, accessed June 6, 2023, http://www.romuplatforma.lt/holokaustas/romu-holokaustas-lietuvoje/; see Agnieška Avin and Anna Pilarczyk-Palaitis, "On the Way to Visibility: The Process of Creating a Cultural Memory of the Genocide of the Lithuanian Roma." *Journal of Baltic Studies* 54, no. 1 (2023): 87–102.

Lincoln rather than Lenin. It was even suggested that medieval Lithuanian campaigns to conquer Muscovy somehow created understandable fears in Russia of resurgent Baltic irredentism, a fanciful use of historic politics.[102]

As the narrative of secessionist radicalism gained ground, the history of Nazi collaboration reared its ugly head in the press. It was in this atmosphere that the rehabilitation controversy of September 1991 came as a rude shock to Lithuanian society. Journalists discovered that there were people who had been involved in the persecution of Jews, had been tried in postwar courts for anti-Soviet activity, and had been mistakenly rehabilitated. Many Lithuanians were taken aback at the Western media's image of thousands of elderly Nazi collaborators walking the streets of Vilnius. It didn't help matters that a major American weekly magazine had published a photo above the caption "Hitler Saluting a Crowd of Lithuanian Supporters in 1939," although the German Nazis depicted saluting the Führer can clearly be seen under the banner: "Dieses Land bleibt ewig deutsch" (This land remains forever German). The fact that the number of problematic rehabilitations of persons repressed during the Soviet regime was less than that implied in American media did little to erase the negative images.[103] Holocaust history was thus enmeshed in a politicized atmosphere from the very beginning of the post-Soviet period and was bound to cause resentment among those Lithuanians who were unlikely to listen to foreigners who understood them so little.

In hindsight, however, the negative publicity was not without the beneficial effect of providing Lithuanian leaders a better understanding of how the Shoah was viewed in the West and they began to act accordingly. On May 8, 1990, the parliament of the Republic of Lithuania published its "Appeal Concerning the Genocide of the Jewish Nation," which condemned the mass murder of the Jews and acknowledged that some Lithuanian citizens were "among the executioners," the first such official statement on the participation of Lithuanians in the Holocaust. An important step in acknowledging this history was President Algirdas Brazauskas's speech to the Knesset during his 1995 visit to Israel in which

---

102 For example, see Alex A. Vardamis, "Those Impatient Lithuanian Nationalists," *Chicago Tribune*, April 3, 1990; and John B. Oakes, "Mr. Bush, Lean on the Lithuanians," *New York Times*, April 21, 1990.

103 Jonathan Alter and Michael Meyer, "An Unpardonable Amnesty," *Newsweek*, September 16, 1991. See Steven Kinzer, "Lithuania Starts to Wipe out Convictions for War Crimes," *New York Times*, September 5, 1991. Cf. the more subdued tone in Marvin Howe's editorial in the *New York Times*, November 17, 1991.

he asked forgiveness for the actions of "those Lithuanians who mercilessly murdered, shot, deported and robbed Jews."[104] In 1999 the Lithuanian Catholic Academy of Sciences published a volume of proceedings on the Church and antisemitism that included articles on the Holocaust. A significant first step, the apologetic tone of some of the contributions nonetheless reflected the tense conversation which the Shoah tended to trigger in Lithuanian society at large.[105] In April 2000 the country's Catholic Bishops' Conference issued a public apology for those "children of the Church who lacked charity towards the persecuted Jews, failed to undertake all possible means to defend them and especially lacked courage to influence those who assisted the Nazis." The bishops acknowledged "past manifestations of antisemitism which burden the memory of the Church."[106] In the following years there were attempts to address outstanding issues related to the war's aftermath on an international stage. In June 2011 the Lithuanian parliament passed, under considerable Western pressure, a law for the restitution of the property of Jewish religious communities, thus beginning to address the problem of compensation even though this has caused some controversy in a country which possessed limited resources for such an expenditure. In April 2013 President Shimon Peres, a Belarusian Litvak by birth, visited Lithuania on a state visit, underscoring the improved ties between the two countries.

Not everyone was enthralled by this attention to Jewish suffering, closer ties to Israel, or the calls for repentance. The president's statement of regret outraged members of the older intelligentsia in particular, some of whom demanded that Jews, in turn, apologize for crimes against the Lithuanian nation during the Soviet occupation and attacked scholars who engaged in what they considered the "blackening of the nation's past." Soon after, the widely read literary journal *Metai* inexplicably published a lengthy screed by the award-winning writer Jonas Mikelinskas that recycled some of the most egregious antisemitic canards, including the claim that some Nazi leaders, including Eichmann, were "full-blooded Jews." Mikelinskas recycled the "double genocide" idea that the collaboration of the Lithuanian rabble in the Nazi murder of the Jews was

---

104 As quoted in Alfonsas Eidintas, *Žydai, lietuviai ir holokaustas*, 402.
105 "Konferencija: 'Katalikų Bažnyčia ir lietuvių-žydų santykiai,'" *LKMA, Metraštis* 14 (1999): 11–330.
106 Published in Josifas Levinsonas, ed. *Šoa (Holokaustas) Lietuvoje: skaitiniai* (Vilnius: Valstybinis Vilniaus Gaono žydų muziejus, 2001), 231–232.

a regrettable but understandable response to the crimes allegedly perpetrated by Jewish collaborators during the first Soviet occupation.[107]

The discussion of "Jewish power" under the Soviets thus took a dangerous turn in the media and among literati. The documentary evidence can easily be manipulated to produce contradictory images.[108] Research on Jews and Soviet power in 1940–1941, even when conducted in a scholarly setting without the noxious antisemitic tropes, is bound to raise fears that examining the ethnic conflicts of the first year of Soviet rule can serve as an excuse for Holocaust murderers. The collaboration of some Jews with Soviet power was not the cause of the Holocaust, although many perpetrators adopted this argument as their singular rationalization for anti-Jewish actions. On the other hand, simply denouncing the Judeo-Bolshevik myth without explanation, or suggesting that research on Jewish participation in the governance of the Lithuanian SSR should be off-limits, only serve to raise suspicions about a cover-up of Soviet crimes, providing a convenient argument for those seeking to evade discussion of Lithuanian participation in the murders of the Jews.[109]

While some Western commentators had urged Lithuanians to own up to the crimes of some of their countrymen during the German occupation, not everyone outside the country welcomed Lithuanian scholarship on the Holocaust. Jews who had survived the war were often less than enthusiastic about what they considered an unwelcome foreign incursion into a narrative of Jewish loss. Joseph A. Melamed, president of the Association of Lithuanian Jews in Israel, made an appeal to Yad Vashem in the fall of 1998 urging the institution not to cooperate with "duplicitous" Lithuanian investigations of the Nazi occupation, claiming that it would inevitably result in insincere "façade painting" rather than genuine research into the mass murder of the Jews.[110]

---

107 See Jonas Mikelinskas, "Teisė likti nesuprastam, arba Mes ir jie, jie ir mes," *Metai* 8–9 (1996): 126–163. Cf. Albinas Gražiūnas, *Lietuva dviejų okupacijų replėse 1940–1944* (Vilnius: Tėvynės sargas, 1996).

108 See above, Chapter 2.

109 For some examples of Lithuanian attitudes during the early 1990s, especially in the provincial press, see Dov Levin, "Lithuanian Attitudes towards the Jewish Minority in the Aftermath of the Holocaust: The Lithuanian Press, 1991–1992," *Holocaust and Genocide Studies* 7, no. 2 (1993): 247–262.

110 Melamed's sharp criticism of Lithuanian commemoration and research on the Holocaust is described in Eidintas, *Byla*, 253–258.

There are emotionally evocative images of the past which frequently reappear in the media and in popular histories. The crowds that threw flowers to invading soldiers represent archetypes; the pictures of Jews welcoming Soviet tanks in June 1940 or those of Lithuanians cheering the German cavalry a year later (as shown in films at the USHMM) are ingrained in the memory banks of the older generation. Real and indelible as they are, the "flower-throwing" images do not shed much light on popular perceptions of occupiers since the context in which people welcome foreign invaders as liberators is far more multifaceted than any photograph can convey.[111] The connection between the two foreign occupations may provide opportunities for political manipulation, but there is no way to ignore firmly rooted collective memories as reflected in the images. Self-perceptions as victims and the stereotypes of the Other as perpetrators are deeply ingrained within the clashing recollections of wartime realities.

Conflicting Agendas:
Institutional Research, Educational Outreach, and the Arts

Scholars of the Holocaust have proposed that "the degree to which a particular country has made progress in . . . recognition of the Holocaust is also the degree to which that country has internalized modern European values," and that "understanding of the Holocaust serves as a barometer of the progress of civil society." If true, then it would seem essential for the Shoah to become part of the national "historical imagination."[112] Since the mid-1990s the Baltic governments have become involved in Holocaust research, driven in part by the call of civic-minded politicians and intelligentsia to confront crimes of the past as a precondition for a healthy democracy. There was also an important practical impetus given the widespread support among Baltic peoples for joining the trans-Atlantic security and European economic structures, such as NATO and

---

111 For instance, it would be problematic to argue that when Czechs welcomed Soviet tanks into Prague in May 1945, they were embracing Stalinism; more likely, they were more concerned with driving out the hated Nazis. The Sudeten Germans' enthusiasm for the German troops entering their towns in October 1938 was of a different order.

112 As stated by Joanna Michlic and John-Paul Himka in the program of the National Convention of the American Association for the Advancement of Slavic Studies (AAASS) in Philadelphia, November 20–23, 2008, session 6–37, "The Memory of the Holocaust in Post-Communist Europe: Similarities and Differences."

the EU. The difficulty of confronting the half-century of foreign domination, a past rife with charges and counter charges of mass crimes and collaboration, and the clueless speculation of some public figures which marked much of the discourse about the murder of the Jews in the Baltic had created international political problems. In May 1998 the three Baltic presidents approved in principle the creation of international commissions to investigate the Soviet and Nazi occupations and publish their findings. The new body in Vilnius, with its rather cumbersome title of the International Commission for the Evaluation of the Crimes of the Nazi and Soviet Occupation Regimes in Lithuania (IHC),[113] was established by presidential decree on September 7 of that year. Emanuelis Zingeris, the only Jewish member of the Seimas, was named chairman of the group which included Lithuanian, American, German, and Russian scholars, as well as several community leaders. The commission was justified with the argument that "due to the repressive legacy of Soviet rule painful problems of the past, such as the Holocaust and other issues, had never been subjected to uncensored public discussion." The government recognized "that for the sake of future generations such historical issues must be addressed, researched and evaluated in compliance with accepted international standards."[114] In line with the sentiments expressed in the aforementioned AASSS convention program, the commission's chairman Zingeris stressed that exposing the crimes of the totalitarian regimes and their collaborators was an important path to strengthening democratic values and civil society.

The project was not universally welcomed. Some Lithuanian émigrés, suspecting (correctly) that the commission would undertake an investigation of native collaboration in the Holocaust, charged that the president's initiative was a Jewish-financed plot, or, at best, a sop to the West under American pressure. The commission was also criticized by some Holocaust survivors in Israel and the Simon Wiesenthal Center, as well as other Jewish organizations in the West as a cynical political gambit intended to facilitate Lithuania's stature as a candidate for inclusion in Western institutions and as an awkward, offensive conflation of Nazism and Communism. However, tackling the relationship

---

113 Recently the agency has styled itself in English with the shorter designation of the International Historical Commission without abandoning its formal title. In Lithuanian it is often referred to as Istorinio teisingumo komisija, which can translate as the Commission for Historical Justice, or also as the Commission for Historical Truth.

114 "The Decree on the Establishment of the Commission," September 7, 1998, IHC Archive (Vilnius).

between the two occupation regimes was inescapable since Soviet rule is tied to the Lithuanian experience of the Nazi occupation in ways both symbolic and substantive; notably, the Nazi and Stalinist atrocities of the first days of the war overlapped in time and space. The Molotov-Ribbentrop Pact and the subsequent period of Soviet-German cooperation also provided a mobilizing historic grievance for the Baltic independence movements whose participants saw no sharp dividing line between the two totalitarian systems. There were legal issues to consider as well: the independence movement had based its argument for the reestablishment of the Lithuanian state as a restoration of sovereignty, which had been suspended but not erased by foreign occupations; hence the period 1940–1990 was to be treated, de jure, as a singular, distinct epoch in Lithuanian history. Nonetheless, the commission's third plenum meeting held on August 29, 1999, committed the body, as both a practical matter and a point of principle, to handle research on the Nazi and Soviet periods separately by creating two distinct working groups in order to "clearly distinguish between the crimes committed by the two occupation regimes and to avoid superficial comparisons during their analysis and evaluation."[115] Following extensive negotiations, a preliminary working arrangement was initiated with representatives of Yad Vashem, with Drs. Yitzhak Arad and Dov Levin participating in the commission's meetings and conferences from 2000 to 2005.

The commission's Nazi crimes sub-commission undertook a number of investigations: antisemitism during the nineteenth and twentieth centuries (before June 1941); the mass murder of Jews during the summer and fall of 1941, including the role of Lithuanian police battalions in the Holocaust; the looting of Jewish assets and property; the persecution and murder of Roma; the mass murder of Soviet POWs; and Nazi persecution and murder of non-Jews. Further research was planned for the problems of forced labor, Lithuania's ghettos, and other aspects of the Nazi occupation.[116] The work of the commission's panel on the Nazi occupation coincided with the ongoing upsurge in Lithuanian academic publications on Jewish history.

To foster public awareness of the crimes of totalitarian regimes, the work of the commission expanded to an outreach program of conferences, Holocaust

---

115 "Mission Statement of the Commission Meeting of November 17, 1998," as well as the "Mission Statement of the meeting of March 2, 1999," IHC Archive (Vilnius).

116 The list of publications and ongoing research projects is available on the commission's website: http://www.komisija.lt.

education, and commemoration, as well as development of school curricula and programs to encourage interethnic tolerance. The commission has concluded a number of agreements with Lithuanian government agencies and educational institutions, including the military and police academies, to facilitate instructional programs on genocide. It has also contributed to the National Holocaust Education Project, an outreach to a new generation of teachers, schoolchildren, students, and soldiers. Nearly five thousand teachers have attended various conferences and seminars, and the IHC has sponsored study trips to Yad Vashem where hundreds of educators have participated in educational programs since 2003. The impact of these programs is difficult to measure. One study maintains that most of the work of teachers committed to Holocaust education is the result of a relatively small and closely knit "community of practice."[117]

In 2002 Lithuania became a member of the Task Force for International Cooperation on Holocaust Education, Remembrance, and Research, now known as the International Holocaust Remembrance Alliance (IHRA). The executive director of the commission participates in the organization's meetings. The IHC also cooperates with the National Fund of the Republic of Austria for Victims of National Socialism and has maintained contacts with the United States Holocaust Memorial Museum. In association with the Auschwitz-Birkenau State Museum the commission implemented the Memorial Sites as a Key for Future Education program, which brought together fifty teachers, museum specialists, and educators from Poland and Lithuania to share experiences and methodological insights. While progress has been made towards involving students in programs such as visiting Holocaust sites, including the Ninth Fort, there has been some resistance by educators who think that the commission's efforts are too focused on the Jews and not enough on ethnic Lithuanians.[118] The IHC has sponsored conferences, most notably "The Holocaust in Lithuania in the Focus of Modern History, Education and Justice," in Vilnius on September 23–25, 2002, the largest such scholarly gathering ever held in the Baltics, which included delegates and scholars from Israel (including the preeminent authority on the Holocaust, Yehuda Bauer), the United States, Germany, Russia, Ukraine, Poland, and other countries.

---

117 Christine Beresniova, *Holocaust Education in Lithuania: Community, Conflict and the Making of Civil Society* (Lanham, MD: Lexington Books, 2017), 139–150; cf. Ellen Cassedy, "'To Transform Ourselves': Lithuanians Look at the Holocaust," *Polin* 25 (2013): 379–394.

118 Beresniova, *Holocaust Education*, 16–17.

Europe-wide educational programs have played a significant role in Holocaust education and awareness. In 2006 the Austrian Gedenkdienst volunteer program celebrated a decade of work with the Jewish Museum which included visiting Lithuanian schools for lectures and programs on tolerance, antisemitism, and the Holocaust.[119] The Office for Democratic Institutions and Human Rights (ODIHR) of the Organization for Security and Cooperation in Europe (OSCE), the Anne Frank House, and the Vilnius Yiddish Institute in 2008 developed a detailed three-step curriculum for secondary schools on the "History of the Jews and Antisemitism." There has been some question of the applicability of popular Western storylines, for example, the case of Anne Frank or the rescue of Danish Jews, which were vastly different experiences from those of Jews in Lithuania. More effective, perhaps, was the special program of publications and essay contests by middle and secondary schools "The Jewish Neighbors of My Grandparents and Great-Grandparents," sponsored by the Remembrance House (Atminties namai) organization, in which students interviewed their own relatives and the still available eyewitnesses as a means of understanding the history of Jewish communities in their locales.[120]

Another institution which has dealt with the Holocaust is the Genocide and Resistance Research Center of Lithuania (LGGRTC) established in 1992. In 1997 the center took control of the Ministry of Culture's Museum of Genocide Victims. The center, which has expanded into a government institution with over 130 historians, research specialists, and support staff, has become the major national institution for the dissemination and commemoration of the crimes of the Soviet occupation in Lithuania. Over the years, the center has been criticized for focusing primarily on Soviet issues and the postwar partisan struggle. In what inevitably struck both Western observers and Lithuanian academics as odd, the ten-volume series titled *The Genocide of the People of Lithuania*, published in 1997–2020, is dedicated solely to the repressions inflicted by the Soviets between 1939 [sic] and 1953.[121] Foreign visitors to the affiliated Museum of Genocide Victims frequently complained that they found few references to the

---

119 Vilna Gaon Jewish State Museum of Lithuania, *Newsletter Special Edition*, November 15, 2006.

120 Linas Vildžiūnas, ed., *Mano senelių ir prosenelių kaimynai žydai* (Vilnius: garnelis, 2002). Cf. the student papers published in Dalia Kuodytė, ed., *Prakalbinta praeitis* (Vilnius: LGGRTC, 2002).

121 Birutė Burauskaitė, ed., *Lietuvos gyventojų genocidas*, 10 vols. (Vilnius: LGGRTC: 1997–2020).

Jews and the Holocaust in exhibits related to the war and occupations. In 2016 the government responded to the political problems stemming from the incongruity of the Center's nomenclature by renaming the institution the Museum of Occupations and Freedom Fights (Okupacijų ir laisvės kovų muziejus).

Both the museum and the LGGRTC encountered criticism because of the insistence of the leadership that both Soviet crimes and the Holocaust constituted genocide, although arguments over what constitutes genocide, a legitimate historical discussion,[122] obscures the real issue: the failure to place the Holocaust at the center of any history of foreign occupation. The Center's historians tasked with exploring the German occupation have made some real progress in addressing the Shoah by publishing a number of well-researched studies on Nazi concentration camp survivors, the Lithuanian police battalions, the 1941 Holocaust in the provinces, the killings in Paneriai, the Vilna Ghetto, rescue, and problems of Holocaust remembrance. The works have appeared in the Center's peer-reviewed journal *Genocidas ir rezistancija* (Genocide and resistance) as well as in books, including the translation of Herman Kruk's weighty memoir of the Vilna Ghetto.[123] In 2020 the center published a documentary study of the fate of Lithuanian Jews in the Stutthof camp.[124] In 2021 Arūnas Bubnys, the center's newly appointed general director and specialist in the history of the German occupation, published, under the auspices of the commission, the most detailed geographic survey to date of the massacres of Lithuanian Jews in the summer and fall of 1941, employing the extensive sources available in the country's archives. The book also listed by name hundreds of individual perpetrators and identified the main police and other units involved in the genocide.[125] A number of problems, which had long bedeviled the institution, came to a head in a political crisis in the spring of 2021 which led to the appointment of Dr. Bubnys to head the Center (as noted below).

Lithuania's Ministry of Culture has sponsored publications memorializing the vanished world of Litvak culture, Jewish life, and the Holocaust and has encouraged these themes in the performing arts as well. In 1990 Jonas Vaitkus

---

122 See, for example, the different perspectives in Subotić, *Yellow Star*, 184ff., and Norman M. Namark, *Stalin's Genocides* (Princeton: Princeton University Press, 2010), 1–29.
123 See the bibliography at genocid.It, accessed November 20, 2019, http://www.genocid.lt/centras/lt/1488/a/.
124 Bubnys and Buchaveckas, *Lietuvos žydai Štuthofo*.
125 Arunas Bubnys, *Holokaustas Lietuvos provincijoje 1941 metais* (Vilnius: margi raštai, 2021).

IMAGE 7.6 Clockwise: Icchokas Meras (1934–2014) at a book signing in July 1968. Renowned Litvak chronicler of the Lithuanian Jewish experience Grigory Kanovich (Grigorijus Kanovičius) (1929–2023), author of *Devilspel*. (Courtesy of Kanovičius family.) Sigitas Parulskis (b. 1965), whose 2012 novel *Tamsa ir partneriai* (The Dark and Partners) was the first major literary depiction of the Holocaust by an ethnic Lithuanian writer.

directed the Lithuanian adaptation of Joshua Sobol's *Ghetto* at the State Academic Drama Theater in Vilnius. In 1994 producer and director Saulius Beržinis presented a documentary on Jewish Vilnius *Goodbye, Jerusalem*, and in 2002 produced another film in which he interviewed the aging participants in the massacres of 1941. In April 1997 an international art festival commemorating the fifty-fifth anniversary of the Vilna Ghetto theater was held in Vilnius.[126] In 2005 director Audrius Juzėnas produced a film version of the Sobol drama *Ghetto*, which in November 2007 won the main prize in the feature film

---

126 As depicted in *Krantai* 3 (1997).

category at the Jewish Eye Film Festival at Ashkelon. One important milestone has been the publication in 2012 of the first Lithuanian-language novel dealing with the massacres of the summer and fall of 1941 by one of the country's premier writers, Sigitas Parulskis. Although literary treatment of the Holocaust in fiction was not new, Parulskis's brutally honest descriptions of atrocities committed by Lithuanian collaborators against Jews were a unique fixture in Lithuanian popular culture.[127] It was a sharp contrast to *Devilspel* by Grigory Kanovich, Lithuania's sole surviving Jewish author with firsthand knowledge of the destruction of Lithuania's shtetls, which concentrated on the personal interactions of Lithuanians and Jews in the fictional town of Mishkine in the summer of 1941 but left the explicit violence off stage.[128]

Wedge Politics and Hate of the Other (1990s–2008)

While academic research, literature, and the arts reflected a new willingness to engage the Shoah within governmental, educational, and cultural institutions, introducing the Holocaust as part of the public's historical imagination has been more difficult. After independence, Lithuania suffered all the problems which afflict the post-Communist states as well as those which are European in scope: a population buffeted by social and economic anxieties; the emergence of an extremist ultranationalist fringe; xenophobia expressed in racist discourse; and even incidents of physical violence. Despite the official attachment to liberal democracy and tolerance, anti-Jewish prejudices still played well, noticeably during times of political turmoil. As the impeachment process of President Rolandas Paksas intensified in 2003–2004, the embattled president embarked on a divisive populist campaign, sometimes accompanied on the stage by Visvaldas Mažonas, a uniformed neo-Nazi. Paksas attempted to rally his political base, the rural and small-town voters most affected by the economic transformation and vulnerable to xenophobic themes, including antisemitic allusions. During the presidential crisis, the nation's mass circulation daily *Respublika*, under editor Vitas Tomkus, published a supplement which could easily have appeared in

---

127 Sigitas Parulskis, *Tamsa ir partneriai* (Vilnius: alma littera, 2012).
128 Grigory Kanovich, *Devilspel*, trans. Yisrael Cohen (Nottingham: Noir Press, 2019). Published in Lithuanian as Grigorijus Kanovicius, *Šėtono apžavai: romanas*, trans. Aldona Paulauskiene (Vilnius: Lietuvos rasytoju sajungos leidykla, 2008).

1930s Germany, replete with anti-American canards, depictions of Jewish world domination, and demonization of the gay community.[129]

Paksas's impeachment and removal in April 2004 eventually restored pro-Western Valdas Adamkus to the presidency, but despite the change in government, problems continued. The internet allowed the extremists access to public discourse. The skinhead metal group "Diktatūra," which stresses the message of "Lithuania for Lithuanians," found some following among the young. An opinion survey published by the Vilmorus polling agency in October 2000 found that when asked to evaluate twenty-five nationalities on a "like-dislike" scale, Lithuanians ranked Israelis (read: Jews) as the second most disliked nationality (the Roma came in first). Poles, Czechs, and Hungarians showed relatively higher tolerance levels. A report from 2006 found that between 1990 and 2005 the number of Lithuanians who asserted that they would not want to live next door to Jews rose from 18% to 31%.[130]

A crucial measure of a society's maturity is the degree of public reaction to hate crimes and incitement. In 2004 authorities took a lenient view of editor Tomkus's antisemitic and antigay ravings in the country's second largest daily newspaper: prosecutors initially imposed a fine, but the verdict was reversed on appeal.[131] On March 11, 2008, as part of the celebrations of the declaration to restore independence, several hundred right-wing extremists, including neo-Nazi skinheads, paraded in central Vilnius, shouting racist and antisemitic slogans. The government's response was tepid: the police took no action and the president's office waited ten days before criticizing the excessive rhetoric of "patriotically inclined youth." Radical nationalist marchers have since continued to parade in public on independence days. One of the youthful far right leaders, Mindaugas Murza, who founded a short-lived "national socialist unity movement" in 1996, was an admirer of the LNP of the 1940s. A member of the Šiauliai city council, Murza was briefly detained by the police for antisemitic

---

129 Vitas Tomkus, "12 laiškų kurie sukrėtė pasaulį," *Respublika*, February 18, 2004.
130 "Polish Public Opinion," CBOS, October 2000, http://cbos.pl/PL/publikacje/public_opinion/2000/10_2000.pdf; Union of Councils for Jews in the Former Soviet Union, "Study Finds Intolerance Rising in Lithuania," February 2, 2006, accessed December 1, 2009, http:///www.ucsj.org/news/study-find-intolerance-rising-in-lithuania.
131 See more about this incident and other examples on the question of current antisemitism in Lithuania as well as its intellectual and political roots in Leonidas Donskis, "Another Word for Uncertainty: Anti-Semitism in Modern Lithuania," accessed July 10, 2021, http://edoc.hu-berlin.de/nordeuropaforum/2006-1/donskis-leonidas-7/PDF/donskis.pdf.

agitation. Even though Lithuanian law provides penalties for hate speech, the enforcement mechanism has been lax. Under pressure, the state has at times shown more strength. In the aftermath of the March 2008 fiasco, the government reacted swiftly when vandals defaced the Vilnius Jewish Center in August of that year.

A Divisive Past 1: Lithuanians, Jewish Partisans, and the War

In June 2007 the Lithuanian procurator's office requested Israeli cooperation in a war crimes investigation concerning the activities of Soviet and Jewish partisans who had been active in eastern Lithuania during the war. One of the persons of interest was Dr. Yitzhak Arad, former director of Yad Vashem, a noted author on the history of the Holocaust in the USSR and a member of the IHC sub-commission on Nazi crimes. The Arad affair embodied the difficulties, distractions, and paradoxes that afflict Lithuania's wartime history and is perhaps one of the most instructive examples of the problems which complicate the introduction of the Holocaust into the public's historical imagination. The inquiry centered on the massacre of thirty-eight villagers in the hamlet of Kaniūkai (Koniuchy) by a predominantly Jewish Soviet partisan unit in January 1944.[132] Not surprisingly the investigation evoked strong foreign protests, outrage among Jews everywhere, and criticism from President Adamkus. The failure of the Lithuanian judiciary to press the prosecution of pro-Nazi collaborators, as evidenced by the delayed process against the former head of the Lithuanian Security Police in Vilnius, Aleksandras Lileikis, and others, gave rise to charges of hypocrisy concerning the motives behind the investigation of anti-fascist partisans. One unfortunate byproduct of the situation was the disruption of the historical commission's research on Nazi war crimes. The Yad Vashem Directorate protested the investigation of a "victim of Nazi oppression" and suspended Israeli participation in the IHC. In solidarity with their Israeli colleague, the commission refused to convene any further meetings of the sub-commission on Nazi crimes until the case was resolved.[133] After an eight-year interruption the commission's

---

132 See above, Chapter 5.
133 Shalev to Zingeris, September 5, 2007; Zingeris to Shalev, September 28, 2007 (author's copy of original).

IMAGE 7.7. Top: Present-day memorial to the Olkinas and Jofė (Joffe) families killed in July 1941. Below: The road to Panemunėlis not far from the grove where Matilda Olkinaitė died. (Courtesy of Karolis Pilypas Liutkevičius.)

research work was reauthorized in October 2012 by President Dalia Grybauskaitė.

The judiciary's insensible move provided much grist for speculation and conspiracy theories about motives. Unwilling to judge Nazi collaborators, the judiciary was pondering a case against Arad, a teenage ghetto survivor who had lost most of his family and had fled to the forests to join the battle against the fascists. It was only too obvious that the scale of the killings at Kaniūkai paled in comparison to Nazi crimes, but clearly, those encouraging the prosecution of Jewish partisans, as well as right-wing commentators who exploited the situation, had chosen their moment well. Despite the damage to Lithuanian-Jewish relations and the country's image abroad, any action by the government to halt the investigations would easily be countered by charges of unconstitutional interference in judicial proceedings. At the same time, inaction risked undoing much of the work in dealing with the legacy of the Holocaust and undermining the goal of enhancing Lithuania's international reputation.

The controversy opened a wound at the most difficult intersection of Lithuanian and Jewish historical imaginations, a place where divided wartime memories are the most difficult to reconcile. Outside Lithuania, the request

IMAGE 7.8. People marching to commemorate the seventy-fifth anniversary of the destruction of the Jews of Molėtai, August 29, 2016, responding to the call by playwright Marius Ivaškevičius to remember the Jews of his hometown. (Inset photo courtesy of Dmitrijus Matvejevas.)

to question Fania Brantsovskaya and Rachel Margolis, two elderly women survivors and former partisans, as witnesses in the Arad case came across as a cruel exercise in harassing the victims.¹³⁴ According to Efraim Zuroff of the Wiesenthal Center in Israel, the questioning of the former partisans amounted to a "deliberate campaign . . . to discredit the brave Jewish heroes of the anti-Nazi resistance and help deflect attention from the infinitely more numerous crimes by Lithuanians against Jews during the Holocaust."¹³⁵ Even some Lithuanians viewed the entire case as a contemptible farce. In September

---

134 Danielle Singer, "Lithuanian Accuses Holocaust Survivors of War Crimes," *Jerusalem Post*, May 29, 2008, 7; Andrew Baker, "Europe's Shameful Honoring of Vilnius," *Forward*, June 26, 2008, https://forward.com/opinion/13641/europe-s-shameful-honoring-of-vilnius-02075/; Adam Mullet, "Adamkus forgives Germany for Nazi Occupation," *Baltic Times*, June 2–July 19, 2008, 4; Dana Gloger, "The Holocaust Survivors Facing War-Crimes Trials," *Jewish Chronicle* (London), June 6, 2006; Lana Gersten and Marc Perelman, "Tensions Mount over Lithuanian Probe," *Forward*, July 3, 2008, https://forward.com/news/13704/tensions-mount-over-lithuanian-probe-02134/; "Prosecution and Persecution: Lithuania Must Stop Blaming the Victims," *Economist*, August 21, 2008.

135 See "Wiesenthal Center Protests Lithuanian Judicial Campaign to Discredit Jewish Heroes of Anti-Nazi Resistance," May 28, 2008, and "Wiesenthal Center: Closure of Fabricated Case against Dr. Arad," September 25, 2008, accessed September 17, 2023, http://www.swcjerusalem.org/oldsite/LITHUANIA_PR.htm.

IMAGE 7.9. Evading history. Memorial in Ukmergė to Juozas Krikštaponis (aka Krištaponis), an officer of the notorious 12th LSD Battaliion which was responsible for mass shootings of Jews and Soviet POWs marking his death as an anti-Soviet partisan in 1945. The municipality refused to remove the monument despite the certification of Krikštaponis's crimes by the Lithuanian Institute of History.

2008, the Lithuanian Prosecutor General's Office closed the case against Dr. Arad in a clumsily worded announcement; this did little to mollify critics. But the Ministry of Justice stubbornly insisted that the investigation of partisan activities as potential war crimes rested on objective legal criteria which allow the prosecution of Soviet occupiers and their collaborators.

A closer study of the history of guerilla warfare in eastern Lithuania reveals a past more confusing and complex than one would deduce from the rhetorical battles it has engendered. The issue of partisan resistance during the 1940s has been particularly vexing in terms of its psychological implications. The anti-fascist guerillas cannot be easily unlinked from their connection to the Soviet cause (although one would think that, given their uniquely desperate circumstances, one can exempt the Jewish fighters as a special case). In Lithuania, the anti-fascist label does not instinctively evoke the positive emotional connotations that it does in the West. The only anti-fascists many Lithuanians had ever met were Red Army soldiers, Soviet partisans, and Stalinist officials among whom were hardliners with nasty reputations. To complicate matters, the Communist-led partisans were in fierce conflict not only with German forces and their collaborators but with the Polish Home Army, a formidable anti-Nazi resistance movement of an Allied government, or in Soviet verbiage, a bona fide member of the anti-Hitlerite coalition.

The perspective of most Lithuanian Jews, especially the elderly survivors, could not be other than radically different. On September 1, 2008, the Lithuanian Jewish community published an open letter to the "leaders of the Lithuanian state" expressing concern on recent antisemitic manifestations but reserving their strongest words on the "persecution of Jewish anti-fascist partisans." "Does Lithuania recognize the victory of the anti-Hitler coalition during the Second World War? Does the Republic of Lithuania recognize the decisions of the Nuremberg trials?" the authors asked.[136] Naturally, most Lithuanians know who won the war, but their memory of the twentieth century, with its negative images of the Stalinist past, is a stumbling block to appreciating the Western/Soviet perspective on the Grand Alliance, creating difficulties when dealing with the historic context in which the Holocaust or, for that matter, any aspect of the war must be located.

To complicate matters further, the usual chronological framework of World War II (1939–1945) has little relevance to Lithuania's majority population: most ethnic Lithuanians who died violently in the twentieth century were killed and/or displaced between 1945 and 1950, a brutal period echoed in the language itself by the term *pokaris* (literally, "the after-war"), which in current parlance is an idiom signifying carnage rather than peace. In locales with small Jewish communities, total violent deaths after V-E Day exceeded those incurred during World War II. In May 1953 Lavrenti Beria reported to the Presidium of the Central Committee of the CPSU that Soviet security forces had "repressed" (that is, killed, deported and/or arrested) more than 276,000 persons in the Lithuanian SSR between 1944 and 1952.[137] This was a statistical understatement of total losses since it omitted the Soviet killings and deportations of June 1941 and excluded certain classes of noncombatants and the pro-regime militias (the "people's defenders") from the list of the casualties of the anti-Soviet guerilla war which, by some estimates, counted thirty-five thousand to forty thousand dead. Postwar deportations alone claimed some 130,000 victims. In the minds of much of the populace, the war began as liberation in 1941 and ended in a "second occupation" in 1944–1945. The latter reality, which may strike some Westerners and especially Russians as offensive, was not a figment of Lithuanian imagination. In the summer of 1944 Lithuanian Communist officials complained to their superiors that Soviet forces often behaved more like conquerors than liberators, listing numerous cases of unprovoked

---

136 "Lietuvos žydų bendruomenė išplatino viešą laišką Lietuvos valstybės vadovams." Simonas Alperavičius, chairman of the Lithuanian Jewish Community, and Tobijas Jafetas, chairman of the Association of Former Ghetto and Concentration Camp Inmates, to Lithuania's president, prime minister, and general procurator, September 1, 2008 (in author's archive).

137 Beria report to the Presidium of the CPSU, May 8, 1953 (author's archive).

shooting, looting, and rape.[138] In any case, many Lithuanians, who evaded Soviet conscription in the summer of 1944 and fled into the forests to join the resistance, believed that it made no more sense to die for Stalin at war's end than it did during the Nazi invasion of 1941.

Decades of the Soviet regime's insistence on the heroism of the Red Army has done little to lessen the widespread aversion to the story of the Great Patriotic War. In the spring of 2005 Baltic cultural and political elites argued over whether their presidents should accept the Russian government's invitation to attend the sixtieth anniversary of Victory Day in Moscow. The majority of the scholars of the Lithuanian Institute of History successfully urged President Adamkus to boycott the festivities, although Latvian president Vaira Viķe-Freiberga broke ranks and took part in the festivities, much to the annoyance of Lithuania's prime minister Andrius Kubilius who remarked that Lithuanians had nothing to celebrate on May 9. The Bronze Soldier riots of April 2007 in Tallinn showed that the memory of wars can indeed turn fatal.[139] The problem is that within such a framework of selective collective memory the significance of the German occupation, and with it that of the Holocaust, is radically diminished. It is not that the Western perspective of World War II is wrong but simply that, for many if not most Lithuanians, it remains irrelevant to their own wartime experience and memories of suffering.

A Divisive Past 2: Flawed Heroes and Contentious Comparisons

In the years which followed the Arad/partisan controversy, new conflicts shaped the "history/cultural wars" in Lithuania. As had happened during the founding of the IHC in 1998, charges of a false symmetry between the Nazi and Stalinist totalitarian systems as an effort to conceal the scope and extent of

---

138 The correspondence is cited in Stončius et al., *16–osios lietuviškosios divizijos*, 116–117.

139 To understand why the statue of a Red Army liberator might grate on Estonians, see Olaf Mertelsman, "Das 'kleinere Übel'? Das Generalkommissariat Estland in estnischen Vergana genheitsdiskurs," in *Reichskommissariat Ostland*, 349–366. Estonia was an outlier: it was the only country in which Jews did not constitute the majority of indigenous victims of the German occupation. For Estonians to conclude that the Nazis were the "lesser evil" needed no ideological predilections, simply a grasp of arithmetic.

IMAGE 7.10. Emanuelis Zingeris, member of the Seimas (parliament), signatory of Lithuania's Declaration of Independence of March 11, 1990, and Chairman of the International Historical Commission. (Officially: The International Commission for the Evaluation of the Crimes of the Nazi and Soviet Occupation Regimes in Lithuania.) (Courtesy of the IHC.)

Lithuanian criminality during the Holocaust were raised again.[140] But the issue eventually also morphed into a storm of charges and countercharges concerning the activities of some anti-Soviet resistance leaders and their relations with the Nazis.

In May 2009 Dr. Dovid Katz of the Vilnius Yiddish Institute attacked what he termed the official Lithuanian "genocide industry," including the historical commission chaired by Lithuania's leading Jewish politician, which, he claimed, had the sole aim of "Holocaust obfuscation." The major point of departure for the controversy was the Prague Declaration of June 3, 2008, signed by the future president of Germany Joachim Gauck, Vaclav Havel, Vytautas Landsbergis, Emanuelis Zingeris, and a number of other European politicians, including former Soviet-bloc dissidents. The declaration called on European institutions to evaluate and condemn the crimes of Communism based on the Nuremberg model and to educate the public on the criminal nature of both Nazism and Communism. Katz claimed that the purpose of placing an equal sign between the two systems was but a crafty attempt to obscure the collaboration of local populations in the Holocaust. In this story, Jewish Lithuanians who disagreed with Katz's position were dismissed as obsequious "show Jews." Efraim Zuroff also attacked the Prague Declaration in the *Jerusalem Post*, citing it as a threat

---

140 The thesis that Holocaust memory has been appropriated by the post-Soviet East European states primarily as a means of criminalizing communism, denigrating wartime anti-fascist movements, and creating a stronger national identity is explored in relation to Lithuania by Subotić, *Yellow Star*, 150–207.

to the "unique status" of the Shoah and warning against "a new and distorted World War II historical narrative." Both authors claimed that Soviet crimes were not genocidal in nature.[141] However, their attack on conflating Communism and Nazism made no mention of scholarly literature on the topic, nor did it explain why the academic historiography of comparative totalitarian systems was somehow illegitimate.[142]

In May 2009 Russia's President Dmitri Medvedev authorized the creation of the Commission to Counteract Attempts to Harm Russia's Interests by Falsifying History, a body dominated by government functionaries rather than historians, a transparent attempt to undermine any critical research into the role of the USSR in World War II.[143] Although the body was disbanded in 2012, in May 2014 the Duma passed a law criminalizing public dissemination of "intentionally false information about the Soviet Union's activities in World War II" and the desecration of "symbols of Russia's military glory,"[144] an obvious attempt to buttress the narrative of the Great Patriotic War and subvert evidence of wartime Stalinist crimes. The debate over the legacy of World War II took a sharp turn at the OSCE Parliamentary Assembly in Vilnius in July 2009 when the Lithuanian delegation successfully proposed a resolution "On Divided Europe Reunited," condemning both Stalinism and Nazism and designating August 23 as a "Europe-Wide Day of Remembrance of the Victims of Stalinism and Nazism." The Greek Communist representative, Costas Alissandrakis, ridiculed the notion of a Soviet occupation of Lithuania and termed any talk of Soviet mass deportations there as "folktales," prompting an angry retort and walkout by Arūnas Valinskas, the speaker of the Seimas. The Russian delegation denounced the resolution and boycotted the vote while Russia's Foreign Ministry denounced the remembrance resolution as an insult.[145]

---

141 Dovid Katz, "Prague's Declaration of Disgrace," *Jewish Chronicle*, May 21, 2009, and more extensively in "Genocide Industry Has Hidden Agenda," *Irish Times*, May 30, 2009. Cf. Efraim Zuroff, "A Combined Day of Commemoration for the Victims of Nazism and Communism?," *Jerusalem Post*, July 12, 2009. Also, cf. Subotić, *Yellow Star*, 38–39.

142 For example, Gellately, *Lenin, Stalin and Hitler*, and the cited studies of Timothy Snyder.

143 Full text is in "Prezident posledit, chtoby istoriya ne obidela Rossiyu," May 19, 2009, https://polit.ru/article/2009/05/19/komissia/.

144 See "Federalnyi zakon o vvedenii otsvetsvennosti za reabilitatsiyu natsizma," May 6, 2014, https://rg.ru/documents/2014/05/07/reabilitacia-dok.html.

145 "A. Valinksas pareikalavo, kad graikų komunistas atsiprašytų už lietuvių tautos įžeidimą," *Lietuvos rytas*, July 3, 2009.

IMAGE 7.11. International Historical Commission programs.
Top: Lithuanian teachers at the IHC-Yad Vashem summer course on the Holocaust, Jerusalem, August 2023. (Courtesy of the IHC.)
Bottom: Teachers and students participating in the local commemorative "Road to Memory" marches to honor victims of the Holocaust at the killing sites. Here marching in the forest of Kurganava near Panevėžys, 2021. (Courtesy of IHC.)

In 2000 one of Lithuania's prominent cultural historians had asserted that the Holocaust simply did not exist in Lithuanian collective memory, a statement that at the time was not far from the truth[146] but which preceded some positive developments in the people's response to Holocaust memory that were to come later. On August 24, 2016, the playwright Marius Ivaškevičius published an emotional confession "I Am Not a Jew," expressing his regret at his own past ignorance of the fate of the Jews and shame at the indifference of his fellow countrymen to the memory and suffering of Holocaust victims. He noted the death of his uncle who perished as an infant in Russia's far north during the deportations but reminded his readers that the commemoration of Lithuanian victims could only acquire real meaning and sincerity "if we showed the same reverence to the Jews who lie in graves near our very homes." He called on Lithuanians to participate in a march to commemorate the seventy-fifth anniversary of the murder of the Jews of his hometown of Molėtai.[147] Ivaškevičius's appeal resonated and, much to his surprise, on the afternoon of August 29, 2016, a crowd of nearly two thousand Lithuanians joined a handful of survivors and other Litvaks in the largest spontaneous demonstration of Holocaust remembrance in the country's history as participants marched on the same fateful route taken by the Jews of Molėtai in 1941. International media reported widely on the event. At the same time, the IHC, local jurisdictions, and schools organized similar demonstrations in other towns on the seventy-fifth anniversary of the genocide of Jews.

The growing public interest in commemorating and memorializing the Holocaust reached Panemunėlis and Rokiškis where the Olkinas family had once lived and worked. In February 1986 a local investigative commission had certified the precise burial place of the "remains of nine Jewish people—victims of the fascists killed in July 1941,"[148] but there had been little public discussion of the fate of the area's Jews. However in November 2016 the Rokiškis amateur theater troupe, including actors from Matilda's hometown, presented a play at the Panemunėlis cultural center that celebrated the Jewish family's life and depicted the crime which marked the community's history. The troupe found the

---

146 Egidijus Aleksandravičius, "Apie atminties archeologiją, kančių kultūrą ir Holokausto prisiminimus," in *Praeitis, istorija ir istorikai*, ed. Egidijus Aleksandravičius (Vilnius: Vaga, 2000).

147 Marius Ivaškevičius, "Aš ne žydas," Delfi, August 24, 2016, https://www.delfi.lt/news/ringas/lit/m-ivaskevicius-as-ne-zydas.d?id=72107298.

148 "Moškėnų tarybinio ūkio kraštotyros organizcijos fašizmo aukų kapinyno nustatymo aktas, November 20, 1986," in Stašys, *Fašizmo aukų kapai*, 5–6.

production difficult. The actors and the audience wept during the performance. In September 2017 the people of Rokiškis and environs erected a memorial at the site with inscriptions in Lithuanian and Hebrew, the language more typical of the post-Soviet era: "The Olkinas and Jofė families were shot in this grove in the year 1941."[149]

In 2015 journalist Rūta Vanagaitė published *Our People* (*Mūsiškiai*) containing a chapter titled "Travels with the Enemy"[150] which recounted the participation of Lithuanians in the Holocaust and included descriptions of visits to killing sites with Nazi hunter Efraim Zuroff. *Our People* raised the subject of the Holocaust to a national conversation, albeit in a different sense than the Molėtai march. The book went through several printings and, unlike the numerous academic studies, inspired a fierce public (and nonacademic) debate exposing the country's social fault lines of Holocaust memory in the process. Professional historians reacted coolly to a journalist's venture into the field but conceded that discussion on the subject was much needed, despite the sharp, even vicious, polemics which it engendered. In general, most Jews wholeheartedly endorsed the book, the liberally inclined intelligentsia either approved with some caveats or saw it as a useful point of departure for dialogue, while right-wing nationalist media condemned it as another blackening of the nation's past. Unfortunately, Vanagaitė's reputation suffered after newspapers publicized her ill-chosen remarks, based on questionable sources, on the torture and death of anti-Soviet resistance leader Adolfas Ramanauskas-Vanagas. The misstatements created a public backlash and dismayed even those historians who initially sympathetic to the author.[151] Despite the writer's fulsome apology, Vanagaitė's publisher

---

149 Laima Vincė, "Nutildyta Mūza. Apie Matildos Olinaitės gyvenimą ir poeziją," January 25, 2019, https://www.bernardinai.lt/2019-01-25-nutildyta-muza-apie-matildos-olkinaites-gyvenima-ir-poezija/; Martyna Šulskutė, "Kad mūsų šešėliai nebūtų už mus didesni: Matildos Olkinaitės ir Holokausto iamžinimas," NARA Journal, December 29, 2022, https://nara.lt/lt/articles-lt/kad-musu-seseliai-nebutu-uz-mus-didesni.

150 Rūta Vanagaitė, *Mūsiškiai* (Vilnius: Alma littera, 2015). Published in English as Rūta Vanagaitė and Efraim Zuroff, *Our People: Discovering Lithuania's Hidden Holocaust* (Lanham, MD: Rowman and Littlefield, 2020).

151 See the discussion of the director of the Lithuanian Institute of History Alvydas Nikžentaitis and Christoph Dieckmann: "Tautinis mitas tai ne paprasta istorija: atviras laiškas vokiečių istorikui," Delfi, October 31, 2021, https://www.delfi.lt/news/ringas/lit/a-nikzentaitis-tautinis-mitas-tai-ne-paprasta-istorija-atviras-laiskas-vokieciu-istorikui.d?id=76220619; cf. Mindaugas Jackevičius, "Vokiečių istorikas įvertino R. Vanagaitės pareiškimus: yra tik vienas kelias pirmyn," Delfi, October 30, 2017, https://www.delfi.lt/news/daily/lithuania/vokieciu-istorikas-ivertino-r-vanagaites-pareiskimus-yra-tik-vienas-kelias-pirmyn.d?id=76199271.

succumbed to the popular outrage and halted the sale of her bestseller. Five years later, the journalist returned to the subject of the Holocaust with the publication of her lengthy interview with Christoph Dieckmann, "How Did It Happen?," which familiarized Lithuanian readers with the major issues of the Holocaust in a nonacademic, straightforward narrative.[152]

The furor over Vanagaitė's comments on Ramanauskas tore at the emotional fabric of Lithuanian imagery of the country's fight for freedom. In 1997 the government posthumously awarded the prestigious Vytis medal of valor to Jonas Noreika, one of the leaders of the postwar anti-Soviet resistance who had been executed by the Soviets in 1947. Soon after, a commemorative plaque citing his heroic role as a partisan leader appeared at the entrance of the Vrublevskis Library of the Lithuanian Academy of Sciences in Vilnius. At the time, few people took notice that Noreika had served as the district chief of Šiauliai in 1941–1943 and had implemented German directives to ghettoize and expropriate the Jews.[153] In 2018, on the seventy-fifth anniversary of the destruction of the Vilna Ghetto, the Jewish community demanded the plaque's removal, their cause supported by Foreign Minister Linas Linkevičius. In April 2019 the plaque was vandalized, but then repaired and once again placed on the building. On July 27, 2019, the panel was removed on orders of the mayor, Remigijus Šimašius, who stated that Noreika's actions against the Jews made any public tribute to the partisan leader unacceptable. The IHRA supported the decision and Jewish American leaders (AJC) commended Šimašius when the mayor visited Washington. Nonetheless, the decision sparked protests, including a rally where antisemitic signs were displayed. On September 9, 2019, a crowd of pro-Noreika demonstrators, in full view of the police and without an official permit, placed a new commemorative plate on the wall of the building.

The controversy inspired contentious litigation in Vilnius. The American lawyer Grant Gochin filed a legal complaint in Vilnius, citing research conducted by his Lithuanian research assistants and demanding that the government officially recognize Noreika's collaboration with the Germans and publicly disavow the insufficiently critical interpretation by the LGGRTC concerning

---

152 Christoph Dieckmann and Rūta Vanagaitė, *Kaip tai įvyko?* (Vilnius: Rūta Vanagaitė, 2020). Available in English: Christoph Dieckmann and Rūta Vanagaitė, *How Did It Happen? Understanding the Holocaust* (Lanham, MD: Rowman and Littlefield, 2021).

153 See above, Chapter 4. Charges that Noreika participated in the murder of the Jews of Plungė have not been established as fact.

MAP 12. Lithuania today. (CIA Factbook.)

Noreika's role in the persecution of the Jews in Šiauliai. In March 2019 the Vilnius district court rejected Gochin's appeal as lacking legal standing and competent argument. Writing history via the courts is a dubious proposition but whatever the legal merits of the case, the LGGRTC's confusing and exculpatory statements by unqualified researchers concerning actions of Lithuanian officials who had engaged in persecution of the Jews met criticism from academics, including the leadership of the Lithuanian Institute of History and scholars of the History Faculty of the University of Vilnius. Parliamentarian and head of the IHC, Emanuelis Zingeris, as well as the IHC's Nazi crimes panel condemned the LGGRTC's ambiguous explanation of Noreika's service under the Germans and reaffirmed the position that had been adopted by the commission in its 2016 meeting, that it "condemns the commemoration in the public sphere of persons . . . [who had] participated in the persecution and/or murder of Jews and other victims during the Nazi occupation regardless of any other activities in which they have engaged in that time or at a later date."[154]

---

154 "A Response to the statement of the Genocide and Resistance Research Centre of Lithuania of March 27, 2019, 'On The Accusations Against Jonas Noreika (General Vėtra),'" Komisija, accessed August 10, 2021, https://www.komisija.lt/en/a-response-to-the-state-

An even more egregious case was the Ukmergė municipality's 1996 construction of a memorial to Juozas Krikštaponis (aka Krištaponis), an officer in the infamous Second (later Twelfth) LSD Battalion,[155] who was killed in action in 1945 after he had joined the anti-Soviet resistance. The controversy came to the fore after President Adamkus's 2002 grant of posthumous promotions to three leaders of the postwar partisan movement, including Krikštaponis. All three had served in police formations under the Germans, although only Krikštaponis was verifiably involved in mass killings. In granting the honor the offices of the president and defense minister had depended on the LGGRTC's less than thorough reports on the men's biographies.[156]

On July 24, 2019, Mayor Šimašius persuaded the Vilnius city council to rename a street honoring Kazys Škirpa despite vocal opposition from right-wing nationalist politicians and activists. Yet no conflict about the past resonates as powerfully as attempts to address the contradictions inherent in the legacy of the postwar resistance which have resonated internationally. On the one hand, expert historical studies have addressed the controversies by examining in detail the makeup of the partisan ranks, as well as the brutal realities of partisan warfare in which atrocities were committed by both the resistance and the Soviet forces. Current academic research will undoubtedly resolve the critical, emotion-laden question of how many Holocaust perpetrators served in the ranks of both the insurgents of June 1941 and the venerated forest brothers of the postwar struggle, although it is obvious that they were a minority.[157] It is also a fact that antisemitic attitudes persisted among the anti-Soviet resistance after 1944, as well as among supporters of Soviet power.[158] However there is no chance that the issue of the postwar partisans will escape the intense "history wars" which have polarized

---

ment-of-the-genocide-and-resistance-research-centre-of-lithuania-of-27–march-2019–on-the-accusations-against-jonas-noreika-general-vetra/.

155 See above, Chapter 6.
156 My thanks to Mindaugas Pocius for providing copies of the correspondence between Jewish community leaders and the Lithuanian Institute of History, as well as of his forthcoming study "Kapitonas Juozas Krikštaponis: Holokausto ir partizaninio pasipriešinimo kolektyvinės atminties susidūrimas."
157 See Mindaugas Pocius, *Kita mėnulio pusė: Lietuvos partizanu kova su kolaboravimu 1944–1953 metais* (Vilnius: LII, 2009); cf. Dainius Noreika, "Skirtingų istorijų sankirtos: Holokaustas, birželio sukilimas ir partizanų karas," in Vareikis, *Holokaustas nacių okupuotose Rytų ir Vakaru valstybėse*, 66–76.
158 See examples in Stončius, *Neapykantos ribos*, 78, 407–409.

both Lithuanian society and international opinion. Official Russian media have exploited the issue of Nazi collaborators in the ranks as more proof of a resurgence of fascism in the Baltics. The fierce attachment of many Lithuanians to the memory of the resistance fighters has energized far-right political groups. Their ire has been intensified by the appearance of memoirs written by granddaughters of collaborators/perpetrators which have resonated among some audiences in Lithuania and, more widely, abroad.[159] The absurd depths to which the recriminations can descend is illustrated by the case of Juozas Lukša-Daumantas, perhaps the best-known leader of the Lithuanian postwar resistance, and his supposed participation in the Lietūkis massacre (see above).

Recent events suggest that the divide over the collective memory of the Holocaust as part of wartime and postwar history will remain a political battleground. In June 2020 the Seimas voted to appoint Dr. Adas Jakubauskas as the director of the LGGRTC. The new head of the agency quickly found himself the object of criticism both for allegedly disregarding the independence of the Center's historians and for the politicization of research into wartime history. The crisis came to a head with Jakubauskas's dismissal of the young researcher Mingailė Jurkutė, allegedly for violating administrative rules. The historians of the Center's staff protested the director's high-handed action, seeing it as an infringement on their academic freedom. On April 1, 2021, the parliament dismissed Jakubauskas from his position and three weeks later appointed in his place Dr. Arūnas Bubnys, the country's leading specialist on the LSD battalions who had authored numerous studies of the German occupation in Lithuania, including a large body of work on the mass murder of the country's Jews. It was obvious that the battle over the center had as much to do with the Holocaust and wartime memory as with administrative incompetence. Jakubauskas admitted as much, charging that he was a victim of "leftist" machinations opposed to his more benign interpretations of the LAF and his defense of the freedom fighters. He urged Lithuanians to "halt the spread of globalist ideas" and follow

---

159 The most reliable and nuanced memoir/study is Šukys, *Siberian Exile*. The account in Rita Gabis, *A Guest at the Shooters' Banquet: My Grandfather's SS Past, My Jewish Family, A Search for the Truth* (New York: Bloomsbury, 2016) is a less scholarly but thoroughly researched and fascinating narrative. Noreika's granddaughter's emotional and more sensational book—Silvia Foti, *The Nazi's Granddaughter: How I Discovered My Grandfather was a War Criminal* (Washington, DC: Regnery, 2021)—is marred by a tendency towards conclusions not always supported by the evidence. Jelena Subotić describes her own emotional reaction to her Serbian grandfather's collaborationist past in *Yellow Star*, xiv-xv.

the example of Poland "which knows how to fight for its values."[160] Vidmantas Valiušaitis, a writer who had popularized an apologetic history of the LAF and whose appointment as chief advisor to the director was a major point of contention, resigned under pressure.

The commemorations surrounding the eightieth anniversary of the events of the summer of 1941 once again illustrated the divides in public memory. On June 4–5, 2021, the Lithuanian Institute of History, Vilnius University, and the Foreign Ministry convened a conference at the Vilnius Town Hall titled "A Divisive Past: The Soviet-German War and Narratives of Mass Violence in East Central Europe." The welcoming remarks by the prime minister, the Speaker of the Seimas, as well as the American, German, and Israeli ambassadors gave official imprimatur to the proceedings. In his concluding keynote address Tomas Venclova reiterated his long-standing appeal to abandon apologetic notions and any ambiguity concerning Lithuanian participation in the Holocaust. The conference stood in contrast (as was the intention of its organizers) to the other gatherings commemorating the anniversary held in the Seimas and many localities which sought to honor the PG and anti-Soviet insurgents of June 1941. It seemed certain that the struggle over the "divisive past" would continue with neither side poised to retreat.

Can Vilnius Remember Vilna?

Whereas Europeans west of the Iron Curtain enjoyed postwar reconstruction and democratic renewal, peoples who were fated to live in the Soviet bloc continued to suffer. According to Ekaterina Makhotina, "the development of Holocaust memory in independent post-Soviet Lithuania cannot be understood or analyzed in isolation from the Soviet period."[161] Open discussion about World War II and the admission of the Holocaust into the historical imagination of the Lithuanian people is a difficult proposition, but not impossible. Achieving this

---

160 ELTA, "Iš LGGRTC atleistas Jakubauskas: politikai spaudė pasmerkti Birželio sukilimo dalyvius ir Lietuvos aktyvistų frontą," accessed July 10, 2021, https://www.delfi.lt/news/daily/lithuania/is-lggrtc-atleistas-jakubauskas-politikai-spaude-pasmerkti-birzelio-sukilimo-dalyvius-ir-lietuvos-aktyvistu-fronta.d?id=86855797. The "values" cited refer to the Polish government's active defense of what it perceives as unjustified allegations of Polish crimes against Jews during the German occupation.

161 Makhotina, "Between 'Suffered' Memory": 210.

IMAGE 7.12. At her apartment in Vilnius: Irena Veisaitė (1928–2020), Holocaust survivor, professor of literature, vice chair of the Lithuanian Open Society Fund, who won numerous awards for her cultural achievements, promotion of tolerance, and defense of human rights. (Courtesy of Artūras Morozovas.)

requires a reorientation of national history to include three key elements: recognition of Jewish life and culture as an integral part of Lithuania's past; the acceptance of the Shoah as a central reality of the modern history of the country and the defining event of the German occupation; and finally, a thorough examination of the behavior of the Lithuanian people during the destruction of the Jews. None of this requires Lithuanians to downplay their own historical experience or to internalize narratives, such as the story of a Soviet "liberation" in 1944, which violate their remembered past and historical common sense. There is no point in questioning the lives of the thousands who found the Soviet impact on their lives worse than what happened to them under the Nazis. The struggle against disinterest in the Holocaust can easily coexist with the acceptance of a past replete with contradictory memories of heroes and villains. However, understanding should not be used as an excuse to evade undertaking the necessary task of confronting the history of the destruction of the Jews. Recognizing the centrality of this history remains the essential task. It may be that some occasions call for "overcoming memory," not in the sense of forgetting but as a practice of de-emphasizing one's own victimization in order to better understand the pain and suffering of the Other. Such an empathetic journey may be emotionally difficult but is essential in overcoming indifference.

Historians have an obligation to constantly remind the public at large that they work with the understanding that our knowledge of the past is constantly evolving even as we accept that which is already known. Scholars engage in dialogue, even disputes, concerning the past, but in open societies these take place under commonly accepted rules of evidence which are expected to be grounded in fact-based investigations of the sources. In some sense, all historians are "revisionists," otherwise historical research would lose its reason for being. This is not always easy to convey to the public. As historian Peter Hayes has pointed out, there is, increasingly, "a gap between what specialists know and what much of the public believes about the Holocaust," or in Paul Levine's words, a growing divide between scholarship and public memory, a "veritable clash between 'town' and 'gown.'"[162]

There are limits to the power of historians working in the academy to positively affect the culture and history wars which have gained momentum in the age of global populist politics. But some questions and answers seem simple enough. Ellen Cassedy, an American Jewish author who traveled to Vilnius to face her own rich and complex Litvak heritage, has written movingly about her encounters with Lithuanians about the Holocaust. "Can Vilnius Remember Vilna?" she asked in one of her recent blogs. One can only hope that the answer will be yes.[163]

---

162 Peter Hayes, *Why? Explaining the Holocaust* (New York: Norton, 2018), 327.

163 Ellen Cassedy, *We Are Here: Memories of the Lithuanian Holocaust* (Lincoln: University of Nebraska Press, 2012). See also Ellen Cassedy, "Can Vilnius Remember Vilna," September 20, 2013, https://reformjudaism.org/blog/can-vilnius-remember-vilna.

Appendixes

Appendix 1

The Jäger Report[1]

The Commander of the Security Police and the SD Kauen [Kaunas]
Einsatzkommando [EK] 3, December 1, 1941
Reich Secret [Classified] 4th copy of 5
Consolidated list of executions carried out in the EK 3 area until December 1, 1941

---

1 The EK3 had been sending reports of its killing actions during the summer of 1941, both in the consolidated *Ereigsnismeldungen* (Operational Situation Reports) and in a more comprehensive account on September 10, 1941. Karl Jäger's oft-quoted meticulous recounting of the genocide forwarded to the RSHA on December 1, 1941, was the most thorough and comprehensive listing of the shooting campaigns. The document was kept in the Russian State Military Archive in Moscow until it was made public in 1963. While there is no doubt as to the document's authenticity, it comes with some limitations. The report contains some minor arithmetical errors. Jäger does not include all the actions carried out by EK 2, nor does he reference the initial killings in the "border zone," nor, for instance, the infamous Yom Kippur Action.

Furthermore, the seeming precision of the statistics, recorded in bookkeeper-like fashion, must be viewed with some caution: the chaotic conditions that characterized some of the actions, as in Marijampolė, make it unlikely that the dead could actually have been counted on the spot with such accuracy. One explanation may be that Jäger simply utilized the lists of Jews counted in July and August 1941 by local officials during the concentration process and assumed that they corresponded to the number of executions. Nonetheless, there is no doubt that Jäger's account gives us the most dependable overall representation of the chronology, venue, and scale of the massacres of the summer and fall of 1941.

There is also the problem of terminology. The report is less than exact regarding the specific identity of the killers. Jäger noted that the killings of July 4 and 6 at the Seventh Fort were carried out by Lithuanian partisans "on my direction and orders," which makes the term "partisan" so elastic as to be functionally meaningless. The personnel of the TDA companies engaged in the shootings were drawn in large part from POWs and deserters of the Red Army's Twenty-Ninth Riflemen's Corps whose participation in the anti-Soviet insurgency cannot be reliably established. In general, the creation of the eight- to ten-man armed German squad as the commanding core of Hamann's Rollkommando, which was filled out by adding men drawn from the TDA units, corresponds to the known facts recorded in other sources. Clearly, the majority of the shooters were Lithuanians. But this ratio was not a hard and fast rule. For example, the "Great Action" in Kaunas of October 28–29, 1941, was not primarily a Rollkommando operation, employing as it did large numbers of Lithuanian police battalion personnel. The number of local auxiliary police (or "partisans" in Jäger's parlance) coopted into the killing operations also varied according to locale. The killings in which the Germans constituted a significant strike force, for example, the case of German Police Battalion Sixty-Five and EK 2 in the Šiauliai region, as well as the selected shootings in Mažeikiai, were not representative of the German-Lithuanian ratio estimated by Jäger.

The security police tasks in Lithuania taken over by Einsatzkommando [EK] 3 [EK 3] on July 2, 1941. (The Wilna [Vilnius] area was taken over by EK 3 on August 9, 1941, the Šiauliai area on October 2, 1941. Until these dates EK 9 operated in Vilnius and EK 2 in Šiauliai.)

On my instructions and orders the following executions were conducted by Lithuanian partisans:

| July 4, 1941 | Kaunas—Seventh Fort | 417 Jewish men, 47 Jewish women | 463 |
| July 6, 1941 | Kaunas—Seventh Fort | 2,514 Jews | 2,514 |

Following the formation of a mobile squad under the command of SS-Obersturmführer Hamann and 8–10 reliable men from the EK 3, the following actions were conducted in cooperation with Lithuanian partisans:

July 7, 1941	Marijampolė	Jews	32
July 8, 1941	Marijampolė	14 Jews, 5 Communist functionaries	19
July 8, 1941	Girkalnis	6 Communist functionaries	[6]
July 9, 1941	Vendžiogala	32 Jewish men, 2 Jewish women, 1 Lithuanian woman, 2 Lithuanian Communists, 1 Russian Communist	38
July 9, 1941	Kaunas—Seventh Fort	21 Jewish men, 3 Jewish women	24
July 14, 1941	Marijampolė	21 Jews, one Russian, 9 Lithuanian Communists	31
July 17, 1941	Babtai	8 Communist functionaries (including 6 Jews)	8
July 18, 1941	Marijampolė	39 Jewish men, 14 Jewish women	53
July 19, 1941	Kaunas—Seventh Fort	17 Jewish men, 2 Jewish women, 4 Lithuanian Communists, 2 Lithuanian Communist women, 1 German Communist	26
July 21, 1941	Panevėžys	59 Jewish men, 11 Jewish women, 1 Lithuanian woman, 1 Pole, 22 Lithuanian Communists, 9 Russian Communists	103
July 22, 1941	Panevėžys	1 Jew	1
July 23, 1941	Kėdainiai	83 Jewish men, 12 Jewish women, 14 Russian Communists, 15 Lithuanian Communists, 1 Russian political officer	125

Appendix 1 | 553

July 25, 1941	Marijampolė	90 Jewish men, 13 Jewish women	103
July 28, 1941	Panevėžys	234 Jewish men, 15 Jewish women, 19 Russian Communists, 20 Lithuanian Communists	288
July 29, 1941	Raseiniai	254 Jews, 3 Lithuanian Communists	257
July 30, 1941	Ariogala	27 Jews, 11 Lithuanian Communists	38
July 31, 1941	Utena	235 Jewish men, 16 Jewish women, 4 Lithuanian Communists, 1 robber/murderer	256
July 11–31, 1941	Vendžiogala	13 Jews, 2 murderers	15

AUGUST

August 1, 1941	Ukmergė	254 Jewish men, 42 Jewish women, 1 Polish Communist, 2 Lithuanian NKVD agents, 1 mayor of Jonava who gave an order to set fire to Jonava	300
August 2, 1941	Kaunas—Fourth Fort	170 Jews, 1 US Jewish man, 1 US Jewish woman, 33 Jewish women, 4 Lithuanian Communists	209
August 4, 1941	Panevėžys	362 Jewish men, 41 Jewish women, 5 Russian Communists, 14 Lithuanian Communists	422
August 5, 1941	Raseiniai	213 Jewish men, 66 Jewish women	279
August 7, 1941	Utena	483 Jewish men, 87 Jewish women, 1 Lithuanian (a robber of corpses of German soldiers)	571
August 8, 1941	Ukmergė	620 Jewish men, 82 Jewish women	702
August 9, 1941	Kaunas—Fourth Fort	484 Jewish men, 50 Jewish women	534
August 11, 1941	Panevėžys	450 Jewish men, 48 Jewish women, 1 Lithuanian Communist, 1 Russian Communist	500
August 13, 1941	Alytus	617 Jewish men, 100 Jewish women, 1 criminal	719 [sic]

Date	Location	Victims	Total
August 14, 1941	Jonava	497 Jewish men, 55 Jewish women	552
August 15–16, 1941	Rokiškis	3,200 Jewish men, Jewish women, and Jewish Children, 5 Lithuanian Communists (plural), 1 Pole, 1 partisan	3,207
August 9–16, 1941	Raseiniai	294 Jewish women, 4 Jewish children	298
June 27–August 16, 1941	Rokiškis	493 Jewish men, 432 Russians, 56 Lithuanians (all active Communists)	981
August 18, 1941	Kaunas—Fourth Fort	698 Jewish men, 402 Jewish women, 1 Polish woman, 711 Jewish intellectuals from Ghetto in reprisal for sabotage	1,812
August 19, 1941	Ukmergė	298 Jewish men, 255 Jewish women, 1 political officer, 88 Jewish children, 1 Russian Communist	645 [sic]
August 22, 1941	Daugavpils	3 Russian Communist, 5 Latvians, including 1 murderer, 1 Russian guardsman, 3 Poles, 3 male gypsies, 1 female Gypsy, 1 Gypsy child, 1 Jewish man, 1 Jewish woman, 1 Armenian man, 2 political officers (prison inspection in Daugavpils)	21 [sic]
August 22, 1941	Agluona	Mental patients: 269 men, 227 women, 48 children	544
August 23, 1941	Panevėžys	1,312 Jewish men, 4,602 Jewish women, 1,609 Jewish children	7,523
August 18–22, 1941	Raseiniai District	466 Jewish men, 440 Jewish women, 1,020 Jewish children	1,926
August 25, 1941	Obeliai	112 Jewish men, 627 Jewish women, 421 Jewish children	1,160
August 25–26, 1941	Šeduva	230 Jewish men, 275 Jewish women, 159 Jewish children	664
August 26, 1941	Zarasai	767 Jewish men, 1,113 Jewish women, 1 Lithuanian Communist, 687 Jewish children, 1 Russian Communist	2,569
August 26, 1941	Pasvalys	402 Jewish men, 738 Jewish women, 209 Jewish children	1,349
August 26, 1941	Kaišiadorys	All Jews, Jewish women, and Jewish children	1,911

Date	Location	Description	Total
August 27, 1941	Prienai	All Jews, Jewish women, and Jewish children	1,078
August 27, 1941	Dagda and Kraslava	212 Jews, 4 Russian POWs	216
August 27, 1941	Joniškis	47 Jewish men, 165 Jewish women, 143 Jewish children	355
August 28, 1941	Vilkija	76 Jewish men, 192 Jewish women, 134 Jewish children	402
August 28, 1941	Kėdainiai	710 Jewish men, 767 Jewish women, 599 Jewish children	2,076
August 29, 1941	Rumšiškės and Žiežmariai	20 Jewish men, 567 Jewish women, 197 Jewish children	784
August 29, 1941	Utena and Molėtai	582 Jewish men, 1,731 Jewish women, 1,469 Jewish children	3,782
August 13–31, 1941	Alytus and environs	233 Jews	233

SEPTEMBER

Date	Location		Description	Total
September 1, 1941	Marijampolė		1,763 Jewish men, 1,812 Jewish women, 1,404 Jewish children, 109 mentally sick, 1 German subject woman citizen married to a Jew, 1 Russian woman	5,090
August 28–September 2, 1941		Darsūniškis	10 Jewish men, 69 Jewish women, 20 Jewish children	99
		Garliava	73 Jewish men, 113 Jewish women, 61 Jewish children	247
		Jonava	112 Jewish men, 1,200 Jewish women, 244 Jewish children	1,556
		Petrašiūnai	30 Jewish men, 72 Jewish women, 23 Jewish children	125
		Jieznas	26 Jewish men, 72 Jewish women, 46 Jewish children	144
		Ariogala	207 Jewish men, 260 Jewish women, 195 Jewish children	662
		Josvainiai	86 Jewish men, 110 Jewish women, 86 Jewish children	282

August 28–September 2, 1941	Babtai	20 Jewish men, 41 Jewish women, 22 Jewish children	83
	Vendžiogala	42 Jewish men, 113 Jewish women, 97 Jewish children	252
	Krakės	448 Jewish men, 476 Jewish women, 97 Jewish children	1,125
September 4, 1941	Pravieniškės	247 Jewish men, 6 Jewish women	253
	Čekiškės	22 Jewish men, 64 Jewish women, 60 Jewish children	146
	Seredžius	6 Jewish men, 61 Jewish women, 126 Jewish children	193
	Veliuona	2 Jewish men, 71 Jewish women, 86 Jewish children	159
	Zapyškis	47 Jewish men, 118 Jewish women, 13 Jewish children	178
September 5, 1941	Ukmergė	1,123 Jewish men, 1,849 Jewish women, 1,737 Jewish children	4,709
August 25–September 6, 1941	Mopping up in: Raseiniai	16 Jewish men, 412 Jewish women, 415 Jewish children	843
	Jurbarkas	Jewish men, Jewish women, Jewish children	412
September 9, 1941	Alytus	287 Jewish men, 640 Jewish women, 352 Jewish children	1,279
September 9, 1941	Butrimonys	67 Jewish men, 370 Jewish women, 303 Jewish children	740
September 10, 1941	Merkinė	223 Jewish men, 355 Jewish women, 276 Jewish children	854
September 10, 1941	Varėna	541 Jewish men, 141 Jewish women, 149 Jewish children	831
Septebmer 11, 1941	Leipalingis	60 Jewish men, 70 Jewish women, 25 Jewish children	155
September 11, 1941	Seirijai	229 Jewish men, 384 Jewish women, 340 Jewish children	953
September 12, 1941	Simnas	68 Jewish men, 197 Jewish women, 149 Jewish children	414
September 11–12, 1941	Užusaliai	Reprisal against inhabitants who fed Russian partisans; some in possession of weapons	43
September 26, 1941	Kaunas—Fourth Fort	412 Jewish men, 615 Jewish women, 581 Jewish children (sick patients and suspected epidemic cases)	1,608

October

October 2, 1941	Žagarė	633 Jewish men, 1,107 Jewish women, 496 Jewish children (as these Jews were being led away a mutiny rose, which was however immediately put down; 150 Jews were shot immediately; 7 partisans wounded)	2,236
October 4, 1941	Kaunas—Ninth Fort	315 Jewish men, 712 Jewish women, 818 Jewish children (reprisal after German police officers were shot at in the ghetto)	1,845
October 29, 1941	Kaunas—Ninth Fort	2,007 Jewish men, 2,920 Jewish women, 4,273 Jewish children (cleansing ghetto of superfluous Jews)	9,200

November

November 3, 1941	Lazdijai	485 Jewish men, 511 Jewish women, 539 Jewish children	1,535
November 15, 1941	Vilkaviškis	36 Jewish men, 48 Jewish women, 31 Jewish children	115
November 25, 1941	Kaunas—Ninth Fort	1,159 Jewish men, 1,600 Jewish women, 175 Jewish children (transferred from Berlin, Munich, and Frankfurt am Main)	2,934
November 29, 1941	Kaunas—Ninth Fort	693 Jewish men, 1,155 Jewish women, 152 Jewish children (transferred from Vienna and Wrocław)	2,000
November 29, 1941	Kaunas—Ninth Fort	17 Jewish men, 1 Jewish woman, for contravention of ghetto law, 1 Reich German who converted to Jewish faith and attended rabbinical school, also 15 terrorists from the Kalinin Group	34

EK 3 detachment in Daugavpils:

July 13–August 21, 1941	Daugavpils	9,012 Jewish men, women, and children, 573 active Communists	9,585

EK 3 DETACHMENT IN VILNIUS:

August 12–September 1, 1941	Vilnius City	425 Jewish men, 19 Jewish women, 8 Communist men, 9 Communist women	461
September 2, 1941	Vilnius City	864 Jewish men, 2,019 Jewish women, 817 Jewish children ("special action" because German soldiers were shot at by Jews)	3,700
September 12, 1941	Vilnius City	993 Jewish men, 1,670 Jewish women, 771 Jewish children	3,334
September 17, 1941	Vilnius City	337 Jewish men, 687 Jewish women, 247 Jewish children, and 4 Lithuanian Communists	1,271
September 20, 1941	Nemenčinė	128 Jewish men, 176 Jewish women, 99 Jewish children	403
September 22, 1941	Naujoji Vilnia	468 Jewish men, 495 Jewish women, 196 Jewish children	1,159
September 24, 1941	Riešė	512 Jewish men, 744 Jewish women, 511 Jewish children	1,767
September 25, 1941	Jašiūnai	215 Jewish men, 229 Jewish women, 131 Jewish children	575
September 27, 1941	Eišiškės	989 Jewish men, 1,636 Jewish women, 821 Jewish children	3,446
September 30, 1941	Trakai	366 Jewish men, 483 Jewish women, 597 Jewish children	1,446
October 4, 1941	Vilnius City	432 Jewish men, 1,115 Jewish women, 436 Jewish children	1,983
October 6, 1941	Semeliškės	213 Jewish men, 359 Jewish women, 390 Jewish children	962
October 9, 1941	Švenčionys	1,169 Jewish men, 1,840 Jewish women, 717 Jewish children	3,726
October 16, 1941	Vilnius City	382 Jewish men, 507 Jewish women, 257 Jewish children	1,146
October 21, 1941	Vilnius City	718 Jewish men, 1,063 Jewish women, 586 Jewish children	2,367
October 25, 1941	Vilnius City	1,776 Jewish women, 812 Jewish children	2,578

October 27, 1941	Vilnius City	946 Jewish men, 184 Jewish women, 73 Jewish children	1,203
October 30, 1941	Vilnius City	382 Jewish men, 789 Jewish women, 362 Jewish children	1,553
November 6, 1941	Vilnius City	340 Jewish men, 749 Jewish women, 252 Jewish children	1,341
November 19, 1941	Vilnius City	76 Jewish men, 77 Jewish women, 18 Jewish children	171
November 19, 1941	Vilnius City	6 POWs, 8 Poles	14
November 20, 1941	Vilnius City	3 POWs	3
November 25, 1941	Vilnius City	9 Jewish men, 46 Jewish women, 8 Jewish children, 1 Pole for possession of arms and other military equipment	64

EK 3 DETACHMENT IN MINSK FROM SEPTEMBER 28, TO OCTOBER 17, 1941:

Pleshchenitsy Byhov Shatsk Bobr Uzda	620 Jewish men, 1,285 Jewish women, 1,126 Jewish children, and 19 Communists	3,050

Prior to EK 3 taking over security police duties, Jews liquidated by pogroms and executions (including partisans): 4,000
Total: 137,346

I can state today that the goal of solving the Jewish problem for Lithuania has been achieved by Einsatzkommando 3. *In Lithuania, there are no more Jews, other than the Work Jews, including their families* [emphasis in original]. They are:

In Šiauliai around 4,500
In Kaunas [around] 15,000
In Vilnius [around] 15,000

I also wanted to kill these Work Jews, including their families, which however brought upon me acrimonious challenges from the Civil Administration (the Reichskommisar) and the army and caused them to issue the prohibition: the Work Jews and their families are not to be shot!

The goal of making Lithuania free of Jews could only be attained through the deployment of a mobile commando with selected men under the leadership of SS First Lieutenant Hamann, who completely and entirely supported my goals and understood the importance of ensuring the cooperation of the Lithuanian partisans and the competent civilian offices.

The implementation of such activities is primarily a question of organization. The decision to systematically make every district free of Jews necessitated an exhaustive preparation of each individual operation and reconnaissance of the prevailing circumstances in the appropriate district. The Jews had to be assembled at one or several locations. Depending on the number, a place for the required pits had to be found and the pits dug. The marching route from the assembly place to the pits amounted on average some 4 to 5 kilometers. The Jews were transported to the place of execution in detachments of 500, at intervals of at least 2 kilometers. The attendant difficulties and nerve-wracking activity occasioned in doing this are shown in a randomly selected example:

<u>In Rokiškis, 3,208 people had to be transported 4.5 kilometers before they could be liquidated</u> [emphasis in original]. To accomplish this task in 24 hours, more than 60 of the 80 available Lithuanian partisans had to be allocated for transportation and cordoning off duty.

The remainder of them, who had to be constantly replaced, carried out the work together with my men. Motor vehicles are only occasionally available. Attempts to escape, which took place every now and then, were prevented exclusively by my men at the risk of their lives. Thus, for example, near Marijampolė, three men of the commando shot down 38 escaping Jews and Communist functionaries on a woodland path without anyone escaping. The marching route to and from the individual operations amounted to 160–200 kilometers. Only by smart usage of the time was it possible to carry out up to five operations in a week and at the same time, to manage nonetheless the work in Kaunas in such a way that no slowdown in the service work took place. The operations in Kaunas itself, where reasonably sufficient trained partisans were available, can be considered as parade shootings compared to the often enormous difficulties that had to be dealt with elsewhere. All the leaders and men of my commando in Kaunas have taken part actively in the large-scale operations. Only one official from the police records department was excused from participation due to illness. I consider the Jewish operations for Einsatzkommando 3 as essentially completed. The still available Work Jews and female Work Jews are urgently required and I can foresee that after winter this manpower will still be most urgently required. I am of the view that sterilization of the male Work Jews should begin immediately to prevent reproduction. Should a Jewish woman nonetheless become pregnant, she is to be liquidated. One of the most important tasks of Einsatzkommando 3, besides the Jewish operations, was the inspection of the mostly overcrowded prisons in the individual locations and cities. On average, in every city in the district, there were 600 people of Lithuanian ethnicity in prison, although there was no actual reason for their incarceration. They were taken into custody because of simple denunciations, etc. by partisans. Many personal accounts were settled in this way. Nobody looked after them. One ought to have been in the prisons and spent a minute in the overcrowded cells, which, in respect to hygiene, defied description. In Jonava—and this is one example of many—16 men, all of whom could have been set free since there was nothing to bring against them, sat for 5 weeks in a dreary cellar room 3 meters long, 3 meters wide and 1.65 meters high. Girls aged 13 to 16 were locked up because they, in order to get work, had applied for admission to the Communist youth. Here it was necessary, through drastic measures, to hammer the proper sense of direction into the heads of the responsible Lithuanian circles. The inhabitants of the prison were assembled in the prison courtyard and checked on the basis of lists and documentation. Those who as a result of harmless offences had been locked up for no reason were assembled in a special group. Those whom we sentenced to 1–3 and 6 months because of their offences were specially separated, as were those who were to be liquidated, such as criminals, Communist functionaries, political officers and other such riffraff. In addition to the announced punishment, some, according to the offence, especially Communist functionaries, received 10 to 40 lashes with the whip, which were meted out immediately. After completion of the examination, the prisoners were led back to their cells. Those who were to be let free were led in formation to the marketplace and there, after a short speech in the presence of many inhabitants, let go. The speech had the following content (it was immediately translated sentence by sentence by an interpreter into Lithuanian and Russian): "If we were Bolsheviks, we would have shot you, but because we are Germans, we give you your freedom." Then followed a severe admonition to abstain from all political activity, to report to the German authorities any hostile activities that came to their attention and to intensively and immediately busy themselves in reconstruction, especially in agriculture. Should one of them again be found guilty of an offence, he would be shot. Then they were released. One cannot imagine the joy, gratitude, and enthusiasm that our measures triggered in those who were freed and in the population. We often had to deflate the enthusiasm with sharp words, when women, children and men with tear-filled eyes sought to kiss our hands and feet.

Signed Jäger
SS-Colonel

Appendix 2

Ghettos in Belarus[1]

The table below shows the approximate number of inmates in restricted Jewish settlements—ghettos and camps—in Belarus that were transferred to Vilnius district in the Generalkommissariat Litauen in April 1942. Current Belarusian names of locales indicated in brackets.

Oszmiana [Ashmyany]	September 1941–April 1943	2,000
Widze [Vidzy]	Early 1942–Fall 1942	1,500
Świr [Svir]	Early November 1941–November 1942	850
Michaliszki [Mikhalishki]	October 1941–March 1943	800
Krewo [Kreva]	October 1941–October 1942	450
Holszany [Halshany]	September 1942–October 1942	450
Kiemieliszki [Kyemyelishki]	October 1941–24 October 1942	350
Soly [Soly]	October 1941–March 1943	300
Bystrzca [Bystritsa]	Fall 1941–October 1942	200
Worniany [Vornyany]	Fall 1941–August 1942	200
Żuprany [Zhuprany]	Fall 1941–Fall 1942	130
Łyntupy [Lyntupy]	Late 1941–December 22, 1942	100
Ostrowiec [Astravyets]	Fall 1941–April 1943	100
Gudogaj [Gudogai]	Fall 1941–Fall 1942	100
Smorgonie [Smarhon, Smorgon]	September 1941–March 1943	n/a

---

1   The situation of the Jews of Belarus is related in some degree to the history of the German occupation in Lithuania. The Litvaks of Belarus maintained close cultural and historic ties to the Jews who came under Lithuanian and Polish rule after the First World War. The Jews of the Vilna region and western Belarus lived as citizens of Poland until 1939. Albert Filbert's murderous EK 9 exterminated the majority of the Litvaks in the western Belarusian shtetls. In October 1941, the Twelfth LSD Battalion arrived from Kaunas and together with German security forces carried out thousands of shootings in Minsk and in Jewish settlements in the region (see Chapter 6). Most of the Belarusian ghettos were abolished by the fall of 1942 although the consolidated Oszmiana ghetto survived until the spring of 1943 when its inmates were murdered at Paneriai.

Sources and Bibliography

Archival Collections

Lithuanian Central State Archive
[Lietuvos centrinis valstybės archyvas], Vilnius

f. 378. Vidaus reikalų ministerijos Valstybės saugumo departamentas [Ministry of the Interior, Department of State Security], 1918–1940.
f. 383. Užsienio reikalų ministerija [Ministry of Foreign Affairs], 1918–1940.
f. 394. Vidaus reikalų ministerijos Policijos departamentas [Ministry of the Interior, Police Department], 1919–1940.
f. 563. Lietuvos tautinės apsaugos "Geležinis vilkas" Vyriausiasis štabas [Lithuanian National Security "Iron Wolf" Staff], 1927–1930.
f. 648. Lietuvos pasiuntinybė Londone [Lithuanian Mission in London], 1920–1990.
f. 922. Lietuvos Respublikos Prezidento kanceliarija [Chancery of the President of the Republic of Lithuania], 1919–1940.
f.1075. Lietuvos kooperatyvų sąjunga "Linas" [Lithuanian Cooperative Society "Linas"], 1940–1941.
f. 1437. Mykolas Sleževičius [Prime Minister Mykolas Sleževičius Collection], 1882–1939.
f. 1556. Zigmas Toliušis (1889–1971) [Populist Political Leader Zigmas Toliusšs Collection], 1912–1944.
f. R-500. Trakų apskrities viršininkas (Der Kreischef von Trakai) [District Chief of Trakai], 1941–1944.
f. R-635. Lietuvos studijų biuras (Studien-Büro Litauen) [Lithuanian Bureau of Studies], 1941–1944.
f. R-660. Lietuvių savisaugos daliu štabas [Lithuanian Self-Defense Forces staff], 1941–1944.
f. R-683. Lietuvos generalinės srities pavienės policijos tarnybos ryšių karininkas prie tvarkos policijos vado Lietuvoje [Lithuanian Generalkommisariat Police Liaison Officer with the Chief of the Order Police in Lithuania], 1941–1944.
f. R-739. Lietuvių aktyvistų frontas [Lithuanian Activist Front], 1940–1941.
f. R-754. Lietuvos TSR Ministrų Taryba [Lithuanian SSR Council of Ministers].
f. R-973. Žydų geto policija (Jüdische Ghetto Polizei) [Jewish Ghetto Police], 1941–1943.
f. R-1436. Alytaus apskrities viršininkas (Der Kreischef. Kreis Alytus) [District Chief of Alytus], 1941–1944.
f. R-1444. Kauno karo komendantūra (Litauische Kommandantur) [Kaunas Military Commandant], 1941.

f. R-1515. Rokiškio apskrities žydų koncentracijos stovykla [Jewish Concentration Camp of Rokiškis District], 1941.

f. R-1534. Kauno apskrities Viršininkas [District Chief of Kaunas].

Lithuanian Special Archive [Lietuvos ypatingasis archyvas], Vilnius

f. 1771. Lietuvos komunistų partijos (LKP) Centro komitetas [Lithuanian Communist Party (LCP) Central Committee].

f. 3377. Partijos istorijos instituto prie LKP CK Marksizmo-leninizmo instituto prie TSKP CK filialas [Institute of Party History of the LCP CC, Institute of Marxism-Leninism of the LCP CC, affiliate of the CPSU CC].

f. K-1. Lietuvos TSR valstybės saugumo komitetas (KGB) [State Security Committee of the Lithuanian SSR (KGB)].

Lithuanian Academy of Sciences Vrublevskis Library, Manuscript Section [Lietuvos mokslų akademijos Vrublevskio bibliotekos Rankraščių skyrius], Vilnius

f. 9. Bendrasis fondas [General Collection].

f. 22. Vilniaus viešosios bibliotekos rankraščių fondų likučiai [Remnants of the Vilnius Public Library Manuscripts Collection].

f. 26. Lietuvos mokslų akademijos darbuotojų disertacijų ir mokslinių darbų rinkinys [Collection of the Dissertations and Scholarly Works of the Employees of the Lithuanian Academy of Sciences].

f. 76. Šiaulių miesto valdyba [Šiauliai City Administration].

f. 159. Hitlerininkų piktadarybėms tirti respublikinės komisijos aktai [Documents of the Republic's Commission to Investigate Nazi Crimes].

Lithuanian State Archive of History [Lietuvos valstybės istorijos archyvas]

f. 1671. Kauno metropolijos kurijos fondas [Kaunas Metropolitanate Curia Collection].

Lithuanian Martynas Mažvydas National Library Rare Books and Manuscript Section [Lietuvos Martyno Mažvydo Nacionalinės bibliotekos Retų knygų ir rankraščiu skyrius].

F223. Kunigo Zenono Ignatavičiaus 1942 metu žiemos dienoraštis 1942.I.3–1942.III.9 [The Winter Diary of Rev. Zenonas Ignatavičius, January 3, 1942–March 9, 1942].

National Archives and Records Administration [NARA], College Park, MD

Captured German Records (Microfilm), Records of German Field Commands: Rear Areas, Occupied Territories, and Others. T501, Roll 2.
US Department of State, Decimal Files. US Mission in Kaunas. M1178. Roll 19.

Hoover Institution Archives. Stanford, California. Turauskas (Edvardas) Papers, 1934–1963.

Box 3, Folder 10: Anicetas Simutis, 1941–1942.
Box 3, Folder 12: Kazys Škirpa, 1939–1943.
Box 3, Folder 15: Antanas Smetona, 1941.
Box 4, Folder 4: A. Koncė, 1941.
Box 5, Folder 3: Lithuanian Activist Front.
Box 7, Folder 9: Lithuanian State Security Department Bulletins, November 1939–June 1940.
Box 8, Folders 8–9: Kazys Škirpa, Memoranda, 1941.
Box 9, Folder 2: World War II, Press Excerpts, 1939–1944.

Yad Vashem, Jerusalem

M. 49.E ZIH (Żydowski Instytut Historyczny) Testimonies, Ada Hirsz.
O.33, M.E. 3541063, File No. 1275.

Centre de Documentation Juive Contemporaine, Paris

CXLIV-430. Rosenberg Collection.

Individual Documents Provided

Avner Shalev to Emanuelis Zingeris, September 5, 2007. Courtesy Emanuelis Zingeris.
Emanuelis Zingeris to Avner Shalev, September 28, 2007. Courtesy Emanuelis Zingeris.
Erich Ehrlinger Report to RSHA, July 1, 1941. Courtesy Christoph Dieckmann.
Fischer-Schweder Case Records, 1957–1958. Courtesy US Department of Justice.
Gladkov Report of March 29, 1941, on Jewish counterrevolutionary organizations. Courtesy Solomonas Atamukas.
Jacob Goldberg's 1948 Memoir (Excerpt) "Fun Letzte Hurban." Courtesy CRH and Associates.
Jonas Grinevičius, "Vilkijoj, Vydūno alėjoj matyta, girdėta." Courtesy Egidijus Saulius Juodis.
Juozas Skvireckas Notes, September 1941. Courtesy Arūnas Streikus.
Karl Jäger to RHSA, December 1, 1941. Courtesy Christoph Dieckmann.
Karl Jäger to RHSA, September 10, 1941. Courtesy Christoph Dieckmann.

Mykolas Krupavičius. "Pro Memoria," November 29, 1945. Courtesy Andrius Kulikauskas.
Krygeris to Tauragė District Chief, July 29, 1941. Courtesy IHC.
Lietuvos TSR paminklų apsaugos ir kraštotyros draugijos Rokiškio skyriaus Moškėnų tarybinio ūkio kraštotyros organizacija, Vladas Stašys, *Fašizmo aukų kapai Kavoliškio miške*, 1987. Courtesy Laima Vincė.
Memorandum to the Ninth Fort Museum in Kaunas, July 2002. Courtesy Sara Ginaitė-Rubinsonienė.
Mission Statement of the Commission, March 2, 1999. Courtesy IHC.
Mission Statement of the Commission, November 17, 1998. Courtesy IHC.
Order No. 1 of Kostas Kalendra, Director of Internal Affairs of the District of Vilnius. Courtesy US Department of Justice.
Šiauliai District Chief Announcement No. 6. Courtesy IHC.
Simonas Alperavičius and Tobijas Jafetas, September 1, 2008. "Lietuvos žydų bendruomenė išplatino viešą laišką Lietuvos valstybės vadovams." Courtesy IHC.
US District Case, Northern District of Ohio vs. Algimantas Dailidė. "Report of Dr. Yitzhak Arad," 1997. Public Record.
Zenonas Ignatavičius Diary, March 10, 1943–July 17, 1944. Courtesy LGGRTC and Lithuanian Institute of History.

Periodicals

Lithuanian Newspapers and Journals

Aidai, 1944–1991.
Aidai/Naujasis židinys, 1991–.
Akiračiai, 1968–.
Apžvalga, 1935–1940.
Aušra, 1931.
Auszra, 1880–.
Į laisvę, 1941–1944.
Krantai, 1989–.
Kregždutė, 1934–1940.
Laisvės kovotojas, 1942–1944.
Lietuvos aidas, 1917–.
Lietuvos rytas, 1990–.
Lietuvos žinios, 1922–1940.
Literatūra ir menas, 1946–.
Mokslo dienos, 1937–1940.
Naujoji Lietuva, 1941–1944.
Naujoji Romuva, 1931–1940.
Nepriklausoma Lietuva, 1942–1944.
Respublika, 1989–.

Tėvynė, 1941–1944.
Vairas, 1929–1940.
Varpas, 1890–.
Verslas, 1932–1940.
Židinys, 1924–1940.
Žvaigždutė, 1923–1940.

Government and Institutional Reports, Published Documents

Anušauskas, Arvydas, ed. *Lietuvos laikinoji vyriausybė: posėdžių protokolai*. Vilnius: LGGRTC, 2001.
Balčiūnas, Juozas, ed. *Lietuvių archyvas: bolševizmo metai*. 4 vols. Kaunas: Studijų biuras, 1942–1943.
Baranauskas, Boleslovas, Evsiejus Rozauskas, and Kazys Rukšėnas, eds. *Nacionalistų talka hitlerininkams*. Vilnius: Mintis, 1970.
Biber, Jevgenija, and Rachel Kostanian, eds. *Vilna Ghetto Posters: Jewish Spiritual Resistance*. Vilnius: The Vilna Gaon Jewish State Museum, 1999.
Brandišauskas, Valentinas, ed. *1941 m. birželio sukilimas: dokumentų rinkinys*. Vilnius: LGGRTC, 2000.
Breslavskienė, Laimutė, Alfonsas Eidintas, Ramutė Jermalavičienė, Leonora Kalasauskienė, Stasė Marcikonienė, et al, eds. *Lietuvos okupacija ir aneksija, 1939–1940: dokumentų rinkinys*. Vilnius: Mintis, 1993.
Burauskaitė, Birutė, ed. *Lietuvos gyventojų genocidas*. 10 vols. Vilnius: LGGRTC: 1997–2020.
CBOS, Polish Public Opinion. October 2000. http://cbos.pl/PL/publikacje/public_opinion/2000/10_2000.pdf.
Dyukov, Aleksandr R., ed. *Nakanune Kholokosta: Front litovskikh aktivistov i sovetskiye repressii v Litve, 1940–1941 gg.: sbornik dokumentov*. Moscow: Fond sodeistviya aktualnym istoricheskim issledovaniyam, "Istoricheskaya pamiat," 2012.
Erslavaitė, Genovaitė, Kazys Rukšėnas, Boleslovas Baranauskas, and Eusiejus Rozauksas, eds. *Masinės žudynės Lietuvoje: dokumentų rinkinys*. Vol. 1. Vilnius: Mintis, 1965.
Erslavaitė, Genovaitė, Boleslovas Baranauskas, and Eusiejus Rozauskas, eds. *Masinės žudynės Lietuvoje*. Vol. 2. Vilnius: Mintis, 1973.
Gudaitis, Leonas, ed. *Lietuvos aneksija: 1940 metų dokumentai*. Vilnius: Periodika, 1990.
Holokausto atlasas Lietuvoje. Accessed April 14, 2022. http://www.holocaustatlas.lt/LT/.
Jewish Virtual Library. The Einsatzgruppen. "The Einsatzgruppen: Operational Situation Report No. 21 USSR (July 13, 1941)." http://www.jewishvirtuallibrary.org/operational-situation-report-ussr-no-21.
Kasparavičius, Algimantas, Česlovas Laurinavičius, and Natalia Lebedeva, eds. *SSSR i Litva v gody vtoroi mirovoi voiny*. Vol. 1, *SSSR i Litovskaya Respublika (mart 1939–avgust 1940 gg.) Sbornik dokumentov*. Vilnius: LII, 2006.

Komisija. "The Decree on the Establishment of the Commission." Accessed September 19, 2013.http://www.komisija.lt/en/body.php?&m=1150456073.

Liekis, Šarūnas. "Documents on the Lithuanian Council in the Central Zionist Archive in Jerusalem." In *A Pragmatic Alliance: Jewish-Lithuanian Political Cooperation at the Beginning of the 20th Century*, edited by Vladas Sirutavičius and Darius Staliūnas, 245–270. Budapest: Central European University Press, 2011.

Liekis, Šarūnas, Lidija Miliakova, and Antony Polonsky. "Prievarta pieš žydus buvusiose Lietuvos-Lenkijos žemėse 1919 m." In *Kai ksenofobija virsta prievarta: lietuvių ir žydų santykių dinamika XIX a. – XX a. pirmojoje pusėje*, edited by Vladas Sirutavičius and Darius Staliūnas, 213–248. Vilnius: Lietuvos istorijos institutas, 2005.

Lietuvos gyventojai: 1923 m. rugsėjo 17 d. gyventojų surašymo duomenys. Kaunas: Lietuvos Respublika, Finansų ministerija, Cent. statistikos biuras, 1924.

Lietuvos statistikos metrastis 1938 11. Kaunas: Centralinis statistikos biuras, 1939.

Lietuvos Respublilkos Seimas. Stenograma. *Lietuvių-žydų santykiai. Istoriniai, teisiniai ir politiniai aspektai*. Vilnius: LRS, 1999.

LGGRTC. "Dėl kunigo Zenono Ignatavičiaus veiklos nacių-sovietų karo metais." May 14, 2019. PDF, author's copy.

———. "Trumpa Holokausto Lietuvoje istorija, istoriografija ir bibliografija." Accessed October 21, 2022. http://www.genocid.lt/centras/lt/1488/a/.

Mallman, Klaus-Michael, Andrej Angrick, Jürgen Matthäus, and Martin Cüppers, eds. *Die "Ereignismeldungen UdSSR" 1941: Dokumente der Einsatzgruppen in der Sowjetunion*. Vol. 1, *für Konrad Kwiet zum 70. Geburtstag*. Darmstadt: WBG, 2011.

Pocius, Mindaugas. ed. *Lietuvos sovietizavimas 1944–1947 m.: VKP(b) CK dokumentai*. Vilnius: LII, 2015.

Royal Institute of International Affairs. *The Baltic States*. London: Oxford University Press, 1938.

Senn, Alfred. E., ed. "Documents: Lithuania in March 1941: An American Diplomat's Report." *Journal of Baltic Studies* 26, no. 2 (1995): 151–158.

Rozauskas, Eusiejus, Boleslovas Baranauskas, and Kazys Rukšėnas, eds. *Documents Accuse*. Vilnius: Gintaras, 1970.

Schalkowsky, Samuel, trans. and ed., with introduction by Samuel Kassow. *The Clandestine History of the Kovno Jewish Ghetto Police*. Bloomington: Indiana University Press in association with USHMM, 2014.

Smetona, Antanas. *Pasakyta parašyta 1935–1940*. Edited by Leonas Sabaliūnas. Vol. 2. Boston: Lithuanian Encyclopedia Press, 1974.

Štaras, Povilas, et al., eds. *Lietuvos liaudis Didžiajame tėvynės kare (1941–1945): dokumentų ir medžiagos rinkinys*. Vilnius: Mintis, 1982.

Stenograma. Praktinis seminaras-diskusija. "Lietuvių ir žydų santykiai. Istoriniai, teisiniai ir politiniai aspektai." genocide.It. Last modified April 23, 1999. http://www.genocid.lt/GRTD/Konferencijos/lietuvi.htm.

Sub-Commission for Evaluation of the Crimes of the Nazi Occupation Regime and the Holocaust. April 11, 2019. "A Response to the Statement of the Genocide and Resistance Research Centre of Lithuania of 27 March 2019: 'On The Accusations

Against Jonas Noreika (General Vėtra).'" Accessed August 10, 2021. https://www.komisija.lt/en/a-response-to-the-statement-of-the-genocide-and-resistance-research-centre-of-lithuania-of-27-march-2019-on-the-accusations-against-jonas-noreika-general-vetra/.

Surblys, Konstantinas, ed. *Lietuvos Liaudies Seimas: Stenogramos ir medžiaga*. Mintis: Vilnius 1985.

———. ed. *Lietuvos Komunistų partija skaičiais 1918–1975*. Mintis: Vilnius, 1976.

Švedienė, Rūta, ed. *Kėdainių kraštas svastikos ir raudonosios žvaigždžių šešėlyje*. Kėdainiai: Spaudvita, 2011.

Tautos Vado Antano Smetonos kalba. Kaunas: Savivaldybė. 1934.

Trial of the Major War Criminals Before the International Military Tribunal. Vol. 37. Nuremberg: IMT, 1949.

UCSJ. "Study Finds Intolerance Rising in Lithuania." February 2, 2006. http://www.ucsj.org/news/study-finds-intolerance-rising-lithuania.

Venclauskas, Linas. "Antisemitizmas Lietuvoje 1939–1940 metais: Valstybės saugumo departamento pranešimai." *Darbai ir dienos* 67 (2017): 293–332.

Published Diaries, Memoirs, and Testimonies

Abramovich, Solomon, and Yakov Zilberg, eds. *Smuggled in Potato Sacks: Stories of the Hidden Children of the Kaunas Ghetto*. London: Valentine Mitchell, 2011.

Adamkus, Valdas. *Likimo vardas-Lietuva: apie laiką, įvykius, žmones*. Kaunas: Santara, 1997.

Alexievich, Svetlana. *Secondhand Time: The Last of the Soviets*. Translated by Bela Shayevich. New York: Random House, 2016.

Arad, Yitzhak. *The Partisan: From the Valley of Death to Mount Zion*. New York: Holocaust Library, 1982.

Audėnas, Juozas. *Paskutinis posėdis: atsiminimai*. New York, Ramovė, 1966.

Bak, Samuel. *Painted in Words: A Memoir*. Bloomington: Indiana University Press, 2001.

Bankier, David, ed. *Expulsion and Extermination: Holocaust Testimonials from Provincial Lithuania*. Translated by Jacob Lampart. Jerusalem: Yad Vashem, 2011.

Beiles, Yudel. *Yudke*. Translated from Lithuanian Vida Urbonavičius-Watkins. Vilnius: baltos lankos, 2001.

Bistrickas, Stasys. *Ir sušaudytieji prabyla*. Vilnius: VPMLL, 1960.

Blynas, Zenonas. *Karo metų dienoraštis 1941–1944*. Edited by Gediminas Rudis. Vilnius: LII, 2007.

Dranseikienė, Aldona. Oral History / Accession Number: 1998.A.0221.110 / RG Number: RG-50.473.0110 (January 13, 2005). Accessed April 4, 2020. https://collections.ushmm.org/search/catalog/irn518532.

Eglinis-Elinas, Mejeris, and Dimitrijus Gelpernas. *Kauno getas ir jo kovotojai*. Vilnius: Mintis, 1969.

Faitelson, Alex. *The Truth and Nothing but the Truth: Jewish Resistance in Lithuania*. New York: Gefen, 2006.
———. *Heroism and Bravery in Lithuania*. Jerusalem: Gefen, 1996.
Foti, Silvia. *The Nazi's Granddaughter: How I Discovered My Grandfather Was a War Criminal*. Washington, DC: Regnery, 2021.
Frome, Frieda. *Some Dare to Dream: Frieda Frome's Escape from Lithuania*. Ames: Iowa State University Press, 1988.
Gabis, Rita. *A Guest at the Shooters' Banquet: My Grandfather's SS Past, My Jewish Family, A Search for the Truth*. New York: Bloomsbury, 2016.
Gerber, Ilya. *Diary from the Kovno Ghetto: August 1942–January 1943*. Translated from the Yiddish by Rebecca Wolpe and edited by Lea Prais. Jerusalem: Yad Vashem, 2021.
Gimbutienė, Marija. *Dienoraštis ir prisiminimai*. Edited by Živilė Gimbutaitė. Kaunas: Naujasis lankas, 2015.
Ginaitė-Rubinsonienė, Sara. *Atminimo knyga: Kauno žydų bendruomenė 1941–1944 metais*. Vilnius: margi raštai, 1999.
Ginsburg, Valdemar. *And Kovno Wept*. Nottinghamshire: Berth Shalom, 1998.
Gordon, Harry. *The Shadow of Death: The Holocaust in Lithuania*. Lexington, KY: University Press of Kentucky, 2000.
Gustainis, Valentinas. *Nuo Griškabūdžio iki Paryžiaus*. Kaunas: Spindulys, 1991.
Holzman, Helene. *Dies Kind soll leben. Die Aufzeichnungen der Helene Holzman*. Edited by Margarete Holzman and Reinhard Kaiser. Frankfurt: Schöffling, 2000.
Ignatavičius, Bruno. "Komunistai Vilkijoje." Ottawa, 1974. Unpublished manuscript.
Ignonis [Ignatavičius], Zenonas. *Praeitis kalba; dienoraštiniai užrašai. Gudija 1941–1944*. Edited by Klemensas Jūra. Brooklyn, NY: Pranciškonų spaustuvė, 1979.
Kairys, Steponas. *Lietuva budo*. New York: Amerikos lietuvių socialdemokratų sąjungos literatūros fondas, 1957.
Kalmanovich, Zelig. *Hope Is Stronger Than Life: Vilna Ghetto Diary*. Translated by Olga Lempert. Vilnius: The Vilna Gaon Museum of Jewish History, 2021.
Kamber, Ilana, Solomonas Abramovičius, and Jakovas Zilbergas, eds. *Išgelbėti bulvių maišuose: 50 Kauno geto vaikų istorijų*. Vilnius: Šiaurės Jeruzalė, 2014.
Kirkel, Rosalyn [Reyzele]. "My Mother Smuggled Me out of the Shavl (Šiauliai) Ghetto: A Hidden Jewish Child during the Holocaust." Wexler Oral History Project. Accessed May 10, 2021. https://www.yiddishbookcenter.org/collections/oral-histories/excerpts/woh-ex-0002669/my-mother-smuggled-me-out-shavl-siauliai-ghetto-hidden-jewish-child-during-holocaust.
Klee, Ernst, Willi Dressen, and Volker Riess, eds. *"The Good Old Days": The Holocaust as Seen by Its Perpetrators and Bystanders*. Old Saybrook: Konecky and Konecky, 1991.
Krėvė, Vincas. *Bolševikų invazija ir liaudies vyriausybė*. Edited by Albertas Zalatorius. Vilnius: Mintis, 1992.
Kruk, Herman. *The Last Days of the Jerusalem of Lithuania: Chronicles from the Vilna Ghetto and the Camps, 1939–1944*. Edited by Benjamin Harshav, translated by Barbara Harshav. New Haven: Yale University Press, 2002.

Lietuvos gyventojų genocide ir rezistencijos tyrimu centras. *Su adata širdyje: getų ir koncentracijos stovyklų kaliniu atsiminimai. With a Needle in the Heart: Memoirs of Former Prisoners of Ghettos and Concentration Camps*. Vilnius: LGGRTC, 2003.

Litinskaya, Zhanna. Interview with Liza Lukinskaya. Centropa Project, February 2005. https://www.centropa.org/biography/liza-lukinskaya.

Lukša, Juozas [pseud. Daumantas, Juozas]. *Partizanai*. 3rd ed. Vilnius: Į laisvę fondas, 1990.

Mackevičius, Mečislovas. *Atsiminimai*. Vilnius: Lietuvos rašytojų sąjungos leidykla, 1997.

Mackonis, Rapolas. *Amžiaus liudininko užrašai*. Edited by Birutė Mackonytė. Vilnius: Lietuvos rašytojų sąjungos leidykla, 2001.

Margolis, Rachel. *A Partisan from Vilna*. Boston: Academic Studies Press, 2010.

Matulaitis, Jurgis. *Užrašai*. Edited by Paulius Subačius, introduction by Vaclovas Aliulis. Vilnius: Aidai, 1998.

Matulionis, Jonas. *Neramios dienos*. Toronto: Litho-Art, 1975.

Milner, Sonja. *Sonja: Survival in War and Peace*. Edited by Goldie Wachsman. New York: Shengold, 1984.

Mishell, William W. *Kaddish for Kovno: Life and Death in a Lithuanian Ghetto, 1941–1945*. Chicago: Chicago Review Press, 1988.

Noreika, Laimonas. "Mano 1941–1942 metai." *Metai* 5–6 (2001): 151–163.

Olkinaitė, Matilda, *Atrakintas dienoraštis: kūrybos rinktinė*. Edited by Mindaugas Kvietkauskas. Vilnius: Lietuvių literatūros ir tautosakos institutas, 2019.

———. *The Unlocked Diary: Collected Works*. Translated by Laima Vincė. Edited by Mindaugas Kvietkauskas. Vilnius: Institute of Lithuanian Literature and Folklore, 2021.

Raštikis, Stasys. *Kovose dėl Lietuvos*. Vol. 2. Los Angeles: Lietuvių dienos, 1957.

Rolnikaitė, Marija. *Turiu papasakoti*. Vilnius: VPMLL, 1963.

Rolnikaitė, Maša. *Turiu papasakoti. Dokumentinė apysaka*. Vilnius: Inter Se, 2021.

Rudaševskis, Icchokas. *Vilniaus geto dienoraštis*. Translation and introduction by Mindaugas Kvietkauskas. Vilnius: Standartų spaustuvė, 2018.

Sakowicz, Kazimierz. *Ponary Diary, 1941–1943: A Bystander's Account of a Mass Murder*. Translated by Laurence Weinbaum, edited by Yitzhak Arad. New Haven: Yale University Press, 2005.

Sandler, David Solly, comp., and Jonathan Boyarin, trans. *The Lithuanian Slaughter of Its Jews: The Testimonies of 121 Jewish Survivors of the Holocaust in Lithuania Recorded by Leyb Koniuchowsky, in Displaced Persons Camps (1946–1948)*. self-pub., 2020.

Šeinius, Ignas. *Raudonasis tvanas*. New York: Talka, 1953.

Škirpa, Kazys. *Sukilimas*. Washington: self-pub., 1973.

Sruoga, Balys. "Dievų miškas." In *Raštai*, edited by Donata Linčiuvienė, 239–565. Vol. 4. Vilnius: Alma Littera, 1994.

———. *Forest of the Gods: Memoirs*. Translated by Aušrinė Byla. Vilnius: Vaga, 1996.

Suckeveris, Abraomas. *Iš Vilniaus geto*. Translated by Asta Baranauskienė and Aurimas Guoga. Vilnius: Versus aureus, 2011.

Šukytė-Grigėnienė, Ona-Genovaitė. Oral History / Accession Number: 2018.455.1 / RG Number: RG-50.030.0989. October 4, 2018. https://collections.ushmm.org/search/catalog/irn628342.

Šuras, Grigorijus. *Užrašai: Vilniaus geto kronika 1941–1944*. Translated by Nijolė Kvaraciejūtė and Algimantas Antanavičius. Vilnius: ERA, 1997.

Švedas, Aurimas, and Irena Veisaitė. *Gyvenimas turėtų būti skaidrus*. Vilnius: Aukso žuvys, 2016.

———. *Life Should be Transparent: Conversations about Lithuania and Europe in the Twentieth Century and Today*. Translated by Karla Gruodis. Budapest: Central European Press, 2020.

Tory, Avraham. *Surviving the Holocaust: The Kovno Ghetto Diary*. Edited by Martin Gilbert, notes by Dina Porat. Cambridge, MA: Harvard University Press, 1990.

Trečiokas [pseud.]. "Atsiminimai iš 9 P. L. D. K. Vytenio pulko gyvenimo." In *Lietuviu archyvas: bolševizmo metai*, edited by J. Balčiūnas, 229–242. Vol. 2. Kaunas: Studijų Biuras, 1942.

Urbšys, Juozas. *Lietuva lemtingaisiais 1939–1940 metais*. Vilnius: Mintis, 1988.

Vaičionis, Juozas. *Iš prisiminimų*. Vilnius: Ciklonas, 2008.

Vaitkus, Mykolas. *Atsiminimai: Milžinų rungtynese, 1940–1944*. Vol. 8. London: Nida, 1972.

Vildžiūnas, Linas. *Mano senelių ir prosenelių kaimynai žydai*. Vilnius: Garnelis, 2002.

Voldemaras, Augustinas. *Pastabos saulėlydžio valandą*, edited by Gediminas Rudis. Vilnius: Mintis, 1992.

Yerushalmi, Eliezer. "The Destruction of the Jews in the Šiauliai Ghetto and Surrounding Towns" [Translated by Andrew Cassel]. JewishGen. Accessed July 22, 2023. https://kehilalinks.jewishgen.org/shavli/YerushalmiUmkum.pdf.

Zeltser, Arkadi, ed. *To Pour out My Bitter Soul: Letter of Jews from the USSR, 1941–1945*. Jerusalem: Yad Vashem, 2016.

Žemelis, Henrikas. "Juodasis Lietuvos istorijos puslapis." *Akiračiai* 5 (1998): 7–9.

Books, Articles, and Unpublished Secondary Sources

Abramowicz, Hirsz. *Profiles of a Lost World: Memoirs of East European Jewish Life before World War II*. Translated Eva Zeitlin Dobkin, edited by Dina Abramowicz and Jeffrey Shandler, and introductions by David E. Fishman and Dina Abramowicz. Detroit: Wayne State University Press, 1999.

Adler, Eliyana R. "Exile and Survival: Lithuanian Jewish Deportees in the Soviet Union." In *That Terrible Summer: 70 Years since the Destruction of the Jewish Communities in Lithuania*, edited by Michael Ben Ya'akov, Gershon Greenberg, and Sigalit Rosmarin, 27–49. Jerusalem: Efrata College, 2013.

———. *In Her Hands: The Education of Jewish Girls in Tsarist Russia*. Detroit: Wayne State University Press, 2011.

Aleksandravičius, Egidijus. *Praeitis, istorija ir istorikai*. Vilnius: Vaga, 2000.

Allen, Charles R., Jr. *Nazi War Criminals among Us*. New York: Jewish Currents, 1963.
Altman, Ilya. "Dokumenty rossiiskikh arkhivov o Kholokoste v Litve." Paper presented at the IHC Conference "The Holocaust in Lithuania in the Focus of Modern History, Education and Justice," Vilnius, September 23–25, 2002.
———. "The Issuance of Visas to War Refugees by Chiune Sugihara as Reflected in the Documents of Russian Archives." *Darbai ir dienos* 67 (2017): 233–234.
Aly, Götz. *Europe against the Jews 1880–1945*. Translated by Jefferson Chase. Metropolitan Books: New York: Metroplitan Books, 2020.
Ambralevičiūtė, Aelita. "Economic Relations between Jewish Traders and Christian Farmers in the Nineteenth-Century Lithuanian Provinces." *Polin* 25 (2013): 71–91.
Anglickienė, Laima. "Svetimas, bet neblogai pažįstamas: žydo įvaizdis lietuvių liaudies kultūroje." *Darbai ir dienos* 34 (2003): 213–234.
Anušauskas, Arvydas. *Lietuvių tautos sovietinis naikinimas: 1940–1958 metais*. Vilnius: Mintis, 1996.
Arad, Yitzhak. "The 'Final Solution' in Lithuania in the Light of German Documentation." *Yad Vashem Studies* 11 (1976): 234–272.
———. *Ghetto in Flames:The Struggle and Destruction of the Jews in Vilna in the Holocaust*. Jerusalem: Ktav Pub. House, 1981.
———. *The Holocaust in the Soviet Union*. Lincoln: University of Nebraska Press, 2009.
Atamukas, Solomonas. *Lietuvos žydų kelias nuo XIV a. iki XXI a. pradžios*. Vilnius: Alma littera, 2007.
Avin, Agnieška, Kirill Kozhanov, and Gopalas Michailovskis. *Litovskone romengiro rakiribnytko archivo / Lietuvos romų sakytinės istorijos archyvas*. Vilnius: Romų visuomenes cetras, 2022.
Avin, Agnieška, and Anna Pilarczyk-Palaitis, "On the Way to Visibility: The Process of Creating a Cultural Memory of the Genocide of the Lithuanian Roma." *Journal of Baltic Studies* 43, no. 1 (2023): 87–102.
Balkelis, Tomas. *War, Revolution, and Nation-Making in Lithuania, 1914–1923*. Oxford: Oxford University Press, 2018.
Balkus, Mindaugas. *Kaip Kovno tapo Kaunu: miesto lituanizavimas 1918–1940 m*. Kaunas: Vytauto Didžiojo universitetas, 2023.
Balys, Jonas. "Antropologinė ir sociologinė žydijos problema." *Akademikas* 2 (1934): 40–42.
Barauskas, Albinas. *Miškų frontuose*. Vaga: 1968.
Barkan, Elazar, Elizabeth A. Cole, and Kai Struve, eds. *Shared History-Divided Memory: Jews and Others in Soviet-Occupied Poland, 1939–1941*. Leipzig: Leipziger Universitätsverlag GMBH, 2007.
Bašinskas, Gediminas. "Lietuvių-žydų konfliktai sovietinės okupacijos pradžioje 1940 metų vasarą: tęstinumai ar lūžiai." *Kai ksenofobija virsta prievarta: lietuvių ir žydų santykių dinamika XIX a. – XX a. pirmojoje pusėje*, edited by Vladas Sirutavičius and Darius Staliūnas, 197–212. Vilnius: LII, 2005.
Batalion, Judy. *The Light of Days: The Untold Story of Women Resistance Fighters in Hitler's Ghettos*. New York: HarperCollins, 2020.

Bauer, Yehuda. *The Death of the Shtetl*. New Haven: Yale University Press, 2009.
Bauman, Zygmunt. *Modernity and the Holocaust*. Ithaca, NY: Cornell University Press, 1992.
Beinfeld, Solon. "Health Care in the Vilna Ghetto." *Holocaust and Genocide Studies* 12, no. 1 (1998): 66–98.
Bendikaitė, Eglė. "'Lai kalba žygiai ir faktai': Panevėžio krašto žydai Nepriklausomybės kovose." In *Iš Panevėžio praeities: Lietuvos nepriklausomybės gynėjai ir puoselėtojai*, edited by Donatas Pilkauskas and Zita Pikelytė, 64–83. Panevėžys: Panevėžio kraštotyros muziejus, 2018.
———. "Dvi ideologijos – vienas judėjimas: sionistinis socializmas nepriklausomoje Lietuvoje." *Darbai ir dienos* 34 (2003): 255–271.
———. "Walking a Thin Line: The Successes and Failures of Socialist Zionism in Lithuania." *Polin* 25 (2013): 207–227.
———. *Sionistinis sąjūdis Lietuvoje*. Vilnius: LII, 2006.
———. "From a Certain Desire or Real Need: The Contexts of Jewish Acculturation in Lithuania after the Failure of National Autonomy in 1925–1940." *Jewish Culture and History* 18, no. 2 (2017): 170–189.
Ben-Naftali, Aya. "Collaboration and Resistance: The Ninth Fort as a Test Case." In *Collaboration and Resistance during the Holocaust: Belarus, Estonia, Latvia and Lithuania*, edited by David Gaunt, Paul A. Levine, and Laura Palosuo, 361–382. Frankfurt am Main: Peter Lang, 2004.
Beresniova, Christine. *Holocaust Education in Lithuania: Community, Conflict and the Making of Civil Society*. Lanham, MD: Lexington Books, 2017.
Binkienė, Sofija. *Ir be ginklo kariai*. Vilnius: Mintis, 1967.
Binkytė, Rūta, Milda Jakulytė-Vasil, and Giedrius Jakubauskas, "The Jewish Village of Degsnė: A Case Study." In *Jewish Space in Central and Eastern Europe*, edited by Larisa Lempertienė and Jurgita Šiaučiūnaitė-Verbickienė, 185–193. Newcastle: Cambridge Scholars Publishing, 2007.
Boruta, Jonas. "Katalikų bažnyčia ir lietuvių-žydų santykiai XIX-XX a." *Lietuvių Katalikų mokslo akademija. Metraštis* 14 (1999): 1–23.
Brandišauskas, Valentinas. "Holokaustas Kėdainių apskrityje." *Genocidas ir rezistencija* 17, no. 1 (2005): 87–99.
———. "Holokaustas Lietuvoje: istoriografinė situacija ir pagrindinės problemos." *Lietuvos Katalikų mokslo akdemija. Metraštis* 14 (1999): 140–150.
———. "Lazdijų apskrities žydų likimas nacistinės okupacijos metais: nuo teisių apribojimo iki žūties." *Genocidas ir rezistencija* 23, no. 1 (2008): 58–75.
———. "Lietuvių ir žydų santykiai 1940–1941 metais." *Darbai ir dienos* 11 (1996): 49–64.
———. "Lietuvos žydų turto likimas Antrojo pasaulinio karo metais." *Genocidas ir rezistencija* 15, no. 1 (2004): 86–107.
———. "Mažeikių apskrities žydų likimas Antrojo pasaulinio karo metais." *Genocidas ir rezistencija* 20, no. 2 (2006): 7–30.
———. *Siekiai atkurti Lietuvos valstybingumą (1940 06 – 1941 09)*. Vilnius: Valstybinis leidybos centras, 1996.

———. "Sukilimo faktografiniai aspektai." (Courtesy Valentinas Brandišauskas).
Braun, Joachim. "Music as Resistance, Music as Survival." In *Collaboration and Resistance during the Holocaust: Belarus, Estonia, Latvia and Lithuania*, edited by David Gaunt, Paul A. Levine, and Laura Palosuo, 361–382. Frankfurt am Main: Peter Lang, 2004.
Brazaitis (Ambrazevičius), Juozas, and Pilypas Narutis. "Lietuvių aktyvistu frontas." In *Lietuvių enciklopedija*, edited by Juozas Girnius, 26–28. Vol. 16. Boston: LE leidykla, 1958.
Bražiūnas, Mantas. "Legalios spaudos ir valdžios santykis Lietuvoje vokiečių okupacijos metais (1941–1944)." *Žurnalistikos tyrimai* 7 (2014): 195–218.
———. "The Darkest Page in the History of Lithuanian Journalism: Anti-Semitism in Legal Press During the Second Half of 1941." *Journalism Research: English Edition* 10 (2016): 127–139.
———. "Žurnalistikos laukas okupuotoje Lietuvoje." PhD diss, University of Vilnius, 2017.
Briedis, Laimonas. *Vilnius: City of Strangers*. Vilnius: baltos lankos, 2009.
Brizgys, Vincentas. "Kunigų seminarija Kaune bolševizmo metais." In *Lietuvių archyvas: bolševizmo metai*. Edited by Juozas Balčiūnas, 56–65. Vol. 1. Kaunas: Studijų Biuras, 1942.
———. *Katalikų Bažnyčia Lietuvoje: pirmoje rusų okupacijoje 1940–1941 m., vokiečių okupacijoje 1941–1944 metais (trumpa apžvalga)*. Chicago: Draugas, 1977.
Browning, Christopher. *Ordinary Men: Reserve Police Battalion 101 and the Final Solution in Poland*. New York: HarperCollins, 1991.
Bubnys, Arūnas. *Lietuvių policijos batalionai 1941–1945*. Vilnius: LGGRTC, 2017.
———. "Lietuvių policijos Šiaulių (14–asis) ir Panevėžio (10–asis) batalionai (1941–1944)." *Genocidas ir rezistencija* 27, no. 1 (2010): 81–90.
———. "Holokaustas Lietuvos provincijoje 1941 m.: žydų žudynės Kauno apskrityje." *Genocidas ir rezistencija* 12, no. 2 (2002): 81–103.
———. "Mažieji Lietuvos žydų getai ir laikinos izoliavimo stovyklos 1941–1943 metais." *Lietuvos istorijos metraštis* (1999): 151–180.
———. "Provokiška Lietuvos valstybės atkūrimo vizija (1940–1944)." In *Lietuvos diplomatija XX amžiuje*, edited by Vytautas Žalys, Raimundas Lopata, and Česlovas Laurinavičius, 132–146. Vilnius: Vaga, 1999.
———. "Šiaulių miesto ir Šiaulių apskrities žydų likimas." In *Šiaulių getas: kalinių sąrašai: 1942*. Edited by Irina Guzenberg and Jevgenija Sedova, 42–71. Vilnius: Valstybinis Vilniaus Gaono Žydų muziejus, 2002.
———. "The Holocaust in Lithuania: An Outline of the Major Stages and their Results." In *The Vanished World of Lithuanian Jews*, edited by Alvydas Nikžentaitis, Stefan Schreiner, and Darius Staliūnas, 205–222. Amsterdam: Rodopi, 2004.
———. "Vilniaus žydų žudynės ir Vilniaus getas (1941–1944)." *Genocidas ir rezistencija* 14, no. 2 (2003): 7–43.
———. "Penktasis lietuvių policijos batalionas." *Genocidas ir rezistencija* 9, no. 1 (2001): 44–50.
———. *Holokaustas Lietuvos provincijoje 1941 metais*. Vilnius: margi raštai, 2021.

———. *Kauno getas 1941–1944*. Vilnius: LGGRTC, 2014.
———. *Lietuvių antinacinė rezistencija 1941–1944*. Vilnius: Komprojektas, 1991.
———. *The Šiauliai Ghetto*. Vilnius: LGGRTC, 2014.
———. *Vokiečių okupuota Lietuva (1941–1944)*. Vilnius: LGGRTC, 1998.
———. *Vokiečių saugumo policijos ir SD Vilniaus Ypatingasis būrys 1941–1944*. Vilnius: LGGRTC, 2019.
Bubnys, Arūnas, and Stanislovas Buchaveckas. *Lietuvos žydai Štuthofo koncentracijos stovykloje 1943–1945 m*. Vilnius: LGGRTC, 2020.
Buchowski, Krzysztof. *Litvomanai ir polonizuotojai: mitai, abipusės nuostatos ir stereotipai lenkų ir lietuvių santykiuose pirmoje ir antroje XX amžiaus pusėje*. Translated by Irena Aleksaitė. Vilnius: baltos lankos, 2012.
Budreckis, Algirdas. *The Lithuanian National Revolt of 1941*. Boston: Lithuanian Encyclopedia Press, 1968.
Bukauskaitė, Evelina. "Gatherings of Jewish Artists in Interwar Lithuania." *Art History and Criticism/Meno istorija ir kritika* 17 (2021): 17–30.
———. "Žydų meninis gyvenimas Lietuvoje 1919–1940m.: tarp autonomijos ir integralumo. Jewish Artistic Life in Lithuania 1919–1940: Between Autonomy and Integrity" [PhD diss. abstract]. Vilnius: Vilniaus dailės akademija, 2021.
Bulavas, Juozas. *Vokiškųjų fašistų okupacinis Lietuvos valdymas 1941–1944 m*. Vilnius: LTSR Mokslų Akademija, 1969.
Buttar, Prit. *Between Giants: The Battle for the Baltics in World War II*. Oxford: Osprey Publishing, 2013.
Casper, Michael Phillips. "Strangers and Sojourners: The Politics of Jewish Belonging in Lithuania, 1914–1940." PhD diss., University of California, Los Angeles, 2019.
Cassedy, Ellen. "Can Vilnius Remember Vilna?" September 20, 2013. Reform Judaism. org, September 20, 2013. https://reformjudaism.org/blog/can-vilnius-remember-vilna.
———. *We Are Here: Memories of the Lithuanian Holocaust*. Lincoln: University of Nebraska Press, 2012.
———. "'To Transform Ourselves': Lithuanians Look at the Holocaust." *Polin* 25 (2013): 379–394.
Černiauskas, Norbertas. *1940. Paskutinė Lietuvos vasara*. Vilnius: Aukso žuvys, 2022.
Černiauskas, Norbertas, Marius Ėmužis, Darius Indrišionis, Kęstutis Kilinskas, et al. "Atviras laiškas Lietuvos gyventojų genocido ir rezistencijos tyrimų centro generaliniam direktoriui prof. dr. Adui Jakubauskui." bernardinai.lt, February 26, 2021, https://www.bernardinai.lt/atviras-laiskas-lietuvos-gyventoju-genocido-ir-rezistencijos-tyrimu-centro-lggrtc-generaliniam-direktoriui-prof-dr-adui-jakubauskui/.
Cohen, Rich. *The Avengers: A Jewish War Story*. New York: A. A. Knopf, 2000.
Damušis, Adolfas. "Profesorius Zenonas Ivinskis." *Į laisvę* 54 (1972): 15–20.
David-Fox, Michael. "Introduction. The People's War: Ordinary People and Regime Strategies in a World of Extremes." *Slavic Review* 75, no. 3 (2016): 551–559.
Davoliūtė, Violeta. "A 'Forgotten' History of Soviet Deportation: The Case of Lithuanian Jews." In *Population Displacement in Lithuania in the Twentieth Century Experiences,*

Identities and Legacies, edited by Tomas Balkelis and Violeta Davoliūtė, 179–210. Brill: Leiden, 2016.

———. "Multidirectional Memory and the Deportation of Lithuanian Jews." *Ethnicity Studies* 2 (2015): 131–149.

Dawidowicz, Lucy. *The War against the Jews 1933–1945.* New York: Bantam, 1975.

Dean, Martin, and Mel Hecker, eds. *Encyclopedia of Camps and Ghettos, 1933–1945.* Vol. 2b. Bloomington: Indiana University Press in association with USHMM, 2012.

Desbois, Patrick. *The Holocaust by Bullets: A Priest's Journey to Uncover the Truth behind the Murder of 1.5 Million Jews.* New York: Palgrave Macmillan, 2008.

Diamond, Ann. "The Translator Who Brought a Lost Jewish Poet's Words to the English-Speaking World." *Smithsonian,* October 24, 2018. https://www.smithsonianmag.com/arts-ulture/translator-brought-jewish-poet-words-english-speaking-world-180970555/.

Dieckmann, Christoph, and Rūta Vanagaitė. *Kaip tai įvyko?* Vilnius: Rūta Vanagaitė, 2020.

———. *How Did It Happen? Understanding the Holocaust.* Lanham, MD: Rowman and Littlefield, 2021.

Dieckmann, Christoph, and Saulius Sužiedėlis. *Lietuvos žydų persekiojimas ir masinės žudynės 1941 m. vasarą ir rudenį: šaltiniai ir analizė / The Persecution and Mass Murder of Lithuanian Jews During Summer and Fall of 1941: Sources and Analysis.* Vilnius: Margi raštai, 2006.

Dieckmann, Christoph, Vytautas Toleikis, and Rimantas Zizas. *Karo belaisvių ir civilių gyventojų žudynės Lietuvoje, 1941–1944 / Murders of Prisoners of War and of Civilian Population in Lithuania, 1941–1944, Totalitarinių režimų nusikaltimai Lietuvoje.* Vilnius: Margi raštai, 2005.

———. "The War and the Killing of the Lithuanian Jews." In *National Socialist Extermination Policies: Contemporary German Perspectives and Controversies,* edited by Ulrich Herbert, 240–273. New York: Berghahn, 2000.

———. "Alytus, 1941–1944: Massenmorde in einer Kleinstadt. Ein Fallbeispiel Deutscher Besatzungspolitik in Litauen." *Lithuanian Foreign Policy Review* 2, no. 8 (2008): 75–104.

———. *Deutsche Besatzungspolitik in Litauen 1941–1944.* 2 vols. Göttingen: Warstein Verlag, 2011.

Dinnerstein, Leonard. *America and the Survivors of the Holocaust.* New York: Columbia University Press, 1982.

Donskis, Leonidas. "Another Word for Uncertainty: Anti-Semitism in Modern Lithuania." edoc-Server Humboldt University. Accessed July 10, 2021. http://edoc.hu-berlin.de/nordeuropaforum/2006-1/donskis-leonidas-7/PDF/donskis.pdf.

Dovydėnas, Liudas. *Mes valdysim pasaulį: atsiminimai.* 2 vols. Woodhaven, NY: Romuva, 1970.

Eidintas, Alfonsas. "The Emigration Policy of the Tautininkai Regime in Lithuania, 1926–1940." *Journal of Baltic Studies* 16, no. 1 (1985): 64–72.

———, ed. *Lietuvos žydų žudynių byla.* Vilnius: Vaga, 2001.

———. *Žydai, lietuviai ir Holokaustas*. Vilnius: Vaga, 2002.
Etkes, Immanuel. *Rabbi Israel Salanter and the Musar Movement: Seeking the Torah of Truth*. Translated by Jonathan Chipman. Philadelphia: Jewish Publication Society, 1993.
Ezergailis, Andrew. *The Holocaust in Latvia 1941–1944*. Riga: Historical Institute of Latvia in association with USHMM, 1996.
Fajnhauz, Dawid. "Konflikty społeczne wśród ludności żydowskiej na Litwie i Białorusi w pierwszej połowie XIX wieku." *Biuletyn Żydowskiego Instytutu Historycznego* 52 (1964): 3–15.
Fishman, David E. "Nuo štadlanų iki masinių partijų: žydų politiniai judėjimai Lietuvoje." In *Lietuvos žydai: istorinė studija*, edited by Vladas Sirutavičius, Darius Staliūnas, and Jurgita Šiaučiūnaitė-Verbickienė, 251–270. Vilnius: baltos lankos, 2012.
———. *The Book Smugglers: Partisans, Poets, and the Race to Save Jewish Treasures from the Nazis*. Lebanon, NH: ForeEdge, 2017.
Frick, David. *Kith, Kin & Neighbors: Communities and Confessions in Seventeenth-Century Wilno*. Ithaca: Cornell University Press, 2013.
Friedman, Karen. "German/Lithuanian Collaboration in the Final Solution 1941–1944." PhD diss., University of Illinois-Chicago, 1994.
Gaigalaitė, Aldona. *Anglijos kapitalas ir Lietuva 1919–1940*. Vilnius: Mokslas, 1986.
Gasparaitis, Siegfried. "'Verrätern wird nur dann vergeben, wenn sie wirklich beweisen können, dass sie mindestens einen Juden liquidiert haben'. Die Front Litauischer Aktivisten (LAF) und die antisowjetischen Austände 1941." *Zeitschrift fur Geschichtswissenschaft* 48 (2001): 886–904.
Garmus, Antanas. "Lietuvos įjungimas į SSSR-Maskvos diktatas." In *Lietuvų archyvas: bolševizmo metai*, edited by Juozas Balčiūnas, 35–46. Vol. 3. Kaunas: n.p., 1942.
Gasche, Malte. "Die Instrumentalisierung des Prähistorie im Reichskommissariat Ostland 1941 bis 1944." In *Reichskommissariat Ostland: Tatort und Erinnerungsobjekt*, edited by Sebastian Lehman, Robert Bohn, and Uwe Danker, 171–187. Paderborn: Ferdinand Schöningh, 2012.
Gellately, Robert. *Lenin, Stalin and Hitler: The Age of Social Catastrophe*. New York: Vintage Books, 2007.
Geniušienė, Giedrė, ed. *Švenčionių krašto žydų tragedija*. Švenčionys: Nalšios muziejus, 2002.
Gerlach, Christian. *Kalkulierte Morde: Die deutsche Wirtschafts- und Vernichtungspolitik in Weissrussland 1941–1944*. Hamburg: Hamburger Edition, 1999.
Gershenson, Olga. *The Phantom Holocaust: Soviet Cinema and Jewish Catastrophe*. New Brunswick: Rutgers University Press, 2013.
Gieczys, Kazimierz. *Bractwa trzeźwości w diecezji żmudzkiej w latach 1858–1864*. Studia Teologiczne 4. Wilno: Księg. św. Wojciecha, 1935.
Ginaitė, Sara. *Žydų tautos tragedijos Lietuvoje pradžia*. Vilnius: Miša, 1994.
———. Review of *Nepokorivvshiesya: Letopis' evreiskogo soprotivleniya*, by Alex (Alter) Faitelson. *Lietuvos istorijos metraštis* 2 (2001): 282–287.

Girnius, Kęstutis. "Lemtingieji 1941–ji metai: Holokausto Lietuvoje prielaidų klausimu." *Naujasis Židinys-Aidai* 2 (2011): 85–100.
Glass, James. *Jewish Resistance during the Holocaust: Moral Uses of Violence and Will.* New York: Palgrave, 2004.
Goldin, Semen. *Russkaya armiya i evrei 1914–1917.* Moscow: Mosty kultury, 2018.
Goldstein, Eric L. "The Social Geography of a *Shtetl*: Jews and Lithuanians in Darbėnai, 1760–1940." In *Jewish Space in Central and Eastern Europe,* edited by Larisa Lempertienė and Jurgita Šiaučiūnaitė-Verbickienė, 27–50. Newcastle: Cambridge Scholars Publishing, 2007.
Goldstein, Jonathan. "Lithuania Honors a Holocaust Rescuer." *Polin* 14 (2001): 249–255.
Gražiūnas, Albinas. *Lietuva dviejų okupacijų replėse 1940–1944.* Vilnius: Tėvynės sargas, 1996.
Grigoravičiūtė, Akvilė. "Jidiš literatūra tarpukario Lietuvoje (1918–1940): savasties paieškos." *Colloquia* 29 (2012): 38–62.
Gringauz, Samuel. "Jewish National Autonomy in Lithuania (1918–1925)." *Jewish Social Studies* 14, no. 3 (1952): 225–246.
———. "The Ghetto as an Experiment of Jewish Social Organization (Three Years of Kovno Ghetto)." *Jewish Social Studies* 11, no. 1 (1949): 3–20.
Gross, Jan T. *Neighbors: The Destruction of the Jewish Community in Jedwabne, Poland.* Princeton: Princeton University Press, 2001.
———. *Polish Society under German Occupation: The Generalgouvernement 1939–1944.* Princeton: Princeton University Press, 1979.
Grunskis, Eugenijus. *Lietuvos gyventojų trėmimai 1940–1941, 1945–1953 metais.* Vilnius: LII, 1996.
Guesnet, François, and Darius Staliūnas. "No Simple Stories: Die litauisch-jüdischen Beziehungen im 19. und 20. Jahrhundert." *Jahrbuch für Antisemitismusforschung* 21 (2012): 17–25.
Gustainis, Valentinas. "Hitlerio užsienio politika." *Vairas* 4 (1933): 424–438.
Gustaitė, Genovaitė. "Vyskupas Jurgis Matulaitis ir žydai Vilniaus vyskupijoje 1918–1925." *Lietuvių Katalikų mokslo akademija. Metraštis* 14 (1999): 105–113.
Gustaitis, Rolandas. *Jews of the Kaišiadorys Region of Lithuania.* Bergenfield, NJ: Avotaynu, 2010.
———. *Kaišiadorių regiono žydai.* Kaišiadorys: Kaišiadorių muziejus, 2006.
Guzenberg, Irina, and Jevgenija Sedova, eds. *Šiaulių getas: kalinių sąrašai:1942.* Vilnius: Valstybinis Vilniaus Gaono Žydų muziejus, 2002.
Hayes, Peter. *Why? Explaining the Holocaust.* New York: Norton, 2017.
He Kissed the Swastika. Vilnius: Mintis, 1964.
Ivaškevičius, Marius. "Aš ne žydas." Delfi, August 24, 2016. https://www.delfi.lt/news/ringas/lit/m-ivaskevicius-as-ne-zydas.d?id=72107298.
Hilberg, Raul. "The Ghetto as a Form of Government." *The Annals of the American Academy of Political and Social Science* 450 (July 1980): 98–112.
———. *The Destruction of the European Jews.* New York: Harper Torchbooks, 1961.

Hroch, Miroslav. *Die Vorkämpfer der nationalen Bewegung bei den kleinen Völkern Europas: eine vergleichende Analyse zur gesellschaftlichen Schichtung der patriotischen Gruppen*. Acta Universitatis Carolinae Philosophica et Historica 24. Prague: Universita Karlova, 1968.

Inaba, Chiharu. "Documents Related to Visas for Life and Historiography of Chiune Sugihara." *Darbai ir dienos* 67 (2017): 263–271.

Ivanovas, Bernaras. "Chiune (Sempo) Sugiharos veiklos Kaune 1930–1940 m. probleminiai aspektai." *Genocidas ir rezistencija* 9, no. 1 (2001): 7–14.

Ivinskis, Zenonas. "Lietuva ir žydai istorijos šviesoje." *Aidai* 1–2 (1972): 31–41.

Jackevičius, Mindaugas. "Vokiečių istorikas įvertino R. Vanagaitės pareiškimus: yra tik vienas kelias pirmyn." Delfi, October 30, 2017. https://www.delfi.lt/news/daily/lithuania/vokieciu-istorikas-ivertino-r-vanagaites-pareiskimus-yra-tik-vienas-kelias-pirmyn.d?id=76199271.

Jacobs, Jack. "The Bund in Vilna, 1918–1939." *Polin* 25 (2013): 263–292.

Jankauskas, Juozas. *1941 m. birželio sukilimas Lietuvoje*. Vilnius: LGGRTC, 2010.

Jankauskas, Pranas. "Lietuviškasis lūžis: kalbų varžybos Kauno savivaldybėje 1918–1928 metais." *Darbai ir dienos* 34 (2003): 33–47.

Janulaitis, Augustinas. *Žydai Lietuvoje: bruožai iš Lietuvos visuomenės istorijos XIV–XIX amž*. Kaunas: A. Janulaitis, 1923.

Jazavita, Simonas. "Dviejų Lietuvos kariuomenės kapitonų likimas dviejų diktatorių pakto fone." Bernardinai, August 26, 2019. https://www.bernardinai.lt/2019-08-26-dvieju-lietuvos-kariuomenes-kapitonu-likimas-dvieju-diktatoriu-pakto-fone/.

———. "Kazio Škirpos geopolitinė Lietuvos vizija ir pastangos ją įgyvendinti 1938–1945." PhD diss., Vytautas Magnus University and Klaipėda University, 2020.

———. "Kazys Škirpa's Geopolitical Vision of Lithuania and the Efforts to Implement It in 1938–1945" [PhD diss. abstract]. Vytautas Magnus University and Klaipėda University, 2020.

Jokubauskas, Vytautas, Jonas Vaičenonis, Vygantas Vareikis, and Hektoras Vitkus. *Valia priešintis: paramilitarizmas ir Lietuvos karinio saugumo problemos*. Klaipėda: Klaipėdos unversiteto Baltijos regiono istorijos ir archeologijos institutas, 2015.

Jonaitis, Leonas. *They Live in Your Midst*. Vilnius: Gintaras, 1972.

Jonušausaks, Laurynas. *Likimo vedami: Lietuvos diplomatinės tarnybos egzilyje veikla, 1940–1991*. Vilnius: LGGRTC, 2003.

Juodis, Egidijus. "Zenonas Ignatavičius, ar galima išlikti žmogumi, kai aplink vien neteisybė, 2020." Dievas ir tėvynė. Accessed May 25, 2021. http://www.prodeoetpatria.lt/index.php/baznycia/21-knygos-tikejimas-baznycia/326-egidijus-juodis-zenonas-ignatavicius.

Juškaitė, Jūratė. "Kultūros istorikė V. Davoliūtė: tremtys buvo sulietuvintos ir 'sukatalikintos.'" Mano Teisės, April 5, 2016. http://manoteises.lt/straipsnis/kulturologe-v-davoliute-tremtys-buvo-sulietuvintos-ir-sukatalikintos/.

Kanovich, Grigory. *Devilspel*. Translated by Yisrael Cohen. Nottingham: Noir Press, 2019.

Kasparavičius, Algimantas. "Lietuviai ir žydai katastrofos išvakarėse." In *Kai ksenofobija virsta prievarta: lietuvių ir žydų santykių dinamika XIX a. – XX a. pirmojoje pusėje*, edited by Vladas Sirutavičius and Darius Staliūnas, 117–156. Vilnius: LII, 2005.

———. "Lietuvių politinės iliuzijos: Lietuvos laikinosios vyriausybės 'politika' ir Holokausto pradžia Lietuvoje." Izb.lt. Accessed June 30, 2018. http://www.lzb.lt/2017/01/11/lietuviu-politines-iliuzijos-lietuvos-laikinosios-vyriausybes-politika-ir-holokausto-pradzia-lietuvoje-1941–metais/.

Kasparavičius, Algis. "From the Lithuanian Press about the Jews during the Nazi Occupation 1941–1942." In *The Shoah (Holocaust) in Lithuania*, edited by Joseph Levinson, 225–228. Vilnius: Vilna Gaon Jewish State Museum, 2006.

Kaubrys, Saulius. "Lietuvos žydų lojalumo raiška: apsisprendimo variacijos 1918–1939 metais." In *Abipusis pažinimas: lietuvių ir žydų kultūriniai saitai*, edited by Jurgita Šiaučiūnaitė-Verbickienė, 105–117. Vilnius: Vilniaus universiteto leidykla, 2010.

———. "Žydų mokyklų tinklas: kiekybinių pokyčių charakteristikos." In *Lietuvos žydai: istorinė studija*, edited by Vladas Sirutavičius, Darius Staliūnas, and Jurgita Šiaučiūnaitė-Verbickienė, 371–385. Vilnius: baltos lankos, 2012.

———. *National Minorities in Lithuania: An Outline*. Translated by Milda Dyke. Vilnius: Vaga, 2002.

Kavaliauskas, Vilius, ed. *Pažadėtoji žemė: Lietuvos žydai kuriant valstybę 1918–1940 m.* Vilnius: Petro ofsetas, 2013.

Kavolis, Vytautas. *Sąmoningumo trajektorijos: lietuvių kultūros modernėjimo aspektai*. Chicago: A & M Publications, 1986.

Kay, Alex J. *Empire of Destruction: A History of Nazi Mass Killing*. New Haven: Yale University Press, 2021.

———. "Transition to Genocide: Einsatzkommando 9 and the Annihilation of Soviet Jewry." *Holocaust and Genocide Studies* 2, no. 3 (2013): 411–442.

Končius, Ignas. *Žemaičio šnekos*. Vilnius: Vaga, 1996.

Končius, Joseph B. *History of Lithuania*. Chicago: Lithuanian-American Community, n.d.

Kopchenova, Irina, Svetlana Amosova, Lara Lempertene, et al, eds. *Evrei na karte Litvy. Birzhai: Problemy sokhraneniiya evreiskogo naslediiya i istoricheskoii pamyati*. Moscow: Sefer, 2015.

Kors, Michael. "Die offizielle Darstellung des Holocaust in der Sowjetzeit (1945–1990)." In *Holocaust in Litauen: Krieg, Judenmorde und Kollaboration im Jahre 1941*, edited by Vincas Bartusevičius, Joachim Tauber und Wolfram Wette, 247–261. Köln: Böhlau, 2003.

Kostanian-Danzig, Rachel. *Spiritual Resistance in the Vilna Ghetto*. Vilnius: Vilna Gaon Jewish State Museum, 2002.

Kotlerman, Ber. "Phillipine Visas-for-Jews from the Perspective of the Unanswered Letters of 1939 to President Quezon." *Darbai ir dienos* 67 (2017): 273–292.

Krausnick, Helmut, and Hans-Heinrich Wilhelm. *Die Truppe des Weltanschauungskrieges: die Einsatzgruppen der Sicherheitspolizei und des SD 1938–1942*. Stuttgart: Deutsche Verlags-Anstalt, 1981.

Krebs, Gerhard. "Germany and Sugihara Chiune: Japanese-Polish Intelligence Cooperation and Counter-Intelligence." *Darbai ir dienos* 67 (2017): 215–230.

Krupavičius, Mykolas. "Lietuvių ir žydų santykiai Hitlerio okupacijos metu." "Partizanai istorija ir dabartis." Accessed June 10, 2021. http://www.partizanai.org/index.php/bendraminciu-straipsniai/251–lietuviu-ir-zydu-santykiai-hitlerio-okupacijos-metu.

Kuodytė, Dalia, ed. *Prakalbinta praeitis*. Vilnius: LGGRT, 2002.

Kuodytė, Dalia, and Rimantas Stankevičius, eds. *Išgelbėję pasaulį . . . Žydų gelbėjimas Lietuvoje (1941–1944)*. Vilnius: LGGRTC, 2001.

Kvietkauskas, Mindaugas. "Mėlynas Matildos talento paukštis." In Matilda Olkinaitė, *Atrakintas dienoraštis: kūrybos rinktinė*, edited by Mindaugas Kvietkauskas, 16–47. Vilnius: Lietuvių literatūros ir tautosakos institutas, 2019.

Kviklys, Bronius. *Lietuvių kova su naciais 1941–1944*. Memmingen: Minties leidinys. 1946.

———. "Vytautas Reivytis." In *Lietuvių enciklopedija*, edited by Juozas Puzinas and Pranas Čepėnas, 92. Vol. 25. Boston: LE leidykla, 1961.

Latvytė-Gustaitienė, Neringa. *Holokaustas Ukmergėje. Holocaust in Ukmergė*. Vilnius: Vilna Gaon State Jewish Museum, 2012.

———. *Holokaustas Trakų apskrityje*. Vilnius: Valstybinis Vilniaus Gaono muziejus, 2002.

Laukaitytė, Regina. *Lietuvos bažnyčios vokiečių okupacijos metais (1941–1944)*. Vilnius: LII, 2010.

———. "Katalikų bažnyčia Lietuvoje 1941–1944: požiūris į žydų genocidą ir krikštą." *Lituanistica* 70 (2007): 1–12.

———. "Lietuvos bažnyčių misijos okupuotose SSSR srityse 1941–1944 m." *Lituanistica* 63 (2005): 1–14.

———. "Žydų religinis gyvenimas Lietuvoje 1944–1956." *Lituanistica* 58 (2012): 295–308.

Lavrinec, Pavel. "Žydų bendruomenė, lietuvių kultūra ir rusų spauda." In *Abipusis pažinimas: lietuvių ir žydų kultūriniai saitai*, edited by Jurgita Šiaučiūnaitė-Verbickienė, 201–227. Vilnius: Vilniaus universiteto leidykla, 2010.

Lazar, Chaim. *Destruction and Resistance: A History of the Partisan Movement in Vilna*. Translated by Galia Eden Barshop. New York: Shengold, 1985.

Leiserowitz, Ruth. "Žydai tapukario Klaipėdos krašte." In *Lietuvos žydai: istorinė studija*, edited by Vladas Sirutavičius, Darius Staliūnas, and Jurgita Šiaučiūnaitė-Verbickienė, 425–431. Vilnius: baltos lankos, 2012.

Lempertienė, Larisa. "Tapukario Lietuvos politinių ir socialinių aktualijų pateikimas žydų dienraštyje *Di Jidiše štime*." In *Abipusis pažinimas: lietuvių ir žydų kultūriniai saitai*, edited by Jurgita Šiaučiūnaitė-Verbickienė, 229–244. Vilnius: Vilniaus universiteto leidykla, 2010.

———. "Žydų spauda ir literatūra." In *Lietuvos žydai: istorinė studija*, edited by Vladas Sirutavičius, Darius Staliūnas, and Jurgita Šiaučiūnaitė-Verbickienė, 219–235. Vilnius: baltos lankos, 2012.

Lenn, Maria. "Nationalism, Democratization and Inter-Ethnic Relations in the Lithuanian State 1988–1992." PhD diss. School of Slavonic and East European Studies, University College, London, 2000.

Levin, Dov. *Baltic Jews under the Soviets 1940–1946*. Jerusalem: The Hebrew University of Jerusalem.

———. "Darsūniškis." JewishGen. Accessed October 29, 2019. https://www.jewishgen.org/yizkor/pinkas_lita/lit_00212.html.

———. "Lithuania." In *The World Reacts to the Holocaust*, edited by David Wyman, 325–353. Baltimore: Johns Hopkins University Press, 1996.

———. "Lithuanian Attitudes towards the Jewish Minority in the Aftermath of the Holocaust: The Lithuanian Press, 1991–1992." *Holocaust and Genocide Studies* 7, no. 2 (1993): 247–262.

———. "The Jews and the Election Campaigns in Lithuania, 1940–1941." *Soviet Jewish Affairs* 10, no. 1 (1980), 39–45.

———. "The Jews and the Socio-Economic Sovietization of Lithuania, 1940–1941 (Part 1)." *Soviet Jewish Affairs* 17, no. 2 (1987): 12–31.

———. "The Jews and the Socio-Economic Sovietization of Lithuania, 1940–1941 (Part 2)." *Soviet Jewish Affairs* 17, no. 3 (1987): 25–38.

———. "The Jews in the Soviet Lithuanian Establishment, 1940–1941." *Soviet Jewish Affairs* 10, no. 2 (1980): 21–37.

———. *Fighting Back: Lithuanian Jewry's Armed Resistance to the Nazis 1941–1945*. Translated by Moshe Kohn and David Cohen. New York: Holmes & Meier, 1985.

———. *The Lesser of Two Evils: Eastern European Jewry under Soviet Rule, 1939–1941*. Translated by Naftali Greenwood. Philadelphia: Jewish Publication Society, 1995.

———. *The Litvaks: A Short History of the Jews in Lithuania*. Jerusalem: Yad Vashem, 2009.

———. *Trumpa žydų istorija Lietuvoje*. Translated by Jonas Morkus. Vilnius: Studija 101, 2000.

Levin, Dov, and Zvie A. Brown. *The Story of an Underground: The Resistance of the Jews of Kovno in the Second World War*. Jerusalem: Gefen, 2014.

Levin, Vladimir. "Socialiniai, ekonominiai, demografiniai bei geografiniai žydų bendruomenės Lietuvoje bruožai." In *Lietuvos žydai: istorinė studija*, edited by Vladas Sirutavičius, Darius Staliūnas, and Jurgita Šiaučiūnaitė-Verbickienė, 153–190. Vilnius: baltos lankos, 2012.

Levine, Hillel. *In Search of Sugihara: The Elusive Japanese Diplomat Who Risked His Life to Rescue 10,000 Jews from the Holocaust*. New York: The Free Press, 1996.

Levinson, Joseph, ed. *The Shoah (Holocaust) in Lithuania*. Vilnius: The Vilna Gaon Jewish State Museum, 2001.

Levinsonas, Josifas, ed. *Skausmo knyga. The Book of Sorrow*. Vilnius: Vaga, 1997.

———, ed. *Šoa (Holokaustas) Lietuvoje: skaitiniai*. Vilnius: Valstybinis Vilniaus Gaono žydų muziejus, 2001.

Liekis, Šarūnas. "Jewish Partisans and Soviet Resistance in Lithuania." In *Collaboration and Resistance During the Holocaust: Belarus, Estonia, Latvia and Lithuania*, edited by David Gaunt, Paul A. Levine, and Laura Palosuo, 459–478. Frankfurt am Main: Peter Lang, 2004.

———. "Lithuanians and Jews in 1914–1918: Motives for Political Cooperation." *Jahrbuch für Antisemitismus* 21 (2012): 115–132.

———. "Soviet Resistance and Jewish Partisans in Lithuania." *Polin* 25 (2013): 331–356.

———. "The Transfer of Vilna District into Lithuania, 1939." *Polin* 14 (2001): 212–222.

———. *A State within a State? Jewish National Autonomy in Lithuania 1918–1925*. Vilnius: Versus Aureus, 2003.

———. *Nineteen Thirty-Nine: The Year That Changed Everything in Lithuania's History*. On the Boundary of Two Worlds: Identity, Freedom and Moral Imagination in the Baltics 20. Amsterdam, Rodopi, 2010.

———. "Jewish Studies in Lithuania since 1990." *Journal of Modern Jewish Studies* 10, no. 1 (2011): 93–100.

Liekis, Šarūnas, and Saulius Sužiedėlis. "Conflicting Memories: The Reception of the Holocaust in Lithuania." In *Bringing the Dark Past to Light: The Reception of the Holocaust in Postcommunist Europe*, edited with an introduction by John-Paul Himka and Joanna Beata Michlic, 319–351. Lincoln: University of Nebraska Press, 2013.

Littman, Sol. *War Criminal on Trial: The Rauca Case*. Toronto: Lester & Orpen Dennys, 1983.

Lohr, Eric. "The Russian Army and the Jews: Mass Deportation, Hostages, and Violence during World War I." *Russian Review* 60, no. 3 (2001): 404–419.

Łossowski, Piotr. "The Ideology of Authoritarian Regimes (The Baltic States 1926–1934–1940)." In *Dictatorships in EastCentral Europe*, edited by Janusz Żarnowski, 181–202. Warsaw: PAN, 1983.

———. *Litwa a sprawy polskie 1939–1940*. Warsaw: PWN, 1982.

Lučinskas, Gintaras. *Vermachto nusikaltimai Dzūkijoje 1941 m. birželį*. Alytus: Gintarinė svajonė, 2011.

Maceina, Antanas. "Tauta ir valstybė." *Naujoji Romuva* 11 (1939): 227–230.

Mačiulis, Dangiras. "'Žydų lavonų klausimas' Lietuvos universitete 1926–1927 metais." *Lietuvos istorijos metraštis* 2 (2002): 159–166.

———. "Žvilgsnis į vieno pogromo anatomiją tarpukario Lietuvoje." In *Kai ksenofobija virsta prievarta: lietuvių ir žydų santykių dinamika XIX a. - XX a. pirmojoje pusėje*, edited by Vladas Sirutavičius and Darius Staliūnas, 181–196. Vilnius: Lietuvos istorijos institutas, 2005.

MacQueen, Michael. "Jews in the Reichskommissariat Ostland, June–December 1941: From White Terror to Holocaust in Lithuania." In *Bitter Legacy: Confronting the Holocaust in the USSR*, edited by Zvi Gitelman, 91–103. Bloomington: Indiana University Press, 1997.

Makhotina, Ekaterina. *Errinerungen an den Krieg – Krieg der Erinnerungen: Litauen und der Zweite Weltkrieg*. Gottingen: Vandoenhoeck & Ruprecht, 2017.

———. "Between 'Suffered' Memory and 'Learned' Memory: The Holocaust and Jewish History in Lithuanian Museums and Memorials After 1990." *Yad Vashem Studies* 41, no. 1 (2016): 207–246.

Maliauskas, Antanas. *Žydai ekonomijos ir visuomenės žvilgsniu*. Kaunas: Saliamono Banaičio spaustuvė, 1914.

Marciński, Franciszek. *Grammatyka polska dla Litwinów uczącyh się jezyka polskiego*. Suwałki: Drukarnia wojewódzka, 1833.

Martinionis, Antanas. *Vietinė rinktinė*. Vilnius: Kardas, 1998.

Maslauskienė, Nijolė. "Lietuvos komunistų tautinė ir socialinė sudėtis, 1939 m. pabaigoje-1940 m. rugsėjo men." *Genocidas ir rezistencija* 5, no. 1 (1999): 77–104.

———. "Lietuvos komunistų sudėtis 1940 spalio-1941 birželio men." *Genocidas ir rezistencija* 6, no. 2 (1999): 20–46.

———. "Valdininkijos šalinimas iš okupuotosios Lietuvos administracijos ir jos keitimas okupantų talkininkais 1940 m. birželio-gruodžio mėn." *Genocidas ir rezistencija* 8, no, 2 (2000): 7–41.

———. "Lietuvos tautinių mažumų įtraukimas į LSSR administraciją ir sovietinės biurokratijos tautiniai santykiai 1940–1941 m." *Genocidas ir rezistencija* 9, no. 1 (2001): 15–43.

Maslauskienė, Nijolė, and Inga Petravičiūtė. *Okupantai ir kolaborantai: Pirmoji sovietinė okupacija (1940–1941)*. Vilnius: margi raštai, 2007.

Matthäus, Jürgen. "Controlled Escalation: Himmler's Men in the Summer of 1941 and the Holocaust in the Occupied Soviet Territories." *Holocaust and Genocide Studies* 21, no. 2 (2007): 218–242.

Medišauskienė, Zita. "Atkarus, bet būtinas: žydai ir bajoriškoji Lietuvos visuomenė," In *Žydų klausimas Lietuvoje XIX a. viduryje*, edited by Vladas Sirutavičius and Darius Staliūnas, 85–106. Vilnius: Lietuvos istorijos institutas, 2004.

Megargee, Geoffrey P., ed. *Encyclopedia of Camps and Ghettos, 1933–1945*. Vol. 1. Bloomington: Indiana University Press in association with USHMM, 2009.

Meras, Icchokas. *Geltonas lopas*. Vilnius: Vaga, 1960.

———. *Lygiosios trunka akimirką*. Vilnius: Vaga, 1963.

———. *Ant ko laikosi pasaulis*. Vilnius: Vaga, 1965.

———. *Stalemate*. Translated by Jonas Zdanys. Seacacus, NJ: Lyle Stuart, 1980.

———. *Striptizas, arba Paryžius-Roma-Paryžius*. Southfield, MI: Ateitis, 1976.

Merkys, Vytautas. "Lietuvos miestų gyventojų tautybės XIX a. pabaigoje, XX a. pradžioje klausimu." *LTSR MA Darbai*, new series A, 2, no. 5 (1958): 85–98.

Mertelsman, Olaf. "Das 'kleinere Übel'? Das Generalkommissariat Estland in estnischen Vergangensheitsdiskurs." In *Reichskommissariat Ostland: Tatort und Erinnerungsobjekt*, edited by Sebastian Lehman, Robert Bohn, and Uwe Danker, 349–366. Paderborn: Ferdinand Schöningh, 2012.

Michlic, Joanna, and John-Paul Himka. Program for the National Convention of the American Association for the Advancement of Slavic Studies (AAASS),

Philadelphia, November 20–23, 2008, Session 6—"The Memory of the Holocaust in Post-Communist Europe: Similarities and Differences."

Mikelinskas, Jonas. "Teisė likti nesuprastam, arba Mes ir jie, jie ir mes." *Metai* 8–9 (1996): 126–163.

Mironas, Vladas. "Tikybos Nepriklausomoje Lietuvoje," In *Pirmasis Nepriklausomos Lietuvos dešimtmetis 1918–1928*, compiled by Vyriausias Lietuvos Nepriklausomybės 10 metų sukaktuvėms ruošti komitetas, 380–390. Kaunas: Šviesa, 1990. Reprint of 1930 ed.

Misiūnas, Romuald J. "Fascist Tendencies in Lithuania." *Slavonic and East European Review* 110 (1970): 88–94.

Misiunas, Romuald J, and Rein Taagepera, *The Baltic States: Years of Dependence*. Berkeley: University of California Press, 1983.

Naimark, Norman. *Stalin's Genocides*. Princeton: Princeton University Press, 2010.

———. *Fires of Hatred: Ethnic Cleansing in Twentieth-Century Europe*. Cambridge, MA: Harvard University Press, 2001.

Needleman, Mallory. "Lithuania under the Soviet Occupation, 1940–41: Observations and Operations by the United States." *MCU Journal* 9, no. 2 (2018): 62–75.

Nikžentaitis, Alvydas. "Tautinis mitas tai ne paprasta istorija: atviras laiškas vokiečių istorikui." Delfi, October 31, 2021. https://www.delfi.lt/news/ringas/lit/a-nikzentaitis-tautinis-mitas-tai-ne-paprasta-istorija-atviras-laiskas-vokieciu-istorikui.d?id=76220619.

Nikžentaitis, Alvydas, Stefan Schreiner, and Darius Staliūnas, eds. *The Vanished World of Lithuanian Jews*. Amsterdam: Rodopi, 2004.

Noreika, Dainius. "Skirtingų istorijų sankirtos: Holokaustas, birželio sukilimas ir partizanų karas." In *Holokaustas nacių okupuotose Rytų ir Vakaru valstybėse: tyrimai ir atmintis / The Holocaust in the Eastern and Western European States Occupied by the Nazis: Studies and Memory*, edited by Vygantas Vareikis, 66–76. Kaunas: Spindulys, 2017.

Parulskis, Sigitas. *Tamsa ir partneriai*. Vilnius: alma littera, 2012.

Pashuto, Vladimir T. *Geroicheskaya borba russkogo naroda za nezavisimost' XIII v.* Moscow: Gos. Izd-vo polit. lit-ry, 1956.

Pažėraitė, Aušra. "Žydų žudynių dalyvių motyvacija," Unpublished report presented to the IHC, n.d.

———. "Musaro sąjūdis." In *Žydai Lietuvoje: Istorija. Kultūra. Paveldas*, compiled by Larisa Lempertienė and Jurgita Šiaučiūnaitė-Verbickienė, 125–129. Vilnius: R. Paknio leidykla, 2009.

———. "Žydų kultūrinių ir politinių orientyrų pokyčiai Aleksandro II laikais." In *Žydų klausimas Lietuvoje XIX a. viduryje*, edited by Vladas Sirutavičius and Darius Staliūnas, 53–84. Vilnius: Lietuvos istorijos institutas, 2004.

Pažėraitė, Aušrelė Kristina. "Išsaugoti sąvastį ar supanašėti? Žydų mokyklų reformos Lietuvoje Nikalojaus laikais." *Darbai ir dienos* 34 (2003): 235–253.

Perrin, Charles. "From Philosemitism to Antisemitism: Jonas Šliūpas, Refugees and the Holocaust." Izb.it. Accessed November 27, 2017. https://www.lzb.lt/wp-content/uploads/2017/11/Jonas-Sliupas-Refugees-and-the-Holocaust.pdf.

———. "Lithuanians in the Shadow of Three Eagles: Vincas Kudirka, Martynas Jankus, Jonas Šliūpas and the Making of Modern Lithuania." PhD diss., Georgia State University, 2013.

Peterson, Edward N. *The American Occupation of Germany: Retreat to Victory*. Detroit: Wayne State University Press, 1977.

Petkus, Viktoras. "Pilietinės drąsos memorandumas. 1942–ieji. Lietuva." bernardinai, November 1, 2015. https://www.bernardinai.lt/2012-11-19-pilietines-drasos-memorandumas-1942-ieji-lietuva/.

Petrukhin, Vladimir. "Rabbanitskiye i karaimskie obshchiny v srednevekovoi Litve: problem nachalnoi istorii." In *Evrei na karte Litvy. Birzhai: Problemy sokhraneniiya evreiskogo naslediiya i istoricheskoii pamyati*, edited by Irina Kopchenova, S. Amosova, L. Dreier, L. Lempertene et al., 59–68. Moscow: Sefer, 2015.

Petuchauskas, Markas. *Price of Concord*. Vilnius: Versus Aureus, 2015.

———. "Kultūros žemynas tilpęs teatre." *Kultūros barai* 1 (2003): 77–81.

Pocius, Mindaugas. "Kapitonas Juozas Krikštaponis: Holokausto ir partizaninio pasipriešinimo kolektyvinės atminties susidūrimas." Unpublished manuscript.

———. *Kita mėnulio pusė: Lietuvos partizanu kova su kolaboravimu 1944–1953 metais*. Vilnius: LII, 2009.

Polonsky, Antony. *The Jews in Poland and Russia*. Vol 1, *1350–1881*. Oxford: The Littman Library of Jewish Civilization, 2010.

Porat, Dina. "The Justice System and Courts of Law in the Ghettos of Lithuania." *Holocaust and Genocide Studies* 12, no. 1 (1998): 49–65.

———. *The Fall of a Sparrow: The Life and Times of Abba Kovner*. Translated and edited by Elizabeth Yuval. Stanford: Stanford University Press, 2010.

———. "The Holocaust in Lithuania: Some Unique Aspects." In *The Final Solution: Origins and Implementation*, edited by David Cesarani, 159–174. London: Routledge, 1994.

———. "The Jewish Councils of the Main Ghettos of Lithuania: A Comparison." In *Modern Judaism* 13, no. 2 (May 1993): 149–163.

Press, Bernhard. *The Murder of the Jews of Latvia 1941–1945*. Translated by Laimdota Mazzarins. Evanston, IL: Northwestern University Press, 2000.

Puławski, Adam. "Posrtrzeganie żydowskich oddziałów partyzanckich przez Armię Krajową i Delegaturę Rządu RP na Kraj." *Pamięć i Sprawiedliwość* 4 (2003): 271–300.

Rakūnas, Algirdas. *Lietuvos liaudies kova prieš hitlerinę okupaciją*. Vilnius: Mintis, 1970.

Radensky, Paul. "Žydų reikalų ministerija ir žydų tautinė autonomija Lietuvoje 1919–1923 metais." *Lietuvos istorijos metraštis* (1995): 84–97.

Rees, Lawrence. "How Curiosity Killed." Historynet, October 8, 2012, https://www.historynet.com/how-curiosity-killed.htm.

Richter, Klaus. "Antisemitismus und litauische Intelligentzija (1900–1914)." *Jahrbuch für Antisemitismusforschung* 21 (2012): 89–114.
Rosin, Josef. *Preserving our Litvak Heritage*. League City, TX: JewishGen, Inc., 2005.
Roskies, David G. "Jewish Cultural Life in the Vilna Ghetto." In *Lithuania and the Jews: The Holocaust Chapter: Symposium Presentations*, 33–44. Washington: Center for Advanced Holocaust Studies, USHMM, 2004.
Rossi, Lauren Faulkner. *Wehrmacht Priests: Nazism and the Nazi War of Annihilation*. Cambridge, MA: Harvard University Press, 2015.
Rubenstein, Joshua, and Ilya Altman, eds. *The Unknown Black Book: The Holocaust in the German-Occupied Soviet Territory*. Bloomington: Indiana University Press in association with USHMM, 2010.
Rudis, Gediminas. "Jungtinis antismetoninės opozicijos sąjūdis 1938–1939 metais." *Lietuvos istorijos metraštis* (1996): 185–215.
———. "Rašytojo atsiminimai apie pirmąjį sovietmetį." Unpublished manuscript.
Rukšėnas, Alfredas. "Kauno 2-asis pagalbinės policijos batalionas ir gyventojų žudynės Baltarusijoje." In *Holokaustas Lietuvoje 1941–1944 m.*, edited by Arūnas Bubnys, 424–469. Vilnius: LGGRTC, 2011.
———. "Kauno Tautinio darbo apsaugos, 2-ojo pagalbinės policijos tarnybų bataliono karių kolektyvinė biografija." PhD diss., Klaipėda University and Lithuanian Institute of History, 2013.
Rukšėnas, Kazys. Hitlerininkų politika Lietuvoje 1941–1944. Phd diss., Lithuanian Academy of Sciences, Institute of History, Vilnius, 1970.
———. "Dėl Lietuvos žydų gelbėjimo hitlerinės okupacijos metais (1941–1945)." *Lietuvos istorijos metrastis* (1978): 36–49.
Ryan, Allan A. *Quiet Neighbors: Prosecuting Nazi War Criminals in America*. San Diego: Harcourt Brace Jovanovich, 1984.
Sakaitė, Viktorija. "Žydų gelbėjimas." *Genocidas ir rezistencija* 2, no. 4 (1998): 81–103.
Sakaitė, Viktorija, comp., and Dalija Epšteinaitė, ed. *Gyvybę ir duoną nešančios rankos / Hands Bringing Life and Bread*. Vol. 3. Vilnius: Vilna Gaon Jewish Museum, 2005.
Sarcevičius, Saulius, Stanislovas Stasiulis, et al. *Nusikaltimų pėdsakai neišnyksta: masinės žudynės Panerių miške 1941–1944 metais*. Vilnius: LII, 2021.
Šarmaitis, Romas. "LKP (b) penktasis suvaziavimas." In *Revoliucinis judėjimas Lietuvje: straipsnių rinkinys*, edited by Romas Šarmaitis, 575–582. Vilnius: VPMLL, 1957.
Šeinius, Ignas. *Siegfried Immerselbe atsijaunina*. Kaunas: Sakalas, 1934.
———. *The Rejuvenation of Siegfried Immerselbe*. Translated by Albinas Baranauskas. New York: Manyland Books, 1965.
Senn, Alfred E. *Lithuania 1940: Revolution from Above*. Amsterdam: Rodopi, 2007.
———. *The Emergence of Modern Lithuania*. New York: Columbia University Press, 1959.
Šetkus, Benediktas. "Valstybinės kalbos mokymas Lietuvos žydų gimnazijose ir progimnazijose 1919–1940 metais." *Istorija* 4 (2017): 67–96.
———. "Kauno žydų gimnazija dėstomąja lietuvių kalba: vokiečių ir žydų konfrontacijos darinys." *Lituanistica* 65, no. 2 (2019): 74–87.

Shaer, Matthew. "The Words of a Young Jewish Poet Provoke Soul Searching in Lithuania." *Smithsonian,* November 2018. https://www.smithsonianmag.com/history/young-jewish-poet-words-provokes-soul-searching-lithuania-holocaust-180970540/.

Shaul, Elisheva. "Jewish Testimonies in Yad Vashem Archives as a Source for the Study of the Holocaust in Lithuania." Paper presented at IHC Conference "The Holocaust in Lithuania in the Focus of Modern History, Education and Justice," Vilnius, September 23–25, 2002.

Shner-Neshamit, Sara. "Lithuanian-Jewish Relations during World War II: History and Rhetoric." In *Bitter Legacy: Confronting the Holocaust in the USSR,* edited by Zvi Gitelman, 167–184. Bloomington: Indiana University Press, 1997.

Shoah Resource Center, Yad Vashem. "From the Diary of Eliezer Yerushalmi: The Ban on Births in the Shavli Ghetto, 1942–1943." Accessed July 23, 2023. https://www.yadvashem.org/odot_pdf/Microsoft%20Word%20-%205385.pdf.

Shochat, Azriel. "Jews, Lithuanians and Russians, 1939–1941." In *Jews and Non-Jews in Eastern Europe, 1918–1945,* edited by Bela Vago and George L. Mosse, 301–314. New York: John Wiley, 1974.

———. "The Beginnings of Antisemitism in Independent Lithuania." *Yad Vashem Studies* 2 (1958): 7–48.

Šiaučiūnaitė-Verbickienė, Jurgita. "Lietuvių ir žydų komunikacija viešojoje erdvėje: pažinimo paieškos." In *Lietuvos žydai: istorinė studija,* edited by Vladas Sirutavičius, Darius Staliūnas, and Jurgita Šiaučiūnaitė-Verbickienė, 387–402. Vilnius: baltos lankos, 2012.

———. "Ocherki istorii evreiskoi obshchiny Birzhaia." In *Evrei na karte Litvy. Birzhai: Problemy sokhraneniiya evreiskogo naslediiya i istoricheskoii pamyati,* edited by Irina Kopchenova, S. Amosova, L. Dreier, L. Lempertene et al..., 69–85. Moscow: Sefer, 2015.

———. "The Jews." In *The Peoples of the Grand Duchy of Lithuania,* edited by Grigorijus Potašenko, 57–68. Vilnius: Aidai, 2002.

———. "Žydų ir lietuvių abipusio pažinimo ir kultūrinio bendradarbiavimo atspirtys tarpukario Lietuvoje: priemonės ir rezultatai." In *Abipusis pažinimas: lietuvių ir žydų kultūriniai saitai,* edited by Jurgita Šiaučiūnaitė-Verbickienė, 16–50. Vilnius: Vilniaus universiteto leidykla, 2010.

———. *Žydai Lietuvos Didžiosios Kunigaikštystės visuomenėje: sambūvio aspektai.* Vilnius: Žara, 2009.

———. "The Jewish Living Space in the Grand Duchy of Lithuania: Tendencies and Ways of Its Formation." In *Jewish Space in Central and Eastern Europe,* edited by Larisa Lempertienė and Jurgita Šiaučiūnaitė-Verbickienė, 7–26. Newcastle: Cambridge Scholars Publishing, 2007.

———. "Vytauto Didžiojo 1388m. privilegija Brastos žydams. Nauji atsakymai į atsakytus klausimus." *Lietuvos istorijos metraštis* 2 (2021): 5–25.

Šikšnianas, Mantas. "Ypatingasis būrys ir masinės žudynės Paneriuose." In *Nusikaltimų pėdsakai neišnyksta: Masinės žudynės Panerių miške 1941–1944 metais,* compiled by Saulius Sarevičius and Stanislovas Stasiulis, edited by Nerijus Šepetys, 24–45. Vilnius: LII, 2021.

———. "Tarp masės ir individo: Vilniaus Ypatingasis būrys 1941–1945 m." *Genocidas ir rezistencija* 39, no. 1 (2016): 93–110.

Sirutavičius, Vladas. "'A Close, but Very Suspicious Stranger': Outbreaks of Antisemitism in Inter-War Lithuania." *Polin* 25 (2013): 245–262.

———. "Antisemitism in Inter-War Lithuania: An Analysis of Two Cases." *Jahrbuch für Antisemitismusforschung* 21 (2012): 133–143.

———. "Antisemitizmo proveržiai." In *Lietuvos žydai: istorinė studija*, edited by Vladas Sirutavičius, Darius Staliūnas, and Jurgita Šiaučiūnaitė-Verbickienė, 403–416. Vilnius: baltos lankos, 2012.

———. "Katalikų Bažnyčia ir modernaus lietuvių antisemitizmo genezė." *Lietuvos Katalikų mokslo akademija. Metraštis* 14 (1999): 69–75.

———. "Valdžios politika žydų atžvilgiu." In *Lietuvos žydai: istorinė studija*, edited by Sirutavičius, Vladas, Darius Staliūnas, and Jurgita Šiaučiūnaitė-Verbickienė, 297–322. Vilnius: baltos lankos, 2012.

Skrupskelienė, Alina, and Česlovas Grincevičius, eds. *Juozas Brazaitis; Raštai*. Vol. 6, *Vienų vieni: rezistencija*. Chicago: Į laisvę fondas, 1985.

Slepyan, Kenneth. "The Soviet Partisan Movement and the Holocaust." *Holocaust and Genocide Studies* 14, no. 1 (2000): 1–27.

———. *Stalin's Guerillas: Soviet Partisans in World War II*. Lawrence, KS: University of Kansas Press, 2006.

Smokowski, Wincenty. "Wspomnienie Trok w 1822 r.1" *Athenaeum* 5 (1841): 157–180.

Snyder, Timothy. "He Welcomed the Nazis and Saved Jews." New York Review, December 21, 2009. http://www.nybooks.com/blogs/nyrblog/2009/dec/21/he-welcomed-the-nazis-and-saved-jews/.

———. *Black Earth: The Holocaust as History and Warning*. New York: Tim Duggan Books, 2015.

———. *Bloodlands: Europe between Stalin and Hitler*. New York: Basic Books, 2010.

———. *The Reconstruction of Nations: Poland, Ukraine, Lithuania, Belarus, 1569–1999*. New Haven: Yale University Press, 2004.

———. "Commemorative Causality." *Modernism/modernity* 20, no. 1 (2013): 77–93.

Solonski, Dov. "A Smile from the Height of the Gallows." In *The Jewish Resistance: The History of the Jewish Partisans in Lithuania and White Russia during the Nazi Occupation 1940–1945*, edited by Lester Eckman and Chaim Lazar, 272–274. New York: Shengold, 1977.

Stahel, David. "Radicalizing Warfare: The German Command and the Failure of Operation Barbarossa." In *Nazi Policy on the Eastern Front, 1941*, edited by Alex J. Kay, Jeff Rutherford, and David Stahel, 19–44. Rochester, NY: University of Rochester Press, 2012.

Staliūnas, Darius. "Antisemitic Tension during the 1905 Revolution in Lithuania." *Jahrbuch für Antisemitismusforschung* 21 (2012): 54–88.

———. "Collaboration of Lithuanians and Jews during the Elections to the First and Second Dumas." In *A Pragmatic Alliance: Jewish-Lithuanian Political Cooperation at *the Beginning of the Twentieth Century*, edited by Darius Staliūnas and Vladas Sirutavičius, 45–75. Budapest: CEU Press, 2011.

———. "Dusetos, Easter 1905: The Story of One Pogrom." *Journal of Baltic Studies* 43, no. 4 (2012): 495–514.

———. "Lietuvių ir žydų politinio bendradarbiavimo epizodai XX a. pradžioje." In *Lietuvos žydai: istorinė studija*, edited by Vladas Sirutavičius, Darius Staliūnas, and Jurgita Šiaučiūnaitė-Verbickienė, 271–282. Vilnius: baltos lankos, 2012.

———. "Lithuanian Antisemitism in the Late Nineteenth and Early Twentieth Centuries." *Polin* 25 (2013): 135–149.

———. "Rusų kalba kaip lietuvių ir žydų komunikacijos priemonė: laikraštis *Naš kraj* (1914)." In *Abipusis pažinimas: lietuvių ir žydų kultūriniai saitai*, edited by Jurgita Šiaučiūnaitė-Verbickienė, 162–181. Vilnius: Vilniaus universiteto leidykla, 2010.

———. "The Lithuanian-Jewish Dialogue in Petrograd in 1917." In *A Pragmatic Alliance: Jewish-Lithuanian Political Cooperation at the Beginning of the Twentieth Century*, edited by Darius Staliūnas and Vladas Sirutavičiius, 231–243. Budapest: CEU Press, 2011.

———. "Žydų istorija lietuviškosios istoriografijos kontekste." In *Abipusis pažinimas: lietuvių ir žydų kultūriniai saitai*, edited by Jurgita Šiaučiūnaitė-Verbickienė, 120–133. Vilnius: Vilniaus universiteto leidykla, 2010.

———. *Enemies for a Day: Antisemitism and Anti-Jewish Violence in Lithuania under the Tsars*. Budapest: CEU Press, 2015.

Stang, Knut. *Kollaboration und Massenmord: die litauische Hilfspolizei, das Rollkommando Hamann und die Ermordung der litauischen Juden*. Frankfurt am Main: Peter Lang, 1996.

Stanislawski, Michael. *Tsar Nicholas I and the Jews: The Transformation of Jewish Society in Russia 1825–1855*. Philadelphia: The Jewish Publication Society of America, 1983.

Stankeras, Petras. *Lietuvių policija 1941–1944 metais*. Vilnius: LGGRTC, 1998.

Stasiulis, Stanislovas. "1941 m. kovo 19 d. LAF atsišaukimas: provokacija, falsifikatas ar tikras dokumentas?" *Lietuvos istorijos studijos* 38 (2016): 72–83.

———. "The Holocaust in Lithuania: The Key Characteristics of Its History, and the Key Issues in Historiography and Cultural Memory." *East European Politics and Societies: and Cultures* 34, no. 1 (February 2020): 264–265.

Statiev, Alexander. "Motivations and Goals of Soviet Deportations in the Western Borderlands." *The Journal of Strategic Studies* 28, no. 6 (2005): 977–1003.

———. Alexander Statiev. "Soviet Partisan Violence against Soviet Civilians: Targeting Their Own." *Europe-Asia Studies* 66, no. 9 (2014): 1525–1552.

———. *The Soviet Counterinsurgency in the Western Borderlands*. Cambridge: Cambridge University Press, 2010.

Stoliarovas, Andriejus. "Lietuvių pagalbinės policijos (apsaugos) 12–asis batalionas." *Karo archyvas* 23, no. 1 (2008): 263–315.

Stončius, Justas, Hektoras Vitkus, and Zigmas Vitkus. *16–osios Lietuviškos šaulių divizijos kariai žydai: istorija ir atminimas*. Klaipėda: Klaipėdos universiteto Baltijos regiono istorijos ir archeologijos institutas, 2021.

———. *Neapykantos ribos: antisemitizas Lietuvoje 1944–1990 metais*. Klaipėda: Klaipėdos universiteto leidykla, 2022.

———. "Žydų verslai Palangoje tarpukario laikotarpiu." In *Palangos žydai: išnykusi miesto bendruomenės dalis*, edited by Hektoras Vitkus, 113–127. Klaipėda: DRUKA, 2017.

Strazhas, Abba. "Das nationale Erwachen des litauischen Volkes und Judenheit." *Acta Universitatis Stockholmiensis-Studia Baltica Stockholmiensia* 2 (1985): 173–185.

Streikus, Arūnas. "Bažnyčios institucija nacių okupacijos laikotarpiu Lietuvoje." komisjia.lt. Accessed May 4, 2021. https://www.komisija.lt/wp-content/uploads/2016/06/A.Streikus_Baznycia-naciu-okupac.-laikotarpiu.pdf.

Strelcovas, Simonas. "Pabėgeliai, vizos, gelbėtojai?" *Darbai ir dienos* 47 (2007): 62–73.

———. *Antrojo Pasaulinio karo pabėgeliai Lietuvoje 1939–1940 metais*. Šiauliai: VšĮ Šiaulių universiteto leidykla, 2010.

———. *Geri, blogi, vargdieniai: Č. Sugihara ir Antrojo pasaulinio karo pabėgeliai Lietuvoje*. Vilnius: Versus, 2018.

Subotić, Jelena. *Yellow Star, Red Star: Holocaust Remembrance after Communism*. Ithaca: Cornell University Press, 2019.

Šukys, Julija. "Ona Šimaitė and the Vilnius Ghetto: An Unwritten Memoir." *Lituanus* 54, no. 2 (2008): 5–25.

———. *Epistophelia: Writing the Life of Ona Šimaitė*. Lincoln: University of Nebraska Press, 2012.

———. *Siberian Exile: Blood, War and a Granddaughter's Reckoning*. Lincoln: University of Nebraska Press, 2017.

Sutton, Karen. *The Massacre of the Jews of Lithuania*. Jerusalem: Gefen, 2008.

Sužiedėlis, Saulius. "The Lithuanian Peasantry of Trans-Niemen Lithuania, 1807–1864: A Study of Social, Economic and Cultural Change." PhD diss., University of Kansas, 1977.

———. "'Listen, the Jews Are Ruling Us Now': Antisemitism and National Conflict During the First Year of Soviet Occupation." *Polin* 25 (2013): 305–333.

———. "Schwierige Erinnerung. Litauen: Holokaust und Opferkonkurrenz." *Osteuropa* 68, no. 6 (2018): 101–114.

———. Review of *Kollaboration und Massenmord: die litauische Hilfspolizei, das Rollkommando Hamann und die Ermordung der litauischen Juden*, by Knut Stang. *Journal of Baltic Studies* 29, no. 1 (1998): 84–88.

———. "A Century After: The 'Great Diet of Vilnius' Revisited." *Journal of Baltic Studies* 38, no. 4 (2007): 419–432.

———. "Foreign Saviors, Native Disciples: Perspectives on Collaboration in Lithuania, 1940–1945." In *Collaboration and Resistance During the Holocaust: Belarus, Estonia, Latvia and Lithuania*, edited by David Gaunt, Paul A. Levine, and Laura Palosuo, 313–359. Frankfurt am Main: Peter Lang, 2004.

———. "Icchokas Meras and the Holocaust: Terror and Salvation in Contemporary Lithuanian Literature." *Lituanus* 27, no. 3 (1981): 5–7.

———. "Lietuvos Katalikų bažnyčia ir Holokaustas kaip istorinių tyrimų objektas." *Lietuvos Katalikų mokslo akademija. Metraštis* 14 (1999): 121–134.

———. "The Historical Sources for Antisemitism in Lithuania and Jewish-Lithuanian Relations during the 1930s." In *The Vanished World of Lithuanian Jews*, edited by Alvydas Nikžentaitis, Stefan Schreiner, and Darius Staliūnas, 119–154. Amsterdam: Rodopi, 2004.

———. "The Military Mobilization Campaigns of 1943 and 1944 in German-Occupied Lithuania: Contrasts in Resistance and Collaboration." *Journal of Baltic Studies* 21, no. 1 (1990): 33–52.

———. "Užnemunės miestų ir miestelių socialekonominės problemos XIX amžiaus pirmojoje pusėje (iki 1864 m. reformos)." In *Lituanistikos instituto 1977 metų suvažiavimo darbai*, edited by Janina K. Reklaitis, 93–105. Chicago: Lituanistikos institutas, 1979.

———. "Vilniaus klausimas ir lietuvių-lenkų konfliktas ketvirto dešimtmečio krizės ir Antrojo pasaulinio karo kontekste." In *Lietuva ir Lenkija XX amžiaus geopolitinėje vaizduotėje*, edited by Anžej Pukšto and Giedrė Milerytė, 155–198. Kaunas: Vytauto Didžiojo universitetas, 2012.

———. "Baltische Erinnerungen und der Vernichtungskrieg 1941–1945." In *Deutsche Besatzung in der Sowjetunion 1941–1944: Vernichtungskrieg, Reaktionen, Erinnerung*, edited by Babette Quinkert and Jörg Morré, 344–363. Paderborn: Ferdinand Schöningh, 2014.

———. "Lithuanian Collaboration during the Second World War: Past Realities, Present Perceptions." In *"Kollaboration" in Nordosteuropa: Erscheinungen und Deutungen im 20. Jahrhundert*, edited by Joachim Tauber, 140–163. Wiesbaden: Harrassowitz Verlag, 2006.

———. "The International Commission for the Evaluation of the Crimes of the Nazi and Soviet Occupation Regimes in Lithuania: successes, challenges, perspectives." *Journal of Baltic Studies* 48, no. 1 (2018): 103–116.

———. "Neighbors, Rivals, Enemies, Victims: Lithuanian Perceptions of Jews in Crisis and War." In *Distrust, Animosity, and Solidarity: Jews and Non-Jews during the Holocaust in the USSR*, edited by Christoph Dieckmann and Arkadi Zeltser, 165–211. Jerusalem: Yad Vashem, 2021.

Svarauskas, Artūras. "Kodėl dalyvauta ir už ką balsuota rinkimuose į Liaudies seimą 1940 metais?" *Lietuvos istorijos metraštis* 2 (2018): 101–128.

———. *Krikščioniškoji demokratija nepriklausomoje Lietuvoje (1918–1940: politinė galia ir jos ribos*. Vilnius: LII, 2014.

Szarota, Tomasz. *U progu zagłady: zajęcia antyżydowskie i pogromy w okupowanej Europie: Warszawa, Paryż, Amsterdam, Antwerpia, Kowno*. Warsaw: Sic!, 2000.

Tarulis, Albertas. "Die Juden im Wirtschaftsleben Litauens." *Osteuropa* 6 (1938): 383–392.

Tatarūnas, Linas. "Žydai Lietuvoje pirmosios sovietų okupacijos metais (1940–1941 m.)" *Istorija* 73, no. 1 (2009): 37–50.

Tauber, Joachim. "Garsden, 24 Juni 1941." *Annaberger Annalen* 5 (1997): 117–134.

———. "Hitler, Stalin und der Antisemitismus in Litauen 1939–1941." *Jahrbuch für Antisemitismusforschung* 21 (2012): 166–182.

———. *Arbeit als Hoffnung: jüdische Ghettos in Litauen 1941–1944*. Quellen und Darstellungen zur Zeitgeschichte 108. Berlin: De Gruyter Oldenbourg, 2015.

Tininis, Vytautas. *Sovietinė Lietuva ir jos veikėjai*. Vilnius: Enciklopedija, 1994.

Tippner, Anja. "Conflicting Memories, Conflicting Stories: Masha Rol'nikaite's Novel and the Soviet Culture of Holocaust Remembrance." *East European Jewish Affairs* 48, no. 3 (2018): 372–390.

———. "The Writings of a Soviet Anne Frank? Masha Rol'nikaite's Holocaust Memoir *I Have to Tell* and Its Place in Soviet Literature." In *Search & Research, Lectures and Papers 19: Representations of the Holocaust in Soviet Literature and Film*, 59–80. Jerusalem: Yad Vashem, 2013.

Toleikis, Vytautas. "Repress, Reassess, Remember: Jewish Heritage in Lithuania." *Eurozine*, November 27, 2008. http://www.eurozine.com/articles/2008-11-27-toleikis-en.html.

———. "Žydai Vyskupo Motiejaus Valančiaus raštuose." *Darbai ir Dienos* 70 (2018): 179–233.

Tomkiewicz, Monika. *Zbrodnia w Ponarach 1941–1944*. Warsaw: Instytut Pamięci Narodowej, 2008.

Trunk, Isaiah. *Judenrat: The Jewish Councils of Eastern Europe under Nazi Occupation*. New York: Macmillan, 1972.

Truska, Liudas. "Litauische Historiographie über den Holocaust in Litauen." In *Holocaust in Litauen: Krieg, Judenmorde und Kollaboration im Jahre 1941*, edited by Vincas Bartusevičius, Joachim Tauber and Wolfram Wette, 264–268. Köln: Böhlau, 2003.

———. *Antanas Smetona ir jo laikai*. Vilnius: Valstybinis leidybos centras, 1996.

———. "Tikros ir primestos kaltės: žydai ir lietuviai pirmuoju sovietmečiu." *Darbai ir dienos* 34 (2003): 285–320.

Truska, Liudas, and Vygantas Vareikis. *Holokausto prielaidos. Antisemitizmas Lietuvoje XIX antroji pusė-1941 birželis. The Preconditions for the Holocaust: Antisemitism in Lithuania. Second Half of the Nineteenth Century–June 1941*. Vilnius: margi raštai, 2004.

Truska, Liudas, Arvydas Anušauskas, and Inga Petravičiūtė. *Sovietinis saugumas Lietuvoje 1940–1953 metais*. Vilnius: LGGRTC, 1999.

USHMM. *Hidden History of the Kovno Ghetto*. Little, Brown and Company: Boston, 1997.

Udrėnas, Nerijus. "Book, Bread, Cross, and Whip: Imperial Russia and the Construction of Lithuanian Identity." PhD diss., Brandeis University, 2000.

Vaičenonis, Jonas. "Prisiekė Adonojo vardu: Žydai pirmosios Lietuvos Respublikos kariuomenėje." *Darbai ir dienos* 34 (2003): 273–283.

Vaišnora, Juozas. "Žydų klausimas." *Židinys* 11 (1937): 418–427.

Valkauskas, Raimundas. "Žydų tautinės autonomijos klausimas." *Lietuvos istorijos studijos* 3 (1996): 57–74.

Valsonokas, Rudolfas. *Klaipėdos problema*. Klaipėda: Rytas, 1932.
van Voren, Robert. *Undigested Past. The Holocaust in Lithuania*. Amsterdam: Rodopi, 2011.
Vanagaitė, Rūta. *Mūsiškiai*. Vilnius: Alma littera, 2015.
Vanagaitė, Rūta, and Efraim Zuroff. *Our People: Discovering Lithuania's Hidden Holocaust*. Lanham, MD: Rowman and Littlefield, 2020.
Vareikis, Vygantas. "Tarp Valančiaus ir Kudirkos: žydų ir lietuvių santykiai katalikiškosios kultūros kontekste." *Lietuvos Katalikų mokslo akademija. Metraštis* 14 (1999): 79–96.
———. "Žemaičiai ir žydai: sugyvenimas, komunikacija, svetimumas." In *Žemaitijos žydų kultūros paveldo atspindžiai*, edited by Hektoras Vitkus and Jolanta Skurdauskienė, 14–34. Klaipėda: Klaipėdos universiteto leidykla, 2019.
Vaskela, Gediminas. "Žydai Lietuvos ūkio struktūroje." In *Lietuvos žydai: istorinė studija*, edited by Vladas Sirutavičius, Darius Staliūnas, and Jurgita Šiaučiūnaitė-Verbickienė, 329–346. Vilnius: baltos lankos, 2012.
———. "Lietuvių ir žydų santykiai visuomenės modernėjimo ir socialinės sferos politinio reguliavimo aspektais (XX a.pirmoji pusė)." In *Žydai Lietuvos ekonominėje-socialinėje struktūroje: tarp tarpininko ir konkurento*, edited by Vladas Sirutavičius and Darus Staliūnas. Vilnius: Lietuvos istorijos institutas, 2006: 133–176.
Veisaitė, Irena. "Pajutau, kad ji man—likimo sesuo." In Matilda Olkinaitė, *Atrakintas dienoraštis: kūrybos rinktinė*, edited by Mindaugas Kvietkauskas, 49–53. Vilnius: Lietuvių literatūros ir tautosakos institutas, 2019.
Venclauskas, Linas, ed. *Šiaurės Kasablanka. Kaunas 1939–1940: Parodos katalogas*. Kaunas: Sugiharos fondas, 2018.
———. "Lietuvos įvaizdžiai antinacinėje lietuvių spaudoje." *Genocidas ir rezistencija* 15, no. 1 (2004): 68–85.
———. "Stereotipų mįslės: antisemitizmas Lietuvos ir Prancūzijos spaudoje 1940–1942 metais." *Darbai ir dienos* 34 (2003): 321–348.
———. *Tekstų byla: lietuvių antisemitinis diskursas nuo XIX a. antros pusės iki 1940 metų*. Vilnius: Versus, 2022.
Verschik, Anna. "The Lithuanian-Language Periodicals *Mūsų garsas* (1924–1925) and *Apžvalga* (1935–1940): A Sociolinguistic Evolution." *Polin* 25 (2013): 293–303.
Vileišis, Petras. [pseud. Ramojus]. *Musu žydai, ir kaip nū anu turime gitiesi*. New York: Lietuwiszkojo Balso, 1886.
Vincė, Laima. "The Silenced Muse: The Life of a Murdered Jewish Lithuanian Poet." *Deep Baltic: Inside the Lands Between*, May 8, 2018. https://deepbaltic.com/2018/05/08/the-silenced-muse-the-life-of-a-murdered-jewish-lithuanian-poet/.
Vitkus, Aleksandras, and Chaimas Bargmanas. *Holokaustas Žemaitijoje: enciklopedinis žinynas* Vilnius: Mokslo ir enciklopedijų leidybos centras, 2016.
———. *Vilkijos getas 1941 metais*. Vilnius: Mokslo ir enciklopedijų leidybos centras, 2019.
Vitkus, Hektoras. "Holokausto atminties raida Lietuvoje." PhD diss., Klaipėda University, 2008.

———. "Memorialinių vietų veiksnys holokausto atminimo kultūroje: sampratos gairės ir tyrimo metodai." *Genocidas ir rezistencija* 9, no. 1 (2006): 86–115.

———. Hektoras Vitkus, "The Use of the Holocaust Memory in Soviet Lithuania: An Ideological Aspect." In *Holokaustas nacių okupuotose Rytų ir Vakarų valstybėse: tyrimai ir atmintis / The Holocaust in the Eastern and Western European States: Occupied by the Nazis: Studies and Memory*, edited by Vygantas Vareikis, 297–310. Kaunas: Spindulys, 2017.

Vitkus, Zigmas. *Atminties miškas: Paneriai istorijoje, kultūroje ir politikoje*. Vilnius: Lapas, 2022.

———. "Smulkiojo verslo lituanizacija tarpukario Lietuvoje: ideologija ir praktika." In *Žydai Lietuvos ekonominėje-socialinėje struktūroje: tarp tarpininko ir konkurento*, edited by Vladas Sirutavičius and Darius Staliūnas, 177–216. Vilnius: LII, 2006.

Vodzinskis, Marcinas. "Chasidai ir *mitnagedai*." In *Žydai Lietuvoje: Istorija. Kultūra. Paveldas*, compiled by Larisa Lempertienė and Jurgita Šiaučiūnaitė-Verbickienė, 121–124. Vilnius: R. Paknio leidykla, 2009.

Vodzinskis, Marcinas. "Socialinis ir kultūrinis bendruomenės modernėjimas." In *Žydai Lietuvoje: Istorija. Kultūra. Paveldas*, compiled by Larisa Lempertienė and Jurgita Šiaučiūnaitė-Verbickienė, 131–133. Vilnius: R. Paknio leidykla, 2009.

Volbikaitė, Goda. "Jidišakalbių literatūrinių sambūrių savikūra tarpukario Kaune: *Vispe ir Mir Aleyn*." *Darbai ir dienos* 57 (2012): 65–84.

Weeks, Theodore. "The Vilnius and Kaunas Ghettos and the Fate of Lithuanian Jewry, 1941–1945." *Polin* 25 (2013): 357–377.

———. *Vilnius between Nations, 1795–2000*. DeKalb, IL: NIU Press, 2015.

Weiss-Wendt, Anton. *Murder without Hatred: Estonians and the Holocaust*. Syracuse: Syracuse University Press, 2009.

Wette, Wolfram. *Karl Jäger: Mörder der litauischen Juden*. Frankfurt am Main: Fischer Taschenbuch Verlag, 2011.

Wierzbicki, Marek. *Polacy i żydzi w zaborze sowieckim: Stosunki polsko-żydowskie na ziemiach pólnocno-wschodnich II RP pod okupacją sowiecką (1939–1941)*. Warsaw: Fronda, 2007.

Yla, Stasys. *Žmonės ir žvėrys dievų miške: kaceto pergyvenimai*. Putnam, CT: Immaculata, 1951.

———. *Komunizmas Lietuvoje*. Edited with an introduction by Nerijus Šepetys. Vilnius: Aidai, 2012.

Zaksas, Irmija. *Rasizmas ir eugenika buržuazinėje Lietuvoje*. Vilnius: VPMLL, 1959.

Zalkin, Mordechai. "Kultūrinės Vilniaus žydų erdvės." In *Lietuvos žydai: istorinė studija*, edited by Vladas Sirutavičius, Darius Staliūnas, and Jurgita Šiaučiūnaitė-Verbickienė, 417–424. Vilnius: baltos lankos, 2012.

———. "Lietuvos žydų bendruomenės kultūrinės transformacijos." In *Lietuvos žydai: istorinė studija*, edited by Vladas Sirutavičius, Darius Staliūnas, and Jurgita Šiaučiūnaitė-Verbickienė, 347–356. Vilnius: baltos lankos, 2012.

———. "Žydų mokyklų idėjinė diferenciacija." In *Lietuvos žyda: istorinė studija*, edited by Vladas Sirutavičius, Darius Staliūnas, and Jurgita Šiaučiūnaitė-Verbickienė, 357–370. Vilnius: baltos lankos, 2012.

———. "'Ant žodžių tilto': žydų susitikimas su lietuvių kultūra tarpukario Lietuvoje." In *Abipusis pažinimas: lietuvių ir žydų kultūriniai saitai*, edited by Jurgita Šiaučiūnaitė-Verbickienė, 53–68. Vilnius: Vilniaus universiteto leidykla, 2010.

———. "Lithuanian Jewry and the Concept of 'East European Jewry.'" *Polin* 25 (2013): 57–70.

———. "Lithuanian Jewry and the Lithuanian National Movement." In *A Pragmatic Alliance: Jewish-Lithuanian Political Cooperation at the Beginning of the 20th Century*, edited by Vladas Sirutavičius and Darius Staliūnas, 21–44. Budapest: CEU Press, 2011.

———. "Sharunas, Prince of Dainava, in a Jewish Gown: The Cultural and Social Role of Hebrew and Yiddish Translations of Lithuanian Literature and Poetry in Interwar Lithuania." *Jahrbuch für Antisemitismusforschung* 21 (2012): 149–165.

———. "Tarp Haskalos ir tradicionalizmo." In *Lietuvos žydai: istorinė studija*, edited by Vladas Sirutavičius, Darius Staliūnas, and Jurgita Šiaučiūnaitė-Verbickienė, 205–217. Vilnius: baltos lankos, 2012.

———. *Modernizing Jewish Education in Nineteenth-Century Eastern Europe: The School as the Shrine of Jewish Enlightenment*. Studies in Jewish History and Culture 50. Leiden: Brill, 2016.

———. "*Mūsų gydytojas*: The Social and Cultural Aspects of the Jewish Medical Doctor in Lithuanian Countryside before the Second World War." In *Jewish Space in Central and Eastern Europe: Day-to-Day History*, edited by Jurgita Šiaučinūnaitė-Verbickienė and Larisa Lempertienė, 175–184. Newcastle: Cambridge Scholars Publishing, 2007.

Žalys, Vytautas. *Kova dėl identiteto: kodėl Lietuvai nesisekė Klaipėdoje tarp 1923–1939. Ringen um Identität. warum Litauen zwischen 1923 und 1939 im Memelgebiet keinen Erfolg hatte*. Lüneburg: Verlag Nordostdeutsches Kulturwerk, 1993.

Žalys, Vytautas, and Alfonsas Eidintas. *Lithuania in European Politics: The Years of the First Republic, 1918–1940*. Edited by Edvardas Tuskenis. New York: St. Martin's Press, 1997.

Zarasų krašto žydų istorija. "Žydų karių, dalyvavusių Lietuvos atvadavime sąjungos Zarasų skyyriaus valdybos nariai." Accessed March 8, 2019. www.zarasu-zydai.lt/index.php/project/zydu-kariu-dalyvavusiu-lietuvos-atvadavime-sajungos-zarasu-skyriaus-valdybos-nariai-1934–m/.

Žeimantas, Vytautas. *Procesas nesibaigia*. Vilnius: Mintis, 1988.

———. *Teisingumas reikalauja*. Vilnius: Mintis, 1984.

Zeltser, Arkadi. *Unwelcome Memory: Holocaust Monuments in the Soviet Union*. Translated from the Russian by A. S. Brown. Jerusalem: Yad Vashem: 2018.

Žepkaitė, Regina. *Vilniaus istorijos atkarpa: 1939 m. spalio 27 d.-1940 m. birželio 15 d*. Vilnius: Mokslas, 1990.

Zingeris, Emanuelis, ed. *Atminties dienos: The Days of Memory*. Vilnius: baltos lankos, 1995.

Zizas, Rimantas. "Bakaloriškių sunaikinimas." In *Lietuva Antrajame pasauliniame kare*, edited by Arvydas Anušauskas and Česlovas Laurinavičius, 489–506. Vilnius: LII, 2007.

———. "Raudonųju partizanų ir Pietryčių Lietuvos kaimų savisaugos ginkluoti konfliktai (Part One)." *Genocidas ir rezistencija* 15, no. 1 (2004): 148–156.

———. "Raudonųju partizanų ir Pietryčių Lietuvos kaimų savisaugos ginkluoti konfliktai (Part Two)." *Genocidas ir rezistencija* 16, no. 2 (2004): 151–159.

———. "Tarpnacionalinė situacija Vokietijos okupuotoje Lietuvoje 1941–1944 metais." In *Epochas jungiantis nacionalizmas: tautos (de)konstravimas tarpukario, sovietmečio ir posovietmečio Lietuvoje*, edited by Česlovas Laurinavičius, 57–130. Vilnius: LII, 2013.

———. "Vietinė savisauga (savigyna) Lietuvoje nacių Vokietijos okupacijos metais (1941–1944)." *Genocidas ir rezistencija* 11, no. 1 (2002): 69–94.

———. "Žudynių Kaniūkuose pedsakais." *Genocidas ir rezistencija* 11, no. 1 (2002): 149–165.

———. *Sovietiniai partizanai Lietuvoje 1941–1944 m*. Vilnius: LII, 2014.

Žukaitė, Veronika. "Bandymai mokyti žydus lietuvių kalbos tarpukario Lietuvoje: mokomųjų priemonių tyrimas." In *Abipusis pažinimas: lietuvių ir žydų kultūriniai saitai*, edited by Jurgita Šiaučiūnaitė-Verbickienė, 312–331. Vilnius: Vilniaus universiteto leidykla.

INDEX

A
Abakonis, Jonas, 100
Ablinga, 160
Abramovičius, Solomonas, 473n186, 476n192
Abramson, Aron, 208
Abramson, Fanya, Lizas's aunt, 230
Abramson, Ida, Lizas's aunt, 230
Abramson, Liza, 8, 128–29, 229–30, 383, 464
Abromovich, Berel M. (Abramovičius, Berelis), 351
Abwehr (German military intelligence), 70n193, 154, 260, 444
Adamkus, Valdas, 92, 531–32, 537, 545
Adutiškis, 250
Africa, 44, 67, 234
Agluona, 554
Aidai, newspaper, 39n96, 566
Aidai/Naujasis židinys, magazine, 135n137, 566
Akiračiai, magazine, 74n207, 92n5, 187n69, 300n117, 438n86, 506n64, 566
Akiva, Zionist youth organization, 83
Akmenė, 223, 249, 354
Alantas, Vytautas (pseud. Jakševičius, Vytautas Benjaminas), 74, 154
Aleksa, Jonas, 416
Aleksandravičius, Egidijus, 509, 541n146
Alekseyevka, 401
Aleksotas, 179, 345, 348, 442
Alexander Jagiellon (Aleksandras Jogailaitis), Grand Duke, 10
Alexander I, Emperor, 16
Alexander II, Emperor, 17
Alexander III, Emperor, 18
Alexievich, Svetlana, 394
Algemayner Yidisher Arbeter Bund (General Jewish Workers' Union). *See* Bund
Algeria, 467
Alimas, Povilas, 234

Alissandrakis, Costas, 539
Aliten. *See* Alytus
Allen, Jr., Charles R., 506
Allies (Western Allies), 38, 363, 379, 401, 451–54, 479–80, 535
Alovė, 214
All-Union Party. *See* AUCP
Alperavičius, Boruchas, 275
Alperavičius, Simonas, 556n136
Alsėdžiai, 249, 422, 424n44, 472
Altman, Ilya, 257n30, 466n170, 467, 469n177, 472n183
Alytus (Olita/Aliten/Alite), xv, 117, 158, 160–61, 174, 192, 214–15, 241, 250, 265–66, 285, 317, 449, 516n94, 518, 553, 555–56
Ambrazevičius-Brazaitis, Juozas, 171, 176, 185, 195–96, 412, 415, 435, 506
America, 126, 138, 152, 467, 501
American Association for the Advancement of Slavic Studies (AAASS), 523n112
American Civil War, xi
American Jewish Joint Distribution Committee (Joint), 48, 49n122, 126
AMO (Anti-Fascist Military Organization), 382. *See also* Jewish Anti-Fascist Committee
Ancoli-Barbasch, Esther, 364
Andrašiūnas, Jonas, 91
Andrijauskas, Alfredas, 3
Anschluss, 74n206
Antanašė estate, 227, 254
Anykščiai, 189, 248
Anykščių šilelis resort, 75
Apžvalga, newspaper, 48, 51, 75, 78–79, 98, 566
Arab-Israeli War, 402
Arad, Yitzhak, 188, 190, 227, 313n149, 321, 325n5, 331, 333–34, 388, 391, 395, 403, 510, 525, 532–35, 537, 566

Arbeter Bund. *See* Bund
Arbeter Shtime, Di, newspaper, 22
Arenstamm, a policeman, 381
Ariogala, 222, 250, 274, 277, 280, 553, 555
Arkis, a Jew from Ylakiai, 233
Armenians, 554
Armia Krajowa (Home Army), 392–93, 395–96, 398, 400, 453, 499, 535
Aronovich, Aron, 392
Aronshtam, Tankhum, 350
Ashkelon, 530
Ashkenazi Jews, 9, 69
Ashmyany (Oszmiana), xi, 324, 331–34, 562
Association of Former Ghetto and Concentration Camp Inmates, 536n136
Association of Jewish Soldiers of Lithuania's Independence Wars (LŽKS), 48, 56, 71, 79, 85–86, 133, 203, 297, 498
Association of Lithuanian Jews, 54, 483, 496, 522
Astravyets (Ostrowiec), 562
Ateitis, journal, 33, 436
Ateitis, organization, 58
Atžalynas, youth paper, 454
AUCP (B) (All-Union Communist Party (Bolsheviks), 105, 113, 489
Audronis, Antanas, 214, 449
Augustovo plan, 384n145
Augustów region, 384
Aukštadvaris, 293, 476
Aukštieji Šančiai, 179, 181, 341, 348
Aukštoji Panemunė, 298
Aunt Janina (Bek's aunt), 341
Auschwitz, 237, 349, 350n55, 359, 457, 514–15, 526
Aušeklis, a Jew from Ylakiai, 233
Aušra, newspaper, 66, 566
Aušra Museum, 352
Aušrotas, Bronius, 154
Austria, 9, 13, 35, 74n206, 307, 339, 415, 443n97, 483, 526–27
Austria-Hungary, 35, 415
Austrian Gedenkdienst volunteer program, 527
Auszra, newspaper, 32n72, 566
Avengers, resistance unit, 390, 392
Avin, Agnieška, 518
Axis states, 73, 153, 392, 511

B
Babrauninkai, 398
Babtai, 250, 267, 270, 347, 552, 556
Bačiūnai, 353–54
Bačkis, Stasys, 151n168
Baisiogala, 280
Bajorai, 253
Bak, Daniela, 377
Bak, Samuel, and his parents, 328n9, 338–39, 341, 375, 377, 473–74
Bakaloriškiai, 400
Baker, Andrew, xii, 534n134
Bakers' Company, 186, 187n69
Balbieriškis, 265, 279
Balbierzyszki, a pharmacist, 369
Balkans, 455
Balkelis, Tomas, 36n84, 38n94, 40n99, 88
Balsienė, Ona, 463n160
Baltics (Baltic States), vii, xiii, xv, 13, 37n91, 43n106, 58n144, 75, 90, 95, 97, 105–6, 122, 134–35, 137, 142n151, 149–50, 153–55, 157, 158n1, 162–63, 165, 178, 191–92, 194, 198, 237, 239, 260, 318, 448–49, 499–500, 503–4, 511, 515, 517, 520, 523–26, 537, 546
Baltic Oil (Baltöl), company, 356
Baltic Sea, 165, 357, 363, 449
Baltic Red Army, 148
Baltic Way, demonstration, 503
Baltoji Vokė, 336
Baltrušaitis, Vladas, 227
Baltruška, Povilas (Baltrushka, Pavel), 108–9
Baltušis-Žemaitis, Feliksas, 401
Balutis, Bronius, 99n30
Balys, Jonas, 69
Baran, Rivka & Shlomo, 484
Baranauskas, Albinas, 72n199
Baranauskas, Boleslovas, 187n69, 197n96, 227n162, 504
Baranavichy, 19
Barauskas, Albinas, 396
Barbarossa, Operation, 157–58, 159n4, 161–62, 208
Barkauskas, J., 299n166
Barzda, a Lieutenant, 275, 277, 298, 443
Basel, 21
Bašinskas, Gediminas, 94n10, 116n83, 146
Batakiai, 248

Index 601

Batory University. *See* Stefan Batory University
Battle of Grunwald, 502n56
Bauer, Yehuda, 92n6, 514, 517, 526
Bavaria, 363, 450
Bayer, Lea, 353–54
Beer, Herta, 363
Begell, William, 327, 330
Begin, Menachem, 132, 465
Beiles, Yudel (Beilesas, Judelis), 304–5, 363, 366n86, 463, 476
Beitar, movement. *See* Betar
Bek's aunt, Janina, 341
Belarus, xv, 3, 10, 13, 17, 20, 22, 39, 70n193, 166, 176, 194, 198, 227, 230, 232, 237, 239, 247, 294, 307, 318, 324, 331, 334–35, 383–84, 388, 390, 393–94, 408, 426–32, 442, 490, 506, 508, 562
Belarusian Communist Party, 111
Belgium, 467
Belgrade, 459
Bellmer, Gevert, 274
Belloc, Hilaire, 69
Bendras žygis, journal, 73n204
Benedictine Convent, 473
Ben-Gurion University, xiii
Ben-Naftali, Aya, 384, 385n146
Beresniova, Christine, 526nn
Berezovki, 230
Beria, Lavrenti, 97n23, 466, 536
Berk, Bluma, 475
Berkė, Z., 287
Berlin, 41, 73, 76, 81, 99, 137–39, 143, 145, 147–50, 152–53, 163n18, 171, 193, 195, 197, 213, 238, 260, 306, 316, 318, 335, 406–8, 459, 461, 468, 507, 557
Bermanas, M., 115
Bermondt-Avalov, Pavel, 37n91
Bermondtists (Bermondtist forces), 37, 452
Bern, 99n30, 138n145, 150, 558
Bernard, a monk, 424
Bernardinai, newspaper, 416n27, 438n85, 542n149
Bernhard Press, publishing house, 95
Bernstein, Leon, 382
Beržinis, Saulius, 423, 529
Betar, radical Zionist youth movement, 126–27, 127n115, 329

Beth Midrash, 272, 282
Bieliatzkin, Simon, 367
Bieliauskas, Feliksas, 109
Bielockis, a doctor, 265
Bikinas, priest, 429
Bikkur-Holim, hospital, 48
Biniakonski, Boria, 337–38
Binkienė, Sofija, 474n187, 477, 501
Birsen. *See* Biržai
Birštonas, 241, 265–66
Biržai (Birże/Birzhai/Birsen/Birzh), xv, 248, 252, 255, 319
Biržiška, Mykolas, 61, 65, 233, 376, 470
Bishops' Conference, 419, 521
Bistrickas, Stasys, 501
Bizauskas, Kazys, 86
Black Sea, 162
Bleiman, Mikhail, 495
Blitzkrieg, 158
Bliumbergas, Nachumas, 281
Bloch, Abraham and Zalman, rabbis, 228
Blumberg, Julius, 56
Blynas, Zenonas, 143n154, 195n91, 196b94, 439n88, 441–45, 514n89
Bobelis, Jurgis, 175–76, 181, 187, 195, 199–200, 203–4, 297, 472
Bobr, 559
Böhme, Hans-Joachim, 163–65, 222
Bolsheviks, x, 22, 37–38, 63, 91–92, 94, 105, 141, 144, 146, 153, 159, 161, 167, 171, 175, 179–82, 195–96, 214, 217, 261, 297, 396, 408, 410, 416–19, 421, 432, 434, 437–38, 452–57, 459, 464, 480, 482–83, 510, 522, 561
Borisevičius, Vincentas, bishop of Telšiai, 420n37, 471, 473, 477
Borisov, 443
Borkowska, Anna, 386
Bortkevičius, Vaitiekus (August Vaitiekus), 241, 282, 285
Boruta, Jonas, 28n59
Boruta, Kazys, 444
Boston, a cloth-weaving factory, 347
Boston, 507
Bramson, Michael (Bramsonas, Mikas), 342
Brandišauskas, Valentinas, 175n44, 181n56, 287n88, 418n32, 421, 425n49, 434, 449n115, 509

Brantsovskaya, Fania, 534
Braška, Povilas, 286
Braun, Joachim, 375n119, 380
Brauns, Moses, 343, 369
Brazauskas, Algirdas, 520
Brazdžionis, Bernardas, 444
Bregšteinas, Mošė, 86
Brendel, Arno, 464
Brent, Jonathan, xiii
Breslau (Wrocław), 306, 557
Brest, 10
Britain, 13n10, 41n102, 80n222, 123, 126, 135, 137, 139, 152–53, 403, 453, 479
British Zone, 481
Brizgys, Vincentas, Bishop, 182, 409–10, 417–19, 420n37, 422, 433, 434n73, 482n9, 501–2, 507
Brown Shirts. *See* SA
Browning, Christopher, 428n54, 439n88
Brunius, Klemensas, 442
Brussels, 22
Bubnys, Arūnas, xii, 138n145, 166n21, 196n95, 208n121, 219n148, 220n149, 222n153, 229n164, 248, 252n16, 273n62, 283, 287n88, 293n98, 293n100, 297n108, 328n12, 351n59, 359n76, 363n84, 428n55, 440n89, 453n130, 488n20, 528, 546
Budelskis, 281
Bulavas, Juozas, 100n31, 503
Bulgaria, 150
Bulvičius, Vytautas, 148
Bumblauskas, Jonas, 116
Bund (General Jewish Workers' Union or Algemayner Yidisher Arbeter Bund), 22, 374, 489
Bundists, 22, 127, 374, 386, 499
Buragas, Petras, 311, 325
Businessmen's Association, 51, 62
Butkūnas, Andrius, 205
Butkus, Petras, 210
Butrimonys, 215, 241, 250, 285, 556
Buvelskis, Vincas, 283
Byelorussia. *See* Belarus
Byhov, 559
Bystrzca (Bystritsa), 562

C
California, 498, 565
Canada, 504
Cape Town, 73
Čaplikas, Kazys, 293
Capuchin monks, 473
Carl, Heinrich, 427, 428n54
Carsten, Gerhard, 221
Casablanca, 466
Cassedy, Ellen, 549
Casper, Michael, 20, 64n172, 509
Caspi-Serebrowitz, Josef, 342, 368
Catherine the Great, Empress, 16
Caucasus (Kaukazas), 314–15, 354
Čekiškės, 279, 556
Čenkus, Stasys, 170
Central Europe, 3, 9–10, 13, 22, 348, 403, 461n155, 511n81, 547
Chaim ben Isaac (Yitzhak) or Chaim of Volozhin, 19–20
Chamberlain, H. Stuart, 71
Chapayev, Vassily, 388
Cheichel, Haykhel, 52
Cheichelis, family, 52
Chervene (Chervyen/Cherven), 176, 508
Chessler, Reubin, 222
Chicago, 505
Chicago Triibune, newspaper, 520n102
Chodakauskas, Tadas, 71
Christian Democrats, 42, 74, 444
CIA Factbook, 544
Čiapas, a worker, 120
Čiurlionis, Mykolas, 472
Chișinău (Kishinev), 29
Čižas, Aleksas, 275
Cohen, Rich, 379
Cold War, 501
Communist International (Third International), 63n168
Communist Youth. *See* Komsomol
Congress Poland, 15
Constituent Assembly (Seimas), 40, 42
Council of Elders, 342, 345–46, 348–50, 385
Council of Lithuania (Vaad Medinat Lite), 12
Courland, 35
Coxe, William, 24

CPSU (Communist Party of the Soviet Union), xiv, 105n37, 536, 564
Cramer, Hans, 241, 342, 345, 372, 456
Cukermanas, Ch., a merchant, 186
Cultural Association of Lithuanian Jews, 496
Curaçao, 466, 469
Curia, 421, 564
Czech Republic, the, 97n24, 443, 523n111, 531

D
Dachau, 359, 363, 366, 470–71, 479
Dagda, 555
Dailidė, Algimantas, 325n5
Dainauskas, Mrs., 475
Dambrauskas, family, 471
Damulevich, 108n50
Damušis, Adolfas, 169n29, 411n19
Danzig, 356, 363
Darbėnai, 27, 28n58, 165–66, 249
Darius, Stepas, 7n14
Darsūniškis, 251, 269–70, 555
Daržininkai, 397–98
Daugavpils, 158, 208, 225, 554, 557
Daugėla, Kazys, 79
Daugeliai, 354
Daugeliškiai/Daugieliszki, 251
Daulius, Juozas. *See* Yla, Stasys (pseud)
Daumantas, Juozas (pseud). *See* Lukša, Juozas
David-Fox, Michael, 79
Death to Fascism, resistance unit, 392, 398
Death to Occupiers, resistance unit, 383n143, 392–93, 399
Dekanozov, Vladimir, 91, 98
Dessler, David Salomon (aka Salk or Salek), 329, 330–32, 337
Didysis Vilniaus seimas (Great Diet of Vilnius). 34
Dieckmann, Christoph, xii, 159n4, 161, 162n14, 162n16, 163n18, 167n25, 187n69, 190n78, 203n108, 297n108, 306n128, 306n130, 317n155, 319n157–58, 414n22, 483n11, 513n87, 517–18, 542n151, 543
Diena, newspaper, 69
Diet, 34, 74, 100–1, 103–4, 116, 118, 174
Diktatūra, metal group, 531

Dinnerstein, Leonard, 512
Displaced Person(s). *See* DP
District Commissariat. *See* GBK
DNB (Deutsches Nachrichtenbüro), 436
Dočkus, Petras, 274–75
Dolskis, Danielius, 87
Dominican Convent, 386
Don, river, 123
Donskis, Leonidas, 74n207, 531n131
Dotnuva, 280
Dov Tam, 119
Dovydėnas, Liudas, 100n31, 174
DP(s) (Displaced Person), 363, 479–82, 484–85, 499, 501, 504–6, 512
Draugelis, Bronius, 289–90
Draznin, I. I., 401, 402n191
Drumont, Edouard, 32
Druskininkai, 192
Dubnow, Simon, 8, 22
Duchy of Warsaw, 18
Dūda, Henrikas, 232, 501
Duksžty (Dūkštas), 248
Duma, 35, 539
Durmashkin, Wolf, 374
Dusetos, 29, 249
Dvariūkai, 224
Dyukov, Aleksandr, 148
Dzhugashvili. *See* Stalin, Joseph

E
Easter, 29, 49, 65
Eastern Europe, 3, 9–10, 13, 19–20, 22, 136, 149, 191, 247, 259, 323, 348, 511n81
Eastern Front, 157, 159, 342n40, 345, 401
East Prussia, 21, 76n215, 154, 169, 222, 355–56, 445
Eglinis-Elinas, Mejeris, 492–93
EG (Einsatzgruppen), xiv, 162–63, 184, 188, 190, 203n111, 204, 206, 238n1, 239, 410, 417
Ehrenburg, Ilya, 401–2, 473n184
Ehrlinger, Erich, 199–201, 204
Eichmann, Adolf, 521
Eidintas, Alfonsas, xii, 42n103, 45n113, 90n1, 101n32, 101n35, 117n87, 125n110, 438n85, 482n9, 483n11, 507nn67–68, 509, 522n110
Einsatzgruppen. *See* EG

Einsatzkommando. *See* EK
Eišiškės (Ejszyszki/Eishyshki/Eischischken/Eishishok), xv, 19, 124, 292–93, 399, 405n1, 558
Eizenstat, Stuart, 498
EK (Einsatzkommando), xiv, 162, 200–1, 204–6, 208, 238n1, 239, 240n4, 254–56, 258–61, 266–67, 271, 273, 282–85, 288, 298–99, 307, 309, 311, 313, 315–16, 319, 551–52, 557–60, 562n1
Elena Nikolayevna, a Russian officer's wife, 175
Elkes, Elkhanan, 341–43, 346, 368, 475
ELTA, news service, 436, 547n160
Emes, Der, newspaper, 125
England, 9, 437
Epstein, Yeshayahu, 498
ERR (Einsatzstab Reichsleiter Rosenberg), 376–77, 447, 473
Eržvilkas, 249
Estonia, vii, 59, 90, 337–38, 349, 355–58, 389, 537n139
EU, xiv, 524
Ežerėnai. *See* Zarasai
Ezherene. *See* Zarasai

F

Faitelson, Aleks (Alex), 187n69, 384n145, 385n146, 515n93
Far East, 127, 467
Feldman-Glazer, Liubovė, 361–62
Feldstein, a veteran, 382
Filbert, Albert, 206, 239, 307, 562n1
Filipow, Boris, 84
Finland, 97n24, 118
Finn, Samuel Joseph, 20
First Republic, vii, 2–3, 7, 35, 44–47, 49, 59, 61, 73, 80, 86–88, 91, 96, 126, 137–38, 143, 151, 153, 171–72, 195n92, 264, 318, 320, 326, 372, 406, 413, 422, 480, 508, 510–11, 518
First World War. *See* World War I
Fischer-Schweder, Bernhard, 163, 164n19–20, 165, 565
Fišas, Strolis, 56
Fishman, David E., 21, 373, 376, 380
Frankfurt am Main, 306, 376, 557
Folkist movement, 48–49

Folksblat, Das, newspaper, 48, 76
Fort IX. *See* Ninth Fort
Fourth Fort, 270n51, 272, 298–99, 553–54, 556
FPO (Fareynikte Partizaner Organizatsye), xiv, 337, 376, 378, 380, 382, 386–90
France, 41n102, 138, 169n29, 448n112, 467, 470, 518
Frank, Anne, 5, 492, 527
Freedom Army. *See* Lithuanian Freedom Army (Lietuvos laisvės armija)
Freedom fighter (Laisvės kovotojas), journal, 456, 566
Freedom Fighters (LLKS), 453, 546
Free Lithuania, resistance unit, 392, 398
Freida, Dr., 72
Frenkel leather factory, 353–54
Fridland, Shimon, 272
Fridmanas, a tailor, 275
Fried, Anatol, 326, 329, 372
Friedlander, Dora, 363
Friedman, Herbert, 484
Friedman, Karen, 512n83
Friends of the Lithuanian Front (Lietuvių Fronto bičiuliai), 506
Frome, Frieda, 45n114, 93, 124
Frumkin, Moshe, 381

G

Galizien, 433
Galvanauskas, Ernestas, 52, 96, 151
Ganz, Elja, 381, 464
Gar, family, 54–55
Gar, Jacob, 55
Gar, Yosif, 203n108
Garfunkel, Leib, 297, 346
Gargždai (Garsden), 163–64, 166n21, 217, 249, 321
Garliava, 250, 267–69, 280, 319n158, 555
Garsden. *See* Gargždai
Gary, Romain, 8
Gauck, Joachim, 538
GBK (Gebietskommissariat), xiv, 240, 243–44, 247–48, 250, 258–59, 279, 283, 288, 307
Gebietskommissar, 240, 245, 279, 290
Gedahnen. *See* Kėdainiai
Gediminas, Grand Duke, 9, 386

Gedvilas, Mečislovas, 96–97, 119, 487
Geleris, Abromas, 220
Geležinis vilkas. *See* Iron Wolf (Wolves) group
Gelgaudiškis, 280–81
Gellately, Robert, viii, 539n142
Gelpernas, Dimitrijus, 492–93
Gelvonai, 254
Gendel, Meir, 255
General Commissariat. *See* GK
General Jewish Workers' Union (Algemayner Yidisher Arbeter Bund). *See* Bund
Genocidas ir rezistancija, journal, 528
Gens, Jacob (Gensas, Jokūbas), 326, 329–35, 337, 353, 367–68, 374, 382, 386–89, 470
Gens, Ephraim (Gensas, Efroimas), 353
Georgenburg. *See* Jurbarkas
Gepneris, Jurgis (aka Hopfner, Jurgis), 221
Gerber, Ilya, 347, 375
German Civil Administration (Zivilverwaltung or ZV), ix, xv, 171, 192–93, 194n89, 197–98, 239–40, 284, 289, 307, 318–20, 422, 447, 559
German military intelligence (Abwehr), 70n193, 154, 260, 444
German news agency (Deutsches Nachrichtenbüro or DNB), 436
German Security Service. *See* SD
Germantas-Meškauskas, Pranas, 154, 177
Gernhardt, Fritz, 203n108
Gerstein, Nina, 376
Gerstein, Yosef, 368
Gershenson, Olga, 494–95
Gertner, Yosef, 219, 267n47
Geruliai, 248, 257, 315
Gerullis, Georg (Gerulis, Jurgis), 70, 154n177
Gestapo, xiv, 154, 195, 201, 222, 225, 252, 255, 278n75, 297, 300, 302, 321, 330, 332, 339, 342, 368, 376, 381, 384–85, 388–89, 413–16, 429, 468, 470. *See also* Tilsit Gestapo
Getz, David, 367
Gewecke, Hans, 243–46, 315, 317, 351, 353, 464
Ghetto 1. *See* Large Ghetto
Ghetto 2. *See* Small Ghetto

Ghetto Manifesto, 385
Gimbutas, Marija, 167–68, 446
Gimbutas's fiancée Jurgis, 168, 446
Ginaitė-Rubinsonienė, Sara, 303, 383n143, 384, 385n146
Ginsburg, Waldemar (Valdemaras), 299, 302, 345, 350
Gira, Liudas, 129
Girėnas, Stasys, 7n14
Girkalnis, 552
Giržadas, Povilas, 283–84
GK (Generalkommissariat), xiv, 194, 247, 258, 273n60, 324, 448n112, 562
Gladkov, Piotr, 95, 124, 126, 127n115, 565
Glass, James, 380n133, 400
Glazer (Glezerytė), Gesa (aka Albina), 383–84
Glazer-Feldman, Liubovė, 361–62
Glazman, Josef, 386, 389
Glickman, David, 303
Glik, Oskar, 339
Glochewski (Hlakauskas), priest, 429
Gluskin, Liuba, 363
Gochin, Grant, 543–44
Göcke, Wilhelm, 348–50
Goebbels, Joseph, 150, 158–59, 394
Goldberg, Isaac Leib, 21
Goldberg (Goldbergas), Jacob (Jakov/Yakov), 182–83, 186, 297, 346, 412–13, 446, 462
Goldman-Liber, Mikhail, 22
Goldstein, Eric L., 27
Goldstein, Shlomo, 186
Gorbachev, Mikhail, 496
Gordon, Harry, 93, 95n15, 114, 288
Gordon, Chaim, 288
Gordon, David, 21
Gordon, Judah Leib, 20
Gordon, Kushel, 288
Gospel of Luke, 433n71
Göring, Hermann Wilhelm, 239, 319
Goštautas, Vaclovas, 220, 283
Gotautas, Bronius, 473
Gräbe, Kurt, 154
Grade, Chaim, 49
Gräfe, Heinz, 154, 413
Grand Duchy of Lithuania, 3, 10–13, 16, 19, 34, 39, 293

Great Action, 2, 282, 303, 343, 348–49, 381, 551n1
Great Britain. *See* Britain
Great Diet of Vilnius (Didysis Vilniaus seimas), 34
Great Synagogue, 376, 492, 498
Great War. *See* World War I
Greene, Sonja, 208
Grigaliūnas-Glovackis, Vincas, 38
Grikevičius, Almantas, 495
Griliks, Ella, 476
Grimmer, Lobe, 363
Grin, Yitzhak, 186
Grinberg, Zalman, 481
Grinevičius, Jonas, 431n66, 445n106, 463n160
Grinfeldas, a Soviet official, 116
Gringauz, Samuel, 136, 366–67, 368n95, 371, 381
Grinkiškis, 280
Grinius, Kazys, 43, 416, 420–21, 471
Grinius, Kazys, Jr., 138
Grinius, Kristina, 471
Grodno, 10, 206, 308
Gross, Jan Tomasz, 213, 460
Grossman, Vassily, 473n184
Grunwald, 502n56
Gruodis, Juozas, 439
Grybas, Vincas, 222
Grybauskaitė, Dalia, 533
Gudogai (Gudogaj), 562
Gudžiūnai, 280
Guesnet, François, 35n83
Gulag, 458, 477
Gunsilius, Wilhelm, 186
Gurvičienė, Fruma, 471
Gurvičienė, Bela and Eta, 471
Gurwicz, Irma, 378
Gustainis, Valentinas, 70
Gustaitis, Rolandas, 273n62
Gypsies, 456, 554. *See also* Roma

H
Hácha, Emil, 97n24
Haifa, 465
Hakarmel, magazine, 20
Hakohen, Adam (pseud). *See* Lebenson, A. D. B.
Halshany (Holszany), 562
HaMaggid, newspaper, 21
Hamann, Joachim, 84n236, 254, 256, 260–61, 263, 266, 270–71, 274, 283–84, 288, 316–17, 321, 512, 515, 551n1, 552, 559
Hamburg, 342, 515
HaMizrachi, Zionist movement, 21
Hana Senesh, ship, 403
Hanau, 485
Handrick, Georg, 203n108
Haolam, magazine, 21
Hasidic movement, 19–20
Hashomer Hatzair, movement, 385–86
Haskalah, movement, 19–21
Havel, Vaclav, 538
Hayes, Peter, 549
Hebraica studies, 376
Hebraism, 20
Hechaluz (He-Halutz), youth movement, 47
Hecker, Mel, xiii
Heleris, Aronas (Heller, Aron), 351
Helsinki, 76
Henkin, Mordechai, Rabbi, 56
Herzl, Theodore, 21, 379
Heydrich, Reinhard, 162
HIAS (Hebrew Immigrant Aid Society), 465
Hilberg, Raul, 191, 323, 379, 510, 514, 517
Himka, John-Paul, 487n16, 523n112
Himmler, Heinrich, 239–40, 324, 348, 354
Hingst, Hans Christian, 307, 325, 328–29
Hitler, Adolf, x, 51, 70, 74, 76–77, 79, 89n256, 97n24, 118, 122, 136–38, 141, 155, 159, 181–82, 194, 196, 220, 239, 319, 345, 385, 402, 406–7, 410, 413, 417–18, 448, 451, 482n9, 505, 520, 536
Hitlerite, 396, 402, 487, 492, 501, 507, 535–36
Hitler Youth (Hitler Jugend), movement, 345
HKP (Heereskraftfahrpark) camp, 338–39, 473
Hlakauskas (Glochewski), priest, 429
Hoduciszki, 250
Hofmekler, Robert W., 377
Hofmekleris, Michelis (Moišė), 375, 377
Holocaust, *passim*

Holocaust Museum. *See* United States Holocaust Memorial Museum
Holszany (Halshany), 562
Holy Synod, 18
Holy Trinity parish, 472
Holzman, Elizabeth, 506
Holzman, Helene, 203
Holzman, Max, 203
Home Army (Armia Krajowa), 392–93, 395–96, 398, 400, 453, 499, 535
Hoover Institution, xiii, 85n245, 99n30, 138n145, 139nn146–47, 153n174, 408n6, 565
Hopfner, Jurgis (born Gepneris, Jurgis), 221
Hörmann, Gustav, 345
Howe, Marvin, 520n103
Hungary, 35, 45, 415

I
Icikovčius, Jankelis, 265
Ignalina, 250
Ignatavičius, Bruno, 120n95, 272n57
Ignatavičius, Zenonas, 426, 428–33, 460n151
IHC (International Historical Commission), vii, xii, xiv, 23, 139n147, 149n166, 248*, 439n87, 518, 524–26, 532, 537–38, 540–41, 544
Į laisvę, journal, 179–80, 182, 436–37, 444, 451–55, 463, 506, 566
Ilgovski, Dovid and Gedal, 87, 133
Impulevičius, Antanas, 428–29
Independence War, 2, 37, 44, 48, 56, 79, 86, 88, 137, 147, 150, 195, 203, 297, 412, 481, 493, 498, 504, 514, 519, 525
Institute for Jewish Research (Yidisher Visnshaftlekher Institut). *See* YIVO
Institute for Research on the Jewish Question (Institut zur Erforschung der Judenfrage), 376
International Red Aid, organization (MOPR), 96
Ioffe, Moses. *See* Jofė, Mauša
Iron Cross, Order of, 222
Iron Curtain, 547
Iron Guard, a Romanian movement, 88
Iron Wolf (Wolves) group (Geležinis vilkas), 43, 62, 194, 444, 563

Iškauskas, Antanas, 192, 290–91
Israel, vii, xii, 17, 30, 46, 54, 132, 366, 402, 465, 471, 490, 496, 499, 505, 509–11, 520–22, 524, 526, 531–34, 547
Israel Salanter (Lipkin), rabbi, 19–20
Italy, 41n102, 62n162, 144, 153, 392
Ivaškevičius, Marius, 534, 541
Ivaškevičius family Archive, 6
Ivinskis, Zenonas, 39n96, 74, 92, 411

J
Jablonskienė, Jadvyga, 471, 477
Jafetas, Tobijas, 536n136
Jäger, Karl, 171n32, 200–1, 203n108, 204, 226, 238, 253–58, 261, 266, 269n49, 270, 273–77, 279, 281, 283, 285n86, 287–89, 291, 293, 296, 298n112, 300, 305–9, 311–12, 315–18, 551n1, 561
Jagiellon, Alexander (Jogailaitis, Aleksandras), Grand Duke of Lithuania, 10
Jakševičius, Vytautas Benjaminas (pseud). *See* Alantas, Vytautas
Jakubauskas, Adas, 546, 547n160
Jakubauskas, Giedrius, 25n52
Jakubėnas, Povilas, 63
Jakulytė-Vasil, Milda, xii, 25n52
Jakys, Pranas (Lukis, Pranas), 164, 170, 243
Jankai, 278, 280
Jankauskas, Juozas, 148n164, 169n29, 171n33
Jankauskas, Pranas, 59n147
Jankowski, a witness, 308
Janulaitis, Augustinas, 18, 508
Japan, 7, 41n102, 127
Jarockis, R., 514n88
Jasaitienė (Jasaitis), Sofija, 471, 472n180
Jasaitis, Domas, 419, 420n37, 471, 472n180
Jašiūnai, 292, 558
Jasukaitis, Jurgis, priest, 424
Jedwabne, 213
Jerusalem, 36n86, 376, 391, 540, 565
Jerusalem Post, newspaper, 534n134, 538, 539n141
Jewish Anti-Fascist Committee, 485–86, 492, 497. *See also* Lithuanian Anti-Jewish Committee
Jewish Committee, 120, 242

Jewish Congress, 38
Jewish Council. *See* Judenrat
Jewish Currents, journal, 509, 510n77
Jewish General Fighting Organization (Yidishe Algemayne Kamfs Organizatsiye), 383
Jewish Joint Distribution Committee. *See* Joint
Jewish-Lithuanian Association for Cultural Cooperation, 65
Jewish Struggle group, resistance unit, 387, 392, 399
Jewish Workers' Union. *See* General Jewish Workers' Union
Jeziorosy. *See* Zarasai
Jieznas, 265–66, 267n45, 271, 279, 555
Joffe (Yoffe), a physician, 218
Jofė, Mauša (Yoffe, Moses), miller, 231, 533, 542
Jofė, Moisiejus (Yoffe, Moses), Soviet official, 489
Joint (American Jewish Joint Distribution Committee), 48, 49n122, 126
Jokūbauskis, Stanislovas, 476
Jonava, 43n107, 223, 250, 267, 281–83, 285, 317, 347, 439, 440n89, 553–55, 560
Joniškėlis, 249, 482
Joniškis, 209–13, 217, 241, 248, 445, 482, 555
Jonuškaitė-Zaunienė, Vincė, 468
Jordan, Fritz, 298–300, 302, 342, 345
Joselevičius, a doctor, 233–34
Josvainiai, 277, 555
Journalist Association, 502
Jovanović, Milivoje, 459
Judaica, xii, 49
Judenrat (Jewish council), 12, 133, 190, 220, 228, 286, 299–1, 306, 308–9, 311, 323, 326, 334–35, 343, 352, 353–54, 367–68, 374
Julijanava, 161
Jung Vilne (Young Vilna), movement, 49, 376
Juodikis, Bronius, 315
Juodis, Egidijus Saulius, 429n57, 431n66, 433n71, 445n106
Juodka, Vytautas, 468
Jūra, Klemensas, 120n95

Jurbarkas (Jurbork/Yurbark/Georgenburg/Yurburg), xv, 221–22, 248, 258, 556
Jurer Rudashevsky, Cilia, 333
Jurevičius, Jonas, 282
Jurgilas, Jonas, 218
Jurgutis, V., 444–45
Jurkūnas, Ignas (pseud. Šeinius, Ignas), 71, 72n199, 90–91, 95n15
Jurkutė, Mingailė, 546
Juzėnas, Audrius, 529

K

Kacas, Aronas (Katz, Aron), 351
Kaczerginski, Schmerke, 365, 376, 379, 382, 389, 486–88
Kailis, 338–39
Kairys, Steponas, 31–33
Kaišadorius. *See* Kaišiadorys
Kaiserwald (Mežaparks), 338, 356–57
Kaišiadorys (Kaišadorius), 250, 256, 271, 273, 279, 347, 473, 554
Kalendra, Kostas, 171n34, 293n99, 472
Kalesninkai, 293
Kaloshin, an official, 489n23
Kalik, Mikhail, 496
Kalinin Group, 306, 557
Kalmanovitch, Zelig, 332n18, 374, 382, 450
Kalniukas, 315
Kalnuotė, 101
Kaltinėnai, 244, 249
Kalvaitis, Antanas, 481
Kalvarija, 498
Kamber, Ilana, 475–76
Kamber, Judita, 475–76
Kamber, Markus, 476
Kaminskas, Mikas, 342
Kaniūkai (Koniuchy), 398–400, 532–33
Kanovich, Grigory (Kanovičius, Grigorijus), 494–95, 497–98, 529–30
Kanovich, Sergey (Kanovičius, Sergejus), xii, 498
Kanovičius family, 529
Kaplan, Abraham, 292
Kaplan, a man from Kovno ghetto, 348
Kaplan, Mordecai, 227
Kaplan, Reyne, 224n156
Kaplanienė (Kaplan), Feigė, 281
Kaplanienė (Kaplan), Ženė, 281

Kaplans, 281
Kaplinski, Shmuel, 379
Karaims, 12–13, 24, 30, 234, 293
Karalius, Vincas, 263, 279
Karkinovsky, Pinia, 384
Karvelis, Petras, 143
Karvelis, Vladas, 401
Kasparavičius, Algimantas, 2, 81n227, 90n1, 97n24
Katz, Aron (Kacas, Aronas), 351
Katz, Dovid, 538
Katz, Menke, 227
Katz, Mrs., 271
Katzenelenbogen, Uriah, 61
Kaubrys, Saulius, 45n112
Kauen. *See* Kaunas
Kaukazas (Caucasus), 314–15, 354
Kaunas (Kauen/Kauno/Kovno/Kovne/Kowno), *passim*
Kaunas Archdiocese, 409, 422, 434n73
Kaunas Brigade, 392–93
Kaunas Curia, 421n38
Kaušėnai, 236–37
Kavoliškis forest, 231
Kay, Alex J., 160n4, 161, 239
Kazlų Rūda, 160, 265, 283, 348, 393
Kėdainiai (Kejdany/Kedaynyay/Gedahnen/Keidan), xv, 21, 127, 222, 250, 274–75, 277, 280, 347, 552, 555
Kelmė, 19, 248, 475, 495
Kempner, Vitka, 387, 389
Kennesaw State University, xiii
Kerbelienė, Hinda (Mrs. Kerbel), 280
Keturakis, Alfonsas, priest, 425
Kerza, Teodoras, 275–76
KGB, xiv, 564. *See also* NKGB
khapuny, kidnappers and looters, 188
Khmelnytski, Bohdan (Chmelnicki), Cossack chieftain, 10
Khrushchev, Nikita, 494
Khrust, member of the Betar Central Committee, 127
Kiduliai, 280, 281n77
Kiel, 260
Kiemeliszki (Kyemyelishki), 562
Kingdom of Poland, 10, 18, 31
King Mindaugas bridge, 340
King Sigismund III Vasa, 10, 12

Kirkel, Rosalyn (Reyzele), 474
Kirkila, Bronius, 181, 438
Kirkutis, Antanas, 274–75
Kiršinas, Vincas, 95
Kishinev (Chișinău), 29
Kittel, Bruno, 316, 336–38, 349, 388
Klaipėda (Kłaijpeda/Memel), xv, 41, 43, 45n113, 51, 57, 62, 68, 73–74, 76–78, 80n222, 88, 163–65, 222, 243
Kleinas, a Jewish official, 119
Kleck, 465
Klimaitis, Algirdas, 184–85, 320–21, 382, 411, 438, 514–15
Klimas, Petras, 99n30, 144, 150
Klimavičius, Vladas, 283
Klooga, 357–58, 364, 381
Knesset, 520
Knezys, Stasys, 170n31
Koganas, Moisiejus Leonas, 96, 115
Komasas, B., a merchant, 186
Komsomol (Communist Youth), 109–21, 128, 164, 169, 173, 189, 213, 215, 225, 390, 441, 445, 561
Koniuchowsky archive, 203n108
Koniuchy. *See* Kaniūkai
Kopchenova, Irina, 252n17
Kopelman, Michael (Moshe), 342
Kopolovičius, Manaškis, 72
Korczak, Rozka, 387
Kostanian-Danzig, Rachel, 374n115
Kovne (Kovno/Kowno). *See* Kaunas
Kovner, Abba, 382, 385, 387, 389, 390, 402, 486
Kovner, Uri Tsvi, 20
Kovno (Kowno). *See* Kaunas
Kovno Ghetto, xi, 136, 190, 230, 298, 300, 302n123, 341, 343–44, 346, 349n55, 363, 365–69, 372, 374, 377, 381–85, 392, 440n89, 446, 455, 460, 468, 470–72, 475–76, 481, 493
Kozlowski, Wacław, 388
Krakės, 222, 250, 274–75, 280, 556
Krakiai deanery, 425
Krantai, magazine, 529n126, 566
Krasauskas, Jurgis, 219
Kraslava, 555
Kravecas, Perecas, 76–77
Kražiai, 249

Kregždutė, magazine, 8, 566
Krekenava, 189, 249
Kremer, Arkadi, 22
Kretinga (Kretynga/ Kretinge/Krottingen), xv, 21, 75, 164–65, 166n21, 170, 217, 243, 248
Kreva (Krewo), 562
Krėvė-Mickevičius, Vincas, 8, 96–99, 103, 115, 360
Kriegsheim, Arno von, 414
Krikštaponis, Juozas (aka Krištaponis, Juozas), 535, 545
Kripas, J., 278n73
Kristallnacht, die, 74
Krištaponis, Juozas. See Krikštaponis, Juozas
Kriūkai, 219, 264, 270, 280–81
Kron. See Kruonis
Krosniūnas, Stasys, 265
Kruglov, Alexander, 516n94
Kruk, Herman, 308n135, 309n136, 311, 326, 328, 330, 332, 358, 368, 370–75, 379, 382, 448, 465, 474, 528
Kruonis (Kron), 54–55, 269
Krupavičius, Mykolas, 409, 416, 481–82
Krygeris, Matas, 197n97, 216–17
Kube, Wilhelm, 432
Kubiliūnas, Petras, 196–97, 199, 321, 397, 416, 419, 446, 481
Kubilius, Andrius, 537
Kudirka, Vincas, 32–33, 82n231
Kudirkos Naumiestis, 174, 219, 250, 278–79
Kukta, V., 468
Kulikauskas, Andrius, xii
Kulvicas, Vladas, 224, 281
Kupiškis, 6, 248, 258, 491
Kurganava, 540
Kuritsky, Motl, 189, 191
Kurliancikas, I., a water works employee, 186
Kuršėnai, 248
Kursk, 401
Kutorga (Kutorgienė), Viktoras, 468, 469n177
Kutorgienė-Buivydaitė (Kutorga), Elena, 167, 374, 468
Kužiai forest, 208, 313
Kvėdarna, 249
Kvetkai, 173
Kviecinskas, Stasys, 195, 297

Kviklys, Bronius, 480
Kybartai, 154, 219, 250
Kyemyelishki (Kiemeliszki), 562
Kymantaite–Čiurlionienė, Sofija, 472

L
Ladiga, Kazys, 340
Ladigienė, Stefanija, 339–40, 462, 470, 477
LAF (Lithuanian Activist Front), x, xiv, 134, 137–53, 155, 164, 169–72, 178–80, 183, 186, 193, 195–96, 209–13, 216, 275, 314, 320, 406–8, 412, 417, 437, 444n103, 452–53, 459, 471, 490, 507, 546–47
Laisvės kovotojas, journal, 456, 566
Laisvoji mintis, magazine, 81, 82n230
Laižuva, 223
Lamp, Pnina, 223
Landsberg, 363, 484
Landsbergienė, Ona, 471
Landsbergis, Vytautas, 471, 538
Landsbergis-Žemkalnis, Vytautas, 187, 411, 471
Langer, Lawrence, 301
Lantos, Thomas, 498
Lapinskas, J., a shoemaker, 256
Large Ghetto, 298, 300, 306, 309, 311, 326
LAS (Lithuanian Activist Movement), 73, 151, 152n171, 408
Lasdien. See Lazdijai
Latsch, a miller, 223
Latvia, vii, 59, 90, 157–58, 160, 233, 338, 355, 358, 408, 537
Latvian Waffen-SS, 348, 350
Lauksargiai (Laukszargen), 217–18
Laurinavičius, Česlovas, 90n1, 97n24, 138n45
Lazdijai (Łoździeje/Lazdiyai/Lasdien/ Lazdei), xvi, 220–21, 250, 286–88, 557
LCP (Lithuanian Communist Party), x, xiv, 43, 57, 68, 94, 96–97, 100–1, 103, 104–8, 110–13, 120, 122, 131, 384, 390, 393–94, 489, 494, 564
LCP Congress, 107–9, 112, 115, 131
LCVA (Lithuanian Central State Archive), xii, xiv, 6, 64n172, 212, 236, 258, 263
League of Nations, 40, 88n253, 144
Lebedeva, Natalia, 90n1, 97n24

Lebenson, A. D. B. (aka Hakohen (pseud), Adam) 20–21
Lechthaler, Franz, 427
Leeb, Wilhelm von, 203
Leibovičius (Leibovich), an engineer, 481
Leibovičius, Mendelis (Leibovitz, Mendel), 351
Leipalingis, 76–77, 285, 556
Lekėčiai, 278–79
Lempert (Lempertienė), Larisa (Lara), xii, 21n46, 25n52, 33n77, 252n17
Lenin, Vladimir, 22, 213, 221, 297, 520
Lentzen, Arnold, 241, 282, 284–86
Lentvaris, 117, 293
Leonas, Petras, 33, 34n78
Leonavičius, Antanas, 222
Levas, Meir, 329
Levickas, Mykolas, 221
Levin, Dov, 94n13, 117n85, 120n96, 132, 135, 190, 270, 466, 510, 522n109, 525
Levin, Mikhail, 398
Levin, Moshe, 350
Levin, Vladimir, 4n4
Levin, Yoyel, 465
Levin, Zvi, 346
Levinas, Emmanuel, 19–20
Levine, Hillel, 467
Levine, Paul, 549
LF (Lithuanian Front), 452, 506
LGGRTC (Research Center on the Genocide and Resistance of the People of Lithuania), xiv, 426n52, 431n64, 514n88, 527–28, 543–46, 547n160
Liaudies Seimas (People's Diet), 34, 74, 100–1, 103–4, 116, 118, 174
Library of Congress, 406n4
Lides, Herzl, 368
Liekis, Algimantas, 515n93
Liekis, Šarūnas, xii, 36, 384n140, 395n172
Liepāja, 356n68
Lietūkis massacre, 108n51, 185–87, 204, 418, 438, 506, 515, 546
Lietuvio žodis, newspaper, 44
Lietuvos aidas, daily, 39, 64, 67, 75, 81, 502, 566
Lietuvos Cukrus, concern, 51
Lietuvos rytas, magazine, 512n82, 539n14, 566

Lietuvos ūkininkas, magazine, 33, 34n78
Lietuvos žinios, daily, 7–8, 64–65, 75, 82, 566
Lifshitz, Jacob Halevi, 21
Lileikis, Aleksandras, 325, 532
Linas, flax producers'cooperative, 50
Linkaičiai armory, 353
Linkevičius, Petras, 313, 481
Linkevičius, Linas, 543
Lincoln, Abraham, 520
Linkuva estate, 182, 224, 249, 252, 419
Lipetz, Abraham and Gusta, 467
Lipzer, Benjamin (Liptzer/Lipcer, Beno), 342, 368, 381
Literatūra ir menas, newspaper, 4n7, 566
Lithuania, *passim*
Lithuanian Activist Front (Lietuvių aktyvistų frontas). *See* LAF
Lithuanian Activist Movement (Lietuvių aktyvistų sajūdis) *See* LAS
Lithuanian Anti-Jewish Committee, 121. *See also* AMO
Lithuanian Businessmen's Association (Lietuvių verslininkų sąjunga), 51, 62
Lithuanian Communist Party. *See* LCP
Lithuanian ELTA news service, 436, 547n160
Lithuanian Freedom Army (LLA), 453
Lithuanian Front (Lietuvių Fronto bičiuliai). *See* LF
Lithuanian Institute of History, xii, 431n64, 461n155, 503, 508–9, 535, 537, 542n151, 544, 545n156, 547, 566
Lithuanian Independence Wars. *See* Independence War
Lithuanian Jewish Congress, 38
Lithuanian Jewish soldiers' (veterans') society (LŽKS). *See* Association of Jewish Soldiers
Lithuanian Journalist Association, 502
Lithuanian Local Force (Lietuvos Vietinė Rinktinė), 460, 461n154, 488
Lithuanian MGB, 490
Lithuanian National Committee (Tautinis Lietuvos komitetas), 151
Lithuanian Nationalist Party (LNP), xiv, 143, 147, 154, 194–95, 406, 436, 441, 443–45, 453, 514, 531

Lithuanian National Socialist Iron Wolf
    Front, 143
Lithuanian People's Army (Lietuvos liaudies
    kariuomenė), 121
Lithuanian Provisional Government
    (Lietuvos laikinoji vyriausybė). See PG
Lithuanian Rabbinical Association, 63
Lithuanian rebels' Citizens' Committee. See
    Vilnius Citizens' Committee
Lithuanian Riflemen's Union (Lietuvos
    šaulių sąjunga), 42, 64, 77, 105, 120, 160,
    186, 209–10, 215, 292n97
Lithuanian Security Police (LSP), 170, 205,
    207, 221, 243, 296n107, 320, 325, 422,
    532
Lithuanian Self-Defense Battalions. See LSD
    Battalions
Lithuanian Union of Freedom Fighters
    (LLKS), 453, 546
Lithuanian Union of Working People
    (Lietuvos Darbo liaudies sąjunga),
    100–1
Lithuanian Writers' Association, 505
Lithuanian Youth Center, 505
Lithuanian Zionist Federation, 47
Lithuania's Jerusalem, newspaper, 497
Littman, Sol, 514
Litvaks, 3, 8–9, 13, 16–17, 20–24, 39, 44–45,
    53, 61, 72, 86–87, 94, 237–38, 246,
    254, 258, 280, 288, 318, 326, 358, 372,
    385–86, 402, 441, 454, 456, 477–79,
    482–83, 492, 498, 508, 521, 528–29,
    541, 549, 562n
Liubetsky, E., 392
Liutkevičius, Karolis Pilypas, 533
Liutkienė (Liutkus), Bronė, 476
Liutkienė (Liutkus), Kazys, 476
Livšinas, J., 61n157
LLA (Lietuvos laisvės armija), 453
LLKS (Lietuvos laisvės kovotojų sąjunga),
    453, 546
LNP (Lietuvių nacionalistų partija). See
    Lithuanian Nationalist Party
Lohse, Hinrich, 194, 318–19, 421
London, 22, 123, 393
Los Angeles Times, newspaper, 514
Lost Shtetl Museum, xii, 3n3, 498
Łoździeje. See Lazdijai

Lozoraitis, Stasys, 138n145, 144, 151,
    152n171, 155
LSD Battalions (Lietuvių savisaugos
    batalionai), 320, 426–28, 439n88, 535,
    545–46, 562n1
LSP (Lietuviu Saugumo policija). See
    Lithuanian Security Police
Lublin, 11, 81, 274, 443
Luria, David, 17
Lurje, Nachmanas, 51n132
Luinienė, Janina, 471
Lukiškės (Lukiszki) prison, 188, 307, 309,
    381, 448
Lukošius, Balys, 292
Lukša, Juozas (pseud. Daumantas), 464,
    515, 546
Lukys, Pranas (Jakys, Pranas), 164n20, 170,
    243
Lutherans, 24
Lutsk, 10
Lviv, 433
Lygumai, 249
Łyntupy (Lyntupy), 562
LŽKS (Lietuvos žydų karių sąjungos). See
    Association of Jewish Soldiers

M
Maccabi, sport clubs, 48, 272
Maceina, Antanas, 74, 138, 147
Mačernis, Vytautas, 8
Mackevičius, Noachas, 117, 411n17
Mackonis, Rapolas, 167, 440–41, 450,
    457–58
Magnus University. See Vytautas Magnus
    University
Maistas, company, 108n51
Maišiagala, 250, 291
Majdanek camp, 350n55, 443n96
Makarov, an officer, 99n29, 117n86
Makhotina, Ekaterina, 491n30, 497,
    502nn56–57, 547
Malašauskas, Jonas, 120
Malenkov, Georgi, 489
Maliauskas, Antanas, 33
Maliauskas, Stasys, 241
Mandatory Palestine, 403
Mandel Center, vii, xiii
Manila, 467

Mannerheim, Carl Gustaf Emil, 118
Mao Zedong, 393
Mapu, Abraham, 21
Marcinkevičius, a laborer, 173
Margiris, resistance unit, 392, 399
Marian Fathers, Congregation of, 69
Marijampolė (Mariampol/Maryampol), xv, 72, 99, 101n35, 219–21, 250, 281, 283–87, 551n1, 552–53, 555
Margolis, Rachel, 399n181, 534
Margolis, Pavel, 345
Markov, Fyodor, 388–89
Martynas Mažvydas National Library of Lithuania, xii, 180, 429n57, 432n67, 564
Marx, Karl, 142
Marxists, 22, 48, 103, 109, 113, 141
Masaryk, Tomàš, 72
Maslauskienė, Nijolė, 101n34, 106n41, 111, 113n61, 127n116, 137n142, 149n166
Matelionis, Juozapas, Rev., 3, 6, 230
Matthäus, Jürgen, xii, 240, 253
Matulaitis, Jurgis, 28, 37n90
Matulionis, Eduardas, 4
Matulionis, Balys, 187
Matulionis, Jonas, 182–84, 199, 412, 416, 446-47
Matulionis, Teofilius, bishop of Kaišiadorys, 426, 473
Matvejevas, Dmitrijus, 534
Matzok, governing body of Zionists, 382
Max, Emil, 222
Mayorov, Nikolai, 489n23
Mazionis, John, 123
Mazoveckis, Becalel, 353–54
Mažeikiai (Mażejki/Mazheikyai/ Mosscheiken/Mazheik), xv, 57, 223, 248, 251–52, 260, 319, 471, 551n1
Mažonas, Visvaldas, 530
Medišauskienė, Zita, 30n65
Medvedev, Dmitri, 539
Meilus, Leonas, 295
Mefitse Haskalah library, 372
Melamed, Joseph A., 522
Mendelsohn, Ezra, 509
Mendelsohn, Moses, 20
Mensheviks, 22, 106
Memel. *See* Klaipėda
Meras, Icchokas, 475, 495–96, 505, 529

Merkinė, 241, 250, 285, 556
Merkys, Antanas, 51–52, 97n23
Merkys, Vytautas, 50n126, 51
Mertelsman, Olaf, 537n139
Metai, journal, 161n12, 521, 522n107
Metalas factory, 169, 181
Mežaparks (Kaiserwald), 338, 356–57
MGB, 490
Miceika, Marijonas, 390
Michaliszki (Mikhalishki), 334, 562
Michalkevičius, Antanas, 398
Michlic, Joanna Beata, 487n16, 523n112
Mickey Mouse, 118
Mickiewicz, Adam, 393
Mickūnai, 291
Miglinas, Simas, 436
Mikelinskas, Jonas, 521
Mikhalishki (Michaliszki), 334, 562
Mikhoels, Solomon, 485, 497
Miklaševičius, Kęstutis, 179
Mikulska, Maria, 473–74
Militia, 116, 226, 232, 278n75, 350, 392, 395, 397–99, 516n94, 536
Millersville University of Pennsylvania, xiii
Milner, Josef, 398
Milner, Sonja, 361
Ministry of Internal Affairs (Vidaus Reikalų Vadyba), 242, 278
Minsk, 17, 176, 394, 426–30, 432, 443, 508, 559, 562n
Mir, 19
Mironas, Prime Minister, 73n204
Mishell, Vera, 363
Mishell, William W., 114, 131, 363, 366
Mishkine, 530
Missenbaum, a German officer, 272
Mitnagedim, 19
Mobile Commando (Mobile Unit). *See* Rollkommando
Mockūnas, Liūtas, 408n6
Mokslo dienos, newspaper, 7n15–16, 566
Molėtai, 79, 256, 534, 541–42, 555
Molk, Y., 225
Molotov, Vyacheslav, 79, 90–91, 97n23, 503, 525
Molotov-Ribbentrop Pact, 79, 503, 525

MOPR, organization (Mezhdunarodnaya organizatsiya pomoshchi revoliutsioneram), 96
Morkūnas, Simonas, 187
Morocco, 467
Morozovas, Artūras, 548
Moscow, 84, 90, 99n29, 103, 105–6, 117, 123, 129n123, 149, 173, 384, 390, 393, 397, 399, 401, 407, 465, 481, 488–89, 492, 494, 496, 503, 519, 537, 551n1
Mošinskienė, Halina, 300n117
Mošinskis, Algirdas, 300n117
Moškėnai, 233n172
Mosscheiken. *See* Mažeikiai
Möst, a dentist, 218
Munich, 306, 381, 481, 483, 557
Murer, Franz, 307, 311, 325, 330, 336
Murza, Mindaugas, 531
Museum of Occupations and Freedom Fights (Okupacijų ir laisvės kovų muziejus), 528
Mushkat, Yosef, 376
Muslims, 12–13, 24
Musninkai, 254
Mussar movement, 19–20
Mussolini, Benito, 118
Mūsų garsas, journal's supplement, 48
Mykolaitis-Putinas, Vincas, 8

N
Naimark, Norman M., xii, 459
Napoleon Bonaparte, 18
Narkompros [Peoples Commissariat of Education), 489
Naroch, 388–90, 393
Nationalist Union (Tautininkų Sąjunga), 43, 52, 70, 75
National Library of Lithuania, xii, 180, 429n57, 432n67, 564
National Socialist German Workers' Party. *See* NSDAP
Natkevičius, Ladas, 84n238, 90, 465
NATO (North Atlantic Treaty Organization), xiv, 523
Natzweiler, 473
Naujaneriai village, 291
Naujasis židinys-Aidai, magazine, 135n137, 566

Naujoji Lietuva, newspaper, 178, 180, 193n84, 440, 449, 458, 566
Naujoji Romuva, newspaper, 74n207, 566
Naujoji Vilnia (Nowa Wilejka), 289, 290–91, 336, 558
Navazelskis, Ina, xiii
NCO (Non-Commissioned Officer), 44, 313, 309, 336, 438
Nebe, Arthur, 188
Negev, xiii
Nemenchuk, Yitzhak, 201, 203n108
Nemenčinė, 288–89, 291, 558
Nemunas, river, 169, 181, 206, 221, 270, 298, 430–31
Nepriklausoma Lietuva, newspaper, 452, 455–57, 566
Neris (Vilija), river, 115, 184–85, 206, 298, 340
Nėris, Salomėja, 129
Netherlands, the, xi, 462, 469
Neugebauer, Rudolf, 336–37
Neum, Walter, 243
Neumann, Ernst, 73
Nevulis, Jurgis, 287–88
New York, xiii, 7n14, 49, 268, 366, 466, 508
New York Times, newspaper, 441, 520nn102–3
Neyman, Georg, 205
Nicholas I, Emperor, 16–17
Nicholas II, Emperor, 18
Nida, seaside resort, 509
Nikžentaitis, Alvydas, xii, 3n3, 338n30, 542n151
Ninth Fort, ix, 2, 154, 183n64, 299–301, 303, 306, 348–49, 363, 381, 384–85, 443n97, 455, 460, 463, 472, 491, 495, 498, 508, 526, 557, 566
NKGB (Narodnyi kommisariat gosudarstvennoi bezopasnosti), xiv, 126, 149
NKVD (Narodnyi kommissariat vnutrennikh del), xiv, 95, 97, 99n29, 105, 107, 112–14, 117, 122, 123n102, 146, 169, 173, 176, 228, 409, 432, 444n101, 466, 504, 508, 553
Nolis, Samuelis, 56
Noreika, Dainius, 545n157
Noreika, Jonas, 62, 244–46, 282, 543–44, 546n159

Noreika, Laimonas, 161, 166, 179
Norkus, Bronius, 204, 271, 287
North America, 501
Norvaiša, Balys, 288, 292
Novoaleksandrovsk. See Zarasai
Nowa Wilejka. See Naujoji Vilnia
Nowe Święciany (Švenčionėliai), 251, 294–95, 335
Novickis, Antanas, 193
NSDAP (Nationalsozialistische Deutsche Arbeiterpartei), xiv, 512
NSKK (Nazionalsozialistisches Kraftfahrkorps), the, 342
Nuremberg Trial, 184, 199n99, 536
Nuremberg Laws, 191, 538
Nyka-Niliūnas, Alfonsas, 8

O

Obeliai, 227, 249, 254, 554
Odesa, 20, 29, 465
ODIHR (Office for Democratic Institutions and Human Rights), 527
Ogiński estate, 249
Old Believer community, 24, 226n161, 285n86, 395, 451
Olita. See Alytus
Olkinas (Olkinaitė), Asna, 5, 230–31
Olkinas, Elijas (Ilia or Ilyushka), 5, 8, 128, 229–30, 383, 464
Olkinas (Olkinaitė), Grunia, 5, 230–31
Olkinas (Olkinaitė), Matilda, 3–9, 86, 127, 227, 229–31, 233, 383, 446, 501, 533
Olkinas (Olkinaitė), Mika, 5, 230–31
Olkinas, Noachas, 5, 230–31
Olympic Games, 76n214
Onuškis, 250, 293
Operation Barbarossa, 157–58, 159n4, 161–62, 208
Order of the Sacred Heart, 472
Organization Todt, 356
Orthodox, 13, 19–20, 44n111, 45–46, 48–49, 94, 106, 130, 374
Oryol (Orel), 391, 401
OSCE (Organization for Security and Co-operation in Europe), 527, 539
Oshima, Hiroshi, 152
Oshry, Efraim, Rabbi, 185n67, 491
Osovsky, Zalman, Rabbi, 184

Ossersee. See Zarasai
Ostman, Eberhard von, 188
Ostrowiec (Astravyets), 562
Oszmiana. See Ashmyany
Ottawa, 120n95
OZE (Obshchestvo okhraneniya zdorovya evreiskogo naseleniya), 48

P

Paberžė, 291
Pabradė, 227, 250
Paežerėliai, 264, 278, 280, 281n77
Pajaujis, Juozas, 73n204
Pajuostė (Pajuostis), 255–56
Pajūris, 218, 244, 249
Paksas, Rolandas, 530–31
Pakruojis, 349, 482
Pakuonis, 269, 280
Palanga (Valteriškė), 69, 75, 81–82, 165, 166n21, 222, 249, 446
Palčiauskas, Kazys, 297–98
Paleckis, Justas, 96, 98, 100, 103, 109, 118, 491–92
Palemonas, 347
Pale of Settlement, 15–16, 18
Palestine, 22, 33, 44, 47–48, 67, 72, 117, 121, 126, 234, 363, 402–3, 447, 465
Paltarokas, Kazimieras, bishop of Panevėžys, 419, 422
Panama Canal, 467
Panemunė, 280, 298
Panemunėlis, 3–9, 227, 229–32, 383, 464, 501, 533, 541
Paneriai (Ponar/Ponary), ix, 206, 268, 289, 304, 307–12, 318, 330, 335–37, 339, 374, 385, 387, 460n152, 487–88, 490–91, 493, 495, 497–99, 501, 513, 528, 562n1
Panevėžys (Ponevezh/ Poniewież/ Poniewiesch), xv, 19, 21, 37–38, 42, 49n126, 56, 71, 101n35, 120, 130, 176, 189, 224, 240, 243, 248, 255–56, 258, 317, 418–19, 422, 489–90, 519, 540, 552–54
Paper Brigade, 365, 376, 387, 389, 470
Papiškės, 330
Parashchenka, a Soviet official, 106
Paris, 99n30, 144, 151n168, 448n112

Paris Peace Conference, 39
Parliament (Seimas), 35, 363, 520–21, 538–39, 544, 546
Parulskis, Sigitas, 529–30
Pashuto, Vladimir T., 502n56
Pasvalys, 248, 256, 554
Pašvitinys, 249
Paukštys, Bronius, Rev., 471–72, 473n184, 477
Pavenčiai, 353–54
Peasant Populists, 42, 452–53, 530
Pennsylvania, xii–xiii
People's Army, 121
People's Government (Liaudies vyriausybė), 96, 98, 103, 118, 124, 457
Peoples Commissariat of Education (Narkompros), 489
People's Commissariat of Internal Affairs. See NKVD
People's Commissariat of State Security. See NKGB
People's Diet (Liaudies Seimas), 34, 74, 100–1, 103–4, 116, 118, 174
Peres, Shimon, 521
Perestroika, 486, 496, 502, 519
Pergalė, journal, 494
Perlmutter, Amos, 515
Pernarava, 275
Perrin, Charles, xiii, 82n231, 435n77
Peshko, A., 293n98
Pessach, a student, 186
Peter Lang, printing house, 512
Petrašiūnai, 473, 555
Petrauskas, 219
Petuchauskas, Markas, 379, 472
PG (Provisional Government), xv, 143, 171–72, 175–76, 178, 181–83, 184n65, 185–87, 191, 193–99, 200, 204, 214, 242n9, 263, 297, 320–21, 406, 408–9, 411–13, 416, 420, 435, 437, 446, 457, 459, 471, 480, 506, 509, 514, 547
Pilionis, Kazys, 215
Pilvelis, Pranas, 77
Pilviškiai, 57, 72, 174, 188, 192
Pitum, Fanny, 183
Pirčiupiai, 400, 455
Pirčiupis, 491
Pius XII, Pope, 434

Plagge, Karl, 338–39
Platakis, Benediktas, 228, 257
Pleshchenitsy, 559
Plokščiai, 263, 281
Plungė (Płungiany/Plungen/Plungyan), xvi, 92, 114, 233–38, 248, 319, 472, 543
Pobedonostsev, Konstantin, 18
Pocienė, Irina, xii
Pocius, Mindaugas, xii, 489–90n23, 545n156
Pohl, Johannes, 376, 379
Pohl, Robert von, 200, 413–15
Poland, vii, 8–10, 12, 15, 18, 31, 39–41, 45, 57–58, 66–67, 71, 79–83, 134–35, 141, 227, 288, 318, 320, 384, 393, 405, 408, 415, 441, 443, 453–55, 457–58, 461n154, 465–66, 468, 489, 506, 516n94, 526, 547, 562n1
Polonsky, Antony, xii, 12
Ponar/Ponary. See Paneriai
Ponevezh. See Panevėžys
Pope Pius XII, 434
Populists (Peasant Populists), 42, 452–53, 530
Porat, Dina, xii, 326, 329, 386n147, 387n153, 509–10
Portugal, 467
Povilaitis, Augustinas, 79, 98
POWs, 170, 177, 253–54, 256, 274, 298–99, 303, 316, 345, 349n53, 356, 362, 390, 392, 395, 427–28, 443, 462–64, 491, 518, 525, 535, 551n1, 555, 559
Pozdnyakov, Nikolai, 84, 98, 109
Požėla, Petras, 252
Prague, 467, 523n111, 538
Pranaitis, Justinas, 28
Prapuolenis, Leonas, 169
Pravieniškės labor camp, 176, 178, 181, 348, 507, 518, 556
Prienai, 250, 256, 263, 265–66, 271, 273, 279, 555
Pripet region, 240
Pročiūnai, 209
Protestants, 13, 44n111
Provisional Government. See PG
Prussia, 13, 19, 21, 41, 76n215, 154, 169, 222, 355–56, 445
Pulmickas, a driver, 256
Pumpėnai, 249, 255

Puodžius, Stasys, 154
Pupko-Krinski, Rachel, 365
Purickis, Juozas, 65
Puronas, Pranas, 296n107
Pušinis, Bronius, 108n51
Pužai, 218
Pyragius, Jonas, 150, 154, 195, 444

Q
Quezon, Manuel Luis, 467n173

R
Rabbinical Association, 63
Rabbinical College of Telshe, 228n163
Rabinovich, Samuel Jacob, 21
Rabinovich, Efraim, 297
Račinskas, Ronaldas, xii
RAD (Reich Labor Service), xv, 208
Radoshkovichi, 189
Radvila. See Radziwiłł
Radviliškis, 224, 248, 353
Radziwiłł, family, 252
Raikishok. See Rokiškis
Raila, Bronys, 141–43, 147
Rainiai, 176, 179, 228–29, 248
Rakiszki. See Rokiškis
Rakštys, Silvestras, 246
Ralys, Kazys, 210, 350
Ramanauskas-Vanagas, Adolfas, 542–43
Rasayn See Raseiniai
Rašė Forest, 423
Raseiniai (Rosienie/Rossieny/Raseinen/
    Rasayn), xvi, 173, 248, 257, 553–54, 556
Raštikis, Stasys, 118, 143, 197n97, 412–13,
    414n22, 415–16
Rathenau, Walter, 74
Rauca, Helmut, 300–3, 343, 381
Raudondvaris, 271
Red Aid, organization (MOPR), 96
Red Army, 4–5, 37, 80, 82–83, 84n239,
    90–91, 94–95, 96–97, 107, 113–14, 119,
    121–22, 130, 132, 135, 141, 144, 148,
    158–60, 162–63, 169–70, 173–74, 176–
    78, 187, 189, 210, 214, 223, 225–28,
    234, 264, 275, 339, 351, 355–56, 363,
    387, 391, 401–2, 419, 474, 476, 479,
    489, 500, 535, 537, 551n1
Red Cross, organization, 90, 168, 420

Reich Labor Service (RAD), xv, 208
Reichstag, 159n3
Reivytis, Vytautas, 195, 263, 265, 267, 278
Rėklaitis, Kazys, 215
Remesa, Gracius, 175
Renteln, Adrian von, 194–97, 239–40, 258,
    307, 397, 416
Respublika, newspaper, 530, 566
Ribbentrop, Joachim von, 79, 150, 152,
    153n174, 503, 525
Ribukai, 249
Richter, Klaus, 34n79, 339, 517
Riehl, Wilhelm Heinrich, 33
Riešė, 291, 336, 558
Rietavas (Ogiński estate), 249
Riga, 174, 203, 208, 337–38, 356, 377, 465
Riflemen's Corps, 121, 170, 321, 401, 551n1
Riflemen's Division, 4, 227, 402
Riflemen's Union (Šaulių sąjunga), 42, 64,
    77, 105, 120, 160, 186, 209–10, 215,
    292n97
Riflemen's Union members (šauliai or
    shaulists), 77, 186, 215, 292n97, 308
Rikhman, Mashe, 114n67
Rimkus, postal official, 431
RKO (Reichskommisssariat Ostland), xv,
    319
Rogow, David, 483
Rokach, Israel, 72
Rokiškis (Rakiszki/Rokishkis/Rokischken/
    Raikishok), xvi, 6–7, 65, 128, 171n32,
    189, 226, 231–32, 233n172, 248,
    253–55, 316, 441–42, 464, 541–42, 554,
    560
Rollkommando (Mobile Commando or
    Mobile Unit), 204, 254, 256–57, 261,
    270, 273–74, 283, 316, 321, 551n1
Rolnikaitė, Marija (Maša), 492, 493n34
Roma People, 518–19, 525, 531. *See also*
    Gypsies
Roman Catholics, 118, 412, 472
Romania, 45, 88
Romanov, dynasty, 18
Rome, 151
Römeris, Mykolas, 75
Ropp, Went von der, 300
Roques (Rocques), Franz von, 203, 414–16
Rosenberg, Alfred, 196n95, 239, 331, 376

Rosenberg Collection, 448n112, 565
Rosenberg Taskforce (ERR or Einsatzstab Reichsleiter Rosenberg), 376–77, 447, 473
Rosenson, Claire, xiii
Rosenthal, Avram, 346
Rosenthal, Emanuel, 346
Rosienie. *See* Raseiniai
Roskies, David, 374n116, 380, 382
Rossi, Lauren Faulkner, 435
Rossieny. *See* Raseiniai
RSDWP Congress, 22
RSHA [Reichssicherheitshauptamt), xv, 154, 162, 163n18, 200, 203n107, 259, 335, 413, 551n1, 565
Rudamina, 250, 286, 291
Rudashevskaja (Rudashevski), Sara, 288, 289n90, 333
Rudashevski, Yitzhak, xii, 332–33, 335, 370–71, 373, 376
Rudashevsky, Cilia (née Jurer), 333
Rudis, Gediminas, xii, 73n203, 96n20, 143n154
Rudnia, 241
Rudniki forest (Rūdninkai), 383n143, 384, 389–90, 392–93, 397–400, 402
Rufkė, an Komsomol activist, 445
Rukšėnas, Alfredas, xii, 248n, 428nn54–55, 439n88
Rukšėnas, Kazys, 197n96, 468n176, 477, 503
Rumšiškės, 250, 267, 273, 276, 555
Runča, Silvestras, 115
Russia, 13, 18, 21–22, 35–36, 39, 81, 91, 99, 108, 114, 124, 134, 140–41, 152–53, 162n14, 216, 415, 419, 426, 433, 505, 520, 526, 539, 541
Russian Civil War, 38
Russian Social Democratic Worker's Party (RSDWP), 22
Russophones, 108, 110, 112, 392

S

SA (Sturmabteilung), xv, 70n193, 260, 342
Šajavičienė (Shayevich), Mina, 280
Sąjūdis, movement, 514, 519
Šakiai (Szaki/Shakyay/Schaken/Shaki), xvi, 21, 32, 43, 72, 116, 219, 250, 262–64, 267, 278–79, 281n77, 491

Sakowicz, Kazimierz, 206–7, 307–9, 311–12
Sakuth, Edwin, 165, 243
Salakas, 248
Salanter, Israel (Lipkin), rabbi, 19–20
Salek (Salk). *See* Dessler, David Salomon
Salesian mission, 473
Šalkauskis, Stasys, 75
Samogitia (Žemaitija), 26, 172, 228, 234, 315, 444–45
Samuel, priest from Petuchauskas, 472
Šančiai, 179, 181, 341, 348
Santara-Šviesa, émigré organization, 505
Sarin, Elis, 492
Šaulys, Jurgis, 99n30, 137, 150–51
Šaulys, Kazimieras, General Vicar, 409, 422
Šavelis, Mejeris, 228
Sayce, Archibald Henry, 33
Schafer, Johannes, 205
Schaken. *See* Šakiai
Schalkowsky, Samuel (Shmuel), 342, 349n55, 372
Schaulen. *See* Šiauliai
Scheinbaum, Yechiel, 387, 389
Schlapobersky (Šlapoberskis), Zadok (Codikas), 274
Schmalleningken (Smalininkai), 221
Schmidt-Hammer, Werner, 165
Schmitz, SS Captain, 300, 302
Schreiber, Nava, 83
Schreiner, Stefan, 3n3, 72n201, 338n30
Schütte, Hans, 407
Schutzmannschaften. *See* LSD Battalions
Schutzstaffel. *See* SS
Schwarz, Paul, 217–18
Schwarze Korps, Das, official newspaper of the SS, 449
Schweinberger, Horst, 205, 309, 381
Schweizer, Richard, 154
Schwintzen. *See* Švenčionys
SD (Sicherheitsdienst), xv, 163–65, 188, 190, 201, 203n111, 207, 218–19, 260, 319, 480n6, 561
Second Republic, 471
Seda, 223, 249
Šeduva, xii, 56, 248, 256, 258, 498, 554
Šeduva Jewish Memorial Fund, 3n3
Segala, Liuba, 127
Šėgžda, Antanas, 439

Seimas, 35, 42–43, 100, 363, 509, 524, 538–39, 546–47
Šeinius, Ignas (pseud). *See* Jurkūnas, Ignas
Seirijai, 250, 285, 556
Self-Defense Battalions. *See* LSD Battalions
Semeliškės, 250, 294, 405n1, 558
Senn, Alfred Erich, 40n99, 123nn103–4, 408n6, 517
Šėras, Eliezeris (Sher, Eliezir), 128
Serbia, 35, 161, 459, 546n159
Serebravičius, Iosifas, 65
Seredžius, 279, 556
Šešupė River, 284
Šėta, 280
Sevastopol, 386
Seventh Fort, 181, 183–84, 190, 197, 200–4, 207, 216, 223, 297, 318, 438, 462, 551–52
Shaer, Matthew, 4
Shaki (Shakyay). *See* Šakiai
Shalev, Avner, 532n133, 565
Shalupayev, A., an official, 293n98
Shatsk, 559
Shaul, Elisheva, 513n85
Shaulists (šauliai), members of the Riflemen's Union, 77, 186, 215, 292n97, 308
Shavl (Shavli). *See* Šiauliai
Sheptytsky, Andrey, Metropolitan, 533
Sheptytsky, Klymentiy, monk, 533
Sher, Eliezir (Šėras, Eliezeris), 128
Sheshkin, Moishe, 294
Shmukler, Yankel, 297, 341
Shoah, vii, xiii, 2–4, 235, 237, 321, 478, 485, 488, 494, 496, 498, 500, 509, 511, 520–21, 523, 528, 530, 539, 548
Shochat, Azriel, 41n101, 136
Shpitz, Levin, Rabbi, 217
Shtrom, Moshe, 186
Shupikov, a Soviet official, 106
Shur, Grigory, 131, 329–31, 332, 336–37, 470
Shvenchyany. *See* Švenčionys
Šiaučiūnaitė-Verbickienė, Jurgita, 10n22, 10n24, 20n45, 21n46, 24n50, 25n52, 47n117, 48n122, 252n17, 510n78
Šiaučiūnas, Pranciškus, 173
Šiaudinė, 280, 281n77
Šiaudviečiai, 491

Šiauliai (Szawle/Shavl/Schaulen/Shavli), xvi, 43n107, 49, 75, 87, 94, 113n65, 116n78, 117–18, 124n107, 128, 133, 208–10, 216, 224, 230, 238, 240, 243–46, 248, 252, 258, 282, 296, 313–15, 317, 324, 326, 351–55, 359, 367–68, 418–19, 424, 436, 464, 471–72, 474–75, 481–82, 531, 543–44, 551n1, 552, 559
Siberia, 4, 131, 413n21
Sicherheitsdienst. *See* SD
Šidlauskas, a Leutenant, 296
Sigismund Vasa, King of Poland and Grand Duke of Lithuania, 10, 12
Šikšnianas, Mantas, 208n121
Šilainiai, 182
Šilalė, 218
Šilavotas, 279
Silesia, 9
Šilinė forest, 225, 248
Šiluva (Ribukai), 249
Šimaitė, Ona, 470–71, 477
Šimašius, Remigijus, 543, 545
Šimkus, Kazys, 154, 302
Simnas, 285, 556
Simoniukštytė, Ausra, 518
Simon Wiesenthal Center, 524, 534
Šimutis, Leonardas, 152
Singer Company, 68
Širvintos, 254, 248
SK (Sonderkommando), 199, 201, 203n108, 204, 207, 310
Skaržinskas, Jurgis, 276, 298
Skaudvilė, 52, 218–19, 248
Škirpa, Kazys, 99–100, 137–39, 143–45, 147, 149–55, 171,406–8, 413, 450–51, 480, 507, 513, 545, 565
Skučas, Kazys, 78, 82, 84, 98
Skvireckas, Juozapas, Archbishop/Metropolitan, 182, 187, 409–10, 417n29, 418, 420–21, 426, 433, 565
Slabada (Slobodka). *See* Vilijampolė
Šlapoberskis (Schlapobersky), Codikas (Zadok), 274
Šlepetys, Jonas, 181n56, 184, 194, 411
Slepyan, Kenneth, 394, 397
Sleževičius, Mykolas, 39, 43
Sliesoraitis, Algirdas, 73n204
Šliūpas, Jonas, 81–82, 434–35

Slobodka (Slabada). *See* Vilijampolė
Slutsk, 427, 428n54, 443
Smalininkai (Schmalleningken), 221
Small Ghetto, 298–300, 303, 305, 309, 311, 313, 326
Smarhon. *See* Smorgonie
SMERSH, Soviet counterintelligence, 481
Smetona, Antanas, 7, 34, 43–44, 47–48, 50, 52, 57, 59, 60n151, 62–64, 67, 70–74, 76, 79, 82, 89, 91, 93–98, 115–16, 118, 121, 126–27, 135, 137–38, 141–43, 146, 151, 153, 232, 264, 406, 412, 457, 509, 511, 565
Šmila, Petras, 173
Smirnov group, resistance unit, 392
Smithsonian, magazine, 4, 5n9, 9
Smokowski, Wincenty, 30
Smolenskin, Peretz, 20
Smorgonie [Smarhon/Smorgon/Smorgony], 335, 562
Sneg (Snieg/Sniegas), Samuel (Shmuel/Šmuelis), Rabbi, 297, 412–13, 415
Sniečkus, Antanas, 97, 124, 394, 397, 399n182, 489, 490, 503, 514
Sniegas, Šmuelis. *See* Sneg, Samuel
Snyder, Timothy, 89, 432–33, 513, 539n142
Soble, Jack, 466
Soblen, Robert, 466
Sobol, Joshua, 529
Social Democrats, 31, 42, 352
Sokol, movement, 443
Solomon Zalman, Elijah ben, Vilna Gaon, 19
Soly, 334–35, 562
Sousa Mendes, Aristides de, 468
Spanish Civil War, 119
Special Platoon (Ypatingasis būrys or YB), 207, 288–89, 291–93, 296, 304, 307, 308n135, 312–13, 321, 339
Spektor, Yitzchak Elchanan, 21
Spielberg, Steven, 500
Sruoga, Balys, 360, 362, 472
Sruoga, Vanda, 472
SS (Schutzstaffel), xv, 154, 161, 163, 199–201, 203–4, 221–22, 228, 239–40, 243, 260–61, 263, 271, 277, 288, 291, 295, 299–300, 307, 309, 316, 324–25, 329, 336, 338–39, 345, 348–51, 354, 356–58, 360, 362–63, 375, 400, 414n22, 428, 433, 449–50, 454–56, 458, 460, 480n6, 488, 506, 515, 552, 559, 561
Stabinis, Mr., 340
Stahel, David, 159n4
Stahlecker, Walter, 163, 184, 188, 190, 199, 203–4, 297–98, 318
Stakauskas, Juozas, 474
Stakliškės, 279
Stalin, Joseph (born Dzhugashvili, Iosif), 79, 82, 89n256, 97, 103, 107, 113, 129n123, 137, 141, 157, 170, 213, 221, 407, 444n101, 466, 487, 491, 502, 505, 537
Stalinist crimes, 2, 123, 127, 148, 158n1, 179, 406, 433, 479, 485, 492, 497, 502, 504, 519, 523n111, 525, 536–37, 539
Staliūnas, Darius, xii, 3n4, 11n26, 17n35, 29n62, 29n64, 30n65, 35n83, 36n85, 56n136, 510n78
Stančikas, Aleksandras, 440n90
Stanford University, xiii, 565
Stang, Knut, 512
Stankeras, Petras, 261n34
Stankevičius, Rimantas, 420n37, 470n178
Stankevičius, Juozas, 439, 440n89
Stankus, Antanas, 314
St. Ann's festival, 213
Saint Anthony of Padua, Church of, 473
Štaras, Povilas, 402n192
Stasiulis, Stanislovas, xiii, 145n156, 208n121, 514n88
Staugaitis, Antanas, 34
Staugaitis, Justinas, 183, 419, 434n76
Štaupas, J., 73n204
St. Bartholomew's Night, 98
St. Casimir Society in Kaunas, 119
Stefan Batory University, 49
Steinberg, Jonathan, 509
St. Francis Church in Vilnius, 188
St. George, 430
St. Joseph's Church, 6
Stöcker, Adolf, 32
Stockholm, xiii
Stončius, Justas, xiii, 70n191, 401n187, 485–86
Storm Trooper Unit. *See* SA
St. Petersburg, 28, 48–49n122
Strashun Library, 49
Streikus, Arūnas, 421n38, 434n74, 565

Strimaitis, Juozas, 470
Strimaitis, Ona, 470
Štromas, Aleksandras, 186, 506
Struggle Group, resistance unit, 387, 392, 399
Sturmabteilung. *See* SA
Stürmer, Der, journal, 75
Stutthof, 356, 358–63, 458, 471, 476, 479, 485, 492, 528
Subačius, 249, 258
Subotić, Jelena, 528n122, 538n140, 546n159
Sudargas, 280, 281n77
Sudeten Germans, 523n111
Sugihara, Chiune, 127, 466–69
Sugihara, Nobuki, 469
Šukys, Julija, xiii, 174n41, 471n178, 546n159
Šukytė-Grigėnienė, Ona-Genovaitė, 231, 232n172, 446n108
Šukytė-Malinauskienė, Eglė, xii
Šumskas, 289, 291
Supreme Committee for the Liberation of Lithuania (VLIK), xv, 453, 481–82
Surviliškis, 280
Sutzkever, Avraham, 49, 309n140, 365, 376, 379–80, 382, 389, 470, 482, 486, 492
Sutzkever, Frydke, 309n140, 389
Suvalkai. *See* Suwałki
Suvalkija (Užnemunė/Suwalszczyzna/Trans-Niemen) region, 18, 28, 72, 219, 283, 285, 393, 473
Suwałki (Suvalkai), xi, 13, 34, 80, 81n226, 149, 516r94
Suwałszczyzna. *See* Suvalkija
Sužiedėlis, Bernardas, 454
Sužiedėlis, Darius, 312, 493
Sužiedėlis, Saulius, 11, 29n61, 31n67, 40, 41n100, 45n112, 162n14, 203n108, 460n152
Svarauskas, Artūras, 74n106, 75n212, 101n33, 118n90
Švedas, Aurimas, xiii, 302n122, 340n35
Švėdasas forest, 189
Švegžda, P., 473
Švėkšna, 166n22, 218, 249
Švenčionėliai (Nowe Święciany), 251, 294–95, 335
Švenčionys (Święcany/Shvenchyany/Schwintzen/Svintsyan), xvi, 22, 227–28, 251, 293–96, 315, 317, 324, 333–35, 388, 391, 558
Švipas, Vladas, 200
Svir (Świr), 562
Svirskaya, Lea, 294–95
Swartendijk, Jan, 469
Sweden, 465, 468
Święcany. *See* Švenčionys
Świr (Svir), 562
Świt, radio station, 456
Szaki. *See* Šakiai
Szarota, Tomasz, 187n69
Szawle. *See* Šiauliai

T
Tacitus, 142n151
Tallinn, 357, 537
Talmud, 19, 21, 28
Tam, Dov, 119
Taryba, Council of Lithuania, 36–37, 41n101
Taškūnas, Vladislovas, 422
Tauber, Joachim, xii, 112n64, 164n19, 324n3, 351n57, 356n68, 461n155, 517
Tauragė (Taurogi/Tauragi/Tauroggen/Tovrig), xvi, 101n32, 166n22, 217–18, 244, 248
Taurai, 116
Tautininkų Sąjunga. *See* Nationalist Union
Tautos žodis, newspaper, 44
TDA battalions (Tautinio darbo apsaugos batalionas), paramilitary units, 154, 200–1, 204–5, 207, 214–15, 224, 239, 256–57, 266–67, 269–71, 273, 275–77, 281–82, 286–87, 291, 298–99, 302–4, 308, 316, 320–21, 426, 438, 440, 442, 445, 551n1
Tec, Nechama, 477
Teilkommando, 208, 251, 288
Telšiai (Telsze/Telshyay/Telschen/Telz), xvi, 19, 68, 95, 176, 183, 228–29, 248, 257, 315, 419, 471, 473
Telz. *See* Telšiai
Terleckas, Antanas, 507
Testament, 19, 33
Teutonic Knights, 141, 452, 454, 502
Tėvynė, journal, 314n151, 436, 567
Third Company, 201, 270, 272, 298, 303, 321, 438, 442

Third International (Communist International), 63n168
Third Lithuania, program, 143
Thomsen, Emil, 164n19
Tijūnaitis, Stasys, 7
Tilsit Gestapo, 154, 163, 165–66, 218–19, 222, 278n75, 321. *See also* Gestapo
Tippner, Anja, 492
Todt Organization, 356
Tokyo, 467
Tomkus, Vitas, 530–31
Torah, the, 19, 221, 225, 379
Tornbaum, Alfred, 299, 302
Tory, Avraham, 297, 301, 335n24, 341n37, 346, 367, 381, 412, 416n25, 417n29
Totleben, Eduard, Count, 274
"Towards Victory," group, 379, 392
Tovrig. *See* Tauragė
Tracken. *See* Trakai
Trakai (Troki/Tracken/Trok), xvii, 10, 30, 116, 119, 251, 273, 292–94, 390, 392, 405, 558
Trakai Brigade, 392
Trans-Niemen region. *See* Suvalkija
Trimitas, journal, 42, 64n171
Tripartite Pact, 150
Trok (Troki). *See* Trakai
Trotskyists, 149
Trotzki, Shaul, 306, 326
Trunk, Isaiah, 323
Truska, Liudas, 60n151, 68n186, 111, 112nn61–62, 137n142, 139n147, 143n152, 143n154, 145n157, 146, 507n67, 509
Tumas-Vaižgantas, Juozas, 6, 61
Turauskas, Edvardas, xiii, 81n227, 138n145, 144, 150–51, 450

U
Uciana. *See* Utena
Ukmergė (Wilkomierz/Ukmerge/Vilkomir), xvi, 38, 127, 248, 254, 257, 491, 535, 545, 553–54, 556
Ukraine, 3, 10, 39, 59, 70n193, 157, 178–79, 240, 499, 511n81, 515, 526
Ulm, 163n18, 164nn19–20
Uniates, 13
Union of Freedom Fighters (LLKS), 453, 546
Union of Lublin, 11
Union to Liberate Vilnius, 67
Union of Working People, 100–1
United Kingdom, the, vii
United Partisan Organization. *See* FPO (Fareynikte Partizaner Organizatsye)
United States, vii, 9, 13, 71, 113, 126, 138, 153, 197n96, 232n171, 234, 366, 453, 468, 504–6, 510, 515, 526
United States Holocaust Memorial Museum in Washington (USHMM), vii, xiii, 54–55, 57, 78, 83, 102, 244, 247–48, 259, 292, 325, 327, 330, 333, 342n39, 343–44, 346, 351, 364–65, 377–78, 423, 475, 482–84, 523, 526
University of Wisconsin, 517
Upyna, 219
Urbaitis, Ignas, 244
Urbšas, Adolfas, 401
Urbšys, Juozas, 84n238, 90, 97n23
US Congress, 498
USHMM. *See* United States Holocaust Memorial Museum
Uspitz, a policeman, 381
USSR, xv, 13n30, 90, 96, 97n23, 103, 122, 127, 130n124, 135n136, 144, 148, 153, 155, 157, 159, 161–62, 172, 190, 213, 238n1, 321, 386, 400–1, 413n21, 417n29, 424, 466, 481n7, 485–86, 491–92, 496, 502–4, 519, 532, 539
Utena (Uciana/Utyana/Utyan), xvi, 225–26, 248, 256, 423, 553, 555
Utyan. *See* Utena
Uvarov, Sergei, 17
Uzda, 559
Užnemunė. *See* Suvalkija
Užpaliai, 249
Užusaliai, 285, 556
Užventis, 249

V
Vaad Medinat Lite (Council of Lithuania) 12
Vabalas, Raimundas, 495
Vabaliai forest, 214
Vabalninkas, 249, 497
Vainutas, 249
Vainutis, Vladas, 233
Vairas, magazine, 70n193, 567

Vaišnora, Juozas, 69
Vaitkus, Jonas, 528
Vaivara camp, 337, 356–58
Vaksman, Sala, 470
Valančius, Motiejus, Bishop, 28
Valinskas, Arūnas, 539
Valiušaitis, Vidmantas, 547
Valkininkai, 293
Valsonok, Rudolph (Valsonokas, Rudolfas), 76n215, 87
Valteriškė. *See* Palanga
Valušienė, Marija, 91n3
Vanagaitė, Rūta, 542–43
Vandžiogala, 250, 270
Varašinskas, Kazys, 190
Varėna, 215, 241, 285, 472, 556
Varpas, journal, 31–32, 567
Vasa, dynasty, 10, 12–13
Vasiljevas, M., 115
Vėbra, Juozas, 169–70
Veisaitė, Irena, xiii, 3–4, 6, 302, 339–40, 345, 462, 470, 548
Vėliučionys estate, 289–91
Veliuona, 215–16, 279, 556
Venclauskas, Linas, xii, 34n79
Venclova, Antanas, 487–88
Venclova, Tomas, 506–7, 547
Vendžiogala, 552–53, 556
Versailles, 481
Verschik, Anna, 47n121, 517
Verslas, magazine, 51n130–32, 52n133–35, 60n152, 62, 70n196, 88n252, 567
verslininkai, 50–52, 60, 62, 75, 115
Vichy regime in France, 517
Videikas, a Communist Party instructor, 214
Viduklė, 249
Viekšniai, 223, 249
Vienna, 20, 306, 342, 557
Veisiejai, 286
Viešvėnai, 229, 249
Vietinė Rinktinė. *See* Lithuanian Local Force
Vievis, 251, 294
Viķe-Freiberga, Vaira, 537
Vilavičius, Aleksandras, 38
Vilčinskas, Balys, 262, 279
Vidzy (Widze), 562
Vileišis, Petras, 32

Vilenchuk, David (Vilenčukas, Dovydas), 471
Vileyka, 239
Vilijampolė (Slabada/Slobodka), 19, 64, 67, 183, 185–87, 190, 204, 285, 297–98, 341, 349–51, 382, 384, 514
Vilija, river. *See* Neris
Vilkaviškis (Wyłkowiszki/Vilkavishkis/ Wilkowischken/Vilkovishk), xvi, 43n107, 57, 188, 192, 250, 466, 557
Vilkienė, Ingrida, xii
Vilkija, 119, 250, 267, 272, 279, 429–31, 445, 463n160, 555
Vilkomir. *See* Ukmergė
Vilkovishk. *See* Vilkaviškis
Vilmorus, polling agency, 531
Vilna (Vilne). *See* Vilnius
Vilna Gaon. *See* Solomon Zalman, Elijah ben
Vilna Gaon Museum of Jewish History, 310, 329, 374n116, 462n158, 470, 472n180, 477, 493, 497, 527n119
Vilna Gaon's Synagogue, 379
Vilna Ghetto, vii, 131, 288, 307, 312–13, 323, 325–27, 328n9, 329–30, 333, 335–39, 349, 358, 365, 367, 369–72, 375–77, 379n129, 381–82, 384–85, 389, 391, 470, 493, 499, 509, 528–29, 543
Vilna Ghetto Posters, exhibit, 376n125, 498, 567
Vilner Emes, newspaper, 125
Vilnius, *passim*
Vilnius Brigade, 390, 392
Vilnius Citizens' Committee, 180, 188, 192, 306, 471
Vilnius City, 109, 307, 325, 558–59
Vilnius City Committee, 489
Vilnius City Council, 545
Vilnius Yiddish Institute, 527, 538
Vincė, Laima, xii, 131n126, 233n172, 566
Vinickis (Vinitskus), Jankelis, 489
Virbalis, 219, 250
Višinskis, Povilas, 34
Viskind, Max, 379
Vitkus, Aleksandras, 229n164
Vitkus, Balys (Vitkaus, Balio), 408, 409n8
Vitkus, Hektoras, 478n2
Vitkus, Zigmas, xiii, 487n17, 490
Vladimir (Volhynia), 10

Vladivostok, 467
Vlasov, Andrei, 349n53
Vlasovites, 349, 354, 395
VLIK (Vyriausias Lietuvos išlaisvinimo komitetas), xv, 453, 481–82
Voldemaras, Augustinas, 67, 91, 118, 143
Voldemarist faction (Voldemarists), 143, 145, 150, 154, 195, 170, 225, 260, 262, 444, 452, 459
Volhynia, 10
Volozhin, 19–20
Volunteer Medal, 304
Vornyany (Worniany), 562
Vort, Das, newspaper, 47
Vrublevskis Library, xiv, 543, 564
VSD (Department of State Security), 72, 81n226
Vukonytė, Nelė, 477
Vygodskis, Jokūbas (Wygodzki, Jakub), 37
Vylius-Vėlavičius, Ignas, 154
Vytautas Magnus University, xii, 58n144, 482n9, 509
Vytautas the Great, Grand Duke, 10, 16, 87, 139–40
Vytis medal, 543
Vyžuonos, 249

W
Waffen-SS, 348, 350, 433, 454
Warsaw, 455–56
Warsaw Ghetto Uprising, 388–89, 499, 506n64
Washington, vii, 94, 98, 342n39, 543
Weeks, Theodore, 517
Wehrmacht, ix, 104, 158–66, 170–71, 181, 186, 190–92, 194, 199–200, 202–4, 208–9, 217, 221, 223–25, 227, 234, 239, 241, 260, 273, 294, 313, 319–20, 338–39, 341, 347, 351, 356, 401, 414n22, 464, 488n20
Weiner, Shraga, 346
Weinreich, Max, 8
Weintraub, Benjamin, 357–58
Weiss, Martin, 288, 292–93, 329, 331–32, 336–37, 339
Weissruthenien, 247
Western Allies, 38, 363, 379, 401, 451–54, 479–80, 535

West Russian Volunteer Army (Bermondtists), 37, 452
white armbands (baltaraiščiai), 170, 173, 177, 183, 185, 189–90, 207, 218, 222–23, 226, 228–32, 236–37, 252, 274, 277, 316, 446, 516
White Terror (Whites), 38, 174n41
Widze (Vidzy), 562
Wiechert, a SS Second Lieutenant, 222
Wiesenthal Center, 524, 534
Wilhelm II, Kaiser, 32
Wilkomierz. *See* Ukmergė
Wilkowischken. *See* Vilkaviškis
Wilna (Wilne). *See* Vilnius
Wisconsin, 517
Wisgardisky-Lewin, Henia, 78, 475
Wittenberg, Yitzhak, 376, 386–89
Wolf, Grigory, 341
Workers' Union. *See* Bund
World War I, 3, 5, 9, 16, 22, 26, 31, 35, 40, 46, 49, 50n128, 123n104, 147, 165, 222, 272, 562n1
World Zionist Organization, 22. *See also* Zionists
Worniany (Vornyany), 562
Writers' Association, 505
Writers' Union, 494
Wrocław (Breslau), 306, 557
Wulff, Horst, 288, 290, 293–94
Wutz, Josef, 447–49, 464
Wygodzki, Jakub (Vygodskis, Jokūbas), 37
Wyłkowiszki. *See* Vilkaviškis

X
XX Amžius, newspaper, 82

Y
Yad Vashem, xii, 346, 354n64, 381n136, 391, 433, 462, 471, 474, 477, 512, 522, 525–26, 532, 540, 565
Yale, 506
YB (Ypatingasis būrys or Special Platoon), 207, 288–89, 291–93, 296, 304, 307, 308n135, 312–13, 321, 339
Yefimov, Dmitry, 490
Yellin, Esther, 473
Yellin, Chaim, 382–84, 473
Yellin, Meir, 199

Yerushalmi, Eliezer, 351, 355
Yidishe Algemayne Kamfs Organizatsiye (Jewish General Fighting Organization), 383
Yidishe/Yiddishe leben, Der, newspaper, 48
Yidishe/Yiddishe Shtime, Di, newspaper, 47–48, 51, 72, 75n211, 76, 82
Yiddishism, 20, 373–74
YIVO (Institute for Jewish Research), xiii, xv, 8, 47n118, 49, 268, 366, 373n112
Yla, Stasys (pseud), 68–69, 362, 485
Ylakiai, 233–34, 238, 249, 319, 497
Yoffe, Moisiejus. *See* Jofė, Mauša
Yom Kippur, 309, 311
Yom Kippur Action, 551n1
Young Vilna (Jung-Vilne) movement, 49, 376
Yunost', literary journal, 496
Yurbark (Yurburg). *See* Jurbarkas

Z

Zaborskaitė, Jolanta, 518
Zacharin, Benjamin, 343
Žagarė, 19, 224, 245–46, 248, 258, 314, 317, 557
Žakavičius, Vytautas, 468
Žakevičius, Stasys Žymantas, 192, 471
Zaksas (Sachs), Haja, 281
Zaksas (Sachs), Reinė, 281
Zaksas (Sachs), Irmija, 69n188, 263, 281
Žalakevičius, Vytautas, 494–95
Žalgiris group, 388
Zalkin, Mordechai, 3n4, 5n10, 20n45, 26, 59, 517
Žalys, Vytautas, xii, 43n103, 76n215, 90n1, 138n145
Zapyškis, 250, 264, 267, 270, 280, 556
Zarasai (Jeziorosy/Zarasyay/Ossersee/Ezherene), xvi, 133, 134n134, 173, 256, 489, 554
Žasliai, 273, 279, 294
Zehnpfenning, Max, 306
Zeideris family, 256
Žeimantas, Vytautas, 501–2
Žeimiai, 274, 280

Želdaf, Joselis, 38
Zelionka, Petras, 438
Želvys, Juozas, 473
Zeltser, Arkadi, xii, 394n170, 402n191, 486
Žemaičių Naumiestis, 249
Žemaičių žemė, newspaper, 172
Žemaitija. *See* Samogitia
Žemaitis, Vladas, 474
Ženauskas, Jonas, 181
Zhukovich, a Rabbi, 126
Zhuprany (Župrany), 562
Židikai, 160, 223
Židinys, magazine, 69n189, 567
Žiežmariai, 251, 273, 279, 336, 405n1, 454, 555
Zimanas, Genrikas (aka Jurgis), 393–94, 397, 399
Zingerienė, Polina, 359, 360n77, 363
Zingeris, Chaimas, 214
Zingeris, Emanuelis, xii, 363, 524, 532n133, 538, 544
Zingeris, Markas, 363
Zionist archive, 36n86
Zionist Congress, 21–22
Zionists, 21–22, 33, 38, 45, 47–49, 63, 67, 80, 83, 94, 106, 126–27, 149, 272, 363, 372, 374, 382–83, 385–87, 465, 485–86, 490, 492
Žiugžda, Juozas, 502
Zivilverwaltung. *See* ZV
Zizas, Rimantas, 390nn159–60, 395n171, 400n184, 454n131
Zokniai, 353–54
Zrolya, a Jew, 173
Žukas, Jonas, 226–27, 253–54
Župrany (Zhuprany), 562
Zuroff, Efraim, 534, 538, 542
Žuvintas (pseud), dissident, 507n68
ZV (Zivilverwaltung), ix, xv, 171, 192–93, 194n89, 197–98, 239–40, 284, 289, 307, 318–20, 422, 447, 559
Žvaginiai, 160
Žvaigždutė, magazine, 7n14, 567
Zwartendijk, Jan, 127, 466, 468
Zwick, Edward, 499